Feminist Literary Theory

FEMINIST LITERARY THEORY

A Reader

Second Edition

Edited by
Mary Eagleton

Blackwell
Publishing

BLACKWELL PUBLISHING
350 Main Street, Malden, MA 02148-5020, USA
9600 Garsington Road, Oxford OX4 2DQ, UK
550 Swanston Street, Carlton, Victoria 3053, Australia

First published 1986
Second edition published 1996

11   2006

Library of Congress Cataloging-in-Publication Data

Feminist literary theory: a reader/edited by Mary Eagleton. — 2nd ed.
    p.   cm.
Includes bibliographical references and index.
ISBN 0-631-19734-6 (pbk)
1. Feminist literary criticism.   I. Eagleton, Mary.
PN98.W64F44   1995
801′.95′082 — dc20   95–13569
                                                                CIP

ISBN-13: 978-0-631-19734-8 (pbk)

A catalogue record for this title is available from the British Library.

Set in 10.5 on 12 pt Ehrhardt
by Pure Tech Corporation, Pondicherry, India
Printed and bound in the United Kingdom
by Athenaeum Press Ltd, Gateshead, Tyne & Wear

The publisher's policy is to use permanent paper from mills that operate a sustainable
forestry policy, and which has been manufactured from pulp processed using
acid-free and elementary chlorine-free practices. Furthermore, the publisher
ensures that the text paper and cover board used have met acceptable
environmental accreditation standards.

For further information on
Blackwell Publishing, visit our website:
www.blackwellpublishing.com

Contents

4   Towards Definitions of Feminist Writing

5 Writing, Reading and Difference

Introduction   284

Extracts from:

6 Locating the Subject

Preface to the Second Edition

In my 1986 preface to the first edition of this *Reader*, I explained that my motivation in producing it had related, largely, to my role as a teacher constructing new courses. I wrote then:

> The idea for this reader sprang directly from the difficulties I faced in putting together those courses. As I sifted through book after book and article after article I became aware not only of the quantity of feminist literary criticism that has been published over the last 15 to 20 years but also of the absence of any introduction to feminist literary theory. The pedagogic problem confronting me was how to fill that gap, how to offer students some understanding of the theoretical context without involving them in endless hours searching through the back numbers of journals.

Clearly the situation has in some ways changed and in other ways been exacerbated since then. Ten years on, the quantity, variety and complexity of feminist literary work seems to have increased exponentially and with that the need for introductory collections for the many students arriving in higher education with a keen level of interest in literary feminism but little knowledge of it. Indeed, these introductions to feminist literary studies are now very readily available. The words quoted above about the lack of them referred to 1982 when I had just begun thinking about the *Reader*. By the time it was published, the first surveys – K. K. Ruthven's *Feminist Literary Studies: An Introduction* (1984) and Toril Moi's *Sexual/Textual Politics: Feminist Literary Theory* (1985) – and the first collections of theoretical essays – Gayle Greene and Coppélia Kahn's *Making a Difference: Feminist Literary Criticism* (1985) and Elaine Showalter's *The New Feminist Criticism: Essays on Women, Literature and Theory* (1986) – had started to appear. Now we enjoy a plethora of readers, surveys, collections of representative essays, retrospective studies, titles with a specific focus, titles with a wide brief, all designed to engage the new reader.

It is still a research necessity, often a pleasure, to hunt through back numbers of journals. However, some of the journal articles I used in 1986 have subsequently been anthologized many times and attained a kind of canonical status: for example, Adrienne Rich's 'Compulsory Heterosexuality and Lesbian Existence'; Bonnie Zimmerman's 'What Has Never Been: An Overview of Lesbian Feminist Literary Criticism'; Barbara Smith's 'Toward a Black Feminist Criticism'. Other critics, already 'stars' or 'emergent stars' in 1986 have continued to shine – Elaine Showalter, Sandra Gilbert, Susan Gubar, Toril Moi, Gayatri Chakravorty Spivak, 'the French'. This process of canonization is both inevitable and worrying. In revising this reader I felt strongly the innate conservatism of the activity. How can one look at the history of feminist literary studies without mentioning Showalter, Gilbert and Gubar, Zimmerman, Moi, . . .: they have been so influential, so central to certain movements or moments. Yet, in so doing, one is reaffirming a handful of particular perspectives and denying access to others. I have tried to respond to this problem in several ways: by raising canon formation as a critical issue, by finding space for non-canonical voices, by discovering extracts which undermine given positions or query the premises and approach of an earlier extract – in short, by trying to open up debates rather than pin them down. However, at the same time, I am aware of the necessary limitations of space; I know that all selections are fashioned through the interests, ignorance and bias of the selector; and I must not fool myself, or the reader, with the fantasy of producing some all-embracing text. The wise reader will both learn from the material and be questioning about it: what are the political and cultural forces that permit us to hear certain voices and not others; whom are we hearing; whom are we not; what are the consequences?

Some of the additions and changes since the first edition respond to research needs. All the extracts are now dated so that arguments can be historically placed and readers can get some sense of how debates shift and develop. An index and a bibliography of the extracts have been included to help access material. Footnotes have been supplemented to give indications of further reading or to point to links across the chapters. Most of the extracts of the first edition are still included. I feel they have stood the test of time. Indeed, as I indicate above, many have now become key texts. Those few extracts that have been omitted lose their place not because of any inadequacy but because the argument has been covered elsewhere.

New material has been introduced throughout the *Reader*. In choosing this material I was not looking for any consensus or party line, rather for differences of viewpoint while at the same time, trying to discern some of the major trends of the last ten years. Three developments in particular have been stressed: firstly, the growing diversity of Black feminisms;

secondly, the continuing influence of and critiques about what has become known as 'French feminism', though the term alone is cause for dispute; thirdly, the fundamental political impact on feminism of postmodernist theories. Moreover, within particular chapters some new emphases have emerged. In the discussion of literary production in chapter 2, I have taken into account a wider sense of the production process with extracts that relate to publishing practices, newspaper reviews, setting up one's own press and the author's relation to her market. In chapter 3 on genre, I have switched the focus away from romance fiction to allow space for a consideration of a larger range of genre fictions and for a fuller appreciation of the political meanings of women's use of different generic forms. In chapter 5, the discussion of difference has broadened to reading alongside writing while the debates about positionality versus identity link with arguments from postmodernism and also with the vexed discussions, given new impetus in the late eighties, concerning the place of men in feminism.

The inclusion of theories of postmodernism has warranted a new chapter, focusing chiefly on postmodernist theories of subjectivity. The postmodernist questioning of, amongst other things, the definition of 'woman' (and, similarly, 'man'), the possibility of a female collectivity, the progressiveness of an egalitarian, humanist ethic, the validity of concepts of truth, identity or a discernible female history radically shook the dominant conventions of Anglo-American feminism during the latter years of the eighties. By the nineties, other critiques had emerged, well able to hold their own with postmodernism but keen to get the political needs of women back at the top of the agenda and willing to re-value the pioneering work of the generation of '68.

Readers of my first edition will know that short extracts have been characteristic of my approach. I appreciate that some readers have been irritated by this, feeling that they were just getting to grips with the argument when it stopped. A few of the new extracts in this edition are longer, particularly where the debate is very dense, but, generally, I have kept to passages which succinctly summarize one or two important points. The aim is to provide readers with a taster – if you want a different metaphor, a snap-shot – and my hope is that they will then pursue further the ideas that interest them. In this wide variety of material – 113 extracts in all – surely all but the most intransigent will find something to absorb or provoke. You can see here the connection with my original pedagogic needs: for large groups of heterogeneous students a teacher needs large amounts of heterogeneous material.

I owe thanks to various people in helping me with this second edition. Firstly, to the teachers and students who have commented on the first edition and told me their likes and dislikes; I have profited greatly over the years from this feedback. In this role, I must especially thank Judy Giles who generously puts at my disposal the insights of her own feminist literary teaching. I am grateful to the Librarian and library staff of the University College of Ripon and York St John for their ready willingness to help with research needs and to Chris Butler and the Research Management Group at the same institution for providing assistance at a vital time. Carol Abel with her exemplary word-processing skills was the embodiment of that assistance and greatly eased my task in the final stages. The friendly chivvying of Simon Prosser at Basil Blackwell both initiated and supported the new edition. My greatest debt is always to David Pierce.

Acknowledgements

We gratefully acknowledge permission to use the following copyright material:

Linda Alcoff: extract from 'Cultural Feminism Versus Post-Structuralism: The Identity Crisis in Feminist Theory' in *Signs*, 13:3 (1988), copyright 1988 by The University of Chicago. All rights reserved. Reprinted by permission of The University of Chicago Press.

Gloria Anzaldúa: extract from *Borderlands/La Frontera: The New Mestiza*, © 1987 by Gloria Anzaldúa. Reprinted by permission of Aunt Lute Books.

Nancy Armstrong: extract from *Desire and Domestic Fiction: A Political History of the Novel*, Copyright © 1987 by Oxford University Press, Inc. Reprinted by permission of the publishers.

Isobel Armstrong: extract from 'Christina Rosetti: Diary of a Feminist Reading' in Sue Roe (ed): *Women Reading Women's Writings* (1987), Copyright © Sue Roe. Reprinted by permission of Harvester Wheatsheaf and of St. Martin's Press, Incorporated.

Margaret Atwood: extract from 'Paradoxes and Dilemmas, the Woman as Writer' in *Women in the Canadian Mosaic*, edited by Gwen Matheson (Peter Martin Associates, 1976). Reprinted by permission of Phoebe Larmore Literary Agency on behalf of the author.

Elizabeth Baines: extract from 'Naming the Fictions', a talk presented to the Women's Writing Conference, © 1986 Elizabeth Baines. Reprinted by permission of the author.

Michèle Barrett: extract from 'Feminism and the Definition of Cultural Politics' in *Feminism, Culture & Politics*, edited by Rosalind Brunt and Caroline Rowan (Lawrence & Wishart Ltd, London, 1982). Reprinted by permission of the publishers. Extract from *Women's Oppression Today*, (London, Verso, 1980), Copyright © 1980, 1986 by Michèle Barrett. Reprinted by kind permission of Verso and the author.

Catherine Belsey: extract from *Critical Practice* (Methuen & Co, 1980), Copyright © Catherine Belsey 1980. Reprinted by permission of Routledge.

Seyla Benhabib: extract from 'Feminism and the Question of Post Modernism' in *The Polity Reader in Gender Studies* (Polity, 1994). Reprinted by permission of Polity Press.

Black Woman Talk Collective: extract from 'Black Woman Talk' reprinted from *Feminist Review* no. 17, © Black Woman Talk Collective. Reprinted by permission of the publishers.

Rachel Bowlby: extract from 'Flight Reservations: The Anglo-American/French Divide in Feminist Criticism' in *Still Crazy After All These Years: Women, Writing and Psychoanalysis* (Routledge, 1992), Copyright © Rachel Bowlby 1992. Reprinted by permission of Routledge.

Rosi Braidotti: extract from *Nomadic Subjects* (Columbia University Press, 1994), Copyright © 1994. Reprinted with permission of the publisher.

Judith Butler: extract from *Gender Trouble: Feminism and the Subversion of Identity* (1990), Copyright © 1990 by Routledge, Chapman & Hall Inc. Reprinted by permission of the publisher, Routledge, New York.

Barbara Christian: 'The Race for Theory' in Linda Kauffman (ed.), *Gender and Theory: Dialogues on Feminist Criticism* (B Blackwell, 1989). Reprinted by permission of Blackwell Publishers.

Hélène Cixous: extract from 'The Laugh of Medusa', in *Signs* 1:4 (1976), translated by K Cohen & P Cohen, copyright 1976 by the University of Chicago. All rights reserved. Extract from 'Castration or Decapitation' in *Signs* 7:1 (1981), Copyright 1981 by the University of Chicago. All rights reserved. Reprinted by permission of the author and of The University of Chicago Press.

Rosalind Coward: extract from *Female Desire: Women's Sexuality Today*, (Grafton Books). Reprinted by permission of HarperCollins Publishers Ltd.

Elizabeth Cowie, Claire Johnston, Cora Kaplan, Mary Kelly, Jacqueline Rose and Marie Yates (The Feminist Anthology Collective): extract from 'Representation vs. Communication' in *No Turning Back: Writings from the Women's Liberation Movement 1975-1980* (First published by The Women's Press, 1981). Reprinted by permission of the authors.

Anne Cranny-Francis: extract from *Feminist Fiction* (Polity, 1990) Copyright © Anne Cranny-Francis 1990. Reprinted by permission of Polity Press.

Jonathan Culler: extract from 'Reading as a Woman' in *On Deconstruction: Theory and Criticism after Structuralism* (London, Routledge, 1983). Reprinted by permission of Routledge.

Mary Ellmann: extracts from *Thinking About Women*, (Macmillan/ Harcourt Brace 1968, Virago 1979), Copyright © 1968 by Mary Ellmann. Reprinted by permission of Macmillan Press Ltd, and Harcourt Brace & Company.

Shoshana Felman: extract from 'Women and Madness: The Critical Phallacy' in *Diacritics* 5:4 (1975). Reprinted by permission of the Johns Hopkins University Press.

Rita Felski: extracts from *Beyond Feminist Aesthetics: Feminist Literature and Social Change* (Cambridge, Mass.: Harvard University Press 1989). Copyright 1989 by Rita Felski. Reprinted by permission of the publishers.

Judith Fetterley: extract from *The Resisting Reader* (Indiana, 1978). Reprinted by permission of Indiana University Press.

Nancy Fraser & Linda J Nicholson: extract from 'Social Criticism without Philosophy: An Encounter between Feminism and Postmodernism' in *Feminism/Postmodernism* edited by Linda J Nicholson (1990). Reprinted by permission of the publisher, Routledge, New York.

Diana Fuss: extract from *Essentially Speaking: Feminism, Nature and Difference* (1989) Copyright © 1989 by Routledge, Chapman & Hall Inc. Reprinted by permission of the publisher, Routledge, New York.

Henry Louis Gates, Jr.: extract from 'Introduction: Writing "Race" and the difference it makes', in Gates (ed.), *'Race' Writing and Difference* (University of Chicago Press, 1986), copyright the University of Chicago, 1985, 1986. Reprinted by permission of the publishers.

Sandra M Gilbert and **Susan Gubar**: extract from *The Madwoman in the Attic: The Woman Writer and the Nineteenth-Century Literary Imagination* (Yale University Press), copyright © 1979 by Yale University, copyright © 1984 by Sandra M Gilbert and Susan Gubar. Reprinted by permission of the publishers. Extract from their Introduction to *Shakespeare's Sisters: Feminist Essays on Women Poets*. Reprinted by Permission of the publisher, Indiana University Press.

Donna Haraway: extracts from 'A Manifesto for Cyborgs: Science, Technology and Socialist Feminism in the 1980s', *Socialist Review* 80, (March/April 1985). Copyright Center for Social Research and Education, 1985. Reprinted by permission of Duke University Press.

Stephen Heath: extract from *The Sexual Fix* (Macmillan, 1982), copyright © 1982 by Stephen Heath. Reprinted by permission of Macmillan Press Ltd.

bell hooks: 'Postmodern Blackness' from *Yearning: Race, Gender and Cultural Politics* (London, Turnaround, 1991) Copyright © Gloria Watkins, 1991. Reprinted by permission of Turnaround.

Luce Irigaray: extract from *This Sex Which Is Not One*, translated from the French by Catherine Porter with Carolyn Burke. Copyright © 1985 by Cornell University Press. Reprinted by permission of the publisher, Cornell University Press.

Rosemary Jackson: extract from *Fantasy: The Literature of Subversion* (Methuen & Co.). Reprinted by permission of Routledge.

Mary Jacobus: extract from *Reading Women: Essays in Feminist Criticism*, Copyright © 1986. Reprinted with permission of the publisher, Columbia University Press. Extract from 'The Buried Letter' in *Women Writing and Writing About Women* edited by Mary Jacobus (Croom Helm). Reprinted by permission of Routledge.

Alice A Jardine: extract from *Gynesis: Configurations of Woman and Modernity*, Copyright © 1985 by Cornell University Press. Reprinted by permission of the publisher, Cornell University Press.

Ann Rosalind Jones: extract from 'Writing the Body: Toward an Understanding of L'Ecriture Feminine' reprinted, in part, from *Feminist Studies*, vol. 7, no. 2 (Summer, 1981): 247–63, here by permission of the publisher, Feminist Studies Inc., c/o Women's Studies Program, University Of Maryland, College Park, MD 20742.

Kadiatu Kanneh: extract from 'Love, Mourning and Metaphor: Terms of Identity' in Isobel Armstrong (ed.) *New Feminist Discourses: Critical Essay on Theories and Texts* (Routledge, 1992) Copyright © Kadiatu Kanneh, 1992. Reprinted by permission of Routledge.

Peggy Kamuf: extract from 'Writing Like a Woman' in Sally McConnell-Ginet et al. (eds) *Women and Language in Literature and Society* (Praeger, 1980). Copyright © 1980 by Praeger Publishers. Reprinted by permission of Greenwood Publishing Group, Inc., Westport, CT.

Cora Kaplan: extract from the Introduction to *Elizabeth Barrett Browning, Aurora Leigh and Other Poems*, (first published by The Women's Press Ltd, 34 Great Sutton Street, London EC1V 0DX, 1978). Reprinted by permission of the author.

Annette Kolodny: extract from 'Dancing Through the Minefield' in *Feminist Studies*, vol. 6, no. 1 (Spring, 1980), © Annette Kolodny, 1980; all rights reserved. Reprinted by permission of the author.

Julia Kristeva: extract from 'A Question of Subjectivity – An Interview' in Philip Rice and Patricia Waugh (eds) *Modern Literary Theory: A Reader* (Edward Arnold, 1989). Reprinted by permission of Hodder Headline. Extract from 'Woman can Never Be Defined' in Elaine Marks and Isabelle de Courtivron (eds): *New French Feminism: An Anthology* (1981). Reprinted by permission of Prentice Hall/Harvester Wheatsheaf and the author. Extract from 'Talking about *Polylogue*' translated by Sean Hand, in Toril Moi (ed.): *French Feminist Thought: A Reader* (B Blackwell, 1987). Reprinted by permission of Blackwell Publishers.

Teresa de Lauretis: extract from 'Upping the Anti (sic) in Feminist Theory' in *Conflicts in Feminism* edited by Marianne Hirsch and Evelyn Fox-Keller (1990). Reprinted by permission of the publisher, Routledge, New York.

Paul Lauter: extract from 'Race and gender in the shaping of the American literary canon', in Judith Newton and Deborah Rosenfelt (eds): *Feminist Criticism and Social Change: Sex, Class and Race in Literature and Culture* (Methuen & Co, 1985). Reprinted by permission of Routledge.

Sarah LeFanu: extract from *In the Chinks of the World Machine: Feminism and Science Fiction*, (first published by The Women's Press Ltd, 1988). Reprinted by permission of the author, The Women's Press Ltd.

Alison Light: extract from 'Feminism and the Literary Critic' in *LTP: Journal of Literature, Teaching, Politics*, reprinted by permission of the author. Extract from *Forever England: Femininity, Literature and Conservatism Between the Wars* (Routledge, London 1991) Copyright © Alison Light 1991. Reprinted by permission of the author and Routledge.

Terry Lovell: extracts from *Consuming Fiction* (London, Verso, 1987), Copyright © 1987 by Verso and Terry Lovell. Reprinted by kind permission of Verso and the author.

Deborah E McDowell: extract from 'New Directions for Black Feminist Criticism', in *Black American Literature Forum*, vol. 14, no. 4, Winter 1980. Copyright © 1980 Indiana State University. Reprinted by permission of the author and the publisher, African American Review.

Nancy K Miller: 'Parables and Politics' from *Paragraph*, vol. 8, 1986. Reprinted by permission of Edinburgh University Press.

Trinh T. Minh-Ha: extract *Woman, Native, Other* (Indiana, 1989), reprinted by permission of Indiana University Press.

Juliet Mitchell: extract from *Women: The Longest Revolution* (Virago Press/Pantheon Books), Copyright © 1966, 1972, 1974, 1975, 1977, 1982, 1983, 1984 by Juliet Mitchell, reprinted by permission of the author and of Pantheon Books, a division of Random House, Inc.

Ellen Moers: extracts from *Literary Women: The Great Writers*. Copyright © 1976, 1977 by Ellen Moers. Used by permission of Doubleday, a division of Bantam Doubleday Dell Publishing Group, Inc., and of Curtis Brown Ltd., New York.

Chandra Talpade Mohanty: 'Under Western Eyes: Feminist Scholarship and Colonial Discourses' from Chandra Talpade Mohanty, Ann Russo and Lourdes Torres (eds), *Third World Women and the Politics of Feministm* (Indiana, 1991). Reprinted by permission of Indiana University Press.

Toril Moi: extract from *Sexual/Textual Politics: Feminist Literary Theory* (Methuen & Co). Reprinted by permission of Routledge.

Lauretta Ngcobo (ed): Editor's Introduction from *Let It Be Told: Essays by Black Women in Britain* (London, Pluto Press, 1987), Copyright to Introduction, © Lauretta Ngcobo 1987. Reprinted by permission of Pluto Press.

Joyce Carol Oates: extract from 'Is There a Female Voice?' in *Gender and Literary Voice, Women & Literature I*, edited by Janet Todd, (New York: Holmes & Meier, 1980) Copyright © 1980 Holmes & Meier Publishers Inc. Reprinted by permission of the publisher.

Carol Ohmann: extract from 'Emily Bronte in the Hands of Male Critics' in *College English*, 32:8, May 1971, Copyright © 1971 by the National Council of Teachers of English. Reprinted by permission of the publisher.

Tillie Olsen: extracts from *Silences*, Copyright © 1965, 1972, 1978 by Tillie Olsen. Used by permission of Delacorte Press/Seymour Lawrence, a division of Bantam Doubleday Dell Publishing Group, Inc., and of the Abner Stein Agency.

Mary Poovey: extract from 'Feminism and Deconstruction' reprinted, in part, from *Feminist Studies*, vol. 14, no. 1 (Spring 1988): 57–63, by permission of the publisher, Feminist Studies, Inc., c/o Women's Studies Program, University of Maryland, College Park, MD 20742.

Janice Radway: extract from 'Women Read the Romance: The Interaction of Text and Context', reprinted, in part, from *Feminist Studies*, vol. 9, no. 1 (Spring 1983): 53–78, reprinted by permission of the publisher, Feminist Studies Inc., c/o Women's Studies Program, University of Maryland, College Park, MD 20742.

Cheri Register: 'American Feminist Literary Criticism: A Bibliographical Introduction' from *Feminist Literary Criticism: Explorations in Theory*, 2nd edition, edited by Josephine Donovan, copyright © 1989 by The University Press of Kentucky. Reprinted by permission of the publishers.

Adrienne Rich: extracts from 'When we Dead Awaken: Writing as Re-Vision' from *On Lies, Secrets, and Silence: Selected Prose 1966-1978* by Adrienne Rich are reprinted by permission of the author and W.W. Norton & Company, Inc. Copyright © 1979 by W. W. Norton & Company Inc. 'Aunt Jennifer's Tigers', 'The Loser', 'Orion', and the lines from 'Snapshots of a Daughter-in-Law' from *Collected Early Poems: 1950-1970* by Adrienne Rich are reprinted by permission of the author and W. W. Norton & Co. Inc. Copyright © 1993 by Adrienne Rich. Copyright © 1967,1963, 1962, 1961, 1960, 1959, 1958, 1957, 1956, 1955, 1954, 1953, 1952, 1951 by Adrienne Rich. Copyright © 1984, 1975, 1971, 1969, 1966 by W. W. Norton & Co. Inc. Extracts from 'Compulsory Heterosexuality and Lesbian Existence' from *Blood, Bread, and Poetry: Selected Prose 1979-1985* by Adrienne Rich, reprinted by permission of the author, W. W. Norton & Co. Inc., and Virago Press. Copyright © 1986 by Adrienne Rich.

Jacqueline Rose: extract from 'Femininity and its Discontents', in *Sexuality in the Field of Vision* (London, Verso, 1986), Copyright © 1986 by Verso and Jacqueline Rose. Reprinted by kind permission of Verso and the author.

K K Ruthven: extract from *Feminist Literary Studies: an Introduction* (Cambridge University Press). Reprinted by permission of the author and publisher.

Robert Scholes: extract from 'Reading like a man' in *Men in Feminism* edited by Alice Jardine and Paul Smith (1987), Copyright © Methuen Inc 1987. Reprinted by permission of the publisher, Routledge, New York.

Susan Sellers (ed.): 'Conversations' from *Writing Differences: Readings from the Seminar of Hélène Cixous* (Open University Press, 1988), Copyright © the Editor and the contributors, 1988. Reprinted by permission of Susan Sellers and the Open University Press.

Elaine Showalter: extract from 'Towards a Feminist Poetics' in *Women Writing and Writing About Women* edited by Mary Jacobus (Croom Helm). Reprinted by permission of Routledge. Extract from *A Literature of Their Own: British Women Novelists from Brontë to Lessing*, (Princeton, 1977/Virago,1978), Copyright © 1977 by Princeton University Press. Reprinted by permission of the author and of Princeton University Press.

Kate Soper: extract from 'Feminism, Humanism and Postmodernism'. This article first appeared in *Radical Philosophy* 55 (Summer, 1990). Reprinted by permission of Radical Philosophy Ltd.

Jane Spencer: extract from *The Rise of the Woman Novelist: From Aphra Behn to Jane Austen* (Blackwell, 1987). Reprinted by permission of Blackwell Publishers.

Domna C Stanton: extract from 'Language and Revolution', in *The Future of Difference*, Hester Eisenstein and Alice Jardine, eds., copyright © 1980 by the Barnard College Women's Center. Reprinted by permission of Rutgers University Press.

Judith Still: extract from 'A Feminine Economy: Some Preliminary Thoughts' in Helen Wilcox et al. (eds): *The Body and the Text: Hélène Cixous, Reading and Teaching* (1990). Copyright © Helen Wilcox, 1990. Reprinted by permission of Harvester Wheatsheaf and of St. Martin's Press, Incorporated.

Janet Todd: extract from *Feminist Literary History* (Polity, 1988), Copyright © Janet Todd 1988. Reprinted by permission of Polity Press.

Alice Walker: extracts from *In Search of Our Mothers' Gardens*, Copyright © 1974 by Alice Walker first published in the UK by The Women's Press, 1984. Reprinted by permission of David Higham Associates on behalf of the author and of Harcourt Brace & Company.

Michelene Wandor: extract from 'The Impact of Feminism on the Theatre' in *Feminist Review*, no. 18. Reprinted by permission of the author.

Ian Watt: extract from *The Rise of the Novel* (Chatto & Windus). Reprinted by permission of Random House UK Ltd.

Patricia Waugh: extract from *Feminine Fictions: Revisiting the Postmodern* (Routledge, 1989) Copyright © Patricia Waugh, 1989. Reprinted by permission of Routledge.

Chris Weedon: extract from *Feminist Practice and Poststructuralist Theory* (Blackwell, 1987). Reprinted by permission of Blackwell Publishers.

Linda R Williams: extract from 'Happy Families? Feminist Reproduction and Matrilineal Thought' in Isobel Armstrong (ed.) *New Feminist Discourses* (Routledge, 1992), Copyright © Linda Willliams 1992. Reprinted by permission of Routledge.

Elizabeth Wilson: extract from *Mirror Writing:An Autobiography* (Virago Press, 1982), copyright © Elizabeth Wilson 1982. Reprinted by permission of the author.

Monique Wittig: extract from 'The Straight Mind' in the collection *The Straight Mind* (Beacon, 1992). Copyright © 1992 by Monique Wittig. Reprinted by permission of Beacon Press.

Women in Publishing: extracts from *Reviewing the Reviews: A Woman's Place on the Book Page* (The Journeyman's Press Ltd, 1987), Copyright © Women in Publishing, 1987. Reprinted by permission of Women in Publishing.

Virginia Woolf: extracts from *A Room of One's Own*, copyright 1929 by Harcourt Brace & Company and renewed 1957 by Leonard Woolf, and from 'Professions for Women' in *The Death of a Moth and Other Essays*, copyright 1942 by Harcourt Brace & Company and renewed 1970 by Marjorie T Parsons, Executrix. Reprinted by permission of the publishers, Chatto & Windus (Random House UK Ltd) and Harcourt Brace & Company.

Bonnie Zimmerman: extract from 'What has Never Been: An Overview of Lesbian Feminist Literary Criticism', reprinted, in part, from *Feminist Studies*, vol. 7, no. 3 (Fall 1981): 451–75, reprinted by permission of the publisher, Feminist Studies Inc., c/o Women's Studies Program, University of Maryland, College Park, MD 20742.

Despite every effort to trace and contact copyright owners prior to publication this has not always been possible. We apologise for any apparent infringement of copyright and if notified, we will be pleased to rectify any errors or omissions at the earliest opportunity.

1

Finding a Female Tradition

INTRODUCTION

Breaking the Silence

It is the women's movement, part of the other movements of our time for a fully human life, that has brought this forum into being; kindling a renewed, in most instances a first-time, interest in the writings and writers of our sex.

Linked with the old, resurrected classics on women, this movement in three years has accumulated a vast new mass of testimony, of new comprehensions as to what it is to be female. Inequities, restrictions, penalties, denials, leechings have been painstakingly and painfully documented; damaging differences in circumstances and treatment from that of males attested to; and limitations, harms, a sense of wrong, voiced.[1]

Tillie Olsen's essay, from which this quotation comes, was first published in 1972 and, later, became part of a volume entitled *Silences*. Both the date and the title are significant. British and American feminist critics in the 1970s were preoccupied with the idea that women writers had been silenced, by and large excluded from literary history. The Olsen quotation exemplifies the key interests of many feminist critics at that time – the desire to rediscover the lost work of women writers, while providing a context that would be supportive of contemporary women writers, and the wish to manifest 'what it is to be female', to declare the experience and perceptions that have been unheard. Aware that critical attention concentrated mostly on male writers, these critics demanded a status and recognition for women authors. But the aim was not simply to fit women into the male-dominated tradition; they also wanted to write the history of a tradition *among* women themselves. The extracts from Ellen Moers and Elaine Showalter, building on the earlier work of Virginia Woolf, reveal the affinity which women writers have felt for each other, the interest – sometimes encouraging, sometimes anxiously competitive – that they have taken in each other's work, the way the writing of one might prepare the ground for another, the problems all faced, and still face, in handling the institutions of literary production. The expansion of feminist literary criticism and of courses about women's writing, and the establishment of feminist publishing houses or feminist lists within existing houses introduced to readers an extensive new area of work: it became increasingly difficult for a teacher to use the 'lack of material' argument to explain the absence of women writers from a course.

Showalter offers two cautionary notes. Firstly, she questions Moers's use of the term 'movement', which suggests a steady and continuous development in women's writing, and mentions the 'holes and hiatuses', the absences, gaps and disruptions which have broken that history. Though no writer ever enjoys continuous critical acclaim, Showalter believes that women writers disappear more easily from literary history, leaving their sisters bereft and struggling to reconstruct the fractured tradition.[2] Secondly, Showalter considers that Patricia Meyer Spacks's concept of a 'female imagination' can confirm the belief in 'a deep, basic, and inevitable difference between male and female ways of perceiving the world'. Such 'essentialist' or 'biologicistic' viewpoints imply that there is something both intrinsic in the experience of being female and common to all women. The danger is that gender is privileged at the expense of class or race and that the approach can too easily become ahistorical and apolitical in the assumption of an unproblematic unity among women, across culture, class and history.[3]

At the same time, Showalter would be among the first to stress that the search for women writers has constituted an important political challenge. To ask the questions – Where are the women writers? What has aided or inhibited their writing? How has criticism responded to their work? – introduces into literary criticism the determinant of gender and exposes literary tradition as a construct. The popular idea that 'talent will out', that 'great' writers will spontaneously and inevitably reveal their quality is shown to be false. To the questioning from Marxist criticism about the class bias of the literary tradition are added feminist queries about its androcentricity. What are proposed by mainstream criticism as impartial and objective academic judgements now look, to feminists, value-laden and ideologically suspect.

Who Belongs to the Female Tradition?

The quotation from Olsen hints at two contradictions that have dogged feminist criticism for many years. On the one hand, how can feminism speak of the relentless silencing of women while at the same time maintaining that there is a formidable tradition to uncover? On the other hand, how can feminism claim a rich plurality of female voices and then produce a rather narrow and homogeneous literary heritage – chiefly that of white, middle-class, heterosexual (or presented as heterosexual) women, living in England and America during the nineteenth and twentieth centuries? This description would apply to many of the critical works produced in America in the late 1960s and throughout the 1970s, books which are, rightly, considered founding texts in feminist literary criticism: Mary Ellmann's *Thinking about Women* (first published 1968), Patricia Meyer Spacks's *The Female Imagination* (1975), Ellen Moers's *Literary Women* (first published in the UK 1977), Elaine Showalter's *A Literature of Their Own: British Women Novelists from Brontë to Lessing* (first published 1977). Lesbians, both Black and white, and heterosexual 'women of colour' criticize white, heterosexual feminists for creating a literary history which is almost as selective and ideologically bound as the male tradition. Sexism is challenged in the white, heterosexual work but heterosexism or homophobia or racism or ethnocentricity may not be. Unpalatable as this may be for white, heterosexual feminists, their failure to recognize difference, the presumption that what is said about white, heterosexual women's writing will count for all women has been repeatedly demonstrated by lesbians and Black women. Black critics, for example, complain that the female stereotypes which so preoccupy white feminists – the Southern belle, or the Angel in the House, or the submissive wife – simply do not apply to them, though they are offered in the criticism as the dominant stereotypes and as widely relevant.[4] Where writing from a different position does exist its place is frequently marginal – the odd paragraph, the single essay.

Bonnie Zimmerman, Adrienne Rich and Alice Walker have had to seek out their own traditions, looking for names, for a history, for foremothers. In doing so they dispute the dominant literary values and expose the heterosexism and racism both within and without the women's movement. Rich's emphasis on the *political* importance of lesbianism and on heterosexuality as an institution challengingly moves the debate beyond the level of liberal pluralism. Lesbianism exists not as 'sexual preference', or an 'alternative life style' but as a fundamental critique of the dominant order and as an organizing principle for women. It is worthwhile comparing Rich's views with the even more challenging thesis of Monique Wittig (Chapter 6).

Rich's essay 'Compulsory Heterosexuality and Lesbian Existence' has provoked much productive debate.[5] All three authors have been frequently discussed, anthologized and, in the cases of Zimmerman and Rich, their essays revised and updated.[6] Yet the problem of defining a literary tradition remains as intractable for Black women and lesbians as it does for white women and heterosexuals. Chris Weedon in her extract examines the key question of definition. The meaning of lesbianism, she maintains, is not fixed or dependent solely on the lifestyle of the author or the subject matter of the text; rather, the meaning 'changes with historical shifts in the discursive construction of female sexuality'. Similarly, to locate a Black tradition, Weedon suggests, may rest on more than the racial origin of the author or major characters. Weedon defines a lesbian tradition and a Black, female tradition as political categories. Thus a lesbian tradition is one which challenges heterosexism; a Black feminist tradition is one which critiques both racism and sexism.[7]

The value of Paul Lauter's essay lies in his close inquiry into the kind of historical shift to which Weedon refers. In his case the focus is the creation in American higher education of the 1920s of a middle-class, male, white, professoriate, which was in a position to determine the content of the American literary canon. In Lauter's view, this group, 'virtually eliminated Black, white female and all working-class writers'. What is also admirable in Lauter's study is his ability to integrate issues of race, gender *and* class. With certain honourable exceptions, American feminist critics have been largely unconcerned with the significance of class as a determinant in women's writing or have seen class as synonymous with race: Black denotes working–class; white denotes middle-class.[8] In Britain, the socialist–feminist perspective has made a more concerted attempt to unite class and gender in an understanding of women's writing. The Marxist-Feminist Literature Collective was a pioneer here and formulated an approach which several members of the collective have developed further in their subsequent individual work. However, a different set of historical and cultural factors has led to an under-representation of matters of race in British literary criticism generally.[9]

New Wine in Old Bottles?

Michèle Barrett alerts us to another problem in creating a female tradition, namely that feminists may continue to employ aesthetic concepts that are compromised and intrinsically linked with the very social order they wish to undermine. Lillian Robinson has made the same point. Commenting on the 1970 Modern Languages Association conference she writes: 'the criticism on display reflected an unexamined acceptance of the methods and values of traditional criticism – except for their sexism, of course.'[10]

To talk of the female tradition of writing can reinforce the canonical view which looks upon literary history as a continuum of significant names. Rather than disrupting the individualistic values by which the mainstream has been created, feminist critics may merely replace a male First Eleven with a female one: so you can study Aphra Behn instead of Dryden, Edith Wharton instead of Henry James, Dorothy Wordsworth instead of William. The very approach which has always seemed to find the majority of women writers lacking is transposed, uncritically, to a separate female tradition, and the humanist ethic which supports that approach is accepted as basically valid, only in need of extending its franchise.

As Barrett indicates, the question of aesthetic value has proved to be as problematic for feminists as it has been for Marxists. The reluctance of some feminists to challenge certain conventional literary concepts, together with their eagerness to establish the importance of women's writing have led feminist literary criticism into the occasional cul-de-sac. Barrett would argue that competition with the male tradition constitutes such a dead-end. Competitive criticism proposes either that women have not reached the standard of men because they have not been allowed to, or, alternatively, that they *have* reached the standard of male writers but their work has not been valued. In either case it is the male-dominated tradition which is taken as the reference point for women's writing. Yet, even if we dispose of the canonical, the problem of aesthetic value remains. Why do we find certain works more pleasurable, relevant, important than others? Barrett would say that the first need is to define the 'we'. Aesthetic value is not universal, or eternal; it does not reside within the text. Rather, it is culturally and historically specific, produced in the act of reading. In one sense feminists instinctively realize this. We recognize that the books we hold dear are not always prized by the literary establishment; hence these books cannot have an intrinsic quality to be perceived by *every* reader.

The practices of publishing and marketing continue to fuel the debate. The rewriting of literary history to include women authors, the production of critical series on key women writers, the editing of weighty volumes of women's writing – most notably Sandra Gilbert and Susan Gubar's *The Norton Anthology of Literature by Women* (1985) – are ambiguous undertakings. They provide the needed focus on women's writing, indicate how restricted literary history has been, but often reaffirm a canonical view of literature.[11] Similarly, the marketing of feminist books has reproduced many of the traditional evaluative epithets – witness, for example, Virago's repeated and unquestioning use of the term 'classic'.

The extracts from Linda Williams, Nancy Miller, Mary Jacobus, and Henry Louis Gates, Jr, engage in different ways with this central question: how can feminist and Black forms of criticism create their own traditions without either being hopelessly marginal or unintentionally imitating the dominant modes? For Williams and Jacobus the matrilineal heritage – so clearly evident in Walker's title, 'In Search of Our Mothers' Gardens' – dangerously substitutes a female paradigm of mother and daughter for the male Oedipal model of father and son. Both Jacobus and Miller use the analogy of letter writing to deconstruct the phrase 'female literary tradition'. For Miller, feminist literary theory needs to 'return to sender' all the accepted assumptions and values of literary criticism; for Jacobus, the female literary tradition is a fluid reading and reinterpretation of 'correspondences', in which the position of the feminist reader is as much in dispute as the meanings of the texts or the relationships between texts. Gates, like Jacobus and Miller, does not abandon wholesale 'the great white Western tradition'. He is opposed to any essentialist Black aesthetic and has been instrumental in introducing deconstructive criticism to Black literary studies. His aim, in the words of Jacques Derrida, is 'to speak the other's language without renouncing [our] own'.

The French Perspective

Despite all the problems and qualifications, Anglo-American criticism rests on the presumption that there definitely is a female tradition, buried like hidden treasure in literary history – Showalter uses a different simile and compares feminist literary tradition to the lost continent of Atlantis rising from the sea – and that the task of the feminist critic is to dig it out, brush it down and exhibit it. As we have already seen from Weedon's and Jacobus's pieces, critics influenced by French deconstructive and psychoanalytical theories are not quite so sure that such an entity exists. Viviane Forrester contends that we cannot know what women are. The feminine is that which has been repressed and women's vision – in Forrester's case with regard to film – is only evident in 'what you don't see', what is absent. While Anglo-American critics are looking for women in history, French women writers, Elaine Marks tells us, are: 'looking for women in the unconscious, which is to say in their own language. "Cherchez la femme" might be one of their implied mottos; where repression is, she is'.[12]

Thus, although we may uncover a whole list of forgotten novels by women or films with female directors, feminists of this school are unwilling to see that as necessarily a female tradition. They want to put the questions that Shoshana Felman asks. Are these novelists and directors speaking as women or are they 'speaking the language of men'? Can they be said to be speaking as women simply because they are born female? For instance, do the female Prime Ministers and Presidents of recent history speak as women or are they, regrettably, ventriloquist dummies for the male voice?

Felman's questions raise a further issue echoed in Gayatri Chakravorty Spivak's work. The problem is not only who is speaking and how is she speaking but to whom is she speaking and on behalf of whom is she speaking. Following Derrida's double focus, Spivak stresses: 'not merely who am I? but who is the other woman? How am I naming her? How does she name me?'. Such questioning relates directly to the problems of constructing a female tradition we looked at earlier. The possibility for some feminists to speak, without awareness, from a highly privileged position must result, in part, from not asking, at its deepest level, the question, 'Who am I?'; the neglect of the non-white, or working-class, or lesbian perspectives must relate to the failure to ask, 'To whom am I speaking?'; and the tendency to universalize, to make claims on behalf of all women, must mean that Felman's anxiety about women as, 'the silent and subordinate object' that is 'spoken for', has not been fully heeded. Spivak extends the context of this argument further beyond our own countries to the women of the 'third world'.[13] How are academic 'first world' feminists and illiterate Indian women to speak together with understanding, without patronage, without exploitation, with a full recognition of both community and diversity?

If Miller evokes Medusa as her mythological figure, both Gates and Spivak turn to Janus. Looking two ways, they want to know both the other language and their own, the colonizer and the colonized. Neither rejects out of hand the historical approach and textual analysis of the Anglo-American critics and it is this perspective that Todd reviews in the final extract. Concerned about deconstruction's dismantling of history 'before a "woman's history" has been described', Todd offers an understanding of feminist literary tradition which is both aware of new critical insights and insistent that women do have a literary past.

Notes

1 Tillie Olsen, *Silences* (London, Virago, 1980), p. 23.

2 A relevant study here is Gaye Tuchman (with Nina E. Fortin), *Edging Women Out: Victorian Novelists, Publishers and Social Change* (London, Routledge, 1989).

3 Spacks's work is again used as an example of possible biologism in Peggy Kamuf's extract in ch. 5.

4 See Deborah E. McDowell, 'New Directions for Black Feminist Criticism', in ch. 4. Also Andrea B. Rushing, 'Images of Black Women in Modern African Poetry: An Overview' in *Sturdy Black Bridges: Visions of Black Women in Literature*, eds Roseann P. Bell, Bettye J. Parker, Beverly Guy-Sheftall (New York, Anchor/Doubleday, 1979). Also Alice Walker, 'A Letter of the Times, or Should this Sado-Masochism Be Saved? in *You Can't Keep a Good Woman Down* (New York, Harcourt Brace Jovanovich, 1982).

5 See Ann Ferguson et al., 'On "Compulsory Heterosexuality and Lesbian Existence": Defining the Issues', in *Signs* vol. 7, no. 1 (Autumn 1981); Alice Echols, 'The New Feminism of Yin and Yang', in *Powers of Desire: the Politics of Sexuality*, eds Ann Snitow, Christine Stansell, Sharon Thompson (New York, Monthly Review Press, 1983); Elizabeth Wilson, 'Forbidden Love', in *Feminist Studies*, vol. 10, no. 2 (Summer, 1984); Maggie Humm, *Feminist Criticism: Women as Contemporary Critics* (Brighton, Sussex, The Harvester Press, 1986); Cora Kaplan, 'Wild Nights: Pleasure/Sexuality/Feminism' in her collection *Sea Changes: Essays on Culture and Feminism* (London, Verso, 1986); the Afterword to Rich's own essay in Adrienne Rich, *Blood, Bread, and Poetry: Selected Prose 1979–1985* (London, Virago, 1986); Paulina Palmer, 'Contemporary Lesbian Feminist Fiction: Texts for Everywoman', *Plotting Change*, ed. Linda Anderson (London, Edward Arnold, 1990).

6 As you will see from the Notes to the Rich extract, the essay was updated for the 1983 reprinting. It was supplemented again when included in her collection, *Blood, Bread, and Poetry*. See note 5 above. Similarly, Zimmerman's material has been updated in her contribution to Sally Munt (ed.), *New Lesbian Criticism* (London, Harvester Wheatsheaf, 1992). Here, in 'Lesbians Like This and That: Notes on Lesbian Criticism for the Nineties', she reviews, not the texts, but the developing issues of lesbian criticism since her own essay of 1981.

7 An extract from the Barbara Smith article to which Weedon refers can be found in ch. 2. The issue of definition is considered again in ch. 4.

8 The honourable exceptions would include the work of Tillie Olsen, Lillian Robinson, Judith Newton, Deborah Rosenfelt. See also Elizabeth Abel's essay 'Race, Class, and Psychoanalysis? Opening Questions', in Marianne Hirsch and Evelyn Fox Keller, (eds) *Conflicts in Feminism* (London, Routledge, 1990) and Donna Landry and Gerald MacLean, *Materialist Feminisms* (Oxford, Blackwell Publishers, 1993).

9 Examples of the work of three of the Collective's members – Cora Kaplan, Mary Jacobus and Michèle Barrett – are included elsewhere in this book. Two notes, however, to refer to the socialist–feminist perspective as being characteristically British rather than American does not

mean that all exponents are British; Cora Kaplan, for example, is American by birth. Furthermore not all members of the Collective have continued to work in this mode. Most notably, Mary Jacobus has deliberately excluded from her collection of essays, *Reading Woman: Essays in Feminist Criticism* (London, Methuen, 1986), any work written before 1978. The examples of her work included in this reader are from the post-1978 period, during which time the major influence on her writing has been post-structuralist and psychoanalytic theory. Finally it is also important to recognize the work of Kaplan and Barrett to redress the race-blindness of much British feminism. See Kaplan's collection *Sea Changes: Essays on Culture and Feminism* (see note 5 above); Michèle Barrett and Mary McIntosh, 'Ethnocentricism and Socialist-Feminist Theory', *Feminist Review*, no. 20. (Summer, 1985).

10 Lillian S. Robinson, *Sex, Class, and Culture* (Bloomington and London, Indiana University Press, 1978), p. xxi.

11 The publication of *The Norton Anthology of Literature by Women* revived in the States all the old arguments about the canon, literary value, aesthetics versus politics etc. See Gail Godwin's review of the volume, 'One Woman Leads to Another' in the *New York Times Book Review*, 28 April 1985; Denis Donoghue, 'A Criticism of One's Own', *Men in Feminism*, eds Alice Jardine and Paul Smith (New York and London, Methuen, 1987).

12 Elaine Marks, 'Women and Literature in France', in *Signs: Journal of Women in Culture and Society*, vol. 3, no. 4 (1978), p. 836.

13 In saying 'our own countries', I refer to the countries in which this text is likely to be published and read. The issues of this paragraph are considered further in ch. 6.

Virginia Woolf

A Room of One's Own

And with Mrs. Behn we turn a very important corner on the road. We leave behind, shut up in their parks among their folios, those solitary great ladies who wrote without audience or criticism, for their own delight alone. We come to town and rub shoulders with ordinary people in the streets. Mrs Behn was a middle-class woman with all the plebeian virtues of humour, vitality and courage; a woman forced by the death of her husband and some unfortunate adventures of her own to make her living by her wits. She had to work on equal terms with men. She made, by working very hard, enough to live on. The importance of that fact outweighs anything that she actually wrote, even the splendid 'A Thousand Martyrs I have made', or 'Love in Fantastic Triumph sat', for here begins the freedom of the mind, or rather the possibility that in the course of time the mind will be free to write what it likes. For now that Aphra Behn had done it, girls could go to their parents and say, You need not give me an allowance; I can make money by my pen. Of course the answer for many years to come was, Yes, by living the life of Aphra Behn! Death would be better! and the door was slammed faster than ever. That profoundly interesting subject, the value that men set upon women's chastity and its effect upon their education, here suggests itself for discussion, and might provide an interesting book if any student at Girton or Newnham cared to go into the matter. Lady Dudley, sitting in diamonds among the midges of a Scottish moor, might serve for frontispiece. Lord Dudley, *The Times* said when Lady Dudley died the other day, 'a man of cultivated taste and many accomplishments, was benevolent and bountiful, but whimsically despotic. He insisted upon his wife's wearing full dress, even at the remotest shooting-lodge in the Highlands; he loaded her with gorgeous jewels', and so on, 'he gave her everything – always excepting any measure of responsibility'. Then Lord Dudley had a stroke and she nursed him and ruled his estates with supreme competence for ever after. That whimsical despotism was in the nineteenth century too.

But to return. Aphra Behn proved that money could be made by writing at the sacrifice, perhaps, of certain agreeable qualities; and so by degrees writing became not merely a sign of folly and a distracted mind, but was of practical importance. A husband might die, or some disaster overtake the family. Hundreds of women began as the eighteenth century drew on to add to their pin money, or to come to the rescue of their families by making translations or writing the innumerable bad novels which have ceased to be recorded even in text-books, but are to be picked up in the fourpenny boxes in the Charing Cross Road.[7] The extreme activity of mind which showed itself in the later eighteenth century among women – the talking, and the meeting, the writing of essays on Shakespeare, the translating of the classics – was founded on the solid fact that women could make money by writing. Money dignifies what is frivolous if unpaid for. It might still be well to sneer at 'blue stockings with an itch for scribbling', but it could not be denied that they could put money in their purses. Thus, towards the end of the eighteenth century a change came about which, if I were rewriting history, I should describe more fully and think of greater importance than the Crusades or the Wars of the Roses. The middle-class woman began to write. For if *Pride and Prejudice* matters, and *Middlemarch* and *Villette* and *Wuthering Heights* matter, then it matters far more than I can prove in an hour's discourse that women generally, and not merely the lonely aristocrat shut up in her country house among her folios and her flatterers, took to writing. Without those forerunners, Jane Austen and the Brontës and George Eliot could no more have written than Shakespeare could have written without Marlowe, or Marlowe without Chaucer, or Chaucer without those forgotten poets who paved the ways and tamed the natural savagery of the tongue. For masterpieces are not single and solitary births; they are the outcome of many years of thinking in common, of thinking by the body of the people, so that the experience of the mass is behind the single voice. Jane Austen should have laid a wreath upon the grave of Fanny Burney, and George Eliot done homage to the robust shade of Eliza Carter[8] – the valiant old woman who tied a bell to her bedstead in order that she might wake early and learn Greek. All women together ought to let flowers fall upon the tomb of Aphra Behn which is, most scandalously but rather appropriately, in Westminster Abbey, for it was she who earned them the right to speak their minds. It is she – shady and amorous as she was – who makes it not quite fantastic for me to say to you tonight: Earn five hundred a year by your wits.

(1929)

Notes

7 *Charing Cross Road*: in London, a centre for second-hand bookshops.
8 *Eliza Carter*: Elizabeth Carter (1717–1806), translator of Epictetus, letter-writer, friend of Dr Johnson and an original 'blue stocking'. The 'blue stockings' were a group of women who hosted evening parties in the 1750s. Eschewing card games and evening dress in favour of literary conversation, they invited eminent men of letters to take part in their discussions. One member of the group, Benjamin Stillingfleet, regulary attended wearing blue worsted stockings instead of black evening clothes, giving rise to the nickname 'blue stocking' for a woman with literary tastes.

ELLEN MOERS

Literary Women

We dwell with satisfaction upon the poet's difference from her predecessors, especially her immediate predecessors: we endeavor to find something that can be isolated in

*order to be enjoyed. Whereas if we approach a poet without this prejudice we shall
often find that not only the best, but the most individual parts of her work may be
those in which the dead poets, her ancestors, assert their immortality most vigorously.*

T. S. Eliot

I

To be a woman writer long meant, may still mean, belonging to a literary
movement apart from but hardly subordinate to the mainstream: an undercurrent, rapid and powerful. The word 'movement' gives an inaccurate idea
of an association often remote and indirect. To use the word George Sand
imposed, and speak of a 'solidarity' of women, would also be misleading, for
writing women have never felt much of a sentimental loyalty to their own
kind – quite the contrary. The harshest criticism of trashy books by lady
writers came from women writers themselves; sometimes, as in the case of
Elizabeth Rigby's famous review of *Jane Eyre*, they denounced books that
were not trashy at all. George Eliot's 'Silly Novels by Lady Novelists' of 1856
is the classic of the genre, as well as one of the funniest pieces of serious
criticism ever written; but long before, in 1789, there was Mary Wollstonecraft's swift dispatch of one of the worst specimens of female pap that she
encountered as a reviewer with the line. 'Pray Miss, write no more!'

Not loyalty but confidence was the resource that women writers drew
from the possession of their own tradition. And it was a confidence that
until very recently could come from no other source. Male writers have
always been able to study their craft in university or coffeehouse, group
themselves into movements or coteries, search out predecessors for guidance
or patronage, collaborate or fight with their contemporaries. But women
through most of the nineteenth century were barred from the universities,
isolated in their own homes, chaperoned in travel, painfully restricted in
friendship. The personal give-and-take of the literary life was closed to them.
Without it, they studied with a special closeness the works written by their
own sex, and developed a sense of easy, almost rude familiarity with the
women who wrote them.

When fame at last propelled Charlotte Brontë to London and gave her the
opportunity to meet her greatest male contemporaries, she exhibited an
awkwardness and timidity in literary society that have become legendary –
except in one encounter, that with Harriet Martineau, to whom she sent a
brusquely confident note soliciting a meeting. 'I could not help feeling a
strong wish to see you,' she wrote; '. . . It would grieve me to lose this chance
of seeing one whose works have so often made her the subject of my
thoughts.' And George Eliot could write in her first letter to Harriet Beecher
Stowe, though they had not and would not ever meet, that she knew her as
a woman as well as a writer, for she had years before taken the liberty, rude
but comprehensible, of reading Mrs. Stowe's intimate correspondence with

another woman. Later Stowe and George Eliot would correspond about the source of Casaubon in *Middlemarch*; their letters provide a tragicomedy of mutual misunderstanding about each other's married life, but they also reveal that there is a human component to literature which a woman writer can more easily discuss with another woman writer, even across an ocean, than she can with the literary man next door.

Emily Dickinson's literary solitude was breached by the incorporeal presence of women writers she knew exclusively but intimately from reading their works and everything she could find about their lives. Jack Capps calls it an 'intimate kinship,' and the phrase is excellent, because it suggests a family relationship which can be either hostile or loving, competitive or supportive, but is always available. Through the closed doors and narrow windows that so often shut on the literary woman's life seeped a whole family of literary relationships for her to exploit: patterns to be followed, deficiencies to be made up, abuses to correct, achievements in works by other women to surpass. What was supplied for the nourishment of male literary production by simple acquaintance was replaced for women writers by the reading of each other's work, reading for intimate reverberation, for what Gertrude Stein called 'a sounding board.'

Take Jane Austen on the one hand, and her contemporaries Wordsworth, Coleridge, and Southey on the other. Wordsworth went to Bristol to meet Coleridge; both were Cambridge men, and they had university friends in common. At Bristol, Wordsworth found Coleridge rooming with an Oxford undergraduate named Southey: they were planning to emigrate to America. Instead, Wordsworth and Coleridge drew close together, settled near each other in the Lake District, and collaborated on a volume which made history, called *Lyrical Ballads*. Meanwhile Jane Austen, almost exactly the same age and from a similar social milieu (had she been a man, she would probably have gone to university), stayed home with her mother at Steventon, Bath, and Chawton. She visited a brother's family now and then, wrote letters to sister and nieces, and read Sarah Harriet Burney, Mrs. Jane West, Anna Maria Porter, Mrs. Anne Grant, Elisabeth Hamilton, Laetitia Matilda Hawkins, Helen Maria Williams, and the rest of the women writers of her day.

'I think I may boast myself to be, with all possible vanity,' she once said, 'the most unlearned and uniformed female who ever dared to be an authoress.' Scholars have industriously scraped together evidence that softens if it does not essentially alter this self-portrait; for Austen of course knew something of the major English writers from Shakespeare to Johnson and read the best poetry of her day. But scholarship has averted its refined and weary eyes from the female fiction that Austen's letters inform us was her daily sustenance in the years that she became one of the greatest writers in the language. Who wants to associate the great Jane Austen, companion of

Shakespeare, with someone named Mary Brunton? Who wants to read or indeed can find a copy of *Self-Control* (1810) by that lady, which Austen was nervous about reading while revising *Sense and Sensibility* for publication and starting *Mansfield Park*, nervous because she was 'always half afraid of finding a clever novel *too clever* – and of finding my own story and my own people all forestalled.' She did, however, read and reread the Brunton book, and said (jokingly), 'I will redeem my credit . . . by writing a close imitation of "Self-Control" . . . I will improve upon it.'

It can be argued that Jane Austen achieved the classical perfection of her fiction because there was a mass of women's novels, excellent, fair, and wretched, for her to study and improve upon. Mary Brunton and the rest of the ladies were her own kind; she was at ease with them. They were her undergraduate fellows in the novel, her literary roommates and incorporeal collaborators, as someone like Walter Scott could never be. Austen's comment on Scott, when she learned he had turned to the then woman-dominated field of fiction, was wickedly female but also half-serious. 'Walter Scott has no business to write novels, especially good ones. – It is not fair. – He has Fame and Profit enough as a Poet, and should not be taking the bread out of other people's mouths. – I do not like him, & do not mean to like Waverley if I can help it – but fear I must.' The fact is that Austen studied Maria Edgeworth more attentively than Scott, and Fanny Burney more than Richardson: and she came closer to meeting Mme de Staël than she did to meeting any of the literary men of her age.

In the case of some women writers, Austen preeminent among them, women's literature has been their major tradition; in the case of others – and I think quality has nothing to do with the difference – it has mattered hardly at all: here Emily Brontë's name comes to mind. In the case of most women writers, women's traditions have been fringe benefits superadded upon the literary associations of period, nation, and class that they shared with their male contemporaries.

In spite of the advent of coeducation, which by rights should have ended this phenomenon, twentieth-century women appear to benefit still from their membership in the wide-spreading family of women writers. Willa Cather, exceptionally well trained to literature in the educational and journalistic institutions of a man's world, found her literary mentor in Sarah Orne Jewett; in that relationship sex easily canceled out the distance between Nebraska and Maine. Even wider incongruities appear in the productive pairings of Jean Rhys and Charlotte Brontë, Carson McCullers and Isak Dinesen, Nathalie Sarraute and Ivy Compton-Burnett. And the last provided, in her first novel, *Dolores*, the oddest exhibit that women's literature has to offer: a groping retrieval of what could be made modern in Austen and Gaskell, necessary to Compton-Burnett's development of her own apparently idiosyncratic fictional manner.

(1977)

Elaine Showalter

A Literature of Their Own: British Women Novelists from
Brontë to Lessing

As the works of dozens of women writers have been rescued from what E. P. Thompson calls 'the enormous condescension of posterity,'[16] and considered in relation to each other, the lost continent of the female tradition has risen like Atlantis from the sea of English literature. It is now becoming clear that, contrary to Mill's theory, women have had a literature of their own all along. The woman novelist, according to Vineta Colby, was 'really neither single nor anomalous,' but she was also more than a 'register and a spokesman for her age.'[17] She was part of a tradition that had its origins before her age, and has carried on through our own.

Many literary historians have begun to reinterpret and revise the study of women writers. Ellen Moers sees women's literature as an international movement, 'apart from, but hardly subordinate to the mainstream: an undercurrent, rapid and powerful. This "movement" began in the late eighteenth century, was multinational, and produced some of the greatest literary works of two centuries, as well as most of the lucrative pot-boilers.'[18] Patricia Meyer Spacks, in *The Female Imagination*, finds that 'for readily discernible historical reasons women have characteristically concerned themselves with matters more or less peripheral to male concerns, or at least slightly skewed from them. The differences between traditional female preoccupations and roles and male ones make a difference in female writing.'[19] Many other critics are beginning to agree that when we look at women writers collectively we can see an imaginative continuum, the recurrence of certain patterns, themes, problems, and images from generation to generation.

This book is an effort to describe the female literary tradition in the English novel from the generation of the Brontës to the present day, and to show how the development of this tradition is similar to the development of any literary subculture. Women have generally been regarded as 'sociological chameleons,' taking on the class, lifestyle, and culture of their male relatives. It can, however, be argued that women themselves have constituted a subculture within the framework of a larger society, and have been unified by values, conventions, experiences, and behaviors impinging on each individual. It is important to see the female literary tradition in these broad terms, in relation to the wider evolution of women's self-awareness and to the ways in which any minority group finds its direction of self-expression relative to a dominant society, because we cannot show a pattern of deliberate progress and accumulation. It is true, as Ellen Moers writes, that 'women studied with a special closeness the works written by their own sex';[20] in terms of influences, borrowings, and affinities, the tradition is strongly marked. But it is also full of holes and hiatuses, because of what Germaine Greer calls the 'phenomenon of the transience of female literary fame'; 'almost uninterruptedly since the Interregnum, a small group of women have enjoyed dazzling literary prestige during their own lifetimes, only to vanish without trace from the records of posterity.'[21] Thus each generation of women writers has found itself, in a sense, without a history, forced to rediscover the past anew, forging again and again the consciousness of their sex. Given this perpetual disruption, and also the self-hatred that has alienated women writers from a sense of collective identity, it does not seem possible to speak of a 'movement.'

I am also uncomfortable with the notion of a 'female imagination.' The theory of a female sensibility revealing itself in an imagery and form specific to women always runs dangerously close to reiterating the familiar stereo-types. It also suggests permanence, a deep, basic, and inevitable difference between male and female ways of perceiving the world. I think that, instead, the female literary tradition comes from the still-evolving relationships between women writers and their society. Moreover, the 'female imagination' cannot be treated by literary historians as a romantic or Freudian abstraction. It is the product of a delicate network of influences operating in time, and it must be analyzed as it expresses itself, in language and in a fixed arrangement of words on a page, a form that itself is subject to a network of influences and conventions, including the operations of the marketplace. In this investigation of the English novel, I am intentionally looking, not at an innate sexual attitude, but at the ways in which the self-awareness of the woman writer has translated itself into a literary form in a specific place and time-span, how this self-awareness has changed and developed, and where it might lead.

I am therefore concerned with the professional writer who wants pay and publication, not with the diarist or letter-writer. This emphasis has required careful consideration of the novelists, as well as the novels, chosen for discussion. When we turn from the overview of the literary tradition to look at the individuals who composed it, a different but interrelated set of motives, drives, and sources becomes prominent. I have needed to ask why women began to write for money and how they negotiated the activity of writing within their families. What was their professional self-image? How was their work received, and what effects did criticism have upon them? What were their experiences as women, and how were these reflected in books? What was their understanding of womanhood? What were their relationships to other women, to men, and to their readers? How did changes in women's status affect their lives and careers? And how did the vocation of writing itself change the women who committed themselves to it? In looking at literary subcultures, such as black, Jewish, Canadian, Anglo-Indian, or even Ameri-can, we can see that they all go through three major phases. First, there is a prolonged phase of *imitation* of the prevailing modes of the dominant tradition, and *internalization* of its standards of art and its views on social roles. Second, there is a phase of *protest* against these standards and values, and *advocacy* of minority rights and values, including a demand for autonomy. Finally, there is a phase of *self-discovery*, a turning inward freed from some of the dependency of opposition, a search for identity.[22] An appropriate terminology for women writers is to call these stages, *Feminine, Feminist*, and *Female*. These are obviously not rigid categories, distinctly separable in time, to which individual writers can be assigned with perfect assurance. The phases overlap; there are feminist elements in feminine writing, and vice versa. One might also find all three phases in the career of a single novelist. Nonetheless, it seems useful to point to periods of crisis when a shift of literary values occurred. In this book I identify the Feminine phase as the period from the appearance of the male pseudonym in the 1840s to the death of George Eliot in 1880; the Feminist phase as 1880 to 1920, or the winning of the vote; and the Female phase as 1920 to the present, but entering a new stage of self-awareness about 1960.

It is important to understand the female subculture not only as what Cynthia Ozick calls 'custodial'[23] – a set of opinions, prejudices, tastes, and values prescribed for a subordinate group to perpetuate its subordination – but also as a thriving and positive entity. Most discussions of women as a subculture have come from historians describing Jacksonian America, but they apply equally well to the situation of early Victorian England. According to Nancy Cott, 'we can view women's group consciousness as a subculture uniquely divided against itself by ties to the dominant culture. While the ties to the dominant culture are the informing and restricting ones, they provoke within the subculture certain strengths as well as weaknesses, enduring values as well as accommodations.'[24] The middle-class ideology of the proper sphere of womanhood, which developed in post-industrial England and America, prescribed a woman who would be a Perfect Lady, an Angel in the House, contentedly submissive to men, but strong in her inner purity and religiosity, queen in her own realm of the Home.[25] Many observers have pointed out that the first professional activities of Victorian women, as social reformers, nurses, governesses, and novelists, either were based in the home or were extensions of the feminine role as teacher, helper, and mother of mankind. In describing the American situation, two historians have seen a subculture emerging from the doctrine of sexual spheres:

> By "subculture" we mean simply "a habit of living" . . . of a minority group which is self-consciously distinct from the dominant activities, expectations, and values of a society. Historians have seen female church groups, reform associations, and philanthropic activity as expressions of this subculture in actual behavior, while a large and rich body of writing by and for women articulated the subculture impulses on the ideational level. Both behavior and thought point to child-rearing, religious activity, education, home life, associ-

ationism, and female communality as components of women's subculture. Female friendships, strikingly intimate and deep in this period, formed the actual bonds.[26]

For women in England, the female subculture came first through a shared and increasingly secretive and ritualized physical experience. Puberty, menstruation, sexual initiation, pregnancy, childbirth, and menopause – the entire female sexual life cycle – constituted a habit of living that had to be concealed. Although these episodes could not be openly discussed or acknowledged, they were accompanied by elaborate rituals and lore, by external codes of fashion and etiquette, and by intense feelings of female solidarity.[27] Women writers were united by their roles as daughters, wives, and mothers; by the internalized doctrines of evangelicalism, with its suspicion of the imagination and its emphasis on duty; and by legal and economic constraints on their mobility. Sometimes they were united in a more immediate way, around a political cause. On the whole these are the implied unities of culture, rather than the active unities of consciousness.

From the beginning, however, women novelists' awareness of each other and of their female audience showed a kind of covert solidarity that sometimes amounted to a genteel conspiracy. Advocating sisterhood, Sarah Ellis, one of the most conservative writers of the first Victorian generation, asked: 'What should we think of a community of slaves, who betrayed each other's interests? of a little band of shipwrecked mariners upon a friendless shore who were false to each other? of the inhabitants of a defenceless nation, who would not unite together in earnestness and good faith against a common enemy?'[28] Mrs. Ellis felt the binding force of the minority experience for women strongly enough to hint, in the prefaces to her widely read treatises on English womanhood, that her female audience would both read the messages between her lines and refrain from betraying what they deciphered. As another conservative novelist, Dinah Mulock Craik, wrote, 'The intricacies of female nature are incomprehensible except to a woman; and any biographer of real womanly feeling, if ever she discovered, would never dream of publishing them.'[29] Few English women writers openly advocated the use of fiction as revenge against a patriarchal society (as did the American novelist Fanny Fern, for example), but many confessed to sentiments of 'maternal feeling, sisterly affection, *esprit de corps*'[30] for their readers. Thus the clergyman's daughter, going to Mudie's for her three-decker novel by another clergyman's daughter, participated in a cultural exchange that had a special personal significance.

(1977)

Notes

16 *The Making of the English Working Class*, New York, 1973, p. 12.
17 Vineta Colby, *The Singular Anomaly: Women Novelists of the Nineteenth Century*, New York, 1970, p. 11.

18 'Women's Lit: Profession and Tradition,' *Columbia Forum 1* (Fall 1972): 27.
19 Spacks, p. 7.
20 Moers, 'Women's Lit.' 28.
21 'Flying Pigs and Double Standards,' *Times Literary Supplement*, (July 26, 1974): 784.
22 For helpful studies of literary subcultures, see Robert A. Bone, *The Negro Novel in America*, New York, 1958; and Northrop Frye, 'Conclusion to *A Literary History of Canada*,' in *The Stubborn Structure: Essays on Criticism and Society*, Ithaca, 1970, pp. 278–312.
23 'Women and Creativity,' p. 442.
24 Nancy F. Cott, introduction to *Root of Bitterness*, New York, 1972, pp. 3–4.
25 For the best discussions of the Victorian feminine ideal, see Françoise Basch, 'Contemporary Ideologies,' in *Relative Creatures*, pp. 3–15; Walter E. Houghton, *The Victorian Frame of Mind*, New Haven, 1957, pp. 341–343; and Alexander Welsh's theory of the Angel in the House in *The City of Dickens*, London, 1971, pp. 164–195.
26 Christine Stansell and Johnny Faragher, 'Women and Their Families on the Overland Trail, 1842–1867,' *Feminist Studies* 11 (1975): 152–153. For an overview of recent historical scholarship on the 'two cultures,' see Barbara Sicherman, 'Review: American History.' *Signs: Journal of Women in Culture and Society* 1 (Winter 1975): 470–484.
27 For a sociological account of patterns of behavior for Victorian women, see Leonore Davidoff, *The Best Circles: Society, Etiquette and the Season*, London, 1973, esp. pp. 48–58, 85–100.
28 Sarah Ellis, *The Daughters of England*, New York, 1844, ch. ix, p. 90.
29 Dinah M. Craik, 'Literary Ghouls,' *Studies from Life*, New York, n.d., p. 13.
30 Letter of October 6, 1851, in *Letters of E. Jewsbury to Jane Welsh Carlyle*, ed. Mrs. Alex Ireland, London, 1892, p. 426. For Fanny Fern, see Ann Douglas Wood, 'The "Scribbling Women" and Fanny Fern: Why Women Wrote,' *American Quarterly* XXIII (Spring 1971): 1–24.

BONNIE ZIMMERMAN

'What Has Never Been: An Overview of Lesbian Feminist Literary Criticism' Feminist Studies

One way in which this unique world view takes shape is as a 'critical consciousness about heterosexist assumptions.'[5] Heterosexism is the set of values and structures that assumes heterosexuality to be the only natural form of sexual and emotional expression, '*the* perceptual screen provided by our [patriarchal] cultural conditioning.'[6] Heterosexist assumptions abound in literary texts, such as feminist literary anthologies, that purport to be open-minded about lesbianism. When authors' biographies make special note of husbands, male mentors, and male companions, even when that author was primarily female-identified, but fail to mention the female companions of prominent lesbian writers – that is heterosexism. When anthologists ignore historically significant lesbian writers such as Renée Vivien and Radclyffe Hall – that is heterosexism. When anthologies include only the heterosexual or nonsexual works of a writer like Katherine Philips or Adrienne Rich who is celebrated for her lesbian or homo-emotional poetry – that is heterosexism. When a topically organized anthology includes sections on wives, mothers, sex objects, young girls, aging women, and liberated women, but not lesbians – that is heterosexism. Heterosexism in feminist anthologies – like the sexism of androcentric collections – serves to obliterate lesbian existence and maintain the lie that women have searched for emotional and sexual fulfilment only through men – or not at all.

Lesbians have also expressed concern that the absence of lesbian material in women's studies journals such as *Feminist Studies*, *Women's Studies*, and *Women and Literature* indicates heterosexism either by omission or by design. Only in 1979 did lesbian-focused articles appear in *Signs* and *Frontiers*. Most lesbian criticism first appeared in alternative, non-establishment lesbian journals, particularly *Sinister Wisdom* and *Conditions*, which are unfamiliar to many feminist scholars. For example, *Signs*' first review article on literary criticism by Elaine Showalter (1975) makes no mention of lesbianism as a theme or potential critical perspective, not even to point out its absence. Annette Kolodny, in the second review article in *Signs* (1976), does call Jane Rule's *Lesbian Images* 'a novelist's challenge to the academy and its accompanying critical community,' and further criticizes the homophobia in then-current biographies, calling for 'candor and sensitivity' in future work.[7] However, neither this nor subsequent review articles familiarize the reader with 'underground' sources of lesbian criticism, some of which had appeared by this time, nor do they explicate lesbianism as a literary theme or critical perspective. Ironically, more articles on lesbian literature have appeared in traditional literary journals than in the women's studies press, just as for years only male critics felt free to mention lesbianism. Possibly, feminist critics continue to feel that they will be identified as 'dykes,' thus invalidating their work.

The perceptual screen of heterosexism is also evident in most of the acclaimed works of feminist literary criticism. None of the current collections of essays – such as *The Authority of Experience* or *Shakespeare's Sisters* – includes even a token article from a lesbian perspective. Ellen Moers' *Literary Women*, germinal work as it is, is homophobic as well as heterosexist. Lesbians, she points out, appear as monsters, grotesques, and freaks in works by Carson McCullers, Djuna Barnes (her reading of *Nightwood* is at the very least questionable), and Diane Arbus, but she seems to concur in this identification rather than call it into question or explain its historical context. Although her so-called defense of unmarried women writers against the 'charge' of lesbianism does criticize the way in which this word has been used as a slur, she neither condemns such antilesbianism nor entertains the possibility that some women writers were, in fact, lesbians. Her chapter on 'Loving Heroinism' is virtually textbook heterosexism, assuming as it does that women writers only articulate love for men.[8] Perceptual blinders also mar *The Female Imagination* by Patricia Meyer Spacks which never uses the word 'lesbian' (except in the index) or 'lover' to describe either the 'sexual ambiguity' of the bond between Jane and Helen in *Jane Eyre*, nor Margaret Anderson's relationship with a 'beloved older woman.' Furthermore, Spacks claims that Gertrude Stein, 'whose life lack[ed] real attachments' (a surprise to Alice B. Toklas), also 'denied whatever is special to women' (which lesbianism is not?).[9] This latter judgment is particularly ominous because heterosexuals often have difficulty accepting that a lesbian, especially a role-playing 'butch,' is in fact a woman. More care is demonstrated by Elaine Showalter who, in *A Literature of Their Own*, uncovers the attitudes toward lesbianism held by nineteenth-century writers Eliza Lynn Linton and Mrs. Humphrey Ward. However, she does not integrate lesbian issues into her discussion of the crucial generation of early twentieth-century writers (Virginia Woolf, Vita Sackville-West, Dorothy Richardson, and Rosamond Lehmann among others; Radclyffe Hall is mentioned, but not *The Well of Loneliness*), all of whom wrote about sexual love between women. Her well-taken point that modern British novelists avoid lesbianism might have been balanced, however, by a mention of Maureen Duffy, Sybille Bedford, or Fay Weldon.[10] Finally, Sandra Gilbert and Susan Gubar's *The Madwoman in the Attic* does not even index lesbianism; the lone reference made in the text is to the possibility that 'Goblin Market' describes 'a covertly (if ambiguously) lesbian world.' The authors' tendency to interpret all pairs of female characters as aspects of the self sometimes serves to mask a relationship that a lesbian reader might interpret as bonding or love between women.[11]

Lesbian critics, who as feminists owe much to these critical texts, have had to turn to other resources, first to develop a lesbian canon, and then to establish a lesbian critical perspective. Barbara Grier who, as Gene Damon, reviewed books for the pioneering lesbian journal *The Ladder*, laid the groundwork for this canon with her incomparable, but largely unknown *The Lesbian in Literature: A Bibliography*.[12] Equally obscure was Jeanette Foster's *Sex Variant Women in Literature*, self-published in 1956 after having been rejected by a university press because of its subject matter. An exhaustive chronological account of every reference to love between women from Sappho and Ruth to the fiction of the fifties, *Sex Variant Women* has proven to be an invaluable starting point for lesbian readers and scholars. Out of print almost immediately after its publication and lost to all but a few intrepid souls, it was finally reprinted by Diana Press in 1975.[13] A further resource and gathering point for lesbian critics was the special issue on lesbian writing and publishing in *Margins*, a review of small press publications, which appeared in 1975, the first issue of a literary journal devoted entirely to lesbian writing. In 1976, its editor, Beth Hodges, produced a second special issue, this time in *Sinister Wisdom*.[14] Along with the growing visibility and solidarity of lesbians within the academic profession, and the increased availability of lesbian literature from feminist and mass-market presses, these two journal issues propelled lesbian feminist literary criticism to the surface.[15]

The literary resources available to lesbian critics form only part of the story, for lesbian criticism is equally rooted in political ideology. Although not all lesbian critics are activists, most have been strongly influenced by the politics of lesbian feminism. These politics travel the continuum from civil rights advocacy to separatism; however, most, if not all, lesbian feminists assume that lesbianism is a healthy lifestyle chosen by women in virtually all eras and all cultures, and thus strive to eliminate the stigma historically attached to lesbianism. One way to remove this stigma is to associate lesbianism with positive and desirable attributes, to divert women's attention away from male values and toward an exclusively female communitas. Thus, the influential Radicalesbians' essay, 'The Woman-Identified Woman,' argues that lesbian feminism assumes 'the primacy of women relating to women, of women creating a new consciousness of and with each other. . . . We see ourselves as prime, find our centers inside of ourselves.'[16] Many lesbian writers and critics have also been influenced profoundly by the politics of separatism which provides a critique of heterosexuality as a political institution rather than a personal choice, 'because relationships between men and women are essentially political, they involve power and dominance.'[17] As we shall see, the notion of 'woman-identification,' that is, the primacy of women bonding with women emotionally and politically, as well as the premises of separatism, that lesbians have a unique and critical place at the margins of patriarchal society, are central to much current lesbian literary criticism.

[. . .]

One of the first tasks of this emerging lesbian criticism has been to provide lesbians with a tradition, even if a retrospective one. Jane Rule, whose *Lesbian Images* appeared about the same time as *Literary Women*, first attempted to establish this tradition.[33] Although her text is problematic, relying overly much on biographical evidence and derivative interpretations and including some questionable writers (such as Dorothy Baker) while omitting others, *Lesbian Images* was a milestone in lesbian criticism. Its importance is partially suggested by the fact that it took five years for another complete book – Faderman's – to appear on lesbian literature. In a review of *Lesbian Images*, I questioned the existence of a lesbian 'great tradition' in literature, but now I think I was wrong.[34] Along with Rule, Dolores Klaich in *Woman Plus Woman* and Louise Bernikow in the introduction to *The World Split Open* have explored the possibility of a lesbian tradition,[35] and recent critics such as Faderman and Cook in particular have begun to define that tradition, who belongs to it, and what links the writers who can be identified as lesbians. Cook's review of lesbian literature and culture in the early twentieth century proposes 'to analyze the literature and attitudes out of which the present lesbian feminist works have emerged, and to examine the continued denials and invalidation of the lesbian experience.'[36] Focusing on the recognized lesbian networks in France and England that included Virginia Woolf, Vita Sackville-West, Ethel Smythe, Gertrude Stein, Radclyffe Hall, Natalie

Barney, and Romaine Brooks, Cook provides an important outline of a lesbian cultural tradition and an insightful analysis of the distortions and denials of homophobic scholars, critics, and biographers.

Faderman's *Surpassing the Love of Men*, like her earlier critical articles, ranges more widely through a literary tradition of romantic love between women (whether or not one calls that 'lesbian') from the sixteenth to the twentieth centuries. Her thesis is that passionate love between women was labeled neither abnormal nor undesirable – probably because women were perceived to be asexual – until the sexologists led by Krafft-Ebing and Havelock Ellis 'morbidified' female friendship around 1900.

Although she does not always clarify the dialectic between idealization and condemnation that is suggested in her text, Faderman's basic theory is quite convincing. Most readers, like myself, will be amazed at the wealth of information about women's same-sex love that Faderman has uncovered. She rescues from heterosexual obscurity Mary Wollstonecraft, Mary Wortley Montagu, Anna Seward, Sarah Orne Jewett, Edith Somerville, 'Michael Field,' and many others, including the Scottish schoolmistresses whose lesbian libel suit inspired Lillian Hellman's *The Children's Hour*. Faderman has also written on the theme of same-sex love and romantic friendship in poems and letters of Emily Dickinson; in novels by Henry James, Oliver Wendell Holmes, and Henry Wadsworth Longfellow; and in popular magazine fiction of the early twentieth century.[37]

Faderman is preeminent among those critics who are attempting to establish a lesbian tradition by rereading writers of the past previously assumed to be heterosexual or 'spinsters.' As songwriter Holly Near expresses it: 'Lady poet of great acclaim/I have been misreading you/I never knew your poems were meant for me.'[38] It is in this area of lesbian scholarship that the most controversy – and some of the most exciting work – occurs. Was Mary Wollstonecraft's passionate love for Fanny Blood, recorded in *Mary, A Fiction*, lesbian? Does Henry James dissect a lesbian relationship in *The Bostonians*? Did Emily Dickinson address many of her love poems to a woman, not a man? How did Virginia Woolf's relationships with Vita Sackville-West and Ethel Smythe affect her literary vision? Not only are some lesbian critics increasingly naming such women and relationships 'lesbian,' they are also suggesting that criticism cannot fail to take into account the influence of sexual and emotional orientation on literary expression.

In the establishment of a self-conscious literary tradition, certain writers have become focal points both for critics and for lesbians in general, who affirm and celebrate their identity by 'naming names,' establishing a sense of historical continuity and community through the knowledge that incontrovertibly great women were also lesbians. Foremost among these heroes (or 'heras') are the women who created the first self-identified lesbian feminist community in Paris during the early years of the twentieth century. With

Natalie Barney at its hub, this circle included such notable writers as Colette, Djuna Barnes, Radclyffe Hall, Renée Vivien, and, peripherally, Gertrude Stein. Contemporary lesbians – literary critics, historians, and layreaders – have been drawn to their mythic and mythmaking presence, seeing in them a vision of lesbian society and culture that may have existed only once before – on the original island of Lesbos.[39] More interest, however, has been paid to their lives so far than to their art. Barnes's portraits of decadent, tormented lesbians and homosexuals in *Nightwood* and silly, salacious ones in *The Ladies Almanack* often prove troublesome to lesbian readers and critics.[40] However, Elaine Marks's perceptive study of French lesbian writers traces a tradition and how it has changed, modified by circumstance and by feminism, from the Sappho of Renée Vivien to the amazons of Monique Wittig.[41]

(1981)

Notes

5 Elly Bulkin, ' "Kissing Against the Light": A Look at Lesbian Poetry,' *Radical Teacher* 10 (December 1978): 8. This article was reprinted in *College English* and *Women's Studies Newsletter*, an expanded version is available from the Lesbian-Feminist Study Clearinghouse, Women's Studies Program, University of Pittsburgh, Pittsburgh, Pennsylvania 15260.

6 Julia Penelope [Stanley], 'The Articulation of Bias: Hoof in Mouth Disease,' paper presented at the 1979 convention of the National Council of Teachers of English, San Francisco, November 1979, pp. 4–5. On the same panel, I presented a paper on 'Heterosexism in Literary Anthologies,' which develops some of the points of this paragraph.

7 Annette Kolodny, 'Literary Criticism: Review Essay,' *Signs* 2, no. 2 (Winter 1976): 416, 419.

8 Ellen Moers, *Literary Women: The Great Writers* (Garden City, N.Y.: Doubleday & Co., 1976), pp. 108–9, 145.

9 Patricia Meyer Spacks, *The Female Imagination* (New York: Avon Books, 1975), pp. 89, 214, 363.

10 Elaine Showalter, *A Literature of Their Own: British Women Novelists From Brontë to Lessing* (Princeton: Princeton University Press, 1977), pp. 178, 229, 316.

11 Sandra M. Gilbert and Susan Gubar, *The Madwoman in the Attic: The Woman Writer and the Nineteenth Century Literary Imagination* (New Haven: Yale University Press, 1979), p. 567. Regarding another issue – their analysis of Emily Dickinson's poem no. 1722 – Nadean Bishop says, 'It is hard to fathom how Sandra Gilbert and Susan Gubar could take this erotic representation of lesbian love-making to be an "image of the chaste moon goddess Diana," who does not have hand or tender tongue or inspire incredulity.' See Nadean Bishop, 'Renunciation in the Bridal Poems of Emily Dickinson,' paper presented at the National Women's Studies Association, Bloomington, Indiana, 16–20 May 1980. One other major critical study, Judith Fetterley's *The Resisting Reader: a Feminist Approach to American Fiction* (Bloomington: Indiana University Press, 1978), is uniquely sensitive to lesbianism in its interpretation of *The Bostonians*.

12 Gene Damon, Jan Watson, and Robin Jordan, *The Lesbian in Literature: A Bibliography* (1967; reprinted, Reno, Nev.: Naiad Press, 1975).

13 Jeannette Foster, *Sex Variant Women in Literature* (1956; reprinted, Baltimore: Diana Press, 1975). See also, Karla Jay, 'The X-Rated Bibliographer: A Spy in the House of Sex,' in *Lavender Culture*, ed. Karla Jay and Allen Young (New York: Harcourt Brace Jovanovich, 1978), pp. 257–61.

14 Beth Hodges, ed., Special Issue on Lesbian Writing and Publishing, *Margins* 23 (August 1975). Beth Hodges, ed., Special Issue on Lesbian Literature and Publishing, *Sinister Wisdom* 2 (Fall 1976).

15 In addition, networks of lesbian critics, teachers, and scholars were established through panels at the Modern Language Association's annual conventions and at the Lesbian Writer's Conference in Chicago, which began in 1974 and continued for several years. Currently, networking continues

through conferences, journals, and other institutionalized outlets. The Lesbian-Feminist Study Clearinghouse reprints articles, bibliographies, and syllabi pertinent to lesbian studies. See note 5 for the address. The Lesbian Herstory Archives collects all material documenting lesbian lives past or present; their address is P.O. Box 1258, New York, New York 10001. *Matrices*, 'A Lesbian-Feminist Research Newsletter,' is a network of information about research projects, reference materials, calls for papers, bibliographies, and so forth. There are several regional editors; the managing editor is Bobby Lacy, 4000 Randolph, Lincoln, Nebraska 68510.

16 Radicalesbians, 'The Woman-Identified Woman,' in *Radical Feminism*, ed. Anne Koedt, Ellen Levine, and Anita Rapone (New York: Quadrangle, 1973). This article is extensively reprinted in women's studies anthologies.

17 Charlotte Bunch, 'Lesbians in Revolt,' in *Lesbianism and the Women's Movement*, ed. Nancy Myron and Charlotte Bunch (Baltimore: Diana Press, 1975), p. 30.

[. . .]

33 Jane Rule, *Lesbian Images* (Garden City, N.Y.: Doubleday & Co., 1975).

34 Bonnie Zimmerman, 'The New Tradition,' *Sinister Wisdom* 2 (Fall 1976): 34–41.

35 Dolores Klaich, *Woman Plus Woman: Attitudes Toward Lesbianism* (New York: William Morrow, 1974); Louise Bernikow, *The World Split Open: Four Centuries of Women Poets in England and America, 1552–1950* (New York: Vintage Books, 1974).

36 Cook, 'Women Alone Stir My Imagination,' p. 720.

37 See Lillian Faderman's articles: 'The Morbidification of Love Between Women by Nineteenth-Century Sexologists,' *Journal of Homosexuality* 4, no. 1 (Fall 1978): 73–90; 'Emily Dickinson's Letters to Sue Gilbert,' *Massachusetts Review* 18, no. 2 (Summer 1977): 197–225; 'Emily Dickinson's Homoerotic Poetry,' *Higginson Journal* 18 (1978): 19–27; 'Female Same-Sex Relationships in Novels by Longfellow, Holmes, and James,' *New England Quarterly* 60, no. 3 (September 1978): 309–32; and 'Lesbian Magazine Fiction in the Early Twentieth Century,' *Journal of Popular Culture* 11, no. 4 (Spring 1978): 800–17.

38 Holly Near, 'Imagine My Surprise,' on *Imagine My Surprise!* (Redwood Records, 1978).

39 See Klaich, chap. 6. Also, see Bertha Harris, 'The More Profound Nationality of their Lesbianism: Lesbian Society in Paris in the 1920s,' *Amazon Expedition* (New York: Times Change Press, 1973), pp. 77–88; and Gayle Rubin's Introduction to Renée Vivien's: *A Woman Appeared to Me*, trans. Jeanette Foster (Reno, Nev.: Naiad Press, 1976).

40 For example, see Lanser, 'Speaking in Tongues.'

41 Marks, 'Lesbian Intertextuality,' in *Homosexualities and French Literature*, ed. George Stambolian and Elaine Marks (Ithaca, N.Y.: Cornell University Press, 1979), pp. 353–77.

ADRIENNE RICH

'Compulsory Heterosexuality and Lesbian Existence'

Biologically men have only one innate orientation – a sexual one that draws them to women – while women have two innate orientations, sexual toward men and reproductive toward their young.[2]

. . . I was a woman terribly vulnerable, critical, using femaleness as a sort of standard or yardstick to measure and discard men. Yes – something like that. I was an Anna who invited defeat from men without ever being conscious of it. (But I am conscious of it. And being conscious of it means I shall leave it all behind me and

become — but what?) I was stuck fast in an emotion common to women of our time, that can turn them bitter, or Lesbian, or solitary. Yes, that Anna during that time was . . .

[Another blank line across the page:][3]

The bias of compulsory heterosexuality, through which lesbian experience is perceived on a scale ranging from deviant to abhorrent, or simply rendered invisible, could be illustrated from many texts other than the two just preceding. The assumption made by Rossi, that women are 'innately' sexually oriented toward men, and that made by Lessing, that the lesbian is simply acting out of her bitterness toward men, are by no means theirs alone; these assumptions are widely current in literature and in the social sciences.

I am concerned here with two other matters as well: first, how and why women's choice of women as passionate comrades, life partners, co-workers, lovers, community, has been crushed, invalidated, forced into hiding and disguise; and second, the virtual or total neglect of lesbian existence in a wide range of writings, including feminist scholarship. Obviously there is a connection here. I believe that much feminist theory and criticism is stranded on this shoal.

My organizing impulse is the belief that it is not enough for feminist thought that specifically lesbian texts exist. Any theory or cultural/political creation that treats lesbian existence as a marginal or less 'natural' phenomenon, as mere 'sexual preference,' or as the mirror image of either heterosexual or male homosexual relations, is profoundly weakened thereby, whatever its other contributions. Feminist theory can no longer afford merely to voice a toleration of 'lesbianism' as an 'alternative life style,' or make token allusion to lesbians. A feminist critique of compulsory heterosexual orientation for women is long overdue. In this exploratory paper, I shall try to show why.

I will begin by way of examples, briefly discussing four books that have appeared in the last few years, written from different viewpoints and political orientations, but all presenting themselves, and favorably reviewed, as feminist.[4] All take as a basic assumption that the social relations of the sexes are disordered and extremely problematic, if not disabling, for women; all seek paths toward change. I have learned more from some of these books than from others, but on this I am clear: each one might have been more accurate, more powerful, more truly a force for change, had the author dealt with lesbian existence as a reality and as a source of knowledge and power available to women, or with the institution of heterosexuality itself as a beachhead of male dominance.[5] In none of them is the question ever raised as to whether, in a different context or other things being equal, women would *choose* heterosexual coupling and marriage; heterosexuality is presumed the 'sexual preference' of 'most women,' either implicitly or explicitly. In none of these books, which concern themselves with mothering, sex roles, relationships, and societal prescriptions for women, is compulsory heterosexuality ever examined as an institution powerfully affecting all these, or the idea of 'preference' or 'innate orientation' even indirectly questioned.

[. . .]

III

I have chosen to use the term *lesbian existence* and *lesbian continuum* because the word *lesbianism* has a clinical and limiting ring. *Lesbian existence* suggests both the fact of the historical presence of lesbians and our continuing creation of the meaning of that existence. I mean the term *lesbian continuum* to include a range – through each woman's life and throughout history – of woman-identified experience, not simply the fact that a woman has had or consciously desired genital sexual experience with another woman. If we expand it to embrace many more forms of primary intensity between and among women, including the sharing of a rich inner life, the bonding against male tyranny, the giving and receiving of practical and political support, if we can also hear in it such associations as *marriage resistance* and the 'haggard' behavior identified by Mary Daly (obsolete meanings: 'intractable,' 'willful,' 'wanton,' and 'unchaste' . . . 'a woman reluctant to yield to wooing')[45] – we begin to grasp breadths of female history and psychology which have lain out of reach as a consequence of limited, mostly clinical, definitions of 'lesbianism.'

Lesbian existence comprises both the breaking of a taboo and the rejection of a compulsory way of life. It is also a direct or indirect attack on male right of access to women. But it is more than these, although we may first begin to perceive it as a form of nay-saying to patriarchy, an act of resistance. It has of course included isolation, self-hatred, breakdown, alcoholism, suicide, and intrawoman violence; we romanticize at our peril what it means to love and act against the grain, and under heavy penalties; and lesbian existence has been lived (unlike, say, Jewish or Catholic existence) without access to any knowledge of a tradition, a continuity, a social underpinning. The destruction of records and memorabilia and letters documenting the realities of lesbian existence must be taken very seriously as a means of keeping heterosexuality compulsory for women, since what has been kept from our knowledge is joy, sensuality, courage, and community, as well as guilt, self-betrayal, and pain.[46]

Lesbians have historically been deprived of a political existence through 'inclusion' as female versions of male homosexuality. To equate lesbian existence with male homosexuality because each is stigmatized is to erase female reality once again. Part of the history of lesbian existence is, obviously, to be found where lesbians, lacking a coherent female community, have shared a kind of social life and common cause with homosexual men. But there are differences: women's lack of economic and cultural privilege relative to men;

qualitative differences in female and male relationships, for example, the patterns of anonymous sex among male homosexuals, and the pronounced ageism in male homosexual standards of sexual attractiveness. I perceive the lesbian experience as being, like motherhood, a profoundly *female* experience, with particular oppressions, meanings, and potentialities we cannot comprehend as long as we simply bracket it with other sexually stigmatized existences. Just as the term 'parenting' serves to conceal the particular and significant reality of being a parent who is actually a mother, the term 'gay' may serve the purpose of blurring the very outlines we need to discern, which are of crucial value for feminism and for the freedom of women as a group.[47]

As the term 'lesbian' has been held to limiting, clinical associations in its patriarchal definition, female friendship and comradeship have been set apart from the erotic, thus limiting the erotic itself. But as we deepen and broaden the range of what we define as lesbian existence, as we delineate a lesbian continuum, we begin to discover the erotic in female terms: as that which is unconfined to any single part of the body or solely to the body itself; as an energy not only diffuse but, as Audre Lorde has described it, omnipresent in 'the sharing of joy, whether physical, emotional, psychic,' and in the sharing of work; as the empowering joy which 'makes us less willing to accept powerlessness, or those other supplied states of being which are not native to me, such as resignation, despair, self-effacement, depression, self-denial.'[48] In another context, writing of women and work, I quoted the autobiographical passage in which the poet H. D. described how her friend Bryher supported her in persisting with the visionary experience which was to shape her mature work:

> . . . I knew that this experience, this writing-on-the-wall before me, could not be shared with anyone except the girl who stood so bravely there beside me. This girl had said without hesitation, "Go on." It was she really who had the detachment and integrity of the Pythoness of Delphi. But it was I, battered and dissociated . . . who was seeing the pictures, and who was reading the writing or granted the inner vision. Or perhaps, in some sense, we were "seeing" it together, for without her, admittedly, I could not have gone on. . . .[49]

If we consider the possibility that all women – from the infant suckling her mother's breast, to the grown woman experiencing orgasmic sensations while suckling her own child, perhaps recalling her mother's milk-smell in her own; to two women, like Virginia Woolf's Chloe and Olivia, who share a laboratory;[50] to the woman dying at ninety, touched and handled by women – exist on a lesbian continuum, we can see ourselves as moving in and out of this continuum, whether we identify ourselves as lesbian or not.

We can then connect aspects of woman identification as diverse as the impudent, intimate girl-friendships of eight-or nine-year olds and the banding together of those women of the twelfth and fifteenth centuries known as

Beguines who 'shared houses, rented to one another, bequeathed houses to their room-mates . . . in cheap subdivided houses in the artisans' area of town,' who 'practiced Christian virtue on their own, dressing and living simply and not associating with men,' who earned their livings as spinners, bakers, nurses, or ran schools for young girls, and who managed – until the Church forced them to disperse – to live independent both of marriage and of conventual restrictions.[51] It allows us to connect these women with the more celebrated 'Lesbians' of the women's school around Sappho of the seventh century B.C.; with the secret sororities and economic networks reported among African women; and with the Chinese marriage resistance sisterhoods – communities of women who refused marriage, or who if married often refused to consummate their marriages and soon left their husbands – the only women in China who were not footbound and who, Agnes Smedley tells us, welcomed the births of daughters and organized successful women's strikes in the silk mills.[52] It allows us to connect and compare disparate individual instances of marriage resistance: for example, the type of autonomy claimed by Emily Dickinson, a nineteenth-century white woman genius, with the strategies available to Zora Neale Hurston, a twentieth-century black woman genius. Dickinson never married, had tenuous intellectual friendships with men, lived self-convented in her genteel father's house in Amherst, and wrote a lifetime of passionate letters to her sister-in-law Sue Gilbert and a smaller group of such letters to her friend Kate Scott Anthon. Hurston married twice but soon left each husband, scrambled her way from Florida to Harlem to Columbia University to Haiti and finally back to Florida, moved in and out of white patronage and poverty, professional success, and failure; her survival relationships were all with women, beginning with her mother. Both of these women in their vastly different circumstances were marriage resisters, committed to their own work and selfhood, and were later charac-terized as 'apolitical.' Both were drawn to men of intellectual quality; for both of them women provided the on-going fascination and sustenance of life.

(1983)

Notes

2 Alice Rossi, 'Children and Work in the Lives of Women' (paper delivered at the University of Arizona, Tucson, February 1976).

3 Doris Lessing, *The Golden Notebook* (New York: Bantam Books [1962] 1977), p. 480.

4 Nancy Chodorow. *The Reproduction of Mothering* (Berkeley: University of California Press, 1978); Dorothy Dinnerstein, *The Mermaid and the Minotaur: Sexual Arrangements and the Human Malaise* (New York: Harper & Row, 1976); Barbara Ehrenreich and Deirdre English, *For Her Own Good: 150 Years of the Experts Advice to Women* (Garden City. N.Y.: Doubleday & Co., Anchor Press, 1978); Jean Baker Miller, *Toward a New Psychology of Women* (Boston: Beacon Press, 1976).

5 I could have chosen many other serious and influential recent books, including anthologies, which would illustrate the same point: e.g., *Our Bodies, Ourselves*, the Boston Women's Health Collective's best-seller (New York: Simon & Schuster, 1976), which devotes a separate (and

inadequate) chapter to lesbians, but whose message is that heterosexuality is most women's life preference; Berenice Carroll, ed., *Liberating Women's History: Theoretical and Critical Essays* (Urbana: University of Illinois Press, 1976), which does not include even a token essay on the lesbian presence in history, though an essay by Linda Gordon, Persis Hunt, et al. notes the use by male historians of 'sexual deviance' as a category to discredit and dismiss Anna Howard Shaw, Jane Addams, and other feminists ('Historical Phallacies, Sexism in American Historical Writing'); and Renate Bridenthal and Claudia Koonz, eds., *Becoming Visible: Women in European History* (Boston: Houghton Mifflin Co., 1977), which contains three mentions of male homosexuality but no materials that I have been able to locate on lesbians. Gerda Lerner, ed., *The Female Experience: An American Documentary* (Indianapolis: Bobbs-Merrill Co., 1977), contains an abridgment of two lesbian/feminist position papers from the contemporary movement but no other documentation of lesbian existence. Lerner does not in her preface, however, how the charge of deviance has been used to fragment women and discourage women's resistance. Linda Gordon, in *Woman's Body, Woman's Right: A Social History of Birth Control in America* (New York: Viking Press, Grossman, 1976), notes accurately that: 'It is not that feminism has produced more lesbians. There have always been many lesbians, despite high levels of repression; and most lesbians experience their sexual preference as innate . . .' (p. 410).

[A. R., 1986: I am glad to update the first annotation in this footnote. *"The New" Our Bodies, Ourselves*, (New York: Simon and Schuster, 1984), contains and expanded chapter on "Loving Women: Lesbian Life and Relationships" and furthermore emphasizes *choices* for women throughout—in terms of sexuality, health care, family, politics, etc.]

[. . .]

45 Daly, *Gyn/Ecology*, p. 15.
46 'In a hostile world in which women are not supposed to survive except in relation with and in service to men, entire communities of women were simply erased. History tends to bury what it seeks to reject' (Blanche W. Cook, ' "Women Alone Stir My Imagination": Lesbianism and the Cultural Tradition,' *Signs: Journal of Women in Culture and Society* 4, no. 4 [Summer 1979]: 719–20). The Lesbian Herstory Archives in New York City is one attempt to preserve contemporary documents on lesbian existence – a project of enormous value and meaning, working against the continuing censorship and obliteration of relationships, networks, communities, in other archives and elsewhere in the culture.
47 [A. R., 1986: The shared historical and spiritual 'crossover' functions of lesbians and gay men in cultures past and present are traced by Judy Grahn in *Another Mother Tongue: Gay Words, Gay Worlds* (Boston: Beacon, 1984). I now think we have much to learn both from the uniquely female aspects of lesbian existence and from the complex 'gay' identity we share with gay men.]
48 Audre Lorde, *Uses of the Erotic: The Erotic as Power* in *Sister Outsider* (Trumansburg, N.Y.: Crossing Press, 1984).
49 Adrienne Rich, 'Conditions for Work: The Common World of Women,' in *On Lies, Secrets, and Silence* (p. 209); H. D., *Tribute to Freud* (Oxford: Carcanet Press, 1971), pp. 50–54.
50 Woolf, *A Room of One's Own*, p. 126.
51 Gracia Clark, 'The Beguines: A Mediaeval Women's Community,' *Quest: A Feminist Quarterly* 1, no. 4 (1975): 73–80.
52 See Denise Paulmé, ed., *Women of Tropical Africa* (Berkeley: University of California Press, 1963), pp. 7, 266–67. Some of these sororities are described as 'a kind of defensive syndicate against the male element' – their aims being 'to offer concerted resistance to an oppressive patriar- chate,' 'independence in relation to one's husband and with regard to motherhood, mutual aid, satisfaction of personal revenge.' See also Audre Lorde, 'Scratching the Surface: Some Notes on Barriers to Women and Loving,' in *Sister Outsider* pp. 45–52; Marjorie Topley, 'Marriage Resistance in Rural Kwangtung,' in *Women in Chinese Society*, ed. M. Wolf and R. Witke (Stanford, Calif.: Stanford University Press, 1978), pp. 67–89; Agnes Smedley, *Portraits of Chinese Women in Revolution*, ed. J. MacKinnon and S. MacKinnon (Old Westbury, N.Y.: Feminist Press, 1976), pp. 103–10.

Alice Walker

'Saving the Life That Is Your Own:
The Importance of Models in the Artist's Life'
In Search of Our Mothers' Gardens

I have often been asked why, in my own life and work, I have felt such a desperate need to know and assimilate the experiences of earlier black women writers, most of them unheard of by you and by me, until quite recently. Why I felt a need to study them and to teach them.

I don't recall the exact moment I set out to explore the works of black women, mainly those in the past, and certainly, in the beginning, I had no desire to teach them. Teaching being for me, at that time, less rewarding than star-gazing on a frigid night. *My discovery of them* – most of them out of print, abandoned, discredited, maligned, nearly lost – came about, as many things of value do, almost by accident. As it turned out – and this should not have surprised me – I found I was in need of something that only one of them could provide.

Mindful that throughout my four years at a prestigious black and then a prestigious white college I had heard not one word about early black women writers, one of my first tasks was simply to determine whether they had existed. After this, I could breathe easier, with more assurance about the profession I myself had chosen.

But the incident that started my search began several years ago: I sat down at my desk one day, in a room of my own, with key and lock, and began preparations for a story about voodoo, a subject that had always fascinated me. Many of the elements of this story I had gathered from a story that my mother several times told me. She had gone, during the Depression, into town to apply for some government surplus food at the local commissary, and had been turned down, in a particularly humiliating way, by the white woman in charge.

My mother always told this story with a most curious expression on her face. She automatically raised her head higher than ever – it was always high – and there was a look of righteousness, a kind of holy *heat* coming from her eyes. She said she had lived to see this same white woman grow old and senile and so badly crippled she had to get about on *two* sticks.

To her, this was clearly the working of God, who, as in the old spiritual, '. . . may not come when you want him, but he's right on time!' To me, hearing the story for about the 50th time, something else was discernible: the possibilities of the story, for fiction.

What, I asked myself, would have happened, if, after the crippled old lady died, it was discovered that someone, my mother perhaps (who would have been mortified at the thought, Christian lady that she is), had voodooed her?

Then, my thoughts sweeping me away into the world of hexes and conjures of centuries past, I wondered how a larger story could be created out of my mother's story; one that would be true to the magnitude of her humiliation and grief, and to the white woman's lack of sensitivity and compassion.

My third quandary was: How could I find out all I needed to know in order to write a story that used *authentic* black witchcraft?

Which brings me back, almost, to the day I became really interested in black women writers. I say 'almost' because one other thing, from my childhood, made the choice of black magic a logical and irresistible one for my story. Aside from my mother's several stories about rootdoctors she had heard of or known, there was the story I had often heard about my crazy Walker aunt.

Many years ago, when my aunt was a meek and obedient girl growing up in a strict, conventionally religious house in the rural South, she had suddenly thrown off her meekness and had run away from home, escorted by a rogue of a man permanently attached elsewhere.

When she was returned home by her father she was declared quite 'mad.' In the backwoods South at the turn of the century, 'madness' of this sort was cured, not by psychiatry, but by powders and by spells. (One may see Scott Joplin's *Treemonisha* to ascertain the role voodoo played among black people of that period.) My aunt's 'madness' was treated by the community conjurer, who promised, and delivered, the desired results. His 'treatment' was a bag of white powder, bought for fifty cents, and sprinkled on the ground around her house, with some of it sewed, I believe, into the bodice of her nightgown.

So when I sat down to write my story about voodoo, my crazy Walker aunt was definitely on my mind.

But she had experienced her temporary craziness so long ago that her story had all the excitement of a might-have-been. I needed, instead of family memories, some hard facts about the *craft* of voodoo, as practiced by Southern blacks in the 19th century. (It never once, fortunately, occurred to me that voodoo was not worthy of the interest I had in it, or was too ridiculous to seriously study.)

I began reading all I could find on the subject of 'The Negro and His Folkways and Superstitions.' There were Botkin and Puckett and others, all white, most racist. How was I to believe anything they wrote, since at least one of them, Puckett, was capable of wondering, in his book, if 'The Negro' had a large enough brain? Who needed *him*, the racist turkey!

Well, I thought, where are the *black* collectors of folklore? Where is the *black* anthropologist? Where is the *black* person who took the time to travel the backroads of the South and collect the information I need: how to cure heart trouble, treat dropsy, hex somebody to death, lock bowels, cause joints to swell, eyes to fall out, and so on. Where was this black person?

And that is when I first saw, in a *footnote* to the white voices of authority, the name of Zora Neale Hurston.

Folklorist, novelist, anthropologist, serious student of voodoo, also all around black woman, with guts enough to take a slide rule and measure random black heads in Harlem; not to prove their inferiority, but to prove that whatever their size, shape, or present condition of servitude, those heads contained all the intelligence anyone could use to get through this world.

Zora Hurston, who went to Barnard to learn how to study what she really wanted to learn: the ways of her own people, and what ancient rituals, customs and beliefs had made them unique.

Zora, of the sandy-colored hair and the daredevil eyes, a girl who escaped poverty and parental neglect by hard work and a sharp eye for the main chance.

Zora, who left the South only to return to look at it again. Who went to rootdoctors from Florida to Louisiana and said, 'Here I am. I want to learn your trade.'

Zora, who had collected all the black folklore I could ever use.

That Zora.

And having found *that* Zora (like a golden key to a storehouse of varied treasure), I was hooked.

What I had discovered, of course, was a model. A model, who, as it happened, provided more than voodoo for my story, more than one of the greatest novels America had produced – though, being America, it did not realize this. She had provided, as if she knew someday I would come along wandering in the wilderness, a nearly complete record of her life. And though her life sprouted an occasional wart, I am eternally grateful for that life, warts and all.

It is not irrelevant, nor is it bragging (except perhaps to gloat a little on the happy relatedness of Zora, my mother, and me), to mention here that the story I wrote, called 'The Revenge of Hannah Kemhuff,' based on my mother's experiences during the Depression, and on Zora Hurston's folklore collection of the 1920s, and on my own response to both out of a contemporary existence, was immediately published and later selected, by a reputable collector of short stories, as one of the *Best Short Stories of 1974*.

I mention it because this story might never have been written, because the very bases of its structure, authentic black folklore, viewed from a black perspective, might have been lost.

Had it been lost, my mother's story would have had no historical underpinning, none I could trust, anyway. I would not have written the story, which I enjoyed writing as much as I've enjoyed writing anything in my life, had I not known that Zora had already done a thorough job of preparing the ground over which I was then moving.

In that story I gathered up the historical and psychological threads of the life my ancestors lived, and in the writing of it I felt joy and strength and my own continuity. I had that wonderful feeling writers get sometimes, not very often, of being *with* a great many people, ancient spirits, all very happy to see me consulting and acknowledging them, and eager to let me know, through the joy of their presence, that indeed, I am not alone.

To take Toni Morrison's statement further, if that is possible, in my own work I write not only what I want to read – understanding fully and indelibly that if I don't do it no one else is so vitally interested, or capable of doing it to my satisfaction – I write all the things I *should have read*.

Consulting, as belatedly discovered models, those writers – most of whom, not surprisingly, are women, who understood that their experience as ordinary human beings was also valuable, and in danger of being misrepresented, distorted, or lost:

Zora Hurston – novelist, essayist, anthropologist, autobiographer.

Jean Toomer – novelist, poet, philosopher, visionary, a man who cared what women felt.

Colette – whose crinkly hair enhances her French, part-black face: novelist, playwright, dancer, essayist, newspaper woman, lover of women, men, small dogs. Fortunate not to have been born in America.

Anaïs Nin, recorder of everything, no matter how minute.

Tillie Olsen, a writer of such generosity and honesty, she literally saves lives . . .

It is, in the end, the saving of lives that we writers are about. Whether we are 'minority' writers or 'majority.' It is simply in our power to do this.

We do it because we care. We care that Vincent Van Gogh mutilated his ear. We care that behind a pile of manure in the yard he destroyed his life. We care that Scott Joplin's music *lives!* We care because we know this: *The life we save is our own.*

(1976)

ALICE WALKER

Title Essay
In Search of Our Mothers' Gardens

What did it mean for a black woman to be an artist in our grandmothers' time? In our great-grandmothers' day? It is a question with an answer cruel enough to stop the blood.

Did you have a genius of a great-great-grandmother who died under some ignorant and depraved white overseer's lash? Or was she required to bake biscuits for a lazy backwater tramp, when she cried out in her soul to paint watercolors of sunsets, or the rain falling on the green and peaceful pasturelands? Or was her body broken and forced to bear children (who were more often than not sold away from her) – eight, ten, fifteen, twenty children – when her one joy was the thought of modeling heroic figures of rebellion, in stone or clay?

How was the creativity of the black woman kept alive, year after year and century after century, when for most of the years black people have been in America, it was a punishable crime for a black person to read or write? And the freedom to paint, to sculpt, to expand the mind with action did not exist. Consider, if you can bear to imagine it, what might have been the result if singing, too, had been forbidden by law. Listen to the voices of Bessie Smith, Billie Holliday, Nine Simone, Roberta Flack, and Aretha Franklin, among others, and imagine those voices muzzled for life. Then you may begin to comprehend the lives of our 'crazy,' 'Sainted' mothers and grandmothers. The agony of the lives of women who might have been Poets, Novelists, Essayists, and Short-Story Writers (over a period of centuries), who died with their real gifts stifled within them.

And, if this were the end of the story, we would have cause to cry out in my paraphrase of Okot p'Bitek's great poem:

> O, my clanswomen
> Let us all cry together!
> Come,
> Let us mourn the death of our mother,
> The death of a Queen
> The ash that was produced
> By a great fire!
> O, this homestead is utterly dead
> Close the gates
> With *lacari* thorns,
> For our mother
> The creator of the Stool is lost!
> And all the young women
> Have perished in the wilderness

But this is not the end of the story, for all the young women – our mothers and grandmothers, *ourselves* – have not perished in the wilderness. And if we ask ourselves why, and search for and find the answer, we will know beyond all efforts to erase it from our minds, just exactly who, and of what, we black American women are.

One example, perhaps the most pathetic, most misunderstood one, can provide a backdrop for our mothers' work: Phillis Wheatley, a slave in the 1700s.

Virginia Woolf, in her book *A Room of One's Own*, wrote that in order for a woman to write fiction she must have two things, certainly: a room of her own (with key and lock) and enough money to support herself.

What then are we to make of Phillis Wheatley, a slave, who owned not even herself? This sickly, frail black girl who required a servant of her own at times – her health was so precarious – and who, had she been white, would have been easily considered the intellectual superior of all the women and most of the men in the society of her day.

Virginia Woolf wrote further, speaking of course not of our Phillis, that 'any woman born with a great gift in the sixteenth century [insert 'eighteenth century,' insert 'black woman,' insert 'born or made a slave'] would certainly have gone crazed, shot herself, or ended her days in some lonely cottage outside the village, half witch, half wizard [insert 'Saint'], feared and mocked at. For it needs little skill and psychology to be sure that a highly gifted girl who had tried to use her gift for poetry would have been so thwarted and hindered by contrary instincts [add 'chains, guns, the lash, the ownership of one's body by someone else, submission to an alien religion'], that she must have lost her health and sanity to a certainty.'

The key words, as they relate to Phillis, are 'contrary instincts.' For when we read the poetry of Phillis Wheatley – as when we read the novels of Nella Larsen or the oddly false-sounding autobiography of that freest of all black women writers, Zora Hurston – evidence of 'contrary instincts' is everywhere. Her loyalties were completely divided, as was, without question, her mind.

But how could this be otherwise? Captured at seven, a slave of wealthy, doting whites, who instilled in her the 'savagery' of the Africa they 'rescued' her from . . . one wonders if she was even able to remember her homeland as she had known it, or as it really was.

Yet, because she did try to use her gift for poetry in a world that made her a slave, she was 'so thwarted and hindered by . . . contrary instincts, that she . . . lost her health. . . .' In the last years of her brief life, burdened not only with the need to express her gift but also with a penniless, friendless 'freedom' and several small children for whom she was forced to do strenuous work to feed, she lost her health, certainly. Suffering from malnutrition and neglect and who knows what mental agonies, Phillis Wheatley died.

So torn by 'contrary instincts' was black, kidnapped, enslaved Phillis that her description of 'the Goddess' – as she poetically called the Liberty she did not have – is ironically, cruelly humorous. And, in fact, has held Phillis up to ridicule for more than a century. It is usually read prior to hanging Phillis's memory as that of a fool. She wrote:

> The Goddess comes, she moves divinely fair,
> Olive and laurel binds her *golden* hair.
> Wherever shines this native of the skies,
> Unnumber'd charms and recent graces rise. [My italics]

It is obvious that Phillis, the slave, combed the 'Goddess's' hair every morning; prior, perhaps, to bringing in the milk, or fixing her mistress's lunch. She took her imagery from the one thing she saw elevated above all others.

With the benefit of hindsight we ask, 'How could she?'

But at last, Phillis, we understand. No more snickering when your stiff, struggling, ambivalent lines are forced on us. We know now that you were not an idiot or a traitor; only a sickly little black girl, snatched from your home and country and made a slave; a woman who still struggled to sing the song that was your gift, although in a land of barbarians who praised you for your bewildered tongue. It is not so much what you sang, as that you kept alive, in so many of our ancestors, *the notion of song.*

(1974)

CHRIS WEEDON

Feminist Practice and Poststructuralist Theory

Similar questions need to be asked of feminist criticism which is concerned with discovering particular women's experience in women's writing. At the present time attempts are being made to describe black and lesbian female experience as expressed in women's writing and to construct traditions of black and lesbian women's writing. As with all traditions, readers assume that texts are connected, that earlier writers influence later ones and that the analysis of such influences comes before the detailed historical location of women's writing within the specific social relations of cultural production, structured by class, gender and race, which produce texts.

The problems facing this approach are at their most extreme in the case of lesbian writing and the construction of a lesbian aesthetic and tradition expressing a lesbian experience. Not only does this project share the problems of approaches which assume that texts express women's experience, it is also faced with the primary problem of defining lesbian texts. In her overview of lesbian-feminist literary criticism, written in 1981, Bonnie Zimmerman addresses the complexities of these issues. She points out that contemporary discourses of lesbianism are wide-ranging. They include the exclusive definition of lesbianism as a sexual practice, the extension of the term lesbian to all 'woman-identified experience' as in the work of Adrienne Rich, or some point between the two. Zimmerman herself endorses Lillian Faderman's definition in *Surpassing the Love of Men* (Faderman, 1981):

> 'Lesbian' describes a relationship in which two women's strongest emotions and affections are directed toward each other. Sexual contact may be part of the relationship to a greater or lesser degree, or it may be entirely absent. By preference the two women spend most of their time together and share most aspects of their lives . . . with each other. (Faderman in Showalter, [*The New Feminist Criticism*] 1985, p. 206)

This definition may indeed serve the interests of current lesbian research and attempts to construct a lesbian tradition. It is important to remember, however, that it is a contemporary definition and that the meaning of lesbianism changes with historical shifts in the discursive construction of female sexuality. The different meanings of lesbianism in the past gave rise to different forms of oppression and resistance, knowledge of which helps to denaturalize the present and sharpen our awareness of the contemporary modes through which gender and sexual power are exercised.

As a group who are socially defined by others in terms of a sexual preference which is not heterosexual and therefore not 'normal', lesbians write from different subject positions than most heterosexual feminists. It is not impossible for heterosexual women to occupy fundamentally anti-heterosexist discourses but this takes a political commitment beyond their own immediate day-to-day interests. While all feminists would agree 'that a woman's identity is not defined only by her relation to a male world and a male literary tradition . . . that powerful bonds between women are a crucial factor in women's lives' (Showalter, 1985, p. 201), this is not enough to counter a heterosexism which is a fundamental structuring principle of discourses of gender and the social practices which they imply.

If it is difficult to decide on the meaning of lesbianism in women, a decision which can only ultimately be political, determined by present and future objectives, the question of what constitutes a lesbian text is equally open to a range of answers: 'This critic will need to consider whether a lesbian text is one written by a lesbian (and if so, how do we determine who is a lesbian?), one written about lesbians (which might be by a heterosexual woman or man), or one that expresses a lesbian 'vision' (which has to be satisfactorily outlined) (Zimmerman in Showalter, 1985, p. 208).

The questions asked by self-defined lesbian critics tend to focus on the relationship between author and text. Zimmerman, for example, assumes that 'the sexual and emotional orientation of a woman profoundly affects her consciousness and thus her creativity' (Showalter, 1985, p. 201). While this is very likely to be the case, we cannot know the intimate details of an author's consciousness; at best we have access to the competing range of subject positions open to her at a particular historical moment. Moreover we cannot look to authorial consciousness for the meaning of a text, since this is always open to plural readings which are themselves the product of specific discursive contexts.

Alternatively lesbianism in fiction can be seen in terms of textual strategies as, for example, in Barbara Smith's exposition of Toni Morrison's *Sula* in the same volume of essays (Showalter, 1985, pp. 168–84). There is a danger, however, of masking important and productive differences by assuming that fiction which contests particular forms of heterosexual practice and family life is necessarily lesbian in its implications.

How we define lesbianism and how we read lesbian texts will depend on how we define our objectives. Bonnie Zimmerman opts for a 'lesbian "essence" that may be located in all these specific historical existences, just as we may speak of a widespread perhaps universal structure of marriage or the family' (Showalter, 1985, pp. 215–16). She stresses, however, that 'differences are as significant as similarities'. If we are searching for positive lesbian role models or for a recognizable lesbian aesthetic, then a fixed concept of lesbianism is important. From a poststructuralist perspective, however, this fixing is always historically specific and temporary and will determine in advance the type of answers we get to our questions. If we want to understand and challenge past and present heterosexism we need to start from the discourses which constitute it and the forms of sexuality, sexual regulation and gendered subjectivity which they construct. We need to look for the possibilities of challenge and resistance to specific modes of heterosexuality. Fictional texts play their part in this process.

Black feminist criticism shares some of the problems faced by lesbian feminist criticism. While there is little debate about whether a text is a black text or a text of colour, this is guaranteed by the author, problems arise over identifying authentic black experience in black women's writing and in constituting an 'identifiable literary tradition' (Barbara Smith in Showalter, 1985, p. 174). Critics can start from the assumption that 'thematically, stylistically, aesthetically and conceptually Black women writers manifest common approaches to the art of creating literature as a direct result of the specific political, social and economic experience they have been obliged to share' (Showalter, 1985, p. 174). Alternatively we can look at black women's writing in its historically produced specificity, attempting to account for the discourses and social practices which have produced individual texts and which may well give rise to similarities between writers but also to differences. The critic of black feminist writing may choose to use existing critical tools, for example, poststructuralism, or as Barbara Smith recommends, reject them and 'write out of her own identity' in an explicitly humanist approach to black consciousness and subjectivity which implicitly restricts white access to black women's writing (p. 175). As with lesbian criticism, the methodology best used by critics of black women's writing is a question of politics. How we read black fiction will determine what insight we can gain from it into the discursive strategies of sexism and racism. As Susan Willis argues in her critical perspective on Black women's writing 'Black women's writing is not a mere collection of motifs and strategies, but a mode of discourse which enables a critical perspective upon the past, the present and sometimes into an emerging future' (Greene and Kahn, [*Making a Difference: Feminist Literary Criticism*] 1985, p. 220).

(1987)

PAUL LAUTER

'Race and Gender in the Shaping of the American Literary Canon:
A Case Study from the Twenties'
Feminist Criticism and Social Change

Demographic factors were also at work, as historian Laurence Veysey has pointed out. The proportion 'of the mature working-age population in America' who were college and university professors and librarians was rising 'spectacularly' in the decades leading to 1920 – especially in relation to older, static learned professionals, like doctors, lawyers and the clergy. Although they constituted only a tiny portion of people at work, professors had enormously larger impact 'as the universities increasingly took over training for a wide variety of prestigious occupations'. In fact, Veysey writes that

> the social effect of intellectual specialization [occurring in universities among other areas of American life] was to transfer authority, most critically over the printed word and what was taught in colleges to sons and daughters of the elite, away from the cultivated professions considered as an entirety and toward a far smaller, specially trained segment within them, those who now earned Ph.D. degrees. . . . Concretely, this meant vesting such authority in a group that, as of 1900, numbered only a few hundred persons spread across the humanistic fields. The immediate effect was thus the intensification of elitism as it was transferred onto a new academic basis. A double requirement was now imposed – intellectual merit, at least of a certain kind, defined far more rigorously, as well as a continuing expectation of social acceptability.[19]

In short, the professoriat exercised increasing control of the definition of a 'literate' reader, including those who were to become the next generation's writers.[20]

The social base of that professoriat was small. The professors, educators, critics, the arbiters of taste of the 1920s, were, for the most part, college-educated white men of Anglo-Saxon or northern European origins. They came, that is, from that tiny, élite portion of the population of the United States which, around the turn of the century, could go to college. Through the first two decades of the new century, this dominant élite had faced a quickening demand for some power and control over their lives from Slavic, Jewish, Mediterranean and Catholic immigrants from Europe, as well as from black immigrants from the rural South. Even women had renewed their demand for the vote, jobs, control over their bodies. The old élite and their allies moved on a variety of fronts, especially during and just after World War I, to set the terms on which these demands would be accommodated. They repressed, in actions like the Prohibition Amendment and the Palmer raids, the political and social, as well as the cultural, institutions of immigrants and of radicals. They reorganized schools and professionalized elementary and secondary school curriculum development, in significant measure as a way to impose middle-class American 'likemindedness' on a heterogeneous, urban, working-class population.[21] Similarly, calling it 'professionalization', they reorganized literary scholarship and teaching in ways that not only asserted a male-centered culture and values for the college-educated leadership, but also enhanced their own authority and status as well.[22]

The Modern Language Association, for example, underwent a major reorganization just after World War I, the effect of which was to concentrate professional influence in the hands of groups of specialists, most of whom met at the annual convention. The convention thus took on much greater significance, practically and symbolically in terms of defining professional leadership. As professionalism replaced gentility, the old all-male 'smoker' at the convention was discontinued. With it also disappeared a female and, on occasion, modestly feminist institution: the ladies' dinner. We do not fully know how, or even in this instance whether, such institutions provided significant support for women scholars, nor do we know what was lost with their disappearance in the 1920s.[23] Clearly, women were left without any significant organizational base within the newly important convention. For when, in 1921, specialized groups were established for MLA conventions, women's roles in them were disproportionately small, minor and largely confined.[24] If the men gave up the social institution that had helped sustain their control, they replaced it with professional authority in the new groups. Not only were women virtually excluded from leadership positions in them and given few opportunities to read papers, but they also appear to have been pushed toward – as men were certainly pushed away from – subject areas considered 'peripheral' to the profession. For example, folk materials and works *by* women became particularly the province *of* women – as papers, dissertation topics and published articles illustrate.[25]

As white women were excluded from the emerging scholarly power structures, and blacks – female or male – were kept almost entirely ghettoized in black colleges, 'their subjects', women and blacks, remained undeveloped in a rapidly developing profession. For example, in the first ten years of its existence, *American Literature* published twenty-four full articles (as distinct from Notes and Queries or Reviews) by women scholars out of a total of 208. Nine of these appeared in the first two volumes, and a number of women published more than once. An article on Dickinson appeared in volume 1, and others in volumes 4 and 6. These apart, the *only* article on a woman writer until volume 10 was one on American comments, mostly by men, on George Sand. In volume 10 one finds a piece, by a male scholar, on Cather, as well as another trying to show that Ann Cotton derived her material from husband John. It is not, I should add, that the journal confined itself to 'major' writers or to authors from the early or mid-nineteenth century. Quite the contrary, it ran pieces on stalwarts like John Pendleton Kennedy, not to speak of *Godey's Ladies' Book*, as well as articles dealing with a number of twentieth-century male authors.

While professionalization was thus erecting institutional barriers against women, their status was being attacked in other ways. Joan Doran Hedrick has shown how the ideology of domesticity and the bogey of 'race suicide', which re-emerged around the turn of the century, was used during the next thirty years to attack women teachers, both the proverbial spinster school-marm and the female college professor.[26] The extent to which such attacks arose from the pressure of job competition, general political conservatism, antisuffrage backlash or other factors is not yet clear. It was true, however, that women had not only been competing more and more effectively for positions in the humanities, but also that the predominance of women students in undergraduate literature courses had long worried the male professoriat. In 1909, for example, the chairman of the MLA's Central Division had devoted his address to the problem of 'Coeducation and literature'. He wondered whether the predominance of women taking literary courses 'may not contribute to shape the opinion that literature is preeminent-ly a study for girls, and tend to discourage some men. . . . This is not yet saying,' he continued, 'that the preference of women turns away that of men. There are many factors to the problem. But it looks that way.' How, he asked, can we deal with the problem that the 'masculine ideal of culture' has largely rejected what the modern languages, and we as its professors, have to offer? 'What may we teachers do more or better than we have done to gain for the humanities as represented by literature a larger place in the notion of masculine culture?'[27]

Something of an answer is provided in an unusually frank way in the *Annual Reports* of Oberlin College for 1919–20. In the section on the faculty, Professor Jelliffe, on behalf of Bibliography, Language, Literature and Art, urged the hiring of an additional teacher of composition. He writes:

> In my opinion the new instructor, when appointed, should be a man. Of sixteen sections in Composition only three are at present being taught by men instructors. This is to discredit, in the opinion of our students, the importance of the subject, for despite the excellent teaching being done by the women of the English faculty, the students are quick to infer that the work is considered by the faculty itself of less importance than that to which the men devote their time.[28]

Such ideas, the institutional processes I have described, and other historical forces outside the scope of the paper, gradually eroded the gains women had made in higher education in the decades immediately following the turn of the century. By the early 1920s, women were earning 16 per cent of all doctorates; that proportion gradually declined (except for the war years) to under 10 per cent in the 1950s. Similarly, the proportion of women in the occupational category of college presidents, professors and instructors rose from 6.4 per cent in 1900 to 32.5 per cent around 1930, but subsequently declined to below 22 per cent by 1960.[29] The proportion of women earning advanced degrees in the modern languages and teaching these subjects in colleges was, of course, always somewhat higher, but the decline affected those fields in a similar way. Because more women were educated in these fields, they were particularly vulnerable in the 1930s to cutbacks ostensibly instituted to preserve jobs for male 'breadwinners' or to nepotism regulations newly coined to spread available positions among the men. Not surprisingly, by the 1950s only 19 per cent of the doctorates being earned in the modern languages were awarded to women,[30] a proportion higher than in fields like sociology, history or biology, but significantly lower than it had been thirty years earlier. As a result, the likelihood of one's encountering a female professor even in literature – and especially at élite male or coeducational institutions – was perhaps even slighter than the chances of encountering a female writer.

Blacks, female or male, faced a color line that professionalization did nothing to dispel. Black professors of literature were, for the most part, separated into their own professional organization, the College Language Association, and into positions at segregated black colleges. The color line persisted in *American Literature* so far as articles on black writers were concerned, until 1971, when the magazine printed its first piece, on James Weldon Johnson. The outlook apparently shared by *American Literature*'s editors comes clearest in a brief review (vol. 10 (1938), pp. 112–13) by Vernon Loggins, then at Columbia, of Benjamin Brawley's collection of *Early Negro American Writers*.

> The volume . . . gives a hint of American Negro literature before Dunbar, but scarcely more than a hint. Yet it should be of practical value in American literature courses in *Negro colleges*. Professor Brawley obviously had such an aim in mind in making the compilation. [Italics mine]

Over the years a few articles appeared on images of blacks in the writings of white authors, but in general, as such reviews and notes on scholarly articles make clear, those interested in black writers were effectively referred to the *Journal of Negro History* or to the *College Language Association Journal*.[31]

Although the existence of such black professional organizations and periodicals reflected the pervasiveness of institutional racism in American life, such black-defined groups and magazines like the *Crisis* had at least the advantage of providing black writers and scholars with outlets for and encouragement of their work. Women, especially white professional writers, faced rather a different problem in this period: one can observe a significant shift in cultural authority from female-defined to male-defined institutions – in symbolic terms, one might say, from women's literary societies to *Esquire* magazine. The analogy may, at first, seem far-fetched, but it is probably more accurate than the cartoon view of women's clubs with which we have lived since the 1920s. In fact, the taste of the older generation of genteel professors and magazine editors largely accorded with that of the female literary clubs; the outlook of the new professoriat and *Esquire*, the *Playboy* of its day, largely coincided, at least with respect to the subjects and writers of fiction, as well as to certain conceptions of male camaraderie and culture.[32] To understand why, we must now turn to the aesthetic theories which helped to shape the canon.

(1983)

Notes

19 Laurence Veysey, 'The humanities, 1860–1920', typescript of paper for volume on the professions, c. 1974, pp. 21, 24.

20 Pattee remarks that 'American literature today is in the hands of college-educated men and women. The professor has molded the producers of it'. See Pattee, *Tradition and Jazz*, p. 237.

21 Barry M. Franklin, 'American curriculum theory and the problem of social control, 1918–1938' (paper presented at the Annual Meeting of the American Educational Research Association, Chicago, 15–19 April 1974), ERIC, ED 092 419. Franklin quotes Edward A. Ross, *Principles of Sociology* (New York: Century, 1920): 'Thoroughly to nationalize a multitudinous people calls for institutions to disseminate certain ideas and ideals. The Tsars relied on the blue-domed Orthodox church in every peasant village to Russify their heterogeneous subjects, while we Americans rely for unity on the "little red school house".'

22 Whatever its ostensible objectives, in practice, professionalization almost invariably worked to the detriment of female practitioners – and often female 'clients' as well. The details of this argument have been most fully worked out for medicine; see, for example, Barbara Ehrenreich and Deirdre English, *Complaints and Disorders: The sexual politics of sickness* (Old Westbury, NY: Feminist Press, 1973), and *For Her Own Good: One hundred and fifty years of the experts' advice to women* (New York: Pantheon, 1979). See also Janice Law Trecker, 'Sex, science and education', *American Quarterly* 26 (October 1974): pp. 352–66; and Margaret W. Rossiter, *Women Scientists in America: Struggles and strategies to 1940* (Baltimore: Johns Hopkins University Press, 1982), especially the chapters titled 'A manly profession', pp. 73–99, which includes a wonderful discussion of the professionally exclusionary function of the male 'smoker', and 'Academic employment: protest and prestige', pp. 160–217.

23 The ladies' dinner had disappeared by 1925. A good deal of work on female cultures of support has recently been published, beginning with Carroll Smith-Rosenberg, 'The female world of love and ritual: relations between women in nineteenth-century America', *Signs* 1 (Autumn 1975), pp. 1–27. In another professional field, history, women apparently felt so excluded from the mainstream and in need of mutual support that in 1929 they formed the Berkshire Conference of Women Historians, an institution extended in the 1970s to include sponsorship of a large conference on women's history. In most academic fields, however, while the proportion of *individual* women obtaining doctorates might have increased or been stable during the 1920s, female-defined *organizations* seem virtually to have disappeared – and with them, I suspect, centers for women's influence.

24 From 1923 on, the MLA gathered in what was called a 'union' meeting, rather than in separate conventions of the Eastern, Central and Pacific divisions – another indication of the new importance of the convention. That year 467 registered as attending the session. Fifty-nine women attended the ladies' dinner; some of the women were probably wives and other women members

probably did not attend. About 24 per cent of the MLA members were female; very likely a smaller proportion attended the convention. Among the divisions and sections there were 37 male chairpersons, and 1 female, Louise Pound, who chaired the Popular Culture section. There were 29 male secretaires, and 1 woman, Helen Sandison, served as secretary for two sections. Of the 108 papers, 6 were delivered by women.

In 1924, 978 persons registered, and 121 women went to the ladies' dinner. There continued to be 1 female chairperson, Louise Pound, and now 43 men. The female secretarial corps had increased to 5, Helen Sandison still serving twice, and 'Mrs Carleton Brown' now serving as secretary for the Phonetics section. Of the 128 papers, 7 were by women.

In *PMLA*, the proportion of women remained, relatively, much higher. In 1924, women were 7 of 47 authors; in 1925, 9 of 47; and in 1926, 11 of 55.

25 For example, of those seven papers delivered by women in the 1924 MLA meeting, two were in Popular Literature, two on Phonetics – where, perhaps not incidentally, women were officers – one in American Literature. Similarly, the entry for American Literature prepared by Norman Foerster for the 1922 American Bibliography (*PMLA*, 1923) contains one paragraph devoted to works about Indian verse, black writers and popular ballads. Four of the scholars cited in this paragraph are women, 5 are men. Otherwise, 58 men and 9 women scholars are cited in the article. Of the 9 women, 2 wrote on women authors, 2 are cobibliographers and 1 wrote on Whittier's love affair.

26 Joan Doran Hedrick, 'Sex, class, and ideology: the declining birthrate in America, 1870–1917', unpublished MS, c. 1974. Hedrick demonstrates that many of the sociologists and educators who developed the idea of utilizing curriculum for social control were involved with the supposed problem of 'race suicide' and active in efforts to restrict immigration as well as to return women to the home.

27 A. G. Canfield, 'Coeducation and literature', *PMLA* 25 (1910), pp. lxxix–lxxx, lxxxiii.

28 *Annual Reports of the President and the Treasurer of Oberlin College for 1919–20* (Oberlin, Ohio: Oberlin College, 10 December 1920), pp. 231–2.

29 Rudolph C. Blitz, 'Women in the professions, 1870–1970', *Monthly Labor Review* 97 (5 May 1974): pp. 37–8. See also Pamela Roby, 'Institutional barriers to women students in higher education', in *Academic Women on the Move*, ed. Alice S Rossi and Ann Calderwood (New York: Russell Sage Foundation, 1973), pp. 37–40; and Michael J. Carter and Susan Boslego Carter, 'Women's recent progress in the professions, or, Women get a ticket to ride after the gravy train has left the station', *Feminist Studies* 7 (Fall 1981), pp. 477–504.

30 Laura Morlock, 'Discipline variation in the status of academic women', in *Academic Women on the Move*, pp. 255–309.

31 In 1951, the Committee on Trends in Research of the American Literature Group circulated a report on research and publications about American authors during 1940–50, together with some notes on publications during the previous decade. For the 1885–1950 period, the report (basing itself on categories established by the *Literary History of the United States*) provided information on ninety-five 'major authors'. Of these, four were black: Charles Chesnutt, Paul Laurence Dunbar, Langston Hughes, Richard Wright – in context a surprisingly 'large' number. Chesnutt is one of the few of the ninety-five about whom no articles are listed for either period; for Dunbar, one three-page article is listed and a 'popular' book; for Hughes, there are four articles, two by Hughes himself. Only Wright had been the subject of a significant number of essays. Among 'minor authors', as defined by *LHUS*, Countee Cullen had two articles, totaling five pages, written about him; W. E. B. DuBois nothing; and James Weldon Johnson, Claude McKay and Jean Toomer, among others, were not even listed. Available in Modern Language Association, American Literature Group Files, University of Wisconsin Memorial Library Archives, Madison, Wisconsin.

32 One suggestive illustration.

I was pleased to get your letter and hear about the hunting. I don't know whether you realize how fortunate you people are to live where the game is still more plentiful than the hunters. It is no fun up here where hunting frequently resembles a shooting duel.

I am vastly amused by the report of the situation of the good and important woman who thought we should have more women on our committees in the American Literature Group.

... Beyond ... [Louise Pound and Constance Rourke] I cannot think of another woman in the country who has contributed sufficiently to be placed on a par with the men on our Board and committees. If you can think of anyone, for heaven's sake jog up my memory. We must by all means keep in the good graces of the unfair sex.

Sculley Bradley to Henry A. Pochmann, 12 January 1938, Modern Language Association, American Literature Group Files, University of Wisconsin Memorial Library Archives, Madison, Wisconsin.

MICHÈLE BARRETT

Women's Oppression Today: Problems in Marxist Feminist Analysis

Although Woolf's account is more systematic than most, we still await a substantial account of *consumption* and reception of texts from the point of view of the ideology of gender (or from any other point of view, one could add). There has been a failure to develop a theory of reading. This is largely, I suspect, because any such analysis would have to confront directly one of the most difficult problems of a materialist aesthetics: the problem of value. Virginia Woolf, it might be noted, simply ignored this problem. Although challenging much of what constituted 'the canon' of great literature of her period, she slides quite unremorsefully into the worst kind of aesthetic league-tabling in much of her criticism. Preoccupation with the question of value ('quality', 'standards') has been detrimental for feminist criticism and appears to have been posed as a choice between two limited options. On the one hand, we have the view exemplified by Virginia Woolf: that women have not reached the achievements of male writers, but that this is to be attributed to the constraints historically inherent in the conditions in which their work was produced and consumed. On the other hand, there is the view that women *have* achieved equally in respect of aesthetic value and we only think otherwise because of the warped and prejudiced response of a predominantly male, and sexist, critical and academic establishment.

This debate is fruitless (although admittedly seductive) in that it reproduces the assumption that aesthetic judgment is independent of social and historical context. Simply to pose the question at this level is to deny what we do already know: that not only are refined details of aesthetic ranking highly culturally specific, but that there is not even any consensus across classes, let alone across cultures, as to which cultural products can legitimately be subjected to such judgments. I am not contending that these observations obviate the problem of aesthetic value, since I believe it to be an urgent task of feminist criticism to take it on in the context of the female literary tradition, but merely that it should not be posed in simplistic terms.

(1980)

HENRY LOUIS GATES, JR

'Writing "Race" and the Difference it Makes'
"Race", Writing, and Difference

We black people tried to write ourselves out of slavery, a slavery even more profound than mere physical bondage. Accepting the challenge of the great white Western tradition, black writers wrote as if their lives depended upon it – and, in a curious sense, their lives did, the "life of the race" in Western discourse. But if blacks accepted this challenge, we also accepted its premises, premises which perhaps concealed a trap. What trap might this be? Let us recall the curious case of M. Edmond Laforest.

In 1915, Edmond Laforest, a prominent member of the Haitian literary movement called La Ronde, made his death a symbolic, if ironic, statement of the curious relation of the marginalized writer to the act of writing in a modern language. Laforest, with an inimitable, if fatal, flair for the grand gesture, stood upon a bridge, calmly tied a Larousse dictionary around his neck, then leapt to his death. While other black writers, before and after Laforest, have been drowned artistically by the weight of various modern languages, Laforest chose to make his death an emblem of this relation of overwhelming indenture.

It is the challenge of the black tradition to critique this relation of indenture, an indenture that obtains for our writers and for our critics. We must master, as Jacques Derrida writes in his essay in this collection, how "to speak the other's language without renouncing [our] own" (p. 333). When we attempt to appropriate, by inversion, "race" as a term for an essence – as did the négritude movement, for example ("We feel, therefore we are," as Léopold Senghor argued of the African) – we yield too much: the basis of a shared humanity. Such gestures, as Anthony Appiah observes in his essay, are futile and dangerous because of their further inscription of new and bizarre stereotypes. How do we meet Derrida's challenge in the discourse of criticism? The Western critical tradition has a canon, as the Western literary tradition does. I once thought it our most important gesture to *master* the canon of criticism, to *imitate* and *apply* it, but I now believe that we must turn to the black tradition itself to develop theories of criticism indigenous to our literatures. Alice Walker's revision of Rebecca Cox Jackson's parable of white interpretation (written in 1836) makes this point most tellingly. Jackson, a Shaker eldress and black visionary, claimed like Jea to have been taught to read by the Lord. She writes in her autobiography that she dreamed a white man came to her house to teach her how to *interpret* and understand the word of God, now that God had taught her to read:

A white man took me by my right hand and led me on the north side of the room, where sat a square table. On it lay a book open. And he said to me. "Thou shall be instructed in this book, from Genesis to Revelations." And then he took me on the west side, where stood a table. And it looked like the first. And said, "Yea, thou shall be instructed from the beginning of creation to the end of time." And then he took me on the east side of the room also, where stood a table and book like the two first, and said, "I will instruct thee – yea, thou shall be instructed from the beginning of all things to the end of all things. Yea, thou shall be well instructed. I will instruct."

And then I awoke, and I saw him as plain as I did in my dream. And after that he taught me daily. And when I would be reading and come to a hard word, I would see him standing by my side and he would teach me the word right. And often, when I would be in meditation and looking into things which was hard to understand, I would find him by me, teaching and giving me understanding. And oh, his labor and care which he had with me often caused me to weep bitterly, when I would see my great ignorance and the great trouble he had to make me understand eternal things. For I was so buried in the depth of the tradition of my forefathers, that it did seem as if I never could be dug up.[17]

In response to Jackson's relation of interpretive indenture to "a white man," Walker, in *The Color Purple*, records an exchange between Celie and Shug about turning away from "the old white man" which soon turns into a conversation about the elimination of "man" as a mediator between a woman and "everything":

You have to git man off your eyeball, before you can see anything a'tall.
   Man corrupt everything, say Shug. He on your box of grits, in your head, and all over the radio. He try to make you think he everywhere. Soon as you think he everywhere, you think he God. But he ain't. Whenever you trying to pray, and man plop himself on the other end of it, tell him to git lost, say Shug.[18]

Celie and Shug's omnipresent "man," of course, echoes the black tradition's epithet for the white power structure, "the man."

For non-Western, so-called noncanonical critics, getting the "man off your eyeball" means using the most sophisticated critical theories and methods available to reappropriate and to define our own "colonial" discourses. We must use these theories and methods insofar as they are relevant to the study of our own literatures. The danger in doing so, however, is best put by Anthony Appiah in his definition of what he calls "the Naipaul fallacy":

It is not necessary to show that African literature is fundamentally the same as European literature in order to show that it can be treated with the same tools; ... nor should we endorse a more sinister line ...: the post- colonial legacy which requires us to show that African literature is worthy of study precisely (but only) because it is fundamentally the same as European literature.[19]

We *must* not, Appiah concludes, ask "the reader to understand Africa by embedding it in European culture" ("S," p. 146).

We must, I believe, analyze the ways in which writing relates to race, how attitudes toward racial differences generate and structure literary texts by us *and* about us. We must determine how critical methods can effectively disclose the traces of ethnic differences in literature. But we must also understand how certain forms of difference and the *languages* we employ to define those supposed differences not only reinforce each other but tend to create and maintain each other. Similarly, and as importantly, we must analyze the language of contemporary criticism itself, recognizing especially that hermeneutic systems are not universal, colorblind, apolitical, or neutral. Whereas some critics wonder aloud, as Appiah notes, about such matters as whether or not "a structuralist poetics is inapplicable in Africa because structuralism is European" ("S," p. 145), the concern of the Third World critic should properly be to understand the ideological subtext which any critical theory reflects and embodies, and the relation which this subtext bears to the production of meaning. No critical theory – be it Marxist, feminist, post-structuralist, Kwame Nkrumah's "consciencism," or whatever – escapes the specificity of value and ideology, no matter how mediated these may be. To attempt to appropriate our own discourses by using Western critical theory uncritically is to substitute one mode of neocolonialism for another. To begin to do this in my own tradition, theorists have turned to the black vernacular tradition – to paraphrase Jackson, they have begun to dig into the depths of the tradition of our foreparents – to isolate the signifying black difference through which to theorize about the so-called discourse of the Other.

(1986)

Notes

17 Rebecca Cox Jackson, "A Dream of Three Books and a Holy One," *Gifts of Power: The Writings of Rebecca Jackson, Black Visionary, Shaker Eldress*, ed. Jean McMahon Humez (Amherst, Mass., 1981), pp. 146, 147.
18 Alice Walker, *The Color Purple* (New York, 1982), p. 179.
19 Anthony Appiah, "Strictures on Structures: The Prospects for a Structuralist Poetics of African Fiction," in *Black Literature and Literary Theory*, ed. Henry Louis Gates, Jr. (New York, 1984), pp. 146, 145; all further references to this work, abbreviated "S," will be included in the text.

NANCY K. MILLER

'Parables and Politics: Feminist Criticism in 1986' Paragraph

Throughout his overview of feminist literary studies, Ruthven complains about and protests against what he calls 'separatist feminism' (13); what he understands to be an exclusive/exclusionist attention to women's writing: 'It would be a pity', he worries, by way of a conclusion:

> if the feminist critique, which has been so successful in identifying androcentric bias against women writers and in making possible a critical discourse free of such prejudices, should be betrayed by a gynocritics developed along separatist lines. For that would simply reproduce the polarity between women's writing and men's which feminist criticism set out to combat in the first place. And it would also make it that much harder next time to persuade men and women that they have far too much to learn from one another to risk going their separate ways. (128)

Since I myself have been dubbed a 'partisan of separatist criticism',[7] I would like in closing to suggest a more accurate and useful way to think about women's writing. I would argue that it is precisely through the processes of recovery, revision and 'revisionary rereading' (Kolodny) which constitute the characteristic gestures of the work on women's writing, that we can learn how to challenge the false continuities ('origins' and influences) of the canon: a collection of texts that might more truthfully be designated as 'men's writing'.[8]

In many ways the reconstruction of feminism, like deconstruction which involves two principles or steps, is a doubled dealing: 'a *reversal* of the classical opposition *and* a general *displacement* of the system'.[9] But the reconstruction sought by feminist literary theory necessarily operates a specific inflection (and displacement) of that set of gestures: the establishment of a female tradition – a move that by its own claims to representation seeks to unsettle the claims of literary history – *and* a steady, Medusa-like gaze from its own genealogies at a tradition that has never thought to think back through its mothers. Put another way, my argument here is that a feminist look at the canon (the system) will reveal the petrification of the gender hierarchies that regulate the institutionalization of literature; and displace the asymmetries those hierarchies install. Contrary to what Ruthven imagines, then, I would argue that by its attention to the questions of feminist literary theory – who reads, who writes, whose interests are served by this reading and writing? – the study of women's writing *returns* separatism from the margins to the nervous 'I' of the dominant beholders. And in my view, meaningful change within the institution will come only from this return to sender that dislocates the universal subject from his place at the centre of the dominant discourse.

The third parable. In the literature of female signature there is a text, a long novel, though that term domesticates the work's explosion of generic re-straints (or rather a kind of Bakhtinian heteroglossia reigns instead), that takes up the question of the pantheon, the canon and the place in it for the woman writer. This work is Germaine de Staël's *Corinne or Italy* (1807). Corinne, the heroine, begins the tour of Rome she has designed to capture the imagination of Oswald, the melancholy Englishman who has come to Italy to recover his health, and recover from the grief brought on by the death of his Father.

Corinne, a poet and improviser whose crowning on the steps of the Capitol dramatically introduces the lovers to each other, takes Oswald first to the Pantheon where one can see 'the busts of the most famous artists: they decorate the niches where the gods of the ancients had been placed' (96).Corinne explains that her deepest desire is to have her place there as well: 'I've already chosen mine, she said, showing him an empty niche' (97).

If we ask again, 'how does the inclusion of women's writing alter our view of the tradition', *Corinne* offers an exemplary set of answers: it rereads the Greek myth through Roman architecture; it incarnates cultural relativism; it articulates the history of Classicism and Romanticism; it politicizes, by making it a question of public display, the notion of genius (Moers); it stages the problem of subjectivity; and dramatizes the question of the artist's relation to the social. The novel had enormous impact on (women) writers in France, England and America. Need I say that it belongs neither to the canon of French literature – though because of Staël's status as an intellectual the novel gets honourable mention – nor to the pantheon of world literature. In other words, the niche still remains empty.

When Corinne realizes she is about to die (young), and is too ill to perform, she has her verses read, in a final theatrical, by a young girl. She also arranges before her death to have her tiny niece, Juliette (the daughter of Oswald and Corinne's English half-sister), learn to speak Italian and play the harp: just like Corinne, but of course with the difference a generation makes. Thus the artist in her lifetime arranges for and underwrites her legacy: what I will call a feminist 'aftertext' (Berg, 219).

Barthes, we know, has argued that the Death of the Author is co-terminous with, if not brought about by, the Birth of the Reader. Although he records the former event with a jubilation feminist critics will not all necessarily share, there is, perhaps, good reason to appropriate and revise the paradigm. For this is our only hope. Confronted with the persistence of the empty niche, it becomes our task to stage the possibility of a different sort of continuity. Not the biological and murderous simplicity that appeals so much to the father and son teams of our cultural paradigms (à la Harold Bloom after Sigmund Freud), but a more complex legacy that like Corinne's passes on its values in life to another generation through reading and its performatives (Berg, 214); and like Lucy Snowe's authorizes its passions from another and finally ambiguous scene of writing.

(1986)

Notes

7 Adrienne Munich, 'Notorious signs, feminist criticism and literary tradition', in *Making a Difference*. In *Reading Woman* Mary Jacobus performs an astute analysis of Ruthven's obsession with separatism:

Ruthven's 'own discourse on feminist criticism retains its imaginary mastery of the discourse of feminism. The measure is separation (feminist criticism as castration) or a reassuring image of wholeness (feminist criticism as the imaginary, narcissistic completion of critical lack): the phallic woman, in short, has something to offer the institution of criticism after all.'

8 There is a proposal on the floor at Dartmouth College, put forward by a man, that the catalogue should accurately designate what is taught. What flows from this is that 'Modern British and American Poetry', for example, would read, 'White European Male Modern British and American Poetry'; and the great works would read: men's writing. In the recorded discussion about the establishment at Barnard College of a Women's Studies Programme and major in 1977, the Professor of Music 'stated that he found it difficult to envision a men's studies programme and therefore found it equally difficult to conceive of a women's studies programme'.

9 The argument continues: 'It is on that condition alone that deconstruction will provide the means of *intervening* in the field of oppositions it criticizes and which is also a field of non-discursive forces' (*Marges*, 392; in Culler, 86). Whether the operations of displacement actually effect an intervention in the scene of non-discursive structures, in the hierarchies of university life, for example, is to my mind the great question of deconstructive criticism as a politics.

MARY JACOBUS

Reading Woman: Essays in Feminist Criticism

"A letter always arrives at its destination": Lacan argues that the letter is always received, always reversed; Derrida argues that Lacan's epistolary law can miss its destination, go astray; Johnson, that its received meaning is always missing, always performed by the reader. Each reading is at once an intervention and an effect of the letter. The woman reader turns the letter a little further. One could say that Charlotte Brontë's *Villette* "reads" Breuer's "Fräulein Anna O."; George Eliot's "The Lifted Veil" both reads and is read by *Studies on Hysteria*; reading "The Yellow Wallpaper" through Wollstonecraft, Wollstonecraft becomes its political unconscious; Irigaray reads George Eliot's *Mill on the Floss*; Kristeva reads Freud's "abjection" of the mother; and so on. But that's not quite all. Feminist reading means reading back into these correspondences the elided "*elle(s)*"; "*elle(s)*" is installed, differentially, between these feminist correspondences, or between feminist and Freudian theory. The system of textual relations or "readings" sketched here is an aspect of a feminist intertextuality which (too easily) gets subsumed under the misleading title of "the female literary tradition" (which tradition, and whose? in what sense literary? in what sense traditional?). The concept of a female literary tradition depends on a linear reading of the relations (usually chronologically conceived) between texts or "letters". Reading back through our mothers and grandmothers (Woolf's model of a female literary tradition) places the feminist reader at the end of a line. Only from this imaginary vantage point (hers) can the feminist literary tradition – the handing on or over of a feminist "address" – be perceived as a signifying chain.

Yet the existence of these chain letters is what makes it possible for the feminist reader to create (and read) her "tradition." She is its reading effect. Matrilinear models of textual relations (relations between texts authored by women) depend on two assumptions – that texts are mothered (what of the father? or, can feminist theory do without Freud?) and that linear descent is constitutive of meaning. To question both assumptions is not to dissolve the (political) category of "women's writing," nor to refuse history, treating all texts as unauthored and existing in an imaginary, chronologically undifferentiated present. Rather, it is to insist that the feminist letter derives its meaning (and its refusal of meaning – its unreadability) from the feminist "plot" or narrative in which it is installed. Feminist literary herstory tells one story, "gynocritics" another, to which post-Lacanian feminist psychoanalysis gives yet a different turn. These feminist discourses argue and interrogate the status claimed for each by their practitioners. Feminist criticism is situated within the exchange that constitutes it, within the differences which divide it from any self or essence, any unified position. Feminist reading thus becomes a reading of the internal difference by which the letter refuses any univocal meaning; but it is also a reading that puts the feminist reader's own position as reader on the line. Taking issue with (as well as from) the mother, the daughter may take a line of her own.

Reading correspondences acknowledges that drawing the line, or closure, can only be an arbitrary and temporary gesture, the placing of an accent here rather than there in the continuing exchange – the movement – of feminist literary criticism which I have chosen to call "Reading Woman." Or, as Irigaray has it, "the one doesn't stir without the other. But we do not move together" ("*Mais ce n'est ensemble que nous mouvons*"). "We" don't make the same moves, but as feminist critics we move only by getting together and by getting across (each other). The correspondence between Wollstonecraft and Irigaray remains unfinished, its itinerary incomplete and its destination deferred. Reading woman goes on from – moves in between – where these women of letters leave off.

(1986)

LINDA R. WILLIAMS

'*Happy Families? Feminist Reproduction and Matrilineal Thought*' New Feminist Discourses

Feminist Family Romances

Mother/daughterhood is then one of the most persistent ways that feminism has articulated women's alternative networks of communication. As metaphor it has profoundly affected our reading of women's literary history, and I want to explore more closely what is at stake in this. It is, I think, not so simple. However strongly this 'pure' bond is asserted, however much it is seen to be a democratic exchange of feeling and information, its intervention as a controlling metaphor in feminist studies, and particularly in feminist criticism, needs to be challenged. From the premiss that women have access to purity of sublime or semiotic communication comes the notion that authentic female communication takes place through matriarchal and matrilineal networks, networks which are purified from the distortions of the symbolic. Hegel's women conceive immaculately because for them no defiling or politicized process of transmission takes place in thought. They 'gather' knowledge in an apparently unmediated way – it is 'exchanged' or absorbed, and therefore not subject to the problems of transmission.

Against this, and with Alice Jardine, I would

> like to avoid the mother/daughter paradigm here (so as not to succumb simply to miming the traditional father/son, master/disciple model), but it is difficult to avoid at this point being positioned by the institution as mothers and daughters. Structures of debt/gift (mothers and increasingly daughters control a lot of money and prestige in the university), structures of our new institutional power over each other, desires and demands for recognition and love – all of these are falling into place in rather familiar ways.[18]

Her 'Notes for an Analysis' is written in anticipation of a 'new kind of feminist intellectual' who 'fully inscribes herself within the ethics of impossibility, concluding by calling for the wiping away of 'the concept of "generation" altogether' when feminist women place themselves 'across the generations'. She suggests an embrace of intra-generational solidarity which would erase the power of differentials bound up in the relationship of debt between mothers and daughters, towards a totality of unified radical feminist intellectuals. It is a pity that such a complex analysis of the contemporaneity of feminism and psychoanalysis ends before suggesting how this embrace of generational forgetting is to take place, and at what point it would resist undifferentiated unity with a dynamic of different, *afamilial* powers.

How, then, can feminism interpret the transmission of ideas, knowledge, systems of thought outside of an Oedipal dynamic? With what language do we currently discuss the channels through which information is passed on? When Hegel writes the offhand 'Women are educated – who knows how?' he invites us to presume that the way in which men are educated is no problem at all. That's obvious – it's women who are the mystery. I want to ask a series of questions about how we pass on information to each other and what we want it to do. What is feminist transmission? Why do we so often employ familial metaphors to interpret our conceptual and scholarly relationships with each other? What are the power relations at stake in setting up feminist networks of thinking which rely on mother-daughter or sisterly ties? Why are we so reluctant to rid ourselves of the family? These questions focus not only on the problem of mother-daughter relations in history or psychoanalysis, but crucially on the way we have interpreted women's *literary* history as a *family* history, glued together by those 'unknowable' feminine relations discussed above: 'the unique bonds that link women in what we might call the secret sisterhood of their literary subculture'.[19] Thus it seems, ironically, that the very force which some writers have drawn upon to signal the breakdown of patriarchal family relations – a feminine communication which disrupts normal epistemologies – has then been used to make coherent an alternative Great (female) Tradition.

Virginia Woolf's famous statement, 'we think back through our mothers if we are women'[20] has engendered a whole family of feminisms dedicated to the recovery of an intellectual matriarchy. As Rachel Bowlby writes, 'Woolf has herself become foremother to a generation of feminists who "think back through our mothers".'[21] What Bowlby is indicating, then, isn't just that Woolf thought that there is a literary history which works matrilineally, but that this has in turn engendered a feminist critical family line. Matriarchal thinking has become a primary feminist characteristic, and its language acts as the freemason's handshake of Gilbert and Gubar's 'secret sisterhood'. I want briefly to outline here the arguments of a few kinswomen who display the family resemblances most strongly. Is it a happy family? I think not. Its members squabble constantly over who mother is. Is she Dale Spender's mother, stable source of a comfortable literary tradition, legitimized and authentic? Is she the sublime, pre-oedipal mother, with whom closeness opens up revolutionary possibilities of disruption?

Dale Spender's *Mothers of the Novel* – dedicated to the author's mother, presumably the grandmother of this text – is an unashamedly evangelical eulogy to 'our' literary matriarchs. Her project is to reclaim the 'treasure chest'[22] of 'women's traditions' which 'we have been missing'.[23] Indeed, her fervent championing of a tradition mothered and reproduced by women – 'it is my contention that women were the mothers of the novel and that any other version of its origin is but a myth of male creation' – is uncannily like that of F. R. Leavis who, in his early work, also occupied an inspired dissident position, championing the canonically repressed. And, like Leavis, what Spender wants to do is to produce an 'authentic' or 'legitimated female tradition',[24] thus exemplifying a feminist critical position which turns to the fecund mother figure as guarantor of a sense of stability and genealogical truth.

Gilbert and Gubar's *The Madwoman in the Attic* is perhaps a more interesting example of matriarchal reading. They take the problem of how creativity is engendered head-on, and partly inherit Harold Bloom's interpretation of literary movement as energized by the anxiety of influence. 'Criticism', for Bloom, 'is the art of knowing the hidden roads that go from poem to poem'[25] – it is the detection of the literary violation of fathers by sons. Writing that 'Poetry (Romance) is Family Romance',[26] Bloom rewrites literary history as the history of Oedipal conflict.

> True poetic history is the story of how poets as poets have suffered other poets, just as any true biography is the story of how anyone suffered his own family – or his own displacement of family into lovers and friends.

Summary – Every poem is a misinterpretation of a parent poem.[27]
For Bloom, imagination is *mis*interpretation; creativity is the deliberate violation of what's come before. A feminism which would assemble all the fragments of women's literary history into 'the career of a single woman artist, a "mother of us all" ',[28] which would conform in part to the notion that female imagination is osmotically communicated through that 'unique bond', would undoubtedly have enormous problems with such a violating tradition. What Gilbert and Gubar want to do is take Bloom's model and strip it of its anxiety as far as literary daughters and mothers are concerned, neatly retaining father as the bad relation. Patriarchal tradition takes on the image of the wicked stepfather in a romance of positive feminine relations: the father remains the one to be killed, and although today's women writers are 'the daughters of too few mothers', nevertheless a dedicated enough act of feminist critical genealogy can trace a whole matriarchal history, putting together the history of 'a woman whom patriarchal poetics dismembered and whom we have tried to remember'. Re-membering thus becomes a process dedicated to unity; fragments of written selves are made to undergo a rite of matrilineal coherence. Remembering phallically assembles fragments into a unity of 'membership'. If patriarchal history was the process of splitting women exogamically from each other, disseminating their powers and dismembering their tradition, certain feminist histories would bring the parts back into the organic whole again. Coherence, progress, growth, community, all combine to produce a stable tradition of women's literary history. The female artist can then begin the struggle which Gilbert and Gubar call 'the anxiety of authorship', 'only by actively seeking a female precursor who, far from representing a threatening force to be denied or killed, proves by example that a revolt against partriarchal literary authority is possible'.[29]

Furthermore, not only has the reintroduction of a sense of tradition restabilized our understanding of women's writing but ironically enough the very fact that women have been able to draw upon matrilineal metaphors has given that tradition the weight of genetic verification. To assert that paternity is undecidable whilst maternity is undeniable is a fairly commonplace idea; as Freud writes in *Moses and Monotheism*,

> this turning from the mother to the father points in addition to a victory of intellectuality over sensuality – that is, an advance in civilization, since

maternity is proved by the evidence of the senses while paternity is a hypothesis, based on an inference and a premiss.[30]

Hélène Cixous, champion of fiction if ever there was one, is, however, quite prepared to denigrate it in contrast with this primary 'fact' of maternity: 'Paternity, which is a fiction, is fiction passing itself off as truth.'[31] To extend this into the metaphorics of writing generations, feminist literary history has reversed and rewritten Cixous' statement as: 'literary maternity, which is a fact, is fact which has historically been passed off as untruth'. Some feminist criticisms have challenged this 'historical passing off' in order to establish a framework within which feminist scholarship is meaningful. Thus in pursuit of matrilineal stability, feminism has been able to deploy the metaphor of the most concrete human given of all: the fact that one is the issue of one's mother. So, patriarchal literary tradition has acted only to render women writers temporary orphans; the happy ending of the family romance is that given sufficiently skilful sleuthing, the truth will out and our true mother will be found.

(1992)

Notes

18 Alice Jardine, 'Notes for an Analysis', in Brennan, op. cit., p. 77.
19 Sandra Gilbert and Susan Gubar, *The Madwoman in the Attic* (New Haven and London, 1979), p. 51.
20 Virginia Woolf, *A Room of One's Own* (1929) (St Albans, 1977), pp. 72–3.
21 Rachel Bowlby, *Virginia Woolf: Feminist Destinations* (Oxford, 1988), p. 25.
22 Dale Spender, *Mothers of the Novel: 100 Good Women Writers Before Jane Austen* (London, 1986), p. 2.
23 ibid., p. 6.
24 ibid., pp. 262–3.
25 Harold Bloom, *The Anxiety of Influence* (Oxford, 1973), p. 96.
26 ibid., p. 95.
27 Bloom, op. cit.
28 Gilbert and Gubar, op. cit., p. 101.
29 ibid., p. 49.
30 Freud, *Moses and Monotheism* (1939 [1934–8]), in Pelican Freud Library vol. 13, *The Origins of Religion*, p. 361.
31 Hélène Cixous and Catherine Clément, *The Newly Born Woman* (1975), trans. Betsy Wing (Manchester, 1986), p. 101.

VIVIANE FORRESTER

'What Women's Eyes See'
New French Feminisms

We don't know what women's vision is. What do women's eyes see? How do they carve, invent, decipher the world? I don't know. I know my own vision, the vision of one woman, but the world seen through the eyes of others? I only know what men's eyes see.

So what do men's eyes see? A crippled world, mutilated, deprived of women's vision. In fact men share our malaise, suffer from the same tragedy: the absence of women particularly in the field of cinema.

If we were responsible for this absence, couldn't they complain about it? 'After all,' they would say, 'we have communicated our images, our vision to you; you are withholding yours. That is why we present a castrated universe, a life whose essential answers are unknown to us. We make films, we attempt to say, to translate, to destroy, to know, to invent, and you condemn us to a monologue that confines us to stale repetition, an isolation such that we are becoming petrified in endless narcissism. We have only fathers. We see only through our own fantasms, our malaise, the tricks we play on you, our renunciations (this network of conventions which replaces you and propagates itself dangerously at every level of our work) and the vacuum created by your absence and the dolls who fill it and whom we have fabricated. And we do not know how you see us. You do not look at us, etc.'

We don't hear such complaints and for obvious reasons. Because this blindness to women's vision, which in fact prohibits any global vision of the world, any vision of the human species, has been fashioned by men for our mutual impoverishment.

How can male directors today not beg women to pick up the camera, to open up unknown areas to them, to liberate them from their redundant vision which is deeply deformed by this lack? Women's vision is what is lacking and this lack not only creates a vacuum but it perverts, alters, annuls every statement. Women's vision is what you don't see; it is withdrawn, concealed. The images, the pictures, the frames, the movements, the rhythms, the abrupt new shots of which we have been deprived, these are the prisoners of women's vision, of a confined vision.

The quality of this vision is not the point – in the hierarchical sense – it is not better (how absurd to speak of a 'better' vision), it is not more efficient, more immediate (certain women will assert that it is, but that's *not* the point); but it is lacking. And this deficiency is suicidal.

Women are going to seize (they are beginning to do so) what they should have acquired naturally at the same time as men did, what men after this bad start should have eventually begged women to undertake: the practice of film making. Women will have to defend themselves against an accumulation of clichés, of sacred routines which men delight in or reject and which will frequently trap women as well. They will need a great deal of concentration and above all of precision. They will have to see, to look, to look at themselves unaffectedly, with a natural gaze that is so difficult to maintain; they will have to dare to see not only their own fantasms, but also, instead of an old catalogue, fresh, new images of a weary world. Why will they be more apt to rid themselves of whatever obstructs men's vision? Because women are the secret to be discovered, they are the fissures. They are the source where no one has been.

(1976)

Translated by Isabelle de Courtivron

SHOSHANA FELMAN

'Women and Madness: The Critical Phallacy'
Diacritics

A question could be raised: if 'the woman' is precisely the Other of any conceivable Western theoretical locus of speech, how can the woman as such be speaking in this book? Who is speaking here, and who is asserting the otherness of the woman? If, as Luce Irigaray suggests, the woman's silence, or the repression of her capacity to speak, are constitutive of philosophy and of theoretical discourse as such, from what theoretical locus is Luce Irigaray herself speaking in order to develop her own theoretical discourse about the woman's exclusion? Is she speaking the language of men, or the silence of women? Is she speaking *as* a woman, or *in place of* the (silent) woman, *for* the woman, *in the name of* the woman? Is it enough to *be* a woman in order to *speak* as a woman? Is 'speaking as a woman' a fact determined by some biological *condition* or by a strategic, theoretical *position*, by anatomy[1] or by culture? What if 'speaking as a woman' were not a simple 'natural' fact, could not be taken for granted? With the increasing number of women and men alike who are currently choosing to share in the rising fortune of female misfortune, it has become all too easy to be a speaker *'for* women.' But what does 'speaking *for* women' imply? What is 'to speak *in the name of* the woman'? What, in a general manner, does 'speech in the name of' mean? Is it not a precise repetition of the oppressive gesture of *representation*, by means of which, throughout the history of logos, man has reduced the woman to the status of a silent and subordinate object, to something inherently *spoken for*? To 'speak in the name of,' to 'speak *for*,' could thus mean, once again, to appropriate and to silence. This important theoretical question about the status of its own discourse and its own 'representation' of women, with which any feminist thought has to cope, is not thought out by Luce Irigaray, and thus remains the blind spot of her critical undertaking.

(1975)

Note

1 Freud has thus pronounced his famous verdict on women: 'Anatomy is destiny,' But this is precisely the focus of the feminist contestation.

GAYATRI CHAKRAVORTY SPIVAK

'French Feminism in an International Frame'
Yale French Studies

A young Sudanese woman in the Faculty of Sociology at a Saudi Arabian University said to me, surprisingly: 'I have written a structural functionalist dissertation on female circumcision in the Sudan.' I was ready to forgive the sexist term 'female circumcision.' We have learned to say 'clitoridectomy' because others more acute than we have pointed out our mistake.

But Structural Functionalism? Where 'integration' is 'social control [which] defines and *enforces . . .* a degree of *solidarity*'? Where 'interaction, seen from the side of the economy,' is defined as 'consist[ing] of the supply of income and wealth applied to purposes strengthening the persistence of cultural patterns?'[1] Structural functionalism takes a 'disinterested' stance on society as functioning structure. Its implicit interest is to applaud a system – in this case sexual – because it functions. A description such as the one below makes it difficult to credit that this young Sudanese woman had taken such an approach to clitoridectomy:

> In Egypt it is only the clitoris which is amputated, and usually not completely. But in the Sudan, the operation consists in the complete removal of all the external genital organs. They cut off the clitoris, the two major outer lips (*labia majora*) and the two minor inner lips (*labia minora*). Then the wound is repaired. The outer opening of the vagina is the only portion left intact, not however without having ensured that, during the process of repairing, some narrowing of the opening is carried out with a few extra stitches. The result is that on the marriage night it is necessary to widen the external opening by slitting one or both ends with a sharp scalpel or razor so that the male organ can be introduced?[2]

In my Sudanese colleague's research I found an allegory of my own ideological victimage:

The 'choice' of English Honors by an upper-class young woman in the Calcutta of the fifties was itself highly overdetermined. Becoming a professor of English in the U.S. fitted in with the 'brain drain.' In due course, a commitment to feminism was the best of a collection of accessible scenarios. The morphology of a feminist theoretical practice came clear through Jacques Derrida's critique of phallocentrism and Luce Irigaray's reading of Freud. (The stumbling 'choice' of French avant-garde criticism by an undistinguished Ivy League Ph.D. working in the Midwest is itself not without ideology-critical interest.) Predictably, I began by identifying the 'female academic' and feminism as such. Gradually I found that there was indeed an area of feminist scholarship in the U.S. that was called 'International Feminism:' the arena usually defined as feminism in England, France, West Germany, Italy, and that part of the Third World most easily accessible to American interests: Latin America. When one attempted to think of so-called Third World women in a broader scope, one found oneself caught, as my Sudanese colleague was caught and held by Structural Functionalism, in a web of information retrieval inspired at best by: 'what can I do *for* them?'

I sensed obscurely that this articulation was part of the problem. I rearticulated the question: What is the constituency of an international feminism? The following fragmentary and anecdotal pages approach the question. The complicity of a few French texts in that attempt could be part both of the problem – the 'West' out to 'know' the 'East' determining a 'westernized Easterner's' symptomatic attempt to 'know her own world'; or of something like a solution, – reversing and displacing (if only by juxtaposing 'some French texts' and a 'certain Calcutta') the ironclad opposition of West and East. As soon as I write this, it seems a hopelessly idealistic restatement of the problem. I am not in a position of choice in this dilemma.

To begin with, an obstinate childhood memory.

I am walking alone in my grandfather's estate on the Bihar-Bengal border one winter afternoon in 1949. Two ancient washerwomen are washing clothes in the river, beating the clothes on the stones. One accuses the other of poaching on her part of the river. I can still hear the cracked derisive voice of the one accused: 'You fool! Is this your river? The river belongs to the Company!' – the East India Company, from whom India passed to England by the Act for the Better Government of India (1858); England had transferred its charge to an Indian Governor-General in 1947. India would become an independent republic in 1950. For these withered women, the land as soil and water to be used rather than a map to be learned still belonged, as it did one hundred and nineteen years before that date, to the East India Company.

I was precocious enough to know that the remark was incorrect. It has taken me thirty-one years and the experience of confronting a nearly inarticulable question to apprehend that their facts were wrong but the fact was right. The Company does still own the land.

I should not consequently patronize and romanticize these women, nor yet entertain a nostalgia for being as they are. The academic feminist must learn to learn from them, to speak to them, to suspect that their access to the political and sexual scene is not merely to be *corrected* by our superior theory and enlightened compassion. Is our insistence upon the especial beauty of the old necessarily to be preferred to a careless acknowledgment of the mutability of sexuality? What of the fact that my distance from those two was, however, micrologically you defined class, class-determined and determining?

How, then, can one learn from and speak to the millions of illiterate rural and urban Indian women who live 'in the pores of' capitalism, inaccessible to the capitalist dynamics that allow us our shared channels of communication, the definition of common enemies? The pioneering books that bring First World feminists news from the Third World are written by privileged informants and can only be deciphered by a trained readership. The distance between 'the informant's world,' her 'own sense of the world she writes about,' and that of the non-specialist feminist is so great that, paradoxically, *pace* the subtleties of reader-response theories, here the distinctions might easily be missed.

This is not the tired nationalist claim that only a native can know the scene. The point that I am trying to make is that, in order to learn enough about Third World women and to develop a different readership, the immense heterogeneity of the field must be appreciated, and the First World feminist must learn to stop feeling privileged *as a woman*.

[. . .]

As soon as one steps out of the classroom, if indeed a 'teacher' ever fully can, the dangers rather than the benefits of academic feminism, French or otherwise, become more insistent. Institutional changes against sexism here or in France may mean nothing or, indirectly, further harm for women in the Third World.[44] This discontinuity ought to be recognized and worked at. Otherwise, the focus remains defined by the investigator as subject. To bring us back to my initial concerns, let me insist that here, the difference between 'French' and 'Anglo-American' feminism is superficial. However unfeasible and inefficient it may sound, I see no way to avoid insisting that there has to be a simultaneous other focus: not merely who am I? but who is the other woman? How am I naming her? How does she name me? Is this part of the problematic I discuss? Indeed, it is the absence of such unfeasible but crucial questions that makes the 'colonized woman' as 'subject' see the investigators as sweet and sympathetic creatures from another planet who are free to come and go; or, depending on her own socialization in the colonizing cultures, see 'feminism' as having a vanguardist class fix, the liberties it fights for as luxuries, finally identifiable with 'free sex' of one kind or another. Wrong, of course. My point has been that there is something equally wrong in our most sophisticated research, our most benevolent impulses.

(1981)

Notes

1 Bert F. Hoselitz, 'Development and the Theory of Social Systems,' in M. Stanley, ed., *Social Development* (New York: Basic Books, 1972), pp. 44, 45. I am grateful to Professor Michael Ryan for drawing my attention to this article.

2 Nawal El Saadawi, *The Hidden Face of Eve: Women in the Arab World* (London: Zed Press, 1980), p. 5.

[. . .]

44 To take the simplest possible American examples, even such innocent triumphs as the hiring of more tenured women or adding feminist sessions at a Convention might lead, since most U.S. universities have dubious investments, and most Convention hotels use Third World female labor in a most oppressive way, to the increasing proletarianization of the women of the less developed countries.

JANET TODD

Feminist Literary History: A Defence

The patriarchal nature of language and culture must inform the tellings of history. This is the genre from which women have been especially excluded and into which they are now entering as objects of study and as writing subjects. Yet there has been in recent years an assault on any notion that a discourse termed historical – or fictional – could denote reality; the result is a problematizing both of history and of the connection of literature and history. In place of history, we are getting histories, different and infinitely numerous itineraries through the past. So, where the eighteenth-and nine-teenth-century novelists seemed to absorb the project of history into fiction, our own age is obsessed with history as a series of fictions. Women are, then, entering history just as the distinction between the historical account and the happening or the something out there is most unstable, when it is becoming clear that that happening has no natural configuration, no necessary articula-tion at all. These developments certainly allow women into the construction of history – they may in fact be connected with their arrival just as the destabilizing of the Renaissance or of modernism may be associated with women's appearance, as Jardine and Gilbert and Gubar have speculated – but they may also allow another kind of marginalization through the idea of the deconstruction of *all* history before a 'women's history' has been described.

So what histories can we use? Not I think the progressive one, neither Whig history nor Chateaubriand's fatalist history, the almost providential retelling of the past to capture a predetermined progress. Some early feminist critical history sounded a little like this, with women writers, especially those labelled as feminist, moving nearer and nearer through time towards a truth we alone had fully grasped. Instead, we should aim for some reconstructions of the past that allow its richness, texture, and strangeness to emerge.

In her introduction to *Tulsa Studies in Women's Literature*, Fall 1986, Shari Benstock celebrates the institution of Gilbert and Gubar's *Norton Anthology*. But in considering the structure of the volume – history, women's history, women's writing – she warns against two assumption: first that of women encased in the more important traditional history, which inevitably turns out to be 'a history of *men*'s accomplishments, of *men*'s concerns (politics, religion, economics, etc.), a record of the development of patriarchy', and, second, that of women existing in a separate female history: 'Women writers (like women) do not have a separate history, do not live lives outside their temporal and spatial circumstances, do not escape cultural, social, and political imperatives'. I believe both her points are true ones, but the opposition she makes here – based of course on the polarization in the *Norton Anthology* – between man's history and a woman's history, even the non-separatist one she proposes, may be limiting. Many studies assume a separation of male public and civic history and female private herstory, with the result that the 'politics, religion and economics' which form male history quickly become men's domain alone and we are in danger of forgetting that history is not gendered, only the telling. What comes forward as women's history, such as changes in fashion of breast feeding, marriage settlements, contraception and the treatment of widows, is profoundly relevant to women's writing, but so are civic events, economic changes and religious and political controversy in which many women played a part and which affected the organization of their lives. Balance is needed. Menstruation is not the *whole* of the female experience.

Nina Baym has warned against the laudable interest in women's private writing; in our enthusiasm for diaries and letters we are in danger of forgetting that women from an early period wrote directly in interventionist modes and wanted to succeed as professional authors. We may be forgetting that women took part in religious struggles, wrote political pamphlets, and in many periods were connected with the government. To some extent it has been the stress on the Victorian domestic woman writer, so much a feature of American feminist criticism of the 1970s, that has pushed the typical woman into retirement and passivity. Even Ruth Perry in her admirable biography of Mary Astell (1986), which fully presents a writing woman engaged with the intellectual and political controversies of her time, can mention in passing that to write for money appeared ill-bred for women until the mid-nineteenth century. It is hard to imagine Fanny Burney and even Jane Austen, both much concerned with the pounds and pence of their enterprise, fitting into this generalization.

Feminist literary criticism should, then, range widely for its history and questions, using and abusing men when necessary, always aware of the partial nature of the historical record and taking as much as possible into account. So we cannot simply ignore the traditional constructed literary history, for example, but we can historicize and so destablize it, just as we can, dimly, start to historicize our own patterns of thought and open up ourselves to criticism from the past. Such openness can occur if we can avoid too quickly establishing limiting continuities and identities between past and present that bully the past and its literature out of their specificity and materiality.

The potential of the historical feminist approach has not yet been fulfilled, an approach that disrupts the canon and all readings and is informed by an apprehension of ideology as material and psychological, but which eschews the tendency towards the single history of psychoanalysis and is wary of the quick assertion that all histories are but rhetoric. It recognizes that empiricism is indeed already theorized but that empirical study still allows challenges on its edges, where theory alone may codify and reify the prejudice of the moment. The historical approach provides tools like any other, but it cannot, in the manner of some of the approaches I have been criticizing, fit texts like a grid. History opens up the possibility of strangeness, while the notion of ideology interposes, in Marilyn L. Williamson's words 'the sexual ideologies of the past between the critic and the text, and in doing so balances the inevitable biases the critic brings to the interpretive process'.[8] What it requires is close literary work which will pry open a history that has been closed to us and which will again be closed to us – albeit with more attractive closure – if we prematurely psychoanalyse, destabilize, or historically generalize on too slim and haphazard a base.

If feminist literary history or historical criticism can keep its integrity, it can gain much from associating outside, and I agree with Alice Jardine, that 'If feminism is to remain radical and not become but patchwork for a patriarchal fabric ripped apart by the twentieth century' it must consider 'what kinds of alliances' it will be able to form 'with the most radical modes of thought produced by that century' (Gynesis, p. 64). Mary Jacobus extends this useful point. She notes that American historical criticism, with its somewhat naïve devotion to pluralism risks turning feminism into yet another ingredient in an existing plurality of literary criticism. Instead, it should constitute a critique of that pluralized mélange.

One form of such a critique could result from the increased critical awareness of historical specificity, as well as a recognition that the separation of surface and implied messages according to our present requirements – our common method of assaulting the past – may represent desire in us rather than in the author. At the very least works of the past should be able to inform us as readers of the differences between present and past perceptions, however flawed our apprehension of them. At the same time we need to learn from the Jacobus kind of approach that language does tell a great deal more than we have been accustomed to hearing. If we stay entirely at the level of theory or unexamined history we may never find 'herstory' at all but remain locked into logical critical extremes, the fallacies committed by both strict empiricists and psychoanalytical theorists.

Feminist literary history can also learn something from the ideas of what has been termed new historicist criticism. This has been much celebrated and abused and is indeed so various that it deserves almost all epithets. But in its more successful manifestations, it does offer a method of specific historical study that takes into account the workings of ideology and the way that the artistic text reproduces that inviting ideology. Criticism can help to caution the reader against this invitation; at the same time, as Jerome J. McGann, a celebrant of the new historicist approach, has argued, work cannot and should not be reduced to pure ideological statement, undifferentiated from any other work, for such a reduction becomes transhistorical:

> all inherited works of literature have it in their power to force a critical engagement with any present form of thought (whether a critical or an ideological form) by virtue of the historical differentials which separate every present from all the past – by virtue of those differentials which draw the present and the past together across the field of concrete and particular differences (*The Romantic Ideology*, p. 14).

(1988)

Note

8 Marilyn L. Williamson, 'Toward a Feminist Literary History', *Signs*, Autumn, 1984.

2

Women and Literary Production

INTRODUCTION

Problems for the Woman Writer

Why are women under-represented as published writers? The extracts by Virginia Woolf, Tillie Olsen and Adrienne Rich point not to a maliciously planned conspiracy by top male publishers to keep women out of print, but to a complex combination of material and ideological factors that inhibit the potential woman writer. The catalogue of material problems is long – inequalities in the educational system, lack of privacy, responsibilities of child-bearing and rearing, domestic obligations – but equally decisive are the restrictions of family and social expectations. Even if women writers solve the material problems that prevent their writing, an anxiety about their chosen role and how they are perceived continues to surface. For many women writers what cannot easily be overcome is an awareness of an oppressive male presence constraining their work; Woolf's irritation about the unsympathetic male reader and Rich's consciousness of following a line of male poets testify to that.[1] Woolf illustrates how deeply entrenched is the problem. Despite her strong belief that 'it is fatal for anyone who writes to think of their sex', despite her privileged position of economic independence and a room of her own, despite her high level of understanding of the issues, she still has to admit, in 'Professions for Women', that she has 'many ghosts to fight, many prejudices to overcome'.

Repeatedly, the woman writer finds herself at a point of tension, aware that her writing both challenges the conventional view of what is appropriate for women and encroaches on what some see as a male preserve. If the woman writer writes about women, she risks the labels of 'partiality', 'narrowness', 'a woman's book'. If she tries to write about her own deepest responses, particularly sexual, she feels anxious at revealing 'the truth about my own experiences as a body' (Woolf), or at 'experiencing myself as a woman' (Rich). The very act of writing is seen as expressing a conflict between 'traditional female functions' and 'the subversive function of the imagination' (Rich).

Rich comments at the end of her extract on the false and polarized definitions which link women with selflessness and altruism and men with a driving egotism that produces art. In an entirely circular way, according to this definition, art is male and men are the 'natural' creators of art. Sandra Gilbert and Susan Gubar also explore this predicament. With what must be among the most memorable opening sentences in literary criticism – 'Is a pen a metaphorical penis?' – they trace that literary history which sees writing as a kind of extension of the male generative act and which confers on the male writer authority, the right to create and control. In trying to negotiate this situation, Gilbert and Gubar believe the woman writer is involved in a complex balancing act between apparent conformity to certain patriarchal literary norms and a trenchant critique, expressing the unacceptable, the authorial rage and desire and antagonism.[2]

The problem for the woman writer lies not only in the production of writing; an equally questionable area is its reception. What Gilbert and Gubar call the 'anxiety of authorship' has been created and maintained in part through the practices of reviewing and literary criticism. 'Phallic' criticism has taken three classic forms.[3] Evident in the extracts already discussed is its tendency to belittle women writers, dismissing them as unfeminine and presumptuous. A second mode, considered in Terry Lovell's *Consuming Fiction* and in the extracts from Women in Publishing and Margaret Atwood, is to ignore or marginalize women's production. What is operating here, Lovell believes, is not a conscious deletion of women's writing, but a set of 'loosely defined rules and codes, which have tended to work against women'. (It could help to refer here to Lauter's extract in chapter 1.) A third strategy is to confine female authors within the bounds of rigid sex stereotyping. When women do attempt to write, they are seen simply as bringing to the major body of established male texts the 'feminine' qualities they are supposed to represent in life generally. The piece from Carol Ohmann and Atwood's section on what she calls the 'Quiller-Couch Syndrome' trace this response from the nineteenth century to the present. Ohmann's work acutely exposes any claims to critical objectivity. The expectation that the author of *Wuthering Heights* was male, and the change in response when the author was revealed as female point to the determining effect of gender in reviewing and criticism.[4]

Perhaps phallic criticism is all that can be expected of one's enemies. But what if the response of one's friends is equally unsatisfactory? Some women writers have complained that feminism has produced its own set of limitations – at worst a kind of prescriptive orthodoxy, at best a list of well-meaning expectations which, nevertheless, no writer could fulfil. With wit and exasperation, Elizabeth Baines, a fiction writer, and Isobel Armstrong, a critic, lament the impossible demands of their audiences. For some, Baines's and Armstrong's writing is clearly not feminist enough.[5] 'Are you sure that what you've been striving for isn't a *phallus*?' the politically correct Feminist Writer asks the fallible, jobbing author in Baines's piece. 'But *I* want to write poetry which men will read,' is the confession extracted from Isobel Armstrong. A sense of 'the-more-feminist-the-more-morally-superior' is a problem to be negotiated in both extracts. Yet, who is to say what *is* a feminist text/reading and how that text/reading is to be produced? Pierre Salesne, who takes part in the Hélène Cixous seminar, would probably equate any prescriptive demands, even feminist prescriptive demands, with 'a certain fantasy of mastery'. The participants in 'Conversations' employ a very different vocabulary. Their aim is not to determine a text but to 'espouse a text', to 'listen to a text', to 'work on a text'; reading is 'a work of love', 'a flowing process of exchange between the reader and the text'. The emphasis is not on control or definition, rather on responsiveness, interaction and a bodily apprehension.[6] Doubtless Baines's Feminist Writer would not be convinced of the political efficacy of this mode of practice.

Possibilities for the Woman Writer

Both Terry Lovell, in her second extract, and Jane Spencer take issue with the claims of Gilbert and Gubar.[7] The emphatic assertions of the male writers whom Gilbert and Gubar quote, speaking so conclusively of the masculine nature of literary production, reveal to Lovell, not a confident and consolidated tradition, but a deep insecurity about femininity and how it might relate to writing. Lovell maintains that in Western culture imaginative writing is not 'male' but 'gender ambiguous' and she supports her argument by setting alongside the male-dominated canon the popular 'feminine' image of creative writing, the involvement of female students in the study of languages and literature, and the centrality of women in the development of the novel.

Lovell's suggestions are important. Most of the work on gender and literary production has looked at the *problems* of female literary production. The marked difference in the number of male and female writers and the prevalence, since the early 1970s, of the debate about gaining access have prompted such an approach. However, it is equally necessary to turn the question on its head and ask, not what has inhibited women's writing, but what has made it possible: historically, there have been more women writers than, say, women sculptors or concert pianists. Lovell's method is to look chiefly at the relationship between social attitudes to writing and the practicalities of production. But other variables, such as literary form, also need to be taken into account. Spencer's comments prompt the question: why is it the novel, *par excellence*, which has been colonized by the woman author? The production of poetry is a domestic activity and yet there are far fewer female poets than male. The theatre is not associated in the popular imagination with 'manliness' and, as students of drama, women are well represented. Yet the public production of theatre seems to determine that women should be under-represented as both playwrights and directors.[8] Even within the novel, as Lovell and Spencer indicate, the situation is double-edged. The woman novelist gains status as a writer during a period when women are losing political power; she creates, and yet is confined by, a certain construction of femininity; she finds a public voice and uses it to praise private virtue.[9] All this indicates that the justifiable complaint about women's exclusion from literary production is but the first line in a complex argument and history.

The Position of the Black Woman Writer

Barbara Smith illustrates how for the Black woman writer problems of literary production are compounded by racism. Black writing by both women and men in the States exists as a 'discrete subcategory of American literature', and reviewing and literary criticism again play their parts in reinforcing certain values and ignoring or discrediting others. Smith appropriately sees literary criticism not simply as a subordinate interpreter of the primary imaginative text but as an important contributor to the possibility of creative writing: it establishes a context in which that writing can be understood. Published in 1977 and often anthologized since, Smith's essay makes the case for a 'non-hostile', (which, of course, need not mean non-critical), 'perceptive', knowledgeable criticism, one which links to the political movement of Black women and provides a method of analysis for Black feminist writing.

It is salutary to read Woolf's 'Judith Shakespeare' story alongside Alice Walker's rewriting of it to appreciate how a Black feminist criticism can introduce a new set of meanings.[10] Towards the end of the Judith Shakespeare extract Woolf makes one of her characteristic rapid developments of an idea, moving within a few lines from the silence of women, to the desire of men to mark, name and possess, to the imperialist claim for the control of land and other people. Set against Woolf's dubious contention that a white *woman* would not wish so to dominate and refashion a Black woman, is Walker's story of the Black poet, Phillis Wheatley, sold into slavery, combing the white mistress's hair and, tragically, finding in the white woman her imagery for godliness. For Woolf, the Black woman enters the argument not as a potential writer – she is white – but as a victim of imperialism. Walker's insertions into Woolf's prose introduce the black woman into history and literary production and in so doing Walker rescues the Black woman from her position as object – whether sympathetically or antagonistically conceived – in the white woman's discourse. She is to become the subject of her own discourse, creating a new imagery and symbolism and constructing, as Smith hopes, a critical framework for the writing of Black women.

The Means of Production

I started this chapter thinking of the individual author sitting at her desk and of what is necessary in the conditions of her life and in her own sense of subjectivity to make writing possible. I broadened the debate to issues of reception in reviewing and literary criticism and to the ideological construction of the author. In what ways are these practices and constructs impregnated by gender? What I should like to focus on, finally, is a further element in the production process, namely the often fraught attempts by feminists to control the printing, publishing and distribution of women's writing and to establish a supportive infrastructure of magazines, journals, writing groups, networks, courses. As early as 1938, Virginia Woolf was voicing this demand for women's control of the means of literary production as a way of avoiding what she refers to as 'adultery of the brain':

> Still, Madam, the private printing press is an actual fact, and not beyond the reach of a moderate income. Typewriters and duplicators are actual facts and even cheaper. By using these cheap and so far unforbidden instruments you can at once rid yourself of the pressure of boards, policies and editors. They will speak your own mind, in your own words, at your own time, at your own length, at your own bidding.[11]

If only Woolf had had desk-top publishing at her disposal.

I term the situation 'fraught' because of the enormity of the task women in literary production set themselves. An absence of funding, mainstream opposition, sometimes lack of necessary skills, political and aesthetic conflicts – the problems are many. Yet just as significant is the combination of conviction, creativity and pragmatism: if you don't know how to print books, you enrol on a course (Jackson). Again, within a generally under-represented category, women, the specific interests and needs of Black women and lesbians are even more marginal and, inevitably, there is no single feminist publishing policy which caters for all groups and all political demands. For instance, the Black Woman Talk Collective interprets the currency of writing by African-American women as a reluctance on the part of British publishers to confront the situation at home; racism is easier to deal with at a distance. Lauretta Ngcobo, on the other hand, views the American input as a valuable stimulus for British publishers to explore the potential British market. Similarly, Ngcobo applauds the attempts of Black teachers to earn for Black writing the status of exam text while Joan Scanlon and Julia Swindells worry about Virago's interest in 'academic feminism, rather than activist feminism'.

In 1991, the managing director of the Women's Press, Ros de Lanerolle was sacked by the Press's chief shareholder, Naim Attallah. In 1993, *Spare Rib* ceased publication. In the same year, Virago celebrated its twentieth anniversary and in the following year three of its directors were made redundant. The ups and downs of the feminist publishing industry relate, in no small measure, to the difficulty of producing a politics while, and through, producing marketable writing. In exploring the history of Virago, Scanlon and Swindells move between feminist politics, commercial writing and the creation of a progressive aesthetics. The cultural paradox within which all this operates is that of an expanding market for women's writing alongside a series of defeats for feminism and women, most notably in areas of social policy. You will recall that we saw a similar paradox at work in Lovell's and Spencer's discussions of the development of the novel.

The full story of the last twenty years of feminist publishing is still to be told.[12] Publishing companies, presses, writing groups, magazines have come and gone; the organization and control of major companies have changed rapidly; little is written down in terms of policy, mission statements, selection criteria, editorial guidelines; certainly nobody doing the job has time to write the history. Most analysis has appeared in valuable, but short, journal and magazine articles. One hopes, though, that someone, somewhere *is* writing a thesis on this aspect of feminist literary production since much knowledge and experience will otherwise be lost.

A second research area also needs further development. At the start of her extract from 'Writing Like a Woman: A Question of Politics', Lovell states: 'The first stage of literary production (I think Lovell refers here to the writing) has been untouched either by technological transformation or by the division of labour'. I suspect that Lovell, if revising her essay today, might want to look again at that sentence. Although word-processing, desk-top publishing, computer networking were underway when Lovell's essay was published in 1983, it is only since then that the less computer literate – I mean myself, not Lovell – have begun to realize dimly the potential impact of technological change on literary production and the implication of that change for gender divisions and for women especially. As Donna Haraway comments:

> Intensifications of hardship experienced world-wide in connection with the social relations of science and technology are severe. But what people are experiencing is not transparently clear, and we lack sufficiently subtle connections for collectively building effective theories of experience. Present efforts – Marxist, psychoanalytic, feminist, anthropological – to clarify even "our" experience are rudimentary.[13]

To paraphrase Haraway, what women are experiencing in, specifically, the communication revolution is not clear. How can women get access to this technology and what, practically, can they do with it to further feminist politics and women's creativity? Haraway herself, when she talks about literary writing, tends to focus on the potential within the multiple meanings and identities of the postmodernist world rather than on the mechanics of production. 'Building effective theories of experience' is difficult when the gaps are so great – between, for instance, the technology of cyberfeminism and the women, still the majority, who mend their press with sticky tape and string or between cyberfeminism and the exploited labour of 'third world' women and men who make the technology.[14]

Notes

1 You can pursue these responses in an interesting group of texts in which women writers talk about their relation to writing. See Anne Stevenson's essay in *Women Writing and Writing About Women*, ed. Mary Jacobus (London and Sydney, Croom Helm, 1979); Michelene Wandor (ed.), *On Gender and Writing* (London, Pandora Press, 1983); Moira Monteith (ed.), *Women's Writing: A Challenge to Theory* (Brighton, Sussex, The Harvester Press Ltd., 1986); Gail Chester and Sigrid Nielson (eds), *In Other Words: Writing as a Feminist* (London, Hutchinson, 1987); Lesley Saunders (ed.), *Glancing Fires* (London, The Women's Press Ltd., 1987); Mary Chamberlain (ed.), *Writing Lives: Conversations between Women Writers* (London, Virago Press, 1988); George Plimpton (ed.), *Women Writers at Work: The Paris Review Interviews* (London, Penguin, 1989); Janet Sternberg (ed.), *The Writer on Her Work* (London, Virago, 1992; Susan Sellers (ed.), *Delighting the Heart: A Notebook by Women Writers* (London, The Women's Press Ltd., 1989).

2 For a historical study of this area see Christine Battersby, *Gender and Genius: Towards a Feminist Aesthetics* (London, The Women's Press, 1989).

3 The term 'phallic' criticism is taken from Mary Ellmann, *Thinking About Women* (New York, Harcourt Brace Jovanovich, 1968), ch. 2.

4 The construction of gender stereotypes in Victorian periodical reviews is discussed also by Elaine Showalter in *A Literature of Their Own: British Women Novelists from Brontë to Lessing* (London, Virago, 1978).

5 See also Eavan Boland's essay, 'The Woman Poet: Her Dilemma' in *Stand Magazine*, Winter 1986–7, in which she describes the contemporary woman poet as caught between a 'debased Romanticism' and a separatist, prescriptive feminism. Some of the issues concerning prescriptive criticism are considered further in ch. 4.

6 A comparative description of the process of reading can be found in Jane Marcus, 'Still Practice, A/Wrested Alphabet', *Feminist Issues in Literary Scholarship*, ed. Shari Benstock, (Bloomington, Indiana University Press, 1987) and Susan Sellers, 'Learning to Read the Feminine', in Helen Wilcox et al. (eds), *The Body and the Text: Hélène Cixous, Reading and Teaching* (London, Harvester Wheatsheaf, 1990). More common in Anglo-American criticism is the notion of feminist reading as either a reading of resistance – see Judith Fetterley, *The Resisting Reader: A Feminist Approach to American Fiction* (Bloomington, Indiana University Press, 1978) – or a revisionary reading – see Adrienne Rich, 'When We Dead Awaken: Writing as Re-Vision', *On Lies, Secrets, and Silence: Selected Prose 1966–1978* (New York, and London W. W. Norton and Co., 1979). Further comment on gendered reading is to be found in ch. 5.

7 Other critics have also queried Gilbert and Gubar's work in a similar vein. See Mary Jacobus, 'Review of *The Madwoman in the Attic: The Woman Writer and the Nineteenth-Century Literary Imagination*', in *Signs: Journal of Women in Culture and Society*, vol. 6, no. 3 (1981), and Toril Moi, *Sexual/Textual Politics: Feminist Literary Theory* (London, Methuen, 1985).

8 See Sue Dunderdale, 'The Status of Women in the British Theatre', in *Drama*, 152, (1984).

9 The relationship between gender and literary form is considered more fully in ch. 3.

10 The extract from Alice Walker to which I refer here is to be found in ch. 1.

11 Virginia Woolf, *Three Guineas* in the combined volume of *A Room of One's Own* and *Three Guineas* ed. Michèle Barrett (London, Penguin, 1993), p. 223.

12 See, for example: Eileen Cadman et al., *Rolling Our Own* (London, Minority Press Group, 1981); Gail Chester and Julienne Dickey (eds.), *Feminism and Censorship* (Bridport, Dorset, Prism Press, 1988); Nicci Gerrard, *Into the Mainstream* (London, Pandora, 1989); Patricia Duncker, *Sisters and Strangers: An Introduction to Contemporary Feminist Fiction* (Oxford, Blackwell, 1992). Look for relevant articles in *Spare Rib*, *Everywoman*, *Trouble and Strife*.

13 Donna Haraway, 'A Manifesto for Cyborgs: Science, Technology, and Socialist Feminism in the 1980s', *Feminism/Postmodernism*, ed. Linda J. Nicholson (London, Routledge, 1990), p. 215.

14 See Gayatri Spivak's comments on the situation of South Korean women workers in a factory owned by the American-based, Control Data Corporation in 'Feminism and Critical Theory', *In Other Worlds: Essays in Cultural Politics* (New York and London, Methuen, 1987).

Virginia Woolf

A Room of One's Own

Let me imagine, since facts are so hard to come by, what would have happened had Shakespeare had a wonderfully gifted sister, called Judith, let us say. Shakespeare himself went, very probably – his mother was an heiress[3] – to the grammar school, where he may have learnt Latin – Ovid, Virgil and Horace – and the elements of grammar and logic. He was, it is well known, a wild boy who poached rabbits, perhaps shot a deer, and had, rather sooner than he should have done, to marry a woman in the neighbourhood, who bore him a child rather quicker than was right. That escapade sent him to seek his fortune in London. He had, it seemed, a taste for the theatre; he began by holding horses at the stage door. Very soon he got work in the theatre, became a successful actor, and lived at the hub of the universe, meeting everybody, knowing everybody, practising his art on the boards, exercising his wits in the streets, and even getting access to the palace of the queen. Meanwhile his extraordinarily gifted sister, let us suppose, remained at home. She was as adventurous, as imaginative, as agog to see the world as he was. But she was not sent to school. She had no chance of learning grammar and logic, let alone of reading Horace and Virgil. She picked up a book now and then, one of her brother's perhaps, and read a few pages. But then her parents came in and told her to mend the stockings or mind the stew and not moon about with books and papers. They would have spoken sharply but kindly, for they were substantial people who knew the conditions of life for a woman and loved their daughter – indeed, more likely than not she was the apple of her father's eye. Perhaps she scribbled some pages up in an apple loft on the sly, but was careful to hide them or set fire to them. Soon, however, before she was out of her teens, she was to be betrothed to the son of a neighbouring wool-stapler. She cried out that marriage was hateful to her, and for that she was severely beaten by her father. Then he ceased to scold her. He begged her instead not to hurt him, not to shame him in this matter of her marriage. He would give her a chain of beads or a fine petticoat, he said; and there were tears in his eyes. How could she disobey him? How could she break his heart? The force of her own gift alone drove her to it. She made up a small parcel of her belongings, let herself down by a rope one summer's night and took the road to London. She was not seventeen. The birds that sang in the hedge were not more musical than she was. She had the quickest fancy, a gift like her brother's, for the tune of words. Like him, she had a taste for the theatre. She stood at the stage door; she wanted to act, she said. Men laughed in her face. The manager – a fat, loose- lipped man – guffawed. He bellowed something about poodles dancing and women acting[4] – no woman, he said, could possibly be an actress. He hinted – you can imagine what. She could get no training in her craft. Could she even seek her dinner in a tavern or roam the streets at midnight? Yet her genius was for fiction and lusted to feed abundantly upon the lives of men and women and the study of their ways. At last – for she was very young, oddly like Shakespeare the poet in her face, with the same grey eyes and rounded brows – at last Nick Greene[5] the actor-manager took pity on her; she found herself with child by that gentleman and so – who shall measure the heat and violence of the poet's heart when caught and tangled in a woman's body? – killed herself one winter's night and lies buried at some cross-roads where the omnibuses now stop outside the Elephant and Castle.

That, more or less, is how the story would run, I think, if a woman in Shakespeare's day had had Shakespeare's genius. But for my part, I agree with the deceased bishop, if such he was – it is unthinkable that any woman in Shakespeare's day should have had Shakespeare's genius. For genius like Shakespeare's is not born among labouring, uneducated, servile people. It was not born in England among the Saxons and the Britons. It is not born today among the working classes. How, then, could it have been born among women whose work began, according to Professor Trevelyan, almost before they were out of the nursery, who were forced to it by their parents and held to it by all the power of law and custom? Yet genius of a sort must have existed among women as it must have existed among the working classes. Now and again an Emily Brontë or a Robert Burns blazes out and proves its presence. But certainly it never got itself on to paper. When, however, one reads of a witch being ducked, of a woman possessed by devils, of a wise woman selling herbs, or even of a very remarkable man who had a mother, then I think we are on the track of a lost novelist, a suppressed poet, of some mute and inglorious[6] Jane Austen, some Emily Brontë who dashed her brains out on the moor or mopped and mowed about the highways crazed with the torture that her gift had put her to. Indeed, I would venture to guess that Anon, who wrote so many poems without signing them, was often a woman. It was a woman Edward Fitzgerald,[7] I think, suggested who made the ballads and the folk-songs, crooning them to her children, beguiling her spinning with them, or the length of the winter's night.

This may be true or it may be false – who can say? – but what is true in it, so it seemed to me, reviewing the story of Shakespeare's sister as I had made it, is that any woman born with a great gift in the sixteenth century would certainly have gone crazed, shot herself, or ended her days in some lonely cottage outside the village, half witch, half wizard, feared and mocked at. For it needs little skill in psychology to be sure that a highly gifted girl who had tried to use her gift for poetry would have been so thwarted and hindered by other people, so tortured and pulled asunder by her own contrary instincts, that she must have lost her health and sanity to a certainty. No girl could have walked to London and stood at a stage door and forced her way into the presence of actor-managers without doing herself a violence and suffering an anguish which may have been irrational – for chastity may be a fetish invented by certain societies for unknown reasons – but were none the less inevitable. Chastity had then, it has even now, a religious importance in a woman's life, and has so wrapped itself round with nerves and instincts that to cut it free and bring it to the light of day demands courage of the rarest. To have lived a free life in London in the sixteenth century would have meant for a woman who was poet and playwright a nervous stress and dilemma which might well have killed her. Had she survived, whatever she had written would have been twisted and deformed, issuing from a strained and morbid imagination. And undoubtedly, I thought, looking at the shelf where there are no plays by women, her work would have gone unsigned. That refuge she would have sought certainly. It was the relic of the sense of chastity that dictated anonymity to women even so late as the nineteenth century. Currer Bell, George Eliot, George Sand,[8] all the victims of inner strife as their writings prove, sought ineffectively to veil themselves by using the name of a man. Thus they did homage to the convention, which if not implanted by the other sex was liberally encouraged by them (the chief glory of a woman is not to be talked of, said Pericles, himself a much-talked-of man), that publicity in women is detestable. Anonymity runs in their blood. The desire to be veiled still possesses them. They are not even now as concerned about the health of their fame as men are, and, speaking generally, will pass a tombstone or a signpost without feeling an irresistible desire to cut their names on it, as Alf, Bert or Chas, must do in obedience to their instinct, which murmurs if it sees a fine woman go by, or even a dog. Ce chien est à moi. And, of course, it may not be a dog, I thought, remembering Parliament Square, the Sieges Allee[9] and other avenues; it may be a piece of land or a man with curly black hair. It is one of the great advantages of being a woman that one can pass even a very fine negress without wishing to make an Englishwoman of her.

[. . .]

But for women, I thought, looking at the empty shelves, these difficulties were infinitely more formidable. In the first place, to have a room of her own, let alone a quiet room or a sound-proof room, was out of the question, unless her parents were exceptionally rich or very noble, even up to the beginning of the nineteenth century. Since her pin money, which depended on the good will of her father, was only enough to keep her clothed, she was debarred from such alleviations as came even to Keats or Tennyson or Carlyle, all poor men, from a walking tour, a little journey to France, from the separate lodging which, even if it were miserable enough, sheltered them from the claims and tyrannies of their families. Such material difficulties were formidable; but much worse were the immaterial. The indifference of the world which Keats and Flaubert and other men of genius have found so hard to bear was in her case not indifference but hostility. The world did not say to her as it said to them, Write if you choose; it makes no difference to me. The world said with a guffaw, Write? What's the good of your writing? Here the psychologists of Newnham and Girton might come to our help, I thought, looking again at the blank spaces on the shelves. For surely it is time that the effect of discouragement upon the mind of the artist should be measured, as I have seen a dairy company measure the effect of ordinary milk and Grade A milk upon the body of the rat. They set two rats in cages side by side, and of the two one was furtive, timid and small, and the other was glossy, bold and big. Now what food do we feed women as artists upon? I asked, remembering, I suppose, that dinner of prunes and custard. To answer that question I had only to open the evening paper and to read that Lord Birkenhead is of opinion – but really I am not going to trouble to copy out Lord Birkenhead's opinion upon the writing of women. What Dean Inge says I will leave in peace. The Harley Street[14] specialist may be allowed to rouse the echoes of Harley Street with his vociferations without raising a hair on my head. I will quote, however, Mr. Oscar Browning, because Mr Oscar Browning was a great figure in Cambridge at one time, and used to examine the students at Girton and Newnham. Mr Oscar Browning was wont to declare 'that the impression left on his mind, after looking over any set of examination papers, was that, irrespective of the marks he might give, the best woman was intellectually the inferior of the worst man.' After saying that Mr Browning went back to his rooms – and it is this sequel that endears him and makes him a human figure of some bulk and majesty – he went back to his rooms and found a stable-boy lying on the sofa – 'a mere skeleton, his cheeks were cavernous and sallow, his teeth were black, and he did not appear to have the full use of his limbs. . . . "That's Arthur" [said Mr Browning]. "He's a dear boy really and most high-minded." '[15] The two pictures always seem to me to complete each other. And happily in this age of biography the two pictures often do complete each other, so that we are able to interpret the opinions of great men not only by what they say, but by what they do.

But though this is possible now, such opinions coming from the lips of important people must have been formidable enough even fifty years ago. Let us suppose that a father from the highest motives did not wish his daughter to leave home and become writer, painter or scholar. 'See what Mr Oscar Browning says,' he would say; and there was not only Mr Oscar Browning; there was the *Saturday Review*; there was Mr Greg – the 'essentials of a woman's being', said Mr Greg emphatically, 'are that *they are supported by, and they minister to, men*'[16] – there was an enormous body of masculine opinion to the effect that nothing could be expected of women intellectually. Even if her father did not read out loud these opinions, any girl could read them for herself; and the reading, even in the nineteenth century, must have lowered her vitality, and told profoundly upon her work. There would always have been that assertion –

you cannot do this, you are incapable of doing that – to protest against, to overcome. Probably for a novelist this germ is no longer of much effect; for there have been women novelists of merit. But for painters it must still have some sting in it; and for musicians, I imagine, is even now active and poisonous in the extreme. The woman composer stands where the actress stood in the time of Shakespeare. Nick Greene, I thought, remembering the story I had made about Shakespeare's sister, said that a woman acting put him in mind of a dog dancing. Johnson repeated the phrase two hundred years later of women preaching. And here, I said, opening a book about music, we have the very words used again in this year of grace, 1928, of women who try to write music. 'Of Mlle Germaine Tailleferre one can only repeat Dr Johnson's dictum concerning a woman preacher, transposed into terms of music. "Sir, a woman's composing is like a dog's walking on his hind legs. It is not done well, but you are surprised to find it done at all." '* So accurately does history repeat itself.

* *A Survey of Contemporary Music*, Cecil Gray, p. 246.

(1929)

Notes

3 *his mother was an heiress*: in the manuscript version Woolf originally named Shakespearer's sister after his mother: 'Let us call her Mary Arden', she wrote. She was an extraordinary child, born around 1564. 'Her father was a small tradesman, perhaps a butcher or a dealer in wool.' See *Women and Fiction*, p. 73.

4 *poodles dancing and women acting*: the reference here is to Samuel Johnson's much-quoted view that a woman preaching was like a dog walking on its hind legs: 'It is not done well; but you are surprised to find it done at all' (from Boswell's *Life of Samuel Johnson*, 31 July 1763).

5 *Nick Greene*: the character of Nicholas Greene, an imaginary poet and critic, had been elaborated in Orlando (1928; Penguin Books, 1993, p. 59ff).

6 *some mute and inglorious*: Woolf refers to Thomas Gray's 'Elegy Written in a Country Church-Yard' (1751) ('Some mute inglorious Milton here may rest'). There are both direct and oblique references to John Milton (1608–74) throughtout *AROO*, who can be understood as representing, for Woolf, the masculine appropriation of writing.

7 *Edward Fitzgerald*: (1809–83) translator of *The Rubáiyát of Omar Khayyám* and Victorian man of letters.

8 *Currer Bell . . . George Sand*: Currer Bell was Charlotte Brontë's (1816–55) pseudonym, under which her early work was published; George Eliot and George Sand were the names under which Mary Ann Evans (1819–80) and Amandine Dupin (1804–76) published.

9 *Ce chien . . . the Sieges Allee*: 'This dog is mine', from Blaise Pascal's (1623–62) *Pensées*. The Siegesallee (Victory Avenue) is in Berlin.

10 *a very fine negress*: Wolff's remark is rather disturbing now. It demonstrates the rare, exoticized status of black women in England at that time, and many years were to pass before an identity of 'black British' people would be accepted. More positively, Woolf's belief that 'as a woman I have no country' (elaborated in *TG*) enables her here to recognize cultural and 'racial' differences without harnessing them to nationalistic dogmas.

[. . .]

15 *He's a dear boy really and most high-minded*: Oscar Browning was a Fellow of King's College, Cambridge; the reference to 'high-minded' Arthur implies a link between misogyny and

homosexuality and might thus be seen as somewhat homophobic on Woolf's part. Jane Marcus has interpreted this in terms of a history in which Sir Leslie Stephen had acted to protect Browning and his nephew, J. K. Stephen, from scandal. Browning had been sacked from Eton, with an implication of sexual scandal, and J. K. Stephen was a favoured pupil there who followed him to Cambridge. Marcus reads Woolf's scorching remarks on Browning as, to some extent at least, a displacement of her anger at the patriarchalism of her father and male relatives. See Jane Marcus, *Virginia Woolf and the Languages of Patriarchy* (Indiana University Press, 1987, pp. 181ff.). Browning recorded his own *Memories of Sixty Years* (1910) and his nephew H. E. Wortham published a biography of him in 1927 (the source of Woolf's anecdote).

16 *they are supported by, and they minister to, men*: Woolf encountered this remark in Barbara Stephen's *Emily Davies and Girton College*, published in 1927. *Two Women*, her review of the book, is reprinted in *WE*, pp. 115–20.

VIRGINIA WOOLF

'Professions for Women'
The Death of the Moth

What could be easier than to write articles and to buy Persian cats with the profits? But wait a moment. Articles have to be about something. Mine, I seem to remember, was about a novel by a famous man. And while I was writing this review, I discovered that if I were going to review books I should need to do battle with a certain phantom. And the phantom was a woman, and when I came to know her better I called her after the heroine of a famous poem, The Angel in the House. It was she who used to come between me and my paper when I was writing reviews. It was she who bothered me and wasted my time and so tormented me that at last I killed her. You who come of a younger and happier generation may not have heard of her – you may not know what I mean by the Angel in the House. I will describe her as shortly as I can. She was intensely sympathetic. She was immensely charming. She was utterly unselfish. She excelled in the difficult arts of family life. She sacrificed herself daily. If there was chicken, she took the leg; if there was a draught she sat in it – in short she was so constituted that she never had a mind or a wish of her own, but preferred to sympathize always with the minds and wishes of others. Above all – I need not say it – she was pure. Her purity was supposed to be her chief beauty – her blushes, her great grace. In those days – the last of Queen Victoria – every house had its Angel. And when I came to write I encountered her with the very first words. The shadow of her wings fell on my page; I heard the rustling of her skirts in the room. Directly, that is to say, I took my pen in my hand to review that novel by a famous man, she slipped behind me and whispered: 'My dear, you are a young woman. You are writing about a book that has been written by a man. Be sympathetic; be tender; flatter; deceive; use all the arts and wiles of our sex. Never let anybody guess that you have a mind of your own. Above all, be pure.' And she made as if to guide my pen. I now record the one act for which

I take some credit to myself, though the credit rightly belongs to some excellent ancestors of mine who left me a certain sum of money – shall we say five hundred pounds a year? – so that it was not necessary for me to depend solely on charm for my living. I turned upon her and caught her by the throat. I did my best to kill her. My excuse, if I were to be had up in a court of law, would be that I acted in self-defence. Had I not killed her she would have killed me. She would have plucked the heart out of my writing. For, as I found, directly I put pen to paper, you cannot review even a novel without having a mind of your own, without expressing what you think to be the truth about human relations, morality, sex. And all these questions, according to the Angel of the House, cannot be dealt with freely and openly by women; they must charm, they must conciliate, they must – to put it bluntly – tell lies if they are to succeed. Thus, whenever I felt the shadow of her wing or the radiance of her halo upon my page, I took up the inkpot and flung it at her. She died hard. Her fictitious nature was of great assistance to her. It is far harder to kill a phantom than a reality. She was always creeping back when I thought I had despatched her. Though I flatter myself that I killed her in the end, the struggle was severe; it took much time that had better have been spent upon learning Greek grammar; or in roaming the world in search of adventures. But it was a real experience; it was an experience that was found to befall all women writers at that time. Killing the Angel in the House was part of the occupation of a woman writer.

[. . .]

I want you to figure to yourselves a girl sitting with a pen in her hand, which for minutes, and indeed for hours, she never dips into the inkpot. The image that comes to my mind when I think of this girl is the image of a fisherman lying sunk in dreams on the verge of a deep lake with a rod held out over the water. She was letting her imagination sweep unchecked round every rock and cranny of the world that lies submerged in the depths of our unconscious being. Now came the experience, the experience that I believe to be far commoner with women writers than with men. The line raced through the girl's fingers. Her imagination had rushed away. It had sought the pools, the depths, the dark places where the largest fish slumber. And then there was a smash. There was an explosion. There was foam and confusion. The imagination had dashed itself against something hard. The girl was roused from her dream. She was indeed in a state of the most acute and difficult distress. To speak without figure she had thought of something, something about the body, about the passions which it was unfitting for her as a woman to say. Men, her reason told her, would be shocked. The consciousness of what men will say of a woman who speaks the truth about her passions had roused her from her artist's state of unconsciousness. She could write no more. The trance was over. Her imagination could work no longer. This I believe to be a very common experience with women writers – they are impeded by the extreme conventionality of the other sex. For though men sensibly allow themselves great freedom in these respects, I doubt that they realize or can control the extreme severity with which they condemn such freedom in women.

These then were two very genuine experiences of my own. These were two of the adventures of my professional life. The first – killing the Angel in the House – I think I solved. She died. But the second, telling the truth about my own experiences as a body, I do not think I solved. I doubt that any woman has solved it yet. The obstacles against her are still immensely powerful – and yet they are very difficult to define. Outwardly, what is simpler than to write books? Outwardly, what obstacles are there for a woman rather than for a man? Inwardly, I think, the case is very different; she has still many ghosts to fight, many prejudices to overcome. Indeed it will be a long time still, I think, before a woman can sit down to write a book without finding a phantom to be slain, a rock to be dashed against. And if this is so in literature, the freest of all professions for women, how is it in the new professions which you are now for the first time entering?

(1942)

TILLIE OLSEN

Silences

Work first:

> Within our bodies we bore the race. Through us it was shaped, fed and clothed.
> . . . Labour more toilsome and unending than that of man was ours. . . . No
> work was too hard, no labour too strenuous to exclude us.[1]

True for most women in most of the world still.

Unclean; taboo. The Devil's Gateway. The three steps behind; the girl babies drowned in the river; the baby strapped to the back. Buried alive with the lord, burned alive on the funeral pyre, burned as witch at the stake. Stoned to death for adultery. Beaten, raped. Bartered. Bought and sold. Concubinage, prostitution, white slavery. The hunt, the sexual prey, 'I am a lost creature, O the poor Clarissa.' Purdah, the veil of Islam, domestic confinement. Illiterate. Denied vision. Excluded, excluded, excluded from council, ritual, activity, learning, language, when there was neither biological nor economic reason to be excluded.

Religion, when all believed. In sorrow shalt thou bring forth children. May thy wife's womb never cease from bearing. Neither was the man created for the woman but the woman for the man. Let the woman learn in silence and in all subjection. Contrary to biological birth fact: Adam's rib. The Jewish male morning prayer: thank God I was not born a woman. Silence in holy places, seated apart, or not permitted entrance at all; castration of boys because women too profane to sing in church.

And for the comparative handful of women born into the privileged class; being, not doing; man does, woman is; to you the world says work, to us it says seem. God is thy law, thou mine. Isolated. Cabin'd, cribb'd, confin'd; the private sphere. Bound feet: corseted, cosseted, bedecked; denied one's body. Powerlessness. Fear of rape, male strength. Fear of aging. Subject to. Fear of expressing capacities. Soft attractive graces; the mirror to magnify man. Marriage as property arrangement. The vices of slaves:[2] dissembling, flattering, manipulating, appeasing.

Bolstering. Vicarious living, infantilization, trivialization. Parasitism, individualism, madness. Shut up, you're only a girl. O Elizabeth, why couldn't you have been born a boy? For twentieth-century woman: roles, discontinuities, part-self, part-time; conflict; imposed 'guilt'; 'a man can give full energy to his profession, a woman cannot.'

How is it that women have not made a fraction of the intellectual, scientific, or artistic-cultural contributions that men have made?

Only in the context of this punitive difference in circumstance, in history, between the sexes; this past, hidden or evident, that (though objectively obsolete – yes, even the toil and the compulsory childbearing obsolete) *continues so terribly, so determiningly to live on, only in this context can the question be answered or my subject here today – the women writer in our century: one out of twelve: – be understood.*

How much it takes to become a writer. Bent (far more common than we assume), circumstances, time, development of craft – but beyond that: how much conviction as to the importance of what one has to say, one's right to say it. And the will, the measureless store of belief in oneself to be able to come to, cleave to, find the form for one's own life comprehensions. Difficult for any male not born into a class that breeds such confidence. Almost impossible for a girl, a woman.

The leeching of belief, of will, the damaging of capacity begin so early. Sparse indeed is the literature on the way of denial to small girl children of the development of their endowment as born human: active, vigorous bodies; exercise of the power to do, to make, to investigate, to invent, to conquer obstacles, to resist violations of the self; to think, create, choose; to attain community, confidence in self. Little has been written on the harms of instilling constant concern with appearance; the need to please, to support; the training in acceptance, deferring. Little has been added in our century to George Eliot's *The Mill on the Floss* on the effect of the differing treatment – 'climate of expectation' – for boys and for girls.

But it is there if one knows how to read for it, and indelibly there in the resulting damage. One – out of twelve.

In the vulnerable girl years, unlike their sisters in the previous century, women writers go to college.[3] The kind of experience it may be for them is stunningly documented in Elaine Showalter's pioneering "Women and the Literary Curriculum."[4] Freshman texts in which women have little place, if at all; language itself, all achievement, anything to do with the human in male terms – *Man in Crises, The Individual and His World*. Three hundred thirteen male writers taught; seventeen women writers: That classic of adolescent rebellion, *A Portrait of the Artist as a Young Man*; and sagas (male) of the quest for identity (but then Erikson, the father of the concept, propounds that identity concerns girls only insofar as making themselves into attractive beings for the right kind of man).[5] Most, *not all*, of the predominantly male literature studied, written by men whose understandings are not universal, but restrictively male (as Mary Ellmann, Kate Millett, and Dolores Schmidt have pointed out); in our time more and more surface, hostile, one-dimensional in portraying women.

In a writer's young years, susceptibility to the vision and style of the great is extreme. Add the aspiration-denying implication, consciously felt or not (although reinforced daily by one's professors and reading) that (as Virginia Woolf noted years ago) women writers, women's experience, and literature written by women are by definition minor. (Mailer will not grant even the minor: 'the one thing a writer has to have is balls.') No wonder that Showalter observes:

> Women [students] are estranged from their own experience and unable to perceive its shape and authenticity, in part because they do not see it mirrored and given resonance in literature. . . . They are expected to identify with masculine experience, which is presented as the human one, and have no faith in the validity of their own perceptions and experiences, rarely seeing them confirmed in literature, or accepted in criticism . . . [They] notoriously lack the happy confidence, the exuberant sense of the value of their individual observations which enables young men to risk making fools of themselves for the sake of an idea.

Harms difficult to work through. Nevertheless, some young women (others are already lost) maintain their ardent intention to write – fed indeed by the very glories of some of this literature that puts them down.

But other invisible worms are finding out the bed of crimson joy.[6] Self-doubt; seriousness, also questioned by the hours agonizing over appearance; concentration shredded into attracting, being attractive; the absorbing real need and love for working with words felt as hypocritical self-delusion ('I'm not truly dedicated'), for what seems (and is) esteemed is being attractive to men. High aim, and accomplishment toward it, discounted by the prevalent attitude that, as girls will probably marry (attitudes not applied to boys who will probably marry), writing is no more than an attainment of a dowry to be spent later according the needs and circumstances within the true vocation: husband and family. The growing acceptance that going on will threaten other needs, to love and be loved; ('a woman has to sacrifice all claims to femininity and family to be a writer').[7]

And the agony – peculiarly mid-century, escaped by their sisters of pre-Freudian, pre-Jungian times – that 'creation and femininity are incompatible.'[8] Anaïs Nin's words.

> The aggressive act of creation; the guilt for creating. I did not want to rival man; to steal man's creation, his thunder. I must protect them, not outshine them.[9]

The acceptance – against one's experienced reality – of the sexist notion that the act of creation is not as inherently natural to a woman as to a man, but rooted instead in unnatural aggression, rivalry, envy, or thwarted sexuality.

And in all the usual college teaching – the English, history, psychology, sociology courses – little to help that young woman understand the source or nature of this inexplicable draining self-doubt, loss of aspiration, of confidence.

It is all there in the extreme in Plath's *Bell Jar* – that (inadequate)[10] portrait of the artist as young woman (significantly, one of the few that we have) – from the precarious sense of vocation to the paralyzing conviction that (in a sense different from what she wrote years later)

> Perfection is terrible. It cannot have children.
> It tamps the womb.

And indeed, in our century as in the last, until very recently almost all distinguished achievement has come from childless women: Willa Cather, Ellen Glasgow, Gertrude Stein, Edith Wharton, Virginia Woolf, Elizabeth Bowen, Katherine Mansfield, Isak Dinesen, Katherine Anne Porter, Dorothy Richardson, Henry Handel Richardson, Susan Glaspell, Dorothy Parker, Lillian Hellman, Eudora Welty, Djuna Barnes, Anaïs Nin, Ivy Compton-Burnett, Zora Neale Hurston, Elizabeth Madox Roberts, Christina Stead, Carson McCullers, Flannery O'Connor, Jean Stafford, May Sarton, Josephine Herbst, Jessamyn West, Janet Frame, Lillian Smith, Iris Murdoch, Joyce Carol Oates, Hannah Green, Lorraine Hansberry.

Most never questioned, or at least accepted (a few sanctified) this different condition for achievement, not imposed on men writers. Few asked the fundamental human equality question regarding it that Elizabeth Mann Borghese, Thomas Mann's daughter, asked when she was eighteen and sent to a psychiatrist for help in getting over an unhappy love affair (revealing also a working ambition to become a great musician although 'women cannot be great musicians'). 'You must choose between your art and fulfillment as a

woman,' the analyst told her, 'between music and family life.' 'Why?' she
asked. 'Why must I choose? No one said to Toscanini or to Bach or my father
that they must choose between their art and personal, family life; fulfillment
as a man. . . . Injustice everywhere.' Not where it is free choice. But where it
is forced because of the circumstances for the sex into which one is born – a
choice men of the same class do not have to make in order to do their work
– that is not choice, that is a coercive working of sexist oppression.[11]

(1978)

Notes

1 Olive Schreiner, *Women and Labour*.
2 Elizabeth Barrett Browning's phrase; other phrases throughout from the Bible, John Milton,
   Richardson's *Clarissa*, Matthew Arnold, Elizabeth Cady Stanton, Virginia Woolf, Viola Klein,
   Mountain Wolf Woman.
3 True almost without exception among the writers who are women in *Twentieth Century Authors*
   and *Contemporary Authors*.
4 *College English*, May 1971. A year later (October 1972), *College English* published an extensive report,
   "Freshman Textbooks," by Jean Mullens. In the 112 most used texts, she found 92.47 percent
   (5,795) of the selections were by men; 7.53 percent (472) by women (One Out of Twelve). Mullens
   deepened Showalter's insights as to the subtly undermining effect on freshman students of the texts'
   contents and language, as well as the minuscule proportion of women writers.
5 In keeping with his 1950s-60s thesis of a distinctly female 'biological, evolutionary need to fulfil
   self through serving others.'
6   O Rose thou art sick./The invisible worm,
               That flies in the night/In the howling storm:
               Has found out thy bed/Of crimson joy:
               And his dark secret love/Does thy life destroy.
                                            William Blake
7 Plath. A letter when a graduate student.
8 *The Diary of Anaïs Nin*, Vol. III, 1939–1944.
9 A statement that would have baffled Austen, the Brontës, Mrs Gaskell, Eliot, Stowe, Alcott, etc.
   The strictures were felt by them in other ways.
10 Inadequate, for the writer being ('muteness is sickness for me') is not portrayed. By contrast, how
   present she is in Plath's own *Letters Home*.
11 'Them lady poets must not marry, pal,' is how John Berryman, poet (himself oft married) expressed
   it. The old patriarchal injunction: 'Woman, this is man's realm. If you insist on invading it, unsex
   yourself – and expect the road to be made difficult.' Furthermore, this very unmarriedness and
   childlessness has been used to discredit women as unfulfilled, inadequate, somehow abnormal.

ADRIENNE RICH

'When We Dead Awaken: Writing as Re-Vision'
On Lies, Secrets, and Silence

I have hesitated to do what I am going to do now, which is to use myself as
an illustration. For one thing, it's a lot easier and less dangerous to talk about
other women writers. But there is something else. Like Virginia Woolf, I am

aware of the women who are not with us here because they are washing the dishes and looking after the children. Nearly fifty years after she spoke, the fact remains largely unchanged. And I am thinking also of women whom she left out of the picture altogether – women who are washing other people's dishes and caring for other people's children, not to mention women who went on the streets last night in order to feed their children. We seem to be special women here, we have liked to think of ourselves as special, and we have known that men would tolerate, even romanticize us as special, as long as our words and actions didn't threaten their privilege of tolerating or rejecting us and our work according to *their* ideas of what a special woman ought to be. An important insight of the radical women's movement has been how divisive and how ultimately destructive is this myth of the special woman, who is also the token woman. Every one of us here in this room has had great luck – we are teachers, writers, academicians; our own gifts could not have been enough, for we all know women whose gifts are buried or aborted. Our struggles can have meaning and our privileges – however precarious under patriarchy – can be justified only if they can help to change the lives of women whose gifts – and whose very being – continue to be thwarted and silenced.

[. . .]

I know that my style was formed first by male poets: by the men I was reading as an undergraduate – Frost, Dylan Thomas, Donne, Auden, MacNiece, Stevens, Yeats. What I chiefly learned from them was craft.[5] But poems are like dreams: in them you put what you don't know you know. Looking back at poems I wrote before I was twenty-one, I'm startled because beneath the conscious craft are glimpses of the split I even then experienced between the girl who wrote poems, who defined herself in writing poems, and the girl who was to define herself by her relationships with men. 'Aunt Jennifer's Tigers' (1951), written while I was a student, looks with deliberate detachment at this split.[6]

> Aunt Jennifer's tigers stride across a screen,
> Bright topaz denizens of a world of green.
> They do not fear the men beneath the tree;
> They pace in sleek chivalric certainty.
> Aunt Jennifer's fingers fluttering through her wool
> Find even the ivory needle hard to pull.
> The massive weight of Uncle's wedding band
> Sits heavily upon Aunt Jennifer's hand.
> When Aunt is dead, her terrified hands will lie
> Still ringed with ordeals she was mastered by.
> The tigers in the panel that she made
> Will go on striding, proud and unafraid.

In writing this poem, composed and apparently cool as it is, I thought I was creating a portrait of an imaginary woman. But this woman suffers from the opposition of her imagination, worked out in tapestry, and her life-style, 'ringed with ordeals she was mastered by.' It was important to me that Aunt Jennifer was a person as distinct from myself as possible – distanced by the formalism of the poem, by its objective, observant tone – even by putting the woman in a different generation.

In those years formalism was part of the strategy – like asbestos gloves, it allowed me to handle materials I couldn't pick up bare-handed. A later strategy was to use the persona of a man, as I did in 'The Loser' (1958):

A man thinks of the woman he once loved: first, after her wedding, and then nearly a decade later.

I

I kissed you, bride and lost, and went
home from that bourgeois sacrament,
your cheek still tasting cold upon
my lips that gave you benison
with all the swagger that they knew –
as losers somehow learn to do.

Your wedding made my eyes ache; soon
the world would be worse off for one

more golden apple dropped to ground
without the least protesting sound,
and you would windfall lie, and we
forget your shimmer on the tree.

Beauty is always wasted: if
not Mignon's song sung to the deaf,
at all events to the unmoved.
A face like yours cannot be loved
long or seriously enough,
Almost, we seem to hold it off.

II

Well, you are tougher than I thought.
Now when the wash with ice hangs taut
this morning of St. Valentine,
I see you strip the squeaking line,
your body weighed against the load,
and all my groans can do no good.

Because you are still beautiful,
though squared and stiffened by the pull
of what nine windy years have done.
You have three daughters, lost a son,

I see all your intelligence
flung into that unwearied stance.

My envy is of no avail.
I turn my head and wish him well
who chafed your beauty into use
and lives forever in a house
lit by the friction of your mind.
You stagger in against the wind.

I finished college, published my first book by a fluke, as it seemed to me, and broke off a love affair. I took a job, lived alone, went on writing, fell in love. I was young, full of energy, and the book seemed to mean that others agreed I was a poet. Because I was also determined to prove that as a woman poet I could also have what was then defined as a 'full' woman's life, I plunged in my early twenties into marriage and had three children before I was thirty. There was nothing overt in the environment to warn me: these were the fifties, and in reaction to the earlier wave of feminism, middle-class women were making careers of domestic perfection, working to send their husbands through professional schools, then retiring to raise large families. People were moving out to the suburbs, technology was going to be the answer to everything, even sex; the family was in its glory. Life was extremely private; women were isolated from each other by the loyalties of marriage. I have a sense that women didn't talk to each other much in the fifties – not about their secret emptinesses, their frustrations. I went on trying to write; my second book and first child appeared in the same month. But by the time that book came out I was already dissatisfied with those poems, which seemed to me mere exercises for poems I hadn't written. The book was praised, however, for its 'gracefulness'; I had a marriage and a child. If there were doubts, if there were periods of null depression or active despairing, these could only mean that I was ungrateful, insatiable, perhaps a monster.

About the time my third child was born, I felt that I had either to consider myself a failed woman and a failed poet, or to try to find some synthesis by which to understand what was happening to me. What frightened me most was the sense of drift, of being pulled along on a current which called itself my destiny, but in which I seemed to be losing touch with whoever I had been, with the girl who had experienced her own will and energy almost ecstatically at times, walking round a city or riding a train at night or typing in a student room. In a poem about my grandmother I wrote (of myself): 'A young girl, thought sleeping, is certified dead' ('Halfway'). I was writing very little, partly from fatigue, that female fatigue of suppressed anger and loss of contact with my own being; partly from the discontinuity of female life with its attention to small chores, errands, work that others constantly undo, small children's constant needs. What I did write was unconvincing to me; my anger and frustration were hard to acknowledge in or out of poems because in fact I cared a great deal about my husband and my children. Trying to look back and understand that time I have tried to analyze the real nature of the conflict. Most, if not all, human lives are full of fantasy – passive day-dreaming which need not be acted on. But to write poetry or fiction, or even to think well, is not to fantasize, or to put fantasies on paper. For a poem to coalesce, for a character or an action to take shape, there has to be an imaginative transformation of reality which is in no way passive. And a certain freedom of the mind is needed – freedom to press on, to enter the currents of your thought like a glider pilot, knowing that your motion can be sustained, that the buoyancy of your attention will not be suddenly snatched away. Moreover, if the imagination is to transcend and transform experience it has to question, to challenge, to conceive of alternatives, perhaps to the very life you are living at that moment. You have to be free to play around with the notion that day might be night, love might be hate; nothing can be too sacred for the imagination to turn into its opposite or to call experimentally by another name. For writing is re-naming. Now, to be maternally with small children all day in the old way, to be with a man in the old way of marriage, requires a holding-back, a putting-aside of that imaginative activity, and demands instead a kind of conservatism. I want to make it clear that I am *not* saying that in order to write well, or think well, it is necessary to become unavailable to others, or to become a devouring ego. This has been the myth of the masculine artist and thinker; and I do not accept it. But to be a female human being trying to fulfill traditional female functions in a traditional way *is* in direct conflict with the subversive function of the imagination. The word traditional is important here. There must be ways, and we will be finding out more and more about them, in which the energy of creation and the energy of relation can be united. But in those years I always felt the conflict as a failure of love in myself. I had thought I was choosing a full life: the life available to most men, in which sexuality, work, and parenthood could coexist. But I felt, at twenty-nine, guilt toward the people closest to me, and guilty toward my own being.

I wanted, then, more than anything, the one thing of which there was never enough: time to think, time to write. The fifties and early sixties were years of rapid revelations: the sit-ins and marches in the South, the Bay of Pigs, the early antiwar movement, raised large questions – questions for which the masculine world of the academy around me seemed to have expert and fluent answers. But I needed to think for myself – about pacifism and dissent and violence, about poetry and society, and about my own relationship to all these things. For about ten years I was reading in fierce snatches, scribbling in notebooks, writing poetry in fragments; I was looking desperately for clues, because if there were no clues then I thought I might be insane, I wrote in a notebook about this time:

Paralyzed by the sense that there exists a mesh of relationships – e.g., between my anger at the children, my sensual life, pacifism, sex (I mean sex in its broadest significance, not merely sexual desire) – an interconnectedness which, if I could see it, make it valid, would give me back myself, make it possible to function lucidly and passionately. Yet I grope in and out among these dark webs.

I think I began at this point to feel that politics was not something 'out there' but something 'in here' and of the essence of my condition.

In the late fifties I was able to write, for the first time, directly about experiencing myself as a woman. The poem was jotted in fragments during children's naps, brief hours in a library, or at 3:00 a.m. after rising with a wakeful child. I despaired of doing any continuous work at this time. Yet I began to feel that my fragments and scraps had a common consciousness and a common theme, one which I would have been very unwilling to put on paper at an earlier time because I had been taught that poetry should be 'universal,' which meant, of course, nonfemale. Until then I had tried very much *not* to identify myself as a female poet. Over two years I wrote a ten-part poem called 'Snapshots of a Daughter-in-Law' (1958–1960), in a longer looser mode than I'd ever trusted myself with before. It was an extraordinary relief to write that poem. It strikes me now as too literary, too dependent on allusion; I hadn't found the courage yet to do without authorities, or even to use the pronoun 'I' – the woman in the poem is always 'she.' One section of it, No. 2, concerns a woman who thinks she is going mad; she is haunted by voices telling her to resist and rebel, voices which she can hear but not obey.

> 2.
> Banging the coffee-pot into the sink
> she hears the angels chiding, and looks out
> past the raked gardens to the sloppy sky.
> Only a week since They said: *Have no patience.*
> The next time it was: *Be insatiable.*
> Then: *Save yourself: others you cannot save.*
> Sometimes she's let the tapstream scald her arm,
> a match burn to her thumbnail
> or held her hand above the kettle's snout
> right in the woolly steam. They are probably angels,
> since nothing hurts her anymore, except
> 'each morning's grit blowing into her eyes.

The poem 'Orion,' written five years later, is a poem of reconnection with a part of myself I had felt I was losing – the active principle, the energetic imagination, the 'half- brother' whom I projected, as I had for many years, into the constellation Orion. It's no accident that the words 'cold and egotistical' appear in this poem, and are applied to myself.

Far back when I went zig-zagging
through tamarack pastures
you were my genius, you
my cast-iron Viking, my helmed
lion-heart king in prison.
Years later now you're young

my fierce half-brother, staring
down from that simplified west
your breast open, your belt dragged down
by an oldfashioned thing, a sword
the last bravado you won't give over
though it weighs you down as you stride

and the stars in it are dim
and maybe have stopped burning.
But you burn, and I know it;
as I throw back my head to take you in
an old transfusion happens again:
divine astronomy is nothing to it.

Indoors I bruise and blunder,
break faith, leave ill enough
alone, a dead child born in the dark.
Night cracks up over the chimney,
pieces of time, frozen geodes
come showering down in the grate.

A man reaches behind my eyes
and finds them empty
a woman's head turns away from my head in the mirror
children are dying my death
and eating crumbs of my life.

Pity is not your forte.
Calmly you ache up there
pinned aloft in your crow's nest,

my speechless pirate!
You take it all for granted
and when I look you back

it's with a starlike eye
shooting its cold and egotistical spear
where it can do least damage.
Breathe deep! No hurt, no pardon
out here in the cold with you
you with your back to the wall.

The choice still seemed to be between 'love' – womanly, maternal love, altruistic love – a love defined and ruled by the weight of an entire culture;

and egotism – a force directed by men into creation, achievement, ambition, often at the expense of others, but justifiably so. For weren't they men, and wasn't that their destiny as womanly, selfless love was ours? We know now that the alternatives are false ones – that the word 'love' is itself in need of re-vision.

(1972)

Notes

5 A.R., 1978: Yet I spent months, at sixteen, memorizing and writing imitations of Millay's sonnets; and in notebooks of that period I find what are obviously attempts to imitate Dickinson's metrics and verbal compression. I knew H. D. only through anthologized lyrics; her epic poetry was not then available to me.

6 A.R., 1978: Texts of poetry quoted herein can be found in A. R. *Poems Selected and New: 1950–1974* (New York: Norton, 1975).

Sandra M. Gilbert and Susan Gubar

The Madwoman in the Attic: The Woman Writer and the Nineteenth-Century Literary Imagination

And the lady of the house was seen only as she appeared in each room, according to the nature of the lord of the room. None saw the whole of her, none but herself. For the light which she was both her mirror and her body. None could tell the whole of her, none but herself.

Laura Riding

Alas! A woman that attempts the pen
Such an intruder on the rights of men,
Such a presumptuous Creature is esteem'd
The fault can by no vertue be redeem'd.

Anne Finch, Countess of Winchilsea

As to all that nonsense Henry and Larry talked about, the necessity of 'I am God'
in order to create (I suppose they mean 'I am God. I am not a woman') . . . this 'I
am God,' which makes creation an act of solitude and pride, this image of God alone
making sky, earth, sea, it is this image which has confused woman.

Anaïs Nin

Is a pen a metaphorical penis? Gerard Manley Hopkins seems to have thought so. In a letter to his friend R. W. Dixon in 1886 he confided a crucial feature of his theory of poetry. The artist's 'most essential quality,' he declared, is 'masterly execution, which is a kind of male gift, and especially marks off men from women, the begetting of one's thought on paper, on verse, or whatever the matter is.' In addition, he noted that 'on better consideration it strikes me that the mastery I speak of is not so much in the mind as a puberty in the life of that quality. The male quality is the creative gift.'[1] Male sexuality, in other words, is not just analogically but actually the essence of literary power. The poet's pen is in some sense (even more than figuratively) a penis.

Eccentric and obscure though he was, Hopkins was articulating a concept central to that Victorian culture of which he was in this case a representative male citizen. But of course the patriarchal notion that the writer 'fathers' his text just as God fathered the world is and has been all-pervasive in Western literary civilization, so much so that, as Edward Said has shown, the metaphor is built into the very word, *author*, with which writer, deity, and *pater familias* are identified. Said's miniature meditation on the word *authority* is worth quoting in full because it summarizes so much that is relevant here:

> *Authority* suggests to me a constellation of linked meanings: not only, as the OED tells us, 'a power to enforce obedience,' or 'a derived or delegated power,' or 'a power to influence action,' or 'a power to inspire belief,' or 'a person whose opinion is accepted': not only those, but a connection as well with *author* – that is, a person who originates or gives existence to something, a begetter, beginner, father, or ancestor, a person also who sets forth written statements. There is still another cluster of meanings: *author* is tied to the past participle *auctus* of the verb *augere*; therefore *auctor*, according to Eric Partridge, is literally an increaser and thus a founder. *Auctoritas* is production, invention, cause, in addition to meaning a right of possession. Finally, it means continuance, or a causing to continue. Taken together these meanings are all grounded in the following notions: (1) that of the power of an individual to initiate, institute, establish – in short, to begin; (2) that this power and its product are an increase over what had been there previously; (3) that the individual wielding this power controls its issue and what is derived therefrom; (4) that authority maintains the continuity of its course.[2]

In conclusion, Said, who is discussing 'The Novel as Beginning Intention,' remarks that 'All four of these [last] abstractions can be used to describe the way in which narrative fiction asserts itself psychologically and aesthetically through the technical efforts of the novelist.' But they can also, of course, be used to describe both the author and the authority of any literary text, a point Hopkins's sexual/aesthetic theory seems to have been designed to elaborate. Indeed, Said himself later observes that a convention of most literary texts is 'that the unity or integrity of the text is maintained by a series of genealogical connections: author – text, beginning-middle-end, text – meaning, reader – interpretation, and so on. *Underneath all these is the imagery of succession, of paternity, or hierarchy*' (italics ours).[3]

There is a sense in which the very notion of paternity is itself, as Stephen Dedalus puts it in *Ulysses*, a 'legal fiction,'[4] a story requiring imagination if not faith. A man cannot verify his fatherhood by either sense or reason, after all; that his child is *his* is in a sense a tale he tells himself to explain the infant's existence. Obviously, the anxiety implicit in such storytelling urgently needs not only the reassurances of male superiority that patriarchal misogyny implies, but also such compensatory fictions of the Word as those embodied in the genealogical imagery Said describes. Thus it is possible to trace the history of this compensatory, sometimes frankly stated and sometimes submerged imagery that elaborates upon what Stephen Dedalus calls the 'mystical estate' of paternity[5] through the works of many literary theoreticians besides Hopkins and Said. Defining poetry as a mirror held up to nature, the mimetic aesthetic that begins with Aristotle and descends through Sidney, Shakespeare, and Johnson implies that the poet, like a lesser God, has made or engendered an alternative, mirror-universe in which he actually seems to enclose or trap shadows of reality. Similarly, Coleridge's Romantic concept of the human 'imagination or esemplastic power' is of a virile, generative force which echoes 'the eternal act of creation in the infinite I AM,' while Ruskin's phallic-sounding 'Penetrative Imagination' is a 'possession-taking faculty' and a 'piercing . . . mind's tongue' that seizes, cuts down, and gets at the root of experience in order 'to throw up what new shoots it will.'[6] In all these aesthetics the poet, like God the Father, is a paternalistic ruler of the fictive world he has created. Shelley called him a 'legislator.' Keats noted, speaking of writers, that 'the antients [*sic*] were Emperors of vast Provinces' though 'each of the moderns' is merely an 'Elector of Hanover.'[7]

In medieval philosophy, the network of connections among sexual, literary, and theological metaphors is equally complex: God the Father both engenders the cosmos and, as Ernst Robert Curtius notes, writes the Book of Nature: both tropes describe a single act of creation.[8] In addition, the Heavenly Author's ultimate eschatological power is made manifest when, as the *Liber Scriptus* of the traditional requiem mass indicates. He writes the Book of Judgment. More recently, male artists like the Earl of Rochester in the seventeenth century and Auguste Renoir in the nineteenth, have frankly defined aesthetics based on male sexual delight. 'I . . . never Rhym'd, but for my Pintle's [penis's] sake,' declares Rochester's witty Timon,[9] and (according to the painter Bridget Riley) Renoir 'is supposed to have said that he painted his paintings with his prick.'[10] Clearly, both these artists believe, with Norman O. Brown, that 'the penis is the head of the body,' and they might both agree too, with John Irwin's suggestion that the relationship 'of the masculine self with the feminine-masculine work is also an autoerotic act . . . a kind of creative onanism in which through the use of the phallic pen on the "pure space" of the virgin page . . . the self is continually spent and wasted. . . .'[11] No doubt it is for all these reasons, moreover, that poets have traditionally used a vocabulary derived from the patriarchal 'family romance' to describe their relations with each other. As Harold Bloom has pointed out, 'from the sons of Homer to the sons of Ben Jonson, poetic influence [has] been described as a filial relationship,' a relationship of '*sonship*.' The fierce struggle at the heart of literary history, says Bloom, is a 'battle between strong equals, father and son as mighty opposites, Laius and Oedipus at the crossroads.'[12]

Though many of these writers use the metaphor of literary paternity in different ways and for different purposes, all seem overwhelmingly to agree that a literary text is not only speech quite literally embodied, but also power mysteriously made manifest, made flesh. In patriarchal Western culture, therefore, the text's author is a father, a progenitor, a procreator, an aesthetic patriarch whose pen is an instrument of generative power like his penis. More, his pen's power, like his penis's power, is not just the ability to generate life but the power to create a posterity to which he lays claim, as, in Said's paraphrase of Partridge, 'an increaser and thus a founder.' In this respect, the pen is truly mightier than its phallic counterpart the sword, and in patriarchy more resonantly sexual. Not only does the writer respond to his muse's quasi-sexual excitation with an outpouring of the aesthetic energy Hopkins called 'the fine delight that fathers thought' – a delight poured seminally from pen to page – but as the author of an enduring text the writer engages the attention of the future in exactly the same way that a king (or father) 'owns' the homage of the present. No sword-wielding general could rule so long or possess so vast a kingdom.

Finally, that such a notion of 'ownership' or possession is embedded in the metaphor of paternity leads to yet another implication of this complex metaphor. For if the author/father is owner of his text and his reader's attention, he is also, of course, owner/possessor of the subjects of his text, that is to say of those figures, scenes, and events – those brain children – he has both incarnated in black and white and 'bound' in cloth or leather. Thus, because he is an *author*, a 'man of letters' is simultaneously, like his divine counterpart, a father, a master or ruler, and an owner: the spiritual type of a patriarch, as we understand that term in Western society.

Where does such an implicitly or explicitly patriarchal theory of literature leave literary women? If the pen is a metaphorical penis, with what organ can females generate texts? The question may seem frivolous, but as our epigraph from Anaïs Nin indicates, both the patriarchal etiology that defines a solitary Father God as the only creator of all things, and the male metaphors of literary creation that depend upon such an etiology, have long 'confused' literary women, readers and writers alike. For what if such a profoundly masculine cosmic Author is the sole legitimate model for all earthly authors? Or worse, what if the male generative power is not just the only legitimate power but the only power there is? That literary theoreticians from Aristotle to Hopkins seemed to believe that this was so no doubt prevented many women from ever 'attempting the pen' – to use Anne Finch's phrase – and caused enormous anxiety in generations of those women who were 'presumptuous' enough to dare such an attempt. Jane Austen's Anne Elliot understates the case when she decorously observes, toward the end of *Persuasion*, that 'men have had every advantage of us in telling their story. Education has been theirs in so much higher a degree; the pen has been in their hands' (II, chap. 11).[13] For, as Anne Finch's complaint suggests, the pen has been defined as not just accidentally but essentially a male 'tool,' and therefore not only inappropriate but actually alien to women. Lacking Austen's demure irony. Finch's passionate protest goes almost as far toward the center of the metaphor of literary paternity as Hopkins's letter to Canon Dixon. Not only is 'a woman that attempts the pen' an intrusive and 'presumptuous Creature,' she is absolutely unredeemable: no virtue can outweigh the 'fault' of her presumption because she has grotesquely crossed boundaries dictated by Nature:

> They tell us, we mistake our sex and way;
> Good breeding, fassion, dancing, dressing, play
> Are the accomplishments we shou'd desire;
> To write, or read, or think, or to enquire
> Wou'd cloud our beauty, and exaust our time,
> And interrupt the conquests of our prime;
> Whilst the dull mannage, of a servile house
> Is held by some, our outmost art and use.[14]

Because they are by definition male activities, this passage implies, writing, reading, and thinking are not only alien but also inimical to 'female' characteristics. One hundred years later, in a famous letter to Charlotte Brontë, Robert Southey rephrased the same notion: 'Literature is not the business of a woman's life, and it cannot be.'[15] It cannot be, the metaphor of literary paternity implies, because it is physiologically as well as sociologically impossible. If male sexuality is integrally associated with the assertive presence of literary power, female sexuality is associated with the absence of such power, with the idea – expressed by the nineteenth- century thinker Otto Weininger – that 'woman has no share in ontological reality.' As we shall see, a further implication of the paternity/creativity metaphor is the notion (implicit both in Weininger and in Southey's letter) that women exist only to be acted on by men, both as literary and as sensual objects. Again one of Anne Finch's poems explores the assumptions submerged in so many literary theories. Addressing three male poets, she exclaims:

> Happy you three! happy the Race of Men!
> Born to inform or to correct the Pen
> To proffitts pleasures freedom and command
> Whilst we beside you but as Cyphers stand
> T increase your Numbers and to swell th' account
> Of your delights which from our charms amount

And sadly are by this distinction taught
That since the Fall (by our seducement wrought)
Our is the greater losse as ours the greater fault.[16]

Since Eve's daughters have fallen so much lower than Adam's sons, this passage says, *all* females are 'Cyphers' – nullities, vacancies – existing merely and punningly to increase male 'Numbers' (either poems or persons) by pleasuring either men's bodies or their minds, their penises or their pens.

In that case, however, devoid of what Richard Chase once called 'the masculine *élan*,' and implicitly rejecting even the slavish consolations of her 'femininity,' a literary woman is doubly a 'Cypher,' for she is really a 'eunuch,' to use the striking figure Germaine Greer applied to all women in patriarchal society. Thus Anthony Burgess recently declared that Jane Austen's novels fail because her writing 'lacks a strong male thrust,' and William Gass lamented that literary women 'lack that blood congested genital drive which energizes every great style.'[17] The assumptions that underlie their statements were articulated more than a century ago by the nineteenth-century editor-critic Rufus Griswold. Introducing an anthology entitled *The Female Poets of America*, Griswold outlined a theory of literary sex roles which builds upon, and clarifies, these grim implications of the metaphor of literary paternity.

> It is less easy to be assured of the genuineness of literary ability in women than in men. The moral nature of women, in its finest and richest development, partakes of some of the qualities of genius; it assumes, at least, the similitude of that which in men is the characteristic or accompaniment of the highest grade of mental inspiration. We are in danger, therefore, of mistaking for the efflorescent energy of creative intelligence, that which is only the exuberance of personal 'feelings unemployed.' . . . The most exquisite susceptibility of the spirit, and the capacity to mirror in dazzling variety the effects which circumstances or surrounding minds work upon it, may be accompanied by *no power to originate, nor even, in any proper sense, to reproduce*. [Italics ours][18]

Since Griswold has actually compiled a collection of poems by women, he plainly does not believe that all women lack reproductive or generative literary power all the time. His gender-definitions imply, however, that when such creative energy appears in a woman it may be anomalous, freakish, because as a 'male' characteristic it is essentially 'unfeminine.'

The converse of these explicit and implicit definitions of 'femininity' may also be true for those who develop literary theories based upon the 'mystical estate' of fatherhood: if a woman lacks generative literary power, then a man who loses or abuses such power becomes like a eunuch – or like a woman. When the imprisoned Marquis de Sade was denied 'any use of pencil, ink, pen, and paper,' declares Roland Barthes, he was figuratively emasculated, for 'the scriptural sperm' could flow no longer, and 'without exercise, without a pen, Sade [became] *bloated*, [became] a eunuch.' Similarly, when Hopkins wanted to explain to R. W. Dixon the aesthetic consequences of a *lack* of male mastery, he seized upon an explanation which developed the implicit parallel between women and cunuchs, declaring that 'if the life' is not 'conveyed into the work and . . . displayed there . . . the product is one of those *hens' eggs* that are good to eat and look just like live ones but never hatch' (italics ours).[19] And when, late in his life, he tried to define his own sense of sterility, his thickening writer's block, he described himself (in the sonnet 'The Fine Delight That Fathers Thought') both as a eunuch and *as a woman*, specifically a woman deserted by male power: 'the widow of an insight lost,' surviving in a diminished 'winter world' that entirely lacks 'the roll, the rise, the carol, the creation' of male generative power, whose 'strong/Spur' is phallically 'live and lancing like the blow pipe flame.' And once again some lines from one of Anne Finch's plaintive protests against male literary hegemony seem to support Hopkins's image of the powerless and sterile woman artist. Remarking in the conclusion of her 'Introduction' to her *Poems* that women are 'to be dull/Expected and designed' she does not repudiate such expectations, but on the contrary admonishes herself, with bitter irony, to *be* dull:

> Be caution'd then my Muse, and still retir'd;
> Nor be dispis'd, aiming to be admir'd:
> Conscious of wants, still with contracted wing.
> To some few friends, and to thy sorrows sing:
> For groves of Lawrell, thou wert never meant;
> Be dark enough thy shades, and be thou there content.[20]

Cut off from generative energy, in a dark and wintry world, Finch seems to be defining herself here not only as a 'Cypher' but as 'the widow of an insight lost.'

(1979)

Notes

Epigraphs: 'In the End,' in *Chelsea* 35:96; 'The Introduction,' in *The Poems of Anne Countess of Winchilsea*, ed. Myra Reynolds (Chicago: University of Chicago Press, 1903), pp. 4–5; *The Diary of Anaïs Nin. Vol. Two. 1934–1939*, ed. Gunther Stuhlmann (New York: The Swallow Press and Harcourt, Brace, 1967), p. 233.

1 *The Correspondence of Gerard Manley Hopkins and Richard Watson Dixon*, ed. C. C. Abbott (London: Oxford University Press, 1935). p. 133.

2 Edward W. Said, *Beginnings: Intention and Method* (New York: Basic Books, 1975), p. 83.

3 Ibid., p. 162. For an analogous use of such imagery of paternity, see Gayatri Chakravorty Spivak's 'Translator's Preface' to Jacques Derrida, *Of Grammatology* (Baltimore: Johns Hopkins University Press, 1976), p. xi: 'to use one of Derrida's structural metaphors, | a preface is | the son or seed . . . caused or engendered by the father (text or meaning).' Also see her discussion of Nietzsche where she considers the 'masculine style of possession' in terms of 'the stylus, the stiletto, the spurs,' p. xxxvi.

4 James Joyce, *Ulysses* (New York: Modern Library, 1934), p. 205.

5 Ibid. The whole of this extraordinarily relevant passage develops this notion further: 'Fatherhood, in the sense of conscious begetting, is unknown to man,' Stephen notes. 'It is a mystical estate, an apostolic succession, from only begetter to only begotten. On that mystery and not on the madonna which the cunning Italian intellect flung to the mob of Europe the church is founded and founded irremovably because founded, like the world, macro- and microcosm, upon the void. Upon incertitude, upon unlikelihood. *Amor matris*, subjective and objective genitive, may be the only true thing in life. Paternity may be a legal fiction' (pp. 204–5).

6 Coleridge, *Biographia Literaria*, chapter 13. John Ruskin, *Modern Painters*, vol. 2. *The Works of John Ruskin*, ed. E. T. Cook and Alexander Wedderburn (London: George Allen, 1903), pp. 250–51. Although Virginia Woolf noted in *A Room of One's Own* that Coleridge thought 'a great mind is androgynous' she added dryly that 'Coleridge certainly did not mean . . . that it is a mind that has any special sympathy with women' (*A Room of One's Own* [New York: Harcourt Brace, 1929], p. 102). Certainly the imaginative power Coleridge describes does not sound 'man-womanly' in Woolf's sense.

7 Shelley, 'A Defense of Poetry.' Keats to John Hamilton Reynolds, 3 February 1818: *The Selected Letters of John Keats*, ed. Lionel Trilling (New York: Doubleday, 1956), p. 121.

8 See E. R. Curtius, *European Literature and the Latin Middle Ages* (New York: Harper Torchbooks, 1963), pp. 305, 306. For further commentary on both Curtius's 'The Symbolism of the Book' and the 'Book of Nature' metaphor itself, see Derrida. *Of Grammatology*, pp. 15–17.

9 'Timon, A Satyr,' in *Poems by John Wilmot Earl of Rochester*, ed. Vivian de Sola Pinto (London: Routledge and Kegan Paul, 1953), p. 99.

10 Bridget Riley, 'The Hermaphrodite,' *Art and Sexual Politics*, ed. Thomas B. Hass and Elizabeth C. Baker (London: Collier Books, 1973), p. 82. Riley comments that she herself would 'interpret this remark as expressing his attitude to his work as a celebration of life.'

11 Norman O. Brown, *Love's Body* (New York: Vintage Books, 1968), p. 134.; John T. Irwin, *Doubling and Incest. Repetition and Revenge* (Baltimore: Johns Hopkins University Press, 1975), p. 163. Irwin also speaks of 'the phallic generative power of the creative imagination' (p. 159).

12 Harold Bloom, *The Anxiety of Influence* (New York: Oxford University Press, 1973), pp. 11, 26.

13 All references to *Persuasion* are to volume and chapter of the text edited by R. W. Chapman, reprinted with an introduction by David Daiches (New York: Norton, 1958).

14 Anne Finch, *Poems of Anne Countess of Winchilsea*, pp. 4–5.

15 Southey to Charlotte Brontë, March 1837. Quoted in Winifred Gérin, *Charlotte Brontë: The Evolution of Genius* (Oxford: Oxford University Press, 1967), p. 110.

16 Finch, *Poems of Anne Countess of Winchilsea*, p. 100. Otto Weininger, *Sex and Character* (London: Heinemann, 1906), p. 286. This sentence is part of an extraordinary passage in which Weininger asserts that 'women have no existence and no essence: they are not, they are nothing,' this because 'woman has no relation to the idea . . . she is neither moral nor anti-moral,' but 'all existence is moral and logical existence.'

17 Richard Chase speaks of the 'masculine *élan*' throughout 'The Brontës, or Myth Domesticated,' in *Forms of Modern Fiction*, ed. William V. O'Connor (Minneapolis: University of Minnesota Press, 1948), pp. 102–13. For a discussion of the 'female eunuch' see Germaine Greer, *The Female Eunuch* (New York: McGraw Hill, 1970). See also Anthony Burgess, 'The Book Is Not For Reading,' *New York Times Book Review*, 4 December 1966, pp. 1, 74, and William Gass, on Norman Mailer's *Genius and Lust*, *New York Times Book Review*, 24 October 1976, p. 2. In this connection, finally, it is interesting (and depressing) to consider that Virginia Woolf evidently defined *herself* as 'a eunuch.' (See Noel Annan, 'Virginia Woolf Fever,' *New York Review*, 20 April 1978, p. 22.)

18 Rufus Griswold, Preface to *The Female Poets of America* (Philadelphia: Carey & Hart, 1849), p. 8.

19 Roland Barthes, *Sade/Fourier/Loyola*, trans. Richard Miller (New York: Hill & Wang, 1976), p. 182; Hopkins, *Correspondence*, p. 133.

20 Finch, *Poems of Anne Countess of Winchilsea*, p. 5.

TERRY LOVELL

Consuming Fiction

It is not possible to offer definite explanations but conspiracy theory will not answer. Rather we may look on literary survival in terms of loosely defined rules or codes, which have tended to work against women. Firstly, it is authors rather than books that survive, with a few notable exceptions such as *Wuthering Heights*. It is the *auteur* who is constructed in literary criticism rather than the text. A single text is seldom enough to establish that status. Once it is established however, *all* the author's texts become worthy of study however flawed any particular one may be, just as all the paintings of a 'great master' will command aesthetic interest and a high price. Writers who, for whatever reason, have a small output will be at a disadvantage. Yet we have seen that women in the nineteenth century typically began their literary apprenticeships later in life than their male colleagues. If and insofar as they were also encumbered with pressing domestic duties, they would have been additionally handicapped.

Secondly, polemical writings usually do not last beyond the moment of controversy. Whenever the 'woman question' is raised, then feminist fiction will be written and earlier feminist fiction rediscovered. Whether or not feminist fiction is always and necessarily tendentious, it will tend to be seen as such when feminism is out of fashion. Books by women which foreground the woman question are likely to be so labelled whatever their literary merits may be. *Red Pottage* may have been a victim of this kind of labelling since, unlike *Daughters of Danaus* or *The Heavenly Twins*, it is not didactic. But it was the only one of Mary Cholmondeley's novels which attracted much notice.

Thirdly, woman-to-woman fiction is coded out of 'literature'. While feminist fiction in the eighteen-nineties was widely read and was not necessarily addressed exclusively to women, women were the preferred readers. Woman-to-woman forms are not permitted to become part of the general stock of 'cultural capital'.

The male producers of new woman fiction, with the exception of Grant Allen, did not fall foul of any of these unwritten rules. A man writing such fiction is not open to the charge of tendentiousness to the same extent as is a woman. He can claim to be disinterested if his fiction seems to support the cause of feminism. But in any case Hardy, Gissing and Meredith did not only write new woman fiction, and they wrote extensively. Their work has survived to become part of the publicly recognized stock of cultural capital.

But while the bulk of that capital is male-produced, women play a major role in its transmission from generation to generation.

(1987)

WOMEN IN PUBLISHING

Reviewing the Reviews: A Woman's Place on the Book Page

We set out to establish what percentage of women authors were reviewed in comparison to men. To do this, we monitored 28 publications – weeklies, monthlies, newspapers, general magazines and literary reviews – for the year 1985. As our research progressed, we realised that it was not just a question of counting the number of men and women authors reviewed in a particular issue. Other considerations, such as positioning on the page and the amount of space devoted to a review, needed to be looked at when evaluating the overall balance between men and women authors.

In our survey, we looked at the following questions:

- How does the space devoted to women's books compare to that devoted to men's?
- Where are reviews of women's books placed on the page?
- Are women reviewers confined mainly to fiction?
- Are there fewer female reviewers?
- Do reviews influence book buyers and librarians, or help to sell books?

As well as analysing the publications, we interviewed the editors of the book pages to find out how they allocated books for review, whether they had any particular policy on reviewing, and what guidelines (if any) they issued to reviewers. We have tried to unravel the mysterious process by which certain books find their way on to the review pages while the vast majority do not. We talked to 25 publishers – mainstream, feminist, paperback and hardback – to find out how they went about targeting review copies of books and whether books by women authors were channelled towards particular publications. As for the booksellers and librarians, to what extent are they influenced by reviews? We asked a number of them whether readers' requests reflected the recommendations of book reviewers. And last, but not least, we talked to the people without whom there would be no books at all – the authors. How do they feel about their treatment by the reviewers? Margaret Forster, Barbara Burford, Andrea Dworkin and Zoë Fairbairns describe their experiences in the claws of the critics.

[. . .]

CHART 2
WHO'S GETTING REVIEWED?

	percentage of books by		
	females	males	unknown
Spare Rib	98.41	1.59	0
Cosmopolitan	67.11	28.95	3.95
Company	64.47	31.58	3.95
Options	57.89	35.09	7.02
Good Housekeeping	57.81	32.81	9.38
She	48.15	39.51	12.35
Woman and Home	45.16	36.56	18.28
School Librarian	38.41	47.83	13.77
City Limits	37.01	62.20	0.79
Fiction Magazine	35.90	64.10	0
Listener	29.22	66.88	3.90
Literary Review	28.90	64.45	6.65
New Statesman	27.49	65.60	7.02
Daily Telegraph	27.17	65.94	6.88
The Times	26.25	68.75	5.00
Punch	21.21	74.24	4.55
New Socialist	20.75	73.58	5.66
Sunday Times	19.80	68.94	11.26
Observer	19.47	74.62	5.91
The Times Literary Supplement	19.38	77.54	3.08
Marxism Today	19.18	64.38	16.44
New Society	18.52	74.07	7.41
Guardian	17.77	75.13	7.11
Spectator	17.76	82.24	0
London Review of Books	16.57	78.00	5.45
Financial Times	15.56	77.78	6.67
Mail on Sunday	14.58	79.17	6.25
The Times Higher Education Supplement	9.54	72.92	17.54

CHART 3
THE SPACE BREAKDOWN

	% Space allotted	
	Female books	Male books
Spare Rib	98.12	1.88
Company	75.51	22.68
Cosmopolitan	72.00	25.90
Good Housekeeping	65.86	31.98
Options	52.70	43.26
Woman and Home	52.30	33.92
She	50.19	39.22
City Limits	40.84	57.96

	Female books	Male books
School Librarian	36.99	47.06
Fiction Magazine	32.76	66.73
Literary Review	29.05	65.92
New Statesman	28.85	65.55
New Socialist	25.11	71.45
Daily Telegraph	23.50	72.25
Punch	23.07	73.20
Observer	20.17	74.77
Listener	18.69	77.21
Times	17.25	78.70
Times Lit Supp	16.99	80.35
Sunday Times	16.93	74.80
Spectator	16.51	83.07
London Review of Books	14.79	79.43
Guardian	13.95	79.43
Marxism Today	13.91	69.01
Financial Times	13.87	80.30
New Society	13.72	76.15
Mail on Sunday	12.75	84.75
The Times Higher Education Supplement	9.58	75.52

*To highlight comparison between female and male, unknowns have been omitted

CHART II
REVIEWING THE REVIEWS

	reviewers			literary editor
	% female	% male	total no.	
Company	100	0	12	F
Cosmopolitan	100	0	12	F
Good Housekeeping	100	0	12	F
Options	100	0	12	F
She	100	0	12	F
Spare Rib	100	0	12	F
Woman and Home	100	0	12	F
New Socialist	51	42	39	M
City Limits	49	51	74	M
Marxism Today	44	56	43	M
School Librarian	43	57	119	–
Punch	38	62	34	M
New Statesman	30	70	91	F
The Times Literary Supplement	27	73	354	M
Observer	25	75	140	M
Fiction Magazine	25	75	16	–
Literary Review	25	75	299	F
London Review of Books	24	76	225	M

Daily Telegraph	21	79	90	M
Mail on Sunday	20	80	44	F
Financial Times	19	81	68	M
Listener	19	81	69	M
The Times	17	83	77	M
New Society	14	86	116	M
Spectator	14	86	81	M
The Times Higher Education Supplement	9	91	180	M
Sunday Times	9	91	211	F
Guardian	9	91	81	M

(1987)

MARGARET ATWOOD

'Paradoxes and Dilemmas, the Woman as Writer'
Women in the Canadian Mosaic

Reviewing and the Absence of an Adequate Critical Vocabulary

Cynthia Ozick, in the American magazine *Ms.*, says, 'For many years, I had noticed that no book of poetry by a woman was ever reviewed without reference to the poet's sex. The curious thing was that, in the two decades of my scrutiny, there were *no* exceptions whatever. It did not matter whether the reviewer was a man or a woman; in every case, the question of the 'feminine sensibility' of the poet was at the center of the reviewers' response. The maleness of male poets, on the other hand, hardly ever seemed to matter.'

Things aren't this bad in Canada, possibly because we were never thoroughly indoctrinated with the Holy Gospel according to the distorters of Freud. Many reviewers manage to get through a review without displaying the kind of bias Ozick is talking about. But that it does occur was demonstrated to me by a project I was involved with at York University in 1971–72.

One of my student groups was attempting to study what we called 'sexual bias in reviewing,' by which we meant not unfavourable reviews, but points being added or subtracted by the reviewer on the basis of the author's sex and supposedly associated characteristics rather than on the basis of the work itself. Our study fell into two parts: (i) a survey of writers, half male, half female, conducted by letter: had they ever experienced sexual bias directed against them in a review?; (ii) the reading of a large number of reviews from a wide range of periodicals and newspapers.

The results of the writers' survey were perhaps predictable. Of the men, none answered Yes, a quarter Maybe, and three-quarters No. Of women, half were Yeses, a quarter Maybes and a quarter Nos. The women replying Yes often wrote long, detailed letters, giving instances and discussing their own attitudes. All the men's letters were short.

This proved only that women were more likely to *feel* they had been discriminated against on the basis of sex. When we got round to the reviews, we discovered they were sometimes justified. Here are the kinds of things we found.

(i) *Assignment of Reviews*. Several of our letter-writers discussed the mechanics of review assignment. Some felt books by women tended to be passed over by book-page editors assigning books for review; others that books by women tended to get assigned to women reviewers. When we started toting up reviews we found that most books in this society are written by men, and so are most reviews. Disproportionately often, books by women were assigned to women reviewers, indicating that books by women fell in the minds of those dishing out the reviews into a special 'female' category. Likewise, women reviewers tended to be reviewing books by women rather than books by men (though because of the preponderance of male reviewers, there were quite a few male-written reviews of books by women).

ii) *The Quiller-Couch Syndrome*. This phrase refers to the turn-of-the-century essay by Quiller-Couch, defining 'masculine' and 'feminine' styles in writing. The 'masculine' style is, of course, bold, forceful, clear, vigorous, etc.; the 'feminine' style is vague, weak, tremulous, pastel, etc. In the list of pairs you can include 'objective' and 'subjective,' 'universal' or 'accurate depiction of society' versus 'confessional,' 'personal,' or even 'narcissistic' and 'neurotic.' It's roughly seventy years since Quiller-Couch's essay, but the 'masculine' group of adjectives is still much more likely to be applied to the work of male writers; female writers are much more likely to get hit with some version of 'the feminine style' or 'feminine sensibility,' whether their work merits it or not.

iii) *The Lady Painter Syndrome, or She Writes Like a Man*. This is a pattern in which good equals male, bad equals female. I call it the Lady Painter Syndrome because of a conversation I had about female painters with a male painter in 1960. 'When she's good,' he said, 'we call her a painter; when she's bad, we call her a lady painter.' 'She writes like a man' is part of the same pattern; it's usually used by a male reviewer who is impressed by a female writer. It's meant as a compliment. See also 'She thinks like a man,' which means the author thinks, unlike most women, who are held to be incapable of objective thought (their province is 'feeling'). Adjectives which often have similar connotations are ones such as 'strong,' 'gutsy,' 'hard,' 'mean,' etc. A hard-hitting piece of writing by a man is liable to be thought of as merely realistic; an equivalent piece by a woman is much more likely to be labelled 'cruel' or 'tough.' The assumption is that women are by nature soft, weak and not very talented, and that if a woman writer happens to be a good writer, she should be deprived of her identity as a female and provided with higher (male) status. Thus the woman writer has, in the minds of such reviewers, two choices. She can be bad but female, a carrier of the 'feminine sensibility' virus; or she can be 'good' in male-adjective terms, but sexless. Badness seems to be ascribed then to a surplus of female hormones, whereas badness in a male writer is usually ascribed to nothing but badness (though a 'bad' male writer is sometimes held, by adjectives implying sterility or impotence, to be deficient in maleness). 'Maleness' is exemplified by the 'good' male writer; 'femaleness,' since it is seen by such reviewers as a handicap or deficiency, is held to be transcended or discarded by the 'good' female one. In other words, there is no critical vocabulary for expressing the concept 'good/female.' Work by a male writer is often spoken of by critics admiring it as having 'balls'; have you ever heard anyone speak admiringly of work by a woman as having 'tits'?

Possible antidotes: Development of a 'good/female' vocabulary (wow, has that ever got womb . . .'); or, preferably, the development of a vocabulary that can treat structures made of words as though they are exactly that, not biological entities possessed of sexual organs.

iv) *Domesticity*. One of our writers noted a (usually male) habit of concentrating on domestic themes in the work of a female writer, ignoring any other topic she might have dealt with, then patronizing her for an excessive interest in domestic themes. We found several instances of reviewers identifying an author as a 'housewife' and consequently dismissing anything she has produced (since, in our society, a 'housewife' is viewed as a relatively brainless and talentless creature). We even found one instance in which the author was called a 'housewife' and put down for writing like one when in fact she was no such thing.

For such reviewers, when a man writes about things like doing the dishes, it's realism; when a woman does, it's an unfortunate feminine genetic limitation.

v) *Sexual Compliment/Put-down*. This syndrome can be summed up as follows:

She: 'How do you like my (design for an airplane/mathematical formula/medical miracle)?'

He: 'You sure have a nice ass.'

In reviewing it usually takes the form of commenting on the cute picture of the (female) author on the cover, coupled with dismissal of her as a writer.

(1976)

CAROL OHMANN

'Emily Brontë in the Hands of Male Critics'
College English

The pseudonyms all the Brontës chose for their joint volumes of poems and for their novels were, Charlotte reported, deliberately selected to admit of ambiguous interpretation. They did not wish to choose names avowedly masculine; they would not call themselves, for example, Charles, Edward, and Alfred. On the other hand, as Charlotte wrote afterwards, 'We did not like to declare ourselves women, because – without at that time suspecting that our mode of writing and thinking was not what is called "feminine" – we had a vague impression that authoresses are liable to be looked on with prejudice; we had noticed how critics sometimes use for their chastisement the weapon of personality, and for their reward, a flattery, which is not true praise.'[2]

Contemporary reviews of *Wuthering Heights*, all five found in Emily Brontë's writing desk and others as well, referred to Ellis Bell as 'he.' 'He' had written a book which, give or take certain differences of emphasis, was declared to be powerful and original. Although an occasional review acknowledged that it was a story of love, its essential subject was taken to be a representation of cruelty, brutality, violence, of human depravity or wickedness in its most extreme forms. Its lack of moral statement or purpose was taken to be either puzzling or censurable. It was awkwardly constructed. But, even so, in spite of the degree to which the reviewers were, variously, displeased, inclined to melancholy, shocked, pained, anguished, disgusted, and sickened, a number of them allowed the novel to be the work of a promising, possibly a great, new writer.

Most of the reviewers simply assumed without comment that the writer's sex was masculine. Two American reviewers did more: they made much of the novelist's sex and found plain evidence of it in the novel itself. Percy Edwin Whipple, in *The North American Review*, found in *Jane Eyre* the signatures of both a male and a female mind.[3] He supposed that two persons had written it, a brother and a sister. To the sister, he attributed certain 'feminine peculiarities': 'elaborate descriptions of dress'; 'the minutiae of the sick-chamber'; and 'various superficial refinements of feeling in regard to the external relations of the sex.' He went on to assert, 'It is true that the noblest and best representations of female character have been produced by men; but there are niceties of thought and emotion in a woman's mind which no man can delineate, but which often escape unawares from a female writer' (356).

From the brother, Whipple derived the novel's clarity and firmness of style, all its charm, and its scenes of profanity, violence, and passion. These scenes, he was virtually certain, were written by the same hand that wrote *Wuthering Heights*. Turning to *Wuthering Heights*, Whipple concentrated on the novel's presentation of Heathcliff, whom he found quintessentially bestial, brutal, indeed monstrous. He did allot a few lines to Heathcliff in love, but without mentioning Catherine. He scored the author of *Wuthering Heights* for 'coarseness' and for being a 'spendthrift of malice and profanity' (358).

George Washington Peck, in *The American Review*, did not overtly theorize on the sex of the author of *Wuthering Heights*. He assumed it to be masculine, then elaborated on the assumption in a rush of comparisons. The novel's language might be that of a Yorkshire farmer or a boatman or of frequenters of 'bar-rooms and steamboat saloons.'[4] He cautioned young ladies against imitating it, lest American social assemblies come to resemble certain scenes in Tammany Hall. The novel's author Peck likened to a 'rough sailor [with] a powerful imagination' (573). He is like a friend of whom one is fond and yet by whom one is continually embarrassed. He is not a gentleman. He would embarrass you with his *gaucheries* whether you were walking down Broadway with him or across the fields of Staten Island or dropping into a shop or store anywhere. Among his eccentricities or faults is a disposition to believe that he understands women. But he does *not* understand them. *He* cannot see *them* as *they* are. He can only see them as he is, and then, just slightly, refine them.

There are not so many reviews of the second edition of *Wuthering Heights*. But there are enough, I think, to show that once the work of Ellis Bell was identified as the work of a woman, critical responses to it changed. Where the novel had been called again and again 'original' in 1847 and 1848, the review in the *Athenaeum* in 1850 began by firmly placing it in a familiar class, and that class was not in the central line of literature. The review in the *Athenaeum* began by categorizing *Wuthering Heights* as a work of 'female genius and female authorship.'[5] The reviewer was really not surprised to learn that *Jane Eyre* and its 'sister-novels' were all written by women. The nature of the novels themselves, together with 'instinct or divination,' had already led the reviewer to that conclusion, which was now simply confirmed by Charlotte Brontë's 'Biographical Notice.' The review quotes a great deal from the 'Notice': Charlotte's description of the isolation of Haworth, her discovery of Emily's poems, the silence that greeted their publication in *Poems by Currer, Ellis, and Acton Bell*, and the deaths of both Emily and Anne. It is on Emily Brontë's *life* that the review spends most of its 2,000 words. References to *Wuthering Heights* are late and few, and then it is grouped not only with *Jane Eyre* but also with *Agnes Grey*. All three are 'characteristic tales' – characteristic of the Bell, that is to say the Brontë, sisters and, more generally, of tales women write. A single sentence is given to *Wuthering Heights* alone: 'To those whose experience of men and manners is neither extensive nor various, the construction of a self-consistent monster is easier than the delineation of an imperfect or inconsistent reality. . . .' The review ends there, repeating still another time its classification of the novel. *Wuthering Heights*, with its 'Biographical Notice,' is a 'more than usually interesting contribution to the history of female authorship in England.'

I don't mean to suggest that this is the first time a reviewer for the *Athenaeum* was ever condescending; the particular terms of the condescension are my point. Emily Brontë the novelist is reduced to Emily Brontë the person, whose fiction in turn is seen to be limited by the experiential limitation of the life. *Wuthering Heights* is an addition to the 'history of female authorship in England.'

There are other consequences that attend the knowledge or the presumption that Ellis Bell is not a man but a woman. Sydney Dobell published a long essay titled 'Currer Bell' in the *Palladium* three months before he could have known on Charlotte's authority that her sister had written *Wuthering Heights*. But he already 'knew' from the intrinsic nature of *Jane Eyre*, *Wuthering Heights*, *Agnes Grey*, and *The Tenant of Wildfell Hall* that they were written by women; indeed, he thought them written by the same woman.[6] Approaching *Wuthering Heights* with that conviction, he stressed the youthfulness of its author. And he likened her to a little bird fluttering its wings against the bars of its cage, only to sink at the last exhausted. Later, when it had more practice writing novels, it would fly freely into the heavens. Dobell stressed also the 'involuntary art' of the novel. (Whipple, you may remember, had said that female authors sometimes wrote well 'unawares.') Finally, Dobell saw the novel primarily as a love story, and for the first time made the heroine Catherine the major focus of interest, but only insofar as she was in love. With Heathcliff, Dobell contended, the 'authoress' was less successful.

It is clear, I hope, in these instances (and the same can be argued of other contemporary responses) that there is a considerable correlation between what readers assume or know the sex of the writer to be and what they actually see, or neglect to see, in 'his' or her work. *Wuthering Heights* is one book to Percy Edwin Whipple and George Washington Peck, who quarrel strenuously with its 'morals' and its taste, but another to the reviewer for the *Athenaeum*, who puts it calmly in its place and discourses on the life of the clergyman's daughter who wrote it. And Peck's rough sailor is born anew as Dobell's piteous birds with wings too young to fly.

(1971)

Notes

2 'Biographical Notice of Ellis and Acton Bell,' *Wuthering Heights: An Authoritative Text with Essays in Criticism*, ed. William M. Sale, Jr. (New York: W. W. Norton, 1963), p. 4. All quotations from *Wuthering Heights* are taken also from this edition.

3 'Novels of the Season,' *The North American Review*, LXVII (1848), 353. K. J. Fielding identifies the reviewer in 'The Brontës and "The North American Review": A Critic's Strange Guesses,' *Brontë Society Transactions*, XIII (1957), 14–18.

4 'Wuthering Heights,' *The American Review*, NS I (1848), 573. Additional reviews of the first edition consulted are the following: *The Athenaeum*, Dec. 25, 1847, 1324–25; *The Atlas*, XXIII (1848), 59; *Britannia*, Jan. 15, 1848; *Douglas Jerrold's Weekly Newspaper*, Jan. 15, 1848; *The Examiner*, Jan. 8, 1848, 21–22; *Godey's Magazine and Lady's Book*, XXXVII (1848), 57; *Graham's Magazine*, XXXIII (1848), 60; *Literary World*, III (1848), 243; *The New Monthly Magazine and Humourist*, LXXXII (1848), 140; *The Quarterly Review*, LXXXIV (1848), 153–185; *The Spectator*, XX (1847), 1217; *Tail's Edinburgh Magazine*, XV (1848), 138–140; *The Union Magazine*, June, 1848, 287; and an unidentified review quoted in full by Charles Simpson in *Emily Brontë* (London: Country Life, 1929). I am indebted for references to reviews of *Wuthering Heights* both to Melvin R. Watson, 'Wuthering Heights and the Critics,' *Trollopian*, III (1949). 243–263 and to Jane Gray Nelson. 'First American Reviews of the Works of Charlotte, Emily, and Anne Brontë,' *BST*, XIV (1964), 39–44. Nelson lists one review that I have not so far seen: *Peterson's Magazine*, June, 1848.

5 *The Athenaeum*, Dec. 28, 1850. All quotations are from pp. 1368–69.

6 'Currer Bell,' *Palladium*, I (1850). Reprinted in *Life and Letters of Sydney Dobell*, ed. E. Jolly (London, 1878), I. 163–186 and in *BST*, V (1918), 210–236. Additional reviews of the second edition consulted are the following: *The Eclectic Review*, XCIII (1851), 222–227: *The Examiner*, Dec. 21, 1850, 815: *The Leader*, Dec. 28, 1850, 953: *The North American Review*, LXXXV (1857), 293–329. The last review, later than the others, appeared in response to Mrs. Gaskell's *Life of Charlotte Brontë*. It implies an apology for the first *North American* review of *Wuthering Heights*. Knowing the lives of the Brontës, the 1857 reviewer finds *Wuthering Heights* peculiar, but he also finds the novel easy to dismiss – its peculiarity or strangeness mirrors the 'distorted fancy' of the writer's life, lived in isolation and deprivation. The novel lies outside normal human experience; it would be inappropriate to bring moral judgment to bear on it. Virtually the same attitude is taken by the reviewer in *The Eclectic Review*. The review in *The Leader*, by G. H. Lewes, is probably the best of the contemporary ones. Still, it would not be difficult to trace in it the operation of sexual prejudice, although the argument would, I think, take more space than I have allotted to any single review here. Charlotte Brontë was quite alert to Lewes's bias, as she revealed in a letter to him dated Nov. 1, 1849. Allan R. Brick gives excerpts from the *Leader* review and comments revealingly on Charlotte Brontë's attitude toward it and toward other early reviews in 'Lewes's Review of *Wuthering Heights*,' *NCF*, XIV (1960), 355–359.

ELIZABETH BAINES

'Naming the Fictions'

Suddenly a new alter-ego entered my life: The Feminist Writer.

She had this thing about Truth: since men's fiction had belied women's experience, then women's fiction must set the record straight.

Now indeed for me the whole point of making fictions – right back to my childhood imaginary friend – had been to counter social 'reality', to expose it as a construct, at best another fiction, at worst a downright lie. But could it be that the Feminist Writer was taking Fiction itself as a record of social reality?

I protested: The truth that Fiction seeks is *emotional* truth; Fiction is intuition. Fiction is dreams!

She countered: Look at that 'intuitive' first published story of yours, colonised by sexism: some dream!

The Left still mistrusts the unconscious, and it's not hard to see why. So the Feminist Writer valued writing that was *conscious*: we women should write consciously out of our gender; Virginia Woolf's notion of androgyny masks colonisation.

I had to agree. Male writers too, I thought, should acknowledge the limitations of their gender.

Ah, but the Feminist Writer wasn't interested in men. She held that, given that fundamentally we can write only out of our own experience, then in the name of honesty we have no business, any of us, representing the experience of the sex that isn't our own. She went further, she put it this way: we women must free ourselves of our traditional concern for the viewpoint of men; men have no *right* to concern themselves in literature with the viewpoint of women.

Well, now I was uneasy. I was beginning to understand about the need for women's space away from men who'd automatically dominate, but wasn't there a philosophical tangle somewhere here? Wasn't it men's ability to disregard the viewpoint of women that was what the patriarchal mess was all about anyway? Didn't this preclude two of the most important elements of Fiction – and indeed the most socially useful – imagination and empathy?

And here again was this concept of Fiction as testimony, confession or reportage. Being honest about who you are intellectually and emotionally had slipped over somehow into proving your credentials, proving your life matched up to your art (and I *thought* we'd all agreed how deceptive our real-life roles can be!).

But she insisted: Art doesn't exist outside life or society. She went on: We Feminist Writers are engaged *with others* in a process of social change. And then she breathed the magic phrase: *Collective Creativity.*

I was enchanted. The notion of a pooling of all our individual consciousnesses and unconsciousnesses, a democratic cross-fertilisation of visions and ideas – well, *that* would surely be a force for social change!

But as it turned out she didn't mean quite that, or only in theory. The Left, after all, finds it hard to trust the Fiction-writer. Such an embarrassingly private enterprise, shutting oneself up in a room, sometimes for six months to a year, without (or so it seems from the outside) reference or deference to anyone else! (As if the writer of fiction were not affected by collective creativity long before she puts pen to paper!) So self-centred, so ivory-tower-ish! Such crass arrogance to commit one's idiosyncratic subjectivity to paper for the rest of the world! It would be no surprise, would it, if the writer of fiction were at best colonised by imperialist and phallocentric thinking, or at worst actually the Enemy Within? So the writer's fiction must be carefully monitored, and if necessary brought into line with agreed reality.

Well, I had to consider this seriously. Of course I'd be glad to have my pernicious tendencies knocked out of me. Of course I'd have been glad not to have made the mistakes of that early story.

But I said, Hang on, writing for me has always been a *rebellion*, this feels too much like conforming. It denies me the fictional authority which has always for me been the whole point of writing!

She didn't like the word *authority*, associated as it was with the patriarch and the imperialist. In a word I'd condemned myself.

She said, Are you sure that what you've been striving for isn't a *phallus*?

Well, I felt dreadful. Really ashamed. Though I managed to whine: But it's all a matter of confidence. If you question my fictions, you damage my confidence, as the patriarchy once did, and I can't write at all without lots of confidence!

And I said, Isn't there also in what you're advocating a dangerous notion of a truer truth, a more objective reality? And isn't 'objectivity' the fallacy of the patriarch and the dictator? Isn't it *you*, after all, who are trading in the notion of a greater authority (than personal subjectivity)?

But she wasn't listening, she was describing ways in which we might improve our work to serve society. She said, Can't you do something about your literary *forms*? We need forms that are more recognisable; this job's too urgent for eccentricity or frills, we must get the message over in the simplest way possible.

I cried: But the form *is* the meaning! Remember, the accessible forms were the ones that couldn't say what we wanted to?

She said, No point in being radical if no-one understands you.

She went on to her next point: We need to create Positive Images.

Which was when I perked up and cried: Ah! So *you too* have dreams?

Well, she tried to deny it. She said she'd rather define it as seeing the need to show how we should live.

I said, *What?* You think that, having spent my whole writing life trying to escape other people's prescriptions for how I should behave, I'd now write conduct books for others?

She shifted her ground. She said, Well, we want to show that, in spite of what has been believed, women *are* positive.

But in fact I'd got her cornered. Within the terms of her own argument she was being inconsistent. She couldn't have it both ways – Fiction as record, *and* Fiction as vision. Not, that is, unless she recognised that the relation between Fiction and social reality is far more complex than she'd so far acknowledged.

(1985)

ISOBEL ARMSTRONG

'Christina Rossetti: Diary of a Feminist Reading'
Women Reading Women's Writing

To begin with, the poem does not have an overtly 'female' content. I was dissatisfied with restricting myself to poems which could be literalised as accounts of women's experience because this circumscribes and isolates women as special cases, culturally and psychologically. What was I permitted to say? It is significant that an oppressive sense of what was 'allowed' hung over me. The sort of individualist feminist criticism I knew then (Kate Millett) pointed to the ideological repression of women expressed in female texts. Barbara Hardy had shaken me by the scruff of the neck with Millett a few years before but I did not want to resolve the poem into a sexual politics of this kind. It seemed to lead me to rage and anger (though I reflect that a little of this would have been useful in confronting my earlier education). It seemed to be a 'vulgar' feminism, like vulgar Marxism. People were beginning to describe women's writing in terms of its claims to an independent tradition. Though I liked the work of Cora Kaplan and Dolores Rosenblatt I was tentative – too much so – about making these claims. Like the cruder feminist individualism it seemed to make women special cases of oppression. But if you do not take this route, how do you prevent yourself from falling into a stodgy impartiality which is not impartiality at all?

I read biography avidly, trying to find out what Christina Rossetti read. If she belonged to a network of texts one could find one's way back to a set of cultural relationships, relationships with some 'central' discourse, which did not trap her into isolation. But in trying to do this I discovered the extraordinary passionate and traumatic story of her love for William Bell Scott and his casually brutal treatment of her, which is proposed in Lorna Morse Packham's biography. I noticed that Geoffrey Grigson's review of the first volume of R. W. Crump's edition (1979) of Rossetti's work in the *Times Literary Supplement* simply ignores Packham's hypotheses. Did he know of them? He prefers a more credible account of her life which is actually more tortuously ingenious. Was I 'allowed' to deal with this agony, and if so, how? My feeling that the biography was important did not seem to match with any form I could write in.

It is interesting that the sense that I was able or 'permitted' to say some things and not others remained as some undefined coercion even in a feminist reading. I believed, and still believe, that one must talk about a politics and simultaneously about language, but how? The politics must be in the form and in the language, I decided, because that frees one to think of structures which must belong to cultural patterns. And since poetry does not simply reproduce, but creates and becomes the materials of cultural forms themselves, this reciprocity seemed promising for the way out of the impasse which makes women the passive object of a special or marginalised experience. It makes the woman poet an agent.

'Winter Rain' is conjured out of rigorous repetition and the iteration of negations. '*Every valley* drinks,/*Every dell* and *hollow*:/ Where the kind rain *sinks* and *sinks* . . .'. It is one of those pastoral lyrics so familiar in English writing that the form is virtually sourceless, speaking out of an idiom so generalised that it comes from everywhere and nowhere. The voice speaks from conventions which are both hidden and obvious. One meets this simultaneous sharing and not sharing in Christina Rossetti's poetry constantly. It is a scrupulous way of marking community with and dissociation from the pastoral tradition which is after all a male preserve. The action of 'fattening' rain appears to follow a conventional course, as it irrigates the concavities of dell and hollow, bursting buds, creating a natural environment for fertility, though the pregnant solidity of 'fattening' works oddly with the diffusing nature of rain. But then comes a systematic deviation into the denial of negatives – 'But for . . . But for . . . no . . . never . . . never . . . no . . . no . . . no . . . never . . . not.' Without rain the natural processes of birth and propagation would cease, the poem says in its 'simplicity'. The frightful matching sterility of land and water, which would not be water but desert, is the final negation. The simple statement of lack goes much further however, questioning expectations about the teleological necessity of recurrence and regularity. What is 'natural' when this is denied?

It seemed that much could be understood when I got to this point. If the teleological order and the 'natural' is being questioned, so implicitly is the cultural. If the 'natural' order which exists in interdependence with the teleological order turns out to be neither natural nor ordered, then a great deal has been said about the coercive force of accepted assumptions. The constant action of doubling, repetition, iteration and duplication seemed to me to create an intransigently restricting order which the poem disrupts by using the processes of order themselves. It was tempting to think in terms of Kristéva's antithesis between the semiotic and the symbolic. The subversive, semiotic freedom of 'fattening' rain, which keels over from the sheer physicality of organic growth to the idea of fattening for slaughter, is in opposition, perhaps, to the repressive abstract patterns of symbolic 'masculine' syntax and repetition. But I was not happy with this. The 'repressive' pattern, if it was that, was overwhelmingly dominant and seemed to be tested in its capacity to sustain itself by showing that it collapsed of itself. There seemed to be a play in and with pattern which made order both restricting *and enabling*. Thus the antithesis between semiotic and symbolic maintained by Kristéva was not sustained, in this poem at least.

The idea that an order could be restricting *and* enabling took me some way for I saw that one could regard the dominant Victorian poetics of expression in a parallel way that seemed both psychoanalytically and politically important. Victorian poetics (Keble is an obvious example) assumes that expression occurs when the barrier of the customary restraints of consciousness is broken. Emotion breaks out of the self into representation. But by the same token, though this is never consciously theorised, the barrier constitutes repression. Each needs, and is predicated on, the other. Though there are significant differences, this does not seem far away from Freud's account of repression as effecting a continual displacement and indeed, creation of energy. I did not wish to use Freud at that time because the two sets of theories don't converge in very important ways, but I am bolder now. We can bring the two theories together. After all, without Freud one would not conceptualise any form of repression. Victorian poetics could be seen as a paradigm for both sexual and political life. I saw that in playing so daringly with the barrier of the symbolic and in recognising the interdependence of expression and repression, Christina Rossetti was both confirming and questioning the limits of both.

Goblin Market, where the 'good' Laura smears the goblins' forbidden fruit on the face of the 'bad' Lizzie, who had been denied the fruit she once bought with a piece of herself, her own hair, took on a new meaning. That there is a market price for the glory of Lizzie's experience which is paid for with one's identity is one gross fact. But we are not asked to 'choose' between a bad and a good girl because there is in reality no *moral* opposition here. The play of desire and restriction, Lizzie and Laura, create one another and the play of opposition is enabling. But Christina Rossetti chooses to distort and intensify the opposition between Laura and Lizzie in this poem because she sees that the play of desire and repression is subjected to a fierce economic and ethical code in their world. The dripping fruit crushed against the faces of both girls, one resisting, one rejoicing, becomes both outrage and orgy, a deliberate demonstration that what is literally 'expressed' here can only be so in the context of violation, abuse, scatological fury and aggression. For a structural condition has been turned into a moral order. The morbid aspect of Victorian culture is in this poem, but, it seems to say, can these facts ever be 'neutral'?

This is something I felt I 'could' say. I took a lecture to America on the problems of full-frontal feminism and its preoccupation with content at the expense of language and form. Elaine Showalter rose in majestic disagreement. She argued that I was colluding with a central academic discourse which always assimilated women to men's concerns. I was too ready to show that Christina Rossetti was part of a dominant Victorian aesthetics of expression. I was not making claims for a feminine tradition. After a long argument I said, 'But *I* want to write poetry which men will read.' 'Ah', said Elaine. She was right to feel that I had not used the sanctions of feminist criticism powerfully. But there is a problem. What can be said about Christina Rossetti ought to be relevant to Tennyson, Browning and Hopkins.

(1987)

HÉLÈNE CIXOUS ET AL.

'Conversations', Writing Differences: Readings from the Seminar of Hélène Cixous

Pierre Salesne: In the early days of the seminar, we worked more closely with theoretical texts. They allowed us to overcome certain obstacles, especially in relation to Freud's work. I think that at that time, it was necessary for us to work on theory to undo in ourselves a certain fantasy of mastery, deconstructing what could otherwise become law and prevent us from getting close to the text. I also think it was in relation to what was happening around us. The seminar has never been outside history. We needed to go back over certain texts in order to reply to the weight of theoretical discourse which threatened the work we were trying to do.

Mara Négron Marreo: In Puerto Rico, literature students are trained in American and European theories of textual analysis. The desire to approach the text as an object characterizes most of these theories. One does a job of dissection on the text. Once all the parts are separated, no one knows how to re-assemble them. We forget that at the beginning there was beginning, a living source. The beating heart of the text is cut open on the operating table. The pulse is silenced.

Sarah Cornell: As far as theory is concerned, we do make use of theoretical tools from the fields of literary criticism, psychoanalysis, linguistics and philosophy, but we don't attempt to reduce the texts in order to make them fit into a so-called academic method or into the fixed framework of any given ideological system. In other words, we wouldn't want to attack the text with theoretical swords and daggers. Instead of keeping the text at a distance or burying it under a discourse of mastery, I'd say we try to approach it, not only with our minds, but also with our hearts and souls, trying to hear, and then say, what the text says to us.

Hélène Cixous: The space we work in qualifies itself by the grouping together of many strangenesses. The texts we work on are strange either because of their language or because of what they say. What binds us together is our belief in the need to ensure that the essence of each strangeness is preserved.

The image this meeting of strangenesses evokes for me is one of movement. When I first encountered the texts of Clarice Lispector I remembered Celan's image of the bottle and the sea: the poem's journey to the reader. Reading Clarice, I witnessed this journey. I saw the map of the world crossed by a voice, a message.

Sometimes in the seminar I feel as if we were replying to the curse of Babel. The biblical curse was finding oneself prey to a multiplicity of languages but I see it as a blessing to be in the midst of so many languages. For languages say different things. And our multiple collectivity makes these differences – this infinite enrichment – apparent to us.

There is a passage in Blanchot where the narrator says 'I espoused him in his language'. What we try to do is to espouse a text in its language. When we translate a text, for example, we don't try to *reduce* it to French. We work to preserve the essence of each different language as it passes from one language to the other.

The work we do is a work of love, comparable to the work of love that can take place between two human beings. To understand the other, it is necessary to go in their language, to make the journey through the other's imaginary. For you are strange to me. In the effort to understand, I bring you back to me, compare you to me. I translate you in me. And what I note is your difference, your strangeness. At that moment, perhaps, through recognition of my own differences, I might perceive something of you.

This movement is like a voyage. Sometimes I have worked on countries poetically. Cambodia is an example. In my mind, I had an imaginary Cambodia composed of everything I had read. But, of course, nothing could render the actual experience of going to Cambodia which is something that passes through the body, through the senses, something which happens between Cambodia and me – my encounter with its smell, its space, the colours of its sky.

I have always thought how much I should like to be able to keep all the various stages of this journey. The pre-journey; the imaginary journey. All the preparations for the journey. The first encounter. The moment of discovery. Then everything we bring back from the encounter.

All these different stages are, in reality, the history of a text. And our reading must be a movement capable of following all the stages of this vast journey from one to the other, to me, to you.

I believe that in order to read – to translate – well, we have to undertake this journey ourselves. We have to go to the country of the text and bring back the earth of which the language is made. And every aspect is important, including the things we don't know, the things we discover.

Sarah Cornell: The etymology of 'to translate' tells us a great deal about what translation actually does. 'Translate' comes from the Latin word *translatus* which is the past participle of *transferre* meaning 'to transfer' or 'to translate'. *Ferre* also gives the idea of 'to carry'. Translation is in fact this process of transferring or carrying across. It creates a bridge from one language to another and thus opens a passageway towards the encounter of the other where he or she dwells, speaks, cries or sings in a different tongue.

Violette Santellani: As a result of participating in the seminar, reading has become a new act. Now when I read, I have the impression of slowing down, of changing down to a lower gear. I am still looking at the text as a place of potential self-discovery, but now I am able to reject earlier positions of evasion and identification to enter the body of the text. The image that comes to mind is that of a mouse exploring all the various threads of a text, examining the different colours and knots of meaning, the patterns and designs, all the dark, shadowy creases and folds.

Sarah Cornell: For me, reading is a flowing process of exchange between the reader and the text. On the one hand, reading means working with the text where the text itself is working consciously or unconsciously. On the other hand, as Hélène wrote in 'Approach to Clarice Lispector',[1] reading is 'letting oneself be read' by the text.

Reading in this way calls for the acceptance of a certain position of non-mastery in order to let oneself go towards the mystery or the unknown in the text. However, I think it's important to point out that 'non-mastery' doesn't mean a total lack of orientation nor a failure to recognize the value of modern theory.

Hélène Cixous: Everything begins with love. If we work on a text we don't love, we are automatically at the wrong distance. This happens in many institutions where, in general, one works on a text as if it were an object, using theoretical instruments. It's perfectly possible to make a machine out of the text, to treat it like a machine and be treated by it like a machine. The contemporary tendency has been to find theoretical instruments, a reading technique which has bridled the text, mastered it like a wild horse with saddle and bridle, enslaving it. I am wary of formalist approaches, those which cut up structure, which impose their systematic grid.

If I set loving the text as a condition, I also set up the possibility that there will be people who will not love some of the text we work on. Some of us won't 'bite' into certain texts, certain texts won't mean anything to us. It doesn't matter. Others amongst us will be called by them and moved to reply.

There are thirty ways into a text. Reading together in this way we bring the text into play. We take a page and everyone comes individually towards it. The text begins to radiate from these approaches. Slowly, we penetrate together to its heart.

I choose to work on the texts that 'touch' me. I use the word deliberately because I believe there is a bodily relationship between reader and text. We work very close to the text, as close to the body of the text as possible; we work phonically, listening to the text, as well as graphically and typographically.

Sometimes I look at the design, the geography of the text, as if it were a map, embodying the world. I look at its legs, its thighs, its belly, as well as its trees and rivers: an immense human and earthly cosmos. I like to work like an ant, crawling the entire length of a text and examining all its details, as well as like a bird that flies over it, or like one of Tsvetaeva's immense ears, listening to its music.

We listen to a text with numerous ears. We hear each other talking with foreign accents and we listen to the foreign accents in the text. Every text has its foreign accents, its strangenesses, and these act like signals, attracting our attention. These strangenesses are our cue. We aren't looking for the author as much as what made the author take the particular path they took, write what they wrote. We're looking for the secret of creation, the same process of creation each one of us is constantly involved with in the process of our lives.

Texts are the witnesses of our proceeding. The text opens up a path which is already ours and yet not altogether ours.

(1988)

Note

1 'Approche de Clarice Lispector', *Poetique*, No. 40, Paris, Editions du Seuil, November 1979, p. 407.

TERRY LOVELL

'Writing Like a Woman: A Question of Politics' The Politics of Theory

Literary Production and Gender

The penetration of capital, and the transformation of literature into a commodity, has been limited to the stages of printing and publishing, and distribution. The first stage of literary production has been untouched either by technological transformation or by the division of labour. Unlike other forms of intellectual work, novel writing has not become institutionalised within the University. In terms of masculine/feminine poles of ideology, novel-writing is deeply ambivalent, like all categories of so-called 'creative writing'. It is paid work, work for breadwinners; and despite recurrent male complaints of female competition, it is dominated by men. Richard Altick estimates that the proportion of female to male novelists remained at about 20%, from 1800–1935.[1] Yet novel-writing is frequently seen as 'feminine' rather than 'masculine'. Even male writers can be found who make this association. John Fowles links all kinds of creativity with femininity. However, this does not mean that he considers it fit work for women. 'There are', he tells us, 'Adam-women and Eve-men; singularly few of the world's great progressive artists and thinkers, have not belonged to the latter category'.[2]

John Fowles' views are of course his own. But I believe he articulates the gender ambiguity of literary production in our culture. However, a recent massive contribution to feminist literary theory has argued the opposite case. Sandra Gilbert and Susan Gubar claim that

> In patriarchal Western culture . . . the text's author is a father, a progenitor, an aesthetic patriarch whose pen is an instrument of generative power like his penis.

They back up their claim with quotations from literary men and women:

> The artist's most essential quality is masterly execution, which is a kind of male gift, and especially marks off men from women . . . (Gerard Manley Hopkins, 1886)

Literature is not the business of a woman's life, and it cannot be . . . (Robert Southey, 1837)

Jane Austen's novels fail because her writing lacks a strong male thrust, (Anthony Burgess)

Literary women lack that blood congested genital drive which energises every great style. (William Gass)[3]

These quotations fail to establish Gilbert and Gubar's claim – in fact they cast doubt upon it. Where femininity and masculinity are strongly marked in culture and ideology, they do not have to be stridently claimed. The writers she quotes protest too much. Their over-insistence paradoxically confirms the gender-ambiguity of 'creative writing' in Western culture, rather than establishing its masculine credentials.

Perhaps this is a further reason for the greater interest which feminism as opposed to socialism has displayed for literature. Literary production has been a contested area vis-à-vis gender in a way in which it has not been for class. I want to argue that this gender ambiguity has made it easier for women and for feminists to breach literary production, but that this has created particular problems for feminist literary theory.

First, though, it is necessary to substantiate my claim that literary production *is* gender ambiguous.

i. I would hazard a guess that there is no strong association among the population at large, of creative writing with 'manliness' – quite the opposite in fact.

ii. The study of literature and languages, through the school system and at university, is heavily dominated by female students.

iii. Women gained access to novel-writing and to other forms of literary work at a time when they were excluded from virtually all other (middle-class) professions except governessing. It was, moreover, the only paid occupation in which they could hope to achieve independence and financial parity with men.[4]

iv. Novel writing is a form of domestic production. Here, home and workplace have never been separated. It is an individual and personalised form of production.

v. Fictional worlds have been largely restricted to the sphere which is conventionally and ideologically assigned to women, or for which women are assumed to have a special responsibility – that of personal relations. . . . the development of the novel has been closely bound up with the social and political position of women . . . there is a fundamental continuity which firmly places them in a private domestic world where emotions and personal relationships are at once the focus of moral value and the core of women's experience. In the novel women are 'prisoners' of feeling and of private life.[5]

Naturally, male writers have struggled against this taint of feminine identification. Hence the sentiments quoted above. They have often done so by denigrating their female colleagues. Women, urged to write, if they must, like ladies, were despised as inferior when they did, attacked as 'unfeminine' when, like Charlotte Brontë, they did not.[6] Certain genres have been marked off as 'lesser' forms, and ceded to women (e.g. romantic fiction). Others have been developed and colonised as vehicles of strident masculinity (the Hemingway-Miller-Mailer school attacked by Kate Millett[7]). More recently, structuralist theory applied to literature has offered a new offensive in the field of literary criticism. Showalter argues that 'The new sciences of the text ... have offered literary critics the opportunity to demonstrate that the work they do is as manly and aggressive as nuclear physics – not intuitive, expressive, feminine'.[8] Where structuralism is allied to Lacanian psychoanalytic theory, the bid to masculinise is strongest. Variants of this approach have consigned the feminine *per se* to absence, silence, incoherence, even madness. Several feminists have attempted to construct theories of feminine identity and a feminist aesthetic upon this marginal territory ceded by a phallocentric theory of language. I believe this to be a mistaken strategy, for it abandons territory which can and ought to be defended against masculine imperialism; coherence, rationality, articulateness.

(1983)

Notes

1 Richard Altick, *The English Common Reader* (Chicago, University of Chicago Press, 1957).
2 John Fowles, *The Aristos* (London, Triad Granada, 1981), p. 157.
3 Sandra M. Gilbert and Susan Gubar, *The Madwoman in the Attic: The Woman Writer and the Nineteenth-Century Literary Imagination* (New Haven, Yale University Press, 1979).
4 Elaine Showalter, *A Literature of Their Own: British Women Novelists From Brontë to Lessing* (London, Virago, 1979).
5 Patricia Stubbs, *Women and Fiction: Feminism and the Novel, 1880–1920* (London, Methuen, 1979), p. x.
6 Showalter, *A Literature of Their Own*.
7 Kate Millett, *Sexual Politics* (London, Virago, 1977).
8 Elaine Showalter, 'Towards a Feminist Poetics', *Women Writing and Writing about Women*, edited by Mary Jacobus (London, Croom Helm, 1979).

JANE SPENCER

The Rise of the Woman Novelist: From Aphra Behn to Jane Austen

Nancy Armstrong has pointed out that feminist analyses of the obstacles to female creativity in patriarchal society may leave women's actual achievements unexplained.[3] To explain why women were sometimes successful and highly acclaimed writers not only in the nineteenth-century but for over 100 years before that, we could postulate that the oppressive ideology excluding women from writing has been neither consistent nor entirely successful. In the eighteenth century we can detect the presence of a view of writing that links it to the feminine role rather than opposing the two. This, as I will show, encouraged the expansion of women's professional writing. But at the same time as encouraging women to write, this feminization of literature defined literature as a special category supposedly outside the political arena, with an influence on the world as indirect as women's was supposed to be. Women's new status as authors did not necessarily mean new powers for women in general. *The Rise of the Woman Novelist*, then, is centrally concerned with the paradox that women writers may well be rising at a time when women's condition in general is deteriorating. My view of women's novels in the eighteenth century is in one sense positive: I am claiming that they occupy a much more important place in the development of the novel than is usually believed, and that they contributed a great deal to women's entry into public discourse. But I am wary of viewing that success as a simple gain: the terms on which women writers were accepted worked in some ways to suppress feminist opposition. Women's writing is not the same thing as women's rights.

[. . .]

By the beginning of the eighteenth century, then, a path was open for the woman writer, but it was full of pitfalls. There were common expectations about women's writing: their main subject would be love, their main interest in their female characters. The idea that women were naturally inclined to virtue, and could exert a salutary moral influence on men, was spreading; and so was the idea that it was through women's tender feelings and their ability to stimulate tender feelings in men, that this influence operated. Hence women writers who wished to claim a special place in literature because of their sex were constrained by the twin requirements of love and morality. The two could be mutually antagonistic. The theme of love could lead to warm, and therefore immoral writing; and on the other hand didacticism could kill romance, a danger that was to be apparent later, in some of the eighteenth-century novels. Women writers had the delicate task of balancing a 'feminine' sensitivity to love with an equally 'feminine' morality.

The women novelists of the eighteenth century inherited a role from the women dramatists of the seventeenth century, but their relationship with those professional predecessors was not always easy. The novel, even more than the pathetic tragedy, allowed for concentration on women's sensibility and women's dilemmas; but the novelists, even more than the earlier dramatists, were affected by the double requirement to delight with romantic love yet instruct according to the strictest of contemporary moral standards. As they tried to fulfil this requirement, they defined their female characters in accordance with the developing ideology of femininity, and though the terms they used changed in line with the century's increasing delicacy, their concerns were similar throughout. Women were defined by their sexuality: and so were women writers. A woman's writing and her life tended to be judged together on the same terms. The woman novelist's sexual behaviour was as much a subject for concern as her heroine's. Her main subject – female sexuality, as controlled by female chastity – was established by the early 1700s. Not only this subject matter but her attitude to it had to be carefully controlled by the ever more onerous demands of proper femininity. Male writers too, of course, were affected by the simultaneous demand for passion and morality so typical of the century: but women writers left it as a demand on their entire selves, not just on their writings.

With these drawbacks, women's empire of wit was founded. It was an empire internally divided by the contradictory demands made by bourgeois society's ideals of femininity, and its attitude to the women who had first won it was deeply ambivalent. But its achievements are worth remembering in themselves and for the legacy they left to us. For as we watch the women novelists of the eighteenth century weighing passion against prudence, sexual attachment against female independence, desire against duty, and morality against romance, we will find them building, out of the contradictions of 'femininity', an identity for themselves as writers and a female tradition in literature.

(1968)

Note

3 See Nancy Armstrong, 'The Rise of Feminine Authority in the Novel', *Novel* 15, no. 2 (Winter, 1982), pp. 127–45.

BARBARA SMITH

'Toward a Black Feminist Criticism' *Conditions: Two*

The role that criticism plays in making a body of literature recognizable and real hardly needs to be explained here. The necessity for non-hostile and perceptive analysis of works written by persons outside the 'mainstream' of white/male cultural rule has been proven by the Black cultural resurgence of the 1960s and '70s and by the even more recent growth of feminist literary scholarship. For books to be real and remembered they have to be talked about. For books to be understood they must be examined in such a way that the basic intentions of the writers are at least considered. Because of racism Black literature has usually been viewed as a discrete subcategory of American literature and there have been Black critics of Black literature who did much to keep it alive long before it caught the attention of whites. Before the advent of specifically feminist criticism in this decade, books by white women, on the other hand, were not clearly perceived as the cultural manifestation of an oppressed people. It took the surfacing of the second wave of the North

American feminist movement to expose the fact that these works contain a stunningly accurate record of the impact of patriarchal values and practice upon the lives of women and more significantly that literature by women provides essential insights into female experience.

In speaking about the current situation of Black women writers, it is important to remember that the existence of a feminist movement was an essential pre-condition to the growth of feminist literature, criticism and women's studies, which focused at the beginning almost entirely upon investigations of literature. The fact that a parallel Black feminist movement has been much slower in evolving cannot help but have impact upon the situation of Black women writers and artists and explains in part why during this very same period we have been so ignored.

There is no political movement to give power or support to those who want to examine Black women's experience through studying our history, literature and culture. There is no political presence that demands a minimal level of consciousness and respect from those who write or talk about our lives. Finally, there is not a developed body of Black feminist political theory whose assumptions could be used in the study of Black women's art. When Black women's books are dealt with at all, it is usually in the context of Black literature which largely ignores the implications of sexual politics. When white women look at Black women's works they are of course ill-equipped to deal with the subtleties of racial politics. A Black feminist approach to literature that embodies the realization that the politics of sex as well as the politics of race and class are crucially interlocking factors in the works of Black women writers is an absolute necessity. Until a Black feminist criticism exists we will not even know what these writers mean. The citations from a variety of critics which follow prove that without a Black feminist critical perspective not only are books by Black women misunderstood, they are destroyed in the process.

Jerry H. Bryant, the *Nation's* white male reviewer of Alice Walker's *In Love & Trouble: Stories of Black Women*, wrote in 1973.

> The subtitle of the collection. 'Stories of Black Women,' is probably an attempt by the publisher to exploit not only black subjects but feminine ones. There is nothing feminist about these stories, however?

Blackness and feminism are to his mind mutually exclusive and peripheral to the act of writing fiction. Bryant of course does not consider that Walker might have titled the work herself, nor did he apparently read the book which unequivocally reveals the author's feminist consciousness.

In *The Negro Novel in America*, a book that Black critics recognize as one of the worst examples of white racist pseudo-scholarship, Robert Bone cavalierly dismisses Ann Petry's classic, *The Street*. He perceives it to be '. . . a superficial social analysis' of how slums victimize their Black inhabitants.[3] He further objects that:

It is an attempt to interpret slum life in terms of *Negro* experience, when a larger frame of reference is required. As Alain Locke has observed, '*Knock on Any Door* is superior to *The Street* because it designates class and environment, rather than mere race and environment, as its antagonist.'[4]

Neither Robert Bone nor Alain Locke, the Black male critic he cites, can recognize that *The Street* is one of the best delineations in literature of how sex, race, *and* class interact to oppress Black women.

In her review of Toni Morrison's *Sula* for the *New York Times Book Review* in 1973, putative feminist Sara Blackburn makes similarly racist comments. She writes:

> . . . Toni Morrison is far too talented to remain only a marvelous recorder of the black side of provincial American life. If she is to maintain the large and serious audience she deserves, she is going to have to address a riskier contemporary reality than this beautiful but nevertheless distanced novel. *And if she does this, it seems to me that she might easily transcend that early and unintentionally limiting classification 'black women writer' and take her place among the most serious, important and talented American novelists now working.*[5] [Italics mine.]

Recognizing Morrison's exquisite gift, Blackburn unashamedly asserts that Morrison is 'too talented' to deal with mere Black folk, particularly those double nonentities, Black women. In order to be accepted as 'serious,' 'important,' 'talented,' and 'American,' she must obviously focus her efforts upon chronicling the doings of white men.

The mishandling of Black women writers by whites is paralleled more often by their not being handled at all, particularly in feminist criticism. Although Elaine Showalter in her review essay on literary criticism for *Signs* states that: 'The best work being produced today [in feminist criticism] is exacting and cosmopolitan,' her essay is neither.[6] If it were, she would not have failed to mention a single Black or Third-World woman writer, whether 'major' or 'minor' to cite her questionable categories. That she also does not even hint that lesbian writers of any color exist renders her purported overview virtually meaningless. Showalter obviously thinks that the identities of being Black and female are mutually exclusive as this statement illustrates.

> Furthermore, there are other literary subcultures (black American novelists, for example) whose history offers a precedent for feminist scholarship to use.[7]

The idea of critics like Showalter *using* Black literature is chilling, a case of barely disguised cultural imperialism. The final insult is that she footnotes the preceding remark by pointing readers to works on Black literature by white males Robert Bone and Roger Rosenblatt!

Two recent works by white women, Ellen Moers' *Literary Women: The Great Writers* and Patricia Meyer Spacks' *The Female Imagination* evidence the same racist flaw.[8] Moers includes the names of four Black and one Puertorriqueña writer in her seventy pages of bibliographical notes and does not deal at all with Third-World women in the body of her book. Spacks refers to a comparison between Negroes (sic) and women in Mary Ellmann's *Thinking About Women* under the index entry, 'blacks, women and,' '*Black Boy* (Wright)' is the preceding entry. Nothing follows. Again there is absolutely no recognition that Black and female identity ever co-exist, specifically in a group of Black women writers. Perhaps one can assume that these women do not know who Black women writers are, that they have had little opportunity like most Americans to learn about them. Perhaps. Their ignorance seems suspiciously selective, however, particularly in the light of the dozens of truly obscure white women writers they are able to unearth. Spacks was herself employed at Wellesley College at the same time that Alice Walker was there teaching one of the first courses on Black women writers in the country.

I am not trying to encourage racist criticism of Black women writers like that of Sara Blackburn, to cite only one example. As a beginning I would at least like to see in print white women's acknowledgement of the contradictions of who and what are being left out of their research and writing.[9]

Black male critics can also *act* as if they do not know that Black women writers exist and are, of course, hampered by an inability to comprehend Black women's experience in sexual as well as racial terms. Unfortunately there are also those who are as virulently sexist in their treatment of Black women writers as their white male counterparts. Darwin Turner's discussion of Zora Neale Hurston in his *In a Minor Chord: Three Afro-American Writers and Their Search for Identity* is a frightening example of the near assassination of a great Black woman writer.[10] His descriptions of her and her work as 'artful,' 'coy,' 'irrational,' 'superficial,' and 'shallow' bear no relationship to the actual quality of her achievements. Turner is completely insensitive to the sexual political dynamics of Hurston's life and writing.

In a recent interview the notoriously misogynist writer, Ishmael Reed, comments in this way upon the low sales of his newest novel:

> . . . but the book only sold 8000 copies. I don't mind giving out the figure: 8000. Maybe if I was one of those young *female* Afro-American writers that are so hot now, I'd sell more. You know, fill my books with ghetto women who can *do no wrong.* . . . But come on, I think I could have sold 8000 copies by myself.[11]

The politics of the situation of Black women are glaringly illuminated by this statement. Neither Reed nor his white male interviewer has the slightest compunction about attacking Black women in print. They need not fear widespread public denunciation since Reed's statement is in perfect agreement with the values of a society that hates Black people, women and Black women. Finally the two of them feel free to base their actions on the premise that Black women are powerless to alter either their political or cultural oppression.

In her introduction to 'A Bibliography of Works Written by American Black Women' Ora Williams quotes some of the reactions of her colleagues toward her efforts to do research on Black women. She writes:

Others have reacted negatively with such statements as, 'I really don't think you are going to find very much written.' 'Have "they" written anything that is any good?' and, 'I wouldn't go overboard with this woman's lib thing.' When discussions touched on the possibility of teaching a course in which emphasis would be on the literature by Black women, one response was, 'Ha, ha. That will certainly be the most nothing course ever offered!'[12]

A remark by Alice Walker capsulizes what all the preceding examples indicate about the position of Black women writers and the reasons for the damaging criticism about them. She responds to her interviewer's question, 'Why do you think that the black woman writer has been so ignored in America? Does she have even more difficulty than the black male writer, who perhaps has just begun to gain recognition?' Walker replies:

There are two reasons why the black woman writer is not taken as seriously as the black male writer. One is that she's a woman. Critics seem unusually ill-equipped to intelligently discuss and analyze the works of black women. Generally, they do not even make the attempt; they prefer, rather, to talk about the lives of black women writers, not about what they write. And, since black women writers are not – it would seem – very likeable – until recently they were the least willing worshippers of male supremacy – comments about them tend to be cruel.[13]

(1977)

Notes

2 Jerry H. Bryant, 'The Outskirts of a New City,' in the *Nation*, 12 November 1973, p. 502.

3 Robert Bone, *The Negro Novel in America* (Yale University Press, New Haven: orig. c. 1958), p. 180.

4 *Ibid. (Knock on Any Door* is a novel by Black writer, Willard Motley.)

5 Sara Blackburn, 'You Still Can't Go Home Again,' in the *New York Times Book Review*, 30 December 1973, p. 3.

6 Elaine Showalter, 'Review Essay: Literary Criticism,' *Signs*, Vol. 1. no. 2 (Winter, 1975), p. 460.

7 *Ibid.*, p. 445.

8 Ellen Moers, Literary Women: The Great Writers (Anchor Books, Garden City. New York: 1977, orig. c. 1976).
Patricia Meyer Spacks, *The Female Imagination* (Avon Books, New York: 1976).

9 An article by Nancy Hoffman, 'White Women, Black Women: Inventing an Adequate Pedagogy,' in *Women's Studies Newsletter*, Vol. 5, nos. 1 & 2 (Spring, 1977), pp. 21–24, gives valuable insights into how white women can approach the writing of Black women.

10 Darwin T. Turner, *In a Minor Chord: Three Afro-American Writers and Their Search for Identity* (Southern Illinois University Press, Carbondale and Edwardsville: c. 1971).

11 John Domini, 'Roots and Racism: An Interview With Ishmael Reed,' in *The Boston Phoenix*, 5 April 1977, p. 20.

12 Ora Williams, 'A Bibliography of Works Written by American Black Women' in *College Language Association Journal*, March 1972, p. 355. There is an expanded book-length version of this bibliography: *American Black Women in the Arts and Social Sciences: A Bibliographic Survey* (The Scarecrow Press, Inc., Metuchen, N.J.: 1973).

13 John O'Brien, ed., *Interviews With Black Writers* (Liveright, New York: c. 1973), p. 201.

BLACK WOMAN TALK COLLECTIVE

'Black Woman Talk'
Feminist Review

Black Woman Talk is a collective of women of Asian and African descent living in Britain. As Black women we feel that the publishing industry has ignored and silenced the views and ideas of Black women living in Britain. It is important for us therefore to restore the lines of communication which have been historically destroyed and to re-establish the links between our scattered and isolated communities.

As Black women we experience oppression due to our sex, race, class and sexual orientation. This is reflected in every area of our lives and the publishing industry is no exception. It is a very powerful medium for communication and it reflects the racism and sexism of this society. The amount of work published for, by and about Black women is totally negligible and Black women's voices have gone unheard. Instead racist and sexist stereotypes have been perpetuated and until now been unchallenged.

More recently, it appears that there is a growing awareness amongst some of the established mainstream and feminist publishers of the need to make Black voices heard. Unfortunately, their enthusiasm to publish works by Black women, particularly from America, seems to stem from their recognition that such books have a lucrative market, rather than any genuine commitment to making publishing accessible to Black women writers in Britain. Afro-American women seem to be the vogue for feminist publishers such as the Women's Press. Such publishers are not only reluctant to hear the voices of Black women in Britain but there is little concern about including Black women in the publishing industry in a way which gives them any decision-making powers at all levels.

Black Woman Talk began as a small group of unemployed women who came together to form a workers' publishing co-operative. We feel there is an urgent need to see more publications available by Black women living in Britain to express our experiences and history. Our own varied experiences in working in Black organizations as well as our varied involvement in creative work such as writing, visual arts, theatre and music places us in contact with Black women who are writing and/or doing visual work. We are all writers and artists who want to see more Black women get access to publishing and the various skills involved in this field.

Black Woman Talk aims to provide a means by which women of Asian and African descent can publish their work, and through the publication of short stories, poetry, political writings, photo-essays, calendars reflect the wide variety of written and visual works produced by us. We would like to encourage more Black women to write and record their life experiences and to provide a greater knowledge and understanding of the lives and history of Black women in the wider community.

We would also like to make alternative materials available for use in schools, libraries and other public information centres.

We will shortly be asking for manuscripts by Black women and as we grow we shall provide employment in a co-operative situation where Black women work with and for other Black women, thus sharing the skills and knowledge we gain, and providing encouragement and advice to other Black women. We would like to extend to cover typesetting and printing in the long term, which would give us greater self-determination and more skills to share.

The existence of *Black Woman Talk* is testimony to the strength of Black Women organizing to create our own means of communication. The international movement of Black women organizing in this way is illustrated by the existence of our sister press in America, Kitchen Table; Women of Color Press, and Kali Press; Third World Women Press in Delhi.

(1984)

LAURETTA NGCOBO

Editor's Introduction
Let It Be Told: Essays by Black Women in Britain

Notwithstanding the general attitudes of mainstream commercial publishers, the picture would be incomplete if no mention were made of certain exceptional developments taking place within the publishing world. Much of it has little to do specifically with Blackwomen writers, but its effects, like ripples in a pool, touch us indirectly. During the past decade and a half there have been changes in the outlook of white, male-dominated publishers which would have rocked the industry were it not so well secured through power, finance and tradition. First the feminist lobby has pressured them into promoting women who, in the main, worked on sufferance within these companies. This, being a case of too little too late for some enterprising women, led to the founding of feminist publishing houses. Initially these too seemed to have no thought for the beleaguered Blackwoman writer, their paramount consideration being to serve the neglected needs of their marginalized fellow white sisters. It has taken the literary cloudburst of Blackwomen's writing from North American to force Britain's feminist presses to look nearer home for Black talent.

Until recently, few publishing houses concerned themselves with Third World writing: the handful who did include Longman, Heinemann and Macmillan, and even they produced almost entirely for the export market. The doors have widened somewhat to admit Blackwomen to the lists of prestigious houses such as Virago, The Women's Press, Zed Press and others. In addition, there is a growing number of small Black companies producing books by our women. One of the oldest is Bogle-L'Ouverture Publications, begun by Jessica Huntley. Another woman who has started her own company, publishing her own work, is Buchi Emecheta. And in 1987 we have seen yet another women's publishing house, Zora Press established by Iyamidè Hazeley and Adeola Solanke. Joining the swelling ranks of committed Black publishers, headed by the now long-established New Beacon Books, are Karnak House, Akira and Karia. We owe a debt to these fledgling Black concerns, as well as to the radical white presses who first provided an outlet for some of our now better known writers.

The books that Blackwomen do write are invariably considered a separate class of writing that is somehow discredited, less authentic, not part of the main body of literature. More often than not, they will be stocked mainly by alternative booksellers. This discrimination means that our books do not easily find their way into schools and universities, for their validity is in doubt. Organizations such as the Association for the Teaching of Caribbean and African and Asian Literature (ATCAL) have been formed by teachers and others with a particular interest in trying to change these prevailing attitudes. Having been in existence for several years, ATCAL has made slow progress in achieving its main aim – to convince the examining bodies to accord examination status to this literature, for it is essential for the young of whatever race to understand the Black experience.

(1987)

CATH JACKSON

'A Press of One's Own'
Trouble and Strife

We were convinced that if we were to be heard, if our words were to be published, we would have to control the process of publishing. And that, for us at that time, meant learning to print. We felt strongly – and with some justification – that on the production floor our words would be changed: not just made not ours but also discarded – simply got rid of. They could be – and were – just thrown away. We had to control the process to get our words out there.

So the three of us [with Cath Jackson, Sheila Shulman and Lilian Mohin were founder members of the Onlywomen Press.] enrolled at Camberwell College of Art to learn printing. We knew a woman who had already done an evening class there, which was how we knew they ran a printing course. But we were the first full-time women students on the course.

SS: To me it was a necessary, physical, material extension of our feminism. It was clear that lesbian feminist writing wasn't getting published. It seemed to us a necessary consequence of being writers. Somewhere too at the back of my head also was Trotsky: the notion that we would be physically making a revolution. In retrospect it was a slightly naive decision because technology was already outstripping us.

LM: We started college in 1974. All the instructors were male and the other students were all young male school leavers – but we hardly had anything to do with them. The tutors took a while to cope, but once they decided we were serious about learning to print, they became immensely helpful. Although they would call us all "the girls" and they refused to tell us apart, even though Deborah is tall and Sheila and I are very short. We had to buy a set of steps which we shared in order to be able to reach the machines.

It was a two-year course, learning print planning and production and the philosophy behind printing. We learned the jargon and the whole process from manufacturing the lead type to setting and printing in lead, offset litho printing and the whole range of modern printing techniques.

Doing the course changed the way we thought about the books we wanted to produce. We became considerably less pompous about our publishing priorities than we might otherwise have been. It taught us about material reality, the mechanics of the real world.

SS: Learning to print made me think much more carefully about how things get done: the difference between thinking something and actually doing it. Before I always thought the world was made of words.

Jacky Bishop joined the group in 1975, as a member of the wider editorial collective.

Jacky Bishop: I was working in accountancy at the time. I'd known Lilian for years through involvement in feminists politics, in the London Women's Liberation Workshop. Back then there was nothing: no lesbian feminist presses, certainly in this country; very little feminism being published anywhere in Britain. But if you wanted something to happen, you went out and did it yourself.

LM: While we were on the course we carried on meeting every week. We used the college equipment to produce several pamphlets of poems as part of our course work, under what was at that time our name: the Women's Press. We did Judith Kazantzis' *'Finding Food'*, work done by Astra, *'Deviation'* by Judith Barrington, *'It'll Take a Long Time'* by Janet Gooch and some of my own poems, *'Cracks'*.

We also taught other women about the production process. It was part of the politics of the press. Later when we got the print business going, we taught women how to print.

JB: I remember sitting in meetings talking politics and binding by hand – literally sewing together – copies of the Astra poetry pamphlet. This was partly because we could not afford to pay to get it bound but more because we wanted to do every part of the process, to make the book ourselves. A few hundred copies could be accommodated by pressing lovers and friends into labour – but they wouldn't do it twice.

LM: We did have some problems at Camberwell. One of the technicians melted down the lead type that I'd set for the Judith Kazantzis pamphlet, '*Finding Food*'. It was his job to proof-read the work that the students had set in type and he took particular exception to one of Judith's poems, a short humourous poem about her husband. He said it was 'against nature'.

We would also take work outside and use the equipment of various sympathetic lefty presses. We printed and published the first ever women's liberation calendar that way and sold it at conferences. It had photographs of various women's liberation movements events taken by feminist photographers. We felt ourselves to be – and were – very much part of the movement and absolutely convinced we were in it together, whatever the political divisions.

SS: We made the plates at a community press in Thornton Heath. The plate-maker, camera and press were all plugged into one multi-socket which they kept in a puddle in the middle of the floor.

LM: There was an informal network of women working in the lefty printing trade – places like Calverts and Bread and Roses. That's often how we were able to use the equipment at these lefty presses, through our contact with the women there. And later there were women-only print shops, like See Red and Women in Print. We talked to each other and helped each other out, but to us at Onlywomen it was less the printing that linked us and more that we were all radical feminists. That first meeting in Islington and the conference we organised later were very much about both feminist printing and publishing.

(1993)

JOAN SCANLON AND JULIA SWINDELLS

'*Bad Apple*' Trouble and Strife

A Man like Maiden

When Virago published Dorothy Richardson's *Pilgrimage* in 1989, Anthony Burgess prefaced his unqualified appreciation of the novel with a characteristically disagreeable and vitriolic attack on the sectional motives of the publishers.

> By no stretch of usage can *Virago* be made not to signify a shrew, a scold, an ill-tempered woman, unless we go back to the etymology – a man-like maiden

(cognate with *virile*) – and the antique meaning – amazon, female warrior – that is close to it. It is an unlovely and aggressive name, even for a militant feminist organisation, and it presides awkwardly over the reissue of a great *roman fleuve* which is too important to be associated with chauvinist sows.

However even as long ago as 1978, Fay Weldon was saying in the *Times Literary Supplement*, that Virago had changed the connotations of the word 'virago', and that it now conjured up the image of 'an industrious and intelligent lady'. That Ursula Owen should quote this on Virago's fifteenth birthday is perhaps significant. She did so as a testimony to Virago's capacity for shifting and broadening the perspective on women's writing. But it is possible to see Fay Weldon's observation in a less celebratory light. What had been potentially disturbing and provocative – 'impudent and shrewish woman' – has already been accommodated to the idea of 'an industrious and intelligent lady'. What had been undeniably connected to a movement, a group, a group-consciousness of women, is moved to the individual writer, 'industrious and intelligent', and 'a lady' at that.

In the Virago *Keepsake* a further shift has taken place; a move from the individual author to the Virago author, a celebration not of the women's movement, or of women's writing, but the survival of the press itself – a recognition of what it stands for, not so much in terms of political achievement, but brand loyalty and quality writing.

Marketing and Radicalism

Carmen Callil, one of the founders of Virago (and now managing director of Chatto and Windus) says:

> 'Virago was founded with two main aims. One was ideological, the other a marketing belief. The idea for a feminist house grew out of the feminist movement which was reborn in this country at the end of the '60s. Virago was set up to publish books which were part of that movement, but its marketing aim was quite specific: we aimed to reach a general audience of women and men who had not heard of, or who disliked and even detested, the idea of feminism' (*The Bookseller*, March 1st, 1986).

Perhaps this model underestimated what would happen to that 'feminism' in the process of moving from those for whom it was part of their political lives and commitment to those who might even detest it. In other words, what the model underestimates or denies is the power of marketing as an ideological process. We could appreciate that it would be good and democratic to have to reckon with it, if we could be sure that in the process, feminism was not being neutralised, not being deprived of its ability to issue a challenge, and yes, to cause some sectors of the community to detest it. The bleakest version of the Virago story, and the consequences of marketability for radicalism, is that it is now the feminist movement, rather than the general public, with whom Virago are at odds.

In the autumn of 1985 Carmen Callil, now chairwoman of Virago, gave a rather odd account of the history of the women's movement in a paper for a Women in Publishing conference in London, in which she explains why women were 'peripheral to the dominant history of the human race'.

> They did not run businesses; they did not control the centre of power in any sphere except the home. This now has changed – for women in the Western world – and I believe that it has changed forever. I believe it to be a central fact for women of our time that there will be no return to the powerlessness of previous generations.

And in 1990, Harriet Spicer, managing director of Virago, assured *The Bookseller* that, while the press might be perceived as publishing less 'right-on' fiction than formerly, its commitments remained unchanged: 'We've remained true to our ideals, of being entertaining and interesting to women'.

This is a far cry from the carefully stated politics of the press as it was repeatedly articulated by Ursula Owen, who left Virago in December 1990 to work for the then Shadow Arts Minister Mark Fisher, and is now on the editorial team of the newly resurrected *Index on Censorship* due to reappear in May 1994. Not only did she insist that the reprint list was an important acknowledgement that the women's liberation movement had not begun with the Ruskin conference in 1969; she was also clear that the need for feminist publishing was inextricably linked to the need for feminism as a political movement, and that women's lives had not yet 'changed that dramatically, except for a few very privileged women who are in the professions':

> What I'd like is a world where you don't need women's publishing companies or women's pages, but I don't see it in my lifetime or my daughter's lifetime or my grandchildren's lifetime. We are playing a small part in what is a very long and difficult process.

The Meaning of Greatness

What is interesting, however, is not just the difference of emphasis manifest amongst the key agents in Virago's inception and development, but the common ground between them. A recurring theme in Virago's own publicity material, and in interviews with the directors, is the need to succeed in the battle for inclusion in school and university curricula. Another commonly articulated belief is in a detectable and significant shift in feminist thinking away from socialist feminism as the 'the central strand of thinking' in the 70s towards a preoccupation with race as a central concern in the present. While it is true that Virago's emphasis on socialist feminism ensured that earlier feminist history was broadened from the story of the Pankhursts to include the stories of suffragists in the mills and factories of the north of England, this breadth of documentation has been less than true of their coverage of the contemporary women's movement. This is not to disparage the contribution which Virago has made to the rewriting of women's history and culture. While it is also true that Virago has sustained a commitment to publishing Black and Asian women's writing, both fiction and non-fiction (including important books such as Amrit Wilson's *Finding a Voice* and *Heart of the Race*, edited by Beverley Bryan, Stella Dadzie and Suzanne Scafe during the 80s) their bias towards another common theme – 'first class writing' – has posed a number of problems, not least in relation to this particular commitment.

Nowhere is it apparent what Virago means by *'great literature'*, 'quality writing' or 'first class prose'. Is this gauged by editorial intuition and sound literary taste – as the critical establishment would have us believe? Or is 'great literature' also subject to the scrutiny which feminism has focussed on other forms of cultural production? The impression one gets from the collective directorial voice of Virago is that the establishment criteria remain the touchstone of aesthetic judgement, but that – some of the time – political criteria prevail instead. So, when Ursula Owen insisted that Virago was not interested in 'the great tradition' as it had been taught in British universities, she proceeded, in the same breath, to endorse its judgements:

> We also wanted to show what women have been writing about in novels over a long period, whether they are considered in "the great tradition" or not. Some of our Virago Modern Classics are great novels: Christina Stead, Willa Cather, and Edith Wharton are great novelists. Some of them are not . . .

This seems to be the central (and shared) confusion at the heart of Virago's editorial policy. Then and now, there appears to be undisputed common ground about what constitutes 'good writing', whereas the agreement about what constitutes politically important writing is likely to be dictated by a different set of criteria, those which are determined by an in-house perception of what is central to feminism at any moment in time, whether it be psychoanalysis, postmodernism – or race. The illusion that feminism of a certain kind is still unmarketable is now articulated, not in terms of the increasingly racist and nationalist climate of the 80s and 90s, but by the apparent refusal of the academy to embrace Virago publications into the curriculum.

Ursula Owen's observation that feminism was not marketable in the '70s, although produced of course with hindsight, nevertheless gives a sort of explanation of how the launching of Virago could be seen as relatively unproblematic in political terms at that time, and certainly courageous in terms of the market. At that stage it appeared that the political project of recovering and discovering women could mesh with Virago's more main-stream commitment (present from the beginning) to publishing works of 'literary merit'. So much so that when Burgess commented on the significances of recovering *Pilgrimage* for the literary canon, he was forced to rant about the 'reductive' political motives of the press. The literary establishment therefore had to acknowledge Virago's role in publishing works that it could not help but recognise as literature, and was rattled enough to complain about the 'appropriation' of these texts for feminism.

It seems that the simplicity which characterised attitudes to the market married well with the *historical* project in those early days. The Women's Press began by reprinting neglected books by women, and when Virago started its own 'classic' reprint list, it became quickly identified with this list. Indeed, it is a common misconception that Virago also began as a reprint publisher, although the first 'Virago Modern Classic', Antonia White's *Frost in May*, did not appear until 1978, five years after the press was launched.

Moving into the Mainstream

It is in the domain of contemporary women's writing and commissioning contemporary writers that this distancing from feminism becomes apparent. Virago's stress on 'women's lives' and embattled positions had suggested a strong commitment to taking risks with new projects. However the need for Virago to create an identity for its original fiction, distinct from that of the Modern Classics, was defined by their marketing director Lennie Goodings, as an attempt to vie with the mainstream paperback publishers: 'We're aiming at the Black Swan, Picador. Faber department. We're saying "trust our editorial judgement." ' If, as Harriet Spicer insists, Virago's conscious strategy, was to be 'specialist and mainstream, and to widen the definition of what is perceived to be mainstream', then they can certainly be said to have succeeded in the latter aim. The question remains, though, what do they mean now in the '90s by 'specialist', and what readership are they referring to when they speak of 'brand loyalty'?

The new-format Virago hard-back fiction, while clearly designed to move away from the historical associations of the elegant green spines, is scarcely a radical departure, but a further bid for recognition as a publisher of literary excellence. These little hardbacks, not dissimilar to the Bodley Head fiction list, urge you to recognise their craftsmanship (sic), and come with the hallmark of liberal male academic approval, with quotes from Oxford literary professors such as John Bayley to reassure us that we are all sophisticated enough in the 1990s to know that women write novels in The Great Tradition too.

The very marketability that 'women's ideas' and 'women's lives' of a certain kind have achieved through the women's presses should lead us at least to enquire about the relationship now between a successful publishing house such as Virago and a generally beleaguered women's movement. In Britain at least, throughout the 80s and early 90s, the women's movement has been struggling against wave against wave of state opposition, implicit and explicit, and a media which has for the most part insisted that we have moved beyond the need for feminism. And yet, women's lists in mainstream publishing and women's studies courses in the academy appear to have boomed. It is also significant that Virago's list is difficult to distinguish from many of the womens (or gender) studies lists of mainstream publishers, such as Routledge or Blackwell. One reason for this may well be that, from the beginning, Virago's non-fiction list has on the whole been dictated by the concerns of academic feminism, rather than activist feminism, and the split between academic feminism and the women's movement has widened enormously over the last fifteen years. Moreover, unlike The Women's Press, Virago has almost exclusively published work by socialist feminists, and has consequently found itself with a large number of post-feminist (not to mention post-social-ist) writers on their hands – in spite of the fact that many of these same women were active in the women's movement in the 70s.

In the early seventies, those feminist presses which inserted themselves into 'the market' were doing so out of political and cultural motives which appeared to operate independently of the marketing process. The media-friendly version of feminism had not been invented; the likes of Naomi Woolf were not in evidence in the 70s. Feminism and marketing were in tension, even perceived as potentially incompatible at that time.

Virago appear to have traversed the 80s clutching the fallasy that radicalism persists independently of contexts; that, whatever the political climate, the 'simple' project of representing women's ideas and women's lives remains a politicized one, even when that project has lost its capacity for generating or reflecting an oppositional position. But writing cannot be separated from the conditions of readership and reception in which it occurs. Virago marked those same fifteenth birthday celebrations with the publication of *Writing Lives*. Their initial manifesto, which they are ostensibly committed to continuing, stated a concern with 'women's lives'. That move from 'women's lives' to writing lives' may be indicative: the general move into writing about writing, and the autobiographies of writers, is disturbingly self-referential. The Virago *Keepsake* marked the latest shift from women writers' lives to Virago writers' lives, and consists of pieces either by Virago writers about each other, or about the experience of writing for Virago.

Writing Lives consists of recorded conversations between women writers. The Virago publicity for the volume asks what Maya Angelou, Molly Keane, Rosamond Lehmann, Rebecca West, Eudora Welty, Paule Marshall, Mary Lavin, Rose Guy and Grace Paley have in common, and answers: 'writing lives' – not feminism, not a relationship to the women's movement, not politics, but writing. Those interested in the lives of women writers, in writing, in 'the literary' (and indeed in the lives off the newly famous) may have been pleased. But some of us were not.

(1994)

3

Gender and Genre

INTRODUCTION

Women and the Novel

Any discussion of gender and literary form is dominated by the need to explain women's special relationship with the novel. Yet even at the end of the 1980s critics could complain that insufficient had been done to account for this important conjunction. Jane Spencer writes in 1986:

> Eighteenth-century England witnessed two remarkable and interconnected literary events: the emergence of the novel and the establishment of the professional woman writer. The first of these has been extensively documented and debated, while the second has been largely ignored.

Nancy Armstrong – her study published the following year – supports Spencer's opinion:

> I know of no history of the English novel that can explain why women began to write respectable fiction near the end of the eighteenth century, became prominent novelists during the nineteenth century, and on this basis achieved the status of artists during the modern period.[1]

Ian Watt's influential work, *The Rise of the Novel: Studies in Defoe, Richardson and Fielding* (1957), established the view that the middle-class woman of the late eighteenth century and nineteenth century had time on her hands and that from the ranks of a leisured, female middle class came not only the women novelists but a wide, female readership. This thesis, which carried conviction for many years, now looks questionable.[2] To Terry Lovell, the separation of Victorian, middle-class society into public and private spheres, the former coded as 'male', the latter as 'female', is less than absolute; Armstrong also feels that this opposition needs to be reappraised. Moreover, Lovell claims that the middle-class woman was extensively occupied with 'the work of surplus consumption' and the production of a 'middle-class gentility'. In this interpretation, her 'leisured' status is disputed.

The combination of public and private significance in the creation of the woman author is notable. Ellen Moers, like Woolf before her, discusses the important role that the novel played in the development of professions for women.[3] Some women novelists earned significant sums of money and an independence they had not previously known. But novel writing seemed appropriate also for those women wishing to preserve a characteristic feminine reticence and the middle-class gentility of which Lovell speaks. The woman novelist could write in the privacy of her own home; indeed, both Virginia Woolf's comments and biographies of women novelists point to the domesticity of the writing arrangements, frequently at a sitting-room or dining-room table. Unlike writing for the theatre there was no need for 'Judith Shakespeare's' unseemly involvement in public life. All negotiations with the publisher could be done by letter or even conducted by a father or husband.

The novel's lack of status and tradition, the belief that it demanded less intellectual rigour than other forms of writing, opened up possibilities for women. At its most disparaging, as Ken Ruthven's extract indicates, novels could be viewed dismissively as the best that women could accomplish: men study classics; women amuse themselves with novels. In a more opportunist way, women might recognize that 'the novel alone was young enough to be soft in [their] hands',[4] that here was a mode without a long history of male authorities. Because the novel's genesis lay partly in forms of writing familiar to women – the diary, the journal, letters – the form could seem more accessible and approachable than a poetry dependent on Greek and Latin allusions. In its content, also, the novel was often considered, and still is, a form particularly fitting for women. Tolstoy may have written novels that range over half of Europe but it was equally possible, as Jane Austen proves, to write novels that go no further than Bath. What happens in the family, in the neighbouring Big House, in the next street or town, has been the staple diet of the novel, and it is the very world that women know so well.

For Woolf, the marking of the nuances of interpersonal relations constitutes women's distinct contribution; the 'training in the observation of character, in the analysis of emotion' becomes an education for novel writing. G. H. Lewes's comment in the Ruthven extract illustrates how some critics have interpreted these attributes as confirmation of women's 'natural' character, which conveniently finds expression in the new literary form. Far more fruitful than Lewes's biologistic stance is to situate the development of the novel and the emergence of the woman novelist within a general feminization of culture in the latter part of the eighteenth century. Both Juliet Mitchell and Nancy Armstrong see links between the development of the novel, the consolidation of bourgeois capitalism, and the creation of a new understanding of the term 'woman'. As Mitchell writes, 'the novel is the prime example of the way women start to create themselves as social subjects under bourgeois capitalism – create themselves as a category: women'. Armstrong puts the same point – 'I will insist that one cannot distinguish the production of the new female ideal either from the rise of the novel or from the rise of the new middle classes in England'. Armstrong's emphasis is on 'female forms of power'. 'In constructing a history of the modern woman, I want to consider the ways in which gender collaborates with class to contain forms of political resistance within liberal discourse.'[5] Mitchell is more concerned with the ambiguity and vulnerability of the position of the woman writer. Using the psychoanalytical approach of French theorist, Jacques Lacan, Mitchell suggests that the woman writer must at once 'be feminine and . . . refuse femininity'; she creates a woman's world within her novels while, at the same time, rejecting that world through the authoritative act of writing. Mitchell sees no alternative for the woman writer. She has to work within the dominant order, what is termed the 'symbolic', for to be outside the dominant order is to be mad or dead. But equally, she must disrupt that symbolic order with a new symbolism. Mary Jacobus poses the problem in similar terms. The tension between Romanticism (feeling, intuition, the imagination), and Reason, (rationalization, order, power) also embodies the dualism of being feminine and refusing femininity.[6]

Subverting the Forms

The comments of Mitchell and Jacobus are suggestive of a critical approach which is common in the gender/genre debate, namely the interest in how the woman writer can *subvert* the male-dominated forms. This can be a conscious aim but is not necessarily so. The disruption may be generated by the psychic and ideological conflicts that are taking place within the text. Rosemary Jackson speaks of Mary Shelley's writing as fantasizing 'a violent attack on the symbolic order' and as a part of a tradition of women Gothic writers whose writings '*subvert* patriarchal society' (my italics). The non-realist forms, which question linear narrative, are thought by Jackson to be an important aspect of that attack on the symbolic order. She sees in Mary Shelley's work no strong narrative line but fragmentary and circular forms which, by leaving the work open and indeterminate, reject an authoritative and definitive resolution.

The opposition of realist and non-realist forms and the attribution of a conservative politics to the realist forms and a progressive politics to the non-realist are central to this line of argument, though the thesis is not without its critics. Compare, for example, the extract from 'Communication vs. Representation' with the comments of Rita Felski. The 'Communication vs. Representation' authors feel that women-centred novels are in many ways closely tied to conventional forms and aesthetic values. Almost always the heroine tells her own story, an autobiographical, confessional mode which can encourage an identification between author, character, and reader that belies the fictive nature of writing. Both the act of writing and the prevalent theme of sexual fulfilment are offered as the problem of the individual woman trying to express her 'true self'. Furthermore, the authors of the extract propose that the interest in women's sexual pleasure in these novels functions not as a radical critique of a society that has no place for women's desire but, more often, as a confirmation of women's position as 'personal, ahistorical, sexual and non-political'. In line with Jackson's argument one could also question the use of a linear narrative. The common structure of these novels is to chart the heroine's progress from unhappy conformity, through adversity to autonomy; 'self-knowledge', 'experience', 'independence' emerge as key words in the publishers' blurbs.

Felski looks at the same texts and, while coming to similar aesthetic conclusions – for example, she, too, believes that readers identify with characters and authors – she interprets the political meanings differently. In these texts she finds a noteworthy 'modification of the notion of individualism as it is exemplified in the male bourgeois autobiography'. Felski considers more positively the emphasis on typical experience and the representative function of the novels: the novels generate for women readers a communal identity *as women*. The unfortunate tone of the 'Communication vs. Representation' piece – rather superior and censorious – means there is no link between the feminist critic and the large number of women who enjoy reading such novels. Felski's emphasis on reception, the 'interactions between texts and readers', makes those links possible, particularly in her suggestion that realist forms and reading for identification may be more politically productive than had previously been thought.[7]

A number of extracts indicate that the woman author's subversive appropriation of a male-dominated form is, at the same time, an appropriation of a public voice. Christine Berg and Philippa Berry consider that the voice of the seventeenth-century women prophets is undermining because it sustains 'a multiplicity of various levels of speech and meaning' and because it relinquishes 'the "I" as the subjective centre of speech'. Using an argument similar to Jackson's, they contend that the refusal of the women prophets to offer a single, constant, rational meaning makes them difficult to assimilate; the spasmodic, irresolute nature of that voice becomes its quality rather than its failing. Moreover, the voice of the women prophets is androgynous. As women speaking the word of God, they refuse to accept sexual difference and encroach on the most sacred areas of male language. Michelene Wandor believes that what is threatening in the woman playwright is that she has the 'control of a multiple set of voices', not simply her own, and that this control is publicly exhibited on the stage. Presumably the woman director would be equally challenging; she too possesses a highly visible level of authority. Though the woman poet is likely to be 'the individual writing in private'

(Wandor) her choice of form may be contentious. Sandra Gilbert and Susan Gubar feel that it is the assertive 'I' of the lyric that is challenging. Yet Cora Kaplan suggests that it is not the lyric but the epic which is the real 'venture into a male stronghold'. We can see how authorial or speaking voice and literary form connect in intricate ways and, especially in the public forms of theatre and the sermon, the modes of production and delivery also become decisive factors.

Gender and Popular Fiction

The final extracts give some indication of the range of popular generic forms in which feminists have taken an interest – utopian writing, romantic and detective fiction, sci-fi – and the variety of feminist critical approaches which have been applied to these forms. Several factors lead to this conjunction of feminism and generic fiction in both its creative and critical guises. For example, Carol Farley Kessler, surveying feminist utopias between 1836–1919, illustrates what an intriguingly ambiguous form utopias can be for both author and reader. On the one hand they are firmly grounded in the material and a profusion of political problems, many of them still familiar to women; on the other, they enjoy the fantasy potential, of which Jackson writes, and which allows the author to move beyond the quotidian. LeFanu sees the same promise in the 'glorious eclecticism' of science fiction. Furthermore, LeFanu suggests certain aspects in the actual production of the writing which can appeal to the novice, female author, providing her with a kind of apprenticeship, a place of safe experimentation. Ursula le Guin, as one illustrious example, came to reflect on the advantages of the marginal in her own development:

> It took me years to realize that I chose to work in such despised, marginal genres as science fiction, fantasy, young adult, precisely because they were excluded from critical, academic, canonical supervision, leaving the artist free.[8]

Le Guin refers here to a traditional notion of literary value. In recent years, however, the development of Cultural Studies, the questioning of the distinction between high and popular culture and feminism's interest in *all* aspects of women's writing have conspired to create women's generic fiction as a legitimate area of exploration for both critic and creative writer.

Utopian writing and sci-fi evidently lend themselves to an interrogation of the existing social order and to the possibility of transformation. Other forms of generic fiction such as romance and detective fiction seem more concerned with re-establishing social norms: the heroine gets her man and lives in happy, heterosexual bliss; the detective captures the crook and crime-free normality returns. Romantic fiction poses particular problems for feminism. Overwhelmingly written by women for women, yet its gender ideology of masterful heroes and doe-eyed heroines is embarrassingly far removed from any feminist ideal of reconstructed male/female relations. The dismissal of this form and its readership by feminists writing in the 1970s – 'dope for dopes' was Germaine Greer's famous summary of the genre – left feminism in the invidious position of having only sneering remarks to make about the form of writing which most women read. To the rescue came a series of critical approaches which allowed critics to scrutinize these texts with full recognition of the reactionary aspects alongside a serious valuing of the significance these texts hold for many women. Represented here are the psychoanalytical critique of Rosalind Coward, the ideological investigation of Ann Barr Snitow and the readership studies of Janice Radway.[9] Psychoanalytical studies look to understand the pleasure of the romance reader. The relish with which the feminist critic debunks the romantic stereotypes and the heady mixture of passion and nostalgia with which she recalls her own adolescent, non-analytical reading may indicate that the pleasure in romance is still there for her too, though in a somewhat differently constituted form.

Both Anne Cranny-Francis and Alison Light relate gender to other discourses – of race, class, imperialism. Cranny-Francis makes a distinction between feminist reworkings of two classic detective figures, the amateur sleuth and the hard-boiled professional, and believes that the first holds a more radical potential for questioning all modes of difference. Light's detailed and subtle study moves carefully between the historical moment, ideological shifts and generic possibilities. As the genre, 'romance', is created in the inter-war period so, Light claims, it moves downmarket: sensationalism, thrills, irrationality become marked as both female and working-class. The *aspiring* woman author could look to crime fiction with its 'apparently masculine qualities of reason and logic' and its proximity to literariness.

Cranny-Francis's list of factors to take into account in a feminist critique of generic fiction provides a helpful summary of material covered in this chapter and it would be a useful exercise to consider each of her points in turn and relate them to the relevant extracts. For example, Light's argument connects chiefly with point three of Cranny-Francis's list. Ann Barr Snitow's work operates in the context of point one . . . and so on. You might want to establish more links and cross-connections for yourself.

Notes

1 Jane Spencer, *The Rise of the Woman Novelist: From Aphra Behn to Jane Austen* (Oxford, Basil Blackwell, 1986), p. vii and Nancy Armstrong, *Desire and Domestic Fiction: A Political History of the Novel* (Oxford, Oxford University Press, 1978), p. 7. Other recent titles in this area include: Dale Spender, *Mothers of the Novel: 100 Good Women Writers before Jane Austen* (London, Pandora Press, 1986); Rosalind Miles, *The Female Form: Women Writers and the Conquest of the Novel* (London, Routledge & Kegan Paul, 1987); Terry Lovell, *Consuming Fiction* (London, Verso, 1987); Gaye Tuchman (with Nina E. Fortin), *Edging Women Out: Victorian Novelists, Publishers, and Social Change* (London, Routledge, 1989).

2 Several recent volumes take issue with aspects of Watt's thesis. See both Lovell, ch. 2 and Armstrong, above.

3 See relevant essays in Michèle Barrett (ed.), *Virginia Woolf: Women and Writing* (London, The Women's Press, 1979); Virginia Woolf, *A Woman's Essays* (ed.) Rachel Bowlby (London, Penguin, 1992).

4 Virginia Woolf, *A Room of One's Own* in the combined volume of *A Room of One's Own* and *Three Guineas* (ed.) Michèle Barrett (London, Penguin, 1993), p. 70.

5 Armstrong, op. cit., p. 26.

6 The ambiguous position of the woman novelist is touched on also in ch. 2.

7 See Gayle Green and Coppélia Kahn (eds) *Changing Subjects: The Making of Feminist Literary Criticism* (London, Routledge, 1993). This is but one example where contributors, in telling the story of their involvement with feminist criticism, repeatedly stress the representative function of their experience. On women-centred novels see also, Rosalind Coward, *Female Desire: Women's Sexuality Today* (London, Paladin, 1984), part IV, 'The True Story of How I Became My Own Person'. This form of writing will be considered further in ch. 4 as these novels are seen by many as a definitive feminist writing.

8 Ursula le Guin, *Dancing At the Edge of the World* (London, Paladin, 1992), p. 234. On science fiction and utopian fiction as social critiques see also Tom Moylan, *Demand the Impossible: Science Fiction and the Utopian Imagination* (London, Methuen, 1986); Lucy Armitt (ed.) *Where No Man Has Gone Before: Women and Science Fiction* (London, Routledge, 1991). Also Sarah Lefanu and Anne Cranny-Francis, included here.

9 Snitow's and Radway's pieces have been published elsewhere. See Ann Snitow, Christine Stansell and Sharon Thompson (eds) *Powers of Desire: The Politics of Sexuality* (New York, Monthly Review Press, 1983); Janice Radway, *Reading the Romance: Women, Patriarchy, and Popular Fiction* (Chapel Hill, University of North Carolina Press, 1984). Also relevant on readers of romantic fiction is Helen Taylor, 'Romantic Readers', in Helen Carr (ed.) *From My Guy to Sci-Fi: Genre and Women's Writing in the Postmodern World* (London, Pandora, 1989). For further studies of psychoanalytical approaches to romantic fiction see, Eileen Phillips (ed.) *The Left and the Erotic* (London, Lawrence & Wishart, 1983); Cora Kaplan, '*The Thorn Birds*: Fiction, Fantasy, Femininity', in her collection *Sea Changes: Essays on Culture and Feminism* (London, Verso, 1986); Alison Light, ' "Returning to Manderley": Romance Fiction, Female Sexuality and Class', *Feminist Review*, no. 16 (Summer 1984).

K. K. RUTHVEN

Feminist Literary Studies: An Introduction

This may surprise people who expect to find the meaning of things in the etymologies of the words which describe them. 'Gender and genre come from the same root', notes the Marxist – Feminist Literature Collective, 'and their connection in literary history is almost as intimate as their etymology.'[77] But argument-from-etymology lost its status as a logical proof long ago, and you can no more prove that genre is intimately connected with gender because both words happen to derive from *genus* ('kind') than you can prove an affinity between Christians and cretins on the grounds of a common origin of those words in *christianus*. The investigation of what Kathleen Blake calls 'gender generics'[78] leads away from names and forms and into those exclusionist practices which, in the past, have obliged women to avail themselves of genres deemed marginal to an androcentric culture, and therefore noncanonical in status. In those centuries when English poetry was seen as an elaborately allusive gloss on various Greek and Latin exemplars, the denial of a classical education to women was bound to have the effect of making them feel somehow unqualified to write the 'learned' poetry preserved in a high-brow print-culture which dissociated itself from such 'vulgar' manifestations of oral culture as the ballad. It is therefore no mere coincidence that women were custodians of the ballad tradition in the crucial period when ballads were first collected and printed. The ballad singer with the oldest and most extensive repertoire was Anna Gordon, whose ballads are called 'stories of a woman's tradition' by David Buchan, and whose immediate sources were all women.[79] According to this construction of the evidence, ballads are old-wives' tales which were able to develop and change in authentically feminine ways mainly because men left them alone. Not until the eighteenth century, when they became the object of antiquarian curiosity, did ballads come under the scrutiny of men who saw it as their duty to 'correct' the transcripts which came their way so that the ballads would look more like publishable poems when they first appeared in print.

That situation cannot be paralleled exactly in a print-culture controlled by male publishers, although the relation of women writers to that most recent of traditional genres, the novel, is not entirely dissimilar. Novels developed as a 'low' form in the eighteenth century, and were not only easier to read than poetry but also suspiciously easy to write. 'There is no species of art which is so free from rigid requirements', George Eliot observed when trying to explain the proliferation of silly novels by lady novelists for lady readers.[80] To think of women as having a special aptitude for writing novels was therefore something of a back-handed compliment, given the low status of a product which, as Jane Austen complained, tended to be thought of as 'only a novel', and therefore as something to be taken no more seriously than women themselves.[81] 'Of all departments of literature, Fiction is the one to which, by nature and by circumstance, women are best adapted', wrote G. H. Lewes when surveying 'the lady novelists' in 1852. 'The domestic experiences which form the bulk of woman's knowledge finds an appropriate form in novels.'[82] With the connection between gender and genre posed in such condescending terms, spirited protests were called for, although few were as memorable as Olive Schreiner's mockery of the belief that 'there must be some inherent connection in the human brain between the ovarian sex function and the art of fiction'.[83]

(1984)

Notes

77 M–FLC, 'Women's writing', p. 31.
78 Blake, 'Pure Tess: Hardy on knowing a woman', *Studies in English literature*, 12 (1982), 700.
79 Buchan, *The ballad and the folk* (London, 1972), p. 64.
80 Eliot, 'Silly novels by lady novelists', p. 324.
81 Austen, *Northanger Abbey* (1818; Oxford, 1923), p. 38.
82 Lewes, 'The lady novelists [1852]', *Women's liberation and literature*, ed. Elaine Showalter (New York, 1971), p. 175.
83 Schreiner, *Woman and labour* (London, 1911), p. 158; Cynthia Ozick writes on 'the Ovarian Theory of Literature', in 'Women and creativity: the demise of the dancing dog [1969]'. *Woman in sexist society*, ed. Gornick and Moran, pp. 309–10.

VIRGINIA WOOLF

A Room of One's Own

Here, then, one had reached the early nineteenth century. And here, for the first time, I found several shelves given up entirely to the works of women. But why, I could not help asking, as I ran my eyes over them, were they, with very few exceptions, all novels? The original impulse was to poetry. The 'supreme head of song'[9] was a poetess. Both in France and in England the women poets precede the women novelists. Moreover, I thought, looking at the four famous names, what had George Eliot in common with Emily Brontë? Did not Charlotte Brontë fail entirely to understand Jane Austen? Save for the possibly relevant fact that not one of them had a child, four more incongruous characters could not have met together in a room – so much so that it is tempting to invent a meeting and a dialogue between them. Yet by some strange force they were all compelled, when they wrote, to write novels. Had it something to do with being born of the middle class, I asked; and with the fact, which Miss Emily Davies a little later was so strikingly to demonstrate, that the middle-class family in the early nineteenth century was possessed only of a single sitting-room between them? If a woman wrote, she would have to write in the common sitting-room. And, as Miss Nightingale was so vehemently to complain, – 'women never have an half hour . . . that they can call their own' – she was always interrupted. Still it would be easier to write prose and fiction there than to write poetry or a play. Less concentration is required. Jane Austen wrote like that to the end of her days. 'How she was able to effect all this', her nephew writes in his Memoir, 'is surprising, for she had no separate study to repair to, and most of the work must have been done in the general sitting-room, subject to all kinds of casual interruptions. She was careful that her occupation should not be suspected by servants or visitors or any persons beyond her own family party.'* Jane Austen hid her manuscripts or covered them with a piece of blotting-paper. Then, again, all the literary training that a woman had in the early nineteenth century was training in the observation of character, in the analysis of emotion. Her sensibility had been educated for centuries by the influences of the common sitting-room. People's feelings were impressed on her; personal relations were always before her eyes. Therefore, when the middle-class woman took to writing, she naturally wrote novels, even though, as seems evident enough, two of the four famous women here named were not by nature novelists. Emily Brontë should have written poetic plays; the overflow of George Eliot's capacious mind should have spread itself when the creative impulse was spent upon history or biography. They wrote novels, however; one may even go further, I said, taking *Pride and Prejudice* from the shelf, and say that they wrote good novels. Without boasting or giving pain to the opposite sex, one may say that *Pride and Prejudice* is a good book. At any rate, one would not have been ashamed to have been caught in the act of writing *Pride and Prejudice*. Yet Jane Austen was glad that a hinge creaked, so that she might hide her manuscript before any one came in. To Jane Austen there was something discreditable in writing *Pride and Prejudice*. And, I wondered, would *Pride and Prejudice* have been a better novel if Jane Austen had not thought it necessary to hide her manuscript from visitors? I read a page or two to see; but I could not find any signs that her circumstances had harmed her work in the slightest. That, perhaps, was the chief miracle about it. Here was a woman about the year 1800 writing without hate, without bitterness, without fear, without protest, without preaching. That was how Shakespeare wrote, I thought, looking at *Antony and Cleopatra*; and when people compare Shakespeare and Jane Austen, they may mean that the minds of both had consumed all impediments; and for that reason we do not know Jane Austen and we do not know Shakespeare, and for that reason Jane Austen pervades every word that she wrote, and so does Shakespeare. If Jane Austen suffered in any way from her circumstances it was in the narrowness of life that was imposed upon her. It was impossible for a woman to go about alone. She never travelled; she never drove through London in an omnibus or had

* *Memoir of Jane Austen*, by her nephew, James Edward Austen-Leigh.

luncheon in a shop by herself. But perhaps it was the nature of Jane Austen not to want what she had not. Her gift and her circumstances matched each other completely. But I doubt whether that was true of Charlotte Brontë, I said, opening *Jane Eyre* and laying it beside *Pride and Prejudice*.

[. . .]

One could not but play for a moment with the thought of what might have happened if Charlotte Brontë had possessed say three hundred a year – but the foolish woman sold the copyright of her novels outright for fifteen hundred pounds; had somehow possessed more knowledge of the busy world, and towns and regions full of life; more practical experience, and intercourse with her kind and acquaintance with a variety of character. In those words she puts her finger exactly not only upon her own defects as a novelist but upon those of her sex at that time. She knew, no one better, how enormously her genius would have profited if it had not spent itself in solitary visions over distant fields; if experience and intercourse and travel had been granted her. But they were not granted; they were withheld; and we must accept the fact that all those good novels, *Villette, Emma, Wuthering Heights, Middlemarch*, were written by women without more experience of life than could enter the house of a respectable clergyman; written too in the common sitting-room of that respectable house and by women so poor that they could not afford to buy more than a few quires of paper at a time upon which to write *Wuthering Heights* or *Jane Eyre*.

Note

9 *supreme head of song*: Woolf quotes Swinburne's *Ave Atque Vale*, for the early Greek woman poet Sappho (b. 612 BC). She wrote hymns and love poems, some of which Swinburne translated.

IAN WATT

The Rise of the Novel: Studies in Defoe, Richardson and Fielding

The distribution of leisure in the period supports and amplifies the picture already given of the composition of the reading public; and it also supplies the best evidence available to explain the increasing part in it played by women readers. For, while many of the nobility and gentry continued their cultural regress from the Elizabethan courtier to Arnold's 'Barbarians', there was a parallel tendency for literature to become a primarily feminine pursuit.

As so often, Addison is an early spokesman of a new trend. He wrote in the *Guardian* (1713): 'There are some reasons why learning is more adapted to the female world than to the male. As in the first place, because they have more spare time on their hands, and lead a more sedentary life . . . There is another reason why those especially who are women of quality, should apply themselves to letters, namely, because their husbands are generally strangers to them.'[1] For the most part quite unashamed strangers, if we can judge by Goldsmith's busy man of affairs, Mr Lofty, in *The Good Natur'd Man* (1768), who proclaims that 'poetry is a pretty thing enough for our wives and daughters; but not for us'.[2]

Women of the upper and middle classes could partake in few of the activities of their menfolk, whether of business or pleasure. It was not usual for them to engage in politics, business, or the administration of their estates, while the main masculine leisure pursuits such as hunting and drinking were also barred. Such women, therefore, had a great deal of leisure, and this leisure was often occupied by omnivorous reading.

Lady Mary Wortley Montagu, for example, was an avid novel reader, asking her daughter to send a list of novels copied down from newspaper advertisements, and adding: 'I doubt not that at least the greater part of these are trash, lumber, etc. However, they will serve to pass away the idle time . . .'[3] Later, and at a definitely lower social level, Mrs Thrale recounted that by her husband's orders she 'was not to *think of the kitchen*' and explained that it was as a result of this enforced leisure that she was 'driven . . . on literature as [her] sole resource'.[4]

Many of the less well-to-do women also had much more leisure than previously. B. L. de Muralt had already found in 1694 that 'even among the common people the husbands seldom make their wives work',[5] and another foreign visitor to England, César de Saussure, observed in 1727 that tradesmen's wives were 'rather lazy, and few do any needlework'.[6] These reports reflect the great increase in feminine leisure which had been made possible by an important economic change. The old household duties of spinning and weaving, making bread, beer, candles, and soap, and many others, were no longer necessary, since most necessities were now manufactured and could be bought at shops and markets. This connection between increased feminine leisure and the development of economic specialization was noted in 1748 by the Swedish traveller, Pehr Kalm, who was surprised to find that in England 'one hardly ever sees a woman here trouble herself in the least about outdoor duties'; even indoors, he discovered, 'weaving and spinning is also in most houses a rare thing, because their many manufacturers save them from the necessity of such'.[7]

Kalm probably conveys a somewhat exaggerated impression of the change, and he is in any case speaking only of the home counties. In rural areas further from London the economy changed much more slowly, and most women certainly continued to devote themselves almost entirely to the multifarious duties of a household that was still largely self-supporting. Nevertheless a great increase in feminine leisure certainly occurred in the early eighteenth century, although it was probably mainly restricted to London, its environs, and the larger provincial towns.

How much of this increased leisure was devoted to reading is difficult to determine. In the towns, and especially in London, innumerable competing entertainments offered themselves: during the season there were plays, operas, masquerades, ridottos, assemblies, drums, while the new wateringplaces and resort towns catered for the summer months of the idle fair. However, even the most ardent devotees of the pleasures of the town must have had some time left for reading; and the many women who did not wish to partake of them, or could not afford to, must have had much more. For those with puritan backgrounds, especially, reading would be a much more unobjectionable resource. Isaac Watts, a very influential early eighteenth-century Dissenter, dwelt luridly on 'all the painful and dismal consequences of lost and wasted time',[8] but he encouraged his charges, very largely feminine, to pass their leisure hours in reading and literary discussions.[9]

(1957)

Notes

1 No. 155.
2 Act II.
3 *Letters and Works*, ed. Thomas (London, 1861), I, p. 203; II, pp. 225–6, 305.
4 *A Sketch of Her Life . . .* , ed. Seeley (London, 1908), p. 22.
5 *Letters Describing the Character and Customs of the English and French Nations* (1726), p. 11.
6 *A Foreign View of England*, trans. Van Muyden (London, 1902), p. 206.
7 *Kalm's Account of His Visit to England . . .*, trans. Lucas (London, 1892), p. 326.
8 'The End of Time', *Life and Choice Works of Isaac Watts*, ed. Harsha (New York, 1857), p. 322.
9 *Improvement of the Mind* (New York, 1885), pp. 51, 82.

TERRY LOVELL

Consuming Fiction

Women as Readers

The differentiation under capitalism of two separate spheres, the public and the private, one masculine, the other feminine, was a prominent feature of the dominant symbolic order by the early nineteenth century in Britain. Feminists have rediscovered this division, and have explored the inner and outer landscapes of the private sphere, the home, within which bourgeois women were at least in theory confined. It should be emphasized that, as they emerged in the eighteenth century, both spheres were bourgeois, although defined and analysed in universal terms as if they were a function of biological sex given by nature. That these divisions were actually developed with the bourgeoisie in mind can be seen in the unselfconscious class double standard of some of this writing, where in the same passage women are ascribed quite contrary qualities when viewed as bourgeois 'ladies' and as working-class 'hands': 'The cerebral organisation of the female is far more delicate than that of a man; the continuity and severity of application needed to acquire real *mastery* in any profession, or over any science, are denied to women, and can never with impunity be attempted by them; mind and health would almost invariably break down. . . . It is clearly a waste of strength, a superfluous extravagance, an economic blunder, to employ a powerful and costly machine to do work which can be done as well by a feebler and a cheaper one. Women and girls are less costly operatives than men. . . .'[32]

The bourgeois public sphere emerged in Europe in the early decades of the eighteenth century in institutions such as the coffee-house.[33] The simultaneous emergence of the bourgeois private sphere is associated with the privitization of family life – the withdrawal of the bourgeois family from public hall to (with)-drawing room, from integrated home and workplace to domestic quarters in the suburbs. This movement of separation and privatization took place at different points in time throughout the nineteenth century, as different industries, and different families within them, rose and prospered. It was neither uniform nor universal. Small family businesses which depended upon family labour continued to be important numerically and economically throughout, and this is one reason why the idea of rigidly defined and separated public and private spheres even for the bourgeoisie must be qualified.[34] In fact it is probably misleading to make an absolute separation between the two, especially where 'private' is conflated with 'personal', as in the writings of Zaretsky.[35] Interpersonal relations are ubiquitous and cannot be confined to the private sphere. They are negotiated in public as well. There are 'intermediate zones' which developed, necessarily, at the time of separation of public from private. Each sphere had its public and private faces. To use Goffman's dramaturgical metaphor,[36] there was a backstage to the public, and a frontstage to the private. Probably the most important decisions and negotiations belonging to the public sphere took place in private, while the bourgeois home itself might provide a semi-public space, open on a carefully restricted basis, to the world of politics and letters in salon culture. This semi-public sphere provided one of the few arenas in which women might gain political influence. Such a role was hazardous for those women who adopted it, and it was only open to married women.

The home, too, had its private and public fronts; backstairs, attics, cellars, as well as front-stairs, parlour, lobby.[37] The very segregation of women in the private sphere created the need, however, for another type of semi-public arena in which the transfer of daughters from one home to another could be negotiated. Jane Austen's world of assemblies, private balls, visiting and the London Season remains one of the most vivid fictional constructions of this carefully chaperoned and vetted intermediate sphere where courtship could be negotiated and within whose confines romantic love could be indulged. The institutions of courtship and the provision of space for its pursuit were a function of the shift from marriages arranged by parents in which the principal parties had only a right of veto, to companionate marriages in which these rights were reversed, and parents held the veto.[38]

The most important condition for the development of a bourgeois private sphere was the increased profitability of the capitalist firm, beyond the point where profits allowed both for the reinvestment necessary for the firm's survival and expansion, and the release of the labour of wives and daughters. But the relationship of women to leisure time is notoriously problematic. Leisure time is defined over against work. Paradigmatically it is the time which is 'free' to be spent in activities which are unpaid, voluntary, and pleasurable. It is also the time and space of consumption rather than production.

It is obvious that consumption requires 'free time'; less obvious that it requires work which may or may not be paid, may or may not be pleasurable. Marx conceptualized the process of capitalist production in terms of his distinction between production and reproduction, the latter taking place in the home and in moments of leisure, in which the wear and tear caused by productive labour is made good, energy restored, in preparation for a further period of productive work. For Marx the value of labour-power (though not of its product) could be measured by the value of the goods and services purchased with the wage and used for purposes of reproduction. What Marx left out of account in this calculus was the labour cost of the processes of reproduction themselves; the labour involved in the acquisition and process-ing of subsistence commodities. It was omitted because it was so hard to see, since it was unpaid and performed by women. The problems posed for Marxism by domestic labour have been explored by Marxist feminists.[39] The debate has focused on the 'necessary labour' of reproduction: childcare, of course, cleaning, cooking, caring generally. But what might be termed 'surplus consumption' also costs labour-time to organize and facilitate. This labour, insofar as it *is* surplus labour, belongs precisely to that grey area which is almost impossible to classify as work or leisure, and in this it differs from 'housework'. Once domestic labour is identified it becomes visible as work. But the work of surplus consumption may not look like work at all. Yet the planning and production of the bourgeois home was and is inordinately time-consuming. The fact that it may give pleasure is not decisive in defining its status. The capitalist producer typically takes pride in the fact that his work is interesting and enjoyable, and that he takes it home with him at night. He would nevertheless resist the implication that it is therefore not real work. Equally its status is not determined by freedom of choice, and in any case these duties were not easily evaded in the nineteenth century among the middle classes.

The work involved in the production of middle-class gentility was visible in its results, on display in the semi-public parts of the home during the 'leisure' activities of entertaining and visiting which functioned to police these duties and enforce compliance to acceptable bourgeois standards. While the more affluent middle-class women had working-class servants to perform the more arduous physical tasks, there is some evidence that many were nevertheless kept busy to a degree and extent that puts the lie to the popular image of the idle lady of leisure.[40]

Ian Watt's assumption that bourgeois women had a near-monopoly of the increasing leisure time *of their class* in the eighteenth century, and that this is why they were such heavy novel readers is questionable even for this early period. Yet it is an assumption still made unthinkingly about women readers today. John Sutherland writes: 'In their adult book choices one suspects that the libraries keep in mind an average user who conforms to the pattern of ratepayer and voter, with a lot of leisure time: women in a word.'[41] It is doubtful whether middle-class women in the twentieth or the nineteenth century had more leisure time than middle-class men. What is true is that the ways available to them of deploying their leisure time were very much more restricted, and that the pattern of work/leisure was less differentiated for women. Women read in their leisure time because reading was cheap, and because it is a leisure activity which is most readily adapted to an undifferentiated work/leisure routine. A novel could be picked up and put down, read as and when, unlike the leisure pursuits of husbands and brothers which typically required blocks of free time which women, once married, did not usually have.

(1987)

Notes

32 W. R. Greg, 'Why are Women Redundant?', *National Review*, April 1862, quoted in Patricia Hollis, ed., *Women in Public: the Women's Movement 1850–1900*, London, 1979, p. 38.

33 Eagleton, *The Functions of Criticism*.

34 Catherine Hall, 'Gender Divisions and Class Formation in the Birmingham Middle Class; 1780–1850', in R. Samuel, ed., *People's History and Socialist Theory*, London, 1981.

35 Eli Zaretsky, *Capitalism, the Family and Personal Life*, London 1976.

36 Erving Goffman, *The Presentation of Self in Everyday Life*, London 1969.

37 Leonore Davidoff, 'Class and Gender in Victorian England', in Judith L. Newton, Mary P. Ryan and Judith R. Walkowitz, eds, *Sex and Class in Women's History*, London 1983.

38 Lawrence Stone, *The Family, Sex and Marriage in England, 1500–1800*, London, 1977.

39 Ellen Malos, ed., *The Politics of Housework*, London 1980.

40 Patricia Branca, *Silent Sisterhood*, London 1975.

41 John Sutherland, *Fiction and the Fiction Industry*, London 1978, p. 19.

ELLEN MOERS

Literary Women

Fanny Burney, now Mme d'Arblay, became pregnant at forty-one and ground out a novel – *Camilla* is her most lifeless production – to support her family. For once in her life, she made the economics of publishing work for her (they were just beginning to be organized to favor the independent author) in the one way that mattered: the acquisition of enough money, all at once, to pay for a house on a little piece of land in the country, which she called Camilla Cottage.

The episode once again is instructive, and shows why novel-writing became the profession of choice for literary women, and even for not particularly literary women whose intelligence and talent might have led them to different kinds of work. Only the novel offered the reward of capital endowment, that lump of money without which middle-class women, whatever their charms, would for long be virtually unmarriageable. Fanny Burney's court post had paid her 200 pounds a year, a wretched sum as Macaulay complained, but probably the highest salary a woman had ever received for respectable work, or would receive for generations to come. *Camilla* made her more than 2,000 pounds, or at least $50,000 in today's money.

The career of journalism, while never so important to English literary women as to French or American, began to open up to a few rare women in England fairly early in the eighteenth century, perhaps because it was so ill paid (almost as poorly paid as translating, which women of George Eliot's caliber would do for a pittance for generations to come). In the nineteenth century Harriet Martineau, for example, held an editorial post for which she received 15 pounds a year; but her first fiction, the *Political Economy* tales which took Martineau not much over two years to write, earned her more than 2,000 pounds.

Charlotte Brontë was dazzled by the first payment from her publishers for *Jane Eyre*: it was 100 pounds, the largest sum of money she had ever seen. There would be five such payments for the novel (probably an unfairly small slice of her publisher's profits) as opposed to the 20 pounds a year Brontë had been earning as a governess. ('My salary is not really more than £16 p.a.,' she wrote a friend in 1841, 'though it is nominally £20, but the expense of washing will be deducted therefrom.' Thus, to arrive at a sense of the real value of a governess' salary, we know that it was five times as much as the cost of laundering a governess' not very extensive wardrobe; we also know that it was about eleven times as much as the price of *Jane Eyre*. Governesses could not afford to buy three-volume novels, or almost anything else.)

The same 20 pounds, on the other hand, was the munificent sum Mrs. Gaskell was paid for a mere short story in 1850. 'I stared,' she wrote, 'and wondered if I was swindling them but I suppose I am not; and Wm has composedly buttoned it up in his pocket.' Through Mrs. Gaskell's letters can be traced the subtle and subtly changing attitudes of a successful literary woman to her husband's absolute control, in principle, over her earnings. Married life, however, as we all know, is a matter of practice as well as principle. By the late 1850s Mrs. Gaskell was paying for her own trips abroad out of the proceeds of her fiction, and in 1865 'I did a terribly grand thing! and a secret thing too!' she wrote Charles Eliot Norton. 'Only you are in

America and can't tell. I bought a house . . . for Mr. Gaskell to retire and for a home for my unmarried daughters.' Including furnishings, the house would cost her 3,000 pounds or so, all to be paid for in the style of Camilla Cottage, by a literary woman's fiction.

The economic system that made novel-writing look particularly attractive to Fanny Burney was subscription publishing: that is, soliciting payment in advance of a guinea and a half direct from readers, whose names were printed at the head of the first edition. Among the three hundred subscribers to *Camilla* were some of the greatest names of the day. And there were three names on the list even better known to posterity than to Fanny Burney, for they were those of the leading women novelists, which is to say the leading novelists, of the next generation: Mrs. Radcliffe, Miss Edgeworth, and Miss Austen of Steventon.

Jane Austen was only twenty when she subscribed to *Camilla*, but then, she was also only twenty when she began 'First Impressions,' the first version of *Pride and Prejudice*, and she had already, in her teens, done a good deal of brilliant apprentice writing in imitation of or satirical reaction to the work of her female predecessors. When *Pride and Prejudice* finally appeared in 1813, women's literature came of age and with it the English novel, for in pure artistry no work in the form has ever surpassed it. It was a remarkable accomplishment of female professionalism, in the mere seventy years or so since *Pamela*, and the mere thirty years or so since *Evelina*.[1] Nor can the two phenomena be separated: the rise of the novel and the rise of women to professional literary status. And ever afterward the makeshift novel, last-born of literary genres, has dominated the literature of the world.

(1977)

Note

1 Whose author was still alive, still writing fiction. Fanny Burney lived to almost ninety, and the posthumous publication of her diaries almost spanned the Victorian age; in the case of her longevity, her life was not characteristic of literary women after her. But her last exemplary act as a woman writer produced yet another manuscript treasure for the Berg Collection: a dozen densely written pages about the operation she underwent for breast cancer in 1811, before the invention of anesthetic.

JULIET MITCHELL

'Femininity, Narrative and Psychoanalysis'
Women: The Longest Revolution

I want to look very briefly at one kind of history: that pre-eminent form of literary narrative, the novel. Roughly speaking, the novel starts with autobiographies written by women in the seventeenth century. There are several famous men novelists, but the vast majority of early novels were written by large numbers of women. These writers were trying to establish what critics today call the 'subject in process'. What they were trying to do was to create a history from a state of flux, a flux in which they were feeling themselves in the process of becoming women within a new bourgeois society. They wrote novels to describe that process – novels which said: 'Here we are: women. What are our lives to be about? Who are we? Domesticity, personal relations, personal intimacies, stories . . .' In the dominant social group, the bourgeoisie, that is essentially what a woman's life was to become under capitalism. The novel is that creation by the woman of the woman, or by the subject who is in the process of becoming woman, of woman under capitalism. Of course it's not a neat homogeneous construction: of course there are points of disruption within it; of course there are points of autocriticism within it. *Wuthering Heights*, for example, is a high point of autocriticism of the novel from within the novel. I shall discuss it soon in that light.

As any society changes its social structure, changes its economic base, artefacts are re-created within it. Literary forms arise as one of the ways in which changing subjects create themselves as subjects within a new social context. The novel is the prime example of the way women start to create themselves as social subjects under bourgeois capitalism – create themselves as a category: women. The novel remains a bourgeois form. Certainly there are also working-class novels, but the dominant form is that represented by the woman within the bourgeoisie. This means that when contemporary Anglo-Saxon feminist critics turn to women writers, resurrect the forgotten texts of these women novelists, they are, in one sense, being completely conformist to a bourgeois tradition. There is nothing wrong with that. It is an important and impressive tradition. We have to know where women are, why women have to write the novel, the story of their own domesticity, the story of their own seclusion within the home and the possibilities and impossibilities provided by that.

This tradition has been attacked by critics such as Julia Kristeva as 'the discourse of the hysteric'. I believe that it has to be the discourse of the hysteric. The woman novelist must be an hysteric. Hysteria is the woman's simultaneous acceptance and refusal of the organisation of sexuality under patriarchal capitalism. It is simultaneously what a woman can do both to be feminine and to refuse femininity, within patriarchal discourse. And I think that is exactly what the novel is; I do not believe there is such a thing as female writing, a 'woman's voice'. There is the hysteric's voice which is *the woman's masculine language* (one has to speak 'masculinely' in a phallocentric world) talking about feminine experience. It's both simultaneously the woman novelist's refusal of the woman's world – she is, after all, a novelist – and her construction from within a masculine world of that woman's world. It touches on both. It touches, therefore, on the importance of bisexuality.

I will say something very briefly about the psychoanalytical theories behind this position of the woman writer who must speak the discourse of the hysteric, who both refuses and is totally trapped within femininity. Then I'll lead on to some of the things that were said earlier about how to disrupt this.

There is much current interest in re-reading Freud in terms of the moment at which sexual division is produced within society: the moment of the castration complex, the moment when the heterogeneously sexual, polymorphously perverse, carnivalesque child has imposed on it the divisions of 'the law'; the one law, the law of patriarchy, the mark of the phallus. At that moment two sexes are psychologically created as the masculine and the not-masculine. At the point in which the phallus is found to be missing in the mother, masculinity is set up as the norm, and femininity is set up as what masculinity is not. What is not there in the mother is what is relevant here; that is what provides the context for language. The expression which fills the gap is, perforce, phallocentric.

In Lacanian thinking this is called the moment of the symbolic. The symbolic is the point of organisation, the point where sexuality is constructed as meaning, where what was heterogeneous, what was not symbolised, becomes organised, becomes created round these two poles, masculine and not-masculine: feminine.

What has gone before can be called the pre-Oedipal, the semiotic, the carnivalesque, the disruptive. Now one can take two positions in relation to that. Either the pre-divided child, the heterogeneous child, the pre-Oedipal child, exists with its own organisation, an organisation of polyvalence, of polyphony. Or alternatively that very notion of heterogeneity, of bisexuality, of pre-Oedipality, of union in a dyadic possibility of child with mother, that image of oneness and heterogeneity as two sides of the same coin, is, in fact, provided by the law, by the symbolic law itself. The question to me has a political dimension to it. If you think that the heterogeneous pre-Oedipal polyvalent world is a separate structure in its own right, then the law is disruptable, the carnival can be held on the church steps. But if this is not the case, if the carnival and the church do not exist independently of each other, the pre-Oedipal and the Oedipal are not separate, discrete states – if, instead, the Oedipal with the castration complex is what defines the pre-Oedipal, then the only way you can challenge the church, challenge both the Oedipal and its pre-Oedipal, is from within an *alternative symbolic universe*. You cannot choose the imaginary, the semiotic, the carnival as an alternative to the symbolic, as an alternative to the law. It is set up by the law precisely as its own ludic space, its own area of imaginary alternative, but not as a symbolic alternative. So that politically speaking, it is only the symbolic, a new symbolism, a new law, that can challenge the dominant law.

Now this does have relevance for the two alternative types of feminist literary criticism which exist today. It was suggested in another paper at this conference that this area of the carnival can also be the area of the feminine. I don't think so. It is just what the patriarchal universe defines as the feminine, the intuitive, the religious, the mystical, the playful, all those things that have been assigned to women – the heterogeneous, the notion that women's sexuality is much more one of a whole body, not so genital, not so phallic. It is not that the carnival cannot be disruptive of the law; but it disrupts only within the terms of that law.

This suggests a criticism of the French school associated with Kristeva, and to me it explains why that school is essentially apolitical. One needs to ask why Kristeva and her colleagues, while producing very interesting ideas, choose exclusively masculine texts and quite often proto-fascist writings as well. Disruption itself can be radical from the right as easily as from the left. This type of disruption is contained within the patriarchal symbolic. To me this is the problem.

I shall just mention some things about *Wuthering Heights* here so that we can use it if we like as a text on which to hang some ideas. I do not want to offer a psychoanalytic reading of this novel; I want to use *Wuthering Heights* simply to illustrate some of the points that I have tried to make here.

Emily Brontë is not writing a carnivalesque query to the patriarchal order; she is clearly working within the terms of a language which has been defined as phallocentric. Yet she is, through a kind of irony, posing questions about patriarchal organisation, and I'll sketch in some of the questions that I think are asked by the novel. First, who tells the story? Emily Brontë's manuscript was stolen from her and presented to a publisher by her sister, Charlotte. It was eventually published under a male pseudonym: Ellis Bell. The author is a woman, writing a private novel; she is published as a man, and acquires some fame and notoriety. She uses two narrators – a man, Lockwood, and a woman, the nurse, Nelly Dean. The whole novel is structured through those two narrators. Lockwood is a parody of the romantic male lover. He is set up as a foppish gentleman from the town who thinks he loves all the things the romantic gentleman is supposed to love, such as solitude, or a heart of gold beneath a fierce exterior. These things are criticised from within the novel, particularly through the character of Isabella, who thinks that Heathcliff is a dark, romantic Gothic hero who will prove to be the true gentleman beneath all his cruelty.

The story of Catherine and Heathcliff is a story of bisexuality, the story of the hysteric. Catherine's father had promised he would bring her back a whip from his visit to Liverpool. Instead he picks up a gypsy child who is fatherless, who never has had and never will have a father's name, who is given just one name: Heathcliff, the name of a brother of Catherine's who had died in infancy. Catherine looks in her father's pocket, finds the whip broken; instead of this whip she gets a brother/lover: Heathcliff.

Heathcliff is what Cathy wants all the rest of her life. She, in fact, makes the conventional feminine choice and marries somebody with whom she cannot be fully united – Edgar Linton. Edgar provides only an illusion of complementarity. I do not mean that they do not have a sexual relation; they have a child whose birth in one sense – the most unimportant – causes Catherine's death. The person that Catherine wants to be 'one' with is Heathcliff. Breaking the incest taboo, she says, 'I *am* Heathcliff, he's more myself than I am.' And Heathcliff says the same of Catherine. Each is the bisexual possibility of the other one, evoking a notion of oneness which is the reverse side of the coin of diverse heterogeneity. This type of 'oneness' can only come with death. Catherine dies; she haunts Heathcliff for twenty years, which is the date when the novel opens: it opens with Lockwood, who is given Heathcliff's dream, thinking (because he is the parodic romantic figure) that he can also get oneness. Heathcliff himself waits the whole stretch of the novel to have his own dream, which is to get back to Catherine. He dies getting back to her. 'Oneness' is the symbolic notion of what happens before the symbolic; it is death and has to be death. The choices for the woman within the novel, within fiction, are either to survive by making the hysteric's ambiguous choice into a femininity which doesn't work (marrying Edgar) or to go for oneness and unity, by suffering death (walking the moors as a ghost with Heathcliff).

I want to end with my beginning, and with a question. I think the novel arose as the form in which women had to construct themselves as women within new social structures; the woman novelist is necessarily the hysteric wanting to repudiate the symbolic definition of sexual difference under patriarchal law, unable to do so because without madness we are all unable to do so. Writing from within that position can be conformist (Mills and Boon romantic novels) or it can be critical (*Wuthering Heights*). I think the novel starts at a point where society is in a state of flux, when the subject is in the process of becoming a woman (or man) as today we understand that identity. If we are today again talking about a type of literary criticism, about a type of text where the subject is not formed under a symbolic law, but within what is seen as a heterogeneous area of the subject-in-process, I would like to end with asking a question: *in the process of becoming what?* I do not think that we can live as human subjects without in some sense taking on a history; for us, it is mainly the history of being men or women under bourgeois capitalism. In deconstructing that history, we can only construct other histories. What are we in the process of becoming?

(1984)

NANCY ARMSTRONG

Desire and Domestic Fiction: A Political History of the Novel

To describe the history of domestic fiction, then, I will argue several points at once: first, that sexuality is a cultural construct and as such has a history:

second, that written representations of the self allowed the modern individual to become an economic and psychological reality; and third, that the modern individual was first and foremost a woman. My argument traces the development of a specific female ideal in eighteenth and nineteenth century conduct books and educational treatises for women, as well as in domestic fiction, all of which often were written by women. I will insist that one cannot distinguish the production of the new female ideal either from the rise of the novel or from the rise of the new middle classes in England. At first, I will demonstrate, writing about the domestic woman afforded a means of contesting the dominant notion of sexuality that understood desirability in terms of the woman's claims to fortune and family name. But then, by the early decades of the nineteenth century, middle-class writers and intellectuals can be seen to take the virtues embodied by the domestic woman and to pit them against working-class culture. It took nothing less than the destruction of a much older concept of the household for industrialization to overcome working-class resistance. In time, following the example of fiction, new kinds of writing – sociological studies of factory and city, as well as new theories of natural history and political economy – established modern domesticity as the only haven from the trials of a heartless economic world. By the 1840s, norms inscribed in the domestic woman had already cut across the categories of status that maintained an earlier, patriarchal model of social relations.[4] The entire surface of social experience had come to mirror those kinds of writing – the novel prominent among them – which represented the existing field of social information as contrasting masculine and feminine spheres.[5]

This book, which links the history of British fiction to the empowering of the middle classes in England through the dissemination of a new female ideal, necessarily challenges existing histories of the novel. For one thing, it insists that the history of the novel cannot be understood apart from the history of sexuality. In dissolving the boundary between those texts that today are considered literature and those that, like the conduct books, are not, my study shows that the distinction between literary and nonliterary was imposed retrospectively by the modern literary institution upon anomalous works of fiction. It shows as well that the domestic novel antedated – was indeed necessarily antecedent to – the way of life it represented. Rather than refer to individuals who already existed as such and who carried on relationships according to novelistic conventions, domestic fiction took great care to distinguish itself from the kinds of fiction that predominated in the eighteenth and nineteenth centuries. Most fiction, which represented identity in terms of region, sect, or faction, could not very well affirm the universality of any particular form of desire. In contrast, domestic fiction unfolded the operations of human desire as if they were independent of political history. And this helped to create the illusion that desire was entirely subjective and therefore essentially different from the politically encodable forms of behavior to which desire gave rise.

At the same time and on the same theoretical grounds, my study of the novel challenges traditional histories of nineteenth century England by questioning the practice of writing separate histories for political and cultural events. Rather than see the rise of the new middle class in terms of the economic changes that solidified its hold over the culture, my reading of materials for and about women shows that the formation of the modern political state – in England at least – was accomplished largely through cultural hegemony. New strategies of representation not only revised the way in which an individual's identity could be understood, but in presuming to discover what was only natural in the self, they also removed subjective experience and sexual practices from their place in history. Our education does much the same thing when it allows us to assume that modern consciousness is a constant of human experience and teaches us to understand modern history in economic terms, even though history itself was not understood in those terms until the beginning of the nineteenth century. We are taught to divide the political world in two and to detach the practices that belong to a female domain from those that govern the marketplace. In this way, we compulsively replicate the symbolic behavior that constituted a private domain of the individual outside and apart from social history.

In actuality, however, the changes that allowed diverse groups of people to make sense of social experience as these mutually exclusive worlds of information constitute a major event in the history of the modern individual. It follows, then, that only those histories that account for the formation of separate spheres – masculine and feminine, political and domestic, social and cultural – can allow us to see what this semiotic behavior had to do with the economic triumph of the new middle classes. In effect, I am arguing, political events cannot be understood apart from women's history, from the history of women's literature, or from changing representations of the household. Nor can a history of the novel be historical if it fails to take into account the history of sexuality. For such a history remains, by definition, locked into categories replicating the semiotic behavior that empowered the middle class in the first place.

(1987)

Notes

4 By "the patriarchal model," I mean specifically the historical phenomenon that linked the political authority of the father over the household to that of the king in a mutually authorizing relationship. On this point, for example, see Gordon J. Schochet, *Patriarchalism in Political Thought* (New York: Basic Books, 1975) and Lawrence Stone, *The Family, Sex, and Marriage in England 1500–1800* (New York: Harper and Row, 1977), pp. 239–40.

5 I draw here on David Musselwhite's argument which implicitly challenges such notions of the politics of the novel as Bakhtin articulates in *The Dialogic Imagination: Four Essays* trans. Michael Holquist (Austin, Univesity of Texas Press, 1981). Rather than view the novel as a form that – like carnival – resisted hegemony, Musselwhite argues that the novel appropriates symbolic practices that would otherwise behave as forms of resistance. I intend to suggest that the politics of the novel are determined, on the one hand, by the genre's tendency to suppress alternative forms of literacy and to

produce the homogenized discourse we know as polite standard English. I will push this argument further and suggest that, on the other hand, the novel's politics depend on how we use the genre today. In writing this book, I am assuming that one may expose the operations of the hegemony by reading the novel as the history of those operations. If there is any truth in this claim, then in adopting the novel's psychologizing strategies, one only perpetuates the great nineteenth century project that suppressed political consciousness. David Musselwhite, "The Novel as Narcotic," *1848: The Sociology of Literature* (Colchester, England: University of Essex, 1978), pp. 208–209.

MARY JACOBUS

'The Buried Letter: Feminism and Romanticism in Villette' Women Writing and Writing About Women

Feminism and Romanticism: 'nothing but hunger, rebellion and rage . . . No fine writing can hide this thoroughly, and it will be fatal to her in the long run' – Arnold's prognosis was wrong (Charlotte Brontë died of pregnancy), but revealingly poses a split between rebellion and 'fine writing'. The divorce of the Romantic Imagination from its revolutionary impulse poses special problems for Victorian Romantics. Where vision had once meant a prophetic denunciation of the *status quo* and the imagining of radical alternatives, it comes to threaten madness or mob-violence. Losing its socially transforming role, it can only turn inwards to self-destructive solipsism. Charlotte Brontë's own mistrust erupts in *Villette* with the fire that flames out during Vashti's performance or in the long-vacation nightmare which drives Lucy to the confessional; while the spectral nun (the Alastor of the Rue Fossette?) has to be laid in order to free Lucy from the burden of the autonomous imagination and allow her to become an economically independent headmistress. There are added complications for a woman writer. The drive to female emancipation, while fuelled by revolutionary energy, had an ultimately conservative aim – successful integration into existing social structures (' "I am a rising character: once an old lady's companion, then a nursery-governess, now a school-teacher" ', Lucy tells Ginevra ironically (XXVII)). Moreover, while the novel's pervasive feminisation of the Romantic Imagination is a triumph, it runs the attendant risk of creating a female ghetto. The annexing of special powers of feeling and intuition to women and its consequences (their relegation to incompetent dependency) has an equally strong Romantic tradition; women, idiots and children, like the debased version of the Romantic poet, become at once privileged and (legally) irresponsible. The problem is illuminated by situating Charlotte Brontë's novels within a specifically feminist tradition. *Villette*'s crushing opposition between Reason and Imagination is also present in Mary Wollstonecraft's writing. *The Rights of Woman* (1791) – directed against the infantilising Rousseauist ideal of feminine 'sensibility' – not only advocates the advantages for women of a rational (rather than sentimental) education, but attempts to insert the author herself into the predominantly male discourse of Enlightenment Reason, or 'sense'. Yet, paradoxically, it is within this shaping Rousseauist sensibility that Mary Wollstonecraft operates as both woman and writer – creating in her two highly autobiographical novels, *Mary* (1788) and *The Wrongs of Woman* (1798), fictions which, even as they anatomise the constitution of femininity within the confines of 'sensibility', cannot escape its informing preoccupations and literary influence.[17] Though their concepts of Reason differ, the same split is felt by Charlotte Brontë. In *Villette*, Reason is the wicked and 'envenomed' step-mother as opposed to the succouring, nourishing, consoling 'daughter of heaven', Imagination (XXI). It is within this primal yet divisive relationship that the novelist herself is constituted as woman and writer – nurtured on Romanticism, fostered by uncongenial Reason. The duality haunts her novel, dividing it as Lucy is divided against herself.

(1979)

Note

17 See Gary Kelly (ed.), *Mary, A Fiction and The Wrongs of Woman* (London, 1976), pp. vii–xxi, and Margaret Walters, 'The Rights and Wrongs of Women' in Juliet Mitchell and Ann Oakley (eds.), *The Rights and Wrongs of Women* (London, 1976), pp. 304–29.

ROSEMARY JACKSON

Fantasy: The Literature of Subversion

Mary Shelley's other prolonged fantasy, *The Last Man*, is even more extreme as a text unable to imagine a resolution of social contradictions except through complete holocaust. Whereas *Frankenstein* depends upon *Political Justice*, *Caleb Williams*, various utopian fantasies, and Coleridge's *Ancient Mariner*, *The Last Man* depends upon a revolutionary political text, Volney's *Ruins of Empires*. This was an anti-despotic publication, brought over from France to be circulated amongst London's Jacobin circles during the 1790s. It celebrates the destruction of patriarchal empire through death's levelling, and many of its powerful, graphic images provide Mary Shelley with dramatic material: 'And now a mournful skeleton is all that subsists of this opulent city, and nothing remains of its powerful government but a vain and obscure remembrance.'[8]

From this revolutionary material, Mary Shelley constructs a remarkable fantasy of cultural annihilation. It is a long, slow-moving narrative, as it tells of a global plague which spreads gradually across the world. Its panorama of decay presents a complete erasure of the human species. Only Verney, the last man (like Frankenstein's creation of a parodic 'first' man, another inversion of Adam), remains to tell the tale of order lapsing into undifferentiation and decay: it is a vast fantasy of entropy. 'One by one we should dwindle into nothingness.' All civilized forms collapse with the plague's levelling: society becomes amorphous. 'I felt as if, from the order of the systematic world, I had plunged into chaos, obscure, contrary, unintelligible.' Through the plague, ordinary life is uncovered and metamorphosed into its opposite.[9]

Verney, as the last man, mourns for the death of culture, weeping over 'the ruins of the boundless continents of the east, and the desolation of the western world.' It is important to distinguish between his voice, as narrator, and Mary Shelley's position, as author. His human (male) lamentation is not hers. In 'dialogue' with his voice of distress is a huge silence: the plague itself, Mary Shelley's fantasy of annihilation of the human. Her writings open an alternative 'tradition', of 'female Gothic'.[10] They fantasize a violent attack upon the symbolic order and it is no accident that so many writers of a Gothic tradition are women: Charlotte and Emily Brontë, Elizabeth Gaskell, Christina Rossetti, Isak Dinesen, Carson McCullers, Sylvia Plath, Angela Carter, all of whom have all employed the fantastic to subvert *patriarchal* society – the symbolic order of modern culture.

A remarkable narrative feature of Mary Shelley's texts is their structural indeterminacy. *The Last Man* is a series of 'fragments', the end being left open. *Frankenstein* is similarly indefinite. Structured like a line of receding mirror images, it moves from the outer tale of Walton, to the inner tale of Frankenstein, to the tale-within-the-tale of the monster's confessions. The reader is progressively seduced from a straightforward epistolary 'realism' into the vortex at the centre where the monster is strangely present (i.e. absent), surrounded by the text's webs of language, 'embedded in the innermost circle . . . like the middle ring of a vast inferno'.[11] The three circles of narrative are not neatly re-situated within each other by the end, but collapse together, as Walton records the progressive vanishing of the monster, its end unknown. This open structure introduces a space within the initial 'closed' realistic form: through the monster, a 'place' has been given to non-human desires.

(1981)

Notes

8 Volney, *Ruins of Empires* (London, undated), p. 4.

9 This anticipates Artaud's metaphorical use of the plague in *The Theatre and its Double*: 'Society's barriers became fluid with the effects of the scourge. Order disappeared. He witnessed the subversion of all morality, the breakdown of all psychology.' (p. 7).

10 Ellen Moers, *Literary Women*, pp 90–110, identifies a tradition of 'female Gothic'. It is surely no coincidence that so many writers and theorists of fantasy as a countercultural form are women – Julia Kristeva, Irène Bessière, Hélène Cixous, Angela Carter. Non-realist narrative forms are increasingly important in feminist writing: no breakthrough of cultural structure seems possible until linear narrative (realism, illusionism, transparent representation) is broken or dissolved'.

11 M. A. Goldberg, 'Moral and Myth in Mrs Shelley's *Frankenstein*', *Keats-Shelley Journal*, 8 (1959), pp. 27–38.

ELIZABETH COWIE ET AL.

'Representation vs. Communication' No Turning Back: Writings from the Women's Liberation Movement 1975–80

The last decade has seen a revival of the women's novel as a first person realistic narrative, a form which is ideologically appropriate to feminism; authors see it as a way of telling women's story for the first time in an undisguised voice. The result has been an identification of author with protagonist, and of both with 'women', a result emphasised when commercial publishers use it as a marketing device, selling women's writing as subversive, sexual autobiography – the autobiography of a gender. The attempt has been to present women for the first time as active, speaking subject; the effect has been to obscure as well as mystify the activity of displacement present in all forms of imaginative writing, the distance between the author and his/her representation which can either be concealed or spoken by the literary text. Where it is spoken by women it always reveals how the meanings of the text are constructed (questions of ideology, realism etc) and also reveals the very specific problems of the history of woman as writers, or what it might mean for them to write at all.

Emotion and sexuality have traditionally dominated the content of women's poetry and fiction, more or less heavily censored (and self-censored) at different periods. A freely chosen sexuality as the symbol or apex of self-realisation is not a new radical demand but a demand as old as the novel (written by men *and* women), whose origin lay precisely in these questions of marriage and sexuality as free individual choice. What happens in this emphasis is that the rejection of woman as, simply, the object of desire in the text and her transformation into the subject of her sexuality, ignores the whole problem of her position as the subject of her own discourse; it assumes that the first resolves the second. The heroine gets what she thinks she wants, her man or her orgasm, and the author is assumed to have her unspoken demand for a voice fulfilled by writing about it. Furthermore, the celebration of a retrieved sexuality ironically confirms the assigning of women to a position as personal, ahistorical, sexual and non-political, therefore also concealing the question of her relationship to precise social and political demands.

Jong's *Fear of Flying* illustrates all that is worst in the 'new' literature, where the woman speaker, deliberately collapsed into the 'real' writer, is represented as an author with writer's block, seeking both sexual gratification and release into prose. A double triumph is equated with liberation. Neither writing nor sexual pleasure as valorised activities are queried in their relation to social and political meanings. Both are complacently offered as individual satisfactions, and silently substituted for a feminist politics.

(1981)

RITA FELSKI

Beyond Feminist Aesthetics: Feminist Literature and Social Change

More examples of this seemingly ambiguous positioning of much feminist writing between autobiography and fiction could easily be found. Recent years have seen the publication of large numbers of feminist texts which are written in an unrelativized first-person perspective, are strongly confessional, and encourage reader identification. This alone does not unambiguously mark the text as autobiography (as Lejeune points out, such features can be imitated by the novel), but they occur within a context of *reception* which encourages an interpretation of the text as the expression, in essence, of the views and experiences of the writing subject. Thus the women's movement has been influential in "personalizing" the literary text by emphasizing its autobio-graphical dimension. Feminist literature is often marketed in such a way as to foreground the persona of the author through the inclusion of photographs and biographical details which link the text to the life and act as a guarantee of its authenticity. Evelyne Keitel, discussing, the reception of feminist confessional literature in West Germany, suggests that it is typically read as a truthful account of the author's experiences which is used as a springboard by readers from which to examine and compare their own experiences. The text is read less for its own sake, as a literary construct, than for its content in relation to its similarities and differences to the reader's own life. Reception, in other words, is strongly functional and often collective; Keitel refers to the use of such texts as Merian's *Der Tod des Märchenprinzen* as a basis for group discussions by women on the subject of their own sexual experiences.[20]

What, then, are the reasons for this blurring of the distinction between autobiography and fiction in feminist literature? Feminist confession exem-plifies the intersection between the autobiographical imperative to communi-cate the truth of unique individuality, and the feminist concern with the representative and intersubjective elements of women's experience. In other words, the shift toward a conception of communal identity which has emerged with new social movements such as feminism brings with it a modification of the notion of individualism as it is exemplified in the male bourgeois autobiography. It is for this reason that Oakley feels free to invent some of the characters in her autobiography, for, as the publisher's blurb states: "In this honest, somewhat painful and absorbing account of her life . . . every woman will find some reflection of her own personality and feelings."[21] The obligation to honest self-depiction which constitutes part of the autobio-graphical contract is here mitigated by the feminist recognition that it is the representative aspects of the author's experience rather than her unique individuality which are important, allowing for the inclusion of fictive but representative episodes distilled from the lives of other women. The fact that the authors discussed write autobiographies explicitly and self-consciously *as women* is of central importance as an indication of the shifting conceptions of cultural identity which are in turn echoed in the changing forms and functions of autobiography.

Keitel has addressed this question in an analysis of the function of contemporary forms of autobiography and autobiographical writing in relation to the self-definition of oppositional subcultures. She points to the emergence of distinctive literary "counter-public spheres" in the 1970s and 1980s, centered on the specific interests and experiences of groups such as women or gays, and reclaiming for literary discourse a representative and mimetic function which has been rendered increasingly problematic since modernism. Much of this literature is primarily concerned not with negation but rather with the affirmation of oppositional values and experiences, serving to identify communal norms which are perceived to bind together members of oppressed groups. In their emphasis on the authenticity of the writing subject and the attempt to generate a process of identification between reader and author, these literary forms can be seen as reiterating certain aspects of the narrative tradition of the eighteenth century, Keitel argues.[22] The autobiographical writing inspired by the women's movement differs, however, from the traditional autobiography of bourgeois individualism, which presents itself as the record of an unusual but exemplary life. Precisely because of this uniqueness, the eighteenth-century autobiography claims a universal significance. Feminist confession, by contrast, is less concerned with unique individuality or notions of essential humanity than with delineating the specific problems and experiences which bind women together. It thus tends to emphasize the ordinary events of a protagonist's life, their typicality in relation to a notion of communal identity. "The legitimation for reporting these experiences lies precisely in their correspondence to other life histories, and all individual traits appear blurred or disguised, in order to emphasize their general validity and applicability."[23]

On the one hand, the autobiographical status of the text is important in guaranteeing its truthfulness as the depiction of the life, and more important, the inner feelings of a particular individual. On the other, it is the *representative* aspects of experience, rather than those that mark the protagonist/narrator as unique, which are emphasized in relation to a notion of a communal female identity. It is for this reason that feminist confession is sometimes deliberately ambiguous in its use of proper names, seeking to minimize the specificity of its content as the depiction of the life of a single individual and to emphasize its exemplary status, while still retaining the claim to historical truthfulness and authenticity which form part of the autobiographical contract. As Oakley writes in *Taking It Like a Woman*, "it would be arrogant to suppose I'm unique; I'm not."[24]

Keitel suggests that this kind of autobiographical writing, precisely because of its combination of "authenticity" and representativeness, has played an important role in the self-definition of social movements in the 1970s and 1980s, serving as an identifying point of reference in much the same way as political theory (the work of Marcuse, for example) was a rallying point for the New Left in the 1960s. By writing autobiographical narratives centered on personal experience, authors avoid "theoretical abstraction"; there exists within contemporary social movements, feminism included, an ambivalence toward theory which extends from a legitimate critique of the kind of arid leftist theorizing which remains oblivious to personal relationships and their exploitative aspects, to an uncritical celebration of "feeling" and a problematic anti-intellectualism. Confessional writing, then, proceeds from the subjective experience of problems and contradictions as encountered in the realm of everyday life. At the same time, however, feminist confession selects out those aspects of experience which are perceived to possess a representative significance in relation to the audience of women it wishes to reach. Through the discussion of, and abstraction from, individual experience in relation to a general problematic of sexual politics, feminist confession thus appropriates some of the functions of political discourse. It is instrumental in the delineation of a group identity through the establishment of norms, formulates elements of a more general feminist critique, and concretizes aspects of the aims and interests of the women's movement: "The lyrical self articulated in these texts always perceives itself as part of a collective, whose experiences constitute its norms and on behalf of whose members it speaks."[25]

[. . .]

Feminist theories of "textual politics" grounded in a modernist aesthetics – for example, the celebration of the writings of Virginia Woolf as radically subversive of patriarchal ideology – are thus open to criticism on the grounds that they continue to draw upon static oppositions between realism and modernism without taking into account the changing social meanings of textual forms. The assumption that the political value of a text can be read off from its aesthetic value as defined by a modernist paradigm, and that a text which employs experimental techniques is therefore more radical in its effects than one which relies on established structures and conventional language, is too simple. Such an assumption takes for granted an equivalence between automatized language and dominant ideology and between experimentalism and oppositionality, an equation which is abstract and ultimately formalist in its failure to theorize the contingent functions of textual forms in relation to socially differentiated publics at particular historical moments. The supposedly revolutionary function of experimental techniques is increasingly questionable in late capitalist society, while the "conservative" status of realism as a closed form which reflects ruling ideologies has been challenged by its reappropriation in new social contexts, for example by oppositional movements such as feminism. It is thus increasingly implausible to claim that aesthetic radicalism equals political radicalism and to ground a feminist politics of the text in an assumption of the inherently subversive effects of stylistic innovation.

Thus I am not in favor of adopting the reductionist and easily criticized position that rejects all aesthetic differences between texts – it would be absurd to deny that *The Waves* is a more formally self-conscious work than an example of feminist confession; but I do suggest that this distinction does not provide sufficient grounds for hailing modernism as a *politically* more radical form vis-à-vis feminist interests without taking into account frameworks of reception as they mediate the potential effects of any particular text in relation to the politics of the women's movement as a whole. Radical impulses are not inherent in the formal properties of texts; they can be realized only through interactions between texts and readers, so that it becomes necessary to situate the modernist text in relation to the interests and expectations of potential audiences. In the context of the women's movement, the necessity and importance of a feminist avant-garde must be balanced against an equal need on the part of oppositional movements for texts which address the particularity of their social experience more explicitly and unambiguously, a need that has often resulted in a preference for realist forms which emphasize the denotative rather than aesthetic dimension of the text. One of the strengths of feminism has been precisely this partial reintegration of literature into the everyday communicative practices of large numbers of women by describing and commenting on women's experiences of gender relations. The political implications of modernism, by contrast, remain somewhat more ambiguous; its conception of the text as a privileged and subversive space which undermines truth and self-identity has a potential tendency to limit direct political effects, precisely because it presupposes the separation of the polysemic artwork from the sphere of everyday social practices. In other words, prevailing conceptions of literature which make it possible to identify the literary text as a site of resistance to ideology by virtue of its formal specificity simultaneously render problematic attempts to harness such an understanding of literary signification to the necessarily more determinate interests of an oppositional politics.

(1989)

Notes

20 Evelyne Keitel, "Verständigungstexte – Form, Funktion, Wirkung," *German Quarterly*, 56, no. 3 (1983): 439.
21 See the back cover of the Fontana 1985 paperback edition.
22 Keitel, "Verständigungstexte," p. 431.

23 Ibid., p. 436.
24 Oakley, *Taking It Like a Woman*, p. 2.
25 Keitel, "Verständigungstexte," p. 447.

CHRISTINE BERG AND PHILIPPA BERRY

' "*Spiritual Whoredom*": *An Essay on Female Prophets in the Seventeenth Century*'
1642: Literature and Power in the Seventeenth Century

The phenomenon of prophecy was of course not restricted to this historical time and place. Nor was prophesying during the revolutionary period the exclusive prerogative of women. Yet it is notable that prophecy in its most exaggerated form – that is, in the form in which it most clearly distinguishes itself from a rational discourse – has much in common with that phenomenon described by Luce Irigaray as 'the language of the feminine', and by Julia Kristeva as the semiotic; while its evident affinities with the discourse of hysteria have frequently been commented upon. We would stress that to confuse such a discourse with a female language, and to see it as articulated merely by women would be a mistake. Freud recognised early on in his career that the phenomenon of hysteria was not restricted exclusively to women. Likewise, a feminine language is one which both sexes may possess. But it does seem clear that the availability of this non-rationalist discursive mode made entry into the domain of politico-religious debate easier for a number of women, whether their contributions to public speech were made within the comparatively narrow confines of a single church or meeting house, or were available and proclaimed within a wider social spectrum. The prophetesses Eleanor Davies, Mary Cary and Anna Trapuel not only published or had their prophesies published by others, they also delivered oracular speeches in various places of public eminence like Parliament or Whitehall. The rough treatment received by many of the prophets of this period (both female and male) as the Revolution progressed – or sought to become more stable – is particularly striking. What emerges, in fact, is an enormous anxiety over the unique phenomenon of prophetic speech, and its refusal satisfactorily to be assimilated into a fixed symbolic order. Yet in what respect exactly did this kind of discourse constitute a threat? We believe that its threat lay precisely in its feminine character. By the sustaining of a multiplicity of various levels of speech and meaning, as well as by relinquishing the 'I' as the subjective centre of speech, the extremist forms of prophetic discourse constitute an extremely dangerous challenge to conventional modes of expression and control within seventeenth century patriarchal society.

[. . .]

Yet it seems clear that the female prophets of the period represented a threat that was in some respects more severe than that of any male prophetic figures of the day. This may in some respects be attributed to the more chaotic nature of many of their prophesyings; but we believe that the anxiety which these women promoted had rather deeper causes which related to the unique nature of the prophetic phenomenon, and to the scarcely admissible possibility that a woman could possess and transmit the word of God. The verbal transmission of the *logos* appears to have been threatening enough – the possibility of a physical *logos* being produced, in the shape of a new Messiah, induced even greater traumas. A number of women in this period proclaimed at different times that they were pregnant with the Christ, announcements which usually prompted rapid precautionary measures by the State. Probably the best known of these, a woman called Mary Adams, was immediately thrown into prison upon making the announcement. It was then proclaimed in a public statement (which suggests that popular interest in the matter had run high) that she had given birth to a monster and committed suicide. What really happened is anybody's guess, but the incident was certainly symptomatic of a deep anxiety about the possession of meaning.

The years between 1640 and 1660 might therefore be described as a period which opens with an excess of revolutionary activity on both the physical and verbal planes, a period characterised not only by Civil War but also by a fierce and bitter debate over the possession of meaning, of the logos. By 1660, however, the revolutionary struggle had failed on both these fronts. It is this tragic failure of course which constitutes the theme of Milton's *Paradise Lost*. In Milton's handling of the figures of Eve and Satan moreover, especially in the scene of temptation in the garden, the possibilities which the revolutionary period had opened up are quite explicitly surveyed. The enormous complexity of this scene seems symptomatic of Milton's own divided attitude to the revolution and its eventual failure. It has often been pointed out that Milton feels a great deal of sympathy for Satan as the failed revolutionary hero par excellence. We would argue that a fairly similar attitude can be traced in his treatment of the character of Eve, who is a figure of tremendous ambiguity within the poem.

Ultimately, however, Milton seems to have been unable to admit women to possession of the *logos*, and so to a specific relation with God. The Knowledge which the fruit of the tree offers Eve is the Knowledge of her body, of her own desire, but the speech which this produces is in the language of the court courtesan. The relationship of Adam and Eve at the end of the poem is hence fundamentally unchanged from that with which it began, as the female is returned to the control of her spouse:

'He for God only, she for God in him'.

What we have been trying to argue in relation to speech of the female prophets, therefore, is that these women and their prophetic activity represented a significant site of resistance in the revolutionary period – resistance against the acceptance of sexual difference and all that implied in the seventeenth century, this refusal of gender hinged upon the vital contemporary question of the possession of meaning or the *logos*. This challenge has of course been posed before, by various women writers and poets, but the threat which it represented became much more acute when the contest was over not only the actual word of God but over the public.

In these utterances, the assumption of gender and of sexual difference is implicitly refused, to be replaced by a peculiarly androgynous mode of speech which is tremendously threatening. When God delivers his word through or across the body of a woman, his masculine integrity and purity is evidently in danger of pollution. At best, the oracles of these women reinstate the feminine within these spheres of religious inspiration and political debate which had long since excluded it. At worst, their prophesying raises the awful, scarcely conceivable possibility that God might actually be a woman.

(1980)

MICHELENE WANDOR

'The Impact of Feminism on the Theatre'
Feminist Review

New Women Playwrights and Problems of Patronage

In the British Alternative Theatre Directory[1] which lists anyone who sends in information about themselves, only 15% of the playwrights are women. However shocking this figure is – compared, for example, to the very large number of women novelists – the situation in performance is even worse. A recent survey shows that about 7% of all plays produced are by women, and of these Agatha Christie accounts for nearly half.[2] Although there are all kinds of constraints on women novelists, even the most misogynist of critics at least acknowledges their importance in the development and achievement of the novel. In theatre there are no female 'classics' to which to point, and there is very little available in print which will testify to the fact that women always have written plays.

There are a number of reasons for women's relative invisibility as playwrights. The first is the perennial problem of publication. As a production process, the core of theatre is its live performance. Commercial success in performance is used as the yardstick by which to judge merit for publication. Since relatively few plays achieve commercial success, relatively few see the light of the printed page, and thus disappear from history. Without a text, plays cannot continue to be produced; and the publication of scripts by, for example Methuen, the largest drama publisher in this country, depends largely on the approval of the theatres which have produced the plays. Thus decisions about publication are essentially (if indirectly) made by theatre directors. This militates against women playwrights' access to print.

The second reason is ideologically more complex, though it is also to do with the live nature of theatre performance, and is connected to the reason why the anomaly of theatre censorship continued to exist for such a long time. The public performance to a live audience is a collective act of communication, akin to that of the public meeting. Theatrical performance is indeed a powerful thing, but there are very few occasions when theatrical performance has incited its audience to commit revolutionary acts en masse. Nevertheless the sense of threat which hovers round the potential subversiveness of theatre has remained with us. What is significant here is the nature of the public and collective voice of theatre, and women have rarely been seen overtly in charge of any kind of public voice. Of course, the woman playwright does not personally stand up and make a speech in her own voice, putting her own views and convictions, but she engages with something which is unconsciously felt as a far greater threat: she provides a text and meanings which others must follow. In her own voice, refracted through the dialogue and structure of the play, she communicates to her audience. She also controls the voices of others. She gives the performers the words which they must speak. Such control of a multiple set of voices, and the public control of an imaginative world (the action on a public stage) makes the woman playwright a far greater threat than the female novelist to the carefully maintained dominance of men as the custodians of public cultural creation. Women novelists still occupy that ambiguous area between private artistic acts (the individual writing in private, being read by another individual in private), and the public production and distribution of their work as commodities on the cultural market. Women playwrights may write in private, but both the collective rehearsal process and the street visibility of the playwright (on hoardings and in theatre advertisements) makes their presence more obvious. It is for this complex of reasons – as well as the male-gendered imaginative bias within plays themselves – that the theatre has been slower than the publishing industry to reflect the impact of feminism on writing.

From the slowly increasing number of women playwrights whose work is now being performed, it might appear that this is changing. Certainly as far as parity of employment goes, the more women playwrights there are, the better. Of course, not all women playwrights are necessarily feminists, and indeed some of the younger women playwrights think they are in a 'postfeminist' age, when all the essential struggles have been fought by their exhausted elder sisters. This is one of the hallmarks of bourgeois feminism.

There is a contradiction between the movement to achieve parity of employment, and the attitude towards the content of writing. Women playwrights who thus occupy a space within bourgeois feminism, or who are not feminists in their lives or work, are more easily taken up by the few liberal moves to increase the number of produced women playwrights. In the past couple of years the public face of women playwrights seems to be represented in two ways. Firstly, by the established, successful, older women playwrights – of whom really only Pam Gems and Caryl Churchill are at all widely known, and secondly, by what looks like a completely new generation (not always young) of women, many of whom are either undeveloped in the craft of writing, or simply throw off easy television-influenced sit-com type plays, or inadequately structured social realism.

In many ways the Royal Court theatre perfectly exemplifies this schizo-phrenia on the part of the theatre world towards writing by women. There is no problem about putting on plays by the already established; they do not need to be proven. It is easy to take a simple patronage attitude to the work of the new and untried, and by such patronage appear to be nobly encoura-ging the development of new writing (an absolutely essential thing) while at the same time implicitly suggesting that such 'primitive' work is part of allowing voices from a ghetto to speak to listeners from the same ghetto. Such patronage is only a problem because the Royal Court is one of the few theatres which has been consistent in encouraging work by women writers. But by veering between the established and the entirely new, they simply slide out of the responsibility of putting on plays by women who are in neither of these categories, but nevertheless are working playwrights. When all theatres make sure that half the plays they put on are by women, the problem of patronage will be on its way out.

So the situation for women playwrights, while briefly improving, could be a matter of fashion. The playwrights currently being performed, if they are not part of a real effort to improve the position of women writers across the board, will merely be token presences of the moment, and perhaps disappear when the novelty of patronizing women's work has worn off. After all, there are already some historical precedents for this. It seems that women playwrights become prominent when there is some kind of fundamental social change which involves morality or sexual ideology: for example, during the Restoration;[3] at the turn of the century, coinciding with the movement for female suffrage;[4] and again in recent years, alongside the new feminism. As the political movements settle and lose their radical or revolutionary momentum, so women recede again from participation in the professional theatre as writers. There is a very real symbiotic relationship between the state of sexual mores, the presence of a feminist movement and the appearance of women playwrights; and the political struggle always comes first. Of course there are continuing flurries and resurgences of energy from women whose feminism or just sheer bloody mindedness makes them choose the theatre. Whether or not there continues to be a vigorous voice from women playwrights will depend to some degree on the state of feminism in a much broader sense. And after that question – of how theatre as an art form, a specific kind of cultural production, relates to politics – there are the vital questions of organization and power.

(1984)

Notes

1 Catherine Itzin, ed., *British Alternative Theatre Directory of Playwrights. Directors and Designers* (London, John Offord, 1983).
2 Conference of Women Theatre Directors and Administrators, *The Status of Women in the British Theatre 1982–1983* (London, WTDA, 1984).
3 Fidelis Morgan, ed., *The Female Wits* (London, Virago, 1981).
4 Jules Holledge, *Innocent Flowers: Women in Edwardian Theatre* (London, Virago, 1981).

SANDRA M. GILBERT AND SUSAN GUBAR

Editors' Introduction
Shakespeare's Sisters: Feminist Essays on Women Poets

Despite a proliferation of literary ancestresses, however, Elizabeth Barrett Browning commented mournfully in 1845 that 'England has had many learned women . . . and yet where are the poetesses? . . . I look everywhere for grandmothers, and see none.'[6] In 1862, moreover, Emily Dickinson, articulating in another way the same distinction between women's prose and women's verse, expressed similar bewilderment. Complaining that

> They shut me up in Prose –
> As when a little Girl
> They put me in the Closet –
> Because they liked me "still" –[7]

she implied a recognition that poetry by women was in some sense inappropriate, unladylike, immodest. And in 1928, as if commenting on both Barrett Browning's comment and Dickinson's complaint, Woolf invented a tragic history for her 'Judith Shakespeare' because she so deeply believed that it is 'the poetry that is still denied outlet.'

Why did these three literary women consider poetry by women somehow forbidden or problematical? Woolf herself, after all, traced the careers of Anne Finch and Margaret Cavendish, admired the 'wild poetry' of the Brontës, noted that Barrett Browning's verse-novel *Aurora Leigh* had poetic virtues no prose work could rival, and spoke almost with awe of Christina Rossetti's 'complex song.'[8] Why, then, did she feel that 'Judith Shakespeare' was 'caught and tangled,' 'denied,' suffocated, self-buried, or not yet born? We can begin to find answers to these questions by briefly reviewing some of the ways in which representative male readers and critics have reacted to poetry by representative women like Barrett Browning and Dickinson.

Introducing *The Selected Poems of Emily Dickinson* in 1959, James Reeves quoted 'a friend' as making a statement which expresses the predominant attitude of many male *literati* toward poetry by women even more succinctly than Woolf's story did: 'A friend who is also a literary critic has suggested, not perhaps quite seriously, that "woman poet" is a contradiction in terms.'[9] In other words, from what Woolf would call the 'masculinist' point of view, the very nature of lyric poetry is inherently incompatible with the nature or essence of femaleness. Remarks by other 'masculinist' readers and critics elaborate on the point. In the midst of favorably reviewing the work of his friend Louise Bogan, for instance, Theodore Roethke detailed the various 'charges most frequently levelled against poetry by women.' Though his statement begins by pretending objectivity, it soon becomes clear that he himself is making such accusations.

> Two of the [most frequent] charges . . . are lack of range – in subject matter, in emotional tone – and lack of a sense of humor. And one could, in individual instances among writers of real talent, add other aesthetic and moral shortcomings; the spinning out; the embroidering of trivial themes; a concern with the mere surfaces of life – that special province of the feminine talent in prose – hiding from the real agonies of the spirit; refusing to face up to what existence is; lyric or religious posturing; running between the boudoir and the altar; stamping a tiny foot against God or lapsing into a sententiousness that implies the author has re-invented integrity; carrying on excessively about Fate, about time; lamenting the lot of the woman; caterwauling; writing the same poem about fifty times, and so on. . . .[10]

Even a cursory reading of this passage reveals its inconsistency: women are taxed for both triviality and sententiousness, for both silly superficiality and melodramatic 'carrying on' about profound subjects. More significant, however, is the fact that Roethke attacks female poets for doing just what male poets do – that is, for writing about God, fate, time, and integrity; for writing obsessively on the same themes or subjects, and so forth. But his language suggests that it is precisely the sex of these literary women that subverts their art. Shaking a Promethean male fist 'against God' is one perfectly reasonable aesthetic strategy, apparently, but stamping a 'tiny' feminine foot is quite another.

Along similar lines, John Crowe Ransom noted without disapproval in a 1956 essay about Emily Dickinson that 'it is common belief among readers (among men readers at least) that the woman poet as a type . . . makes flights into nature rather too easily and upon errands which do not have metaphysical importance enough to justify so radical a strategy.'[11] Elsewhere in the same essay, describing Dickinson as 'a little home-keeping person' he speculated that 'hardly . . . more' than 'one out of seventeen' of her 1,775 poems are destined to become 'public property,' and observed that her life 'was a humdrum affair of little distinction,' although 'in her Protestant community the gentle spinsters had their assured and useful place in the family circle, they had what was virtually a vocation.'[12] (But how, he seemed to wonder, could someone with so humdrum a social destiny have written great poetry?) Equally concerned with the problematical relationship between Dickinson's poetry and her femaleness – with, that is, what seemed to be an irreconcilable conflict between her 'gentle' spinsterhood and her fierce art – R. P. Blackmur decided in 1937 that 'she was neither a professional poet nor an amateur; she was a private poet who wrote indefatigably, as some women cook or knit. Her gift for words and the cultural predicament of her time drove her to poetry instead of antimacassars.'[13]

Even in 1971, male readers of Dickinson brooded upon this apparent dichotomy of poetry and femininity. John Cody's *After Great Pain* perceptively analyzes the suffering that many of Dickinson's critics and biographers have refused to acknowledge. But his conclusion emphasizes what he too sees as the incompatibility between womanly fulfillment and passionate art.

> Had Mrs. Dickinson been warm and affectionate, more intelligent, effective, and admirable, Emily Dickinson early in life would probably have identified with her, become domestic, and adopted the conventional woman's role. She would then have become a church member, been active in community affairs, married, and had children. The creative potentiality would of course still have been there, but would she have discovered it? What motivation to write could have replaced the incentive given by suffering and loneliness? If in spite of her wifely and motherly duties, she had still felt the need to express herself in verse, what would her subject matter have been? Would art have sprung from fulfillment, gratification, and completeness as abundantly as it did from longing, frustration, and deprivation?[14]

Interestingly, these questions restate an apparently very different position taken by Ransom fifteen years earlier: 'Most probably [Dickinson's] poems would not have amounted to much if the author had not finally had her own romance, enabling her to fulfill herself like any other woman.' Though Ransom speaks of the presence and 'fulfillment' of 'romance,' while Cody discusses its tormenting absence, neither imagines that poetry itself could possibly constitute a woman's fulfillment. On the contrary, both assume that the art of a woman poet must in some sense arise from 'romantic' feelings (in the popular, sentimental sense), arise either in response to a real romance or as compensation for a missing one.

In view of this critical obsession with womanly 'fulfillment' – clearly a nineteenth-century notion redefined by twentieth-century thinkers for their own purposes – it is not surprising to find out that when poetry by women *has* been praised it has usually been praised for being 'feminine,' just as it has been blamed for being deficient in 'femininity.' Elizabeth Barrett Browning, for instance, the most frequently analyzed, criticized, praised, and blamed woman poet of her day, was typically admired 'because of her understanding of the depth, tenderness, and humility of the love which is given by women,'[15] and because 'she was a poet in every fibre of her but adorably feminine. . . .'[16] As the 'Shakespeare of her sex,'[17] moreover, she was especially respected for being 'pure and lovely' in her 'private life,' since 'the lives of women of genius have been so frequently sullied by sin . . . that their intellectual gifts are [usually] a curse rather than a blessing.'[18] Significantly, however, when Barrett Browning attempted unromantic, 'unfeminine' political verse in *Poems Before Congress*, her collection of 1860, at least one critic decided that she had been 'seized with a . . . fit of insanity,' explaining that 'to bless and not to curse is a woman's function. . . .'[19]

As this capsule review of *ad feminam* criticism suggests, there is evidently something about lyric poetry by women that invites meditations on female fulfillment or, alternatively, on female insanity. In devising a story for 'Judith Shakespeare,' Woolf herself was after all driven to construct a violent plot that ends with her suicidal heroine's burial beneath a bus-stop near the Elephant and Castle. Symbolically speaking, Woolf suggests, modern London, with its technological fumes and its patriarchal roar, grows from the grim crossroads where this mythic woman poet lies dead. And as if to reinforce the morbid ferocity of such imagery, Woolf adds that whenever, reading history or listening to gossip, we hear of witches and magical wise women, 'I think we are on the track of . . . a suppressed poet . . . who dashed her brains out on the moor or mopped and mowed about the highways crazed with the torture that her gift had put her to.' For though 'the original [literary] impulse was to poetry,' and 'the "supreme head of song" was a poetess,' literary women in England and America have almost universally elected to write novels rather than poems for fear of precisely the madness Woolf attributes to Judith Shakespeare. 'Sure the poore woman is a little distracted,' she quotes a contemporary of Margaret Cavendish's as remarking: 'Shee could never be soe rediculous else as to venture at writeing books and in verse too, if I should not sleep this fortnight I should not come to that.'[20] In other words, while the woman novelist, safely shut in prose, may fantasize about freedom with a certain impunity (since she constructs purely fictional alternatives to the difficult reality she inhabits), it appears that the woman poet must in some sense become her own heroine, and that in enacting the diabolical role of witch or wise woman she literally or figuratively risks a melodramatic death at the crossroads of tradition and genre, society and art.

Without pretending to exhaust a profoundly controversial subject, we should note here that there are a number of generic differences between novel-writing and verse-writing which do support the kinds of distinctions Woolf's story implies. For one thing, as we noted earlier, novel-writing is a useful (because lucrative) occupation, while poetry, except perhaps for the narrative poetry of Byron and Scott, has traditionally had little monetary value. That novel-writing was and is conceivably an occupation to live by has always, however, caused it to seem less intellectually or spiritually valuable than verse-writing, of all possible literary occupations the one to which European culture has traditionally assigned the highest status. Certainly when Walter Pater in 1868 defined the disinterested ecstasy of art for his contemporaries by noting that 'art comes to you proposing frankly to give nothing but the highest quality to your moments as they pass, and simply for those moments' sake,' he was speaking of what he earlier called 'the poetic passion,' alluding to works like the Odes of Keats rather than the novels of Thackeray or George Eliot. Verse-writing – the product of mysterious 'inspiration,' divine afflatus, bardic ritual – has historically been a holy vocation.[21] Before the nineteenth century the poet had a nearly priestly role, and 'he' had a wholly priestly role after Romantic thinkers had appropriated the vocabulary of theology for the realm of aesthetics. But if in Western culture women cannot be priests, then how – since poets are priests – can they be poets? The question may sound sophistic, but there is a good deal of evidence that it was and has been consciously or unconsciously asked, by men and women alike, as often as women suffering from 'the poetic passion' have appeared in the antechambers of literature.

As Woolf shows, though, novel-writing is not just a 'lesser' and therefore more suitably female occupation because it is commercial rather than aesthetic, practical rather than priestly. Where novel-writing depends upon reportorial observation, verse-writing has traditionally required aristocratic education. 'Learn . . . for ancient rules a just esteem;/To copy Nature is to copy them,' Alexander Pope admonished aspiring critics and (by implication) poets in 1709, noting that 'Nature and Homer' are 'the same.'[22] As if dutifully acquiescing, even the fiery iconoclast Percy Bysshe Shelley assiduously translated Aeschylus and other Greek 'masters.' As Western society defines 'him,' the lyric poet must have aesthetic models, must in a sense speak the esoteric language of literary forms. She or he cannot simply record or describe the phenomena of nature and society, for literary theorists have long believed that, in poetry, nature must be mediated through tradition – that is, through an education in 'ancient rules.' But of course, as so many women writers learned with dismay, the traditional classics of Greek and Latin – meaning the distilled Platonic essence of Western literature, history, philosophy – constituted what George Eliot called 'spheres of masculine learning' inalterably closed to women except under the most extraordinary circumstances. Interestingly, only Barrett Browning, of all the major women poets, was enabled – by her invalid seclusion, her sacrifice of ordinary pleasures – seriously to study 'the ancients.' Like Shelley, she translated Aeschylus' *Prometheus Bound*, and she went even further, producing an unusually learned study of the little-known Greek Christian poets. What is most interesting about Barrett Browning's skill as a classicist, however, is the fact that it was barely noticed in her own day and has been almost completely forgotten in ours.

Suzanne Juhasz has recently and persuasively spoken of the 'double bind' of the woman poet,[23] but it seems almost as if there is a sort of triple bind here. On the one hand, the woman poet who learns a 'just esteem' for Homer is ignored or even mocked – as, say, the eighteenth-century 'Blue Stockings' were. On the other hand, the woman poet who does not (because she is not allowed to) study Homer is held in contempt. On the third hand, however, whatever alternative tradition the woman poet attempts to substitute for 'ancient rules' is subtly devalued. Ransom, for instance, asserts that Dickinson's meters, learned from 'her father's hymnbook,' are all based upon 'Folk Line, the popular form of verse and the oldest in our language,' adding that 'the great classics of this meter are the English ballads and Mother Goose.' Our instinctive sense that this is a backhanded compliment is confirmed when he remarks that 'Folk Line is disadvantageous . . . if it denies to the poet the use of English Pentameter,' which is 'the staple of what we may call the studied or "university" poetry, and . . . is capable of containing and formalizing many kinds of substantive content which would be too complex for Folk Line. Emily Dickinson appears never to have tried it.'[24] If we read 'pentameter' here as a substitute for 'ancient rules,' then we can see that once again 'woman' and 'poet' are being defined as contradictory terms.

Finally, and perhaps most crucially, where the novel allows – even encourages – just the self-effacing withdrawal society has traditionally fostered in women, the lyric poem is in some sense the utterance of a strong and assertive 'I.' Artists from Shakespeare to Dickinson, Yeats, and T. S. Eliot have of course qualified this 'I,' emphasizing, as Eliot does, the 'extinction of personality' involved in a poet's construction of an artful, masklike persona, or insisting, as Dickinson did, that the speaker of poems is a 'supposed person.'[25] But, nevertheless, the central self that speaks or sings a poem must be forcefully defined, whether 'she' 'he' is real or imaginary. If the novelist, therefore, inevitably sees herself from the *outside*, as an object, a character, a small figure in a large pattern, the lyric poet must be continually aware of herself from the *inside*, as a subject, a speaker: she must be, that is, assertive, authoritative, radiant with powerful feelings while at the same time absorbed in her own consciousness – and hence, by definition, profoundly 'unwomanly,' even freakish. For the woman poet, in other words, the contradictions between her vocation and her gender might well become insupportable, impelling her to deny one or the other, even (as in the case of 'Judith Shakespeare') driving her to suicide. For, as Woolf puts it, 'who shall measure the heat and violence of the poet's heart when caught and tangled in a woman's body?'

(1979)

Notes

6 *The Letters of Elizabeth Barrett Browning*, ed. Frederick G. Kenyon (2 vols. in I, New York: Macmillan, 1899), I, 230–32. Compare Woolf's 'For we think back through our mothers if we are women. It is useless to go to the great men writers for help, however much one may go to them for pleasure' (*A Room*, p. 79).
7 Thomas Johnson, ed., *The Complete Poems of Emily Dickinson* (Boston: Little, Brown, 1960), #613.
8 See especially 'Aurora Leigh' and 'I am Christina Rossetti' in *The Second Common Reader* (New York: Harcourt Brace, 1932), pp. 182–92 and 214–21.
9 Reprinted in Richard B. Sewall, ed., *Emily Dickinson: A Collection of Critical Essays* (Englewood Cliffs, N.J.: Prentice-Hall, 1963), p. 120. In fairness to Reeves, we should note that he quotes this statement in order to dispute it.
10 Theodore Roethke. 'The Poetry of Louise Bogan,' *Selected Prose of Theodore Roethke*, ed. Ralph J. Mills. Jr. (Seattle: University of Washington Press, 1965), pp. 133–34.
11 'Emily Dickinson: A Poet Restored,' in Sewall, p. 92.
12 Ibid., p. 89.
13 Quoted in Reeves, p. 119.
14 John Cody, *After Great Pain: The Inner Life of Emily Dickinson* (Cambridge, Mass.: The Belknap Press of Harvard University Press, 1971), p. 495.
15 Gardner B. Taplin, *The Life of Elizabeth Barrett Browning* (New Haven: Yale University Press, 1957), p. 417.
16 *The Edinburgh Review*, vol. 189 (1899), 420–39.
17 Samuel B. Holcombe, 'Death of Mrs. Browning,' *The Southern Literary Messenger*, 33 (1861), 412–17.
18 *The Christian Examiner*, vol. 72 (1862), 65–88.
19 'Poetic Aberrations,' *Blackwood's*, vol. 87 (1860), 490–94.
20 *A Room*, p. 65.
21 See Pater, 'Conclusion' to *The Renaissance*, and, for a general discussion of the poet as priest, M. H. Abrams, *Natural Supernaturalism* (New York: Norton, 1971).
22 See Pope, 'An Essay on Criticism,' Part I, II. 135–40.
23 Suzanne Juhasz, *Naked and Fiery Forms: Modern American Poetry by Women. A New Tradition* (New York: Harper & Row, 1976), 'The Double Bind of the Woman Poet,' pp. 1–6.
24 Ransom, ibid.; Sewall, pp. 99–100.
25 See T. S. Eliot, 'Tradition and the Individual Talent,' and Emily Dickinson, letter to T. W. Higginson, July 1892, in *The Letters of Emily Dickinson*. Thomas Johnson, ed. (Cambridge, Mass.: The Belknap Press of Harvard University Press, 1958), vol. II, p. 412.

CORA KAPLAN

Editor's Introduction
Aurora Leigh and Other Poems

In the opening of Book V of *Aurora Leigh* there is a long discursive section on the poet's vocation where the author dismisses the lyric mode – ballad, pastoral and Barrett Browning's own favourite, the sonnet – as static forms: the poet 'can stand/Like Atlas in the sonnet and support/His own heavens pregnant with dynastic stars;/But then he must stand still, nor take a step.' The move into epic poetry chipped at her reputation in establishment circles, but enhanced her popularity. It was a venture into a male stronghold; epic and dramatic verse are associated with the Classicists and with Shakespeare, Milton, Shelley and Tennyson, and later, Browning. In 1893 the influential critic Edmund Gosse wrote that women have achieved nothing 'in the great solid branches of poetry in epic, in tragedy, in didactic and philosophical verse. . . . The reason is apparently that the artistic nature is not strongly developed in her.' This typical retrospective judgment may be a clue to *Aurora Leigh*'s modern oblivion, and one reason why such an important and diverse poet as Barrett Browning is now known almost exclusively as the author of *Sonnets from the Portuguese* (1850), her brilliant series of love lyrics to her husband. Twentieth-century male poet-critics echo Gosse's belief that women's voice in poetry, as in life, should be confined to the lyric. How can one account then for a sustained narrative poem that is both didactic and philosophical as well as passionate and female, an unmannerly intervention in the 'high' patriarchal discourse of bourgeois culture? *Aurora Leigh* makes few apologies for this rude eruption into the after-dinner subjects that go with the port and cigars. Barrett Browning knew less about 'this live throbbing age,/That brawls, cheats, maddens, calculates, aspires,' than Mrs Gaskell. But it is the latter, in *Mary Barton*, who intervenes with the authorial voice to offer a timid sop to male expertise: 'I am not sure if I can express myself in the technical terms of either masters or workmen. . . .'

The taboo, it is stronger than prejudice, against women's entry into public discourse as speakers or writers, was in grave danger of being definitively broken in the mid-nineteenth century as more and more educated, literate women entered the arena as imaginative writers, social critics and reformers. The oppression of women within the dominant class was in no way as materially brutal as the oppression of women of the working class, but it had its own rationale and articulation. The mid-century saw the development of a liberal 'separate but equal' argument which sometimes tangled with, sometimes included the definition of women's sphere and the development of the cult of true womanhood. The publicity given on the woman question hardly dented the continued elaboration of mores and manners which ensured that daughters were marriageable, i.e. virgins. Patriarchal dominance involved the suppression of women's speech outside the home and a rigorous censorship of what she could read or write. All the major women writers were both vulnerable to and sensitive about charges of 'coarseness'. The Brontë sisters, Sand and Barrett Browning were labelled coarse by their critics, and, occasionally, by other women. Sexual impurity, even in thought, was *the* unforgivable sin, the social lever through which Victorian culture controlled its females, and kept them from an alliance with their looser lived working-class sisters.

The debates on the woman question which took up so many pages of leading British periodicals between 1830 and 1860 should not be seen as marginal to a male-dominated ruling class, increasingly threatened from below by an organising proletariat. Caught between this and the need to accommodate a limited demand for equity from informed women of their own class, they were equally committed to the absolute necessity of maintaining social control over females, and its corollary, the sexual division of labour. To get a sense of the space and importance given to the issue, one only has to leaf through the major quarterlies for a given year. The winter 1857 issue of the *North British Review* had both a substantial review of *Aurora Leigh* and a long review article dealing with eight books, titled 'The Employment of Women', which ranges from an abrupt dismissal of Margaret Fuller's *Woman in the Nineteenth Century* for its romantic obscurity, to a serious discussion of Anna Jameson's *The Communion of Labour*, a work which argued that middle-class women should be 'employed' in ameliorating the condition of the female poor. In support of Mrs Jameson the article quotes both Tennyson's *The Princess* and *Aurora Leigh*.

The right to write was closely connected with every wider choice that women might wish to make. In an age characterised by the importance of the popular press as the place of ideological production and the spread of female literacy, it was of prime importance to warn women off questioning traditional sexual morality. Public writing and public speech, closely allied, were both real and symbolic acts of self-determination for women. Barrett Browning uses the phrase 'I write' four times in the first two stanzas of Book I, emphasising the connection between the first person narrative and the 'act' of women's speech; between the expression of woman's feelings and thoughts and the legitimate professional exercise of that expression. Barrett Browning makes the link between women's intervention into political debate and her role as imaginative writer quite clear in her defence of Harriet Beecher Stowe's *Uncle Tom's Cabin*. She rejoices in Stowe's success as 'a woman and a human being' and pushes the message home to her timid female corres-pondent:

> Oh, and is it possible that you think a woman has no business with questions like the question of slavery? Then she had better use a pen no more. She had better subside into slavery and concubinage herself I think as in the times of old, shut herself up with the Penelopes in the "women's apartment", and take no rank among thinkers and speakers.

Writing is a skilled task learnt at the expense of 'Long green days/Worn bare of grass and sunshine, – long calm nights/From which the silken sleeps were fretted out . . . with no amateur's/Irreverent haste and busy idleness/I set myself to art!' *Aurora Leigh* enters, however tentatively, into debates on *all* the forbidden subjects. In the first person epic voice of a major poet, it breaks a very specific silence, almost a gentlemen's agreement between women authors and the arbiters of high culture in Victorian England, that allowed women to write if only they would shut up about it.

(1978)

CAROL FARLEY KESSLER

Editor's Introduction
Daring to Dream: Utopian Stories by United States Women
1836–1919

Of the 12 feminist Utopias published during this period but not included in this collection, two short stories – 'The Rappite's Economy'[1] and 'Transcendental Fruitlands'[2] – and one novel – *World War I Ourland*[3] – are satiric Utopias; a fourth – the African eutopia *Liberia*[4] – is the only work before 1900 to consider race. All of these reveal the hegemony of patriarchal ideology, particularly in the control of women's labor. Rebecca Harding Davis in 'The Harmonists' decries one man's power to maintain in a 'communist village' a 'utopia of prophets and poets,' who appear to a visitor as 'gross men' and 'poor withered women' with 'faded and tired' faces showing a 'curious vacancy'.[5] Louisa May Alcott in 'Transcendental Wild Oats' wryly describes 'the most ideal of all these castles in Spain,' where to the question posed by Mrs Lamb – 'are there any beasts of burden on the place?' – another – seeing how overworked she was – responded, 'Only one woman!' Fruitlands fails: 'The world was not ready for Utopia yet' and Mrs Lamb wonders to her disappointed husband, 'Don't you think Apple Slump would be a better name for it, dear?'[6] In each short story, women supply the labor to achieve a man's ideal and in both cases, the ideal fails to materialize as anticipated. (In two novels, Alcott shows women's co-operative ventures succeeding – four young women in *An Old-fashioned Girl* who share rooms, and the heterogeneous community of women concluding *Work*.)[7] Editor of *Godey's Lady's Book*, Sarah Josepha Hale in *Liberia; or Mr. Peyton's Experiments* provides yet another version of female labor in the service of male ideology. Black Keziah, indomitable manager of Mr Peyton's household, directs the labor of her husband Polydore in several of Mr Peyton's experiments to provide his 'servants' with an economic basis for living outside slavery. (Though racist by 1980s standards, for its time Hale's novel shows a measure of sympathy.) Hale, Davis, and Alcott all subscribe to the concept of women's moral guardianship of society. Gilman however, as noted above, saw women and men as both degenerate and remediable.

Several other works, while predominantly eutopian, use bad marriages to show how social regulation of woman's sexuality works to her disadvantage. First the marriage 'bargain' is shown corrupt: 'The man wants a housekeeper, the woman a home';[8] he married her to 'be stunning,' she him for money, called 'the god of civilization'.[9] Both exchange of services and exchange of objects – especially when one object is a person – do not work. Second, such corrupt marriages set eutopian sexual arrangements in relief: the freedom of exotic bronze-skinned women to select their sexual partners on a tropic island where mates 'strive to please each other' make a 'civilized' mate's demand to be pleased the more objectionable.[10] Third, the children resulting from such corrupt marriages receive inadequate financial support: a deserted mother of three small children tries taking in boarders as a livelihood, but crying infants drive boarders away. Then her husband abducts her son.[11]

To correct men's control of women's labour and sexuality, feminist eutopias of this period suggest several possibilities: paid work, education, suffrage, and co-operation. 'A New Society' envisioned by a Lowell 'mill girl' paid equal wages regardless of sex, limited the work day to eight hours, and required three hours daily of mental or manual labor, whichever was not a person's means of livelihood.[12] In general both women and men work with access to the full range of jobs.[13] A short story called 'Friend Island' boasts a sea-captain heroine: 'a true sea-woman of that elder time when woman's superiority to man had not been so long recognized'.[14] The story is her reminiscence of a sentient island, an early science-fiction tale that anticipates 1970s strategies for demonstrating interrelationships among human, animal, plant, and earth.

A second strategy for avoiding control is education – for daughters as well as sons,[15] especially to make 'an honorable living' instead of submitting to 'the best we can get' in a marriage.[16] And such self-sufficient women would of course keep their own names when they married.[17]

A third strategy, suffrage, is far more emphasized by subsequent histories of women than by Utopists: of the 59 Utopias appearing before 1920, only 14 or 24 per cent favor suffrage, though 10 more consider political issues, including general activity and office holding. Typical of a feminist viewpoint is a passage from Mary Theresa Shelhamer's *Life and Labor in the Spirit World* (1885):

> She should have a voice in the affairs of the country under whose laws she lives
> and educates her children. . . . Some people pretend to fear that when women
> vote they will have no time for domestic affairs, and the institution of the home
> itself will be destroyed. . . . From the fuss made . . . one would think it took a
> week to put a small slip of paper into a medium-sized box. Why, we have
> known of men who could put in half a dozen in less than half that time, and
> no one suspects women to be less clever than men.[18]

The passage is interesting for its acknowledgment of popular fears that women would no longer perform traditional domestic roles once they were admitted to the political sphere reserved for men. Many accepted the view that women, family, and home were the calm center in a raging storm of social flux, that to permit change there would ensure complete social chaos. (One anti-feminist Utopia *Pantaletta* showed women's political control to be a comedy of error.[19] Shelhamer ridicules this popular fear at the same time that she assumes the sexes to be equally clever, such equality of intelligence more readily assumed however in Utopian fiction than by the public at large. Women Utopists ignore woman's traditional restriction to the home and thereby imply that integrating the public and private spheres for women will be no more disastrous than for men.[20]

More important than suffrage in feminist eutopias are co-operative or communitarian solutions to social control: some 54 per cent (32) for this period include such solutions. They take two forms – co-operative services or self-sufficient experimental communities. The earlier of two communitarian examples is *A New Aristocracy*, of 'brain and heart,' to be established in Idlewild, New York, upon a Parisian suburban model.[21] As in works by Howland and Graul (Selections 5 and 12), independent wealth makes possible the establishment of a factory, with workers' cottages and cultural buildings.[22] *Other Worlds* describes a society called 'The Colony,' to which members contribute an entry fee and work to support the Colony (compare Selection 8, Mason, 1889). Members own stock in their Colony, and enjoy its services. For example, a Nursery with a professionally trained staff cares for children, thus the single parent and a working couple are assured of responsible childrearing.[23] Such child care service is the major focus of *Reinstern* ('pure star'), 'a planet as yet undiscovered by your astronomers, who waste lifetimes searching with telescopes for what inner vision will readily disclose when you allow the real self to predominate'.[24] This eutopia presents an apprentice system to educate young adults for shared parenting, such training believed prerequisite to marriage.[25] Parents of each sex receive 'equal honors, salaries, and privileges,'[26] but biological parents are not solely responsible for children and systematically receive support appropriate to their children's ages. *Moving the Mountain*, another eutopia having co-operative services, also includes detailed nursery and child garden arrangements.[27] In addition by the 1940s apartment residences for self-supporting women had become common in the United States with facilities to provide food hygienically and knowledgeably! (Gilman was particularly outraged by 'the waste of private housekeeping' and devoted the novel *What Diantha Did* (1910) to demonstrating an alternative.)[28]

Two points emerging from this group of eutopias are especially salient for the concerns of Utopias during the 1970s. First, the observation that the 'nowhere' of Utopia can be the 'somewhere' of 'inner vision' marks the 1970s recognition of Utopia as a state of mind showing a spiritual or religious motive to underlie Utopia.[29] Some nineteenth-century Utopists called this visionary 'nowhere' by more theological names: 'heaven' (Selection 6, Phelps, 1883) or the 'spirit world'.[30] Several recent analysts of current Utopias by women consider these to be intrinsically spiritual.[31] In fact some would see women's liberation itself as a 'spiritual quest.'[32] Second, on a more mundane level, the domestic labor typically a concern of these communitarian eutopias before 1920 currently receives broadly based investigation in research, as well as visionary alternative solution in Utopia. Economists, historians, and anthropologists provide studies of women's triple labor loads: unpaid child-care and housekeeping work added to underpaid salaried work.[33] That 1970s eutopias completely restructure society to remove from women this triple burden should not surprise us. It is worth noting that the particular domestic solutions envisioned in Utopias before 1920 have not come to pass, but the domestic problems that we now seek to address were accurately forecast. Utopias, though not blueprints, can be harbingers.

(1984)

Notes

1 Rebecca Harding Davis, 'The Harmonists', *The Atlantic Monthly*, 17 (1866).

2 Louisa May Alcott, 'Transcendental Wild Oats: A Chapter from an Unwritten Romance', *The Independent*, 25 (1873).

3 Charlotte Perkins Gilman, 'With Her in Ourland', *The Forerunner*, 6 (1916).

4 Sarah Josepha Hale, *Liberia: or Mr Peyton's Experiments* (New York, Harpers and Brothers, 1853).

5 Davis, 'The Harmonists', pp. 531, 533, 535, 537.

6 Davis, 'The Harmonists', pp. 1570, 1571.

7 Louisa May Alcott, *An Old-Fashioned Girl* (Boston, Roberts, 1870), ch. 13: 'The Sunny Side'; *Work: A Story of Experience* (1873; rpt New York, Shocken. 1977), ch. 20.

8 Mary Theresa Shelhamer, *Life and Labor in the Spirit World. Being a Description of the Localities, Employments. Surroundings, and Conditions of the Spheres* (Boston: Colby & Rich, 1885), p. 12.

9 Mrs M. A. Weeks Pittock, *The God of Civilization: A Romance* (Chicago, Eureka, 1890), ch. 22

10 Pittock, *The God of Civilization*, ch. 12, p. 60.

11 Lena Jane Fry, *Other Worlds: A Story Concerning the Wealth Earned by American Citizens and Showing How It Can Be Secured to Them Instead of to the Trusts* (Chicago: author, 1905), chs 12, 15.

12 Betsey Chamberlain (Tabitha pseud.), 'A New Society', *The Lowell Offering I* (1841).

13 Shelhamer, *Life and Labor*; Eloise O. Randall Richberg, *Reinstern* (Cincinnati, Editor Publishing, 1900); Fry, *Other Worlds*; Charlotte Perkins Gilman, *Moving the Mountain. The Forerunner*, 2, 1911; Charlotte Perkins Gilman, *Herland, The Forerunner*, 6 (1915).

14 Gertrude Barrows Bennett (Francis Stevens pseud.), 'Friend Island', *All-Story Weekly*, 7 September 1918, p. 126.

15 Chamberlain, 'A New Society'.

16 Shelhamer, *Life and Labor*.

17 Fry, *Other Worlds*, ch. 28; Gilman, *Herland*, pp. 118ff.

18 Shelhamer, *Life and Labor*, p. 13.

19 Mrs J. Wood, *Pantaletta: A Romance of Sheheland* (New York, American News Company, 1882).

20 For background, see Barbara Welter, 'Anti-Intellectualism and the American Woman, 1800–1860,' in *Dimity Convictions: The American Woman in the Nineteenth Century* (Athens, Ohio, Ohio University Press, 1976), pp. 71–82; Julia Ward Howe, ed., *Sex and Education* (1874; rpt New York, Arno, 1972), a collection of articles responding to Dr Edward H. Clarke, *Sex in Education* (1873).

21 Alice Elinor Bartlett (Arnold Birch pseud.), *A New Aristocracy* (New York, Bartlett, 1891).

22 Bartlett, *A New Aristocracy*, pp. 306–9.

23 Fry, *Other Worlds*.

24 Richberg, *Reinstern*, p. 10.

25 Richberg, *Reinstern*, pp. 19–20.

26 Richberg, *Reinstern*, pp. 23–4.

27 Gilman, *Moving The Mountain*, ch. 4.

28 Charlotte Perkins Gilman, 'The Waste of Private Housekeeping,' *Annals of the American Academy of Political and Social Science* (July 1913): 91–5; *What Diantha Did* (New York, Charlton, 1910).

29 Thea Alexander, *2150 AD* (Temple, Arizona, Macro Books, 1971); Dorothy Bryant, *The Comforter* (San Francisco, D. M. Bryant, 1971); Mary Station, *From the Legend of Biel* (New York, Ace, 1975); Marge Piercy, *Woman on the Edge of Time* (New York, Knopf, 1976).

30 Shelhamer, *Life and Labor*.

31 See Lee Cullen Khanna, 'Women's Worlds: New Directions in Utopian Fiction,' *Alternative Futures*, 4 (2–3) 1981: 58–9; also Carol Pearson and Katherine Pope, *The Female Hero in American and British Literature* (New York: Bowker, 1981), pp. 260–5.

32 Carol P. Christ, *Diving Deep and Surfacing: Women Writers on Spiritual Quest* (Boston, Beacon Press, 1980), esp. pp. 1–12; Carol P. Christ and Judith Plaskow, eds, *Womanspirit Rising: A Feminist Reader in Religion* (San Francisco, Harper & Row, 1979), esp. pp. 1–17, 43–52, 217–19.

33 For examples, see John Kenneth Galbraith, 'The Economics of the American Housewife,' *Atlantic* 232 (August 1973): 78–83; Delores Hayden, *The Grand Domestic Revolution: A History of Feminist Designs for American Homes, Neighbourhoods and Cities* (Cambridge, Mass., MIT Press, 1981); Eleanor Leacock, 'History, Development, and the Division of Labor by Sex: Implications for Organization,' *Signs: Journal of Women in Culture and Society*, 7 (1981): 474–91; Bettina Berch, *The Endless Day: The Political Economy of Women and Work* (New York, Harcourt Brace Jovanovich, 1982); Susan Strasser, *Never Done: A History of American Housework* (New York: Pantheon, 1982).

SARAH LeFANU

In the Chinks of the World Machine: Feminism and Science Fiction

What, then, *does* challenge the sexual status quo? I believe it has been challenged profoundly by the growth of feminism over the last twenty years. The feminist intervention in science fiction has not been an easy one: writers have had to struggle not only against the weight of the male bias of the form but also against the weight of a cultural and political male hegemony that underpins the form itself. However, women writers have been able to draw on the possibilities opened up by an important strand within science fiction that is in opposition to the dominant ideology, that, rather than celebrating imperialistic and militaristic glory, is subversive, satirical, iconoclastic. To quote Amis again, 'science fiction's most important use . . . is a means of dramatising social enquiry, as providing a fictional mode in which cultural tendencies can be isolated and judged.'[3]

One of the major theoretical projects of the second wave of feminism is the investigation of gender and sexuality as social constructs, thus posing a challenge to notions of a natural law regulating feminine behaviour and an innate femaleness that describes and circumscribes 'woman'. Feminism has drawn on a variety of theories and practices in this endeavour, from an emphasis on consciousness-raising as a means of transposing the experience of oppression from an individual to a wider, social level, to a development of psychoanalytic theory that explores the creation of the gendered subject within language and culture. Questions of class and race have pushed feminism further from the experience of individual oppression into a wider political arena. The stock conventions of science fiction – time travel, alternate worlds, entropy, relativism, the search for a unified field theory – can be used metaphorically and metonymically as powerful ways of exploring the construction of 'woman'. Feminist SF, then, is part of science fiction while struggling against it.

In the following pages I shall describe the fruits of this marriage between feminist politics and science fiction. The freedom that SF offers from the constraints of realism has an obvious appeal and has been exploited by mainstream writers such as Margaret Atwood and Marge Piercy. Its glorious eclecticism, with its mingling of the rational discourse of science with the pre-rational language of the unconscious – for SF borrows from horror, mythology and fairy tale – offers a means of exploring the myriad ways in which we are constructed as women.

Further, science fiction offers women new ways of writing. Despite the growing popularity of the trilogy – an unnerving prospect for the writer as she starts out – there is still a privileged place for the short story within the body of SF. What is perhaps most remarkable is the fluidity of form that SF allows: the set length of the novel does not dominate. Writers can let themselves experiment, writing and rewriting in short story, novella or novel form. More than in any other form of fiction there is an easy flow between writers and readers. Professional writers often start out as fans, writing in fanzines or producing their own. One does not have to be a professional in order to be read. Ideas, themes and characters are borrowed, elaborated, reworked by different people in different forms. One example of this is the elaboration of the Kirk/Spock relationship in *Star Trek* produced and written in a series of fanzines entirely by women. Another is Suzette Haden Elgin's Ozark Centre for Language Studies, where, amongst other things, she is developing the study of Láadan, the women's language of her novels *Native Tongue* and *The Judas Rose*. Writers, C.J. Cherryh being one example, may invent a universe and then invite other writers to share it. There are many collaborations in SF, such as in the rather unappealingly named Sime/Gen novels of Jacqueline Lichtenberg and Jean Lorrah, and between Cynthia Felice and Connie Willis. And the numerous SF conventions bring together writers, fans and artists from all over the world.

All this leads to a breakdown of the conventional hierarchies between writers and readers, and challenges the conventional authority of the single author. Such an anti-authoritarian style has, potentially, a particular interest for women, for whom writing requires not just self-confidence, but the confidence necessary to break through what can be seen as a male-dominated world of ordered discourse, into a male-dominated world of professionalism.

(1988)

Note

3 Kingsley Amis, *New Maps of Hell*, p. 54.

ROSALIND COWARD

Female Desire: Women's Sexuality Today

In the adoration of the powerful male, we have the adoration of the father by the small child. This adoration is based on the father as all-powerful, before disillusionment and the struggle for autonomy set in. Sometimes the patriarchal nature of the fantasy becomes explicit:

> His words hit her physically, so forcibly did they remind her of her father: he had been the only person who had ever used that word to describe the colour of her hair. And now to hear Stephen do so – the man she loved, who could only see her as a machine – was more than she could bear. Eyes blinded by tears, she ran out.

Roberta Leigh

The way in which these men are portrayed certainly involves a journey back to a world before any struggle for autonomy has occurred. It isn't even an adolescent fantasy; it's pre-adolescent, very nearly pre-conscious. As a fantasy, it represents the adoration of a person on whom your welfare depends, the exaggerated evaluation which children experience before the process of becoming a separate person begins. As the child becomes more independent there's invariably a re-estimation of the parent, perhaps even a disillusionment. The parent who is no longer omnipotent in the child's welfare is no longer seen as omnipotent in the world. The child begins the difficult process of recognizing social valuation as well as personal valuation of the parents. The struggle for autonomy also brings its problems. By adolescence, there's usually a full-scale struggle for independence. Power which might previously have been adored – after all, it ensured the welfare of a dependent child – becomes controlling and suffocating for a child struggling to become independent. The power of one person is seen as depriving another of autonomy. Especially for women, the relationship to patriarchal authority is bound to be hazardous. Men have power and authority only if women's equality is denied.

But in the fantasies represented by these novels, the power of men is adored. The qualities desired are age, power, detachment, the control of other people's welfare. And the novels never really admit any criticism of this power. Occasionally the heroines 'protest' their right to gainful employment, or rebel against the tyranny of the loved men. But in the end they succumb to that form of power. And what attracted them in the first place were precisely all the attributes of the unreconstructed patriarch. The qualities which make these men so desirable are, actually, the qualities which feminists have chosen to ridicule: power (the desire to dominate others); privilege (the exploitation of others); emotional distance (the inability to communicate); and singular love for the heroine (the inability to relate to anyone other than the sexual partner).

It is interesting to realize that obstacles do exist in the way of the heroine's adoration of her man. But the obstacles are never the criticisms or ambiguity which a woman might really feel towards that kind of man. The obstacles come from the outside, from material circumstances or misunderstandings. The work of the narrative is to remove these misunderstandings and obstacles, one by one. Instead of contradictory feelings towards such men, or feelings of suffocation, we have a number of frustrating circumstances which are finally cleared away to allow for the heroine safely to feel her respect and love for the man. In other words, these fantasies admit a belief that everything would be all right between the sexes were it not for a series of foolish misperceptions and misunderstandings.

There are a number of other factors which indicate a powerful infantile fantasy at work. For instance, there's the jealousy to which the heroine is invariably exposed. A rival for the hero's affections is almost obligatory, and the rival is usually better suited by class or by temperament. The crunch point in the narrative often comes when the heroine sees the hero and the other woman embracing, or meets the other two together. When the narrative is resolved, we discover that the hero was thinking about our heroine all along. He was either seeking consolation in another's arms, or was taken in by some scheming type. A satisfactory resolution of this obstacle is the discovery that the hero was after all loyal to the heroine, at least with the emotions if not the body.

The obliteration of a rival is another standard component of an infantile fantasy. The sight of the hero in another's arms is reminiscent of Freud's accounts of one of the forms taken by infantile jealousy provoked by the sight of the parents embracing. The child sees this and is jealous, seeking in fantasy to obliterate the intruding parent. Common childhood fantasies are of obliterating that parent and taking her/his place, becoming the rightful and only recipient of the other parent's love. In pulp romance, the disappointments based on discovering that others have claims on the loved one's attention are obliterated. There aren't really obstacles to total monomaniacal love, only temporary frustrations which the narrative then removes.

There is another significant way in which these narrative fantasies are regressive. It is the way in which sexual desire is portrayed. The hero's power is not only reminiscent of the father's perfection before the fall, so to speak; the power also works to absolve the women from any responsibility for the sexual engagement. Heroes are usually established as either sexually active (lots of girlfriends) or as almost untouchable. In the first case, the heroes are the objects of intense sexual interest, and have active sexual lives but refuse to settle down. In the end it is the overwhelming nature of their special desire for the heroine which is eventually secured. She alone has kindled the overwhelming desire that is going to end in marriage. The 'untouchable' syndrome is really very similar. In these cases, the hero is remote, too good for sexual intrigue, better still a priest – someone, in short, who ought not to feel sexual passion. The heroine alone awakens his desire. The desire he feels for her is so great that he has to come off his pedestal, gather her in his arms and crush her to his chest.

All the frustrations and delays integral to a good romance only heighten this outcome, where the hero's desire is made suddenly explicit. The hero's desire is so great that it borders on the uncontrollable. One journalist called it the 'bruised lips' syndrome, and it is certainly the case that the uncontrollable desire has close resemblances with descriptions of rape. The heroine keeps her blouse buttoned up only with the greatest difficulty until they can breathlessly mutter the marriage vows at each other and bring the novel to a satisfactory close: ' "Please put your dress on," he murmured huskily, "so we can go talk to your parents about our wedding" ' (Janet Dailey).

This fantasy is the ultimate expression of passive sexuality. The heroine may well be 'in love' with the hero. She may well adore him and admire him. But her *desire* is only ever triggered as a response, crushed out of her, as it were, as a series of low moans. Again psychoanalytic writing is illuminating about this kind of fantasy. It represents the projection of active desires by yourself on to another person, who then becomes responsible for that desire.

[. . .]

One thing about these fantasies, though, is that however passive the female, she is not actually powerless. The conclusion of marriage isn't necessary so much for reasons of morality, but because these fantasies are very obviously about a certain transfer of power, from the man to the woman. The woman is not annihilated by her subordination to the patriarch; she also assumes some power over him since his great power is finally harnessed to one woman – the heroine. Indeed, there are often other elements in romantic novels where the men are rendered helpless and dependent, like children. There's often a scene where the hero falls ill, suffers from hallucinations in the desert, or is even injured:

The human frailty of Stephen Brandon's sickness – even though momentary – robbed Julia of her awesome fear with which she had regarded him. One could not see a man prostrate and not feel sorry for him; and sympathy – however fleeting – left change in its wake.

Roberta Leigh

Rendering the hero ill, dependent, or injured is a narrative device which crops up all over the place. There's a common theme in fiction and films of women being attracted to cripples, or having fantasies about nursing men through illness during which the man suddenly realizes that 'what he's been feeling is love'. Dick Francis's racing thrillers, which are extremely popular with women, have this theme of male mutilation down to a fine art. We can be sure that if the hero isn't brutalized within the first few pages, he'll certainly get shot, beaten up or fall off his horse pretty soon. Now, all this is extremely interesting; it points to a push for power in female fantasy.

In romantic fiction, the hero is made dependent only 'fleetingly', as Roberta Leigh would undoubtedly have it. But this momentary impotence allows the woman to acquire power, the power of a mother caring for a child. And the concluding marriage is the symbol of the woman achieving power. The men are castrated and then restored. The power which the heroine achieves is the power of the mother; the daughter has taken the mother's place.

(1984)

ANN BARR SNITOW

'*Mass Market Romance: Pornography for Women is Different*'
Radical History Review

III

What is the Harlequin romance formula? The novels have no plot in the usual sense. All tension and problems arise from the fact that the Harlequin world is inhabited by two species incapable of communicating with each other, male and female. In this sense these Pollyanna books have their own dream-like truth: our culture produces a pathological experience of sex difference. The sexes have different needs and interests, certainly different experiences. They find each other utterly mystifying.

Since all action in the novels is described from the female point of view, the reader identifies with the heroine's efforts to decode the erratic gesture of 'dark, tall and gravely handsome'[6] men, all mysterious strangers or powerful bosses. In a sense the usual relationship is reversed: woman is subject, man, object. There are more descriptions of his body than of hers ('Dark trousers fitted closely to lean hips and long muscular legs . . .') though her clothes are always minutely observed. He is the unknowable other, a sexual icon whose magic is maleness. The books are permeated by phallic worship. Male is good, male is exciting, without further points of reference. Cruelty, callousness, coldness, menace, are all equated with maleness and treated as a necessary part of the package: 'It was an arrogant remark, but Sara had long since admitted his arrogance as part of his attraction.'[7] She, on the other hand, is the subject, the one whose thoughts the reader knows, whose constant reevaluation of male moods and actions make up the story line.

The heroine is not involved in any overt adventure beyond trying to respond appropriately to male energy without losing her virginity. Virginity is a given here; sex means marriage and marriage, promised at the end, means, finally, there can be sex.

While the heroine waits for the hero's next move, her time is filled by tourism and by descriptions of consumer items: furniture, clothes, and gourmet foods. In *Writers Market* (1977) Harlequin Enterprises stipulates: 'Emphasis on travel.' (The exception is the occasional hospital novel. Like foreign places, hospitals offer removal from the household, heightened emotional states, and a supply of strangers.) Several of the books have passages that probably come straight out of guide books, but the *particular* setting is not the point, only that it is exotic, a place elsewhere.[8]

More space is filled by the question of what to wear. 'She rummaged in her cases, discarding item after item, and eventually brought out a pair of purple cotton jeans and a matching shift. They were not new. She had bought them a couple of years ago. But fortunately her figure had changed little, and apart from a slight shrinkage in the pants which made them rather tighter than she would have liked, they looked serviceable.'[9] Several things are going on here: the effort to find the right clothes for the occasion, the problem of staying thin, the problem of piecing together outfits from things that are not new. Finally, there is that shrinkage, a signal to the experienced Harlequin reader that the heroine, innocent as her intent may be in putting on jeans that are a little too tight, is wearing something revealing and will certainly be seen and noted by the hero in this vulnerable, passive act of self-exposure. (More about the pornographic aspects later. In any other titillating novel one would suspect a pun when tight pants are 'serviceable' but in the context of the absolutely flat Harlequin style one might well be wrong. More, too, about this style later on.)

Though clothes are the number one filler in Harlequins, food and furniture are also important and usually described in the language of women's magazines:[10] croissants are served hot and crispy and are 'crusty brown,'[11] while snapper is 'filleted, crumbed and fried in butter' and tomato soup is 'topped with grated cheese and parsley'[12] (this last a useful, practical suggestion anyone could try).

Harlequins revitalize daily routines by insisting that a woman combing her hair, a woman reaching up to put a plate on a high shelf (so that her knees show beneath the hem, if only there were a viewer), a woman doing what women do all day, is in a constant state of potential sexuality. You never can tell when you may be seen and being seen is a precious opportunity. Harlequin romances alternate between scenes of the hero and heroine together in which she does a lot of social lying to save face, pretending to be unaffected by the hero's presence while her body melts or shivers, and scenes in which the heroine is essentially alone, living in a cloud of absorption, preparing mentally and physically for the next contact.

The heroine is alone. Sometimes there is another woman, a competitor who is often more overtly aware of her sexuality than the heroine, but she is a shadow on the horizon. Sometimes there are potentially friendly females living in the next bungalow or working with the patient in the next bed, but they, too, are shadowy, not important to the real story, which consists entirely of an emotionally isolated woman trying to keep her virginity and her head when the only person she ever really talks to is the hero, whose motives and feelings are unclear: 'She saw his words as a warning and would have liked to know whether he meant [them] to be.'[13]

The heroine gets her man at the end, first, because she is an old-fashioned girl (this is a code for no premarital sex) and, second, because the hero gets ample opportunity to see her perform well in a number of female helping roles. In the course of a Harlequin romance, most heroines demonstrate passionate motherliness, good cooking, patience in adversity, efficient planning, and a good clothes sense, though these are skills and emotional capacities produced in emergencies, and are not, as in real life, a part of an invisible, glamorless work routine.

Though the heroines are pliable (they are rarely given particularized character traits; they are all Everywoman and can fit in comfortably with the life-style of the strong-willed heroes be they doctors, lawyers, or marine biologists doing experiments on tropical islands), it is still amazing that these novels end in marriage. After one hundred and fifty pages of mystification, unreadable looks, 'hints of cruelty'[14] and wordless coldness, the thirty-page denouement is powerless to dispel the earlier impression of menace. Why should this heroine marry this man? And, one can ask with equal reason, why should this hero marry this woman? These endings do not ring true, but no doubt this is precisely their strength. A taste for psychological or social realism is unlikely to provide a Harlequin reader with a sustaining fantasy of rescue, of glamour, or of change. The Harlequin ending offers the impossible. It is pleasing to think that appearances are deceptive, that male coldness, absence, boredom, are not what they seem. The hero *seems* to be a horrible roué; he *seems* to be a hopeless, moody cripple; he *seems* to be cruel and unkind; or he *seems* to be indifferent to the heroine and interested only in his work; but always, at the end a rational explanation of all this appears. In spite of his coldness or preoccupation, the hero really loves the heroine and wants to marry her.

In fact, the Harlequin formula glorifies the distance between the sexes. Distance becomes titillating. The heroine's sexual inexperience adds to this excitement. What is this thing that awaits her on the other side of distance and mystery? Not knowing may be more sexy than finding out.

Or perhaps the heroes are really fathers – obscure, forbidden objects of desire. Whatever they are, it is more exciting to wonder about them than to know them. In romanticized sexuality the pleasure lies in the distance itself. Waiting, anticipation, anxiety – these represent the high point of sexual experience.

Perhaps there is pleasure, too, in returning again and again to that breathless, ambivalent, nervous state *before* certainty or satiety. Insofar as women's great adventure, the one they are socially sanctioned to seek, is romance, adventurousness takes women always back to the first phase in love. Unlike work, which holds out the possible pleasures of development, of the exercise of faculties, sometimes even of advancement, the Harlequin form of romance depends on the heroine's being in a state of passivity, of not knowing. Once the heroine knows the hero loves her, the story is over. Nothing interesting remains. Harlequin statements in *Writers Market* stress 'upbeat ending essential here' (1977). Here at least is a reliable product that reproduces for women the most interesting phase in the love/marriage cycle and knows just when to stop.

IV

What is the world view implied by the Harlequin romance formula? What are its implicit values? The novels present no overt moral superstructure. Female virginity is certainly an ideal, but an ideal without a history, without parental figures to support it or religious convictions to give it a context. Nor can one say money is a value; rather it is a given, rarely mentioned. Travel and work, though glamorous, are not really goals for the heroine either. They are holding patterns while she awaits love.

Of course, the highest good is the couple. All outside events are subordinated to the psychodrama of its formation. But the heroine must struggle to form the couple without appearing to do so. Her most marketable virtue is her blandness. And she is always proud when she manages to keep a calm façade. She lies constantly to hide her desires, to protect her reputation. She tries to cover up all signs of sexual feeling, upset, any extreme of emotion. She values being an ordinary woman and acting like one. (Indeed, for women, being ordinary and being attractive are equated in these novels. Heroes are of course expected to have a little more dash and sometimes sport scars.) Finally, the heroine's value system includes the given that men are all right, that they will turn into husbands, despite appearances to the contrary.

The world of Harlequin novels has no past. (At most, occasionally the plot requires a flashback.) Old people hardly appear except as benevolent peripheral presences. Young women have no visible parents, no ties to a before. Everyone is young though the hero is always quite a bit older than the heroine. Is this why there are no parents, because the lover is really *in loco parentis?*

Harlequins make no reference to a specific ethnic group or religion. (In this they differ from a new popular mass form, the family saga, which is dense with ethnic detail, national identity, *roots*.) Harlequins are aggressively secular: Christmas is always the tinsel not the religious Christmas. One might expect to find romance linked, if only sentimentally, to nature, to universal categories, to first and last things. Harlequins assiduously avoid this particular shortcut to emotion (while of course exploiting others). They reduce awe of the unknown to a speculation on the intentions of the cold, mean stranger and generally strip romance of its spiritual, transcendent aspect.

At the other extreme from the transcendent, Harlequins also avoid all mention of local peculiarities beyond the merely scenic. They reduce the allure of difference, of travel, to a mere travelogue. The couple is alone. There is no society, no context, only surroundings. Is this what the nuclear family feels like to many women? Or is this, once again, a fantasy of safety and seclusion, while in actuality the family is being invaded continually and is under pressures it cannot control?

The denatured quality of Harlequins is convenient for building an audience: anyone can identify. Or, rather, anyone can identify with the fantasy that places all the characters in an upper-class, polite environment familiar not in experience but in the ladies' magazines and on television. The realities of class – workers in dull jobs, poverty, real productive relations, social divisions of labor – are all, of course, entirely foreign to the world of the Harlequin. There are servants in the novels lest the heroine, like the reader, be left to do all the housework, but they are always loyal and glad to help. Heroines have familiar service jobs – they are teachers, nurses, nursery-maids – but the formula finds a way around depicting the limitations of these jobs. The heroine can do the work ordinary women do while still seeming glamorous to the reader either because of *where* the heroine does her work or how she is rescued from doing it.

All fiction is a closed system in many respects, its language mainlining into areas of our conscious and subconscious selves by routes that by-pass many of the things we know or believe about the real world of our daily experience. This by-passing is a form of pleasure, one of art's pleasing tricks. As Fred Kerner, Harlequin's director of publishing, said when describing the formula to prospective authors in *The Writer*: 'The fantasy must have the same appeal that all of us discovered when we were first exposed to fairy tales as children.'[15] I do not wish to imply that I would like to remove a Harlequin romance from the hands of its readers to replace it with an improving novel that includes a realistically written catalogue of woman's griefs under capitalism and in the family. My purpose here is diagnostic. A description of the pared-down Harlequin formula raises the question: What is it about this *particular* formula that makes it so suggestive, so popular, with such a large female readership, all living under capitalism, most living – or yearning to live – in some form of the family?

Harlequins fill a vacuum created by social conditions. When women try to picture excitement, the society offers them one vision, romance. When women try to imagine companionship, the society offers them one vision, male, sexual companionship. When women try to fantasize about success, mastery, the society offers them one vision, the power to attract a man. When women try to fantasize about sex, the society offers them taboos on most of its imaginable expressions except those that deal directly with arousing and satisfying men. When women try to project a unique self, the society offers them very few attractive images. True completion for women is nearly always presented as social, domestic, sexual.

One of our culture's most intense myths, the ideal of an individual who is brave and complete in isolation, is for men only. Women are grounded, enmeshed in civilization, in social connection, in family and in love (a condition a feminist culture might well define as desirable) while all our culture's rich myths of individualism are essentially closed to them. Their one socially acceptable moment of transcendence is romance. This involves a constant return in imagination to those short moments in the female life cycle, courtship. With the exception of the occasional gourmet meal, which the heroine is often too nervous to eat, all other potential sources of pleasure are rigidly excluded from Harlequin romances. They reinforce the prevailing cultural code: pleasure for women is men. The ideal of romance presented in these books is a hungry monster that has gobbled up and digested all sorts of human pleasures.

There is another way in which Harlequin romances gloss over and obscure complex social relations: they are a static representation of a quickly changing situation – women's role in late capitalism. They offer a comfortably fixed image of the exchange between men and women at the very moment when the social actuality is confusing, shifting, frightening. The average American marriage now lasts about five years. A rape takes place every twelve minutes. While the social ferment of the sixties gave rise to the Gothic form in cheap fiction – family dramas that were claustrophic and anti-erotic compensations for an explosion of mobility and sexuality – in the seventies we have the blander Harlequins, novels that are picaresque and titillating, written for people who have so entirely suffered and absorbed the disappearance of the ideal of home that they don't want to hear about it any more. They want instead to read about premarital hopefulness.

Harlequin romances make bridges between contradictions; they soothe ambivalence. A brutal male sexuality is magically converted to romance; the war between men and women who cannot communicate ends in truce. Stereotyped female roles are charged with an unlikely glamour, and women's daily routines are revitalized by the pretense that they hide an ongoing sexual drama.

In a fine piece about modern Gothic romances, Joanna Russ points out that in these novels, ' "Occupation: Housewife" is simultaneously avoided, glamorized, and vindicated.'[16] Female skills are exalted: it is good to nurture, good to observe every change in expression of the people around you, important to worry about how you look. As Russ says, the feminine mystique is defended and women are promised all sorts of psychological rewards for remaining loyal to it. Though in other respects, Gothics are very different from Harlequins, they are the same in this: both pretend that nothing has happened to unsettle the old, conventional bargain between the sexes. Small surface concessions are made to a new female independence (several researchers, misreading I believe, claim that the new heroines are brave and more interested in jobs than families[17]) but the novels mention the new female feistiness only to finally reassure readers that *plus ça change, plus c'est la même chose*. Independence is always presented as a mere counter in the sexual game, like a hairdo or any other flirtatious gesture; sexual feeling utterly defeats its early stirrings.

In fact, in Harlequin romances, sexual feeling is probably the main point. Like sex itself, the novels are set in an eternal present in which the actual present, a time of disturbing disruptions between the sexes, is dissolved and only a comfortable timeless, universal battle remains. The hero wants sex; the heroine wants it, too, but can only enjoy it after the love promise has finally been made and the ring is on her finger.

(1979)

Notes

6 Rachel Lindsay, *Prescription for Love* (Toronto: Harlequin Books, 1977), p. 10.

7 Rebecca Stratton, *The Sign of the Ram* (Toronto: Harlequin Books, 1977), pp. 56, 147.

8 Here is an example of this sort of travelogue prose: 'There was something to appeal to all age groups in the thousand acre park in the heart of the city – golf for the energetic, lawn bowling for the more sedate, a zoo for the children's pleasure, and even secluded walks through giant cedars for lovers – but Cori thought of none of these things as Greg drove to a parking place bordering the Inlet.' Graham, *Mason's Ridge*, p. 25.

9 Anne Mather, *Born Out of Love* (Toronto: Harlequin Books, 1977), p. 42.

10 See Joanna Russ, 'Somebody's Trying to Kill Me and I Think It's My Husband: The Modern Gothic.' *Journal of Popular Culture* 6, no. 4 (Spring 1973) 1: 666–91.

11 Mather, *Born Out of Love*, p. 42.

12 Daphne Clair, *A Streak of Gold* (Toronto: Harlequin Books, 1978), p. 118.

13 Lindsay, *Prescription for Love*, p. 13.

14 Stratton, *The Sign of the Ram*, p. 66. The adjectives 'cruel' and 'satanic' are commonly used for heroes.

15 May 1977, p. 18.

16 Russ, 'Somebody's Trying to Kill Me,' p. 675.

17 See for example, Josephine A. Ruggiero and Louise C. Weston, 'Sex Role Characterizations of Women in Modern Gothic Novels,' *Pacific Sociological Review* 20, no. 2 (April 1977): 279–300.

JANICE A. RADWAY

'Women Read the Romance: The Interaction of Text and Context' Feminist Studies

Dorothy Evans lives and works in the community of Smithton, as do most of her regular customers. A city of about 112,000 inhabitants, Smithton is located five miles due east of the state's second largest city, in a metropolitan area with a total population of over 1 million. Dot was forty-eight years old at the time of the survey, the wife of a journeyman plumber, and the mother of three children in their twenties. She is extremely bright and articulate and, while not a proclaimed feminist, holds some beliefs about women that might be labeled as such. Although she did not work outside the home when her children were young and does not now believe that a woman needs a career to be fulfilled, she feels women should have the opportunity to work and be paid equally with men. Dot also believes that women should have the right to abortion, though she admits that her deep religious convictions would prevent her from seeking one herself. She is not disturbed by the Equal Rights Amendment and can and does converse eloquently about the oppression women have endured for years at the hands of men. Despite her opinions, however, she believes implicitly in the value of true romance and thoroughly enjoys discovering again and again that women can find men who will love them as they wish to be loved. Although most of her regular customers are more conservative than Dot in the sense that they do not advocate political measures to redress past grievances, they are quite aware that men commonly think themselves superior to women and often mistreat them as a result.

In general, Dot's customers are married, middle-class mothers with at least a high school education.[11] More than 60 percent of the women were between the ages of twenty-five and forty-four at the time of the study, a fact that duplicates fairly closely Harlequin's finding that the majority of its readers is between twenty-five and forty-nine.[12] Silhouette Books has also recently reported that 65 percent of the romance market is below the age of 40.[13] Exactly 50 percent of the Smithton women have high school diplomas, while 32 percent report completing at least some college work. Again, this seems to suggest that the interview group is fairly representative, for Silhouette also indicates that 45 percent of the romance market has attended at least some college. The employment status and family income of Dot's customers also seem to duplicate those of the audience mapped by the publishing houses. Forty-two percent of the Smithton women, for instance, work part-time outside the home. Harlequin claims that 49 percent of its audience is similarly employed. The Smithton women report slightly higher incomes than those of the average Harlequin reader (43 percent of the Smithton women have incomes of $15,000 to $24,999, 33 percent have incomes of $25,000 to $49,999 – the average income of the Harlequin reader is $15,000 to $20,000), but the difference is not enough to change the general sociological status of the group.

In one respect, however, Dot and her customers may be unusual, although it is difficult to say for sure because corroborative data from other sources are sadly lacking. Although almost 70 percent of the women claim to read books other than romances, 37 percent nonetheless report reading from five to nine romances each week. Even though more than one-half read less (from one to four romances a week), when the figures are converted to monthly totals they indicate that one-half the Smithton women read between four and sixteen romances a month, while 40 percent read more than twenty. This particular group is obviously obsessed with romantic fiction. The most recent comprehensive survey of American book readers and their habits has discovered that romance readers tend to read more books within their favorite category than do other category readers, but these readers apparently read substantially fewer than the Smithton group. Yankelovich, Skelly, and White found in their 1978 study that 21 percent of the total book reading public had read *at least* one gothic or romance in the last six months.[14] The average number of romantic novels read by this group in the last six months was only nine. Thus, while it is probably true that romance readers are repetitive consumers, most apparently do not read as consistently or as constantly as Dot and her customers. Romances undoubtedly play a more significant role, then, in the lives of the Smithton women than they do in those of occasional romance readers. Nevertheless, even this latter group appears to demonstrate a marked desire for, if not dependency upon, the fantasy they offer.

When asked why they read romances, the Smithton women overwhelmingly cite escape or relaxation as their goal. They use the word 'escape,' however, both literally and figuratively. On the one hand, they value their romances highly because the act of reading them literally draws the women away from their present surroundings. Because they must produce the meaning of the story by attending closely to the words on the page, they find that their attention is withdrawn from concerns that plague them in reality. One woman remarked with a note of triumph in her voice: 'My body may be in that room, but I'm not!' She and her sister readers see their romance reading as a legitimate way of denying a present reality that occasionally becomes too onerous to bear. This particular means of escape is better than television viewing for these women, because the cultural value attached to books permits them to overcome the guilt they feel about avoiding their responsibilities. They believe that reading of any kind is, by nature, educational.[15] They insist accordingly that they also read to learn.[16]

On the other hand, the Smithton readers are quite willing to acknowledge that the romances which so preoccupy them are little more than fantasies or fairy tales that always end happily. They readily admit in fact that the characters and events discovered in the pages of the typical romance do not resemble the people and occurrences they must deal with in their daily lives. On the basis of the following comments, made in response to a question about what romances 'do' better than other novels available today, one can conclude that it is precisely the unreal, fantastic shape of the story that makes their literal escape even more complete and gratifying. Although these are only a few of the remarks given in response to the undirected question, they are representative of the group's general sentiment.

> Romances hold my interest and do not leave me depressed or up in the air at the end like many modern day books tend to do. Romances also just make me feel good reading them as I identify with the heroines.

> The kind of books I mainly read are very different from everyday living. That's why I read them. Newspapers, etc., I find boring because all you read is sad news. I can get enough of that on TV news. I like stories that take your mind off everyday matters.

> Different than everyday life.

> Everyone is always under so much pressure. They like books that let them escape.

> Because it is an escape, and we can dream. And pretend that it is our life.

> I'm able to escape the harsh world a few hours a day.

> It is a way of escaping from everyday living.

> They always seem an escape and they usually turn out the way you wish life really was.

> I enjoy reading because it offers me a small vacation from everyday life and an interesting and amusing way to pass the time.

These few comments all hint at a certain sadness that many of the Smithton women seem to share because life has not given them all that it once promised. A deep-seated sense of betrayal also lurks behind their deceptively simple expressions of a need to believe in a fairy tale. Although they have not elaborated in these comments, many of the women explained in the interviews that despite their disappointments, they feel refreshed and strengthened by their vicarious participation in a fantasy relationship where the heroine is frequently treated as they themselves would most like to be loved.

[. . .]

In fact, the Smithton readers do not believe the books are identical, nor do they approve of all the romances they read. They have elaborated a complex distinction between 'good' and 'bad' romances and they have accordingly experimented with various techniques that they hoped would enable them to identify bad romances before they paid for a book that would only offend them. Some tried to decode titles and cover blurbs by looking for key words serving as clues to the book's tone; others refused to buy romances by authors they didn't recognize; still others read several pages *including the ending* before they bought the book. Now, however, most of the people in the Smithton group have been freed from the need to rely on these inexact predictions because Dot Evans shares their perceptions and evaluations of the category and can alert them to unusually successful romantic fantasies while steering them away from those they call 'disgusting perversions.'

When the Smithton readers' comments about good and bad romances are combined with the conclusions drawn from an analysis of twenty of their favorite books and an equal number of those they classify as particularly inadequate, an illuminating picture of the fantasy fueling the romance-reading experience develops.[21] To begin with, Dot and her readers will not tolerate any story in which the heroine is seriously abused by men. They find multiple rapes especially distressing and dislike books in which a woman is brutally hurt by a man only to fall desperately in love with him in the last four pages. The Smithton women are also offended by explicit sexual description and scrupulously avoid the work of authors like Rosemary Rogers and Judith Krantz who deal in what they call 'perversions' and 'promiscuity.' They also do not like romances that overtly perpetuate the double standard by excusing the hero's simultaneous involvement with several women. They insist, one reader commented, on 'one woman – one man.' They also seem to dislike any kind of detailed description of male genitalia, although the women enjoy suggestive descriptions of how the hero is emotionally aroused to an overpowering desire for the heroine. Their preferences seem to confirm Beatrice Faust's argument in *Women, Sex, and Pornography* that women are not interested in the visual display characteristic of male pornography, but prefer process-oriented materials detailing the development of deep emotional connection between two individuals.[22]

According to Dot and her customers, the quality of the *ideal* romantic fantasy is directly dependent on the character of the heroine and the manner in which the hero treats her. The plot, of course, must always focus on a series of obstacles to the final declaration of love between the two principals. However, a good romance involves an unusually bright and determined woman and a man who is spectacularly masculine, but at the same time capable of remarkable empathy and tenderness. Although they enjoy the usual chronicle of misunderstandings and mistakes which inevitably leads to the heroine's belief that the hero intends to harm her, the Smithton readers prefer stories that combine a much-understated version of this continuing antagonism with a picture of a gradually developing love. They most wish to participate in the slow process by which two people become acquainted, explore each other's foibles, wonder about the other's feelings, and eventually 'discover' that they are loved by the other.

(1983)

Notes

11 Table 1 Select Demographic Data: Customers of Dorothy Evans

Category	Responses	Number	%
Age	(42) Less than 25	2	5
	25–44	26	62
	45–54	12	28
	55 and older	2	5
Marital Status	(40) Single	3	8
	Married	33	82
	Widowed/separated	4	10
Parental Status	(40) Children	35	88
	No children	4	12
Age at Marriage	Mean – 19.9		
	Median – 19.2		
Educational Level	(40) High school diploma	21	53
	1–3 years of college	10	25
	College degree	8	20
Work Status	(40) Full or part time	18	45
	Child or home care	17	43
Family Income	(38) $14.999 or below	2	5
	15,000–24,999	18	47
	25,000–49,999	14	37
	50,000 +	4	11
Church Attendance	(40) Once or more a week	15	38
	1–3 times per month	8	20
	A few times per year	9	22
	Not in two (2) years	8	20

Note: (40) indicates the number of responses per questionnaire category. A total of 42 responses per category is the maximum possible. Percent calculations are all rounded to the nearest whole number.

12 Quoted by Barbara Brotman. 'Ah, Romance! Harlequin Has an Affair for Its Readers,' *Chicago Tribune*, 2 June 1980. All other details about the Harlequin audience have been taken from this

article. Similar information was also given by Harlequin to Margaret Jensen, whose dissertation, 'Women and Romantic Fiction: A Case Study of Harlequin Enterprises, Romances, and Readers' (Ph.D. dissertation, McMaster University, Hamilton, Ontario, 1980), is the only other study I know of to attempt an investigation of romance readers. Because Jensen encountered the same problems in trying to assemble a representative sample, she relied on interviews with randomly selected readers at a used bookstore. However, the similarity of her findings to those in my study indicates that the lack of statistical representativeness in the case of real readers does not necessarily preclude applying those readers' attitudes and opinions more generally to a large portion of the audience for romantic fiction.

13 See Brotman. All other details about the Silhouette audience have been drawn from Brotman's article. The similarity of the Smithton readers to other segments of the romance audience is explored in greater depth in my book. However, the only other available study of romance readers which includes some statistics, Peter H. Mann's *The Romantic Novel: A Survey of Reading Habits* (London: Mills & Boon, 1969), indicates that the British audience for such fiction has included in the past more older women as well as younger, unmarried readers than are represented in my sample. However, Mann's survey raises suspicions because it was sponsored by the company that markets the novels and because its findings are represented in such a polemical form. For an analysis of Mann's work, see Jensen, 389–92.

14 Yankelovich, Skelly and White, Inc., *The 1978 Consumer Research Study on Reading and Bookpurchasing*, prepared for the Book Industry Study Group, October 1978, 122. Unfortunately, it is impossible to determine from the Yankelovich study findings what proportion of the group of romance readers consumed a number similar to that read by the Smithton women. Also, because the interviewers distinguished between gothics and romances on the one hand and historicals on the other, the figures are probably not comparable. Indeed, the average of nine may be low since some of the regular 'historical' readers may actually be readers of romances.

15 The Smithton readers are not avid television watchers. Ten of the women, for instance, claimed to watch television less than three hours per week. Fourteen indicated that they watch four to seven hours a week, while eleven claimed eight to fourteen hours of weekly viewing. Only four said they watch an average of fifteen to twenty hours a week, while only one admitted viewing twenty-one or more hours a week. When asked how often they watch soap operas, twenty-four of the Smithton women checked 'never,' five selected 'rarely,' seven chose 'sometimes,' and four checked 'often.' Two refused to answer the question.

16 The Smithton readers' constant emphasis on the educational value of romances was one of the most interesting aspects of our conversations, and chapter 3 of *Reading the Romance* discusses it in depth. Although their citation of the instructional value of romances to a college professor interviewer may well be a form of self-justification, the women also provided ample evidence that they do in fact learn and remember facts about geography, historical customs, and dress from the books they read. Their emphasis on this aspect of their reading, I might add, seems to betoken a profound curiosity and longing to know more about the exciting world beyond their suburban homes.

[. . .]

21 Ten of the twenty books in the sample for the ideal romance were drawn from the Smithton group's answers to requests that they list their three favorite romances and authors. The following books received the highest number of individual citations: *The Flame and the Flower* (1972), *Shanna* (1977), *The Wolf and the Dove* (1974), and *Ashes in the Wind* (1979), all by Kathleen Woodiwiss; *The Proud Breed* (1978) by Celeste DeBlasis; *Moonstruck Madness* (1977) by Laurie McBain; *Visions of the Damned* (1979) by Jacqueline Marten; *Fires of Winter* (1980) by Joanna Lindsey; and *Ride the Thunder* (1980) by Janet Dailey. I also added *Summer of the Dragon* (1979) by Elizabeth Peters because she was heavily cited as a favorite author although none of her titles were specifically singled out. Three more titles were added because they were each voluntarily cited in the oral interviews more than five times. These included *The Black Lyon* (1980) by Jude Deveraux, *The Fulfillment* (1980) by LaVyrie Spencer, and *The Diplomatic Lover* (1971) by Elsie Lee. Because Dot gave very high ratings in her newsletter to the following, these last seven were added: *Green Lady* (1981) by Leigh Ellis; *Dreamtide*

(1981) by Katherine Kent; *Made for Each Other* (1981) by Parris Afton Bonds; *Miss Hungerford's Handsome Hero* (1981) by Noel Vreeland Carter; *The Sea Treasure* (1979) by Elisabeth Barr; *Moonlight Variations* (1981) by Florence Stevenson; and *Nightway* (1981) by Janet Dailey.
Because I did not include a formal query in the questionnaire about particularly bad romances, I drew the twenty titles from oral interviews and from Dot's newsletter reviews. All of the following were orally cited as 'terrible' books, labeled by Dot as part of 'the garbage dump,' or given less than her 'excellent' or 'better' ratings: *Alyx* (1977) by Lolah Burford: *Winter Dreams* by Brenda Trent; *A Second Chance at Love* (1981) by Margaret Ripy; *High Fashion* (1981) by Victoria Kelrich; *Captive Splendors* (1980) by Fern Michaels; *Bride of the Baja* (1980) by Jocelyn Wilde; *The Second Sunrise* (1981) by Francesca Greer; *Adora* (1980) by Bertrice Small; *Desire's Legacy* (1981) by Elizabeth Bright; *The Court of the Flowering Peach* (1981) by Janette Radcliffe; *Savannah* (1981) by Helen Jean Burn; *Passion's Blazing Triumph* (1980) by Melissa Hepburne; *Purity's Passion* (1977) by Janette Seymour; *The Wanton Fires* (1979) by Meriol Trevor; and *Bitter Eden* (1979) by Sharon Salvato. Four novels by Rosemary Rogers were included in the sample because her work was cited repeatedly by the Smithton women as the worst produced within the generic category. The titles were *Sweet Savage Love* (1974), *Dark Fires* (1975), *Wicked Loving Lies* (1976), and *The Insiders* (1979).
22 See Faust, passim.

ALISON LIGHT

Forever England: Femininity, Literature and Conservatism Between the Wars

The question of 'genre' is a useful one to raise, however. In the first place it reminds us of the modernity of many of these critical adjudications; in the second, of the modernity of many of the forms themselves, and finally, that the shaping of bestselling forms of fiction into a recognisable typology, which took significantly new commercial impetus in the period between the wars, altered the conditions for all writers. Once it became possible for readers to ask for a 'detective story' or a 'romance', 'an Edgar Wallace' or 'a Georgette Heyer', and to know what to expect, any writer, and especially those aiming at a broad readership, was up against the question of genre and could expect to be measured in some way against those categories. Moreover, they were categories which frequently confirmed the expectation that particular forms of writing spoke especially to women or to men.

The meanings of romance and of 'romantic' as terms of literary description became more narrowly specialised between the wars, coming to signify only those love-stories, aimed ostensibly at a wholly female readership, which deal primarily with the trials and tribulations of heterosexual desire, and end happily in marriage. At the same time, there is a sense in which, as part of the creation of this 'genre', romance went downmarket as it was boosted by the growth in forms of 'mass entertainment' in the period and its commercialisation made it a bestselling form for a much larger group of readers. Cheaper paperback editions and a plethora of new fiction weeklies for working women and girls (or 'books' as they called them), including *Peg's Paper* (1919), *Red Star* (1929), *Secrets* (1932) and *Oracle* (1933), offered them a staple of 'really grand stories', especially romances, 'that will make you eager to draw up your chair to the fire and have a real good read'.[8] Whereas before the war 'leisure' might be seen as primarily the property of the 'leisured', that is, wealthy, classes, a new market of 'leisure consumers' amongst the working classes was in the process of being created. Those women's magazines wishing to dissociate themselves from this cheap entertainment, laid their stress not on fiction (which was a mere sideline) but on 'services' to readers (the range of 'experts' to deal with readers' problems which the new *Good Housekeeping* introduced, for example), on household management and 'constructive' uses of free time.[9]

Film, and especially Hollywood cinema, together with the spate of film magazines which became a craze in the late 1920s and '30s, made romance even more visible as the major form for a more heterogeneous class of audience.[10] And for many critics of the new forms of mass entertainment, it was romance which provided the model of all that was meretricious about the popular cultural forms of modernity: the creation of a reader or viewer whose individuality is effaced as they abandon themselves to the screen or to the 'tide of cheap, easy fiction', 'waiting passively to be stimulated'.[11] What might strike the reader now examining these criticisms is how much the descriptions echo traditional views of feminine sexuality as a whole, and can be readily collapsed into a vocabulary of distaste for the lower-class woman in particular. It is as though these new audiences and readerships can only be forgiven if they are seen as experiencing a kind of moral and intellectual violation against their will; if they enjoy it, they must be, like the fictions, 'cheap and easy'. The language in which F. R. Leavis condemns the experience of cinema in his attack on mass culture conjures up again a debased, because feminine, position:

> [Films] provide now the main form of recreation in the civilised world; and they involve surrender, under conditions of hypnotic receptivity, to the cheapest of emotional appeals.[12]

Progressive bourgeois women writers, and university women, were in the van of the attack on this lower class of fiction, of which Q. D. Leavis's pioneering study of 1932, *Fiction and the Reading Public*, is only the best-known example. Rebecca West deplored 'Marie Corelli's incurably commonplace mind' (whilst generously admitting that if 'she had a mind like a milliner's apprentice', she was nevertheless 'something more than a milliner's apprentice').[13] In her review of Ethel M. Dell's *Charles Rex*, West advised the critic who was trying to understand the appeal of best sellers to remember that

> whistles can be made sounding certain notes which are clearly audible to dogs and other of the lower animals, though man is incapable of hearing them.[14]

Storm Jameson (an admirer of the Leavises and an English graduate herself) lamented a fiction 'infected with film technique' and feeding 'herd prejudice', in which

Deep calls to deep, and the writer's thought is sucked into the immense vacuum created in women's minds by a civilisation in which they have either nothing much to do or too much (too much machine-minding).[15]

The inclusion of that last sympathetic parenthesis suggests how far 'empty' leisure was no longer the sign of the aristocratic or idle, wealthy woman but of the worker; increasingly a new pressure is felt to differentiate the cultural pleasures of women who might count themselves in the middle classes, not just from the excesses of the class above, but from the reading and viewing of those below.

When Virginia Woolf in 1929 looked forward to the day when women's writing 'would no longer be the dumping ground for the personal emotions',[16] her version of feminism was in keeping with a horror of 'gush' or 'tosh', of the emotionality with which the pre-war bourgeois woman had been burdened, and whose rejection was now de rigueur. Many writers of fiction adopted a tone of irony toward the emotions which would have caused consternation to their mothers. E. M. Delafield, for example, was typical of her flippant generation in wryly asking the rhetorical question of her readers which presupposed their own disavowal of such things:

Imagination, emotionalism, sensationalism, what woman is not the victim of these insidious and fatally unpractical emotions?'

(*The Way Things Are*, p. 336)

The revelation of inner desires and emotional depths was traumatic not just for 'severely political' or public women,[17] however, but for all those aiming at a modern female respectability, different both from the image of bourgeois femininity in the past and from a contemporary sexuality displayed across more proletarian forms. We might speculate that the modern bourgeois woman between the wars retreats from the visibly erotic or from displays of femininity, as the working classes become more publicly sexualised. Certainly, with intensity of feeling and expressivity such thorough bad taste, many writers left romance well alone or found ways of writing from a less 'feminine' position in the culture.[18]

Crime fiction, for example, was one place within the more popular literatures that 'middlebrow' and 'highbrow' could meet, and where both men and women of the middle classes could be united in despising romantic literature. No 'shopgirl, factory girl, skivvy or housewife'[19] was likely to read Christie, but if she did, it was surely with a sense of its superiority to Bertha Ruck, *Peg's Paper* or Mills & Boon, if only because it did not advertise its femininity. Regardless of how many women wrote detective fiction between the wars, it was still considered to be a masculine form, mainly read by men.[20] Neither gushy nor confessional, the crime story laid a stress on those apparently masculine qualities of reason and logic; its modernist emphasis was upon surface, form and contemplation – the antithesis of romance's depth, substance and emotional involvement. It is an opposition maintained with a superb lack of self-consciousness by some critics today:

> the sort of mind that likes well-made plots is not likely to go in for formless romance and affection as well – murder (in fiction, at least) conforms to disciplines that love does not.[21]

Given the inferiority afforded to 'formless romance', writing detective fiction was, and is, for many women writers not only a way of claiming the 'unfeminine' qualities of orderliness and control, but also of attempting to avoid the 'stigma' of gender altogether. As crime fiction included university dons and 'highbrows' amongst its authors, there was always a meagre portion of cultural *cachet* which writers like Dorothy L. Sayers were only too happy to seize upon. Detective stories (so the argument runs), because of their emphasis upon cerebration, if nothing else, take more 'work' than other popular forms of novel, are closer to 'real novels', and thereby occupy a more elevated position amongst the 'pulp' fictions.[22] Dorothy L. Sayers was the first of many crime writers who sought to 'improve' the detective story, turn it from a mere crossword puzzle into a 'proper' novel: romance writers, on the other hand, were usually content to 'entertain'.

(1991)

Notes

8 From *Miracle*, 1938, cited by Cynthia White, *Women's Magazines 1693–1968* (Michael Joseph, 1970), p. 98.

9 White, *Women's Magazines*, discusses some of these shifts. Kirsten Drotner, *More Next Week! English Children and Their Magazines 1751–1945* (Aarhus University, Aarhus, 1985) offers a thoughtful analysis of the growth of new markets for women's fiction; Asa Briggs, *Mass Entertainment* (Griffin, London, 1960) and W. H. Fraser, *The Coming of the Mass Market 1850–1914* (Macmillan, London, 1981) provide an overview and some statistics. There is as yet no critical history of the development of forms of romance fiction in the late nineteenth and early twentieth century, or indeed a study of the reading of working women on a par with Louis James's *Fiction for the Working Man 1830–1850* (Oxford University Press, Oxford, 1963); Rachel Anderson, *The Purple Heart Throbs: The Sub-literature of Love* (Hodder & Stoughton, London, 1974) is a mainly descriptive account of popular writers like Marie Corelli and Elinor Glyn; Mirabel Cecil, *Heroines in Love 1750–1974* (Michael Joseph, London, 1974) and Nicola Beauman, *A Very Great Profession: The Woman's Novel 1914–39* (Virago, London, 1983) are also helpful; Helen Taylor also provides a helpful retrospective on contemporary feminist debates about popular romance in 'Romantic readers', in H. Carr (ed.), *From My Guy to Sci-Fi: Genre and Women's Writing in the Postmodern World* (Pandora, London, 1989).

10 See Billie Melman, *Women and the Popular Imagination: Flappers and Nymphs* (Macmillan, London, 1988); A. Huyssen, 'Mass culture as woman: modernism's Other', in T. Modleski (ed.), *Studies in Entertainment – Critical Approaches to Mass Culture* (Indiana University, Bloomington, 1986). Film-going does not seem to have been seen as respectable until the late 1930s, and then it might be pilloried as 'suburban'.

11 Storm Jameson, 'Novels and novelists' and 'Apology for my life', in *Civil Journey* (Cassell, London, 1939), p. 83 and p. 19.

12 F. R. Leavis, *Mass Civilisation and Minority Culture* (Minority Press, Cambridge, 1930), p. 10. For Leavis the 'industrialisation' of literature is at once a 'levelling down' in class terms and a hybridisation: a kind of anarchy which de-centres all systems of discrimination. This is 'the plight of culture': 'The landmarks have shifted, multiplied and crowded upon one another, the distinctions and dividing lines have blurred away, the boundaries are gone and the arts and literatures of different countries and periods have flowed together' (p. 19). Fears about modernity as a cultural miscegenation -- the threat to 'the Anglo-Saxon race' – surface in the singling out of jazz ('negro' music) by many critics. Storm Jameson, for example, maintains that bestsellers left audiences 'where they found them, confused by the noise of saxophones' (*Civil Journey*, p. 82).

13 'The Tosh Horse', in *The Strange Necessity* (Virago, London, 1987), p. 321.

14 ibid., p. 323.

15 Jameson, *Civil Journey*, pp. 18; 82; 84.

16 'Women and fiction' first appeared in *The Forum*, March 1929 and then in *Granite and Rainbow* (Hogarth Press, London, 1958); reprinted in Michèle Barrett (ed.), *Virginia Woolf: Women and Writing* (Women's Press, London, 1979), p. 51.

17 See Steedman, 'Women's biography and autobiography: forms of history, histories of forms' in Carr, *From My Guy to Sci-Fi*.

18 Even *Eve*, a high-society magazine for women, declared after the war that 'there has been a slump in sentimentalism' and 'misty-eyed emotionality' was dead: Cecil, *Heroines in Love*, p. 151. Of course romance came back, but differently.

19 Beauman, *A Very Great Profession*, p. 183.

20 See, for example, George Orwell's assumptions in 'Bookshop memories' (November 1936), in *The Collected Essays, Journalism and Letters of George Orwell*, vol. 1 (Penguin, Harmondsworth, 1970), p. 275.

21 G. C. Ramsey, *Agatha Christie: Mistress of Mystery* (Collins, London, 1968), p. 52.

22 The same divisions between 'high' and 'low' operate within the genre too: P. D. James, now published in large paperback format by Faber & Faber, appears more literary and more respectable than the other bestselling British 'queen of crime', Ruth Rendell. Their relation is rather like that which obtained between Sayers and Christie.

ANNE CRANNY-FRANCIS

Feminist Fiction: Feminist Uses of Generic Fiction

So why the feminist incursion into the detective fiction genre? Why have feminist writers, that is, writers working within a feminist framework, with a feminist ideology, textually constructing a feminist reading position for their readers, chosen to write detective fiction? The answer to this question is partly answered at the conclusion of Marcia Muller's story 'The Broken Men'. Her detective, Sharon McCone has solved the mystery surrounding the death of a clown and the story ends with her musing on the social function of clowning:

> What was it, I thought, that John had said to me about clowns when we were playing gin in the dressing room at the pavilion? Something to the effect that they were all funny but, more important, that they all made people take a look at their own foibles. John Tilby and Elliot Larson – in a sense both broken men like Gary Fitzgerald had been – knew more about those foibles than most people. Maybe there was a way they could continue to turn that sad knowledge into laughter.

(Muller, ['The Broken Men' in Greenburg and Prozini, eds, *Academy Mystery Novellas Volume 1*, Chicago] 1985, p. 221)

Muller concludes her text with the self-referentiality characteristic of the feminist generic texts analysed in previous chapters. Like them, detective fiction can be a means of examining contemporary social issues, including the nature of contemporary gender ideologies. Detective fiction may make a society look at its own foibles, at the ideological discourses which structure social practices and individual interactions, the constructions of social institutions and individual subjectivity. If detective fiction truly detects, it might offer social criticism and self-knowledge along with its entertainment – just like the carnivalesque clowns of Muller's story.

For feminist writers this self-knowledge must include an awareness of the way that the individual subject is constructed through the negotiation of a number of ideologies, including race and class as well as gender. If the detective novel is to do more than extend the idealist construction of women as Woman, it must engage with women's negotiation of a matrix of ideological discourses and so reveal the differences between women, as well as their similarities. Both *Murder in the English Department* [London, The Women's Press, 1982] and *Murder in the Collective* [London, The Women's Press, 1987] address this complex task. In Miner's novel the influence of class background on the individual is considered in some depth. The detective, Nan Weaver renegotiates her relationship with her own working-class background in the course of the novel. It is also interesting that this book has been criticized for its representation of class in that it does not adopt an unequivocal pro-working-class line. In fact, Miner achieves a more complex and interesting, and realistic, end; to have a woman who has fled her working-class background reconsider that decision, not because of her own actions, but because she recognizes the dignity and autonomy of a working-class woman (her sister) who has successfully negotiated the compromises attendant on her acceptance of that class status. At the party to celebrate Adams's release she is the most uncomfortable participant, the working-class emigre who watches from the outside as working-class and middle-class individuals interact on the basis of mutual respect. When Weaver drives off into the sunset at the conclusion of the novel, unsure of her future, Miner signifies that her narrative is not resolved; the negotiation continues. The resolution of this novel cannot be constructed in terms of a simple acceptance of bourgeois individualism, nor of an essentially bourgeois representation of working-class life (itself the construction of working-class emigres). The reading position of Miner's novel produces a complex understanding of both the similarities between women, the product of their construction by (patriarchal) gender ideology, and of their differences which are a function of their individual negotiation of (bourgeois) class ideology. In *Murder in the Collective* Wilson achieves a similar complexity, with the negotiation of (white supremacist) race ideology seen as a crucial difference between the women represented in the novel.

Many of the female detective novels written in the hard-boiled format do not address issues of difference. Their achievement is to develop a radical female characterization, the competent, caring, professional woman, one who breaks the virgin/whore dichotomy of traditional female characterization. The narrative of bourgeois individualism is left entirely unchallenged in the text, along with its assumptions about race. Certainly the traditional male-oriented detective narrative stands as a discursive referent for these texts, but it inflects similarly the ideologies of race and class. In other words, it does seem that a distinction must be made between those texts which address only gender ideology and so may be termed critical and provisionally radical, and those which cross-reference the negotiation of gender ideology with the ideologies of race and class and so challenge the idealist conceptualization of women (as Woman, without race, without class) and so may be termed radical or subversive. The hard-boiled revisions tend to fall into the first category; the amateur detective revisions into the second. So perhaps it is not so surprising to find that books in the first category are published by a variety of mainstream publishers, whilst those in the second category line up on the bookshelf in the familiar striped livery of the Women's Press.

[. . .]

In summary, then, this study of feminist revisions of generic fiction points to a series of issues which must be addressed when evaluating such fiction:

1 Genre fiction is encoded with ideological discourses which articulate the socio-historical formation in which the particular text is written.

2 These discourses are coded into the conventions of the genre.

3 A historical study of the development of the genre enables the critic to identify the discourses coded into particular conventions, and into the (socio-historically determined) modifications of conventions.

4 Feminist writers are using generic fiction both to describe or reveal (sometimes in the representational or story level of the text, sometimes in the dialogue which constitutes the feminist reading position of the text) the naturalization of patriarchal subject positions and causal sequences or narratives, and to explore the use of fiction as ideological practice.

5 The major strategy employed by feminist writers is the construction within the text of a feminist reading position; that is, a position at which the contradictions within the text are explained if the reader sees them from the perspective of a feminist discourse.

6 Construction of this reading position may involve changing to some extent the conventions of the genre, reworking them to express a changed socio-historical (discursive) formation; and it may involve voicing a patriarchal discourse which is then contextualized or placed in dialogue with other discourses.

7 In constructing this reading position, however, feminist writers have to be constantly aware that conservative (patriarchal) discourses are coded into generic conventions and that these discourses may subvert the feminist discourse and reading position they are constructing in the text.

8 In some woman-centred texts writers (who may or may not be feminist) concentrate their attention on the representational or story level of the text; that is, they tell stories about the oppression of women in which women are the major characters, but they pay little attention to other semiotic practices of their texts. The result is that these texts can still position readers in terms of a patriarchal discourse, even if oppositional voices are sometimes heard.

9 Other feminist writers work comprehensively with the semiotic practices of the text to construct a reading position at which the discourses operating in the text, coded into narrative(s) and generic conventions, are aligned by a feminist discourse to be mutually explicable.

10 Feminist writers working at this comprehensive level have also to be aware that texts are often constructed from not only more than one narrative, but also more than one genre: horror within science fiction as in *Alien* and *The Word for World is Forest*, romance within utopian fiction as in *Looking Backward* and *Woman on the Edge of Time*, fantasy within detective fiction as in the earliest stories of Edgar Allan Poe. In this case the writer must be aware of the dialogic nature of the text, and take account of the encoded discourses of all these textual conventions, as well as the semiotic significance of the particular generic mix in constructing a feminist reading position. I have not dealt with the mixing of genres at any length in this study since it demands a full-length analysis in its own right (it is basically a complication of the dialogic model of semiotic practice used in my analysis of separate genres). As Derrida argues, one can never not mix genres; texts almost inevitably carry traces of other genres, in the very process defining themselves as primarily texts not of that trace genre(s) (Derrida, ['The Law of Genre', *Glyph* 7] 1980). But the traces must be taken into account, since they too encode discourses of various kinds.

(1990)

4

Towards Definitions of Feminist Writing

INTRODUCTION

Defining Feminist Imaginative Writing

How would a reader recognize an example of feminist imaginative writing? Are there certain definable characteristics that mark 'x' as a feminist and 'y' as a non-feminist text? Leaving aside for a moment all the problems around the word 'tradition', can we say that a tradition of women's writing is one of *feminist* writing? Or if this seems too all-embracing a definition, can we at least establish that the writing of declared feminists must be feminist? In short, is authorial intention everything? On the other hand, does the feminism lie in interpretation; could feminists agree on a definitive list of books that are more open than others to a feminist reading? Perhaps the nature of the readership is the key. Are the women-centred novels Rosalind Coward mentions to be categorized as 'feminist' because lots of feminists read them? Or can the problem ultimately resolve itself as one of content? Does the placing of women's experience, ideas, visions, achievements at the centre of a piece of writing, or, as in Michèle Barrett's example, an art exhibition, make that work feminist?

The extracts from Coward and Barrett prove that these problems are not open to easy solutions. Both agree that we cannot take 'women's' writing to be a synonym for 'feminist' writing: feminism is 'an alignment of political interests' (Barrett), which some women writers may adopt and others not. But Coward claims further that: 'Feminism can never be the product of the identity of women's experiences and interests – there is no such unity. While Barrett agrees that an emphasis on female experience does not *necessarily* make the work feminist, she is uneasy about Coward's sweeping rejection: 'it is not possible to conceive of a feminist art that could be detached from a shared experience of oppression.'

Equally, an examination of authorial intention raises more questions than answers. Books conceived with the most laudable political motives can prove, on reading, to be lame and unconvincing. Conversely, books from authors with no particular sympathy for feminism are widely read by feminists and prove a rich vein for feminist criticism; much of Doris Lessing's work would illustrate this point. Readers too are unreliable guides. Coward makes clear that women-centred novels do not become feminist simply because feminists read them. On the other hand, Barrett believes that it was precisely the audience's 'reading' of *The Dinner Party* that made the event, rather than the specific work, feminist: 'In this sense, although I disputed the claims of *The Dinner Party* to be an *intrinsically* feminist work I would not dispute that it is a feminist event. But this is because its meaning has been constructed, collectively, as such.'[1]

The problems of definition are tangibly illustrated in the difficulties which face feminist and left-wing book shops in arranging their stock. Should they adopt a separatist policy and have a special section for women's writing? Should there be sub-sections for the work of lesbians and 'women of colour'? Are all the books in a women's section feminist? Are the excluded books by male authors all closed to a feminist interpretation? The apparently innocuous task of putting books on shelves is curiously transformed into a political dilemma. And this is but one visible example from a production process – financing, publishing, marketing, distribution – that is charged with contradictions. Feminists weigh the conflicting appeals of an all-women minority press, politically committed but publishing on a very small scale, and a mainstream company for which feminism is ultimately a marketable commodity but which has a wide distribution network; they ponder the gap between the desire for radical change and the necessary involvement of feminist publishing houses in capitalism; they query the intensive, populist and – at times – sensationalist marketing of some women's writing: is this a sign of being incorporated or a sign of a widening feminist interest?[2]

Defining Feminist Literary Criticism

A similar set of questions has been put concerning feminist literary criticism. What makes it distinctive from other forms of criticism? How should it relate to non-feminist criticism or to the practice of imaginative writing? Should feminist critics have a common political position and critical method? Are there critical methods which assist feminist politics and others which would hinder? Deborah McDowell's introductory paragraph again shows the impossibility of precise definition though, strangely, she does not seem to see this looseness of terminology as generating any theoretical problems.[3]

Prescriptive Criticism   Cheri Register's response, to establish a 'prescriptive' feminist critics, has been a common one, though not all have been as programmatic. Register starts from a position with which no feminist would disagree. She recognizes the political nature of writing; she wants to link feminist criticism with the women's movement; and she is equally wary of 'ivory tower academism' and political ranting. There is an energy and enthusiasm in the writing, an eagerness to raise issues and a healthy disregard for 'objective' judgements. But what she proposes is a highly dogmatic form of criticism, couched in authoritarian language – we keep being told what we should do, what is correct, or what is impermissible – and she offers a reductive analysis of the relationship between writing and politics. 'To earn feminist approval, literature must perform one or more of the following functions', illustrates the approach. What is interesting about Register's essay is that she is tentatively aware of some of the dangers in what she advocates and frequently qualifies her demands, and yet is unable finally to resolve the contradictions inherent in her argument. For example, she asserts that feminist writing should 'express female experience authentically', but also that 'authors should not feel obligated to offer an exact representation of their own lives'; she quotes, approvingly, Wendy Martin's suggestion that literature should provide role-models who are 'self-actualizing, whose identities are not dependent on men', but then stresses that 'characters should not be idealized beyond plausibility'; she suggests that 'concrete political issues' have a place in 'feminist-approved literature', but immediately adds that that place 'must be consistent with the demands for authenticity and subjectivity . . .'.

These brief quotations indicate that a crucial concept in prescriptive criticism is the belief in 'authenticity' and in the revelation of a 'true' female identity. Indeed, a whole series of terms – 'experience', 'truth', 'authentic', 'identity', 'realistic' – operates as either connecting or interchangeable buzz-words in the debate. The author herself must be 'authentic', telling the entire and unvarnished truth about her experiences and perceptions. Register quotes Erica Jong's condemnation of a poet who 'has not really looked into herself and told it true'. Secondly, the text should express a 'representative' female experience which we, the readers, can accept as an 'authentic reflection' of our lives. And each individual woman should be struggling to find her own 'true' identity, for which task strong, independent female characters may provide inspiring role-models. The intimation is that, hitherto, we have been presented with 'false' realities, 'false' images, 'unrepresentative' models, and that these, like dead skins, should be shed to find the 'true' reality and the 'authentic' selves at the core of our beings.

The reductive nature of prescriptive criticism lies partly in its seeing literature as 'a straight reflection of ideology' with the feminist writer simply replacing 'an incorrect patriarchal reading with one "more" correct and equally prescriptive' (Light). Writers critical of prescriptive criticism contend that there is no 'true' reality waiting to be revealed and, thus, fiction cannot offer that to the reader. Alison Light looks to texts not for coherence but for the contradictions and ambiguities that allow us a 'plurality of readings'.[4] Nor is there a simple and direct channel of communication from author to text to reader. Even if the authorial intention was to present a feminist message, there is no guarantee that the reader would receive the text in that way.

Furthermore, as Cora Kaplan and Elizabeth Wilson argue, the search for a hidden but autonomous and unified identity is alluring and yet futile. They see identity as unresolved and inconsistent, what Kaplan calls 'the inherently unstable and split character of all human subjectivity'. Thus to look, in either life or literature, for strong women as role-models is, according to this critique, unsatisfactory. The image of the strong woman is too simple, too resolved and one-dimensional; it 'allows for no moment of weakness, and cannot reflect the diversity and complexity of our desires' (Wilson). Instead of being inspired by such images women can feel inadequate in comparison. In these triumphant, achieving, heroic characterizations, where is there any place for all my failings, and impure motives. Whereas critics such as McDowell and Register understandably look for firm foundations in trying to establish the basic premises of feminist and Black feminist criticism, others find a rejection of the definitive opens their thinking to the ambiguities of lived experience.

Playful Pluralism At the opposite extreme to prescriptive criticism is Annette Kolodny's 'playful pluralism'. Concerned about both reductive readings and the wholesale rejection of non-feminist criticism, Kolodny suggests that feminist criticism should be viewed as *one* reading among many, taking part in an 'ongoing dialogue of competing potential possibilities'. She sees feminist criticism as useful 'in recognizing the particular achievements of woman-as-author' and 'in conscientiously decoding woman-as-sign'. This pluralism will not lead to chaos, Kolodny argues, but will prevent critics from claiming that their work is 'either exhaustive or definitive'. And it will not simply reproduce the bourgeois appeal to pluralism because this version will stress, rather than deny, 'the power of ideology'. However, Toril Moi worries whether Kolodny's brand of feminist criticism is not 'throwing the baby out with the bathwater'. If we accept an endless plurality of readings will we, in so doing, endorse the existence of 'the most "masculinist" of criticism'? For instance, would Kolodny look upon my fourth-form English language text book, which explained rhythm as 'the pulsating sounds that incite natives to kill', as simply an aspect of the pluarity of interpretation? Moi is not looking for a prescriptive criticism, but she does see the need for a more analytical and evaluative approach than the one Kolodny suggests, and that means closely examining critical theory to ensure that the methods and tools we use genuinely aid the development of a feminist politics.

Gynocriticism Elaine Showalter has looked at critical theory and seen in it, even in feminist literary theory, an alarming attachment to the 'male theoretician' and to 'male texts and films'. The names she finds suspect – Althusser, Barthes, Macherey and Lacan – are, presumably, the very ones Cora Kaplan has found most useful when she writes of her interest in 'Marxist and feminist appropriations of psychoanalytic and structuralist theories'. The contrasting responses clearly expose the problematic relationship of feminist literary criticism to other critical theories. Are the non-feminist theories all to be rejected as irrevocably androcentric and male-dominated or can they be transformed and used for the benefit of feminism? Or, to make a further distinction, can we say that *some* male-centred theories are useful to feminism while others are not? Showalter sees no place for the adaptation of 'male models and theories' or, indeed, for 'the angry or loving fixation on male literature'. She proposes instead 'gynocriticism' which will 'construct a female framework for the analysis of women's literature' and 'develop new models based on the study of female experience'. Showalter's essay was first published in 1979. By the mid eighties not only was Showalter herself engaging in critical debate with male theorists but all the concepts on which she had built her definition of gynocriticism had themselves come into dispute.[5]

Gynesis In opposition to Showalter's 'gynocriticism' Alice Jardine has coined the word 'gynesis'.[6] Gynesis is but one manifestation from a series of critical practices – linguistic, postmodernist, psychoanalytic – that has rendered increasingly impossible the act of definition. As meanings have become unstable and proliferating, any definition becomes not only elusive but impermissible if one sees definition as linked to control. Gynocriticism will happily speak of female experience, culture and history – terms which gynesis finds questionable. The concepts which prescriptive criticism employs as self-evidently meaningful would be, for Jardine, the prompting for endless, deconstructive debates. Gynocriticism is concerned with women as real, historical persons, assigned by patriarchy to a female subculture, a place of both exclusion and autonomy. Gynesis does not see women's space as an empirically proven place within culture (the harem, for example), or within history (the female tradition, for instance); rather it discovers the 'feminine' or 'woman' as a gap, an absence, a 'nonknowledge' that has escaped the 'master narratives'. Yet both positions would agree that whoever, whatever this 'woman' is, she has the power to trouble and destabilize the dominant order.

Feminism itself has been profoundly unsettled by postmodernist thought. The meaning of feminism and feminist writing is uncertain if the project of feminist Enlightenment is no longer valid, if history as either progress or struggle no longer exists, if terms like 'woman' and 'gender' carry no collective understanding. Much of the contemporary work on feminism and postmodernism seems trapped in a battle of antitheses. Do we see 'woman' as sign or historical figure? Mary Poovey, for instance, debates 'woman' as 'a position within a dominant, binary symbolic order' but also discusses 'concrete historical women'. Similarly, Julia Kristeva's dismissal of 'being a woman' as 'absurd and obscurantist' is qualified by the word 'almost'. Here, Kristeva recognizes the political struggles in which women, identified *as women*, are necessarily still involved. Does feminism operate within the parameters of the hegemonic or does it hold a transformative potential? Kristeva talks of this issue in terms of uniting 'negativity' with the 'ethical penchant in the women's struggle'. Can women function as a group or is this identity riven by unbridgeable difference? Both extracts from Poovey and Nancy Fraser and Linda J. Nicholson stress the false collectivity of the term 'women' which so often in practice excludes particular groups of women. Thus Fraser and Nicholson want to replace 'unitary notions of woman and feminine gender identity with plural and complexly constructed conceptions of social identity'. What is the productive political practice for postmodern feminism? If there are no oppositional blocks, then Fraser and Nicholson suggest a 'patchwork of overlapping alliances'.

Negotiating the Minefield

At the same time as I summarize the material in terms of these antitheses, I am thinking of Rachel Bowlby's warning about 'simple, homologous opposi- tions'. Using Moi's *Sexual/Textual Politics* and Jardine's *Gynesis: Configura- tions of Woman and Modernity*, Bowlby illustrates how even authors who are highly conscious of both theory and politics can have theoretical and political blind-spots. Moi and Jardine, Bowlby believes, construct their own texts in the very binary hierarchies they deprecate: French and American criticism emerge as separately defined modes, the French evidently superior to the American. As rapidly as we deconstruct our premises, we reconstruct more. There never is a point where all is laid bare, luminously transparent to both author and reader.

This dense network of charge and counter-charge, positionings and reposi- tionings, alliances and oppositions operates within feminist criticism and between feminism and other critical discourses. Feminists actively involved in critical theory do not look upon theorizing as essentially 'male'. Indeed, they see certain male-dominated theories as malleable and helpful to feminism. To the Showalter of gynocriticism this synthesizing process is 'a revisionism which becomes a kind of homage'.[7] While Marxist-feminists or feminists working in the Lacanian tradition see themselves as engaged in a principled critical dialogue with the male theoreticians, Showalter views their work as, at times, dangerously complicit and insufficiently women-centred. In their turn, Marxist, psychoanalytical and post-structuralist feminists have com- plained that a lack of theoretical sophistication in some feminist criticism has, unwittingly, drawn feminism into theoretical positions that do no service to the feminist cause. Register's prescriptive criticism, for instance, reads in many ways like a feminist equivalent to socialist realism. Instead of writing placing itself at the service of the workers' revolution, it is now at the service of feminist liberation; instead of developing class solidarity, writing now promotes sisterhood; instead of introducing working-class characters, writing should 'serve as a forum for women'. In both cases, inspirational role-models and writing with the specific intention of raising consciousness are stressed. For Cora Kaplan and Elizabeth Wilson it is the continuing influence in feminist criticism of Romantic aesthetic theory that is questionable. Kaplan feels that the Romantic view of writers as 'the conscious, constant and triumphant sources of the meanings they produce' is still prevalent in feminism; Wilson views the 'longing for utopias and reconstructed selves' as a sign of feminism's failure to analyse 'political romanticism'. Finally, Moi takes issue with what she sees as Showalter's uncritical acceptance of humanism and empiricism.[8] Showalter's rejection of 'male' theory is, ultimately, a rejection of only some 'male' theories and an unperceived acquiescence with others; the charge of complicity is returned.

The two final extracts from Barbara Christian and bell hooks link to issues of race the debates of feminism and theory. Some of the points made by Christian indicate the continuing currency of earlier responses – the concern about prescriptiveness, the wish to prioritize Black women's imaginative writing, the political import of theory as a controlling and defining mechanism. Christian does not actually name the particular critical theories to which she objects, though it seems that the pseudo-scientism of structuralism is one target. hooks explicitly is discussing postmodernism and here takes issue with Fraser and Nicholson's conviction that postmodernism provides a methodology open to subordinated groups: indeed, Fraser and Nicholson actually name hooks as one of their examples.[9] There may be a rhetoric of 'Otherness', hooks believes, but that rhetoric is rarely made concrete by actually recognizing 'a critical black presence in the culture and in most scholarship and writing on postmodernism'. Invisible to whites, resisted by Blacks, where is the Black woman interested in theory to find her audience? Fraser and Nicholson's image of 'a tapestry composed of threads of many different hues' – it sounds somewhat like Joseph's amazing techni-colour dream coat and a little like Kolodny's 'playful pluralism' – is, perhaps, an *aspiration* to set aside Christian and hook's more grounded perception of an academic élite of, largely, male, white theorists for whom theory signifies power, status and an institutional base.

Notes

1 Michèle Barrett, 'Feminism and the Definition of Cultural Politics' in *Feminism, Culture and Politics*, eds Rosalind Brunt and Caroline Rowan (London, Lawrence and Wishart, 1982), p. 57.

2 Ch. 2 contains further references on aspects of production.

3 'What is feminist literary criticism?' is precisely the question Toril Moi addresses in her essay 'Feminist Literary Criticism', in *Modern Literary Theory: A Comparative Introduction*, eds Ann Jefferson and David Robey (London, Batsford, 1987). In a very different way the question is answered by Adrienne Rich in 'Toward a More Feminist Criticism', *Blood, Bread, and Poetry: Selected Prose 1979–1985* (London, Virago, 1986). The extract from Chris Weedon in ch. 1 is also relevant.

4 An earlier and more extensive exploration of this idea in relation to Kate Millett's work, as Light indicates, is to be found in Cora Kaplan, 'Radical Feminism and Literature: Rethinking Millett's *Sexual Politics*', now anthologized in Kaplan's collection of essays *Sea Changes: Essays on Culture and Feminism* (London, Verso, 1986). There are some indications that a rather more sympathetic

reassessment of Millet's work is underway. See Maggie Humm, *Feminist Criticism: Women as Contemporary Critics* (Brighton, Harvester Wheatsheaf, 1986), and *A Reader's Guide to Contemporary Feminist Literary Criticism* (London, Harvester Wheatsheaf, 1994); Anne Jones, 'Feminism I: Sexual Politics', in *Literary Theory at Work: Three Texts* ed. Douglas Tallack, (London, Batsford, 1987); Catherine Belsey and Jane Moore, 'Introduction to the Story so Far', *The Feminist Reader: Essays in Gender and the Politics of Literary Criticism* (London, Macmillan, 1989).

5 See Showalter's 'Critical Cross-Dressing; Male Feminists and the Woman of the Year', in Alice Jardine and Paul Smith (eds), *Men in Feminism* (New York and London, Methuen, 1987).

6 Showalter, in turn, responds to 'gynesis' in 'Women's Time, Women's Space: Writing the History of Feminist Criticism', in Shari Benstock (ed.), *Feminist Issues in Literary Scholarship* (Bloomington and Indianapolis, Indiana University Press, 1987). See also Toril Moi's comments on Jardine in 'Feminism and Postmodernism: Recent Feminist Criticism in the United States' in Terry Lovell (ed.) *British Feminist Thought: A Reader* (Oxford, Blackwell, 1990).

7 Elaine Showalter, 'Feminist Criticism in the Wilderness', in *The New Feminist Criticism: Essays on Women, Literature and Theory* (London, Virago, 1986), p. 247.

8 For another clear critique of feminism's sympathy with humanism see Peggy Kamuf, 'Replacing Feminist Criticism', Mary Eagleton (ed.), *Feminist Literary Criticism* (London, Longman, 1991).

9 Ch. 6 provides a fuller consideration of postmoderninst ideas. The following offer good introductions to post-structuralist and postmodernist thought: Chris Weedon, *Feminist Practice and Poststructuralist Theory* (Oxford, Basil Blackwell, 1987); special issues of *Feminist Studies*, vol. 14, no. 1 (Spring 1988); Patricia Waugh, *Feminist Fictions: Revisiting the Postmodern* (London and New York, Routledge, 1989): Patricia Waugh (ed.), *A Reader in Postmodernism* (London, Edward Arnold, 1992).

ROSALIND COWARD

' *"This Novel Changes Lives": Are Women's Novels Feminist*
Novels? A Response to Rebecca O'Rourke's Article
"Summer Reading" '
Feminist Review

Women-centred Writing

It is just not possible to say that women-centred writings have any necessary relationship to feminism. Women-centred novels are by no means a new phenomenon. The Mills and Boon romantic novels are written by, read by, marketed for and are all about women. Yet nothing could be further from the aims of feminism than these fantasies based on the sexual, racial and class submission which so frequently characterise these novels. The plots and elements of these novels are frequently so predictable that cynics have suggested that Mills and Boon's treasured authors might well be computers. Yet the extraordinary rigidity of the formula of the novels, where the heroine invariably finds material success through sexual submission and marriage, does not prevent these publishers having a larger sales than Pan and Penguin. The average print run for each novel is 115,000. While Mills and Boon may have a highly individual market, their formulae are not so radically different from romance fiction in general. Such immensely popular writers as Mary Stewart and Georgette Heyer invariably have the experience of the heroine at the centre, and concentrate on the vagaries of her emotions as the principal substance of the novel. In the cinema, the equivalent of the romantic novel is melodrama, and melodrama is often promoted as 'women's pictures', suggesting that they are directed towards women as well as being about women. Indeed it would not be stretching credibility too far to suggest that the consciousness of the individual heroine has been a principal narrative device of the English novel in the last century, a fact which may well have contributed to the relative presence of women writers in this field.

While this all shows how misguided it would be to mark a book of interest to feminism because of the centrality it attributes to women's experiences, it could be argued that what we loosely call feminist novels are qualitatively different. But to make such a claim it would be necessary to specify in what way 'women-centred' writing, allying itself with feminist politics, did mark itself out as different. Some of the so-called feminist novels like *The Women's Room* and *A Piece of the Night* do make explicit their allegiance to the women's liberation movement. However, many of the others in roughly the same genre do not. *Fear of Flying, Kinflicks* and *Loose Change* all fall into this category.

Yet the encounter with the milieu and aspirations of feminism often forms a central element in the narrative of these novels. And, the practice of consciousness raising – the reconstruction of personal histories within a group of women – sometimes forms the structure of the novel. Then there is a further category. Here we find novels like Kate Millett's *Sita* whose feminist commitment is guaranteed not so much by the content of the book as by the other theoretical and political writings of the author. And finally there is a whole host of novels which are adopted as honorary 'feminist novels', taking in such different writers as Doris Lessing, Fay Weldon and Alison Lurie. Their writings deal not so much with the milieu of contemporary feminism as with charting the experience of women's oppression.

Now, there is a certain convention within all these novels which does clearly mark them off from the romance genre for example. One striking feature is the frequency with which we meet with the quasi-autobiographical structure. *The Women's Room, Fear of Flying, Kinflicks, Sita* all foreground the writer, struggling to turn her experience into literature, even if this figure loiters in the background in god-like omnipotence as in *The Women's Room*. Moreover the 'voice' of the central protagonist, if not presenting itself directly as the author's voice, frequently offers itself as 'representative' of women in general, firstly claiming sexual experience as a vital terrain of all women's experience, sometimes also making generalities as to the oppressive nature of that experience. The distinctiveness of the genre has attracted attention; a Sunday Times colour supplement heading shows one response to the self-consciously 'representative' nature of these novels:

> Liberating the Libido. Getting sex straight was an essential first step along the noisy road to liberation; writing about it could be the next leap forward. Books by women surveying sex, and novels by women whose heroines savour sex are selling like hotdogs in America beating men into second place and turning the authoresses into millionairesses at the drop of a hard sell dust jacket.

I have raised this here in order to show that we do have a recognizable group of novels whose roots are, in a variety of ways, in the women's liberation movement but that their relation to feminism is not the necessary outcome of taking women's experience as central. But other questions arise in relation to this statement, questions as to whether the 'representativeness' which these novels claim is simply a reflection of 'feminist consciousness', or a propaganda device towards such a consciousness, or whether we have to be more cautious in analysing their structure and effects.

The Commercial Success of the Novels that Change Lives

Rebecca seems to imply that the widespread success of these novels can be attributed to a widespread diffusion of 'feminist consciousness'. In fact the disparity between the print runs of these novels and political texts gives rise to the exactly opposite suspicion in more cynical minds. Perhaps the kind of writing involved in *Kinflicks* or *The Women's Room* corresponds more closely to the structures of popular fiction rather than satisfying the incipient feminism of the population. The fact is that the space occupied by these novels is not so radically different from the conventional structures which make up the 'novelistic'. In other words that space of themes, modes of writing, hierarchies of appropriate statements which constitute these 'feminist novels' is not so utterly unlike those of popular fiction in general. We can isolate several aspects of this correspondence.

A dominant element in contemporary fiction has been that of the 'confessional' novel – the structuring of the novel, and the significant events of the narrative, around the voice of a principal protagonist describing her/his life. Novels like J. D. Salinger's *Catcher in the Rye* or *Lucky Jim* by Kingsley Amis bear an exceptionally strong resemblance to feminist works such as Alice Monroe's *Lives of Girls and Women* in this respect. But the similarity does not end here. For this structure has increasingly been characterized by the absolute centrality given to the experience of adolescence and young adulthood. In particular the experiences of this period have come to be almost synonymous with sexual experience. In drawing attention to the reception of feminist writers by the bourgeois press, I have already hinted how this preoccupation with the confession of sexual experience is one of the most characteristic features of contemporary feminist writings. Like the confessional novel in general, the novels by feminists also present the experience of sexuality as the significant experience of the novel. Whereas in romantic fiction (and indeed quite often in 'the classics') it was the events leading to marriage, or events disrupting love, which occupied the position of significant events, increasingly sexual experience is becoming sufficient.

Certain points can be made about the confessional form of these novels and their preoccupation with sexuality. An obvious point is that speaking about sexuality, and a preoccupation with sexuality, is not in and of itself progressive. Feminists have been involved for too long now in the analysis of images and ideologies to be conned into thinking that accounts of sexuality are progressive just because they take women's sexuality as their central concern. Criticism of pornography, which frequently highlights the sexual experiences of women, is just one example of representations of sexuality which feminists have actually contested.

It has been suggested that the centrality which the confession of sexuality has assumed and which is now an integral part of our culture does not in fact represent a radical break with the past. Michel Foucault (1978) for example has suggested that it represents a continuation of certain practices of dealing with sexuality which have been part of western culture for several centuries. He argues that sexuality has never been 'repressed' as such but has been the object of a variety of discourses for several centuries. In the past these discourses were frequently directed towards a control or negation of certain sexual practices, as with the medical and educational discourses of the Victorian period: they nevertheless had sexuality as their object. In Catholic countries, he suggests that the practice of the church confessional was taken over into scientific and social discourses, where once again sexuality became an object to be interrogated, spoken about, controlled. Again and again however, whatever the explicit aim of the discourses, sexuality was taken to be the element which revealed the 'true' and 'essential' nature of people. Foucault sees within this concern with sexuality the workings of power; the identity of the subject is found through discourses which multiply areas of pleasure and attention only to control, classify, subject. To deny a sudden rupture in the history of sexuality – from repression to liberation – does not mean that we have to go along with Foucault in suggesting that there have not been radical changes in the representations of sexuality themselves. For women, discourses on sexuality have changed importantly. The equation of female sexuality with the illicit and disgusting is no longer a dominant representation, and the possibilities of sexual enjoyment no longer focussed on motherhood, are changes for which feminism has fought.

Nevertheless these ideas are useful in this context. They indicate how the centrality which sexuality has assumed in the novel, either coyly in romantic preoccupations or explicitly in the confession of sexual experiences, has definite correspondences with other social practices. Within the novel, the 'confession' has appeared, structured by traditions, specific to the novel. In particular it has been influenced by the importance of narrative, which organizes a series of events or experiences as significant and progressing towards a meaningful conclusion. This space of time, or narrative, is one in which the central character or characters undergo an experience or series of experiences which radically affect their lives or transform their attitudes. The effect of this structure is to create a distinct ideology of knowledge and indeed life – that experience brings knowledge and possibly wisdom. But where women have been, and are, the central focus of the novel, a variation occurs. That variation is that the only space where knowledge or understanding for women is produced is across sexual experience – love, marriage, divorce or just sex. In romance for example, the significant space is that of encounter, love, (possibly) a hindrance and marriage; understanding is finding the proper mate. It is rare to find a novel such as Jane Austen's *Emma* where the sentimental lesson is combined with an intellectual lesson, that of discretion. An examination of novelistic practices – customs of the single central character, 'realistic' writing, the delineation of time as progressive and significant – would require a lengthy article but it is sufficient to bring them forward here to indicate that women centred novels are *not* the product of a feminist audience. Nor can we say that the structures of the realist novel are neutral and that they can just be filled with a feminist content. Indeed, it could be argued that the emergence of this particular form of 'women's writing' with its emphasis on sexual experience as the source of significant experience, might have the effect of confirming women as bearers of sentiment, experience and romance (albeit disillusioned).

It is quite clear that there are compelling similarities between 'novels that change lives' and contemporary fictional conventions, which should warn us against any simple designation of these novels as feminist. This does not mean that we cannot say anything about the emergence of this group of novels in their specificity, nor does it mean that there is nothing progressive about these novels. First of all, it is clear that female sexuality (as distinct from just female emotions) is becoming more and more an object to be interrogated, in a variety of social practices – film, sociological, psychological and 'sexological' studies. The novel's own history – its confessional form, and its highlighting of sexual events as significant time – make it particularly responsive to this preoccupation. And this preoccupation undoubtedly at a certain level represents a response to a problem: what is female sexual pleasure? Thus, though feminist writing may well be compromised by its uncritical use of the conventional forms of the novel, it is also an important presence in a popular form of fiction.

But it would also be limited to suggest that all the novels which we loosely designate feminist never escape beyond defining women entirely by their sexuality. Occasionally some go beyond the limits of the conventional novelistic forms and preoccupations. Doris Lessing and Fay Weldon, for example, both occasionally disrupt the conventions of the central narrative voice or character, and their writings suddenly become a myriad of historical, social and sexual concerns which do not 'belong' to an individual subjectivity. Where sexuality is treated as political this is occasionally the outcome and is one of the most interesting aspects of novels like these.

It is by paying attention to practices of writing, conventions of genre and their relation to other forms of writing, that we can differentiate between novels and assess their political effects. And it is only in conjunction with an analysis of the conventions internal to the text that we can understand marketing strategies.

Publishing Practices and Women-centred Novels

Rebecca O'Rourke suggests that commercial publishers are cashing in on feminism. I have already suggested that we cannot designate many of the novels she discusses as feminist in any simple sense. And a cursory glance at the marketing of these 'women-centred' novels by commercial publishers confirms my view that they are often directed towards the popular fiction market. Look at the difference between the 'sensationalist' cover of *Kinflicks* (a cover which many found incongruous with the content of the book) and the restful paintings which characterize the publications of the feminist publishing groups – paintings which lay claim for the novels as 'classics'.

There are undoubtedly important considerations in the relationship between commercial publishing groups and political movements, both socialist
and feminist. You would have to be blind not to notice how the publication
by commercial publishing houses of 'women's studies' texts has proliferated.
These sections clearly have a commercial viability but their existence is no
less the product of hard fought battles of feminists within more conventional
publishing groups. The kinds of numbers printed of 'academic' feminist
books are minimal compared with say *Kinflicks*, (about 4,000 versus 50,000),
but the issue seems to be similar. It is just not enough to regret the profits of
commercial firms. In fact such profits should be welcomed if they encourage
groups with a mass market to invest in other such books. The question is
much rather what is the relationship of the practice of reading, both of fiction
and non-fiction, with political movements, in what way are texts effective,
and, most importantly, which ones are. The passive relation which Rebecca
assumes (that is, that these novels simply provide pleasure for the already
converted) would surely be a cause for pessimism.

(1980)

MICHÈLE BARRETT

'Feminism and the Definition of Cultural Politics'
Feminism, Culture and Politics

II. When Is Women's Art Feminist Art?

This leads to a second problem. This is the question asked by Rosalind
Coward in her article 'Are Women's Novels Feminist Novels?'.[1] Although
Coward's piece is directed towards one particular review article on feminist
fiction, her argument is in fact a generalized critique of a major (if not the
main) tendency in feminist literary criticism. She argues that feminists have
emphasized the unity and continuity of women's creative work and have
tended to confuse feminist art with, simply, women's art. Coward rejects this
conflation of the two, and she suggests that the current popularity of
'women's fiction' is not necessarily feminist at all. Feminism, she argues, is
an alignment of political interests and not a shared female experience; hence
a tradition of women's art is of no particular importance.

This goes right to the nub of a number of controversial questions about
feminism and culture. Is the recovery of women's artistic work of the past an
integral part of our developing feminist project, or merely a sentimental
resuscitation of marginalia better left in the obscurity to which establishment
criticism has consigned it? What do we gain by elevating traditional crafts
such as embroidery and knitting to the status of art objects and hanging them
in galleries? What is the meaning of an art exhibition where the objects

displayed are kitchen utensils or the careful record of a child's upbringing? How should we react to art that claims to be based on a 'female language' or on an artistic rendering of the female body and genitalia? In what sense might these various imaginative comments on women's experience be seen as 'feminist' art? Is a work of art feminist because the artist says it is, or the collective who produced it announce their feminist principles of work?

These questions were crystallized for me in a thought-provoking way by Judy Chicago's exhibition *The Dinner Party*, and although this has not yet been shown in Britain I want to use it to illustrate some points. The leaflet accompanying the show states that ' . . . the goal of *The Dinner Party* is to ensure that women's achievements become a permanent part of our culture', and the scale of the exhibition matches this monumental aspiration.

The central conception is a triangular dining-table, along the sides of which are placed symbolic representations of thirty-nine women: pre-Christian goddesses; historical figures such as Sappho and Boadaceia; women like the suffragist Susan B. Anthony and the artist Georgia O'Keefe. (This dining-table echoes the 'last supper' so significant to our male-dominated Christian culture.) Each of the figures at the table has a place setting of a runner, cutlery, goblet and plate, whose different designs evoke her particular character. From these thirty-nine women the names of 999 less resoundingly famous, but still reasonably well-known, women radiate in inscriptions on the 'heritage floor'. Surrounding this central focus of the exhibition are banners designed for the entrance, documentation of the five year's work by Judy Chicago and her team of helpers, an exhibition of china-painting, and a display of congratulatory telegrams from feminist artists all over the world.

The size of the exhibition – completely devoted to women's achievements – is, literally, spectacular. When I saw it an entire floor of the San Francisco Museum of Modern Art had been given over to it. The dining-table itself totals nearly 150 feet in length, each woman's place setting using about three and a half feet of space. The combination of this impressive scale and the lavish, beautiful, solid, ceramics and embroidery made the experience of being there an obviously moving one for many women. Never before, it seemed, had women taken over the cultural arena in such a flamboyant and confident way. The atmosphere, too, was wonderful – bringing back all the most positive and sisterly dimensions of a large women's liberation conference since there were so many feminists there.

The experience of being there was for me a striking one and I warmed immediately to the project. It conveyed a real sense of women's achievements and perhaps we too frequently refuse to take pride in them. The feeling of straightforward gender-congratulation was a new and welcome one. Yet in other respects the exhibition was extremely disturbing.

First, it was clear from the documentation that Judy Chicago had not only conceived the project but had directed the work of her many assistants with a positively dictatorial zeal. The principles of collective work vaunted here were not so much the ones I might recognize as feminist but an attempt to recreate the 'school' or studio of an 'Artistic Genius' like Michelangelo. Although hundreds of people gave much time and work to the project it is Judy Chicago personally who has, apparently not unwillingly, made an international reputation from it.

Second, we have to question whether it is necessarily progress to retrieve embroidery and china-painting from the inglorious role of women's drudgery (or at best 'craft') and re-allocate them to the realm of 'high art'. This is undoubtedly the aim of the show, and it one that is fraught with problems. What has happened to previous radical artists who attempted to challenge prevailing definitions of the 'appropriate' contents of art galleries? This is not a reactionary question, for the answer is that by and large their iconoclasm has been effectively dampened by a versatile establishment and so their challenge to the institution has been converted into artistic novelty. To sail into the establishment without seeing this as a problem is to beg the question of what 'art' is and how it differs from other forms of work. It is not enough simply to get what women do recognized as 'art'.

Third, I found the uncritical exercise of ranking 'great women' rather disturbing. There is something rather crude in deeming (to take some British examples of the figures used) the composer Ethel Smythe and the writer Virginia Woolf as worthy of individual places at the dining-table, while Jane Austen and Dorothy Wordsworth merit only an inscription on the floor. The heroines of feminism are here graded, ranked according to a set of criteria that are highly subjective. (On what grounds was it decided that Eleanor of Acquitaine made a greater contribution to feminism than the Virgin Mary? Is there not something bizarre in ranking Emily Dickinson with the Primordial Goddess?) The list of names in the catalogue is studded with epithets like 'pioneer', 'prizewinning', 'cultural leader' and 'eminent intellectual' – all of them terms of evaluation which we have developed a critical stance towards. The search for heroines and role models, for the great women of history, is one which raises a number of difficulties.

Finally, there are the problems surrounding how these women are represented in the exhibition. It is, perhaps, unsurprising and even appropriate that mythological goddesses are symbolized through renderings of clitoral and vaginal imagery. We have little to know them by. But for other women, of whose lives and beliefs we know far more (since they are historical rather than mythological figures), the inevitable vaginal imagery is less appropriate. Less appropriate! I was in fact horrified to see a 'Virginia Woolf' whose image to me represented a reading of her life and work which contradicted all she had ever stood for. There she sits: a genital sculpture in deep relief (about four inches high) resting on a runner of pale lemon gauze with the odd blue wave embroidered on it. Gone is Woolf's theory of androgyny and love of gender ambiguity; gone the polemical public voice; gone the complex symbolic abstractions of her writing. I found this exclusive emphasis on genitalia, and the sentimentality of the trappings, a complete betrayal – as was the 'Emily Dickinson' whose vagina is trimmed with a white lace effect over the palest pink. Very few of our celebrated sisters manage to escape this dreadful posthumous fate. Ethel Smythe appears here as a rather fine grand piano on a background of grey pin-stripe, but this, one fears, is attributable to Chicago's perceptions of her as a dyke. It is in fact typical of Chicago's somewhat biologistic approach to feminism that various of her protagonists are credited for creating a 'female form' of art or literature in itself a controversial achievement since the possible existence of 'female' forms of art has yet to be established. The notion that some forms of art are intrinsically female (or male) is a dubious one.

All these reservations about *The Dinner Party* have a bearing on the problem of what can be said to be feminist art. This particular case is of interest in that Chicago's claims for the exhibition – that it serves her project of securing artistic recognition for women's achievements – crystallize one specific approach to feminist cultural politics. Her argument that women's art is systematically excluded from the artistic establishment is demonstrated by the fact that after an immensely popular American tour the show went into storage rather than on to Europe.

But problems still remain in (i) the difficulty of arriving at a consensus among feminists as to what constitutes 'feminist' art and (ii) the fact that the use of women's lives, histories and experience does not necessarily ensure the coherent, feminist, reading of Chicago's work that the artist appears to desire. In this sense the case of *The Dinner Party* does seem to me to illustrate the truth of Rosalind Coward's warning that women's art is not necessarily feminist art. Feminist art is not the same as any art which emphasizes women's experience.

We cannot, however, completely separate feminist art from women's experience and hence I would not go so far as Rosalind Coward when she writes:

> Feminism can never be the product of the identity of women's experiences and interests – there is no such unity. Feminism must always be the alignment of women in a political movement with particular political aims and objectives. It is a grouping unified by its *political interests*, not by its common experiences.[2]

Whatever the problems of basing feminism on the experience shared by women, far greater problems arise in attempting completely to divorce feminism (as a political project) from women's experience. This leads to the position that women's shared experience of oppression plays no significant part in the construction of a feminist cultural politics, which in turn must lead to the conclusion that feminist art could equally well be developed by (for instance) a man. Although an emphasis on women's experience, or the fact of female authorship, or indeed a concern with the female body, is not enough to make a work of art feminist I do not see how feminism can ever take women to be a dispensable category. So although I agree than an emphasis on women is not a sufficient condition to make cultural production feminist it must at least be a *necessary* condition. Put another way, feminist art could be seen as a category *within* a tradition of women's art but I fail to see how it could be generated outside it. It may be that in general women's art is only indirectly useful or inspiring to feminism, but it is not possible to conceive of a feminist art that could be detached from a shared experience of oppression.

(1982)

Notes

1 Rosalind Coward, ' "This Novel Changes Lives": Are Women's Novels Feminist Novels? A Response to Rebecca O'Rourke's Article "Summer Reading" ', *Feminist Review*, 5 (1980). See previous extract.
2 Coward, ' "This Novel Changes Lives" ', p. 63.

Deborah E. McDowell

'New Directions for Black Feminist Criticism'
Black American Literature Forum

Despite the shortcomings of Smith's article, she raises critical issues on which Black feminist critics can build. There are many tasks ahead of these critics, not the least of which is to attempt to formulate some clear definitions of what Black feminist criticism is. I use the term in this paper simply to refer to Black female critics who analyze the works of Black female writers from a feminist or political perspective. But the term can also apply to any criticism written by a Black woman regardless of her subject or perspective – a book written by a male from a feminist or political perspective, a book written by a Black woman or about Black women authors in general, or any writings by women.[23]

In addition to defining the methodology. Black feminist critics need to determine the extent to which their criticism intersects with that of white feminist critics. Barbara Smith and others have rightfully challenged white women scholars to become more accountable to Black and Third World women writers, but will that require white women to use a different set of critical tools when studying Black woman writers? Are white women's theories predicated upon culturally-specific values and assumptions? Andrea Benton Rushing has attempted to answer these questions in her series of articles on images of Black women in literature. She maintains, for example, that critical categories of women, based on analyses of white women characters, are Euro-American in derivation and hence inappropriate to a consideration of Black women characters.[24] Such distinctions are necessary and, if held uniformly, can materially alter the shape of Black feminist scholarship.

Regardless of which theoretical framework Black feminist critics choose, they must have an informed handle on Black literature and Black culture in general. Such a grounding can give this scholarship more texture and completeness and perhaps prevent some of the problems that have had a vitiating effect on the criticism.

This footing in Black history and culture serves as a basis for the study of the literature. Termed 'contextual,' by theoreticians, this approach is often frowned upon if not dismissed entirely by critics who insist exclusively upon textual and linguistic analysis. Its limitations notwithstanding, I firmly believe that the contextual approach to Black women's literature exposes the conditions under which literature is produced, published, and reviewed. This approach is not only useful but necessary to Black feminist critics.

To those working with Black women writers prior to 1940, the contextual approach is especially useful. In researching Jessie Fauset, Nella Larsen, and Zora Neale Hurston, for example, it is useful to determine what the prevalent attitudes about Black women were during the time that they wrote. There is much information in the Black 'little' magazines published during the Harlem Renaissance. An examination of *The Messenger*, for instance, reveals that the dominant social attitudes about Black women were strikingly consistent with traditional middle class expectations of women. *The Messenger* ran a monthly symposium for some time entitled 'Negro Womanhood's Greatest Needs.' While a few female contributors stressed the importance of women being equal to men socially, professionally, and economically, the majority emphasized that a woman's place was in the home. It was her duty 'to cling to the home [since] great men and women evolve from the environment of the hearthstone.'[25]

One of the most startling entries came from a woman who wrote:

the New Negro Woman, with her head erect and spirit undaunted is resolutely marching forward, ever conscious of her historic and noble mission of doing her bit toward the liberation of her people in particular and the human race in general. Upon her shoulders rests the big task to create and keep alive, in the breast of black men, a holy and consuming passion to break with the slave traditions of the past; to spurn and overcome the fatal, insidious inferiority complex of the present, which . . . bobs up ever and anon, to arrest the progress of the New Negro Manhood Movement; and to fight with increasing vigor, with dauntless courage, unrelenting zeal and intelligent vision for the attainment of the stature of a full man, a free race and a new world.[26]

Not only does the contributor charge Black women with a formidable task, but she also sees her solely in relation to Black men.

This information enhances our understanding of what Fauset, Larsen, and Hurston confronted in attempting to offer alternative images of Black women. Moreover, it helps to clarify certain textual problems and ambiguities of their work. Though Fauset and Hurston, for example, explored feminist concerns, they leaned toward ambivalence. Fauset is especially alternately forthright and cagey, radical and traditional, on issues which confront women. Her first novel, *There Is Confusion* (1924), is flawed by an unanticipated and abrupt reversal in characterization that brings the central female character more in line with a feminine norm. Similarly, in her last novel, *Seraph on the Swanee* (1948), Zora Neale Hurston depicts a female character who shows promise for growth and change, for a departure from the conventional expectations of womanhood, but who, in the end, apotheosizes marriage, motherhood, and domestic servitude.

These two examples alone clearly capture the tension between social pressure and artistic integrity which is felt, to some extent, by all women writers. As Tillie Olsen points out, the fear of reprisal from the publishing and critical arenas is a looming obstacle to the woman writer's coming into her own authentic voice. 'Fear – the need to please, to be safe – in the literary realm too. Founded fear. Power is still in the hands of men. Power of validation, publication, approval, reputation. . . .'[27]

While insisting on the validity, usefulness, and necessity of contextual approaches to Black women's literature, the Black feminist critic must not ignore the importance of rigorous textual analysis. I am aware of many feminist critics' stubborn resistance to the certainly methodology handed down by white men. Although the resistance is certainly politically consistent and logical, I agree with Annette Kolodny that feminist criticism would be 'shortsighted if it summarily rejected all the inherited tools of critical analysis simply because they are male and western.' We should, rather, salvage what we find useful in past methodologies, reject what we do not, and, where necessary, move toward 'inventing new methods of analysis.'[28] Particularly useful is Lillian Robinson's suggestion that 'A radical kind of textual criticism . . . could usefully study the way the texture of sentences, choice of metaphors, patterns of exposition and narrative relate to [feminist] ideology.'[29]

This rigorous textual analysis involves, as Barbara Smith recommends, isolating as many thematic, stylistic, and linguistic commonalities among Black women writers as possible. Among contemporary Black female novelists, the thematic parallels are legion. In Alice Walker and Toni Morrison, for example, the theme of the thwarted female artist figures prominently.[30] Pauline Breedlove in Morrison's *The Bluest Eye*, for example, is obsessed with ordering things:

Jars on shelves at canning, peach pits on the step, sticks, stones, leaves. . . .
Whatever portable plurality she found, she organized into neat lines, according

to their size, shape or gradations of color. . . . She missed without knowing what she missed paints and crayons.[31]

*

Similarly, Eva Peace in *Sula* is forever ordering the pleats in her dress. And Sula's strange and destructive behavior is explained as 'the consequence of an idle imagination.'

Had she paints, clay, or knew the discipline of the dance, or strings; had she anything to engage her tremendous curiosity and her gift for metaphor, she might have exchanged the restlessness and preoccupation with whim for an activity that provided her with all she yearned for. And like any artist with no form, she became dangerous.[32]

Likewise, Meridian's mother in Alice Walker's novel, *Meridian*, makes artificial flowers and prayer pillows too small for kneeling.

The use of 'clothing as iconography'[33] is central to writings by Black women. For example, in one of Jessie Fauset's early short stories. 'The Sleeper Wakes' (1920), Amy, the protagonist, is associated with pink clothing (suggesting innocence and immaturity) while she is blinded by fairy-tale notions of love and marriage. However, after she declares her independence from her racist and sexist husband, Amy no longer wears pink. The imagery of clothing is abundant in Zora Neale Hurston's *Their Eyes Were Watching God* (1937). Janie's apron, her silks and satins, her head scarves, and finally her overalls all symbolize various stages of her journey from captivity to liberation. Finally, in Alice Walker's *Meridian*, Meridian's railroad cap and dungarees are emblems of her rejection of conventional images and expectations of womanhood.

A final theme that recurs in the novels of Black women writers is the motif of the journey. Though one can also find this same motif in the works of Black male writers, they do not use it in the same way as do Black female writers.[34] For example, the journey of the Black male character in works by Black men takes him underground. It is a 'descent into the underworld,'[35] and is primarily political and social in its implications. Ralph Ellison's *Invisible Man*, Imamu Amiri Baraka's *The System of Dante's Hell*, and Richard Wright's 'The Man Who Lived Underground' exemplify this quest. The Black female's journey, on the other hand, though at times touching the political and social, is basically a personal and psychological journey. The female character in the works of Black women is in a state of becoming 'part of an evolutionary spiral, moving from victimization to consciousness.'[36] The heroines in Zora Neale Hurston's *Their Eyes Were Watching God*, in Alice Walker's *Meridian*, and in Toni Cade Bambara's *The Salt Eaters* are emblematic of this distinction.

Even though isolating such thematic and imagistic commonalities should continue to be one of the Black feminist critic's most urgent tasks, she should beware of generalizing on the basis of too few examples. If one argues authoritatively for the existence of a Black female 'consciousness' or 'vision' or 'literary tradition,' one must be sure that the parallels found recur with enough consistency to support these generalizations. Further, Black feminist critics should not become obsessed in searching for common themes and images in Black women's works. As I pointed out earlier, investigating the question of 'female' language is critical and may well be among the most challenging jobs awaiting the Black feminist critic. The growing body of research on gender-specific uses of language might aid these critics. In fact wherever possible, feminist critics should draw on the scholarship of feminists in other disciplines.

An equally challenging and necessary task ahead of the Black feminist critic is a thoroughgoing examination of the works of Black male writers. In her introduction to *Midnight Birds*, Mary Helen Washington argues for the importance of giving Black women writers their due first. She writes:

> Black women are searching for a specific language, specific symbols, specific images with which to record their lives, and, even though they can claim a rightful place in the Afro-American tradition and the feminist tradition of women writers, it is also clear that, for purposes of liberation, black women writers will first insist on their own name, their own space.[37]

I likewise believe that the immediate concern of Black feminist critics must be to develop a fuller understanding of Black women writers who have not received the critical attention Black male writers have. Yet, I cannot advocate indefinitely such a separatist position, for the countless thematic, stylistic and imagistic parallels between Black male and female writers must be examined. Black feminist critics should explore these parallels in an effort to determine the ways in which these commonalities are manifested differently in Black women's writing and the ways in which they coincide with writings by Black men.

Of course, there are feminist critics who are already examining Black male writers, but much of the scholarship has been limited to discussions of the negative images of Black women found in the works of these authors.[38] Although this scholarship served an important function in pioneering Black feminist critics, it has virtually run its course. Feminist critics run the risk of plunging their work into cliche and triviality if they continue merely to focus on how Black men treat Black women in literature. Hortense Spillers offers a more sophisticated approach to this issue in her discussion of the power of language and myth in female relations in James Baldwin's *If Beale Street Could Talk*. One of Spillers's most cogent points is that 'woman-freedom or its negation, is tied to the assertions of myth, or ways of saying things.'[39]

Black feminist criticism is a knotty issue, and while I have attempted to describe it, to call for clearer definition of its methodology, to offer warnings of its limitations, I await the day when Black feminist criticism will expand to embrace other modes of critical inquiry. In other words, I am philosophically opposed to what Annis Pratt calls 'methodolatry.' Wole Soyinka has offered one of the most cogent defenses against critical absolutism. He explains:

> The danger which a literary ideology poses is the act of consecration and of course excommunication. Thanks to the tendency of the modern consumer mind to facilitate digestion by putting in strict categories what are essentially fluid operations of the creative mind upon social and natural phenomena, the formulation of a literary ideology tends to congeal sooner or later into instant capsules which, administered also to the writer, may end by asphyxiating the creative process.[40]

Whether or not Black feminist criticism will or should remain a separatist enterprise is a debatable point. Black feminist critics ought to move from this issue to consider the specific language of Black women's literature, to describe the ways Black women writers employ literary devices in a distinct way, and to compare the way Black women writers create their own mythic structures. If they focus on these and other pertinent issues, Black feminist critics will have laid the cornerstone for a sound, thorough articulation of the Black feminist aesthetic.

(1980)

Notes

23 I am borrowing here from Kolodny who makes similar statements in 'Some Notes Defining a "Feminist Literary Criticism," ' p. 75.

24 Andrea Benton Rushing, 'Images of Black Women in Afro-American Poetry,' in *The Afro-American Woman: Struggles and Images*, ed. Sharon Harley and Rosalyn Terborg-Penn (Port Washington, NY: Kennikat Press, 1978), pp. 74–84. She argues that few of the stereotypic traits which Mary Ellmann describes in *Thinking About Women* 'seem appropriate to Afro-American images of black women.' See also her 'Images of Black Women in Modern African Poetry: An Overview,' in *Sturdy Black Bridges: Visions of Black Women in Literature* (New York: Anchor Press- Doubleday, 1979), pp. 18–24. Rushing argues similarly that Mary Ann Ferguson's categories of women (the submissive wife, the mother angel or 'mom,' the woman on a pedestal, for example) cannot be applied to Black women characters whose cultural imperatives are different from white women's.

25 *The Messenger*, 9 (April 1927), 109.

26 *The Messenger*, 5 (July 1923), 757.

27 Tillie Olsen, *Silences* (New York: Delacorte Press, 1978), p. 257.

28 Kolodny, 'Some Notes,' p. 89.

29 Robinson, 'Dwelling in Decencies: Radical Criticism and the Feminist Perspectives,' in *Feminist Criticism*, ed. Cheryl Brown and Karen Olson (New Jersey: The Scarecrow Press, 1978), p. 35.

30 For a discussion of Toni Morrison's frustrated female artists see Renita Weems, 'Artists Without Art Form: A Look at One Black Woman's World of Unrevered Black Women,' *Conditions: Five*, 2 (Autumn 1979), 48–58. See also Alice Walker's classic essay, 'In Search of Our Mothers' Gardens,' *Ms.*, May 1974, for a discussion of Black women's creativity in general.

31 Toni Morrison, *The Bluest Eye* (New York: Pocket Books – Simon and Schuster, 1970), pp. 88–89.

32 Toni Morrison, *Sula* (New York: Bantam Books, 1980), p. 105.

33 Kolodny, 'Some Notes on Defining a "Feminist Literary Criticism," ' p. 86.

34 In an NEH Summer Seminar at Yale University, Summer 1980, Carolyn Naylor of Santa Clara University suggested this to me.

35 For a discussion of this idea see Michael G. Cooke, 'The Descent into the Underworld and Modern Black Fiction,' *Iowa Review*, 5 (Fall 1974), 72–90.

36 Mary Helen Washington, *Midnight B.rds* (Garden City, NY: Anchor Press-Doubleday, 1980), p. 43.

37 Washington, p. xvii.

38 See Saundra Towns, 'The Black Woman as Whore: Genesis of the Myth,' *The Black Position*, 3 (1974), 39, 59, and Sylvia Keady, 'Richard Wright's Women Characters and Inequality,' *Black American Literature Forum*, 10 (1976), 124–128, for example.

39 'The Politics of Intimacy: A Discussion,' in *Sturdy Black Bridges*, p. 88.

40 Wole Soyinka, *Myth, Literature and the African World* (London: Cambridge University Press, 1976), p. 61.

Cheri Register

'American Feminist Literary Criticism: A Bibliographical Introduction'
Feminist Literary Criticism

Can feminists establish themselves as objective literary critics, given their political orientation?

The opponents of Phallic Criticism doubt whether any form of criticism can be truly objective; methods that appear to be non-ideological are actually supporting the status quo.[57] Nancy Hoffman thinks it not only impossible, but even undesirable, to create a feminist criticism that is totally objective. Her classroom method integrates objective distance and emotional involvement.[58] Feminist critics recognize that theirs is a specialized, highly political type of analysis, only one of many to which literature might be subjected. There are, however, varying opinions about feminist criticism's place in the spectrum that ranges between ivory tower academism and political activism. Lillian Robinson speaks from the political end:

> Some people are trying to make an honest woman out of the feminist critic, to claim that every "worthwhile" department should stock one. I am not terribly interested in whether feminism becomes a respectable part of academic criticism; I am very much concerned that feminist critics become a useful part of the women's movement.[59]

Because of its origin in the women's liberation movement, feminist criticism values literature that is of some use to the movement. Prescriptive Criticism, then, is best defined in terms of the ways in which literature can serve the cause of liberation. To earn feminist approval, literature must perform one or more of the following functions: (1) serve as a forum for women; (2) help to achieve cultural androgyny; (3) provide role-methods; (4) promote sisterhood; and (5) augment consciousness-raising. I would like to discuss these functions one by one.

In order to be useful as a *forum*, literature must allow forthright and honest self-expression, writing which is not constrained by pre-existing standards that may be alien to female culture. Virginia Woolf's first directive to female writers was: 'Above all, you must illumine your own soul with its profundities and its shallows, and its vanities and its generosities, and say what your beauty means to you or your plainness.' She regretted that the female author of the nineteenth century wrote with 'a mind which was slightly pulled from the straight, and made to alter its clear vision in deference to external authority.'[60] Ellen Morgan renews Woolf's advice: 'Feminist criticism should, I believe, encourage an art true to women's experience and not filtered through a male perspective or constricted to fit male standards.'[61] On the other hand, authors should not feel obligated to offer an exact representation of their own lives, but rather 'the fictional myths *growing out of their lives* and told by themselves for themselves.'[62] The arts must help people understand what female experience is, 'what it's like, what you think, how it operates. What it feels like to be us.'[63] Before literature can begin to perform the other functions, however, it must express female experience authentically, in all its variety. The emphasis on variety is apparent in the course syllabi in the *Female Studies* series. The works selected represent various ages, classes, and races of women. Tillie Olsen's 'Women: A List Out of Which to Read,' which appears in cumulative fashion in the *Women's Studies Newsletter* (Old Westbury, New York: The Feminist Press), is an example of a growing tendency on the part of feminist critics and teachers to seek out materials that will compass the totality of the female life experience.

Once literature begins to serve as a forum, illuminating female experience, it can assist in humanizing and equilibrating the culture's value system, which has historically served predominantly male interests. That is, it can help to bring about *cultural androgyny*. Carolyn Heilbrun has reintroduced Woolf's 'androgyny' into the vocabulary of literary criticism in her book *Toward a Recognition of Androgyny* (New York: Alfred A. Knopf, 1973).[64] Other feminist critics agree that a 'female impulse' in literature is necessary for the achievement of cultural androgyny. Firestone expresses it succinctly: The 'development of "female" art . . . is progressive: an exploration of strictly female reality is a necessary step to correct the warp in a sexually biased culture. It is only after we have integrated the dark side of the moon into our world view that we can begin to talk seriously of universal culture.'[65] Of course, a pluralistic society like the one that exists in the United States must also draw on the experiences of its ethnic and regional groups if it is to be truly balanced.

Feminists often emphasize that they are not simply seeking more room for women in the present social order. They want a new social order founded on 'humanistic' values, some of which are traditionally 'female' and not respected in contemporary society. Those traditionally 'male' values that feminists believe harmful to the common good – excessive competition, for example – would be de-emphasized. Therefore, a female literary personage with 'masculine' characteristics does not necessarily meet with feminist approval. Ellen Harold, writing about Emma Peel, the heroine of 'The Avengers,' a British television series shown in the United States, comments: 'What is truly said is that, though she is equal to a man and superior to most men, the measure of her competence is a strictly *macho* one – her capacity for violence. As an attempt at an emancipated woman she leaves something to be desired, for both men and women need new standards against which to measure themselves.'[66]

A literary work should provide *role-models*, instill a positive sense of feminine identity by portraying women who are 'self-actualizing, whose identities are not dependent on men.'[67] This function is particularly crucial in children's literature. In *Dick and Jane as Victims*, Women on Words and Images find fault with elementary school readers for reserving active mastery skills for boys – that is, creativity, ingenuity, adventurousness, curiosity, perseverance, bravery, autonomy – and describing girls as passive, docile, dependent, incompetent, and self-effacing. Adult women who are re-examining their lives may also depend on literature to introduce new possibilities and to help them evaluate the alternatives open to them. 'We cannot live in a certain way, we cannot see ourselves as the people we wish to be, until we perceive the wished-for life and self in our imaginations.'[68] To compensate for the death of satisfactory fictional role-models, feminist teachers are enlarging the definition of literature to include biography, autobiography, and memoirs. The syllabus for the Women's Biography Course offered at California State University in Sonoma illustrates the urgency of the search for role-models.[69]

It is important to note here that although female readers need literary models to emulate, characters should not be idealized beyond plausibility. The demand for authenticity supercedes all other requirements. Mary Anne Ferguson assigns works like Tillie Olsen's *Tell Me a Riddle* and Willa Cather's *My Antonia* to help her students 'realize that liberation involves hard choices; that it begins and ends with the self; that self-knowledge depends upon contact with the real world.'[70]

Literature should show women involved in activities that are not traditionally 'feminine', to speed the dissolution of rigid sex roles. It is not enough, however, to simply place a female character in a new occupation, with no corresponding change in her personality and behavior. Marion Meade describes the effects of the women's liberation movement on television heroines: although a few series feature female doctors or lawyers or television producers, the women's behavior and their relationships with men follow the familiar stereotyped pattern. They are caricatures, not realistic women, she says.[71]

The feminist movement in America is seeking to create a feeling of *sisterhood*, a new sense of community among women, in order to overcome group self-hatred, the animosity that many women feel for others of their sex as a result of isolation, competition for male attention, and belief in female inferiority. Virginia Woolf noticed the dearth of gratifying woman-to-woman relationships in literature:

> "Chloe liked Olivia," I read. And then it struck me how immense a change was there. Chloe liked Olivia perhaps for the first time in literature. Cleopatra did not like Octavia. And how completely *Antony and Cleopatra* would have been altered had she done so! . . . All these relationships between women, I thought, rapidly recalling the splendid gallery of fictitious women, are too simple. So much has been left out, unattempted.[72]

In addition to testing new female-female (and female-male) relationships, a literary work can serve the cause of sisterhood by recounting experiences that the reader can identify as her own, experiences that are, perhaps, shared by many women. She will feel a common bond with the author and other readers who have similar reactions to the book. This is vital for adolescent readers, says Susan Koppelman Cornillon:

> We are all aware of the agony of adolescence in our culture, the evasive fumblings as we attempt to communicate about our fears and our needs and our anxieties without actually ever mentioning to anyone what they really are: the creation of elaborate private symbologies that enable us to grieve about our pimples, our sexual fantasies, our masturbation, the strange changes happening to our bodies. But boys outgrow this secretiveness soon – because there is a vast wealth of literature for them to stumble on, both great and popular, classical and contemporary, pious and lewd, that assures them that, indeed, they are normal. Or even better, their suffering is portrayed as a prerequisite for maturity, if not a prelude to greatness.[73]

Literature might also enable a reader to emphasize with women whose subjective accounts of female reality differ from her own.

> Loving someone is wanting to know them. Insofar as we are able to learn and know of each other, we can acknowledge, and even in part assimilate into our own imaginative life, the thousand differences that have always been used as wedges to drive us apart. So that the experience of all women everywhere becomes, in a sense, our communal property, a heritage we bestow upon each other, the knowledge of what it has meant to be female, a woman in this man's world.[74]

In order to augment *consciousness-raising*, literature should provide realistic insights into female personality development, self-perception, interpersonal relationships, and other 'private' or 'internal' consequences of sexism. The reader can then note recurring problems and generalize from them with the aid of factual information about the status of women from other sources.[75] Feminist critics are far more concerned with exposing these private effects than with raising concrete issues, such as job discrimination and lack of child care facilities. In this age of mass communications, public forums, and official investigative committees, fiction is no longer the most effective means of arousing concern about measurable social problems. That is not to say that concrete political issues have no place in feminist-approved literature. But their presence must be consistent with the demands for authenticity and subjectivity prerequisite to an effective integration of the personal and the political. In disparaging didactic feminist poetry, Erica Jong noted, 'We all claim to believe that political oppression and personal feelings are related, and yet a great deal of the self-consciously polemical poetry that has come out of the Women's Movement reads like a generalized rant and it lacks any sort of psychological grounding. The poet has not really looked into herself and told it true. She has been content to echo simplistic slogans.'[76] Likewise, a fictional account of job discrimination that covers only the material consequences will not suffice. If the protagonist is, indeed, fully characterized, we will also see the private or psychic effects of discrimination. Ellen Morgan values a subtle rendering of both types of problems in which 'neo-feminist consciousness informs the novel as light informs a painting, rather than appearing as subject matter.'[77]

There is a precedent for this sort of personalized polemic in black literature. James Baldwin's novels are not single-issue tracts, but rather in-depth studies of individual examples of black humanity. Ralph Ellison's *Invisible Man* was successful not because it exposed conditions that were completely foreign to whites in America, but because it appealed to common, multiracial feelings of insignificance and alienation, showing how much more intense they are when institutionalized. Perhaps the difference between this and the muckraking and Socialist literatures of the early twentieth century is due to the fact that the victims have become the authors.[78]

Factual information about discrimination should be carefully integrated into a story with a larger focus, so that its presence seems natural. Joyce Nower warns, however, against condemning the author who merely translates position papers into fiction: 'A woman artist who writes a lousy story on a woman active in the Movement, or involved in getting an abortion, should be accorded the respect of critical appraisal: a lousy writer but important in that she is trying to use new materials.'[79] Ellen Morgan concurs: 'The capacity to teach and to delight which some of this work has would suggest that critical standards which deny literary legitimacy and value to [propagandistic] writing may be inadequate tools for [its] evaluation.'[80]

No feminist critic insists that a fictional work include political analysis.[81] The author need only describe the problems and offer some solutions, if the character herself can find them. The remaining tasks involved in conscious-ness-raising are left to the reader: to compare the problems encountered by female literary characters with her own, to explain similarities in terms of causes, and to decide on appropriate political action. Literature can thus augment the face-to-face consciousness-raising that is fundamental to the American women's liberation movement.

There is a potential conflict between the consciousness-raising function and the role-model function. A work that offers a thorough literary description of women's oppression may also feature a 'heroine' who is thoroughly oppressed and therefore unlikely to be emulated by female readers. Erica Jong, for one, is dissatisfied with 'all those so-called feminist novels in which women are depicted as helpless victims.'[82] The ideal feminist fictional work is one that fulfills all five functions in equilibrium. Rather than being driven to mental breakdown or suicide or immobility, the heroines of new feminist fiction will somehow manage to resist destruction, perhaps with the support and confidence of other women. Their outlook and behavior will presage a new social order that integrates the best aspects of 'female culture' with selected 'male' values.

(1975)

Notes

57 Lillian Robinson and Lise Vogel, 'Modernism and History,' *Images of Women in Fiction*, ed. Koppelman Cornillon, pp. 278–305; and Fraya Katz Stoker. 'The Other Criticism: Feminism vs. Formalism,' ibid., pp. 313–25.

58 Hoffman, 'A Class of Our Own,' pp. 14–27.

59 Robinson, 'Dwelling in Decencies,' p. 889.

60 Woolf, *A Room of One's Own*, pp. 93, 77.

61 Ellen Morgan to author, February 13, 1972.

62 Russ, 'What Can a Heroine Do?' p. 19.

63 Millett, 'Notes on the Making of *Three Lives*,' p. 2.

64 See also Carolyn Heilbrun, 'The Masculine Wilderness of the American Novel,' *Saturday Review*, January 29, 1972, pp. 41–44.

65 Firestone, *Dialectic of Sex*, p. 167.

66 Harold, 'A Look at Some Old Favorites,' pp. 44–45.

67 Martin, 'The Feminine Mystique in American Fiction,' p. 33.

68 Michele Murray, 'Introduction' to *A House of Good Proportion. Images of Women in Literature*, ed. Murray (New York: Simon and Schuster, 1973), p. 19.

69 *Female Studies VII*, ed. Rosenfelt, pp. 82–85.

70 Quoted in Showalter, 'Introduction: Teaching about Women, 1971,' p. x.

71 Marion Meade, 'On the Trail of the Liberated TV Heroine,' *Aphra* 2 (Spring 1971): 30–34.

72 Woolf, *A Room of One's Own*, p. 86.

73 Susan Koppelman Cornillon, 'The Fiction of Fiction,' *Images of Women in Fiction*, ed. Koppelman Cornillon, p. 115.

74 Millett, 'Introduction' to 'Prostitution: A Quartet,' p. 23. See also Hoffman, 'A Class of Our Own.'

75 See Morgan's critique of Alix Kates Schulman, *Memoirs of an Ex-Prom Queen* (New York: Alfred A. Knopf, 1972) in 'Humanbecoming,' pp. 197–204.

76 Erica Jong, 'Visionary Anger' (a review of Adrienne Rich, *Diving Into the Wreck*) *Ms*, July 1973, p. 31.

77 Morgan, 'Humanbecoming,' p. 197.

78 For a discussion of this earlier literature see Walter B. Rideout, *The Radical Novel in the United States, 1900–1954: Some Interrelations of Literature and Society* (Cambridge: Harvard University Press, 1956).

79 Joyce Nower to author, March 7, 1972.

80 Morgan, 'Humanbecoming,' p. 187.

81 With the possible exception of Kate Millett. In *Sexual Politics*, p. 139, she criticizes Virginia Woolf for not explaining the causes of Rhoda's suicidal misery in *The Waves*, but in 'Notes on the Making of *Three Lives*,' written two years later, she says that she would now rather *express* female experience than analyze it.

82 Jong, 'Visionary Anger,' p. 34.

ALISON LIGHT

'Feminism and the Literary Critic' LTP: Journal of Literature, Teaching, Politics

Kate Millett's *Sexual Politics* (1970) was for me in many ways the starting point from which to move toward a feminist literary criticism. Crucially, Millett chose to use literary texts as the key source of illustrations for her arguments as to the dominant political organisation of all social formations, as casebook evidence, that is, for the development of a radical feminist theory of patriarchy. This theory in turn depended upon a particular notion of ideology and of the relation between literature and politics which has been extremely influential and has informed many other aspects of feminist discussion ever since.[1]

Sexual Politics attempts a far-reaching analysis of patriarchy, traced across cultures and history as the primary political institution, the expression of the distribution of political power according to an original sexual division of labour. Patriarchy is thus envisaged as the hierarchical institutionalisation of the unequal roles and status given to the two biological genders – 'the birthright priority whereby male rules females' (Millett, 1972 edition, p. 25). Ideology then is posited as the system of ideas and values which works to maintain the psychological, emotional, and social consent of the State's subjects to such a form of government. It is a kind of conditioning agent which, like the family in Millett's analysis, 'mediating between the individual and the social structure' (p. 33), is both a mirror and a restatement of the ways in which patriarchy functions to degrade and subordinate the female. Patriarchal ideology ensures the socialisation of individuals according to already given and thus 'stereotyped lines of sex category' (p. 26). It promotes, and elsewhere in Millett's text often *is*, the false consciousness which works continually to misrepresent women and their lives.

Consequently for Millett, literature, together with all other cultural products of this patriarchal consciousness, is proposed as ideological because it teaches, amongst other things, the acceptance of those sex roles. Male writers, by virtue of their gender, must reproduce the sexual politics of the real world in the little worlds of their fiction. Thus, in her section 'The Literary Reflection', Millett takes four twentieth century authors: Lawrence, Miller, Mailer, and Genet to provide her with 'instances of sexual description' (p. 23) which she sees as merely reproducing the normative values of a patriarchal sexual politics.

The task of the feminist critic becomes, as Millett demonstrates with her full scholarly apparatus, a matter of the exposure of that 'sexism' which will have been expressed with different amounts of force in every literary text. The acts of reading and criticising are seen in terms either of a succumbing to or a resisting of the ideological onslaughts of the text; the feminist literary critic, as cultural revolutionary, then, works to free the text from its ideological burden, leaving both the work and the author liberated, able at last to be properly acclaimed as examples of 'distinguished moral and intellectual integrity' (p. xii).

But Millett's polemic begs many questions, questions which I was beginning to ask myself, in a fairly untheorised way, when I started my postgraduate course. What for example would happen if different authors were chosen, those for whom, like Joyce and Forster, an exploration of female consciousness was central to their narratives? Where is history in Millett's account – either in relation to the ideas of sexuality she sees expressed in a text, or in terms of the developing literary genre itself? How indeed, since Millett only looks at novels, would other genres be accessible to this analysis, especially those which don't produce a coherent narrative at all? And what about the meaning of sexuality in different texts by the same authors? Of course Millett's choice of authors was a particularly loaded one, but even so wasn't it possible to produce different readings of the same novels she discusses?

In fact my first reading of *Sexual Politics* was not as a feminist, but as a budding (and suitably pompous) literary critic in the sixth form. I used Millett as another, decidedly eccentric, authority on *Sons and Lovers*, my A level text. Against her insistence on seeing the novel as Lawrence's autobiography, and the arrogant Paul Morel as simply his mouthpiece, I had scrawled exasperated comments in the margin – 'But we see this!' and 'Lawrence shows us!' In my own reading at seventeen I identified desperately with Miriam, and contrived to reject Paul even though I was well aware that I was often reading against the grain. My objections, however, point to my recognition that if Lawrence *is* Paul, he is also Paul's mother and girl-friends, and if, as Millett does, we take their part, we haven't somehow escaped Lawrence but exposed the way in which novels, as constructs of the imagination, might be attempts at 'ungendering', and, however unsuccessful, at dispersing or even at transgressing the gendered experience of an author and its usual restraints. I suspected that it was these displacements, contradictions, and tensions which I enjoyed in following a narrative – but in any case Millett's analysis brought me no nearer to understanding where the pleasure, which I took to be the main motivation in reading, lay.

Further, in seeing each text as autobiography, Millett of course needs the authoritative narrative voice which she finds in her narrowly-selected authors. Ironically Millett is here aligned with much traditional literary criticism, and she leaves the literary establishment free to continue to scapegoat such authors as fanatical exceptions to the rule of 'objective' genius, without having to examine its own practice.

Millett's position, with its stress on literature as a straight reflection of ideology, it appeared, necessarily left little room for the specifically literary at all. There is no discussion of what the demands of writing may be, of how one text is read and written through another, or of how reading, writing, and criticising, as different activities, are situated in history and – as Millett's own feminism suggests – engaged with differently by different individuals or groups. For Millett finally resists the logic of her own intervention, and, in exposing the false consensus of earlier readings, wants not a plurality of readings but to replace an incorrect patriarchal reading with one 'more' correct and equally prescriptive. Far from her readings opening out and liberating the reader, criticism operates as a mode of gaining access and control, an appropriation of an incontrovertible, but this time 'feminist', truth.

The dissatisfaction I felt with a feminist literary criticism which focused on an exposure of sexist ideology as content involved, at least in part, a sense of the dependence of Millett's radical feminist politics upon those very established values and categories – whether sexual, social, or literary – which it was attempting to subvert. Millett's emphasis on an unmediated ideology functioning as a reflex of State power, her slippage towards biologistic definitions of gender positions, her refusal of the literary where it might engage with a notion of the unconscious, were not simply produced by a radical feminist politics, but were – and still are – necessary and mutually supportive parts of the whole package.

Feminism to me, and especially my experience of consciousness-raising, meant precisely that socialisation, whether into femininity or masculinity, was never successfully achieved, and it was this possibility of unconscious resistance which gave room for political mobilisation. Women's (and men's) relation to any ideology was lived in the midst of contradictions – ideology was not a blanket of ignorance thrown over the heads of fully conscious and grown human beings.

Millett's cultural politics, on the other hand, seemed to me to keep both culture and politics the property of the enlightened few. For if the text is ideology's dupe, and the feminist critic its only hope, where does that leave the rest of us ordinary women in the struggle for a cultural politics? In Millett's programme we can only go back to 'the limited role alloted to the female' which 'tends to arrest her at the level of biological experience' (p. 26). Not surprisingly then there are few women's voices in Kate Millett's *Sexual Politics*, except, of course, her own.

It's only fair to say that my re-reading of Millett last year left me feeling pained and confused, since however unsatisfactory I felt her textual analyses to be, they were in a crucial way infinitely preferable to all those of traditional literary criticism: they validated my anger as a feminist, they recognised that as a woman I had been relegated, misrepresented, and often excluded by 'culture', and that some kind of struggle around the practices of art and literary criticism was possible. And it needs to be remembered that this culture and its dominant values were being forcefully asserted elsewhere in the university. Indeed, if I found the prospect of three years spent league-tabling authors a profoundly depressing one, that had as much to do with my own attachment to the concepts of Art and Genius, to the universalizing values of literary criticism, as with a dislike of the feminist strategy itself. I was afraid to take on my 'cultural heritage'. As a feminist my pleasure in these authors could never be the same again, but I had no way of using that sense of alienation, no way of making it productive, trapped as I was inside the standards of a literary criticism which made me feel at best 'original' and at worst highly 'subjective'.

(1983)

Note

1 For an extended discussion of this see Cora Kaplan, 'Radical Feminism and Literature: Rethinking Millett's *Sexual Politics*', *Red Letters*, No. 9 (1979).

CORA KAPLAN

'*Speaking/ Writing/ Feminism*' *On Gender and Writing*

In the early stages of thinking about women and writing I had, in common with other feminists, talked mostly about the ways in which women were denied access to something I have called 'full' subjectivity. While any term so abstract evokes more meaning than it can possibly contain in a given context, what I was working towards was a description of a position within culture where women could, without impediment, exist as speaking subjects. I now think that this way of posing the question of writing/speaking and subjectivity is misleading. It assumes, for instance, that *men* write from a realised and realisable autonomy in which they are, in fact, not fantasy, the conscious, constant and triumphant sources of the meanings they produce. This assumption is part of an unreconstructed romantic definition of the poet as it was most eloquently expressed in Wordsworth's 1800 introduction to *Lyrical Ballads*. Here the poet has a universalised access to experience of all kinds, feels things more deeply, and expresses those feelings 'recollected in tranquillity' for all men. It did not take much thought to point out how difficult it was for women to appropriate this romantic definition of genius and transcendence, given the contemporary restraints on their experience and the contempt in which their gender-specific feelings were held. A more interesting question was about the status of the definition itself which even today has enormous currency within traditional literary criticism. How far was it an ideological fiction? In what sense could any writing or writer – widen the thing defined, the romantics did – any *actor* in history *be* that romantic subject? For if one were to accept a modern re-working of the romantic definition of the creative process, then as a feminist 'full subjectivity' would become a political goal for feminism, as well as a precondition for all acts of struggle and intervention, writing included.

In the last few years I have come round to a very different perspective on the problem, drawn from Marxist and feminist appropriations of psychoanalytic and structuralist theories, but confirmed, I think, by my own and other women's fragmented experience of writing and identity. Rather than approach women's difficulty in positioning themselves as writers as a question of barred access to some durable psychic state to which all humans should and can aspire, we might instead see their experience as foregrounding the inherently unstable and split character of all human subjectivity. Within contemporary western culture the act of writing and the romantic ideologies of individual agency and power are tightly bound together, although that which is written frequently resists and exposes this unity of the self as ideology. At both the psychic and social level, always intertwined, women's subordinate place within culture makes them less able to embrace or be held by romantic individualism with all its pleasures and dangers. The instability of 'femininity' as female identity is a specific instability, an eccentric relation to the construction of sexual difference, but it also points to the fractured and fluctuant condition of all consciously held identity, the impossibility of a will-full, unified and cohered subject.

Romantic ideologies of the subject suppress this crucial and potentially hopeful incoherence, or make its absence a sign of weakness and thus an occasion for mourning or reparation. Feminism has been caught up far too often in this elegiac mood, even when on other fronts it has mounted an impressive critique of Western rationalism as a phallocratic discourse of power. One option within feminism to combat the seeming weakness which inheres in women's split subjectivity has been to reassert an economy of control, to deny the constant effect of unconscious processes in utterance and practice, and to pose an unproblematic rationalism for women themselves, a feminist psyche in control of femininity. For myself, this avenue is closed, if only because it makes me feel so demoralised, a not-good-enough feminist as I was a not-good-enough daughter. I would rather see subjectivity as always in process and contradiction, even female subjectivity, structured, divided and denigrated through the matrices of sexual difference. I see this understanding as part of a more optimistic political scenario than the ones I have been part of, one that can and ought to lead to a politics which will no longer overvalue control, rationality and individual power, and which, instead, tries to understand human desire, struggle and agency as they are mobilised through a more complicated, less finished and less heroic psychic schema.

(1983)

ELIZABETH WILSON

Mirror Writing: An Autobiography

I did not enter the women's movement in search of an identity. Political activity simply presented itself to me as an imperative and as an escape, a liberation from the privatised obsessions of the search for identity.

The radical movements of the late sixties and of the seventies did, though, raise the question of personal identity in a way no political movement had raised it before. Earlier socialists may have tried to raise questions of the personal life, but only now was a culture already saturated with the individualism of popularised psychotherapies awaiting the revolution of everyday life. Changed consciousness had become a necessary part of revolutionary change.

Yet this heightened and fractured sense of individual identity – a key feature of modern Western culture – which charged the radical movements with power, has also acted as a brake upon them. For it has become ever more chancy for revolutionaries to rely on the once powerful appeal of solidarity with a class or group. We failed to develop a collective subjectivity.

Feminists found this too. At first it seemed enough for women to speak out. If they did this, they would find themselves, and find themselves together. Many of the journals and books of the movement have names that suggest this, for instance *Women's Voice – Another Voice – Call to Women*, and if there is a typical literary form of feminism it is the fragmented, intimate form of confessional, personal testimony, autobiography, the diary, 'telling it like it was'.

The idea that women need only throw off their oppression for a 'real' self to appear is, nonetheless, oversimplified. Can we really say that our socially constructed 'feminine' identity is merely a husk to be discarded as we bite into the kernel, or a chrysalis the butterfly breaks out of? Women have spoken out, have given testimony as if the 'truth' of their experiences were transparent and straightforward. But – is it?

Feminists have turned to testimonies written by women who were not or could not be part of any movement. In many such testimonies a woman's identity is built, initially at least, out of pain and suffering, out of false experience. We thrill, as if someone had drawn the edge of a razor across our flesh, to the way in which Jean Rhys tears off a layer of skin to reveal her raw experience as victim of male cruelty and indifference. We sink towards madness with Doris Lessing at the pain of that same cruelty turned on women who dare to be 'free'. Kate Millett tells of the same pain, which she hoped to escape in the women's movement, but which returned to torment her from within feminism itself.

Some women speak of the moment of optimism when at last they have thrown off the role of victim and martyr. Some go further still in finding a new identity in the women's movement.

Yet women are offered only a collective identity 'in the movement'. A new identity is assumed but remains amorphously within 'sisterhood'. The 'movement' is a vague, formless conception of the celebration of womenness, an essence of womanhood; sometimes it is described as an endless dance in which women-loving-women sing as they circle in the weaving hand-in-hand of an embrace of all by all in which all individuality, all difference – all identity – is dissolved. Anja Meulenbelt writes of this moment:

> I dance in the crowd to the witch music . . . Or just look, at women whom I have begun to find so beautiful, who dance close together in couples, who dance in groups, with swinging hair and shining eyes, proud of what they are. Grown up and now stronger than those people who had no need to fight oppression. I am in love, I think, with a species . . . I dance with old friends and new ones, my body supple . . . I feel beautiful among women, am beautiful . . . It is as if I have come home . . . Back in mother's arms . . .[8]

Thus have women tried to construct a collective identity out of a shared experience of collective oppression. For many women, the moment of commitment to the women's movement must also have seemed like the birth of a new *individual* identity: 'I am a feminist.' Yet an emphasis on the moment of collective identification, although necessary, is not enough. It can become static. It does not develop the idea of identity as process, and it also in a curious way is blind to what each of us *as an individual* brings with us into the movement. For all its emphasis on the truth of experience, it ignores – although perhaps necessarily in seeking a basis for solidarity and sisterhood – our sense of individuality and of an unique past, an unique self.

Yet we carry this unique identity forward with us in the movement, after the moment of collective identification. What comes after the moment when we say: 'I am a feminist'? How do we develop a collective subjectivity that allows for differnece and diversity?

Feminists have written an enormous amount about stereotypic constructions of 'femininity'. There has also been a popular stereotypic construction of 'feminist' (dungarees – no make up – hates men – angry). But what do those feminists do who reject equally both these images from the dominant culture? Perhaps, instead of dwelling so obsessively on how femininity gets inside our heads, feminists should have thought more about how to construct a plurality of positive images of women. As it is, women have fallen back on to the notion of the 'strong woman'. But however good it is to be strong, we feel ambivalent about the strong, powerful woman, since this too is an image that allows for no moment of weakness, and cannot reflect the diversity and complexity of our desires. Women who have sought to identify with 'strong women' in the movement have sometimes been so disappointed when these turned out not to be super-human after all that they have even turned against feminism itself.

This is a form of romanticism. The contemporary radical sexual liberation movements were supposed to be grounded in a rejection of romanticism. Yet the rejection of romanticism at the individual level, at the level of personalised romantic love, was over-emphasised at the expense of any real examination of political romanticism – the longing for utopias and reconstructed selves, and the longing for the pure, revolutionary moment. That political romanticism can easily give way to a 'left wing melancholy' which stresses the inescapable awfulness of the 'society of the spectacle', our destiny as victims, the impossibility of escape.

Even more dangerously, in hard times we seek out 'my identity' not in the clamour of revolutionary affirmation on the streets, but in the cover of small, enclosed spaces. We seek it, if we are lucky, in the haunts of the new hedonism, in the hushed hour of the analytic couch, in the jacuzzi baths, in the cult of the body beautiful, in the discos and restaurants of the glittering metropolis – Manhattan heaven. If we are less privileged we may seek it in the harsh consolation of cult churches or even in the rhetoric of fascism with its deliberate, seductive elevation of the irrational, its call to the unconscious. Socialist and revolutionary movements seem somehow to have lost their ability to give the individual an enhanced identity within the powerful safety of the movement. They have come to be seen, all too often, as a submission to conformity, which is the opposite of what they were intended to be.

Feminists and radicals need some powerful sense of identity as both collective and individualised. There is not one tyrannical identity to which all must approximate, but a group insistence on the value of difference. The testimony of consciousness raising, and of those 'women's' literary forms of diary, autobiography and confession, do not suggest an identical experience of the world, although the testimony has made possible the identification of points of similarity which have formed the basis for collective politics.

(1982)

Note

8 Meulenbelt, Anja (1980) *The Shame is Over* (London: The Women's Press).

Annette Kolodny

'Dancing Through the Minefield: Some Observations on the Theory, Practice and Politics of a Feminist Literary Criticism'
Feminist Studies

What distinguishes our work from those similarly oriented 'social conscious-ness' critiques, it is said, is its lack of systematic coherence. Pitted against, for example, psychoanalytic or Marxist readings, which owe a decisive share of their persuasiveness to their apparent internal consistency as a system, the aggregate of feminist literary criticism appears woefully deficient in system, and painfully lacking in program. It is, in fact, from all quarters, the most telling defect alleged against us, the most explosive threat in the minefield. And my own earlier observation that, as of 1976, feminist literary criticism appeared 'more like a set of interchangeable strategies than any coherent school or shared goal orientation,' has been taken by some as an indictment, by others as a statement of impatience. Neither was intended. I felt then, as I do now, that this would 'prove both its strength *and* its weakness,'[48] in the sense that the apparent disarray would leave us vulnerable to the kind of objection I've just alluded to; while the fact of our diversity would finally place us securely where, all along, we should have been: camped out, on the far side of the minefield, with the other pluralists and pluralisms.

In our heart of hearts, of course, most critics are really structuralists (whether or not they accept the label) because what we are seeking are patterns (or structures) that can order and explain the otherwise inchoate; thus, we invent, or believe we discover, relational patternings in the texts we read which promise transcendence from difficulty and perplexity to clarity and coherence. But, as I've tried to argue in these pages, to the imputed 'truth' or 'accuracy' of these findings, the feminist must oppose the painfully obvious truism that what is attended to in a literary work, and hence what is reported about it, is often determined not so much by the work itself as by the critical technique or aesthetic criteria through which it is filtered or, rather, read and decoded. All the feminist is asserting, then, is her own equivalent right to liberate new (and perhaps different) significances from these same texts; and, at the same time, her right to choose which features of a text she takes as relevant because she is, after all, asking new and different questions of it. In the process, she claims neither definitiveness nor structural completeness for her different readings and reading systems, but only their usefulness in recognizing the particular achievements of woman-as-author and their applicability in conscientiously decoding woman-as-sign.

That these alternate foci of critical attentiveness will render alternate readings or interpretations of the same text – even among feminists – should be no cause for alarm. Such developments illustrate only the pluralist contention that, 'in approaching a text of any complexity . . . the reader must choose to emphasize certain aspects which seem to him crucial' and that, 'in fact, the variety of readings which we have for many works is a function of the selection of crucial aspects made by a variety of readers.' Robert Scholes, from whom I've been quoting, goes so far as to assert that 'there is no single "right" reading for any complex literary work,' and, following the Russian formalist school, he observes that 'we do not speak of readings that are simply true or false, but of readings that are more or less rich, strategies that are more or less appropriate.'[49] Because those who share the term 'feminist' nonetheless practice a diversity of critical strategies, leading, in some cases, to quite different readings, we must acknowledge among ourselves that sister critics, 'having chosen to tell a different story, may in their interpretation identify different aspects of the meanings conveyed by the same passage.'[50]

Adopting a 'pluralist' label does not mean, however, that we cease to disagree; it means only that we entertain the possibility that different readings, even of the same text, may be differently useful, even illuminating, within different contexts of inquiry. It means, in effect, that we enter a dialectical process of examining, testing, even trying out the contexts – be they prior critical assumptions or explicitly stated ideological stances (or some combination of the two) – that led to the disparate readings. Not all will be equally acceptable to every one of us, of course, and even those prior assumptions or ideologies that are acceptable may call for further refinement and/or clarification. But, at the very least, because we will have grappled with the assumptions that led to it, we will be better able to articulate *why* we find a particular reading or interpretation adequate or inadequate. This kind of dialectical process, moreover, not only makes us more fully aware of what criticism is, and how it functions; it also gives us access to its future possibilities, making us conscious, as R. P. Blackmur put it, 'of what we have done,' 'of what can be done next, or done again,'[51] or, I would add, of what can be done differently. To put it still another way: just because we will no longer tolerate the specifically sexist omissions and oversights of earlier critical schools and methods does not mean that, in their stead, we must establish our own 'party line.'

In my view, our purpose is not and should not be the formulation of any single reading method or potentially procrustean set of critical procedures nor, even less, the generation of prescriptive categories for some dreamed of nonsexist literary canon.[52] Instead, as I see it, our task is to initiate nothing less than a playful pluralism, responsive to the possibilities of multiple critical schools and methods, but captive of none, recognizing that the many tools needed for our analysis will necessarily be largely inherited and only partly of our own making. Only by employing a plurality of methods will we protect ourselves from the temptation of so oversimplifying any text – and especially those particularly offensive to us – that we render ourselves unresponsive to what Scholes has called 'its various systems of meaning and their interaction.'[53] Any text we deem worthy of our critical attention is usually, after all, a locus of many and varied kinds of (personal, thematic, stylistic, structural, rhetorical, etc.) relationships. So, whether we tend to treat a text as a *mimesis*, in which words are taken to be recreating or representing viable worlds; or whether we prefer to treat a text as a kind of equation of communication, in which decipherable messages are passed from writers to readers; and whether we locate meaning as inherent in the text, the act of reading, or in some collaboration between reader and text – whatever our predilection, let us not generate from it a straitjacket that limits the scope of possible analysis. Rather, let us generate an ongoing dialogue of competing potential possibilities – among feminists and, as well, between feminist and nonfeminist critics.

The difficulty of what I describe does not escape me. The very idea of pluralism seems to threaten a kind of chaos for the future of literary inquiry while, at the same time, it seems to deny the hope of establishing some basic conceptual model which can organize all data – the hope which always begins any analytical exercise. My effort here, however, has been to demonstrate the essential delusions that inform such objections: If literary inquiry has historically escaped chaos by establishing canons, then it has only substituted one mode of arbitrary action for another – and, in this case, at the expense of half the population. And if feminists openly acknowledge ourselves as pluralists, then we do not give up the search for patterns of opposition and connection – probably the basis of thinking itself; what we give up is simply the arrogance of claiming that our work is either exhaustive or definitive. (It is, after all, the identical arrogance we are asking our nonfeminist colleagues to abandon.) If this kind of pluralism appears to threaten both the present coherence of and the inherited aesthetic criteria for a canon of 'greats,' then, as I have earlier argued, it is precisely that threat which, alone, can free us from the prejudices, the strictures, and the blind spots of the past. In feminist hands, I would add, it is less a threat than a promise.

What unites and repeatedly invigorates feminist literary criticism, then, is neither dogma nor method, but, as I have indicated earlier, an acute and impassioned *attentiveness* to the ways in which primarily male structures of power are inscribed (or encoded) within our literary inheritance; the consequences of that encoding for women – as characters, as readers, and as writers; and, with that, a shared analytic *concern* for the implications of that encoding not only for a better understanding of the past, but also for an improved reordering of the present and future as well. If that *concern* identifies feminist literary criticism as one of the many academic arms of the larger women's movement, then that *attentiveness*, within the halls of academe, poses no less a challenge for change, generating, as it does, the three propositions explored here. The critical pluralism that inevitably follows upon those three propositions, however, bears little resemblance to what Robinson has called 'the greatest bourgeois theme of all, the myth of pluralism, with its consequent rejection of ideological commitment as "too simple" to embrace the (necessarily complex) truth.'[54] Only ideological commitment could have gotten us to enter the minefield, putting in jeopardy our careers and our livelihood. Only the power of ideology to transform our conceptual worlds, and the inspiration of that ideology to liberate long-suppressed energies and emotions, can account for our willingness to take on critical tasks that, in an earlier decade, would have been 'abandoned in despair or apathy.'[55] The fact of differences among us proves only that, despite our shared commitments, we have nonetheless refused to shy away from complexity, preferring rather to openly disagree than to give up either intellectual honesty or hard-won insights.

Finally, I would argue, pluralism informs feminist literary inquiry not simply as a description of what already exists but, more importantly, as the only critical stance consistent with the current status of the larger women's movement. Segmented and variously focused, the different women's organizations neither espouse any single system of analysis nor, as a result, express any wholly shared, consistently articulated ideology. The ensuing loss in effective organization and political clout is a serious one, but it has not been paralyzing; in spite of our differences, we have united to *act* in areas of clear mutual concern (the push for the Equal Rights Amendment is probably the most obvious example). The trade-off, as I see it, has made possible an ongoing and educative dialectic of analysis and proferred solutions, protecting us thereby from the inviting traps of reductionism and dogma. And so long as this dialogue remains active, both our politics and our criticism will be free of dogma – but never, I hope, of feminist ideology, in all its variety. For, 'whatever else ideologies may be – projections of unacknowledged fears, disguises for ulterior motives, phatic expressions of group solidarity' (and the women's movement, to date, has certainly been all of these, and more) – whatever ideologies express, they are, as Geertz astutely observes, 'most distinctively, maps of problematic social reality and matrices for the creation of collective conscience.' And despite the fact that 'ideological advocates ... tend as much to obscure as to clarify the true nature of the problems involved,' as Geertz notes, 'they at least call attention to their existence and, by polarizing issues, make continued neglect more difficult. Without Marxist attack, there would have been no labor reform; without Black Nationalists, no deliberate speed.'[56] Without Seneca Falls, I would add, no enfranchisement of women, and without 'consciousness raising,' no feminist literary criticism nor, even less, women's studies.

(1980)

Notes

48 Annette Kolodny. 'Literary Criticism,' Review Essay in *Signs* 2, no. 2 (Winter 1976): 420.

49 Scholes, *Structuralism in Literature*, p. 144–45. These comments appear within his explication of Tzvetan Todorov's theory of reading.

50 I borrow this concise phrasing of pluralistic modesty from M. H. Abrams's 'The Deconstructive Angel,' *Critical Inquiry* 3, no. 3 (Spring 1977): 427. Indications of the pluralism that was to mark feminist inquiry were to be found in the diversity of essays collected by Susan Koppelman Cornillon for her early and ground breaking anthology, *Images of Women in Fiction: Feminist Perspectives* (Bowling Green, Ohio: Bowling Green University Popular Press, 1972).

51 R. P. Blackmur, 'A Burden for Critics,' *The Hudson Review* 1 (1948): 171. Blackmur, of course, was referring to the way in which criticism makes us unconscious of how art functions; I use his wording here because I am arguing that that same awareness must also be focused on the critical act itself. 'Consciousness,' he avers, 'is the way we feel the critic's burden.'

52 I have earlier elaborated my objection to prescriptive categories for literature in 'The Feminist as Literary Critic,' Critical Response in *Critical Inquiry* 2, no. 4 (Summer 1976): 827–28.

53 Scholes, *Structuralism in Literature*, pp. 151–52.

54 Lillian Robinson, 'Dwelling in Decencies: Radical Criticism and the Feminist Perspective,' *College English* 32, no. 8 (May 1971); reprinted in *Sex, Class, and Culture*, p. 11.

55 'Ideology bridges the emotional gap between things as they are and as one would have them be, thus insuring the performance of roles that might otherwise be abandoned in despair or apathy,' comments Geertz in 'Ideology as a Cultural System,' p. 205.

56 Ibid., p. 205. 220.

Elaine Showalter

'Toward a Feminist Poetics'
Women Writing and Writing About Women

The Feminist Critique: Hardy

Let us take briefly as an example of the way a feminist critique might proceed, Thomas Hardy's *The Mayor of Casterbridge*, which begins with the famous scene of the drunken Michael Henchard selling his wife and infant daughter for five guineas at a country fair. In his study of Hardy, Irving Howe has praised the brilliance and power of this opening scene:

> To shake loose from one's wife; to discard that drooping rag of a woman, with her mute complaints and maddening passivity; to escape not by a slinking abandonment but through the public sale of her body to a stranger, as horses are sold at a fair; and thus to wrest, through sheer amoral wilfulness, a second chance out of life – it is with this stroke, so insidiously attractive to male fantasy, that *The Mayor of Casterbridge* begins.[8]

It is obvious that a woman, unless she has been indoctrinated into being very deeply identified indeed with male culture, will have a different experience of this scene. I quote Howe first to indicate how the fantasies of the male critic distort the text; for Hardy tells us very little about the relationship of Michael and Susan Henchard, and what we see in the early scenes does not suggest that she is drooping, complaining or passive. Her role, however, is a passive one; severely constrained by her womanhood, and further burdened by her child, there is no way that *she* can wrest a second chance out of life. She cannot master events, but only accommodate herself to them.

What Howe, like other male critics of Hardy, conveniently overlooks about the novel is that Henchard sells not only his wife but his child, a child who can only be female. Patriarchal societies do not readily sell their sons, but their daughters are all for sale sooner or later. Hardy wished to make the sale of the daughter emphatic and central; in early drafts of the novel Henchard has two daughters and sells only one, but Hardy revised to make it clearer that Henchard is symbolically selling his entire share in the world of women. Having severed his bonds with this female community of love and loyalty, Henchard has chosen to live in the male community, to define his human relationships by the male code of paternity, money and legal contract. His tragedy lies in realising the inadequacy of this system, and in his inability to repossess the loving bonds he comes desperately to need.

The emotional centre of *The Mayor of Casterbridge* is neither Henchard's relationship to his wife, nor his superficial romance with Lucetta Templeman, but his slow appreciation of the strength and dignity of his wife's daughter, Elizabeth-Jane. Like the other women in the book, she is governed by her own heart – man-made laws are not important to her until she is taught by Henchard himself to value legality, paternity, external definitions, and thus in the end to reject him. A self-proclaimed 'women-hater', a man who has felt at best a 'supercilious pity' for womankind, Henchard is humbled and 'unmanned' by the collapse of his own virile façade, the loss of his mayor's chain, his master's authority, his father's rights. But in Henchard's alleged weakness and 'womanishness', breaking through in moments of tenderness, Hardy is really showing us the man at his best. Thus Hardy's female characters in *The Mayor of Casterbridge*, as in his other novels, are somewhat idealised and melancholy projections of a repressed male self.

As we see in this analysis, one of the problems of the feminist critique is that it is male-oriented. If we study stereotypes of women, the sexism of male critics, and the limited roles women play in literary history, we are not learning what women have felt and experienced, but only what men have thought women should be. In some fields of specialisation, this may require a long apprenticeship to the male theoretician, whether he be Althusser, Barthes, Macherey or Lacan; and then an application of the theory of signs or myths or the unconscious to male texts or films. The temporal and intellectual investment one makes in such a process increases resistance to questioning it, and to seeing its historical and ideological boundaries. The critique also has a tendency to naturalise women's victimisation, by making it the inevitable and obsessive topic of discussion. One sees, moreover, in works like Elizabeth Hardwick's *Seduction and Betrayal*, the bittersweet moral distinctions the critic makes between women merely betrayed by men, like Hetty in *Adam Bede*, and the heroines who make careers out of betrayal, like Hester Prynne in *The Scarlet Letter*. This comes dangerously close to a celebration of the opportunities of victimisation, the seduction *of* betrayal.[9]

Gynocritics and Female Culture

In contrast to this angry or loving fixation on male literature, the programme of gynocritics is to construct a female framework for the analysis of women's literature, to develop new models based on the study of female experience, rather than to adapt male models and theories. Gynocritics begins at the point when we free ourselves from the linear absolutes of male literary history, stop trying to fit women between the lines of the male tradition, and focus instead on the newly visible world of female culture. This is comparable to the ethnographer's effort to render the experience of the 'muted' female half of a society, which is described in Shirley Ardener's collection, *Perceiving Women*.[10] Gynocritics is related to feminist research in history, anthropology, psychology and sociology, all of which have developed hypotheses of a female subculture including not only the ascribed status, and the internalised constructs of femininity, but also the occupations, interactions and consciousness of women. Anthropologists study the female subculture in the relationships between women, as mothers, daughters, sisters and friends; in sexuality, reproduction and ideas about the body; and in rites of initiation and passage, purification ceremonies, myths and taboos. Michelle Rosaldo writes in *Woman, Culture, and Society*,

> the very symbolic and social conceptions that appear to set women apart and to circumscribe their activities may be used by women as a basis for female solidarity and worth. When men live apart from women, they in fact cannot control them, and unwittingly they may provide them with the symbols and social resources on which to build a society of their own.[11]

Thus in some women's literature, feminine values penetrate and undermine the masculine systems which contain them; and women have imaginatively engaged the myths of the Amazons, and the fantasies of a separate female society, in genres from Victorian poetry to contemporary science fiction.

In the past two years, pioneering work by four young American feminist scholars has given us some new ways to interpret the culture of nineteenth-century American women, and the literature which was its primary expressive form. Carroll Smith-Rosenberg's essay 'The Female World of Love and Ritual' examines several archives of letters between women, and outlines the homosocial emotional world of the nineteenth century. Nancy Cott's *The Bonds of Woman-*

hood: Woman's Sphere in New England 1780–1835 explores the paradox of a cultural bondage, a legacy of pain and submission, which none the less generates a sisterly solidarity, a bond of shared experience, loyalty and compassion. Ann Douglas's ambitious book, *The Feminization of American Culture*, boldly locates the genesis of American mass culture in the sentimental literature of women and clergymen, two allied and 'disestablished' post-industrial groups. These three are social historians; but Nina Auerbach's *Communities of Women: An Idea in Fiction* seeks the bonds of womanhood in women's literature, ranging from the matriarchal households of Louisa May Alcott and Mrs Gaskell to the women's schools and colleges of Dorothy Sayers, Sylvia Plath and Muriel Spark. Historical and literary studies like these, based on English women, are badly needed; and the manuscript and archival sources for them are both abundant and untouched.[12]

(1979)

Notes

8 Irving Howe, *Thomas Hardy* (London, 1968), p. 84. For a more detailed discussion of this problem, see my essay 'The Unmanning of the Mayor of Casterbridge' in Dale Kramer (ed.), *Critical Approaches to Hardy* (London, 1979).

9 Elizabeth Hardwick, *Seduction and Betrayal* (New York, 1974).

10 Shirley Ardener (ed.), *Perceiving Women* (London, 1975).

11 'Women, Culture, and Society: A Theoretical Overview' in Louise Lamphere and Michelle Rosaldo (eds.), *Women, Culture and Society* (Stanford, 1974), p. 39.

12 Carroll Smith-Rosenberg. 'The Female World of Love and Ritual: Relations Between Women in Nineteenth-Century America', *Signs: Journal of Women in Culture and Society*, vol. 1 (Autumn 1975), pp. 1–30; Nancy Cott, *The Bonds of Womanhood* (New Haven, 1977); Ann Douglas, *The Feminization of American Culture* (New York, 1977); Nina Auerbach, *Communities of Women* (Cambridge, Mass., 1978).

TORIL MOI

Sexual/ Textual Politics: Feminist Literary Theory

Arguing that feminist criticism is a fundamentally 'suspicious' approach to literature, Kolodny sees the principal task of the feminist critic as that of examining the validity of our aesthetic judgments: 'What ends do those judgments serve, the feminist asks; and what conceptions of the world or ideological stances do they (even if unwittingly) help to perpetuate?' (15). This is surely one of her most valuable insights.

The problem arises when she proceeds from this to a wholesale recommendation of *pluralism* as the appropriate feminist stance. Feminist criticism lacks systematic coherence, she argues, and this fact ('the fact of our diversity'), should 'place us securely where, all along, we should have been: camped out, on the far side of the minefield, with the other pluralists and pluralisms' (17). Feminists cannot and indeed should not provide that 'internal consistency as a system' that Kolodny ascribes to psychoanalysis and Marxism. In her discourse, these two theoretical formations come to figure as monolithically oppressive blocks towering over the diversified, anti-authoritarian feminist field. But it is not only untrue that Marxism and psychoanalysis offer such a unified theoretical field; it is also surely doubtful that feminist criticism is *that* diversified.[2] Kolodny acknowledges that feminist politics is the basis for feminist criticism; so that though we may argue over what constitutes proper feminist politics and theory, that debate nevertheless takes place within a feminist political framework, much like debates within contemporary Marxism. Without common political ground, there can simply be no recognizable *feminist* criticism. In this context, Kolodny's 'pluralist' approach risks throwing the baby out with the bathwater:

> Adopting a "pluralist" label does not mean, however, that we cease to disagree; it means only that we entertain the possibility that different readings, even of the same text, may be differently useful, even illuminating, within different contexts of inquiry.
>
> (18)

But if we wax pluralistic enough to acknowledge the feminist position as just one among many 'useful' approaches, we also implicitly grant the most 'masculinist' of criticism the right of existence: it just *might* be 'useful' in a very different context from ours.

Kolodny's intervention in the theoretical debate pays too little attention to the role of politics in critical theory. When she states, correctly, that 'If feminist criticism calls anything into question, it must be that dog-eared myth of intellectual neutrality' (21), she still seems not to recognize that even critical theory carries with it its own political implications. Feminist criticism cannot just

> initiate nothing less than a playful pluralism, responsive to the possibilities of multiple critical schools and methods, but captive of none, recognizing that the many tools needed for our analysis will necessarily be largely inherited and only partly of our own making.
>
> (19)

Feminists must surely also conduct a political and theoretical evaluation of the various methods and tools on offer, to make sure that they don't backfire on us.

[. . .]

In the first article, Showalter distinguishes between two forms of feminist criticism. The first type is concerned with woman as reader, which Showalter labels 'feminist critique'. The second type deals with woman as writer, and Showalter calls this 'gynocritics'. 'Feminist critique' deals with works by male authors, and Showalter tells us that this form of criticism is a 'historically grounded inquiry which probes the ideological assumptions of literary phenomena' (25). This sort of 'suspicious' approach to the literary text seems however to be largely absent from Showalter's second category, since among the primary concerns of 'gynocritics' we find 'the history, themes, genres and structures of literature by women' as well as the 'psychodynamics of female creativity' and 'studies of particular writers and works' (25). There is no indication here that the feminist critic concerned with women as writers should bring other than sympathetic, identity seeking approaches to bear on works written by women. The 'hermeneutics of suspicion', which assumes that the text is not, or not only, what it pretends to be, and therefore searches for underlying contradictions and conflicts as well as absences and silences in the text, seems to be reserved for texts written by men. The feminist critic, in other words, must realize that the woman-produced text will occupy a totally different status from the 'male' text.

Showalter writes:

> One of the problems of the feminist critique is that it is male-oriented. If we study stereotypes of women, the sexism of male critics, and the limited roles women play in literary history, we are not learning what women have felt and experienced, but only what men have thought women should be.
>
> (27)

The implication is not only that the feminist critic should turn to 'gyno-critics', the study of women's writings, precisely in order to learn 'what women have felt and experienced', but also that this experience is directly available in the texts written by women. The text, in other words, has disappeared, or become the transparent medium through which 'experience' can be seized. This view of texts as transmitting authentic 'human' experience is, as we have seen, a traditional emphasis of Western patriarchal humanism. In Showalter's case, this humanist position is also tinged by a good portion of empiricism. She rejects theory as a male invention that apparently can only be used on men's texts (27–8). 'Gynocritics' frees itself from pandering to male values and seeks to 'focus ... on the newly visible world of female culture' (28). This search for the 'muted' female culture can best be carried out by applying anthropological theories to the female author and her work: 'Gynocritics is related to feminist research in history, anthropology, psychology and sociology, all of which have developed hypotheses of a female subculture' (28). The feminist critic, in other words, should attend to historical, anthropological, psychological and sociological aspects of the 'female' text; in short, it would seem, to everything but the text as a signifying process. The only influences Showalter appears to recognize as constitutive of the text are of an empirical, extra-literary sort. This attitude, coupled with her fear of 'male' theory and general appeal to 'human' experience, has the unfortunate effect of drawing her perilously close to the male critical hierarchy whose patriarchal values she opposes.

(1985)

Note

2 Lukács, Brecht, Stalin, Trotsky, Benjamin, Gramsci and Althusser are all considered Marxists, and psychoanalysis comprises names as divergent as Freud, Adler, Jung, Reich, Horney, Fromm, Klein and Lacan.

Alice A. Jardine

Gynesis: Configurations of Woman and Modernity

Gynesis

These new ways have not surfaced in a void. Over the past century, those master (European) narratives history, philosophy, religion which have determined our sense of legitimacy in the West have undergone a series of crises in legitimation. It is widely recognized that legitimacy is part of that judicial domain which, historically, has determined the right to govern, the succession of kings, the link between father and son, the necessary paternal fiction, the ability to decide who is the father – in patriarchal culture. The crises experienced by the major Western narratives have not, therefore, been gender-neutral. They are crises in the narratives invented by men.

Going back to analyze those narratives and their crises has meant going back to the Greek philosophies in which they are grounded and, most particularly, to the originary relationships posited between the *techné* and *physis, time* and *space*, and all the dualistic oppositions that determine our ways of thinking. And rethinking those oppositions has meant, among other things, putting their "obligatory connotations" into discursive circulation, making those connotations explicit in order, one would hope, to put them into question. For example, the *techné* and time have connoted the male; *physis* and space the female. To think new relationships between the *techné* and *physis*, time and space, and so on, within an atmosphere of crisis, has required backing away from all that has defined and immobilized the possibilities of their relationships in the history of Western philosophy, requestioning the major topics of that philosophy: Man, the Subject, Truth, History, Meaning. At the forefront of this rethinking has been a rejection by and within those narratives of what seem to have been the strongest pillars of their history: Anthropomorphism, Humanism, and Truth. And again, it is in France that, in my opinion, this rethinking has taken its strongest conceptual leaps, as "philosophy," "history," and "literature" have attempted to account for the crisis-in-narrative that is modernity.

In general, this has brought about, within the master narratives in the West, a vast self-exploration, a questioning and turning back upon their own discourse, in an attempt to create a new *space* or *spacing within themselves* for survivals (of different kinds). In France, such rethinking has involved, above all, a reincorporation and reconceptualization of that which has been the master narratives' own "nonknowledge," what has eluded them, what has engulfed them. This other-than-themselves is almost always a "space" of some kind (over which the narrative has lost control), and this space has been coded as *feminine*, as *woman*. It is upon this process that I am insisting in this study: the transformation of woman and the feminine into verbs at the interior of those narratives that are today experiencing a crisis in legitimation.

To designate that process, I have suggested what I hope will be a believable neologism: *gynesis* – the putting into discourse of "woman" as that *process* diagnosed in France as intrinsic to the condition of modernity; indeed, the valorization of the feminine, woman, and her obligatory, that is, histori- cal connotations, as somehow intrinsic to new and necessary modes of thinking, writing, speaking. The object produced by this process is neither a person nor a thing, but a horizon, that toward which the process is tending: a *gynema*. This *gynema* is a reading effect, a woman-in-effect that is never stable and has no identity. Its appearance in a written text is perhaps noticed only by the feminist reader – either when it becomes insistently "feminine" or when women (as defined metaphysically, historically) seem magically to reappear within the discourse. This tear in the fabric produces in the (feminist) reader a state of uncertainty and sometimes of distrust – especially when the faltering narrative in which it is embedded has been articulated by a man from within a nonetheless still-existent discipline. When it appears in women theorists' discourse, it would seem to be less troubling. The still existent slippages in signification among feminine, woman, women, and what I am calling *gynesis* and *gynema* are dismissed (at least in the United States and increasingly by male feminist critics) as irrelevant *because* it is a woman speaking.

I have tried to introduce here briefly some of the reasons why feminists may not want to qualify, too rapidly, major texts of modernity in the West, especially in France, as necessarily feminist or antifeminist, most particularly when they are texts signed by women. I hope I have begun to convey, as well, how important I think it is for feminist theoreticians in France, England, the United States, and (especially) elsewhere to rethink the history, impact, place for, and possible future directions of contemporary interpretive modes with regard to feminist theory. For if, as I have only begun to suggest, modernity represents a perhaps unavoidable and, in any case, new kind of discursivity on, about, as woman, a valorization and speaking of woman, and if contemporary feminists are going to take modernity and its theorists seriously, then feminist theory must address some new and complex questions – questions that form the matrix of the pages to follow.

Are gynesis and feminism in contradiction, or do they overlap and interact with each other, perhaps even render each other inevitable, in some way? In what sense do certain of the texts of gynesis reintroduce very familiar representations of women in spite of themselves? To what extent is the process designated as feminine by those texts absolutely dependent on those representations? When we posit that process as one incarnated by *women*, are we not falling back into the anthropomorphic (or gynomorphic?) images thinkers of modernity have been trying to disintegrate?

On the other hand, in what ways do some of the major texts in question exceed those familiar representations of women? How do women theorists' texts of gynesis differ from those of male theorists; or French texts of gynesis from American ones? If the gynesis seemingly intrinsic to modernity is but the product of male fantasy, does that necessarily mean it offers no radical tools for women? How might these texts offer new ways of connecting the most radical insights of feminism to the larger questions facing the West as it moves toward a new century?

Most important, if modernity and feminism are not to become mutually exclusive and, at the same time, if feminism is not to compromise the quality of its attention to female stereotyping of whatever kind, what could be new strategies for asking new kinds of questions?

(1985)

MARY POOVEY

'Feminism and Deconstruction'
Feminist Studies

So we are back to the problem with which I began. Is it possible to be a woman if one accepts the philosophical program of deconstruction, or must a deconstructive critic be a "woman"? By way of proposing my answer to this question, I want to outline what I see as the positive contributions deconstruction makes to a feminism that is interested not only in the idea of "woman" but also in the concrete, class-and race-specific facts of historical women. I will conclude with an analysis of the limitations of deconstruction and some suggestions about how and why feminism must finally use deconstructive strategies to demystify the category of "woman" whose seductive appeal threatens to prevent some kinds of questions from being asked.

From the perspective of a feminist interested in history and such social determinants as race and class, the primary contribution of deconstruction is not its recuperative program but the project of demystification. Because deconstruction reveals the figurative nature of all ideology, it can expose the artifice inherent in such categories as "nature" and gender. This, in turn, opens the possibility for (although, as I will argue in a moment, it does not presuppose or mandate) a genuinely historical practice – one that could analyze and deconstruct the specific articulations and institutionalizations of these categories, their interdependence, and the uneven processes by which they have been deployed and altered. Given this emphasis, deconstructive strategies could enable feminists to write a history of the various contradictions within institutional definitions of woman that would show how these contradictions have opened the possibility for change. The fact that the nineteenth-century legal principle of "coverture," for example, institutionalized the married woman as *the* normative "woman" meant that unmarried women enjoyed rights which "naturally" belonged to men. Despite other institutional and ideological constraints upon their behavior, this contradiction within the category "woman" facilitated the entry of increasing numbers of (middle-class) women into waged work, *and* it helped expose the artificiality of an opposition that aligned legal and property rights with sex.

The second contribution deconstruction can make is to challenge hierarchical and oppositional logic. Because the practice of deconstruction transforms binary oppositions into an economy in which terms circulate rather than remain fixed, it could (although it does not usually or necessarily) mobilize another ordering system in which the construction of false unities intrinsic to binary oppositions would not prevail. In other words, in its demystifying mode, deconstruction does not simply offer an alternative hierarchy of binary oppositions; it problematizes and opens to scrutiny the very nature of identity and oppositional logic and therefore makes visible the artifice necessary to establish, legislate, and maintain hierarchical thinking. Given this emphasis, deconstructive strategies could enable us to chart more accurately the multiple determinants that figure in any individual's social position and (relative) power and oppression. All women may currently occupy the position "woman," for example, but they do not occupy it in the same way. Women of color in a white-ruled society face different obstacles than do white women, and they may share more important problems with men of color than with their white "sisters." By deconstructing the term "woman" into a set of independent variables, this strategy can show how consolidating all women into a falsely unified "woman" has helped mask the operations of power that actually divide women's interests as much as unite them.

Deconstruction's third contribution is the idea of the "in-between." Even as an ad hoc strategy, the "in-between" constitutes one tool for dismantling binary thinking. Once the binary construct is revealed to be artificial, the identity of the two, apparently fixed terms and the rigidity of the "structure" that prevents other possibilities from being formulated could be destabilized. Such a strategy would not abolish either the hierarchical thinking that lurks within binary oppositions or power more generally conceived. But it would enable us to rethink "power" (along with identity) so as to perceive its fragmentary quality. We could then see (and make the most of) the power various groups of women do currently wield and expose the limitations of the power that seems to be (but is not) the "property" of some unified ruling group.[17]

Thus, just to provide one more concrete example, deconstruction provides the tools for exposing the fact that the opposition between the "sexes," like the definitions of "women" and "men," is a social construction, not a reflection or articulation of biological fact. In so doing, deconstruction sets up the possibility that the supposedly fixed opposition of masculine/feminine might lose its social prominence because we could begin to recognize that there is no necessary connection between anatomical sexuality and gender stereotypes or roles. This, in turn, might legitimate behaviors that do not seem to "derive from" sex (boys might be allowed to be more nurturing, for example). This social liberation of the concept from its natural "referent" might, in turn, open the door for examining even the fixity of the anatomical categories upon which the binary opposition seems to be based. Instead of relegating all biological variants into the two categories, "male" and "female" (with "abnormal" absorbing everything that is "left over"), this practice might enable us both to multiply the categories *of* sex and to detach reproduction from sex – a hitherto unthinkable concept increasingly made possible by new reproductive technologies. Such a focus on the social construction of sexual identity goes beyond the more common understanding of social construction many feminists now endorse, because it deconstructs not only the relationship between women and certain social roles but also the very term "woman." Such a reconceptualization of sex and the individual is the radical – and logical – extension of deconstruction's program. It would challenge the very basis of our current social organization. In so doing, it would necessarily feel like a loss, but it might also create the conditions of possibility for as yet unimagined organizations of human potential.

This brave new world of the reconceptualized subject may be implied by deconstruction, but it does not follow necessarily from its current practice. Indeed, as it is most typically practiced – both in its recuperative and its demystifying modes – deconstruction tends to work against the kinds of historically specific, political practices to which I have just alluded. It must be obvious to anyone familiar with deconstruction today that its politics, when they are visible, are most typically conservative. One reason for this is the popularity of what I have called deconstruction's recuperative project. I have already suggested that the particular formulation of the subversive position as a "feminine" language allows for the kind of biologism all too compatible with conservative arguments about female nature. Beyond this, however, the relegation of the "feminine" to a unified *position* has two limiting consequences. On the one hand, it subordinates the diversity of the real historical women who occupy that position to the likeness they share by virtue of their placement as "other." And on the other hand, it works against any analysis of who comes to occupy that position, why certain groups occupy it at various times, or the relationships among those groups. Just to give one example of this second problem, the deconstructive project can be (and has been) used to analyze the marginalization of peoples of color as well as women, and the recuperative emphasis of deconstruction has been invoked to describe the subversive operations of black "signifyin(g)" or "jive."[18]

Yet although this emphasis on placement and subversive languages undoubtedly provides a vocabulary for conceptualizing the positive effects of difference and therefore for undermining negative stereotypes, it does not facilitate our understanding of the relationship between women and blacks, for example, nor does it account for the specific kinds of oppression or subversiveness women or blacks (or black women) may suffer or exercise when assigned to that position. In providing no tools for analyzing specificity, moreover, the recuperative mode of deconstruction provides no model of change. If we cannot describe why a particular group came to occupy the position of "other" or how its tenure in that position differs from the effect such positioning has on other groups, we have no basis upon which to posit or by which to predict any other state of affairs. We have no basis, in other words, for political analysis or action.

The more fundamental limitation of deconstruction follows from the reluctance of deconstructive critics to examine the artifice – and historical specificity – of their own practice. To committed deconstructive critics, everything seems subject to deconstruction's dismantling gaze except deconstruction itself. Insofar as it purports to be a master strategy instead of the methodological counterpart to a historically specific conceptualization of language and meaning, deconstruction – even in its demystifying mode – participates in the very process it claims to expose. The very project of deconstructing binary logic is inextricably bound to a preoccupation with the *structures* of language and conceptualization, after all, instead of, for example, an interest in the social relations or institutions by which language and ideas (including deconstruction) are produced, distributed, and reinforced. As long as it is viewed only according to its own implicit definition – as an ahistorical master strategy – deconstruction must remain outside of politics, because no stable position (other than its own) can exist. This gives deconstruction an apparently unassailable hold on the conceptualization of meaning. But this, I suggest, is not because deconstruction is "true" or because it *necessarily* superseded politics but only because it has refused the historicizing tendency it contains but has not so far turned upon itself.

My original problem, then, returns with a vengeance born of my political commitment to the future as well as the present. Because of its ability to dismantle binary logic and deconstruct identity, I do think deconstruction has provided and continues to offer an essential tool for feminist analysis. But in order for this double-edged blade not to reproduce the system it purports to cut apart, deconstruction itself must be historicized and subjected to the same kind of scrutiny with which it has dismantled Western metaphysics. As part of this historicizing project, we should examine the extent to which deconstruction's feminization of philosophy is implicated in the feminization – and appropriation – of other practices traditionally considered masculine (and therefore unacceptably explicit in their aggression). I would also like to see some analysis of the kinds of questions deconstruction precludes by conceptualizing its questions in terms of structures and play and more analysis of the political interests deconstruction currently serves – as well as the interests in which it could be enlisted.[19] Ultimately, my prediction is that feminists practicing deconstructive and other poststructuralist techniques from an explicitly political position will so completely rewrite deconstruction as to leave it behind, for all intents and purposes, as part of the historicization of structuralism already underway in several disciplines.

For the present, however, and looking toward the future, I propose that materialist feminists need to pursue two projects simultaneously. On the one hand, we need to recognize that "woman" *is* currently both a position within a dominant, binary symbolic order *and* that the position is arbitrarily (and falsely) unified. On the other hand, we need to remember that there *are* concrete historical women whose differences reveal the inadequacy of this unified category in the present and the past. The multiple positions real women occupy – the positions dictated by race, for example, or by class or sexual preference – should alert us to the inadequacy of binary logic and unitary selves without making us forget that this logic *has* dictated (and still does) some aspects of women's social treatment. At the same time, however, this emphasis must also lead us to question the ahistorical nature of what has been taken as the basis of feminism. For, if the position "woman" *is* falsely unified and if one's identity is *not* given (solely or necessarily) by anatomy, then woman – or even women – cannot remain a legitimate rallying point for political actions. Real historical women have been (and are) oppressed, and the ways and means of that oppression need to be analyzed and fought. But at the same time, we need to be ready to abandon the binary thinking that has stabilized women as a group that *could* be collectively (although not uniformly) oppressed.

I suggest, then, that materialist feminists need to do battle on two fronts. We must recognize that what (most) women now share is a positional similarity that masquerades as a natural likeness and that has historically underwritten oppression, *and* we must be willing to give up the illusory similarity of nature that reinforces binary logic even though such a move threatens to jeopardize what seems "special" about women. My argument is that the structural similarity that pretends to reflect nature masks the operation of other kinds of difference (class and race, for example) precisely by constructing a "nature" that seems desirable, because it gives women what seems to be (but is not) a naturally constructive and politically subversive role. In the long run, materialist feminists will need to write not only the history of women's oppression but also the future of gender difference(s). We will need to turn from campaigns that reproduce the essentialism of sex difference to projects that call into question the very essentialism upon which our history has been based. In this sense, conceptualizing the issue in terms of real women is part of the solution, but it is also part of the problem. Deconstruction is a critical component of the political work I am outlining here, but unless it is deployed upon itself, it will trap us in a practice that once more glorifies the "feminine" instead of giving us the means to explode binary logic and make the social construction of (sexed) identities a project of pressing political concern. If deconstruction took feminism seriously, it wouldn't look like deconstruction anymore. If feminism took deconstruction at its word, we could begin to dismantle the system that assigns to all women a single identity and a marginal place.

(1988)

Notes

17 See Brown and Adams, 47.
18 See esp. Hortense J. Spillers, "Interstices: A Small Drama of Words," in *Pleasure and Danger: Exploring Female Sexuality*, ed. Carol S. Vance (Boston: Routledge & Kegan Paul, 1984), 73–100.
19 See Bartkowski, 76–77.

JULIA KRISTEVA

'Woman Can Never Be Defined'
New French Feminisms

Julia Kristeva: The belief that "one is a woman" is almost as absurd and obscurantist as the belief that "one is a man." I say "almost" because there are still many goals which women can achieve: freedom of abortion and contraception, day-care centers for children, equality on the job, etc. Therefore, we must use "we are women" as an advertisement or slogan for our demands. On a deeper level, however, a woman cannot "be"; it is something which does not even belong in the order of *being*. It follows that a feminist practice can only be negative, at odds with what already exists so that we may say "that's not it" and "that's still not it." In "woman" I see something that cannot be represented, something that is not said, something above and beyond nomenclatures and ideologies. There are certain "men" who are familiar with this phenomenon; it is what some modern texts never stop signifying: testing the limits of language and sociality – the law and its transgression, mastery and (sexual) pleasure – without reserving one for males and the other for females, on the condition that it is never mentioned. From this point of view, it seems that certain feminist demands revive a kind of naive romanticism, a belief in identity (the reverse of phallocratism), if we compare them to the experience of both poles of sexual difference as is found in the economy of Joycian or Artaudian prose or in modern music – Cage, Stockhausen.[3] I pay close attention to the particular aspect of the work of the avant-garde which dissolves identity, even sexual identities; and in my theoretical formulations I try to go against metaphysical theories that censure what I just labeled "a woman" – this is what, I think, makes my research that of a woman. Perhaps I should add something here, and it's not contradictory to what I just said. Because of the decisive role that women play in the reproduction of the species, and because of the privileged relationship between father and daughter, a woman takes social constraints even more seriously, has fewer tendencies toward anarchism, and is more mindful of ethics. This may explain why our negativity is not Nietzschean anger. If my work aims at broadcasting to the public precisely what this society censures in the avant-garde practice, then, I think, my work obeys ethical exigencies of this type. The whole problem is to know whether this ethical penchant in the woman's struggle will remain separated from negativity; in which case the ethical penchant will degenerate into conformity, and negativity will degenerate into esoteric perversion. The problem is on the agenda of the women's movement. But without the movement, no work of any woman would ever really be possible.

(1974)

Note

3 James Joyce, Antonin Artaud, John Cage, Karlheinz Stockhausen: writers and musicians included in the avant-garde canon. – Tr.

NANCY FRASER AND LINDA J. NICHOLSON

'Social Criticism Without Philosophy: An Encounter between Feminism and Postmodernism' Feminism/Postmodernism

On the other hand, the practice of feminist politics in the 1980s has generated a new set of pressures which have worked against metanarratives. In recent years, poor and working-class women, women of color, and lesbians have finally won a wider hearing for their objections to feminist theories which fail to illuminate their lives and address their problems. They have exposed the earlier quasi-metanarratives, with their assumptions of universal female dependence and confinement to the domestic sphere, as false extrapolations from the experience of the white, middle-class, heterosexual women who dominated the beginnings of the second wave. For example, writers like Bell Hooks, Gloria Joseph, Audre Lord, Maria Lugones, and Elizabeth Spelman have unmasked the implicit reference to white Anglo women in many classic feminist texts. Likewise, Adrienne Rich and Marilyn Frye have exposed the heterosexist bias of much mainstream feminist theory.[17] Thus, as the class, sexual, racial, and ethnic awareness of the movement has altered, so has the preferred conception of theory. It has become clear that quasi-metanarratives hamper rather than promote sisterhood, since they elide differences among women and among the forms of sexism to which different women are differentially subject. Likewise, it is increasingly apparent that such theories hinder alliances with other progressive movements, since they tend to occlude axes of domination other than gender. In sum, there is growing interest among feminists in modes of theorizing which are attentive to differences and to cultural and historical specificity.

In general, then, feminist scholarship of the 1980s evinces some conflicting tendencies. On the one hand, there is decreasing interest in grand social theories as scholarship has become more localized, issue-oriented, and explicitly fallibilistic. On the other hand, essentialist vestiges persist in the continued use of ahistorical categories like gender identity without reflection as to how, when, and why such categories originated and were modified over time. This tension is symptomatically expressed in the current fascination, on the part of U.S. feminists, with French psychoanalytic feminisms: The latter propositionally decry essentialism even as they performatively enact it.[18] More generally, feminist scholarship has remained insufficiently attentive to the *theoretical* prerequisites of dealing with diversity, despite widespread commitment to accepting it politically.

By criticizing lingering essentialism in contemporary feminist theory, we hope to encourage such theory to become more consistently postmodern. This is not, however, to recommend merely any form of postmodernism. On the contrary, as we have shown, the version developed by Jean-François Lyotard offers a weak and inadequate conception of social criticism without philosophy. It rules out genres of criticism, such as large historical narrative and historically situated social theory, which feminists rightly regard as indispensable. But it does not follow from Lyotard's shortcomings that criticism without philosophy is in principle incompatible with criticism with social force. Rather, as we argue next, a robust postmodern-feminist paradigm of social criticism without philosophy is possible.

Toward a Postmodern Feminism

How can we combine a postmodernist incredulity toward metanarratives with the social-critical power of feminism? How can we conceive a version of criticism without philosophy which is robust enough to handle the tough job of analyzing sexism in all its endless variety and monotonous similarity?

A first step is to recognize, *contra* Lyotard, that postmodern critique need forswear neither large historical narratives nor analyses of societal macrostructures. This point is important for feminists, since sexism has a long history and is deeply and pervasively embedded in contemporary societies. Thus, postmodern feminists need not abandon the large theoretical tools needed to address large political problems. There is nothing self-contradictory in the idea of a postmodern theory.

However, if postmodern-feminist critique must remain theoretical, not just any kind of theory will do. Rather, theory here would be explicitly historical, attuned to the cultural specificity of different societies and periods and to that of different groups within societies and periods. Thus, the categories of postmodern-feminist theory would be inflected by temporality, with historically specific institutional categories like the modern, restricted, male-headed, nuclear family taking precedence over ahistorical, functionalist categories like reproduction and mothering. Where categories of the latter sort were not eschewed altogether, they would be genealogized, that is, framed by a historical narrative and rendered temporally and culturally specific.

Moreover, postmodern-feminist theory would be nonuniversalist. When its focus became cross-cultural or transepochal, its mode of attention would be comparativist rather than universalizing, attuned to changes and contrasts instead of to covering laws. Finally, postmodern-feminist theory would dispense with the idea of a subject of history. It would replace unitary notions of woman and feminine gender identity with plural and complexly constructed conceptions of social identity, treating gender as one relevant strand among others, attending also to class, race, ethnicity, age, and sexual orientation.

In general, postmodern-feminist theory would be pragmatic and fallibilistic. It would tailor its methods and categories to the specific task at hand, using multiple categories when appropriate and forswearing the metaphysical comfort of a single feminist method or feminist epistemology. In short, this theory would look more like a tapestry composed of threads of many different hues than one woven in a single color.

The most important advantage of this sort of theory would be its usefulness for contemporary feminist political practice. Such practice is increasingly a matter of alliances rather than one of unity around a universally shared interest or identity. It recognizes that the diversity of women's needs and experiences means that no single solution, on issues like child care, social security, and housing, can be adequate for all. Thus, the underlying premise of this practice is that, while some women share some common interests and face some common enemies, such commonalities are by no means universal; rather, they are interlaced with differences, even with conflicts. This, then, is a practice made up of a patchwork of overlapping alliances, not one circumscribable by an essential definition. One might best speak of it in the plural as the practice of feminisms. In a sense, this practice is in advance of much contemporary feminist theory. It is already implicitly postmodern. It would find its most appropriate and useful theoretical expression in a postmodern-feminist form of critical inquiry. Such inquiry would be the theoretical counterpart of a broader, richer, more complex, and multilayered feminist solidarity, the sort of solidarity which is essential for overcoming the oppression of women in its "endless variety and monotonous similarity."

(1990)

Notes

17 Marilyn Frye, *The Politics of Reality: Essays in Feminist Theory* (Trumansburg, NY: The Crossing Press, 1983); Bell Hooks, *Feminist Theory from Margin to Center* (Boston: South End Press, 1984); Gloria Joseph, "The Incompatible Menage à Trois: Marxism, Feminism and Racism," *Women and Revolution*, ed. Lydia Sargent (Boston: South End Press, 1981), pp. 91–107; Audre Lord, "An Open Letter to Mary Daly," *This Bridge Called My Back: Writings by Radical Women of Color*, ed. Cherrie Moraga and Gloria Anzaldúa (Watertown, MA: Persephone Press, 1981), pp. 94–97; Maria C. Lugones and Elizabeth V. Spelman, "Have We Got a Theory for You! Feminist Theory, Cultural Imperialism and the Demand for the Woman's Voice," *Hypatia, Women's Studies International Forum*, Vol. 6, No. 6, 1983, pp. 578–581; Adrienne Rich, "Compulsory Heterosexuality and Lesbian Existence," *Signs: Journal of Women in Culture and Society*, Vol. 5, No. 4, Summer 1980, pp. 631–660; Elizabeth Spelman, "Theories of Race and Gender: The Erasure of Black Women," *Quest*, Vol. 5, No. 4, 1980/81, pp. 36–62.

18 See, for example, Hélène Cixous, "The Laugh of the Medusa," trans. Keith Cohen and Paula Cohen, *New French Feminisms*, ed. Elaine Marks and Isabelle de Courtivron (New York: Schocken Books, 1981), pp. 245–261; Hélène Cixous and Catherine Clément, *The Newly Born Woman*, trans. Betsy Wing (Minneapolis: University of Minnesota Press, 1986); Luce Irigaray, *Speculum of the Other Woman* (Ithaca, NY: Cornell University Press, 1985) and *This Sex Which Is Not One* (Ithaca, NY: Cornell University Press, 1985); Julia Kristeva, *Desire in Language: A Semiotic Approach to Literature and Art*, ed. Leon S. Roudiez (New York: Columbia University Press, 1980) and "Women's Time," trans. Alice Jardine and Harry Blake, *Signs: Journal of Women in Culture and Society* Vol. 7, No. 1, Autumn 1981, pp. 13–35. See also the critical discussions by Ann Rosalind Jones, "Writing the Body: Toward an Understanding of l'Ecriture Féminine," *The New Feminist Criticism: Essays on Women, Literature and Theory*, ed. Elaine Showalter (New York: Pantheon Books, 1985), and Toril Moi, *Sexual/Textual Politics: Feminist Literary Theory* (London: Methuen, 1985).

RACHEL BOWLBY

'Flight Reservations: The Anglo–American / French Divide in Feminist Criticism' Still Crazy After All These Years: Women, Writing and Psychoanalysis

Toril Moi's *Sexual/Textual Politics* does not belong autobiographically to the transatlantic mode, since the author is a Norwegian who was working at the time of writing in Britain.[8] But it is organised around the same type of contrast between American and French modes of feminist literary criticism, through long sections dealing with each. The book is a model of lucid exposition and argument, and it rapidly and deservedly established itself as an indispensable text for both students and teachers of literary theory.

Running through Moi's readings of different critical texts is a double criterion of political efficacy and distance from conventional liberal humanism, and it is in theoretical terms identified as French that American critics are found wanting: they tend to be confined to traditional conceptions of literature as the immediate transcription of experience, and of the transcription of female experience as the mark of genuine women's literature. Such an approach, as she argues, cannot accommodate a theory of representation. It takes 'man' and 'woman' as naturally given rather than symbolic categories, and in viewing language as a transparent medium, it reduces and refuses the complexity of the literary text. And so the book's title indicates its departure in a 'textual' direction away from what must now be seen as the too literalising argument of Kate Millett's diatribe against male authors in *Sexual Politics*: necessary as a first bash in 1969, but lacking in the analytically more complex tools that feminist criticism has subsequently acquired.[9]

As the proportion of interrogative sentences would suggest on its own, Alice Jardine's *Gynesis: Configurations of Woman and Modernity* is a less expository text than Toril Moi's. Jardine sets out to question both the apparent ease with which Franco-American feminist differences are articulated, and the facility with which the term 'feminist' is transported between the two countries, given its different connotations in each one. The book's neologistic title invokes what Jardine perceives as a constantly recurring focus of postmodernist enquiry in fiction and philosophy. 'Gynesis' would be:

> The putting into discourse of 'woman' as that *process* diagnosed in France as intrinsic to the condition of modernity; indeed, the valorization of the feminine, woman, and her obligatory, that is, historical connotations, as somehow intrinsic to new and necessary models of thinking, writing, speaking.[10]

Or again:

> *Gynesis*: a new kind of writing on the woman's body, a map of new spaces yet to be explored, with 'woman' supplying the only directions, the only images, upon which Postmodern Man feels he can rely.[11]

'Gynesis' in this sense of an exploration of textual spaces 'gendered feminine' is located or 'diagnosed' in male writers ranging from Derrida, Lacan and Deleuze to Lyotard, Baudrillard, Goux and Sollers, all of whose theoretical or fictional undoings of 'the paternal metaphor' underpinning western discourse turn out to revolve around and explore the question of femininity.

Like Toril Moi, Alice Jardine is interested in modernist or postmodernist writing, and she links its emergence to the 'crisis in legitimation' more or less evident in western society since the beginning of the twentieth century. The loss of phallogocentric guarantees is precisely the moment at which the feminine becomes an open question: not a straightforward alternative to masculinity, or a known identity, but a virtual point towards or around which new kinds of question will cluster.

Gynesis has little to say about the issue of women's adequate representation in literature: this would be the falsely universalising, realistic criterion rejected also by Moi. But Jardine's text does frequently refer to the problematic relation between this fluid 'gynesis' located in modern writing and a female personage variously invoked as 'the feminine reader' or 'the woman reader', to whom are attributed sceptical, common-sense responses to the theoretical propositions of 'gynesis'. In effect, it is as if this 'feminist reader' is none other than the pragmatic American whose simple formulations have to be corrected and complicated by French sophistication, just as in the earlier quotation Jardine declared that her 'questions themselves' were American, but their 'structure' was French.[12] Despite the alleged interactions and mutual transformations, 'gynesis' and 'feminism' remain as distinct and opposed in Jardine's text as the French or American modes to which they are related.

The final chapter compares French and American postmodernist fiction by men, as represented in particular texts by Philippe Sollers, Thomas Pynchon and John Hawkes. While both the French writer and the Americans are concerned with the questions of interpretation, textuality and femininity, the differences, for Jardine, are crucial. Concluding the analysis of the American writers, she states:

> This is a thematization of gynesis very different from the conceptual, textual, constitutive process of gynesis inherent to modernity as diagnosed in France. The 'woman-in-effect' in American male fiction, throughout its thematization of gynesis, is as far from the most radical tenets of modernity as it is close to the conceptual foundations of, among other things, (Anglo-)American feminist thought itself.[13]

The polarisation here between 'thematization' and 'gynesis' as 'process' reproduces what it accuses in the text, and comes precariously close to the type of static binary opposition – such as 'form versus content' – from which postmodernist and feminist thought, in the different and connected ways which Jardine's book so well describes, is said to have moved on.

Even in Jardine's own account, the opposition sometimes looks forced or arbitrary. The following paragraph says why the French fictional mode is better:

> The 'she' haunting much of the most important contemporary writing by men in France is at times angelic, at times monstrous. But 'she' is always seen, above

all, as that which must be explored through an erotic merging at the interior of language, through a radical dismemberment of the textual body, a female body. *Woman*, as identity, may eventually reappear within the boundaries of that exploration, but never for long, usually separated from it, and always with duplicity.[14]

The 'she' as angel/monster, as ghostlike ('haunting') as dismembered body, and as duplicitous sounds uncannily familiar from somewhere. Without more specification of the difference, this could equally be read as the usual list of accusation levelled against a misogynist text, and thus as proof not of Sollers' difference, but of the fact that he remains locked in the conventional masculine fantasies of femininity which are attributed to the American writers.

It would seem, then, that however strong the assertion to the contrary, there is a tendency for the differences between American and French critical modes to be fixed into simple, homologous oppositions between stasis and process, theme and text, pragmatism and theory, realism and (post)modernism. This effect is reinforced by the representation of American feminist aims as outmoded or displaced by the passing of the universalising, egalitarian politics identified with pre-twentieth-century ideals. The universalising logic according to which women claim their rights as political subjects equal to men must now, apparently, be seen as part of a bygone stage of feminist debate; but it is also assumed to be the position from which Jardine's 'feminist reader' would put her questions to the French theoretical texts that come her way.

(1988)

Notes

8 Toril Moi, *Sexual/Textual Politics: Feminist Literary Theory* (London: Methuen, 'New Accents', 1985).

9 Ibid., pp. 24–31.

10 Jardine, op. cit., p. 25

11 Ibid., p. 52.

12 Ibid., p. 18.

13 Ibid., p. 257.

14 Ibid., p. 246.

Barbara Christian

'The Race for Theory' *Gender and Theory: Dialogues on Feminist Criticism*

I have seized this occasion to break the silence among those of us, critics, as we are now called, who have been intimidated, devalued by what I call the race for theory. I have become convinced that there has been a take-over in the literary world by Western philosophers from the old literary elite, the neutral humanists. Philosophers have been able to effect such a take-over because so much of the literature of the West has become pallid, laden with despair, self-indulgent, and disconnected. The New Philosophers, eager to understand a world that is today fast escaping their political control, have redefined literature so that the distinctions implied by that term, that is, the distinctions between everything written and those things written to evoke feeling as well as to express thought, have been blurred. They have changed literary critical language to suit their own purposes as philosophers, and they have re-invented the meaning of theory.

My first response to this realization was to ignore it. Perhaps, in spite of the egocentrism of this trend, some good might come of it. I had, I felt, more pressing and interesting things to do, such as reading and studying the history and literature of black women, a history that had been totally ignored, a contemporary literature bursting with originality, passion, insight, and beauty. But unfortunately it is difficult to ignore this new take-over, theory has become a commodity because that helps determine whether we are hired or promoted in academic institutions – worse, whether we are heard at all. Due to this new orientation, works (a word which evokes labor) have become texts. Critics are no longer concerned with literature, but with other critics' texts, for the critic yearning for attention has displaced the writer and has conceived of himself as the center. Interestingly in the first part of this century, at least in England and America, the critic was usually also a writer of poetry, plays, or novels. But today, as a new generation of professionals develops, he or she is increasingly an academic. Activities such as teaching or writing one's response to specific works of literature have, among this group, become subordinated to one primary thrust, that moment when one creates a theory, thus fixing a constellation of ideas for a time at least, a fixing which no doubt will be replaced in another month or so by somebody else's competing theory as the race accelerates. Perhaps because those who have effected the take- over have the power (although they deny it) first of all to be published, and thereby to determine the ideas which are deemed valuable, some of our most daring and potentially radical critics (and by *our* I mean black, women, Third World) have been influenced, even co-opted, into speaking a language and defining their discussion in terms alien to and opposed to our needs and orientation. At least so far, the creative writers I study have resisted this language.[1]

For people of color have always theorized – but in forms quite different from the Western form of abstract logic. And I am inclined to say that our theorizing (and I intentionally use the verb rather than the noun) is often in narrative forms, in the stories we create, in riddles and proverbs, in the play with language, since dynamic rather than fixed ideas seem more to our liking. How else have we managed to survive with such spiritedness the assault on our bodies, social institutions, countries, our very humanity? And women, at least the women I grew up around, continuously speculated about the nature of life through pithy language that unmasked the power relations of their world. It is this language, and the grace and pleasure with which they played with it, that I find celebrated, refined, critiqued in the works of writers like Toni Morrison and Alice Walker. My folk, in other words, have always been a race of theory – though more in the form of the hieroglyph, a written figure which is both sensual and abstract, both beautiful and communicative. In my own work I try to illuminate and explain these hieroglyphs, which is, I think, an activity quite different from the creating of the hieroglyphs themselves. As the Buddhists would say, the finger pointing at the moon is not the moon.

In this discussion, however, I am more concerned with the issue raised by my first use of the term, *the race for theory*, in relation to its academic hegemony, and possibly of its inappropriateness to the energetic emerging literatures in the world today. The pervasiveness of this academic hegemony is an issue continually spoken about – but usually in hidden groups, lest we, who are disturbed by it, appear ignorant to the reigning academic elite. Among the folk who speak in muted tones are people of color, feminists, radical critics, creative writers, who have struggled for much longer than a decade to make their voices, their various voices, heard, and for whom literature is not an occasion for discourse among critics but is necessary nourishment for their people and one way by which they come to understand their lives better. Clichéd though this may be, it bears, I think, repeating here.

The race for theory, with its linguistic jargon, its emphasis on quoting its prophets, its tendency towards 'Biblical' exegesis, its refusal even to mention specific works of creative writers, far less contemporary ones, its preoccupations with mechanical analyses of language, graphs, algebraic equations, its gross generalizations about culture, has silenced many of us to the extent that some of us feel we can no longer discuss our own literature, while others have developed intense writing blocks and are puzzled by the incomprehensibility of the language set adrift in literary circles. There have been, in the last year, any number of occasions on which I had to convince literary critics who have pioneered entire new areas of critical inquiry that they did have something to say. Some of us are continually harassed to invent wholesale theories regardless of the complexity of the literature we study. I, for one, am tired of being asked to produce a black feminist literary theory as if I were a mechanical man. For I believe such theory is prescriptive – it ought to have some relationship to practice. Since I can count on one hand the number of people attempting to be black feminist literary critics in the world today, I consider it presumptuous of me to invent a theory of how we *ought* to read. Instead, I think we need to read the works of our writers in our various ways and remain open to the intricacies of the intersection of language, class, race, and gender in the literature. And it would help if we share our process, that is, our practice, as much as possible since, finally, our work *is* a collective endeavor.

The insidious quality of this race for theory is symbolized for me by a term like 'Minority Discourse'[2] – a label that is borrowed from the reigning theory of the day but which is untrue to the literatures being produced by our writers, for many of our literatures (certainly Afro-American literature) are central, not minor. I have used the passive voice in my last sentence construction, contrary to the rules of Black English, which like all languages has a particular value system, since I have not placed responsibility on any particular person or group. But that is precisely because this new ideology has become so prevalent among us that it behaves like so many of the other ideologies with which we have had to contend. It appears to have neither head nor center. At the least though, we can say that the terms 'minority' and 'discourse' are located firmly in a Western dualistic or 'binary' frame which sees the rest of the world as minor, and tries to convince the rest of the world that it *is* major, usually through force and then through language, even as it claims many of the ideas that we, its 'historical' other, have known and spoken about for so long. For many of us have never conceived of ourselves only as somebody's *other*.

Let me not give the impression that by objecting to the race for theory I ally myself with or agree with the neutral humanists who see literature as pure expression and will not admit to the obvious control of its production, value, and distribution by those who have power, who deny, in other words, that literature is, of necessity, political. I am studying an entire body of literature that has been denigrated for centuries by such terms as *political*. For an entire century Afro-American writers, from Charles Chestnutt in the nineteenth century through Richard Wright in the 1930s, Imamu Baraka in the 1960s, Alice Walker in the 1970s, have protested the literary hierarchy of dominance which declares when literature is literature, when literature is great, depending on what it thinks is to its advantage. The Black Arts Movement of the 1960s, out of which Black Studies, the Feminist Literary Movement of the 1970s, and Women's Studies grew, articulated precisely those issues, which came *not* from the declarations of the New Western Philosophers but from these groups' reflections on their own lives. That Western scholars have long believed their ideas to be universal has been strongly opposed by many such groups. Some of my colleagues do not see black critical writers of previous decades as eloquent enough. Clearly they have not read Wright's 'A blueprint for Negro Writing', Ellison's *Shadow and Act*, Chesnutt's resignation from being a writer, or Alice Walker's 'In search of Zora Neale Hurston'.[3] There are two reasons for this general ignorance of what our writer-critics have said. One is that black writing has been generally ignored in the USA. Since we, as Toni Morrison has put it, are seen as a discredited people, it is no surprise, then, that our creations are also discredited. But this is also due to the fact that until recently, dominant critics in the Western world have also been creative writers who have had access to the upper-middle-class institutions of education and, until recently, our writers have decidedly been excluded from these institutions and in fact have often been opposed to them. Because of the academic world's general ignorance about the literature of black people, and of women, whose work too has been discredited, it is not surprising that so many of our critics think that the position arguing that literature is political begins with these New Philosophers. Unfortunately, many of our young critics do not investigate the reasons *why* that statement – literature is political – is now acceptable when before it was not; nor do we look to our own antecedents for the sophisticated arguments upon which we can build in order to change the tendency of any established Western idea to become hegemonic.

For I feel that the new emphasis on literary critical theory is as hegemonic as the world which it attacks. I see the language it creates as one which mystifies rather than clarifies our condition, making it possible for a few people who know that particular language to control the critical scene – that language surfaced, interestingly enough, just when the literature of peoples of color, of black women, of Latin Americans, of Africans, began to move to 'the center'. Such words as *center* and *periphery* are themselves instructive. *Discourse, canon, texts,* words as Latinate as the tradition from which they come, are quite familiar to me. Because I went to a Catholic Mission school in the West Indies I must confess that I cannot hear the word 'canon' without smelling incense, that the word 'text' immediately brings back agonizing memories of Biblical exegesis, that 'discourse' reeks for me of metaphysics forced down my throat in those courses that traced *world* philosophy from Aristotle through Thomas Aquinas to Heidegger. 'Periphery' too is a word I heard throughout my childhood, for if anything was seen as being at the periphery, it was those small Caribbean islands which had neither land mass nor military power. Still I noted how intensely important this periphery was, for US troups were continually invading one island or another if any change in political control even seemed to be occurring. As I lived among folk for whom language was an absolutely necessary way of validating our existence, I was told that the minds of the world lived only in the small continent of Europe. The metaphysical language of the New Philosophy, then, I must admit, is repulsive to me and is one reason why I raced from philosophy to literature, since the latter seemed to me to have the possibilities of rendering the world as large and as complicated as I experienced it, as sensual as I knew it was. In literature I sensed the possibility of the integration of feeling/knowledge, rather than the split between the abstract and the emotional in which Western philosophy inevitably indulged.

Now I am being told that philosophers are the ones who write literature, that authors are dead, irrelevant, mere vessels through which these narratives ooze, that they do not work nor have they the faintest idea what they are doing; rather, they produce texts as disembodied as the angels. I am frankly astonished that scholars who call themselves marxists or post-marxists could seriously use such metaphysical language even as they attempt to deconstruct the philosophical tradition from which their language comes. And as a student of literature, I am appalled by the sheer ugliness of the language, its lack of clarity, its unnecessarily complicated sentence constructions, its lack of pleasurableness, its alienating quality. It is the kind of writing for which composition teachers would give a freshman a resounding F.

Because I am a curious person, however, I postponed readings of black women writers I was working on and read some of the prophets of this new literary orientation. These writers did announce their dissatisfaction with some of the cornerstone ideas of their own tradition, a dissatisfaction with which I was born. But in their attempt to change the orientation of Western scholarship, they, as usual, concentrated on themselves and were not in the slightest interested in the worlds they had ignored or controlled. Again I was supposed to know *them*, while they were not at all interested in knowing *me*. Instead they sought to 'deconstruct' the tradition to which they belonged even as they used the same forms, style, language of that tradition, forms that necessarily embody its values. And increasingly as I read them and saw their substitution of their philosophical writings for literary ones, I began to have the uneasy feeling that their folk were not producing any literature worth mentioning. For they always harkened back to the masterpieces of the past, again reifying the very texts they said they were deconstructing. Increasingly, as *their* way, *their* terms, *their* approaches remained central and became the means by which one defined literary critics, many of my own peers who had previously been concentrating on dealing with the other side of the equation, the reclamation and discussion of past and *present* Third World literatures, were diverted into continually discussing the new literary theory.

From my point of view as a critic of contemporary Afro-American women's writing, this orientation is extremely problematic. In attempting to find the deep structures in the literary tradition, a major preoccupation of the new New Criticism, many of us have become obsessed with the nature of reading itself to the extent that we have stopped writing about literature being written today. Since I am slightly paranoid, it has begun to occur to me that the literature being produced *is* precisely one of the reasons why this new philosophical-literary-critical theory of relativity is so prominent. In other words, the literature of blacks, women of South America and Africa, etc., as overtly 'political' literature, was being pre-empted by a new Western concept which proclaimed that reality does not exist, that everything is relative, and that every text is silent about something – which indeed it must necessarily be.

(1989)

Notes

This essay is reprinted (with changes) with permission from Barbara Christian and first appeared in *Cultural Critique* 6 (Spring 1987): 51–63.

1 For another view of the debate this 'privileged' approach to Afro-American texts has engendered, see Joyce A. Joyce, ' "Who the Cap Fit:" unconsciousness and unconscionableness in the criticism of Houston A. Baker, Jr, and Henry Louis Gates, Jr', *New Literary History* 18 (1987): 371–84. I had not read Joyce's essay before I wrote my own. Clearly there are differences between Joyce's view and my own.

2 This paper was originally written for a conference at the University of California at Berkeley entitled 'Minority Discourse', and held on 29–31 May 1986.

3 See Ellison 1964; Farnsworth 1969; Gayle 1971; Jones, L. 1966; Neal 1971: pp. 357–74; Walker 1975; Wright 1937.

bELL hOOKS

'Postmodern Blackness'
Yearning: Race, Gender and Cultural Politics

Postmodernist discourses are often exclusionary even as they call attention to, appropriate even, the experience of "difference" and "Otherness" to provide oppositional political meaning, legitimacy, and immediacy when they are accused of lacking concrete relevance. Very few African-American intellectuals have talked or written about postmodernism. At a dinner party I talked about trying to grapple with the significance of postmodernism for contemporary black experience. It was one of those social gatherings where only one other black person was present. The setting quickly became a field of contestation. I was told by the other black person that I was wasting my time, that "this stuff does not relate in any way to what's happening with black people." Speaking in the presence of a group of white onlookers, staring at us as though this encounter were staged for their benefit, we engaged in a passionate discussion about black experience. Apparently, no one sympathized with my insistence that racism is perpetuated when blackness is associated solely with concrete gut level experience conceived as either opposing or having no connection to abstract thinking and the production of critical theory. The idea that there is no meaningful connection between black experience and critical thinking about aesthetics or culture must be continually interrogated.

My defense of postmodernism and its relevance to black folks sounded good, but I worried that I lacked conviction, largely because I approach the subject cautiously and with suspicion.

Disturbed not so much by the "sense" of postmodernism but by the conventional language used when it is written or talked about and by those who speak it, I find myself on the outside of the discourse looking in. As a discursive practice it is dominated primarily by the voices of white male intellectuals and/or academic elites who speak to and about one another with coded familiarity. Reading and studying their writing to understand postmodernism in its multiple manifestations, I appreciate it but feel little inclination to ally myself with the academic hierarchy and exclusivity pervasive in the movement today.

Critical of most writing on postmodernism, I perhaps am more conscious of the way in which the focus on "Otherness and difference" that is often alluded to in these works seems to have little concrete impact as an analysis or standpoint that might change the nature and direction of postmodernist theory. Since much of this theory has been constructed in reaction to and against high modernism, there is seldom any mention of black experience or writings by black people in this work, specifically black women (though in more recent work one may see a reference to Cornel West, the black male scholar who has most engaged postmodernist discourse). Even if an aspect of black culture is the subject of postmodern critical writing, the works cited will usually be those of black men. A work that comes immediately to mind is Andrew Ross's chapter "Hip, and the Long Front of Color" in *No Respect: Intellectuals and Popular Culture*; while it is an interesting reading, it constructs black culture as though black women have had no role in black cultural production. At the end of Meaghan Morris' discussion of postmodernism in her collection of essays *The Pirate's Fiance: Feminism and Postmodernism*, she provides a bibliography of works by women, identifying them as important contributions to a discourse on postmodernism that offer new insight as well as challenging male theoretical hegemony. Even though many of the works do not directly address postmodernism, they address similar concerns. There are no references to works by black women.

The failure to recognize a critical black presence in the culture and in most scholarship and writing on postmodernism compels a black reader, particularly a black female reader, to interrogate her interest in a subject where those who discuss and write about it seem not to know black women exist or even to consider the possibility that we might be somewhere writing or saying something that should be listened to, or producing art that should be seen, heard, approached with intellectual seriousness. This is especially the case with works that go on and on about the way in which postmodernist discourse has opened up a theoretical terrain where "difference and Otherness" can be considered legitimate issues in the academy. Confronting both the absence of recognition of black female presence that much postmodernist theory re-inscribes and the resistance on the part of most black folks to hearing about real connection between postmodernism and black experience, I enter a discourse, a practice, where there may be no ready audience for my words, no clear listener, uncertain then, that my voice can or will be heard.

During the sixties, black power movement was influenced by perspectives that could easily be labeled modernist. Certainly many of the ways black folks addressed issues of identity conformed to a modernist universalizing agenda. There was little critique of patriarchy as a master narrative among black militants. Despite the fact that black power ideology reflected a modernist sensibility, these elements were soon rendered irrelevant as militant protest was stifled by a powerful, repressive postmodern state. The period directly after the black power movement was a time when major news magazines carried articles with cocky headlines like "Whatever Happened to Black America?" This response was an ironic reply to the aggressive, unmet demand by decentered, marginalized black subjects who had at least momentarily successfully demanded a hearing, who had made it possible for black liberation to be on the national political agenda. In the wake of the black power movement, after so many rebels were slaughtered and lost, many of these voices were silenced by a repressive state; others became inarticulate. It has become necessary to find new avenues to transmit the messages of black liberation struggle, new ways to talk about racism and other politics of domination. Radical postmodernist practice, most powerfully conceptualized as a "politics of difference," should incorporate the voices of displaced, marginalized, exploited, and oppressed black people. It is sadly ironic that the contemporary discourse which talks the most about heterogeneity, the decentered subject, declaring breakthroughs that allow recognition of Otherness, still directs its critical voice primarily to a specialized audience that shares a common language rooted in the very master narratives it claims to challenge. If radical postmodernist thinking is to have a transformative impact, then a critical break with the notion of "authority" as "mastery over" must not simply be a rhetorical device. It must be reflected in habits of being, including styles of writing as well as chosen subject matter. Third world nationals, elites, and white critics who passively absorb white supremacist thinking, and therefore never notice or look at black people on the streets or at their jobs, who render us invisible with their gaze in all areas of daily life, are not likely to produce liberatory theory that will challenge racist domination, or promote a breakdown in traditional ways of seeing and thinking about reality, ways of constructing aesthetic theory and practice. From a different standpoint, Robert Storr makes a similar critique in the global issue of *Art in America* when he asserts:

> To be sure, much postmodernist critical inquiry has centered
> precisely on the issues of "difference" and "Otherness." On the
> purely theoretical plane the exploration of these concepts has
> produced some important results, but in the absence of any
> sustained research into what artists of color and others outside
> the mainstream might be up to, such discussions become

rootless instead of radical. Endless second guessing about the latent imperialism of intruding upon other cultures only compounded matters, preventing or excusing these theorists from investigating what black, Hispanic, Asian and Native American artists were actually doing.

Without adequate concrete knowledge of and contact with the non-white "Other," white theorists may move in discursive theoretical directions that are threatening and potentially disruptive of that critical practice which would support radical liberation struggle.

(1991)

5

Writing, Reading and Difference

INTRODUCTION

Three American Responses

The first three extracts in this chapter – all by American women – illustrate three classic positions in the debate about whether women write differently from men. Joyce Carol Oates appeals for an individual style, for a sexless writing, beyond definitions of 'male' and 'female'. To have a 'male' or 'female' style is 'symptomatic of inferior art' where the female style might degenerate into mere propaganda on women's issues. Against this Oates offers what is, at root, an idealist view of literature as the expression of an individual authorial voice which 'transcends' the material and the political, 'even while being fueled by them'. At the same time she realizes, with resignation, that a 'sex-determined voice' is probably the best that criticism will offer the woman writer.[1]

Ellen Moers, looking at the use of bird metaphors in women's writing, concludes that there *is* something distinctive in the way women writers have used certain images. The tendency in Moers's argument is to see a link between particular metaphors and the social and historical position of women writers and women characters: so, given what we know of the restricted lifestyle of middle-class women in the nineteenth century, the caged bird metaphor in *Jane Eyre* is appropriate – almost predictable. But what is confusing in Moers's writing is the interchangeable use she makes of the terms 'feminine' and 'female': the recurrent references in women's writing to 'the little hard nut, the living stone' constitute 'a feminine metaphor'; the caged bird metaphor 'truly deserves the adjective female'.[2] The convention in feminist writing has been to use 'feminine' to refer to the cultural construction of women and 'female' to refer to biology. Though it generally appears that Moers is talking about culture rather than biology, there are occasions when her use of 'female' instead of 'feminine' suggests that she is attributing to women some innate propensity to certain images or forms of language.[3] This confusion of terminology poses a particular problem in understanding French feminist writing since the adjective *féminin* does not translate easily into English.[4]

Moers's method of textual analysis, searching for distinctive imagery, tones or stylistic devices, has been a common one in American criticism. Feminists involved in this work do not feel that they are in pursuit of 'inferior art' (Oates). On the contrary, they look upon the search for a female style as a further stage in uncovering a female tradition, in exploring the interconnections between women writers, and in establishing the methodology which Elaine Showalter terms 'gynocriticism' (see chapter 4). They are eager to find conclusive similarities in women's writing but reluctant to make extravagant claims; their work often contends that we need more stylistic analysis to substantiate fully any proposition.[5] But it seems unlikely that criticism will ever discern a definitive female style. The differences between women writers always seem to outnumber the similarities. Moreover, there is no way of knowing whether the common factors are due to the writer's sex, their shared class or racial background, the demands of the literary form they all employ, or to any one of a dozen or more factors. As Annette Kolodny warns, the thesis can operate as a self-fulfilling prophecy. If the explicit aim is to find stylistic similarities in women's writing, it is not surprising if, in that mass of material, some similarities are actually discovered.[6]

Mary Ellmann offers a different approach. She does not write of 'male' and 'female' but of 'masculine' and 'feminine' modes of writing, characterizing the 'masculine' in terms of an authority apparently absent in the so-called 'feminine'. Crucially, she presents this masculine voice as not necessarily the prerogative of the male writer, nor is the feminine voice possible only for women. Thus, in Simone de Beauvoir she discovers an adherence to the tone of authority which disappoints her, but in Norman Mailer, a delightful exhilarating abuse of it. It is in writing which expresses the 'disruption of authority' or the 'disruption of the rational' that Ellmann finds the characteristics of 'what were previously considered feminine habits of thought'; there is an advantage, therefore, in the woman writer allying herself with 'a literature at odds with authority'. Rashness, daring, mockery, 'sudden alternations of the reckless and the sly, the wildly voluble and the laconic' are the stylistic qualities that can undercut the 'established masculine mode' – and are, of course, precisely the qualities which Ellmann's own writing embodies.

Textuality or Sexuality

In several ways Ellmann's remarks foreshadow, with striking prescience, recent developments in critical theory, particularly in post-structuralist and psychoanalytic thinking. For critics of these persuasions, the important issue, in Mary Jacobus's felicitous expression, is 'not the sexuality of the text but the textuality of sex' – in other words, the question is not 'is this a male text or a female text?' but 'how is masculinity and femininity produced in this text?' Peggy Kamuf and Jacobus fear that in looking for the difference of women's writing, presumably with the laudable aim of illustrating its quality and uniqueness, one gets caught up in a form of biological determinism. Thus, the 'distinctiveness' of women's writing becomes, merely and obviously, that it is writing produced by women. In addition, the emphasis on the author's name and sexual identity plays, with alarming ease, into the hands of the dominant order and its concepts of identity and meaning: 'the father's name and the index of sexual identity' (Kamuf); 'the woman author as origin and her life as the primary locus of meaning' (Jacobus). What starts as a radical move to focus on the specificity of women can be undermined and incorporated.

Though describing certain common themes and styles in women's writing, Julia Kristeva is cautious about any contention 'that a specifically female writing exists'. This is partly because, as indicated above, any similarities in women's (or men's) writing could be produced by a wide variety of factors and partly because, like Kamuf and Jacobus, Kristeva does not subscribe to the notion of a fixed sexual identity; on the contrary, she views sexual identity as 'constantly remade and reborn through the impetus provided by a play of signs'. Where she does suggests differences – for example, that in women's writing the emotion exceeds the expression or that women's writing shows less interest in composition – she makes clear that these are differences of degree – 'more often than in texts by men' – rather than absolute differences and that they are the product of a complicated interplay between unconscious forces and linguistic signs. Just as interesting to Kristeva is that which the woman writer does not say, cannot say, 'the speech of non-being' and this interest finds an echo in Jacobus's preoccupation with 'the gaps, the absences, the unsayable or unrepresentable of discourse'. This 'unspoken' is characterized as 'the feminine' – a gap in phallocentric culture for Jacobus; 'a "space" of some kind (over which the narrative has lost control)' for Alice Jardine (chapter 4.); for others, a potential at the margins.

If the sex of the author cannot guarantee anything about the writing, what about the sex of the reader? Do men and women read differently? Do you have to be a woman to read as a feminist? If reading 'as a woman' is a position rather than an identity does the reader's sex have any significance at all? Judith Fetterley's extract belongs to that period when American feminist criticism was preoccupied with the canon, finding women's place within it and, in Fetterley's case, considering its deleterious effect on the woman reader. As Jonathan Culler indicates, Fetterley's objection is not to negative images of women 'but to the way in which the dramatic structure of these stories induces women to participate in a vision of woman as the obstacle to freedom'. In Fetterley's view, the woman reader of the male-authored text is coerced into a position of 'immasculation'; the narrative strategies require her to identify with 'a male point of view'. Her necessary defence is to become 'a resisting reader'. As we can see from the opening sentence of Culler's extract, his critical distinction is to separate the idea of reading 'as a woman' from the idea of 'being a woman'. Women can read 'as men' – indeed, that is the significance of the reference to Fetterley – while men can, similarly, read 'as women'.[7] You will notice how the argument on reading parallels the debate on writing. Just as the role of the sex-identified author (male or female) is challenged by a concern with textuality (masculine or feminine), so the sex-identified reader is replaced by an emphasis on reading positions ('as a woman'; 'as a man') that are unrelated to sexual identity.

Or are they? Jacobus's query about the continuity between 'life' and 'text' refers as much to the act of reading as writing and the nature, significance and articulation of the continuity has provoked intense debate. Robert Scholes replies to Culler through an interchange with Jacques Derrida and he compares Derrida's claim to write 'from a feminine place' with Culler's argument about 'reading as a woman'. Scholes's worry about the dismissal of women's experience as a validating factor, what Jacobus calls 'life', is a political concern. The rejection could be a way of diminishing women's authority to speak/read 'as members of a class who share that experience' (notice that Scholes sees Derrida's comments as a put-down); is it also an opportunity for men to usurp that speaking/reading position? Scholes's conclusion is that women abandon at their peril concepts of experience and authority, though the deployment of such terms needs now to be more theoretically aware than in the gynocritical model.[8]

The Politics of Difference

When Virginia Woolf refers to Dorothy Richardson's sentence as 'of a more elastic fibre than the old, capable of stretching to the extreme, of suspending the frailest particles, of enveloping the vaguest shapes', her aim is to valorize the difference she perceives. Stephen Heath notices a problem in this mode of thinking:

> To lay the emphasis on difference and the specificity of woman (as of men) in the paradigm male/female is a gesture within the terms of the existing system, for which, precisely, women are different *from* men.

According to binary thinking the male and the masculine constitutes the norm, the positive and the superior; the female and the feminine is the aberration, the negative, the inferior. As Luce Irigaray suggests, 'the feminine finds itself defined as lack, deficiency, or as imitation and negative image of the subject'. In extolling the female, the woman writer does not break the pattern of patriarchal binary thought whereby the female is defined in relation to the male but continues to operate 'within the terms of the existing system'.

Difference as binary opposition is largely acceptable to the dominant order. Indeed, there is a long tradition of reactionary argument which enthusiastically discusses sexual difference in language. At its best, this tradition will label women's language as subjective, emotional or impressionistic; at its worst, as bitchy or gossip, marked by the inconsequential. The implicit rider to this definition is that 'male' language is authoritative, rational, appropriate for serious public platforms, and that if women wish to improve their position, then they must become adept in the use of this language. But this is not to say that the appeal to sexual difference is always reactionary in nature. The writers and critics we are considering here are well aware of how meaning can be differently constituted and take on new levels of significance. Thus, Jacobus can at once warn against the incipient biologism of the category 'women's writing' and, at the same time, recognize it as 'strategically and politically important'; Heath can also see in sexual difference 'a powerful and necessary mode of struggle and action'; and Irigaray can advise that 'one must assume the feminine role deliberately'. In this context, the feminine is not a natural predisposition for women but the conscious utilization of a decon-structive method: Irigaray calls it 'mimicry'. Irigaray stresses that this is a perilous undertaking: 'to try to recover the place of her [woman's] exploitation by discourse, without allowing herself to be simply reduced to it'. Rosi Braidotti explains Irigaray's discrimination methodology as follows:

> . . . how can we nourish and develop what is most innovative and subversive in women's thought, while avoiding the classic traps awaiting the feminine: mimetism, dependency, denigration, hysteria, aporia? How can we speak, think and create, within structures that are misogynist and seem to feed off the exclusion of the feminine? How can one be a conceptual thinker and not be contaminated by the 'femino-phobic' nature of theoretical thought?[9]

For Hélène Cixous and Irigaray the creative lies not in difference as opposition but in difference as multiplicity and heterogeneity. As Cixous says, 'you can't talk about *a* female sexuality, uniform, homogenous, classifiable into codes' ('Medusa'). Similarly, Irigaray in prioritizing touch over sight emphasizes the fluid oscillation and permeation of self-touching against the 'centrism' of phallic order. Cixous focuses on movement, abundance and openness. There is an expansive, jubilant creativity when she speaks of 'infinite richness' or the 'inexhaustible' or 'luminous torrents'. Far from the feminine being defined in relation to the masculine, it is, in Cixous's terms, that which escapes being 'theorized, enclosed, coded'. Both draw connections between the feminine practice of language and what Irigaray terms the 'disruptive excess' of female desire. On speaking, Cixous comments, 'Speak of her pleasure and, God knows, she has something to say about that, so that she gets to unblock a sexuality that's just as much feminine as masculine . . .' ('Castration'). On writing, she exhorts, 'Write! Writing is for you, you are for you; your body is yours, take it' ('Medusa'). The variety, the exuberance, the plenitude of writing, links with the full orgasmic overflowing of female pleasure, 'jouissance'. Because female desire, what women want, is so repressed or so misrepresented in a phallocentric society, its expression becomes a vital location for deconstructing that control.

The extracts from Judith Still, Frances Jaffer (quoted by Rachel Blau Du Plessis) and Catherine Clément indicate some of the problems and possibilities in women's use of a 'position of mastery' ('Castration') and of a 'feminine economy of generosity' (Still) and how these problems and possibilities manifest themselves in the institutional context of education. Still's suggestion is that a feminine economy of openness can have implications for how we act as teachers, critics and readers: she advocates 'reading in a motherly, creative fashion'. This view contrasts with Jaffer's satirical evocation of the masculine, phallic economy of criticism – 'lean, dry, terse, powerful, strong, spare, linear, focused, explosive'. As Cixous ('Castration or Decapitation?') and Jaffer demonstrate women's sexual/textual body is, in conservative terms, notably inadequate – 'soft, moist, blurred, padded, irregular, going round in circles'. But Clément's equally sharp and satirical extract raises important questions. Is it impossible, politically that is, for women to adopt the position of mastery implied in the public platform and the use of a rational discourse? Surely the rational and the analytic can serve women? Why is heckling permissible and rhetoric not? We can see the connection here with Irigaray's comments and Braidotti's gloss on them. Women try to be heard 'within structures that are misogynist' (Braidotti). If they speak the feminine they risk self-destruction; if they use a 'position of mastery' they risk incorporation.

Connection and Dis-Connection

Ann Rosalind Jones and Kadiatu Kanneh in their critiques of French feminism are considering specifically the work of Cixous and Irigaray and what became known from the mid seventies as l'écriture féminine or 'writing the body'. Their extracts are characteristic of those critiques which perceive in this form of French feminism a kind of biological determinism, an idealizing of the female body and an absence of close attention to the mediation of the body in varied cultural and historical contexts. Jones argues that l'écriture féminine renders the female body 'too unproblematically pleasurable and totalized an entity'. Do all women find pleasure in their bodies? Do all women – lesbian and heterosexual, women of different races or different classes – find pleasure in the same way. Are women directly in touch with their bodies or is that contact socially constructed? Is this pleasure necessarily politically progressive? Cixous's profuse, creative woman could be read as a revised version of a fecund Mother Earth with all the reactionary connotations of 'natural' womanhood. Both Jones and Kanneh also find problems with generalized references to social forces and with how those forces relate to the construction of the female body and the practice of writing. Thus, Cixous's comments on the 'imbecilic capitalist machinery' and 'smug-faced readers, managing editors, and big bosses' hardly get beyond abuse to an analysis of the mechanisms at play.

Stephen Heath, in his remarks on Virginia Woolf, talks about what he calls 'the sexual fix'. Woolf claims that 'it is fatal for anyone who writes to think of their sex' and then produces, as Heath indicates, 'a quite different position in the writing itself'. Her language carries a history and range of meanings contrary to her overt intentions. Kanneh discerns a similar process in the language of Cixous and Irigaray. While ostensibly liberating and proliferating meaning, they also 'lock all women into a history free-floating between images of black subjection and imperialist domination'. Kanneh points out in Cixous's 'Medusa', the metaphors of black and white, darkness and light and the references to a 'unique empire', 'that other limitless country', 'the Dark Continent'. Differences are established in terms of gender but in respect to race and class there is a 'flagrant fluidity of metaphor' which fails to recognize women's diverse positions and histories. Repeatedly, such critiques of *l'écriture féminine* praise the astute and multi-layered explorations of the unconscious, admire the Utopian vision but search for a more materially aware politics.

The history of French feminism's reception into the English and American markets is a story in itself.[10] The striking combination of theoretical complexity and the intensely impassioned, in the French examples, 'disconnects', in Domna Stanton's word, from the dominant empirical and materialist traditions of English and American feminism. For the Anglo-Americans the 'otherness' of French feminism and its radical questioning of precepts and practices is, in about equal measure, attractive and alarming. Gynocriticism, the major Anglo-American mode, holds little currency in French circles. The concern with a tradition of women writers, with the woman author's social position, with the problems of production finds scant emphasis in the work of French feminists: indeed, as many critics have pointed out, women writers themselves barely feature.

On the other hand, as we have already seen in Rachel Bowlby's remarks (chapter 4), the construction of French and Anglo-American feminisms as two monolithic and oppositional blocks has never been either true or helpful. For instance, the comments from the editorial collective of *Questions féministes* discuss concepts and vocabulary familiar to any Anglo-American audience: 'social mediation'; 'socio-historical contexts'; 'social beings'. Both 'French' and 'Anglo-American' have always been more complicated terms than some commentaries would suggest and the fact that one finds Anglo-American practitioners of French feminism and vice versa indicates that we are not talking about fixed national identities but a transatlantic traffic in critical ideas. A series of qualifications is necessary: for instance, French feminism is more than *l'écriture féminine*; French feminists are not adequately represented by the limited number of texts in translation and the excessive critical focus on certain key essays; Anglo-American feminism has never been as blunt and theoretically unsophisticated as some would indicate. Finally, just as we doubt the opposition of 'French' and 'Anglo-American', can we now begin to question the synchrony of 'Anglo-American'? In that hyphen lies another set of presumptions ripe for deconstruction.

Notes

1 Elaine Showalter responds to Oates and writers of a similar opinion in 'Women Who Write Are Women', *The New York Times Book Review*, 16 December 1984.

2 Ellen Moers, *Literary Women* (London, The Women's Press, 1978), p. 244.

3 Mary Poovey defines this problem: '. . . these strategies were feminine, not in the sense that they were "natural" to women . . . but in the sense that they characterized women's learned or internalized responses to the objective female social situation . . .'. *The Proper Lady and the Woman Writer: Ideology as Style in the Works of Mary Wollstonecraft, Mary Shelley and Jane Austen* (Chicago and London, The University of Chicago Press, 1984), p. 43. I realize that I am here accepting as given a distinction between sex and gender, biology and construct which is very much in dispute. See, for instance, the work of Judith Butler. However, whatever conceptual framework one uses, the slippages in Moers's terminology remain a problem.

4 Toril Moi makes this point in *Sexual/Textual Politics: Feminist Literary Theory* (London, Methuen, 1985), p. 97 and Nicole Ward Jouve in *White Woman Speaks With Forked Tongue: Criticism as Autobiography* (London, Routledge, 1991), p. 84. See also Judith Still, 'A Feminine Economy: Some Preliminary Thoughts', in Helen Wilcox et al. (eds) *The Body and the Text: Hélène Cixous, Reading and Teaching* (Hertfordshire, Harvester Wheatsheaf, 1990).

5 See, for example, the extract from Deborah McDowell in ch. 4. See also Josephine Donovan, 'Feminist Style Criticism' in *Images of Women in Fiction: Feminist Perspectives* ed. Susan Koppleman Cornillon (Bowling Green, Ohio, Bowling Green University Press, 1972), and Annette Kolodny, 'Some Notes on Defining a "Feminist Literary Criticism", in *Critical Inquiry* vol. 2, no. 1 (Autumn, 1975).

6 Kolodny (1975), p. 78.

7 This suggestion, implicit in Culler, of the *equivalence* of the reading positions is one that has been disputed by other critics who focus on the power imbalance between men and women. See Tania Modleski, 'Feminism and the Power of Interpretation: Some Critical Readings', in Teresa de Lauretis (ed.) *Feminist Studies/Critical Studies* (London, Macmillan, 1988). Note also that the comments from Shoshana Felman to which Culler refers are to be found in ch. 1.

8 For further study of gendered reading, see: Nelly Furman, 'Textual Feminism', in *Women and Language in Literature and Society*, eds Sally McConnell-Ginet, Ruth Barker, Nelly Furman (New York, Praeger Publishers, 1980); *Gender and Reading: Essays on Readers, Texts, and Contexts* (Baltimore and London, The Johns Hopkins University Press, 1986); Diana Fuss, 'Reading Like a Feminist', *Essentially Speaking: Feminism, Nature and Difference* (New York and London, Routledge, 1989); Sara Mills (ed.) *Gendering the Reader* (Hertfordshire, Harvester Wheatsheaf, 1994). References to gendered reading can also be found in ch. 2. A further contextualizing of Scholes's position can be found in Christopher Norris, *The Truth About Postmodernism* (Oxford, Blackwell, 1993).

9 Rosi Braidotti, 'Radical Philosophies of Sexual Difference: Luce Irigaray', in *The Polity Reader in Gender Studies* (Cambridge, Polity Press, 1994), p. 63. For further explication of Irigaray see the work of Margaret Whitford: 'Rereading Irigaray', in Teresa Brennan (ed.) *Between Feminism and Psychoanalysis* (London, Routledge, 1989); *The Irigaray Reader* (Oxford, Blackwell, 1991); *Luce Irigaray: Philosopher in the Feminine* (London, Routledge, 1991), especially the chapter 'Subjectivity in Language'.

10 This story is beginning to be told in, for example, the relevant essays of Bowlby. See also Nicole Ward Jouve, op. cit., and Kelly Oliver, *Reading Kristeva: Unraveling the Double-bind* (Bloomington and Indianapolis, Indiana University Press, 1993), ch. 7.

Joyce Carol Oates

'Is There a Female Voice? Joyce Carol Oates Replies'
Gender and Literary Voice

If there is a distinctly 'female' voice – if there is a distinctly 'male' voice – surely this is symptomatic of inferior art?

For a practicing writer, for a practicing artist of any kind, 'sociology,' 'politics,' and even 'biology' are subordinate to matters of personal vision, and even to matters of craftsmanship. Content cannot make serious art. Good intentions cannot make serious art. 'Characters with whom women identify' don't make serious art. No one would confuse propaganda with art, nor should one confuse – however generously, however charitably – propagandistic impulses with the impulses of art. To me, the concepts embodied in the title of your journal simply don't have the same weight. 'Women' refers to a sociological, political, and biological phenomenon (or class, or function, or stereotype); 'literature' refers to something that always transcends these categories *even while being fueled by them*. A feminist 'theme' doesn't make a sentimental, weak, cliché-ridden work valuable; a non-or even anti-feminist 'theme' doesn't make a serious work valueless, even for women. Unfair, perhaps, unjust – but inevitable. Content is simply raw material. Women's problems – women's insights – women's very special adventures: these are material: and what matters in serious art is ultimately the skill of execution and the uniqueness of vision. My personal and political sympathy for feminist literature keeps me silent (I mean in my role as a reviewer of new books) when confronted with amateurish and stereotypical works by women. Having little to say that would be welcomed (to put it mildly) I think it is most prudent to say nothing at all, or discuss a work's interesting and valuable *content*. As if fiction were a matter of content and not of language.

Then again – how am I to feel when discussed in the *Harvard Guide to Contemporary American Literature* under the great lump 'Women Writers,' the only works of mine analyzed being those that deal explicitly with *women's problems* – the rest of my books (in fact, the great majority of my books) ignored, as if they had never been written? What should a serious woman writer feel? Insult . . . hurt . . . anger . . .   frustration . . . indifference . . . amusement? Or gratitude for having been recognized at all, even if it is only as a 'woman writer' (and I stress the *only*, though not with much reproach). Attempting to rise out of categories (and there are many besides that of 'women'), the writer is thrown back, by critics frequently as well-intentioned as not. No response is adequate, or feels genuine. Of course the serious artistic voice is one of individual *style*, and it is sexless; but perhaps to have a sex-determined voice, or to be believed to have one, is, after all, better than to have no voice at all.

(1980)

ELLEN MOERS

Literary Women

Is the bird merely a species of the littleness metaphor? Or are birds chosen because they are tortured, as little girls are tortured, by boys like John Reed, who 'twisted the necks of the pigeons, killed the little peachicks. . . .'? Or because bird-victims can be ministered to by girl-victims – as in the scene where Jane, a prisoner in the nursery, tugs at the window sash to put out a few crumbs from her meager breakfast for the benefit of 'a little hungry robin, which came and chirruped on the twigs of the leafless cherry-tree nailed against the wall near the casement' – a metaphor which draws as much on the crucifixion as on country winters. Or is it because birds are beautiful and exotic creatures, symbols of half-promised, half-forbidden sensual delights, like the bird of paradise painted 'nestling in a wreath of convolvuli and rosebuds' on the china teaplate which Jane begs to take in her hands and examine closely, but is 'deemed unworthy of such a privilege'?

Because birds are soft and round and sensuous, because they palpitate and flutter when held in the hands, and especially because they sing, birds are universal emblems of love.

> My heart is like a singing bird
> Whose nest is in a watered shoot:

proclaims Christina Rossetti in her best-known poem, because 'the birthday of my life/Is come, my love is come to me.' Indeed, without birds, those patterns of animal monogamy, the Jane Eyre/Rochester love affair could not advance from romantic beginning to marital consummation. They meet on an icy moonlit road: Rochester, fierce and virile on a black horse, but lamed; and Jane – ' "Childish and slender creature! It seemed as if a linnet had hopped to my foot and proposed to bear me on its tiny wing." ' She peers at him through wide, inquisitive eyes 'like an eager bird'; she struggles in his arms 'like a wild frantic bird'; and when at last they are united, Rochester in his maimed blindness is like 'a royal eagle, chained to a perch, . . . forced to entreat a sparrow to become its purveyor.'

[. . .]

Of all creatures, birds alone can fly all the way to heaven – yet they are caged. Birds alone can sing more beautifully than human voices – yet they are unheeded, or silenced. It is only when we hear the woman as well as the poet in Christina Rossetti that we sense the full force of her metaphor in 'A Royal Princess':

> Me, poor dove that must not coo –
> eagle that must not soar.

It is only when we explore the agonizing splits in the meaning to a girl of the bird itself – freedom against sexual fulfillment, love that also means murder by the hunter – that we can respond fully to 'A White Heron,' the poignant tale by Sarah Orne Jewett.

Whenever a girl stands at a window, as Jane Eyre does, and looks toward the winding white road that vanishes over the horizon, she yearns for the wings of liberty: 'for liberty I gasped; for liberty I uttered a prayer; it seemed scattered on the wind then faintly blowing.' Boys too gasp for liberty, but boys do not receive, they only send such valentines to young ladies as Mary Russell Mitford describes in *Our Village* as a sample of the newest in London taste: 'a raised group of roses and heartsease, executed on a kind of paper cut-work, which, on being lifted up, turned into a cage enclosing a dove – tender emblem!'

From Mary Wollstonecraft's *Maria* – to Brontë's *Jane Eyre* – to Anne Frank's *Diary of a Young Girl* – I find that the caged bird makes a metaphor that truly deserves the adjective female. And I am not at all surprised by George Eliot's and Virginia Woolf's delight in Mrs. Browning's version of the caged bird metaphor in *Aurora Leigh*. The heroine's spinster aunt, that pattern of English propriety, had lived, Aurora says,

> A sort of cage-bird life, born in a cage,
> Accounting that to leap from perch to perch
> Was act and joy enough for any bird.
> Dear heaven, how silly are the things that live
> In thickets, and eat berries!
>   I alas,
> A wild bird scarcely fledged, was brought to her cage,
> And she was there to meet me. Very kind.
> Bring the clean water, give out the fresh seed.

So in *Jane Eyre*, when Rochester proposes an illicit sexual union, Jane fights to get free of the man she loves, but will not have on the wrong terms. ' "Jane, be still," ' he says, ' "don't struggle so, like a wild, frantic bird. . . ." ' Her reply is touched with Brontë pomposity, but there is also Brontë wit in her use of a metaphor hallowed with female associations: ' "I am no bird; and no net ensnares me; I am a free human being with an independent will, which I now exert to leave you." ' In Brontë's work, both aspirations – to female freedom and moral freedom – are served by the bird metaphor, free flying.

(1978)

MARY ELLMANN

Thinking About Women

(1)

A generalization is in order at this point. Perhaps a third of future humanity
will at some time during the course of their lives need an organ transplant.
Terminal patients, victims of fatal accidents, condemned criminals who might
be persuaded to will their healthy organs to society, and suicides, who number
22,000 a year in the United States, all die anyway. It will be a tragic waste if
their organs are not made available to patients whose lives could be prolonged.
With certain obvious qualifications, obtaining these organs involves questions
of legal and social machinery rather than basic morality. We have not yet run
quite full tilt into the moral dilemma.[1]

(2)

I know nothing of the circumstances surrounding Herbert Blau's resignation
from the Lincoln Center Repertory Company, but it is a melancholy decision
for which we all bear some measure of responsibility. Blau's tenure with the
company was far from distinguished; it is hard to think of a single play
produced by him at the Vivian Beaumont that stimulated any real excitement,
expectation, or sense of adventure. But given the quality of the man himself
and of his past work, we must surely look to other causes than artistic
inadequacy for some clue to his failure.[2]

(3)

Whether the 'newer kind of shorter fiction' – be it a stylized snapshot as in
Robbe-Grillet's 'The Secret Room' or a 'near-novel' as in Flannery O'Connor's 'Wise Blood' – marks a genuine departure is a moot point. The stories
gathered by Mr. Marcus may represent a rear-guard action, an after-life of
the novel and the long tales of Conrad or Henry James. It is too early to tell.
My own hunch is that the future of imaginative form lies elsewhere, in works
part philosophic, part poetic, part autobiographical. It is, I think, the writings
of Blake, of Nietzsche, of such solitary masters as Elias Canetti and Ernst
Bloch, that contain the seeds of the next major literary genre. If the act of
fiction is to reassert its claims on the adult mind, it will have to embody more
knowledge, more intensity of thought and an awareness of language more in
tune with that of Wittgenstein and Lévi-Strauss. What is, just now, more old-
fashioned than a novel?[3]

The first statement sets off with an exemplary firmness, which opens the
door for a bold prediction in turn. This prediction hurries past its own *perhaps*
to appal the reader: must *a third* of all his descendants undergo this surgery?
But to frighten is a subordinate effect of authority. Its chief effect is rather

one of confidence, reason, adjustment and efficacy. These appear in the third sentence and come to an incomparable climax in the words *all die anyway.* How calmly the dead are found dead here! But no, there is regret – men may hang themselves anyway, but to bury their kidneys with them is a 'tragic waste.' In fact, the statement alienates the reader from the (defensible) goal of organ transplantation: why go to such lengths to keep bodies alive in a society habituated to accident, crime, capital punishment and despair?

But this is admittedly an extreme instance of the idiom. The topic, surgery, is in itself extreme. Only an exceptional self-confidence and aggressive purpose enable the surgeon to invade the body, which has for civilized laymen (except in moments of rage or hatred) a profound sanctity. One has to think of surgery as a virtuous barbarity, and expect barbaric terms to intrude upon explanations of its legitimate point of view. The second and third statements are more representative, however, in that they apply themselves to matters of no practical or physical urgency, and yet advance themselves along the same rhetorical route of authority as does the first statement. What units the second and third is again the sensation of firmness, directness, confidence. They seem to me fair examples of critical prose now in this country, of an established masculine mode of speaking competently on esthetic issues. Particularly in the second passage, the decision with which even dull phrases are delivered makes them work. This decision dwindles somewhat in the third (where the *moot point* and the *hunch* are drains upon it), but here too the certainty with which even a predictable point is made establishes the effect of validity. 'What is, just now, more old-fashioned than a novel?' For a moment, while he bears the weight of this question, the reader is subdued, and cannot at once remember that in fact nothing is, just now, more old-fashioned than the question itself.

[. . .]

Unexpectedly, as though one found that some frivolous expenditure was practical after all, in this new idiom women writers move about with an ease they could not feel before. Again, I am not speaking of those who relentlessly prolong our evening with Elizabeth Barrett Browning (they will *not* get up and say, 'Enough of this lucrative distress. Call me a cab.'). Instead, I hope to define the way in which it is now possible for women to write well. Quite simply, having not had physical or intellectual authority before, they have no reason to resist a literature at odds with authority. There are, of course, those who prefer instead to wear hand-me-downs, to borrow now the certitude of the nineteenth century. One might say that the defect of Simone de Beauvoir is the authority of her prose: the absence of hesitation in hesitant times amounts to a presence, a tangible deficiency, a sense of obtuseness.

In better work by women now, while sentiment is avoided as stigmatic (as the inimical mark of their sex in others' minds), authority too is skirted –

again, as in Mailer and Svevo, by deliberate rashness or by ironic constraint. The tenor of Mary McCarthy's remarks on *Macbeth* is rather different from that of E. E. Stoll's:

> He is a general and has just won a battle; he enters the scene making a remark about the weather. "So fair and foul a day I have not seen." On this flat note Macbeth's character tone is set. "Terrible weather we're having." "The sun can't seem to make up its mind." "Is it hot/cold/wet enough for you?" A commonplace man who talks in commonplaces, a golfer, one might guess, on the Scottish fairways, Macbeth is the only Shakespeare hero who corresponds to a bourgeois type: a murderous Babbitt, let us say.
>
> Macbeth has absolutely no feeling for others except envy, a common middle-class trait. He *envies* the murdered Duncan his rest, which is a strange way of looking at your victim.[4]

At once a comical and a suicidal wit: the intention of wit exceeds that of justice or plausibility. What is said is said more naturally and more quickly than what Stoll says, and the opinion of Macbeth is engaging. But wrong. One doesn't for a minute *accept* Macbeth as the general, the golfer, the Eisenhower. And the Babbitt reference is quite dead, like a hemline of the late thirties. The point of view is feminine, in the pejorative sense, not only in its wifely depreciation of Macbeth (Lady Macbeth's 'good sense' is later preferred to Macbeth's 'simple panic'), but also in its social narrowness. In its determination to make Macbeth middle-class, the criticism is middle-class itself. It is hard to imagine a more philistine conception of envy than that 'common middle-class trait.' But it is the rashness of the judgment which redeems it, its daring, its mocking diminution of a subject which God knows had taken on an institutionalized grandeur.[5] The rashness links Mary McCarthy, for all their disagreements, with Norman Mailer; the diminution with Svevo, and with now.

(1968)

Notes

1 Roy L. Walford, M.D., 'A Matter of Life and Death,' *Atlantic*, August 1967, p. 70.
2 Robert Brustein, 'Saturn Eats His Children,' *New Republic*, January 28, 1967, p. 34.
3 George Steiner, 'The Search for New Genres,' *Book Week*, December 11, 1966, p. 16.
4 Mary McCarthy, 'General Macbeth,' *Harper's*, June 1962, pp. 35 and 37.
5 It is perhaps necessary to distinguish between varieties of rashness. The rashness of Mary McCarthy, which ousts conventional attitudes, is not the rashness, say, of Rebecca West: 'We were not alone. The house was packed with little girls, aged from twelve to sixteen, in the care of two or three nuns. They were, like any gathering of their kind in any part of the world, more comfortable to look at than an English girls' school. They were apparently waiting quite calmly to grow up. They expected it, and so did the people looking after them. There was no panic on anybody's part. There were none of the unhappy results which follow the English attempt to make all children look insipid and docile, and show no signs whatsoever that they will ever develop into adults. There were no little girls with poked chins and straight hair, aggressively proud of being

plain, nor were there pretty girls making a desperate precocious proclamation of their femininity. But, of course, in a country where there is very little homosexuality, it is easy for girls to grow up into womanhood.' (*Black Lamb and Grey Falcon*, Vol. I, p. 163.)

The final generalization is the clue: a person is obviously rash to allow herself to say anything so simple-silly. But the rashness is placid and auntlike. In the end, it reiterates an old point of view rather than risking a new one.

PEGGY KAMUF

'Writing Like a Woman'
Women and Language in Literature and Society

The opening chapter of Patricia Meyer Spacks's *The Female Imagination* is on theorists (Simone de Beauvoir, Mary Ellmann, and Kate Millett), and it concludes in this fashion: "So what is a woman to do, setting out to write about women? She can imitate men in her writing, or strive for an impersonality beyond sex, but finally she must write as a woman: what other way is there?"[3] Spacks's study puts together readings of a list of literary works by women in order to determine how, in her phrase, one "writes as a woman." However, by limiting the field to works whose authors are women, the critic finally gets caught in the kind of biological determinism, which, in other contexts, is recognized as a primary instance of antifeminist sexism. Consider, for example, this passage from the prologue:

> Surely the mind has a sex, minds *learn* their sex – and it is no derogation of the female variety to say so. At any rate, for readily discernible historical reasons women have characteristically concerned themselves with matters more or less peripheral to male concerns, or at least slightly skewed from them. The differences between traditional female preoccupations and roles and male ones make a difference in female writing. Even if a woman wishes to demonstrate her essential identity with male interests and ideas, the necessity of making the demonstration, contradicting the stereotype, allies her initially with her sisters. And the complex nature of the sisterhood emerges in the books it has produced.[4]

Spacks's concept of female writing is one which must expand to include the works of a woman (de Beauvoir is her primary example) "who wishes to demonstrate her essential identity with male interests and ideas." Although the author sets out with a statement of faith in a psychological or cultural differentiation which can be characterized sexually ("Surely the mind has a sex . . ."), she abandons this intuition without a second thought when she must account for a woman who, by her own reckoning, has a "male" mind. By adopting the biological distinction of male/female to define a cultural phenomenon, the critic demonstrates the impossibility of limiting that definition to what it "is" for, as it turns out, it "is" also what it "is not." By "female writing," we discover, Spacks quite banally understands works signed by biologically determined females of the species.

If the inaugural gesture of this feminist criticism is the reduction of the literary work to its signature and to the tautological assumption that a feminine "identity" is one which signs itself with a feminine name, then it will be able to produce only tautological statements of dubious value: women's writing is writing signed by women. Western culture has, of course, traditionally reserved a separate category for the intellectual or cultural productions of women, intimating their special status as exceptions within those realms where to "think male thoughts" is not to be distinguished from thinking in universals. Coming out of that tradition, we are also formed in the cult of the individual and the temptation which results to explain to ourselves artistic and intellectual productions as expressions, simple and direct, of individual experience. However, if these are principles establishing the grounds of a practice of feminist criticism, then that practice must be prepared to ally itself with the fundamental assumptions of patriarchy which relies on the same principles.

If, on the other hand, by "feminist" one understands a way of reading texts that points to the masks of truth with which phallocentrism hides its fictions, then one place to begin such a reading is by looking behind the mask of the proper name, the sign that secures our patriarchal heritage: the father's name and the index of sexual identity.

(1980)

Notes

3 Patricia Meyer Spacks, *The Female Imagination* (New York: Knopf, 1975), p. 35.
4 Ibid., p. 7.

MARY JACOBUS

Reading Woman: Essays in Feminist Criticism

And yet the question "Is there a woman in the text?" remains a central one – perhaps *the* central one – for feminist critics, and it is impossible to answer it without theory of some kind. The respective answers given by Anglo-American and French criticism are defined, in part at least, by the inherent paradox of "theory." In America the flight toward empiricism takes the form of an insistence on "woman's experience" as the ground of difference in writing. "Women's writing," "the woman reader," "female culture" occupy an almost unchallenged position of authority in feminist critical discourse of this kind. The assumption is of an unbroken continuity between "life" and "text" – a mimetic relation whereby women's writing, reading, or culture, instead of being produced, reflect a knowable reality.[27] Just as one can identify a woman biologically (the unstated argument would run), so one can with a little extra labor identify a woman's text, a woman reader, the essence of female culture. Of course the category of "women's writing" remains as strategically and politically important in classroom, curriculum, or interpretive community as the specificity of women's oppression is to the women's movement. And yet to leave the question there, with an easy recourse to the female signature or to female being, is either to beg it or to biologize it. To insist, for instance, that *Frankenstein* reflects Mary Shelley's experience of the trauma of parturition and postpartum depression may tell us about women's lives, but it reduces the text itself to a monstrous symptom. Equally, to see it as the product of "bibliogenesis" – a feminist rereading of *Paradise Lost* that, in exposing its misogynist politics, makes the monster's fall an image of woman's fall into the hell of sexuality – rewrites the novel in the image not of books but of female experience.[28] Feminist interpretations such as these have no option but to posit the woman author as origin and her life as the primary locus of meaning.

By contrast, the French insistence on *écriture féminine* – on woman as a writing-effect instead of an origin – asserts not the sexuality of the text but the textuality of sex. Gender difference, produced, not innate, becomes a matter of the structuring of a genderless libido in and through patriarchal discourse. Language itself would at once repress multiplicity and heterogeneity – true difference – by the tyranny of hierarchical oppositions (man/woman) and simultaneously work to overthrow that tyranny by interrogating the limits of meaning. The "feminine," in this scheme, is to be located in the gaps, the absences, the unsayable or unrepresentable of discourse and representation.[29] The feminine text becomes the elusive, phantasmal inhabitant of phallocentric discourse, as Gradiva *rediviva* haunts Freud's *Delusions and Dreams*, or, for the skeptical Girard, the narcissistic woman exercises her illusory power over the theory of narcissism. And yet, in its claim that women must write the body, that only the eruption of female jouissance can revolutionize discourse and challenge the Law of the Father, *écriture féminine* seems – however metaphorically – to be reaching not so much for essentialism (as it is often accused of doing) as for the conditions of representability. The theoretical abstraction of a "marked" writing that can't be observed at the level of the sentence but only glimpsed as an alternative libidinal economy almost invariably gives rise to gender-specific images of voice, touch, anatomy; to biologistic images of milk or jouissance. How else, after all, could the not-yet-written forms of *écriture féminine* represent themselves to our understanding? Not essentialism but representationalism is the French equivalent of Anglo-American empiricism – an alternative response to the indeterminacy and impenetrability of theory. If the woman in the text is "there," she is also "not there" – certainly not its object, not necessarily even its author. That may be why the heroine of feminist critical theory is not the silenced Irma, victim of Freudian theory, but the hysterical Dora whose body is her text and whose refusal to be the object of Freudian discourse makes her the subject of her own. Perhaps the question that feminist critics should ask themselves is not "Is there a woman in this text?" but rather: "*Is there a text in this woman?*"

(1986)

Notes

27 See Jonathan Culler's discussion of the concept of "the woman reader" in *On Deconstruction*, pp. 44–64.

28 See the respective readings of Frankenstein by Ellen Moers. "Female Gothic," in Levine and Knoepflmacher, *The Endurance of Frankenstein*, pp. 77–87, and by Gilbert and Gubar, "Horror's Twin: Mary Shelley's Monstrous Eve," *The Madwoman in the Attic*, pp. 213–47.

29 See, for instance, Hélène Cixous, "The Laugh of the Medusa," in Marks and de Courtivron, *New French Feminisms*, pp. 245–64, and "Castration or Decapitation," Annette Kuhn, trans., *Signs* (Autumn 1981), 7(1): 41–55; Luce Irigaray, "When Our Lips Speak Together," and "The Power of Discourse and the Subordination of the Feminine," in *This Sex Which Is Not One*. Catherine Porter, trans. (Ithaca: Cornell University Press, 1985), pp. 205–18, 68–85. For a recent critique of *écriture féminine*, see also Ann Rosalind Jones, "Writing the Body: Toward an Understanding of *L'Écriture Féminine*," *Feminist Studies* (Summer 1981), 7(2): 247–63, reprinted in Elaine Showalter, ed., *The New Feminist Criticism: Essays on Women, Literature, and Theory* (New York: Pantheon Books, 1985), pp. 361–77.

JULIA KRISTEVA

'Talking about Polylogue'
French Feminist Thought: A Reader

Julia Kristeva: If we confine ourselves to the *radical* nature of what is today called 'writing', that is, if we submit meaning and the speaking subject in language to a radical examination and then reconstitute them in a more polyvalent than fragile manner, there is nothing in either past or recent publications by women that permits us to claim that a specifically female writing exists. If it is true that the unconscious ignores negation and time, and is woven instead from displacement and condensation (hinted at by the metaphors of 'language' or 'matheme'), I should say that writing ignores sex or gender and displaces its difference in the discreet workings of language and signification (which are necessarily ideological and historical). Knots of desire are created as a result. This is one way, among others, of reacting to the radical split that constitutes the speaking subject. This eternally premature baby, prematurely separated from the world of the mother and the world of things, remedies the situation by using an invincible weapon: linguistic symbolization. Such a method deals with this fundamental change characterizing the speaking subject not by positing the existence of an *other* (another person or sex, which would give us psychological humanism) or an *Other* (the absolute signifier, God) but by constructing a network where drives, signifiers and meanings join together and split asunder in a dynamic and enigmatic process. As a result, a strange body comes into being, one that is neither man nor woman, young nor old. It made Freud dream of sublimation, and the Christians of angels, and it continues to put to modern rationality the embarrassing question of an identity that is sexual (among other things), and which is constantly remade and reborn through the impetus provided by a play of signs. The hasty attempt to contain the radical nature of this experience within a sexual identity is perhaps sometimes a means of modernizing or simply marketing an evasion of its most trenchant features.

On the other hand, in books written by women, we can eventually discern certain stylistic and thematic elements, on the basis of which we can then try to isolate a relationship to writing that is peculiar to women. But in speaking of these characteristics, for the moment I find it difficult to say if they are produced by something specific to women, by socio-cultural marginality, or more simply by one particular structure (for example hysteria) promoted by present market conditions from among the whole range of potential female qualities.

As regards the themes to be found in texts by women, they invite us to see, touch and smell a body made of organs, whether they are exhibited with satisfaction or horror. It is as if the effects giving rise to inter-subjective relations and social projects (rules over by the phallus which is nowadays so disparaged) were here reduced to the level of secretions and intestines, carefully disguised by the culture of the past but now on open display. Moreover, these female writings, even at their most optimistic, seem underpinned by a lack of belief in any project, goal or meaning. It is as if no single Other could sustain their abrasive dissatisfaction, but that, paradoxically, without entertaining any illusions they call upon a host of others to fill this vacuum. This gives writings by women a content that is always psychological and often dissenting, disillusioned or apocalyptic – something all too easily interpreted as being political criticism. The epistolary genre or memoirs, as well as their offshoots, lend themselves best to this tendency. Finally, a great number of texts by women seem to be concerned at the moment with reformulating love. The Western conception of love (Christian or courtly love patronized by the combined figures of Christ and the Virgin Mary) today fails to satisfy the needs and desires of a woman's body. Feminism is the result of a crisis in religion which has shown up at its nodal point: namely its conception of love. We are not surprised, then, to read of women who proclaim another sort of love, whether for another woman or for children. This brings us into the obscure realm of primary narcissism or the archaic relationship which a woman has with her mother (an area over which Christianity has publicly drawn a veil or which it has carefully dismissed).[4]

As for the style of women's writings, I am struck by two permanent features. First, every time I read a text by a woman, I am left with the impression that the notion of the signifier as a network of distinctive marks is insufficient. It is

insufficient because each of these marks is charged not only with a discrimi-
nating value which is the bearer of signification, but also with a drive or an
emotional force which does not signify as such but which remains latent in
the phonic invocation or in the·gesture of writing. It is as if this emotional
charge so overwhelmed the signifier as to impregnate it with emotion and so
abolish its neutral status; but, being unaware of its own existence, it did not
cross the threshold of signification or find a sign with which to designate
itself. This holds as much for more modest writings as for those called risqué,
where the expression (more often that in texts by men) falls short of the
emotional charge which gives rise to it. Poetic language has always shared
similar features, but female writings probably introduce into the day-to-day
style of a particular age this abolition of the neutrality of the signifier that
operates in close conjunction with a delusive and deluded signified. On the
other hand, and perhaps as a consequence of this, women's writings exhibit a
striking lack of interest (some would say lack of ability) in the art of
composition. They fail to orchestrate signifiers as one might with musical
staves. When a woman tries her hand at the architectonics of the word
perfected by Mallarmé or Joyce, it generally leads to one of two things: either
the art of composition gets bogged down in an artificially imposed structure
that smacks of word-play or crossword puzzles, a sort of candid and
consequently self-invalidating pataphysics; or else – and this is the solution
which seems to me the more interesting – silence, and the unspoken, riddled
with repetition, weave an evanescent canvas. This is where Blanchot saw the
'poverty of language' revealed and where some women articulate, through
their sparing use of words and their elliptical syntax, a lacuna that is
congenital to our monological culture: the speech of non-being . . .

(1977)
Translated by Seán Hand

Note

4 I return to this in detail in my article, 'Héréthique de l'amour', *Tel Quel*, 74 (Winter 1977, pp. 30–49)
(reprinted as 'Stabat Mater' in *Histoires d'amour* (Paris: Denoël, 1983), tr. by Léon S. Roudiez as
'Stabat Mater' in *The Kristeva Reader*, ed. Toril Moi (Oxford: Blackwell, 1986, pp. 160–86)).

JUDITH FETTERLEY

The Resisting Reader

In "A Woman's Map of Lyric Poetry," Elizabeth Hampsten, after quoting in
full Thomas Campion's "My Sweetest Lesbia," asks, "And Lesbia, what's in
it for her?"[6] The answer to this question is the subject of Hampsten's essay
and the answer is, of course, nothing. But implicit in her question is another

answer – a great deal, for someone. As Lillian Robinson reminds us, "and, always, *cui bono* – who profits?"[7] The questions of who profits, and how, are crucial because the attempt to answer them leads directly to an understanding of the function of literary sexual politics. Function is often best known by effect. Though one of the most persistent of literary stereotypes is the castrating bitch, the cultural reality is not the emasculation of men by women but the *immasculation* of women by men. As readers and teachers and scholars, women are taught to think as men, to identify with a male point of view, and to accept as normal and legitimate a male system of values, one of whose central principles is misogyny.

One of the earliest statements of the phenomenon of immasculation, serving indeed as a position paper, is Elaine Showalter's "Women and the Literary Curriculum." In the opening part of her article, Showalter imaginatively recreates the literary curriculum the average young woman entering college confronts:

> In her freshman year she would probably study literature and composition, and the texts in her course would be selected for their timeliness, or their relevance, or their power to involve the reader, rather than for their absolute standing in the literary canon. Thus she might be assigned any one of the texts which have recently been advertised for Freshman English: an anthology of essays, perhaps such as *The Responsible Man*, "for the student who wants literature relevant to the world in which he lives," or *Conditions of Men*, or *Man in Crisis: Perspectives on The Individual and His World*, or again, *Representative Men: Cult Heroes of Our Time*, in which thirty-three men represent such categories of heroism as the writer, the poet, the dramatist, the artist, and the guru, and the only two women included are the Actress Elizabeth Taylor and The Existential Heroine Jacqueline Onassis. . . . By the end of her freshman year, a woman student would have learned something about intellectual neutrality; she would be learning, in fact, how to think like a man.[8]

Showalter's analysis of the process of immasculation raises a central question: "What are the effects of this long apprenticeship in negative capability on the self-image and the self-confidence of women students?" And the answer is self-hatred and self-doubt: "Women are estranged from their own experience and unable to perceive its shape and authenticity. . . . they are expected to identify as readers with a masculine experience and perspective, which is presented as the human one. . . . Since they have no faith in the validity of their own perceptions and experiences, rarely seeing them confirmed in literature, or accepted in criticism, can we wonder that women students are so often timid, cautious, and insecure when we exhort them to 'think for themselves'?"[9]

The experience of immasculation is also the focus of Lee Edwards' article, "Women, Energy, and *Middlemarch*." Summarizing her experience, Edwards concludes:

Thus, like most women, I have gone through my entire education – as both student and teacher – as a schizophrenic, and I do not use this term lightly, for madness is the bizarre but logical conclusion of our education. Imagining myself male, I attempted to create myself male. Although I knew the case was otherwise, it seemed I could do nothing to make this other critically real.

Edwards extends her analysis by linking this condition to the effects of the stereotypical presentation of women in literature:

I said simply, and for the most part silently that, since neither those women nor any women whose acquaintances I had made in fiction had much to do with the life I led or wanted to lead, I was not female. Alien from the women I saw most frequently imagined, I mentally arranged them in rows labelled respectively insipid heroines, sexy survivors, and demonic destroyers. As organizer I stood somewhere else, alone perhaps, but hopefully above them.[10]

Intellectually male, sexually female, one is in effect no one, nowhere, immasculated.

Clearly, then, the first act of the feminist critic must be to become a resisting rather than an assenting reader and, by this refusal to assent, to begin the process of exorcizing the male mind that has been implanted in us. The consequence of this exorcism is the capacity for what Adrienne Rich describes as re-vision – "the act of looking back, of seeing with fresh eyes, of entering an old text from a new critical direction." And the consequence, in turn, of this re-vision is that books will no longer be read as they have been read and thus will lose their power to bind us unknowingly to their designs. While women obviously cannot rewrite literary works so that they become ours by virtue of reflecting our reality, we can accurately name the reality they do reflect and so change literary criticism from a closed conversation to an active dialogue.

In making available to women this power of naming reality, feminist criticism is revolutionary. The significance of such power is evident if one considers the strength of the taboos against it:

I permit no woman to teach . . . she is to keep silent.

St. Paul

By Talmudic law a man could divorce a wife whose voice could be heard next door. From there to Shakespeare: "Her voice was ever soft,/Gentle, and low-an excellent thing in woman." And to Yeats: "The women that I picked spoke sweet and low/And yet gave tongue." And to Samuel Beckett, guessing at the last torture, The Worst: "a woman's voice perhaps, I hadn't thought of that, they might engage a soprano."

Mary Ellmann[11]

The experience of the class in which I voiced my discontent still haunts my nightmares. Until my face froze and my brain congealed, I was called prude and, worse yet, insensitive, since I willfully misread the play in the interest of proving a point false both to the work and in itself.

Lee Edwards[12]

The experience Edwards describes of attempting to communicate her reading of the character of Shakespeare's Cleopatra is a common memory for most of us who have become feminist critics. Many of us never spoke; those of us who did speak were usually quickly silenced. The need to keep certain things from being thought and said reveals to us their importance. Feminist criticism represents the discovery/recovery of a voice, a unique and uniquely powerful voice capable of canceling out those other voices, so movingly described in Sylvia Plath's *The Bell Jar*, which spoke about us and to us and at us but never for us.

(1978)

Notes

6 *College English* 34 (1973), 1075.
7 "Dwelling in Decencies: Radical Criticism and the Feminist Perspective," *College English* 32 (1971), 887; reprinted in *Sex, Class, and Culture* (Bloomington: Indiana University Press, 1978), p. 16.
8 *College English* 32 (1971), 855.
9 Ibid., 856–57.
10 *Massachusetts Review* 13 (1972), 226, 227.
11 *Thinking About Women* (New York: Harcourt Brace Jovanovich, 1968), pp. 149–50.
12 Edwards, p. 230.

JONATHAN CULLER

'Reading as a Woman'
On Deconstruction: Theory and Criticism after Structuralism

As Heilbrun suggests, reading as a woman is not necessarily what occurs when a woman reads: women can read, and have read, as men. Feminist readings are not produced by recording what happens in the mental life of a female reader as she encounters the words of *The Mayor of Casterbridge*, though they do rely heavily on the notion of the experience of the woman reader. Shoshana Felman asks, "Is it enough to be a woman in order to speak as a woman? Is 'speaking as a woman' determined by some biological condition or by a strategic, theoretical position, by anatomy or by culture?" ("Women and Madness: The Critical Phallacy," p. 3). The same question applies to "reading as a woman."

To ask a woman to read as a woman is in fact a double or divided request. It appeals to the condition of being a woman as if it were a given and simultaneously urges that this condition be created or achieved. Reading as a woman is not simply, as Felman's disjunctions might seem to imply, a theoretical position, for it appeals to a sexual identity defined as essential and privileges experiences associated with that identity. Even the most sophisticated theorists make this appeal – to a condition or experience deemed more basic than the theoretical position it is used to justify. "As a female reader, I am haunted rather by another question," writes Gayatri Spivak, adducing her sex as the ground for a question ("Finding Feminist Readings," p. 82). Even the most radical French theorists, who would deny any positive or distinctive identity to woman and see *le féminin* as any force that disrupts the symbolic structures of Western thought, always have moments, in developing a theoretical position, when they speak as women, when they rely on the fact that they *are* women. Feminist critics are fond of quoting Virginia Woolf's remark that women's "inheritance," what they are given, is "the difference of view, the difference of standard"; but the question then becomes, what is the difference? It is never given as such but must be produced. Difference is produced by differing. Despite the decisive and necessary appeal to the authority of women's experience and of a female reader's experience, feminist criticism is in fact concerned, as Elaine Showalter astutely puts it, "with the way in which the *hypothesis* of a female reader changes our apprehension of a given text, awakening us to the significance of its sexual codes" ("Towards a Feminist Poetics," p. 25, my italics).[7]

Showalter's notion of the *hypothesis* of a female reader marks the double or divided structure of "experience" in reader-oriented criticism. Much male response criticism conceals this structure – in which experience is posited as a given yet deferred as something to be achieved – by asserting that readers simply do in fact have a certain experience. This structure emerges explicitly in a good deal of feminist criticism which takes up the problem that women do not always read or have not always read as women: they have been alienated from an experience appropriate to their condition as women.[8] With the shift to the hypothesis of a female reader, we move to a second moment or level of feminist criticism's dealings with the reader. In the first moment, criticism appeals to experience as a given that can ground or justify a reading. At the second level the problem is precisely that women have not been reading as women. "What is crucial here," writes Kolodny, "is that reading is a *learned* activity which, like many other learned interpretive strategies in our society, is inevitably sex-coded and gender-inflected" ("Reply to Commentaries," p. 588). Women "are expected to identify," writes Showalter, "with a masculine experience and perspective, which is presented as the human one" ("Women and the Literary Curriculum," p. 856). They have been constituted as subjects by discourses that have not identified or promoted the possibility of reading "as a woman." In its second moment, feminist criticism undertakes, through the postulate of a woman reader, to bring about a new experience of reading and to make readers – men and women – question the literary and political assumptions on which their reading has been based.

In feminist criticism of the first sort, women readers identify with the concerns of women characters; in the second case, the problem is precisely that women are led to identify with male characters, against their own interests as women. Judith Fetterley, in a book on the woman reader and American fiction, argues that "the major works of American fiction constitute a series of designs upon the female reader." Most of this literature "insists on its universality at the same time that it defines that universality in specifically male terms" (*The Resisting Reader*, p. xii). One of the founding works of American literature, for instance, is "The Legend of Sleepy Hollow." The figure of Rip Van Winkle, writes Leslie Fiedler, 'presides over the birth of the American imagination; and it is fitting that our first successful homegrown legend should memorialize, however playfully, the flight of the dreamer from the shrew' (*Love and Death in the American Novel*, p. xx). It is fitting because, ever since then, novels seen as archetypally American – investigating or articulating a distinctively American experience – have rung the changes on this basic schema, in which the protagonist struggles against constricting, civilizing, oppressive forces embodied by woman. The typical protagonist, continues Fiedler, the protagonist seen as embodying the universal American dream, has been "a man on the run, harried into the forest and out to sea, down the river or into combat – anywhere to avoid 'civilization,' which is to say, the confrontation of a man and a woman which leads to the fall to sex, marriage, and responsibility."

Confronting such plots, the woman reader, like other readers, is powerfully impelled by the structure of the novel to identify with a hero who makes woman the enemy. In "The Legend of Sleepy Hollow," where Dame Van Winkle represents everything one might wish to escape and Rip the success of a fantasy, Fetterley argues that "what is essentially a simple act of identification when the reader of the story is male becomes a tangle of contradictions when the reader is female" (*The Resisting Reader*, p. 9). "In such fictions the female reader is co-opted into participation in an experience from which she is explicitly excluded; she is asked to identify with a selfhood that defines itself in opposition to her; she is required to identify against herself" (p. xii).

One should emphasize that Fetterley is not objecting to unflattering literary representations of women but to the way in which the dramatic structure of these stories induces women to participate in a vision of woman as the obstacle to freedom. Catherine in *A Farewell to Arms* is an appealing character, but her role is clear: her death prevents Frederic Henry from coming to feel the burdens she fears she imposes, while consolidating his investment in an idyllic love and in his vision of himself as a "victim of cosmic antagonism" (p. xvi). "If we weep at the end of the book," Fetterley concludes, "it is not for Catherine but for Frederic Henry. All our tears are ultimately for men, because in the world of *A Farewell to Arms* male life is what counts. And the message to women reading this classic love story and experiencing its image of the female ideal is clear and simple: the only good woman is a dead one, and even then there are questions" (p. 71). Whether or not the message is quite this simple, it is certainly true that the reader must adopt the perspective of Frederic Henry to enjoy the pathos of the ending.

Fetterley's account of the predicament of the woman reader – seduced and betrayed by devious male texts – is an attempt to change reading: "Feminist criticism is a political act whose aim is not simply to interpret the world but to change it by changing the consciousness of those who read and their relation to what they read" (p. viii). The first act of a feminist critic is "to become a resisting rather than an assenting reader and, by this refusal to assent, to begin the process of exorcizing the male mind that has been implanted in us" (p. xxii).

(1982)

Notes

7 Feminists criticism is, of course, concerned with other issues as well, particularly the distinctiveness of women's writing and the achievements of women writers. The problems of reading as a woman and of writing as a woman are in many respects similar, but concentration on the latter leads feminist criticism into areas that do not concern me here, such as the establishment of a criticism focused on women writers that parallels criticism focused on male writers. Gynocriticism, says, Showalter, who has been one of the principal advocates of this activity, is concerned "with woman as the producer of textual meaning, with the history, themes, genres, and structures of literature by women. Its subjects include the psychodynamics of female creativity; linguistics and the problem of a female language; the trajectory of the individual or collective female literary career; literary history; and, of course, studies of particular writers and works" ("Towards a Feminist Poetics," p. 25). For work of this kind, see Sandra Gilbert and Susan Gubar, *The Madwoman in the Attic*, and the collection edited by Sally McConnell-Ginet, Ruth Borker, and Nelly Furman, *Women and Language in Literature and Society* (New York: Praeger, 1980).

8 The analogy with social class is instructive: progressive political writing appeals to the proletariat's experience of oppression, but usually the problem for a political movement is precisely that the members of a class do not have the experience their situation would warrant. The most insidious oppression alienates a group from its own interests as a group and encourages it to identify with the interests of the oppressors, so that political struggles must first awaken a group to its interests and its "experience."

ROBERT SCHOLES

'Reading Like a Man'
Men in Feminism

Derrida is troubled by the same problems, which he addresses in a light and impromptu manner at the end of the conference from which I quoted him earlier. Here are three short passages from his final remarks:

In other words if we consider for example what is called a writing man – for example me, to the extent that I'm supposed to be a man – then writing on woman should be less writing on woman than writing from or on the basis of (*depuis*) what comes to me from a feminine place.

Following Culler, we can rewrite this as a comment on reading:

> If we consider for example what is called a reading man – for example me, to the extent that I'm supposed to be a man – then reading as a woman should be less reading as a woman than reading from or on the basis of what comes to me from a feminine place.

Yes, possibly, but where is this "feminine place" and on what basis does a man have access to it? In deconstructive terms it is the trace of femininity that inevitably is inscribed in something defined as *not* feminine. But to reason in this way is to give the trace a positive status as a place or locus of the feminine. The "feminine place" here is perhaps not strictly deconstructive but Jungian. Still, one must wonder exactly what does come from this feminine place and how it might be recognized or authenticated as feminine. Derrida's awareness of the problem is suggested by his immediate restatement of it in terms of – of all things – voice.

> . . . I too have learned from the *écoute* of women, from listening to the degree I can to a certain feminine voice.

Of special interest here is the qualification – "to the degree I can." What is it, we must ask, that sets limits to Derrida's ability to hear "a certain feminine voice"? Why does he need to suggest that he hears this voice less well than he hears other (presumably masculine) voices? What can it be other than his own membership in the class of males, with all that implies in the way of experience? At some level the concept of *experience*, which was earlier dismissed and replaced by the more docile and vulnerable concept of *essence*, is returning to trouble this text also.

Quite properly Derrida wants to complicate the question of gender, to deconstruct it,

> Because it's not such a simple thing when we say that whoever bears a masculine proper name, is anatomically male, etc., is a man. This feminine voice can pass through trajectories that are extremely multiple . . . In other words, on the other side, and even in the most feminist women, the masculine voice is not silent. (p. 32).

After these words the text indicates "LAUGHTER." This laughter I read as symptomatic. Feminism and feminists have, however gently and gracefully, been put in their place – again. Whenever women speak up, it is the phallogocentric male voice speaking through them. And when they read actively and aggressively as members of the class, woman, are they then reading through male eyes as well? Or are they finally reading as women conscious of their own experience as members of a class who share that experience?

To put the problem another way, is there any difference between reading *as* a woman and reading *like* a woman? Can Mary actually read *as* a woman because she *is* a woman, or can she only read *like* a woman because no individual can ever be a woman? To put the question still another way, can John read *as* a woman or only *like* a woman? If neither John nor Mary can really read *as* a woman, and either one can read *like* a woman, then what's the difference between John and Mary? My own feeling is that until no one notices or cares about the difference we had better not pretend it isn't there. Above all, I think no man should seek in any way to diminish the authority which the experience of women gives them in speaking about that experience, and I believe that women should be very wary of critical systems that deny or diminish that authority.

Experience, of course, sets limits even as it confers authority. If some irreducible minimum of space or time separates us from our own experience, it is also true that this separation is never complete. We are subjects constructed by our experience and truly carry traces of that experience in our minds and on our bodies. Those of us who are male cannot deny this either. With the best will in the world we shall never read as women and perhaps not even like women. For me, born when I was born and living where I have lived, the very best I can do is to be conscious of the ground upon which I stand: to read not as but like a man.

(1987)

Stephen Heath

The Sexual Fix

There is a passage towards the end of *A Room of One's Own* in which Virginia Woolf sums up something of her thinking as regards the introduction of determinations of sex into writing:

> Even so, the very first sentence that I would write here, I said, crossing over to the writing-table and taking up the page headed Women and Fiction, is that it is fatal for anyone who writes to think of their sex. It is fatal to be a man or woman pure and simple; one must be woman-manly or man-womanly. It is fatal for a woman to lay the least stress on any grievance; to plead even with justice any cause; in any way to speak consciously as a woman. And fatal is no figure of speech; for anything written with that conscious bias is doomed to death. It ceases to be fertilized. Brilliant and effective, powerful and masterly, as it may

appear for a day or two, it must wither at nightfall; it cannot grow in the minds of others. Some collaboration has to take place in the mind between the woman and the man before the art of creation can be accomplished. Some marriage of opposites has to be consummated. The whole of the mind must lie wide open if we are to get the sense that the writer is communicating his experience with perfect fullness. There must be freedom and there must be peace. Not a wheel must grate, not a light glimmer. The curtains must be close drawn. The writer, I thought, once his experience is over, must lie back and let his mind celebrate its nuptials in darkness. He must not look or question what is being done. Rather, he must pluck the petals from a rose or watch the swans float calmly down the river.[1]

'It is fatal for anyone who writes to think of their sex.' That proposition reverses Cixous's emphasis on the need specifically to pose sex, woman, her wants, female pleasure, writing that. Suppose in turn we re-reverse it: it is fatal for anyone who writes – reads, speaks, takes up language – not to think of their sex, not to bring into reflection their sexual positioning and its effects in language, speech, discourse, writing.

Reading the Woolf passage, we can grasp something of the difficulties, the meshes of sex in language. The thesis is clear – it is fatal for anyone who writes to think of their sex, one must be woman-manly or man-womanly – but it is not clear that we are not given a quite different position in the writing itself. 'Some marriage of opposites has to be consummated', for example. 'Consummated' is already a whole sexual history: 'consummate', 'to complete marriage by sexual intercourse', as the OED defines it, giving 1540 as the date for its first appearance; a legality, the law of marriage, a male scenario. How is consummation defined? The legal procedures for the invalidation of marriages from the seventeenth century on are explicit: by penetration and emission (in France there existed an extraordinary and extreme procedure known as '*congrès*' under which judges could order trial consummations before witnesses, the husband or wife against whom the demand for annulment was made having to defend themselves by demonstrating that they could actually manage intercourse). Woolf is writing discursively here in a male-defined position; the 'marriage of opposites' is one-sided in its representation – creation as consummation, a finality, an end, penetration and climax, male climax. After which, 'when his experience is over', the writer 'must lie back and let his mind celebrate its nuptials in darkness'. Perhaps it might be said that here exactly Woolf does bring in the balance, shifts to different terms, elements of a potentially female position, lying back, as earlier, more evidently, she has stressed that 'the mind must lie wide open'. But this 'female position' is equally male, part of the same scenario: the penetrating active man, the receptive passive woman. The marriage in the writing is one single order with its two given sides, its two specified positions. The very notion of 'opposites' is from within that order: man and woman, male and female, complement one another, with the latter derived as the difference from the former, so many essential female qualities in counterpart to his essential and defining maleness. Working with marriage, consummation, opposites, man and woman added together, Woolf is returned, even against the possibilities of her thesis, to what is a representation that assigns women to a certain place as woman, in relation to a certain domination and evaluation from men, the place of man.

[. . .]

It is fatal for anyone who writes to think of their sex but, even as she sets out that thesis, Woolf is caught up in a web of words and images and ways of writing that brings with them a position, a sexual stance, a certain representation. Cixous's question, how is female pleasure to be written? Or, how is the fatality – the historical fatality, the fix – of this position of 'sexuality', male and female, the man and the woman, the one and the other, the difference, to be broken, written away from?

This is an important area of theoretical discussion and literary practice today, most notably from the perspective of feminism and in terms of the possibility of the development of a specifically woman's language. 'Woman's desire would not speak the same language as man's'[2] (this and following quotations are from French feminist writers, Cixous herself, Michèle Montrelay and, as here, Luce Irigaray); the point now is to achieve an authentic language of that desire – and thus to write thinking of one's sex.

In this context, a number of theses and arguments are advanced and made as regards the relation of woman and language:

– The woman is more naturally a writer, since close to the mother tongue, close to creation: 'it is the woman who is more the writer, by the very fact that she creates an idiom; and the poet well knows that it is the mother tongue he speaks and no other';[3] woman's pleasure being in excess and at the expense of the phallus, the phallic order of the signifier, it is like a process of writing (understanding the latter as a play in language, the disturbance of fixed meanings): 'female pleasure can be seen as *writing* . . . this pleasure and the literary text (which is also written like an orgasm produced from within discourse) are the effect of the same murder of the signifier'.[4]

– The woman is close to the body, the source of writing: 'it is obvious that a woman does not write like a man, because she speaks with the body, writing is from the body'.[5] Writing resembles the body and the sexual division of male and female is expressed in the difference of women's writing: 'a feminine textual body can be recognized by the fact that it is always without end, has no finish, which moreover is what makes the feminine text very often difficult to read'.[6] Against 'the "I" of phallocratic language'[7] (this formulation in fact taken from an American feminist, Mary Daly), erect and single, the 'two lips' of the female sex in a female language, constantly moving and plural.

– A woman's writing is anti-theory, has no metalanguage ('cannot describe itself from outside or in formal terms'[8]), it has no place for 'the concept as such', is 'fluid' in style, breaking syntax and developing towards a new syntax of 'auto-affection'[9] (the 'two lips' of the female sex are perpetually joining in embrace), with 'neither subject nor object'.[10]

Clearly what these theses and arguments do is to assert a very powerful sexual determination in language and language use, and in particular to valorize sexual difference as male/female, female versus male, by an appeal to signs and correspondences of a femininity, a femaleness – flow, liquid, lips, holes – as well as to specifically women's experiences – menstruation, pregnancy, and so on. All of which, of course, bears first on literary production, women writing, but equally on literary reception, women reading and their literary criticism. Thus an English critic, Gillian Beer, follows the idea of the feminine textual body as being without end exactly when she talks in connection with Virginia Woolf of how 'the eschewing of plot is an aspect of her feminism. The avoidance of narrative climax is a way of getting outside the fixing properties of event';[11] and Woolf herself, despite her fatal-to-think-of-one's-sex stress, could praise her contemporary fellow-novelist Dorothy Richardson for her invention of 'a woman's sentence', 'the psychological sentence of the feminine gender' – 'of a more elastic fibre than the old, capable of stretching to the extreme, of suspending the frailest particles, of enveloping the vaguest shapes'.[12]

Problems quickly emerge however. To lay the emphasis on difference and the specificity of women (as of men) in the paradigm male/female is a gesture within the terms of the existing system, for which, precisely, women are different *from* men. Patriarchy, men in its order, has never said anything but that women are – the woman, the female, is – different: they are not men. Lawrence's novels, for instance, are full of 'pure man'/'pure woman', 'male soul'/'female soul', the antithesis derived from and justifying the reign of the phallus. Different as female to male, women are readily pinned to and identified with their sex, their bodies, a biology (the poet Ezra Pound: 'the female/Is an element, the female/Is a chaos/An octopus/A biological process'[13]): woman as the female animal, as sexuality, in every sense a sex object. The signs and correspondences claimed are none other than those of the system itself: women as fluid, flowing (Lawrence, regretting the rise of 'the modern woman': 'But women used to know better . . . Women used to see themselves as a softly flowing stream of attraction and desire and beauty, soft quiet rivers of energy and peace'[14]); women as maternity (Lawrence again can argue *for* matriarchy, meaning by the latter 'full self-responsibility as mothers and heads of the family',[15] leaving men alone to get on with 'the life of society').

And so the litany of difference has gone on and continues, attributing ('recognizing', as it would say) 'qualities' (often defects as far as its view of women – woman is concerned). 'If the male orgasm is in some sort "consonantic", is not the female orgasm "vocalic"?'[16] At school, as we were guided through Palgrave's

Golden Treasury of English Poetry, we were much taken with liquid vowels and hard consonants but were not quite together enough to make the obvious connections which only a French psychoanalyst today could so felicitously spell out for us (and doubtless tomorrow we will be reminded that men are active and women passive verbs – or is it transitive and intransitive?). 'Feminine in its lack of restraint, its wordiness, and the utter absence of feeling for form',[17] wrote Arnold Bennett of George Eliot's style; 'feminine forgetfulness of one's self',[18] added his contemporary Walter Pater writing generally; while David Holbrook sums up the tradition within which such remarks are automatically made with his recent unsparing praise for 'the female elements of intuition, creativity, and sympathy'.[19] A pat on the back from the solid men and women can be sent happily clucking back to the farmyard, to what Lawrence calls 'the lovely henny surety, the hensureness which is the real bliss of every female'.[20]

Difference, that is, is difficult, speedily comes round to an essence of woman and man, male and female, a kind of anthropologico-biological nature. But men and women are not simply given biologically; they are given in history and culture, in a social practice and representation that includes biological determinations, shaping and defining them in its process. The appeal to an 'undeniable' biological reality as essential definition is always itself a form of social representation, within a particular structure of assumption and argument. It is this appeal indeed that is made by the existing system and its 'sexuality', which holds to the clear identity – determined and fixed, rooted in nature – of the man and the woman, with the latter the difference, and runs over from there into an elaborate account of 'masculine' and 'feminine' modes of behaviour, characteristics, styles – the whole gamut of 'qualities' that the theses and arguments on the relations of woman and language uncannily reproduce (compare the idea of a breakdown of syntax, a writing with 'neither subject nor object', never-ending, an 'elastic' sentence 'enveloping the vaguest shapes', with Bennett's 'feminine in its lack of restraint, its wordiness, and the utter absence of feeling for form'; the whole idea of resemblance to the body is that of the system: women are like – *are* – their bodies which then specify their nature, define them essentially, their condition for ever).

This is difficult again, however, in that in a given situation the appeal to difference can be a powerful and necessary mode of struggle and action, can take the force of an alternative representation, turning difference against the order of the same that it is used to support (the single identity of man and woman from him); thus, for example, the reappropriation of the question of 'what does a woman want?', at once a question in the system *and* a moment of trouble that can be brought round against it, as its contradiction. The attempt to distinguish specifically feminine elements of writing, to develop a specifically female language, can clearly become important as a basis for movement and challenge and transformation. Virginia Woolf can perfectly well lay down that it is fatal to think of one's sex (as though there were one sex that one was, an absolute identity of sex) and at the same time praise Richardson's 'woman's sentence', this having a precise radical value, 'only in the sense that it is used to describe a woman's mind by a writer who is neither proud nor afraid of anything that she may discover in the psychology of her sex'. A critic such as Gillian Beer can perfectly well reverse Arnold Bennett's commonplace about the feminine inability to manage form into a feminist valuation of Woolf's eschewing of plot and narrative climax, inasmuch as in the context in which Woolf writes the latter are exactly strategies of the system, part of its novelistic resolution.

(1982)

Notes

1 Virginia Woolf, *A Room of One's Own* (1929) (St Albans and London: Granada, 1977), p. 99.
2 Luce Irigaray, *Ce Sexe qui n'en est pas un* (Paris: Seuil, 1977) p. 25.
3 Eugénie Lemoine-Luccioni, 'Ecrire', *Sorcières* no. 7, p. 14.
4 Michèle Montrelay, *L'Ombre et le nom*, pp. 80–1.
5 Hélène Cixous, 'Quelques questions à Hélène Cixous', *Les Cahiers du GRIF* no. 13 (October 1976), p. 20.
6 H. Cixous, 'Le sexe ou la tête', *Les Cahiers du GRIF* no. 13 (October 1976), p. 14.
7 Mary Daly, *Gyn/Ecology* (London: The Women's Press, 1979), p. 327.
8 Luce Irigaray, 'Woman's Exile', *Ideology and Consciousness* no. 1 (May 1977), p. 65.
9 Irigaray, *Ce Sexe*, p. 130 ('I'm trying to say that the female sex would be, above all, made up of *"two lips"*. . . these *"two lips"* are *always joined in an embrace*' 'Woman's Exile', pp. 64–5).
10 ibid. p. 132. Translations of French feminist texts, including one or two pieces by Irigaray, can be found in *New French Feminisms* ed. Elaine Marks and Isabelle de Courtivron (Amherst: University of Massachusetts Press, 1980).
11 Gillian Beer, 'Beyond Determinism: George Eliot and Virginia Woolf', in *Women Writing and Writing About Women* (London: Croom Helm, 1979), p. 95.
12 Virginia Woolf, 'Romance and the Heart' (1923), *Contemporary Writers* (London: Hogarth, 1965), pp. 124–5.
13 Ezra Pound, Canto XXIX, *The Cantos of Ezra Pound* (London: Faber & Faber, 1968), p. 149.
14 D. H. Lawrence, 'Do Women Change?' (1929), *Phoenix* II, p. 541.
15 D. H. Lawrence, 'Matriarchy' (1928), *Phoenix* II, p. 552.
16 Jean-Louis Tristani, *Le Stade du respir* (Paris: Minuit, 1978), p. 36.
17 Arnold Bennett, *The Journals of Arnold Bennett* ed. Newman Flower (London: Cassell, 1932), vol. 1, p. 6.
18 Walter Pater, *Plato and Platonism* (1893) (London: Macmillan, 1920), p. 281.
19 Holbrook, *The Masks of Hate*, p. 237.
20 D. H. Lawrence, 'Cocksure Women and Hensure Men' (1929), *Phoenix* II, p. 555.

LUCE IRIGARAY

'The Powers of Discourse and the Subordination of the Feminine' This Sex Which Is Not One

But as we have already seen, even with the help of linguistics, psychoanalysis cannot solve the problem of the articulation of the female sex in discourse. Even though Freud's theory, through an effect of dress-rehearsal – at least as far as the relation between the sexes is concerned – shows clearly the function of the feminine in that scene. *What remains to be done, then, is to work at 'destroying' the discursive mechanism.* Which is not a simple undertaking. . . . For how can we introduce ourselves into such a tightly-woven systematicity?

There is, in an initial phase, perhaps only one 'path', the one historically assigned to the feminine: that of *mimicry*. One must assume the feminine role deliberately. Which means already to convert a form of subordination into an affirmation, and thus to begin to thwart it. Whereas a direct feminine challenge to this condition means demanding to speak as a (masculine), 'subject', that is, it means to postulate a relation to the intelligible that would maintain sexual indifference.

To play with mimesis is thus, for a woman, to try to recover the place of her exploitation by discourse, without allowing herself to be simply reduced to it. It means to resubmit herself – inasmuch as she is on the side of the 'perceptible', of 'matter' – to 'ideas', in particular to ideas about herself, that are elaborated in/by a masculine logic, but so as to make 'visible', by an effect of playful repetition, what was supposed to remain invisible: the cover-up of a possible operation of the feminine in language. It also means 'to unveil' the fact that, if women are such good mimics, it is because they are not simply resorbed in this function. *They also remain elsewhere*: another case of the persistence of 'matter', but also of 'sexual pleasure'.

Elsewhere of 'matter': if women can play with mimesis, it is because they are capable of bringing new nourishment to its operation. Because they have always nourished this operation? Is not the 'first' stake in mimesis that of re-producing (from) nature? Of giving it form in order to appropriate it for oneself? As guardians of 'nature', are not women the ones who maintain, thus who make possible, the resource of mimesis of men? For the logos?

It is here, of course, that the hypothesis of a reversal – within the phallic order – is always possible. Re-semblance cannot do without red blood. Mother-matter-nature must go on forever nourishing speculation. But this re-source is also rejected as the waste product of reflection, cast outside as what resists it: as madness. Besides the ambivalence that the nourishing phallic mother attracts to herself, this function leaves woman's sexual pleasure aside.

That *'elsewhere' of female pleasure* might rather be sought first in the place where it sustains ek-stasy in the transcendental. The place where it serves as security for a narcissism extrapolated into the 'God' of men. It can play this role only at the price of its ultimate withdrawal from prospection, of its 'virginity' unsuited for the representation of self. Feminine pleasure has to remain inarticulate in language, in its own language, if it is not to threaten the underpinnings of logical operations. And so what is most strictly forbidden to women today is that they should attempt to express their own pleasure.

That 'elsewhere' of feminine pleasure can be found only at the price of *crossing back through the mirror that subtends all speculation*. For this pleasure is not simply situated in a process of reflection or mimesis, nor on one side of this process or the other: neither on the near side, the empirical realm that is opaque to all language, nor on the far side, the self-sufficient infinite of the God of men. Instead, it refers all these categories and ruptures back to the necessities of the self-representation of phallic desire in discourse. A playful crossing, and an unsettling one, which would allow woman to rediscover the place of her 'self-affection'. Of her 'god', we might say. A god to which one can obviously not have recourse – unless its *duality* is granted – without leading the feminine right back into the phallocratic economy.

Does this retraversal of discourse in order to rediscover a 'feminine' place suppose a certain work on/ of language?

It is surely not a matter of interpreting the operation of discourse while remaining within the same type of utterance as the one that guarantees discursive coherence. This is moreover the danger of every statement, every discussion, *about Speculum*. And, more generally speaking, of every discussion *about* the question of woman. For to speak *of* or *about* woman may always boil down to, or be understood as, a recuperation of the feminine within a logic that maintains it in repression, censorship, nonrecognition.

In other words, the issue is not one of elaborating a new theory of which woman would be the *subject* or the *object*, but of jamming the theoretical machinery itself, of suspending its pretension to the production of a truth and of a meaning that are excessively univocal. Which presupposes that women do not aspire simply to be men's equals in knowledge. That they do not claim to be rivalling men in constructing a logic of the feminine that would still take onto-theologic as its model, but that they are rather attempting to wrest this question away from the economy of the logos. They should not put it, then, in the form 'What is woman?' but rather, repeating/interpreting the way in which, within discourse, the feminine finds itself defined as lack, deficiency, or as imitation and negative image of the subject, they should signify that with respect to this logic a *disruptive excess* is possible on the feminine side.

An excess that exceeds common sense only on condition that the feminine not renounce its 'style'. Which, of course, is not a style at all, according to the traditional way of looking at things.

This 'style', or 'writing', of women tends to put the torch to fetish words, proper terms, well-constructed forms. This 'style' does not privilege sight; instead, it takes each figure back to its source, which is among other things *tactile*. It comes back in touch with itself in that origin without ever constituting in it, constituting itself in it, as some sort of unity. *Simultaneity* is its 'proper' aspect – a proper(ty) that is never fixed in the possible identity-to-self of some form or other. It is always *fluid*, without neglecting the characteristics of fluids that are difficult to idealize: those rubbings between two infinitely near neighbours that create a dynamics. Its 'style' resists and explodes every firmly established form, figure, idea or concept. Which does not mean that it lacks style, as we might be led to believe by a discursivity that cannot conceive of it. But its 'style' cannot be upheld as a thesis, cannot be the object of a position.

And even the motifs of 'self-touching', of 'proximity', isolated as such or reduced to utterances, could effectively pass for an attempt to appropriate the feminine to discourse. We would still have to ascertain whether 'touching oneself', that (self-) touching, the desire for the proximate rather than for (the) proper(ty), and so on, might not imply a mode of exchange irreducible to any *centring*, any *centrism*, given the way the 'self-touching' of female 'self-affection' comes into play as a rebounding from one to the other without any possibility of interruption, and given that, in this interplay, proximity confounds any adequation, any appropriation.

But of course if these were only 'motifs' without any work on and/or with language, the discursive economy could remain intact. How, then, are we to try to redefine this language work that would leave space for the feminine? Let us say that every dichotomizing – and at the same time redoubling – break, including the one between enunciation and statement (*énoncé*), has to be disrupted. Nothing is ever to be *posited* that is not also reversed and caught up again in the *supplementarity of this reversal*. To put it another way: there would no longer be either a right side or a wrong side of discourse, or even of texts, but each passing from one to the other would make audible and comprehensible even what resists the recto-verso structure that shores up common sense. If this is to be practised for every meaning posited – for every word, *énoncé*, sentence, but also of course for every phoneme, every letter – we need to proceed in such a way that linear reading is no longer possible: that is, the retroactive impact of the end of each word, *énoncé*, or sentence upon its beginning must be taken into consideration in order to undo the power of its teleological effect, including its deferred action. That would hold good also for the opposition between structures of horizontality and verticality that are at work in language.

What allows us to proceed in this way is that we interpret, at each 'moment', the *specular make-up* of discourse, that is, the self-reflecting (stratifiable) organization of the subject in that discourse. An organization that maintains, among other things, the break between what is perceptible and what is intelligible, and thus maintains the submission, subordination, and exploitation of the 'feminine'.

This language work would thus attempt to thwart any manipulation of discourse that would also leave discourse intact. Not, necessarily, in the *énoncé*, but in its *autological presuppositions*. Its function would thus be to *cast phallocentrism, phallocratism*, loose from its moorings in order to return the masculine to its own language, leaving open the possibility of a different language. Which means that the masculine would no longer be 'everything'. That it could no longer, all by itself, define, circumvene, circumscribe, the properties of any thing and everything. That the right to define every value – including the abusive privilege of appropriation – would no longer belong to it.

(1977)

Translated by Catherine Porter (with Carolyn Burke)

HÉLÈNE CIXOUS

'The Laugh of the Medusa'
New French Feminisms

I shall speak about women's writing: about *what it will do*. Woman must write her self: must write about women and bring women to writing, from which they have been driven away as violently as from their bodies – for the same reasons, by the same law, with the same fatal goal. Woman must put herself into the text – as into the world and into history – by her own movement.

The future must no longer be determined by the past. I do not deny that the effects of the past are still with us. But I refuse to strengthen them by repeating them, to confer upon them an irremovability the equivalent of destiny, to confuse the biological and the cultural. Anticipation is imperative.

Since these reflections are taking shape in an area just on the point of being discovered, they necessarily bear the mark of our time – a time during which the new breaks away from the old, and, more precisely, the (feminine) new from the old (*la nouvelle de l'ancien*). Thus, as there are no grounds for establishing a discourse, but rather an arid millennial ground to break, what I say has at least two sides and two aims: to break up, to destroy; and to foresee the unforeseeable, to project.

I write this as a woman, toward women. When I say 'woman,' I'm speaking of woman in her inevitable struggle against conventional man; and of a universal woman subject who must bring women to their senses and to their meaning in history. But first it must be said that in spite of the enormity of the repression that has kept them in the 'dark' – that dark which people have been trying to make them accept as their attribute – there is, at this time, no general woman, no one typical woman. What they have *in common* I will say. But what strikes me is the infinite richness of their individual constitutions: you can't talk about *a* female sexuality, uniform, homogeneous, classifiable into codes – any more than you can talk about one unconscious resembling another. Women's imaginary is inexhaustible, like music, painting, writing: their stream of phantasms is incredible.

I have been amazed more than once by a description a woman gave me of a world all her own which she had been secretly haunting since early childhood. A world of searching, the elaboration of a knowledge, on the basis of a systematic experimentation with the bodily functions, a passionate and precise interrogation of her erotogeneity. This practice, extraordinarily rich and inventive, in particular as concerns masturbation, is prolonged or accompanied by a production of forms, a veritable aesthetic activity, each stage of rapture inscribing a resonant vision, a composition, something beautiful. Beauty will no longer be forbidden.

I wished that that woman would write and proclaim this unique empire so that other women, other unacknowledged sovereigns, might exclaim: I, too, overflow; my desires have invented new desires, my body knows unheard-of songs. Time and again I, too, have felt so full of luminous torrents that I could burst – burst with forms much more beautiful than those which are put up in frames and sold for a stinking fortune. And I, too, said nothing, showed nothing; I didn't open my mouth, I didn't repaint my half of the world. I was ashamed. I was afraid, and I swallowed my shame and my fear. I said to myself: You are mad! What's the meaning of these waves, these floods, these outbursts? Where is the ebullient, infinite woman who, immersed as she was in her naiveté, kept in the dark about herself, led into self-disdain by the great arm of parental-conjugal phallocentrism, hasn't been ashamed of her strength? Who, surprised and horrified by the fantastic tumult of her drives (for she was made to believe that a well-adjusted normal woman has a . . . divine composure), hasn't accused herself of being a monster? Who, feeling a funny desire stirring inside her (to sing, to write, to dare to speak, in short, to bring out something new), hasn't thought she was sick? Well, her shameful sickness is that she resists death, that she makes trouble.

And why don't you write? Write! Writing is for you, you are for you; your body is yours, take it. I know why you haven't written. (And why I didn't write before the age of twenty-seven.) Because writing is at once too high, too great for you, it's reserved for the great – that is for 'great men'; and it's 'silly.' Besides, you've written a little, but in secret. And it wasn't good, because it was in secret, and because you punished yourself for writing, because you didn't go all the way, or because you wrote, irresistibly, as when we would masturbate in secret, not to go further, but to attenuate the tension a bit, just enough to take the edge off. And then as soon as we come, we go and make ourselves feel guilty – so as to be forgiven; or to forget, to bury it until the next time.

Write, let no one hold you back, let nothing stop you: not man; not the imbecilic capitalist machinery, in which publishing houses are the crafty, obsequious relayers of imperatives handed down by an economy that works against us and off our backs; and not *yourself*. Smug-faced readers, managing editors, and big bosses don't like the true texts of women – female-sexed texts. That kind scares them.

I write woman: woman must write woman. And man, man. So only an oblique consideration will be found here of man; it's up to him to say where his masculinity and femininity are at: this will concern us once men have opened their eyes and seen themselves clearly.[1]

Now women return from afar, from always: from 'without,' from the heath where witches are kept alive; from below, from beyond 'culture'; from their childhood which men have been trying desperately to make them forget, condemning it to 'eternal rest.' The little girls and their 'ill-mannered' bodies immured, well-preserved, intact unto themselves, in the mirror. Frigidified. But are they ever seething underneath! What an effort it takes – there's no end to it – for the sex cops to bar their threatening return. Such a display of forces on both sides that the struggle has for centuries been immobilized in the trembling equilibrium of a deadlock.

(1976)
Translated by Keith Cohen and Paula Cohen

Note

1 Men still have everything to say about their sexuality, and everything to write. For what they have said so far, for the most part, stems from the opposition activity/passivity from the power relation between a fantasized obligatory virility meant to invade, to colonize, and the consequential phantasm of woman as a 'dark continent' to penetrate and to 'pacify.' (We know what 'pacify' means in terms of scotomizing the other and misrecognizing the self.) Conquering her, they've made haste to depart from her borders, to get out of sight, out of body. The way man has of getting out of himself and into her whom he takes not for the other but for his own, deprives him, he knows, of his own bodily territory. One can understand how man, confusing himself with his penis and rushing in for the attack, might feel resentment and fear of being 'taken' by the woman, of being lost in her, absorbed or alone.

Hélène Cixous

'Castration or Decapitation?'
Signs: Journal of Women in Culture and Society

But first she would have to *speak*, start speaking, stop saying that she has nothing to say! Stop learning in school that women are created to listen, to believe, to make no discoveries. Dare to speak her piece about giving, the possibility of a giving that doesn't take away, but *gives*. Speak of her pleasure and, God knows, she has something to say about that, so that she gets to unblock a sexuality that's just as much feminine as masculine, "de-phallocentralize" the body, relieve man of his phallus, return him to an erogenous field and a libido that isn't stupidly organized round that monument, but appears shifting, diffused, taking on all the others of oneself. Very difficult: first we have to get rid of the systems of censorship that bear down on every attempt to speak in the feminine. We have to get rid of and also explain what all knowledge brings with it as its burden of power: to show in what ways, culturally, knowledge is the accomplice of power: that whoever stands in the place of knowledge is always getting a dividend of power: show that all thinking until now has been ruled by this dividend, this surplus value of power that comes back to him who knows. Take the philosophers, take their position of mastery, and you'll see that there is not a soul who dares to make an advance in thought, into the as-yet-unthought, without shuddering at the idea that he is under the surveillance of the ancestors, the grandfathers, the tyrants of the concept, without thinking that there behind your back is always the famous Name-of-the-Father, who knows whether or not you're writing whatever it is you have to write without any spelling mistakes.

Now, I think that what women will have to do and what they will do, right from the moment they venture to speak what they have to say, will of necessity bring about a shift in metalanguage. And I think we're completely crushed, expecially in places like universities, by the highly repressive operations of metalanguage, the operations, that is, of the commentary on the commentary, the code, the operation that sees to it that the moment women open their mouths – women more often than men – they are immediately asked in whose name and from what theoretical standpoint they are speaking, who is their master and where they are coming from: they have, in short, to salute . . . and show their identity papers. There's work to be done against *class*, against categorization, against classification – classes. "Doing classes" in France means doing military service. There's work to be done against military service, against all schools, against the pervasive masculine urge to judge, diagnose, digest, name . . . not so much in the sense of the loving precision of poetic naming as in that of the repressive censorship of philosophical nomination/conceptualization.

Women who write have for the most part until now considered themselves to be writing not as women but as writers. Such women may declare that sexual difference means nothing, that there's no attributable difference between masculine and feminine writing. . . . What does it mean to "take no position"? When someone says "I'm not political" we all know what that means! It's just another way of saying: "My politics are someone else's!" And it's exactly the case with writing! Most women are like this: they do someone else's – man's – writing, and in their innocence sustain it and give it voice, and end up producing writing that's in effect masculine. Great care must be taken in working on feminine writing not to get trapped by names: to be signed with a woman's name doesn't necessarily make a piece of writing feminine. It could quite well be masculine writing, and conversely, the fact that a piece of writing is signed with a man's name does not in itself exclude femininity. It's rare, but you can sometimes find femininity in writings signed by men: it does happen.

Which texts appear to be woman-texts and are recognized as such today, what can this mean, how might they be read?[4] In my opinion, the writing being done now that I see emerging around me won't only be of the kinds that exist in print today, though they will always be with us, but will be something else as well. In particular we ought to be prepared for what I call the "affirmation of the difference," not a kind of wake about the corpse of the mummified woman, nor a fantasy of woman's decapitation, but something different: a step forward, an adventure, an exploration of woman's powers: of her power, her potency, her ever-dreaded strength, of the regions of femininity. Things are starting to be written, things that will constitute a feminine Imaginary, the site, that is, of identifications of an ego no longer given over to an image defined by the masculine ("like the woman I love, I mean a dead woman"), but rather inventing forms for women on the march, or as I prefer to fantasize. "in flight," so that instead of lying down, women will go forward by leaps in search of themselves.

There is work to be done on female sexual pleasure and on the production of an unconscious that would no longer be the classic unconscious. The unconscious is always cultural and when it talks it tells you your old stories, it tells you the old stories you've heard before because it consists of the repressed of culture. But it's also always shaped by the forceful return of a libido that doesn't give up that easily, and also by what is strange, what is outside culture, by a language which is a savage tongue that can make itself understood quite well. This is why, I think, *political* and not just literary work is started as soon as writing gets done by women that goes beyond the bounds of censorship, reading, the gaze, the masculine command, in that cheeky risk taking women can get into when they set out into the unknown to look for themselves.

This is how I would define a feminine textual body: as a *female libidinal economy*, a regime, energies, a system of spending not necessarily carved out by culture. A feminine textual body is recognized by the fact that it is always endless, without ending: there's no closure, it doesn't stop, and it's this that very often makes the feminine text difficult to read. For we've learned to read books that basically pose the word "end." But this one doesn't finish, a feminine text goes on and on and at a certain moment the volume comes to an end but the writing continues and for the reader this means being thrust into the void. These are texts that work on the beginning but not on the origin. The origin is a masculine myth: I always want to know where I come from. The question "Where do children come from?" is basically a masculine, much more than a feminine, question. The quest for origins, illustrated by Oedipus, doesn't haunt a feminine unconscious. Rather it's the beginning, or beginnings, the manner of beginning, not promptly with the phallus in order to close with the phallus, but starting on all sides at once, that makes a feminine writing. A feminine text starts on all sides at once, starts twenty times, thirty times, over.

(1981)
Translated by Annette Kuhn

Notes

4 There follows in the original a passage in which several categories of women's writing existing at the time (1975) are listed and discussed. These include: " 'the little girl's story.' where the little girl is getting even for a bad childhood," "texts of a return to a woman's own body," and texts which were a critical success, "ones about madwomen, deranged, sick women." The passage is omitted here, at the author's request, on the grounds that such a categorization is outdated, and that the situation with regard to women's writing is very much different now than it was five or six years ago (translator's note).

JUDITH STILL

'A Feminine Economy: Some Preliminary Thoughts'
The Body and the Text: Hélène Cixous, Reading and Teaching

Ecriture féminine is related to the idea of an *économie féminine* in that both display a different relation to 'the other'. Whereas a masculine economy requires strict delineation of property (from the ownership of one's body onwards to the onwership of the fruits of one's labour and so on), a feminine economy is one (of proximity) of taking the other into oneself and being taken into the other also. A feminine economy is about mutual knowing and knowing again (re-cognition in those senses only). *Ecriture féminine* therefore should be a writing shot through (like shot silk) with otherness. Does this require it to be 'difficult' (since we are trained in conservative forms), modernist, expressionist, James-Joyce writing? If so, much contemporary women's writing (especially black women's writing) fails.[16]

Categorisation, whether deriving from pretensions to scientific rigour, from claims to an aesthetic sensibility, or from the espousal of political priorities, inevitably involves establishing some kind of hierarchy – whether explicit or implicit. Cixous' 'Castration or decapitation' suggests that this kind of activity is part of *l'Empire du Propre*.[17] But 'feminist' criticism usually has explicit political priorities, and very often measures texts against a previously-established ideal model, or, at the very least, has a check list of criteria by which it can award points to (and take them off) the text under scrutiny. The work of earlier feminist writers, such as that of Simone de Beauvoir, is often judged, and found lacking, by recent feminist readers – on the grounds, for example, that it is too dependent on male criteria (form and content).[18] But a founding Mother can be excused on account of the times in which she was writing. Someone writing in the 1980s has no such historical escape route.

I wish to argue against always reading in terms of measuring against a standard and in favour of reading in a motherly, creative fashion. That is to say that not only should 'creative' writing be open to the other, but that reading should be too. In a sense this is only to reiterate the point that reading is writing as writing is reading. Cixous' own readings and writings often demonstrate this point. However, she is also associated with the assertion that *écriture féminine* is to be found in very few places. I do not wish to deny the necessary aggressive elements in mothering, reading or creating! I simply wish to privilege (of course!) the reconstructive over the critical, the generous over the calculated. I would argue (following the theoretical hints by Cixous) that the *féminin(e)* is not chosen for us, as Annie Leclerc suggests when she says we are wombs/vaginas/breasts, end of argument. Leclerc should be supplemented with Christine Delphy's analysis.[19] Femininity is not a fixed content which females can only accept or deny (and to which males have no access), but a complex construct involving many 'others' to that which presents itself as universal 'man' – a construct which is influenced by (though not absolutely determined by) relations of production, ideological state apparatuses and the like. Before there is a same time as we take our place within the masculine) in different ways. That *économie féminine* which is a theoretical extreme or poetic utopia can still inform our practice, showing that the (masculine) economy of rational (i.e. calculated) profit maximisation is not universal and inevitable in all spheres of exchange. As readers and teachers – both positions of would-be mastery – the feminine economy of generosity, as opposed to a Hegelian seeking of recognition (*reconnaissance* – also gratitude), can influence our practice. A search for feminines in texts can be a celebration of what we find as well as an analysis of the interplay of all the various differences; it need not involve a marking down of those works judged as insufficiently feminine nor a fetishisation of any one particular mode of discourse or practice.

(1990)

Notes

16 Here I am thinking in particular of institutional questions such as access to education and (colonial) education in a language other than the mother tongue. These questions relate to class as well as race.

17 'Castration or decapitation', translated by Annette Kuhn, *Signs*, vol. 7, no. 1, 1981.

18 See, for example, Mary Evans, *Simone de Beauvoir: A Feminist Mandarin* (London: Tavistock, 1985); Judith Okely, *Simone de Beauvoir: A re-reading* (London: Virago, 1986); T. Moi, 'She came to stay' review of Evans and Okely, *Paragraph*, vol. 8, 1986, 110–20.

19 See A. Leclerc, *Parole de femme* (Paris: Livre de Poche, 1974); some extracts have been translated in *New French Feminisms* edited by Elaine Marks and Isabelle de Courtivron (Hemel Hempstead: Harvester Wheatsheaf, 1980), and in *French Connections* edited by Claire Duchen (London: Hutchinson, 1987). C. Delphy's critique of Leclerc is in 'Protofeminism and antifeminism' in *Close to Home: A materialist analysis of women's oppression*, translated and edited by Diana Leonard (London: Hutchinson, 1984).

FRANCES JAFFER

*Quoted by Bachel Blau DuPlessis 'For the Etruscans:
Sexual Difference and Artistic Production – The Debate over a
Female Aesthetic'
The Future of Difference*

April 28

The Body, and its language, which is of course, all language. These notions of writing from the neck up. All that fear, almost terror, of the women at Barnard, of being caught in the old stereotype – woman/body, mother/nature, an inferior kind of mind, and flee it sisters deny it don't be trapped by our own feminism.

But that male body, how IT dominates the culture, the environment, the language. Since 3,000 B.C. in Sumeria, Tiamat's monsters again and again, and every myth an effort to keep the sun rising. Save the sun, everybody, from the watery deeps, the dark underneath it must go – Into – Every night into such dangers, such soft inchoate darkness, what will become of it, will it rise again will it will it rise again? The language of criticism: 'lean, dry, terse, powerful, strong, spare, linear, focused, explosive' – god forbid it should be 'limp'!! But – 'soft, moist, blurred, padded, irregular, going around in circles,' and other descriptions of *our* bodies – the very *abyss* of aesthetic judgment, danger, the wasteland for artists! That limp dick – an entire civilization based on it, help the sun rise, watch out for the dark underground, focus focus focus, keep it high, let it soar, let it transcend, let it aspire to Godhead.

(1980)

CATHERINE CLEMENT

*'Enslaved Enclave'
New French Feminisms*

'*Bravo, sir.*' A woman, among the others, sends forth this salutation from the balcony. It tumbles, falls. To speak, then, and still worse, to put oneself in a public position of theoretical premeditation, is to assume the position of 'the man.' That explains the shouts, mimicking, gestures, and, soon, the piercing cries of 'Hey, hey'; though theory and articulated speech are inadmissible, shouted speech is allowed. In other words, more seriously and irremediably: that would mean that dialectics, for example – but there is nothing else – would be inaccessible to women, and it then becomes impossible to understand all contradiction and hence, all struggle. That would mean that by their nature – innate or acquired in oppression – women could not use thought to help free themselves: that the only scansion of violence permitted them is obtuse, unthinking in its expression. That would mean that language is always masculine, that it is determined according to sex, and that discursiveness is not an integral part of feminine discourse. Even if somewhere it is true that rhetoric and vocabulary are formed by centuries of male cultural domination, to renounce the exercise of thought, to give it to them, is *to perpetuate*, as always when it is a matter of 'not being part of the system.' 'Be a feminist and shout'; an unchanged variant of 'Be beautiful and keep your tongue.'

(1981)

Translated by Marilyn R. Schuster

ANN ROSALIND JONES

'*Writing the Body: Toward An Understanding of L'Ecriture Féminine' Feminist Studies*

Can the body be the source of a new discourse? Is it possible, assuming an unmediated and *jouissant* (or, more likely, a positively reconstructed) sense of one's body, to move from that state of unconscious excitation directly to a written female text?

Madeleine Gagnon says yes, in *La Venue à l'écriture*, written with Cixous in 1977. Her view is that women, free from the self-limiting economy of male libido ('I will come once and once only, through one organ alone; once it's up and over, that's it; so I must beware, save up, avoid premature overflow'), have a greater spontaneity and abundance in body and language both:

> We have never been the masters of others or of ourselves. We don't have to confront ourselves in order to free ourselves. We don't have to keep watch on ourselves, or to set up some other erected self in order to understand ourselves. All we have to do is let the body flow, from the inside; all we have to do is erase . . . whatever may hinder or harm the new forms of writing; we retain whatever fits, whatever suits us. Whereas man confronts himself constantly. He pits himself against and stumbles over his erected self.[25]

But psychoanalytic theory and social experience both suggest that the leap from body to language is especially difficult for women.[26] Lacanian theory holds that a girl's introduction into language (the symbolic order represented by the father and built on phallic/non-phallic oppositions) is complex, because she cannot identify directly with the positive poles of that order. And in many preliterate and postliterate cultures, taboos against female speech are enforced: injunctions to silence, mockery of women's chatter or 'women's books' abound. The turn taking in early consciousness-raising groups in the

United States was meant precisely to overcome the verbal hesitancy induced in women by a society in which men have had the first and the last word. Moreover, for women with jobs, husbands or lovers, children, activist political commitments, finding the time and justification to write at all presents an enormous practical and ideological problem.[27] We are more likely to write, and to read each other's writing, if we begin by working against the concrete difficulties and the prejudices surrounding women's writing than if we simplify and idealize the process by locating writing as a spontaneous outpouring from the body.

Calls for a verbal return to nature seem especially surprising coming from women who are otherwise (and rightly!) suspicious of language as penetrated by phallocentric dogma. True, conventional narrative techniques, as well as grammar and syntax, imply the unified viewpoint and mastery of outer reality that men have claimed for themselves. But literary modes and language itself cannot be the only targets for transformation; the *context* for women's discourses needs to be thought through and broadened out. A woman may experience *jouissance* in a private relationship to her own body, but she writes for others. Who writes? Who reads? Who makes women's texts available to women? What do women want to read about other women's experience? To take a stance as a woman poet or novelist is to enter into a role criss-crossed with questions of authority, of audience, of the modes of publication and distribution. I believe that we are more indebted to the 'body' of earlier women writers and to feminist publishers and booksellers than to any woman writer's libidinal/body flow. The novelist Christiane Rochefort sums up with amusing directness the conflicting public forces and voices that create the dilemma of the French woman who wants to write:

> Well. So here you are now, sitting at your writing table, alone, not allowing anybody anymore to interfere. Are you free?
>
> First, after this long quest, you are swimming in a terrible soup of values – for, to be safe, you had to refuse the so-called female values, which are not female but a social scheme, and to identify with male values, which are not male but an appropriation by men – or an attribution to men – of all human values, mixed up with the anti-values of domination-violence-oppression and the like. In this mixture, where is your real identity?
>
> Second, you are supposed to write in certain forms, preferably: I mean you feel that in certain forms you are not too much seen as a usurper. Novels. Minor poetry, in which case you will be stigmatized in French by the name of 'poetesse': not everybody can afford it. . . .
>
> You are supposed, too, to write *about* certain things: house, children, love. Until recently there was in France a so-called *littérature féminine*.
>
> Maybe you don't want to write *about*, but to write, period. And of course, you don't want to obey this social order. So, you tend to react against it. It is not easy to be genuine.[28]

Whatever the difficulties, women are inventing new kinds of writing. But as Irigaray's erudition and plays with the speaking voice show (as do Cixous's mischievous puns and citations of languages from Greek through German to Portuguese, and Wittig's fantastic neologisms and revision of conventional genres), they are doing so deliberately, on a level of feminist theory and literary self-consciousness that goes far beyond the body and the unconscious. That is also how they need to be read. It takes a thoroughgoing familiarity with *male* figureheads of Western culture to recognize the intertextual games played by all these writers; their work shows that a resistance to culture is always built, at first, of bits and pieces of that culture, however they are disassembled, criticized, and transcended. Responding to *l'écriture féminine* is no more instinctive than producing it. Women's writing will be more accessible to writers and readers alike if we recognize it as a conscious response to socioliterary realities, rather than accept it as an overflow of one woman's unmediated communication with her body. Eventually, certainly, the practice of women writers will transform what we can see and understand in a literary text; but even a woman setting out to write about her body will do so against and through her socioliterary mothers, midwives, and sisters. We need to recognize, too, that there is nothing universal about French versions of *écriture féminine*. The speaking, singing, tale telling, and writing of women in cultures besides that of the Ile de France need to be looked at and understood in their social context if we are to fill in an adequate and genuinely empowering picture of women's creativity.

But I risk, after all this, overstating the case against *féminité* and *l'écriture féminine*, and that would mean a real loss. American feminists can appropriate two important elements, at least, from the French position: the critique of phallocentrism in all the material and ideological forms it has taken, and the call for new representations of women's consciousness. It is not enough to uncover old heroines or to imagine new ones. Like the French, we need to examine the words, the syntax, the genres, the archaic and elitist attitudes toward language and representation that have limited women's self-knowledge and expression during the long centuries of patriarchy. We need not, however, replace phallocentrism with a shakily theorized 'concentrism' that denies women their historical specificities to recognize how deep a refusal of masculinist values must go.[29] If we remember that what women really share is an oppression on all levels, although it affects us each in different ways – if we can translate *féminité* into a concerted attack not only on language, but also directly upon the sociosexual arrangements that keep us from our own potentials and from each other – then we are on our way to becoming 'les jeunes nées' envisioned by French feminisms at their best.

(1981)

Notes

25 Madeleine Gagnon, 'Corps I,' *New French Feminisms*, p. 180. See Chantal Chawaf for a similar statement, in 'La Chair linguistique,' *New French Feminisms*, pp. 177–78.

26 Cora Kaplan combines psychoanalytic and anthropological accounts of women's hesitations to speak, in 'Language and Gender,' *Papers on Patriarchy* (Brighton, England: Women's Publishing Collective, 1976). Similarly, Sandra M. Gilbert and Susan Gubar demonstrate how socially derived ambivalence toward the role of writer has acted upon women's writing in English, in *The Madwoman in the Attic: The Woman Writer and the Nineteenth-Century Literary Imagination* (New Haven: Yale University Press, 1979).

27 See Tillie Olsen's *Silences* (New York: Delacorte, 1979) for a discussion of the practical demands and self-doubts that have hindered women's writing, especially 'The Writer Woman: One out of Twelve.' pp. 177–258.

28 Christiane Rochefort, 'Are Women Writers Still Monsters?' a speech given at the University of Wisconsin, Madison, Wis., February 1975, translated in *New French Feminisms*, pp. 185–86.

29 'Concentrism' is Elaine Showalter's term, used in a speech, 'Feminist Literary Theory and Other Impossibilities,' given at the Smith College Conference on Feminist Literary Criticism, Northampton, Mass., October 25, 1980.

KADIATU KANNEH

'Love, Mourning and Metaphor: Terms of Identity' New Feminist Discourses

The privileging of the body in the writing of Cixous and Irigaray as the focal point for a radical subversion is in many ways, however, a dangerous political move. It is undeniably crucial to revalorize the female body, to rescue it from the vilification which, for centuries, has been practised against it through oppressive codes and institutions. When men are degrading women sexually, hating them carnally and violently, it is positive to reclaim and revalue the female body. To see the body as a source of potential power and intense pleasure is a needed reaction to the kind of anti-female sadism which is explored by Benoîte Groult in 'Night Porters',[32] and is the sad fate of the heroine in *The Story of O*. It is highly important, however, to determine which aspects of this femininity should be held up for celebration, and to sort out just what would be the political ramifications of such a move.

Lacan's insistence that there is no feminine outside language is useful here in that it marks out the difficulties into which Cixous and Irigaray fall. Cixous's description in 'The Laugh of the Medusa' of the painful moment of a woman speaking in public is an example of the dubious valorizations upon which she relies. The description concentrates upon the interplay of language and body which is the peculiarly feminine mode of discourse: 'She doesn't "speak", she throws her trembling body forward; she lets go of herself, she flies; all of her passes into her voice, and it's with her body that she vitally support the "logic" of her speech.'[33] Here the woman is seen bursting from the 'snare of silence' and flying free in the *jouissance* of her own natural self-expression, a form of expression which spills out of the definite structures of 'masculine' discourse: 'Her speech, even when "theoretical" or political is never simple or linear or "objectified", generalized.' There is another way of reading this moment, however, which would be to examine the causes for such a manner of public address from a social viewpoint. Surely, this tremor which seizes the woman from the depths of her lungs, this irresistible use of the body to complement the unmanageable ripple of her voice, is an accurate account not of an inherent feminine essence but of the direct results of social marginalization and intolerable sexual visibility. Not conditioned to wear mastery in a public scene or to forget the role of her body in a voyeuristic male society, the female public speaker acts, in this prototypical case, with a shivering uncertainty, handling the language of politico-theoretical discourse with stumbling skill. Celebrating this part of feminine activity and so following the rallying cry of Marguerite Duras, 'We must move on to the rhetoric of women, one that is anchored in the organism, in the body',[34] Cixous runs on the same tracks as the 'Wages for Housework' campaign which, finding women incarcerated in the kitchen, rushes to sing the kitchen's praise.

This same danger recurs throughout 'The Laugh of the Medusa', where women's supposed empathy with nature, their removal from the construction of civilizations and their innate maternal instinct – 'In women there is always more or less of the mother who makes everything all right, who nourishes' – are merely valorizations of spaces into which women have been coerced by dint of a social world which will not tolerate women as law-givers. This quotation from *Questions Féministes*, which Deborah Cameron includes in her *Feminism and Linguistic Theory*, adequately pinpoints the risk that women run by celebrating an area of 'femininity' which is merely the very point of ineffectiveness outside and beneath social control to which they have been driven: 'To advocate a direct relation to the body is therefore not subversive because it is equivalent to denying the reality and the strength of social mediations, the very same ones that oppress us in our bodies.'[35]

Determinism through body language – the self at the centre of the orgasm and its roots in the unconscious – relies upon a belief in a pre-linguistic reality, a way of experiencing and understanding the self which is prior to the symbolic. The falsity of this search and its prescription for a Utopian future is evident in Simone de Beauvoir's *Memoirs of a Dutiful Daughter*, in which she recalls the bliss of a childhood perception uninitiated into words:

> White was only rarely totally white, and the blackness of evil was relieved by lighter touches; I saw greys and half-tones everywhere. Only as soon as I tried to define their muted shapes, I had to use words, and found myself in a world of bony-structured concepts.[36]

The memory here is of an understanding which is wholly informed by the senses, which runs intuitively with a flow of sensation that needs no translation into a socially conceptual language. Simone de Beauvoir imagines a period where her body articulated lights and shadows, safety and fear, joy and pain through a dreamtime in tune with the flooding naunces of life. Language arrives as a dam against the flow, where meaning comes up against more concrete definitions. However, this passage upon a mode of experience which is born with the body has a neutrality to the social world and history which has already placed white in direct opposition to black and qualified each according to the scale which is lodged in Western ideology: white as a purity far superior to 'the blackness of evil'. This recalls Jacqueline Rose's intimation (*Sexuality in the Field of Vision*) that 'the effects of the unconscious are tied to the key fantasies operating at the heart of institutions'. Seeping into de Beauvoir's 'pre-linguistic' experience and already forming her conceptions are the institutionalized values appraised by Sista Roots in her poem 'Dictionary Black', which apprehends the loaded metaphors of a deeply racist

> A Darky is a Negro
> Not fair–atrocious–evil
> And the Prince of Darkness
> Is the Devil . . .
> . . . So I turn to 'white'
> All sweetness and light[17]

The spine of white culture also supports Hélène Cixous's 'The Laugh of the Medusa', the work being animated from within the nerve centre of a Western post-colonial backbone. Cixous consistently upholds her argument that women inhabit a pre-civilizational world which is closer to the pulse of nature and the rhythms of sensuality, a world which can be found in the germinating moments of childhood sexuality, by drawing a sustained analogy with black Africa. She stakes a claim for a true female identity by linking women's position with that of people outside Western culture, people whose land and bodies have suffered systematic vilification, thrown under a cloak of fear and mystery: 'they can be taught that their territory is black: because you are Africa, you are black. Your continent is dark. Dark is dangerous.' The principle for revaluing such a space is to celebrate its apparent 'natural' qualities: 'We the precocious, we the repressed of culture, our lovely mouths gagged with pollen, our wind knocked out of us, we the labyrinths, the ladders, the trampled spaces, the bevies . . . we are black and we are beautiful.'[38]

This reference to African peoples in order to underline the position of women outside history and culture, beyond the self-conscious, adult world of reason and politics, is in indirect collusion with the deliberate policies of the Western colonial countries which aim to wipe out the achievements and the intricate pasts of the colonized. Ngũgĩ Wa Thiong'o (in *Decolonizing the Mind*) attacks just this Eurocentric myopia in Western philosophy, for instance 'Hegel with his Africa comparable to a land of childhood still enveloped in the dark mantle of the night as far as the development of self-conscious history was concerned'.[39]

If we apply this approach to the white feminist practice of hoarding accounts of black subjectivity in order to mark out a common linguistic ground we face a tricky political situation which pivots itself on questions of language, experience and identity. The fusion of metaphor and body, identity and experience is both a political choice and a historical coercion which, I believe, cannot be either swept aside by poetic licence or blindly embraced as immutable. Cixous legitimizes her use of black historical metaphors, based on references to colonialism, slavery and racism, by claiming that, 'In woman, personal history blends together with the history of all women, as well as national and world history.' The call for a feminine culture which sees itself as separate from the history of wars and colonialisms is validated by the assertion that women had nothing to do with all of this: 'This is known by the colonised people of yesterday, the workers, the nations, the species off whose backs the history of *men* has made its gold' (my emphasis).[40]

Liberating the female body from language creates flesh out of words. Desire explodes the social, sex subverses and recreates the political. Upholding a female experience which cannot – biologically/physically – slide into the male and yet can slide racially and class-wise, Cixous and Irigaray legitimize a flagrant fluidity of metaphor. The question of who owns which metaphor is tied closely into an ongoing struggle over the past, over history, which will inevitably be a matter of eclectic analogy and constructions of fantasy. However, this eclecticism has definite political meaning in that the oppressions of the present are very often fixed in ways of perceiving the body – through race – as a personification of the past. The unconscious use of geography and time in understanding identity through the body is made conscious by Cixous's defiant attempts to disengage the specificity of historical metaphor, releasing women from the grip of time and placing a radical feminine identity beyond the tyrannies of race and class, 'so as to prevent the class struggle, or any other struggle for the liberation of a class or people, from operating as a form of repression, pretext for postponing the inevitable'. The joyous fervour with which Cixous cries for the blowing up of the past, of history and of political struggles outside the unconscious and the body relies on her understanding of difference as variations of sensual pleasure between women. Her drive to unlock women from a history she labels as exclusively male manages to lock all women into a history free-floating between images of black subjection and imperialist domination. Sensuality and the body suck in figurations of power drawn from colonial ideas of land and nature. Female masturbation is a 'unique empire', the unconscious is 'that other limitless country', and 'the Dark Continent' of the female psyche 'is neither dark nor unexplorable'.

The idea that women should ignore the divisions between themselves and sweep together across class, race and national boundaries to create a post-historical Utopian home, bypasses the knowledge that racial oppression has always created the body from obsessive fantasies of biology and environment. The power of Cixous's metaphors comes precisely from their continuing life in present ideologies of race. Black women are not in a position to bypass the histories and divisions, both of class and race, which block the development of a unified feminist movement.

(1992)

Notes

32 Marks and de Courtivron (eds), op. cit., pp. 68–75.
33 Cixous, 'The Laugh of the Medusa', p. 251.
34 From an interview with the Marguerite Duras by Susan Husserl-Kapit in *Signs*, Winter 1975, in Marks and de Courtivron (eds), op. cit., p. 238.
35 Quoted by Deborah Cameron (ed.), *Feminism and Linguistic Theory* (Macmillan, London, 1985), p. 130.
36 Quoted in Cameron (ed.), op. cit., p. 138.
37 Rhonda Cobham and Merle Collins, eds, *Watchers and Seekers* (The Women's Press Ltd, London, 1987), pp. 109–11.
38 Cixous, 'The Laugh of the Medusa', p. 248.
39 Ngũgĩ Wa Thiong'o, *Decolonizing the Mind* (James Currey and Heinemann, London, 1987), p. 16.
40 Cixous, 'The Laugh of the Medusa', p. 258.

DOMNA C. STANTON

'Language and Revolution: The Franco-American Dis-Connection' The Future of Difference

No less disturbing is the facile rejection of *écriture féminine* as too intellectual and elitist to be feminist. Admittedly, our understanding of Cixous, Kristeva, Irigaray, and others requires knowledge of philosophy, linguistics, and psychoanalytic theory. Even more, one must be willing to decipher dense texts replete with plays on words and devoid of normal syntactical construc-tions. Through their very mode of writing, however, these texts are striving to practice what they preach by subverting the syntax, the semantics, and even the Cartesian logic of the Logos. As Kristeva has written, '. . . playful language ergo disrupted law, violated, pluralized, maintained solely to allow a poly-valent, poly-logic game which leads to a conflagration of the essence of the Law. . . .'[35] We American feminists tend to consider such wordplay virtuosic and exhibitionistic. We ignore the paradoxical disjunction between *what* we say and *how* we say it, and thus we continue to speak *about* subverting the patriarchal order in pellucid rationalistic discourse. Indeed, the charge of intellectualism and elitism directed at *écriture féminine* is connected to a serious lack of awareness about the nature of our own critical practice that verges on bad faith. Viewed within their specific contexts, Anglo-American feminist empiricism is certainly not any less intellectual than *écriture féminine*. The opposite could in fact be argued: for *écriture féminine* not only combines theory with a subjectivism that confounds the protocols of scholarly discourse, it also strives to break the phallologic boundaries between critical analysis, essay, fiction, and poetry. Moreover, those who maintain that *écriture féminine* is not feminist because it appropriates concepts from such 'seminal' thinkers as Saussure, Freud, Lacan, and Derrida choose to forget that it was not feminists but Anglo-American patriarchs who founded, and trained us in, the biographical, thematic, stylistic, sociohistorical, or Marxist literary criticism that we unquestioningly practice. Instead of blinding ourselves to the academic origins and present boundaries of our critical discourse, we should acknowledge that, when compared to the work of other women in our society, feminist scholarship is fundamentally both intellectual and privileged. That admission, however, should not be the cause for futile self-flagellation. Nor should it compound the existing, nefarious tendency to assign intellectuality, the capacity for abstraction and speculation, and the use of rigorous modes of analysis to the male, and intuitiveness, sensibility, and emotionality to the female – a type of thinking which validates traditional stereotypes, reinforces the tyranny of the binary, and thus strengthens the phallologocentric order. Rather, we should celebrate our own and all women's heterogeneous contributions to the demolition of the old and the building of a new order of thought and being.

This is not to suggest, however, that the presuppositions and goals of *écriture féminine* should be espoused without serious examination. American and French women should interrogate the premise that the global subversion of the Logos can be achieved through language, and we should question the proposition that there *can* exist a locus outside of the symbolic order from which woman might speak her difference. In *Les Guérillères* (1969), for example, Monique Wittig endorsed the notion that there is no reality outside the symbolic.[36] But whereas in that epic work she argued 'that in the first place the vocabulary of every language is to be examined, modified, turned upside down, that every word must be screened,'[37] in her recent paper 'The Straight Mind,' Wittig insists that emphasis on language has made French women writers lose sight of material reality[38] – a view which many American feminists might echo. We should also point out that French theorizing on the subversion of the Logos has tended to replace, and not merely to supplement, the kind of political activism which Americans consider crucial to their self-definition as feminists. Last, and as some recent French texts seem to confirm, a dis-connection with the *real* can lead to a regressive mystification of the 'feminine' and may yield nothing more than a new 'lingo,' a code doomed to repetition and extinction.[39]

(1980)

Notes

35 Kristeva, 'Un Nouveau type d'intellectuel: Le Dissident,' *Tel Quel* 74 ['Recherches féminines'] (Winter 1977): 5. '. . . Language enjouée donc loi bouleversée, violée, pluralisée, maintenue uniquement pour permettre un jeu polyvalent, polylogique, qui conduit à l'embrasement de l'être de la loi. . . .'

36 Monique Wittig, *Les Guérillères* (New York: Avon Books, 1973), trans. David Le Lay, p. 134.

37 Ibid.

38 See 'The Straight Mind,' *Questions féministes* 7 (December 1979); and *Feminist Issues* 1, 1 (Summer 1980).

39 In my view, this danger is immanent in the recurring identification of the female in *écriture féminine* with madness, antireason, primitive darkness, mystery, self- diffusion, and self-irridation, traits which represents a revalorization of traditional 'feminine' stereotypes. I discuss this problem briefly in 'Parole et écriture: Women's Studies, USA,' *Tel Quel* 71–73 (Autumn 1977): 126. Françoise Colin, an editor of *Les Cahiers du GRIF*, has noted the danger signals of a new female 'lingo' and stressed the need for multiplicity and heterogeneity in 'polyglo(u)ssons' in *Les Cahiers du GRIF* 12 ['Parlez-vous française?: femmes et langages I'] (June 1976): 3–9.

EDITORIAL COLLECTIVE OF QUESTIONS FEMINISTES

'Variations on Common Themes'
New French Feminisms

Otherness and the Identity-Body

Some women declare that 'language must be shattered,' because language is supposed to be male as it is a conveyor of, among other things, male chauvinism. They claim for themselves 'another' language, that, in its new form, would be closer to woman's lived experience, a lived experience in the center of which the Body is frequently placed. Hence the watchwords: 'liberate-the-body' and 'speak-the-body.' It is legitimate to expose the oppression, the mutilation, the 'functionalization' and the 'objectivation'[2] of the female body, but it is also dangerous to place the body at the center of a search for female identity. Furthermore, the themes of Otherness and of the Body merge together, because the most visible difference between men and women, and the only one that we know for sure to be permanent (barring mutations) is indeed the difference in body. This difference has been used as a pretext to 'justify' full power of one sex over the other.

When a group is in power it propagates the reigning ideology, it imposes categories. The group in power, which always needs to justify its domination, condemns those that it oppresses to being different: he or she cannot be treated equally because – Therefore colonized people are generally 'lazy' and 'incapable' of producing anything from their head themselves, etc. Such 'differences' are not explained by specific historical circumstances because history evolves and can bring about resolutions. For the oppressor, it is safer to speak of natural differences that are invariable by definition. That is the basis of racist and sexist ideologies. And thus a status of inferiority is inextricably bound to a status of difference.

Now, after centuries of men constantly repeating that *we* were different, here are women screaming, as if they were afraid of not being heard and as if it were an exciting discovery: 'We are different!' Are you going fishing? No, I am going fishing.

The very theme of difference, whatever the differences are represented to be, is useful to the oppressing group: as long as such a group holds power, any difference established between itself and other groups validates the only difference of importance, namely, having power while others do not. The fact that blacks have 'a sense of rhythm' while whites do not is irrelevant and does not change the balance of power. On the contrary, any allegedly natural feature attributed to an oppressed group is used to imprison this group within the boundaries of a Nature which, since the group is oppressed, ideological confusion labels 'nature of oppressed person.' In the present context, since oppression is not over, to demand the right to Difference without analyzing its social character is to give back to the enemy an effective weapon.

To advocate a 'woman's language' and a means of expression that would be specifically feminine seems to us equally illusory. First, the so-called explored language extolled by some women writers seems to be linked, if not in its content at least by its style, to a trend propagated by literary schools governed by male masters. This language is therefore as academic and as 'masculine' as other languages. Secondly, it is at times said that woman's language is closer to the body, to sexual pleasure, to direct sensations, and so on, which means that the body could express itself directly without social mediation and that, moreover, this closeness to the body and to nature would be subversive. In our opinion, there is no such thing as a direct relation to the body. To advocate a direct relation to the body is therefore not subversive because it is equivalent to denying the reality and the strength of social mediations, the very same ones that oppress us in our bodies. At most, one would advocate a different socialization of the body, but without searching for a true and eternal nature, for this search takes us away from the most effective struggle against the socio-historical contexts in which human beings are and will always be trapped. If there is one natural characteristic of human beings, it is that human beings are by nature social beings.

(1981)

Translated by Yvonne Rochette-Ozzello

Note

2 The tendency to 'nominalize' is characteristic of contemporary theoretical discourse in France and corresponds to the preoccupation with process. – Tr.

6

Locating the Subject

INTRODUCTION

What is the Subject?

The reference to 'the subject' in this title can be understood in at least three ways. Firstly, it suggests the human subject and our concepts of what it means to be called, or to name oneself, 'a woman' or 'a man'. Linked with this is the notion of a *collective* subject, 'women': feminists, as we all know, speak frequently about women as a group, some even use the term 'class', with common needs and purposes. These categories – let us focus particularly on 'woman' and 'women' – have been much debated in recent years and the theorists mentioned in the first three extracts give some indication of the range of subject disciplines (here is a second meaning of the term 'subject') which have been preoccupied with this topic: for instance, psychoanalysis (Freud and Lacan); linguistics (Saussure and Beneviste); philosophy (Derrida); politics and ideology (Althusser). Feminism necessarily interrelates with these disciplines in trying to explore its specific focus on woman/women. The third meaning of 'subject' to consider here is subject as a discourse. We can think of feminism itself as a subject, a subject of inquiry, and ask what are the implications of this preoccupation with the human subject for the political and intellectual practice of feminism. The varied theoretical inputs listed above have been drawn together in the critique of postmodernism and you will recall that we began to consider in chapter 4 some of the issues in the on-going dialogue between feminism and postmodernism: the mutability of the subject; the relation between collectivity and difference; the gap between a postmodernist and an historical/materialist view of woman. The extracts in this chapter will take the arguments further.

Julia Kristeva's and Jacqueline Rose's extracts can be read, to an extent, as defences of psychoanalysis and testimonies to its usefulness for feminism. Kristeva comments on the instability of language, meaning and subjectivity and coins the phrase 'subject in process' to convey the sense of the subject as incomplete, always becoming, never stable. Similarly, Rose mentions the 'failure' of identity. This 'failure' is not to be interpreted as the inadequacy of certain individuals to achieve full subjecthood but rather 'the resistance to identity at the very heart of psychic life', thus a 'failure' common to us all. Rose sees in this interpretation the possibility of a link between feminism and psychoanalysis. Psychoanalysis, like feminism, 'becomes one of the few places in our culture where it is recognized as more than a fact of individual pathology that most women do not painlessly slip into their roles as women, if indeed they do at all'. Kristeva and Rose appreciate that there are both psychological and political arguments to bring to this figure of the fragmented, unrealized female subject. To function, the individual needs to attain 'a certain type of stability' (Kristeva). This stability is an illusion, frequently challenged, but a vital illusion to maintain our everyday living. Moreover, to encourage political change, women may need a different sense of subjecthood, one which sees women as capable and purposeful. Feminism has to negotiate a passage between psychoanalysis and politics and, in Rose's view, the idea of the subject as at odds with social norms offers a useful point of disjunction for any radical politics. It is an inconsistency in the social fabric which feminism can exploit.[1]

The implication of Rose's reference to Louis Althusser is made clearer in Catherine Belsey's extract. Again using insights from psychoanalysis and linguistics Belsey explores the construction of the individual through and in language. In Belsey's opinion, I am not an autonomous fully-formed individual who decides, periodically, to use language as a tool to express my views about the world. On the contrary, 'the subject is constructed in language and discourse': language makes me rather more than I make language. For Althusser the individual takes up the subject-positions which language and cultural norms permit her to adopt. Althusser uses the term 'interpellation' to describe the process by which ideology 'calls' or 'hails' the individual to her subject-position. Belsey, in quoting Althusser, reveals yet a further meaning of the term 'subject': the subject is 'also a *subjected being* who submits to the authority of the social formation'. Kristeva too explores this sense of accountability on the part of the subject – indeed both use a legal metaphor – when she writes that 'our identities are constantly called into question, brought to trial, over-ruled'. Neither Althusser nor Kristeva would present the subject as merely a powerless victim of controlling forces. However, Althusser is interested in how ideology works and how individuals, *apparently* freely, adopt positions which in many respects are not in their interests. Thus, as Rose indicates, Lacan's psychoanalytical theories were open to a political reinterpretation by Althusser and both perspective offer possibilities for feminists interested in the creation of, specifically, the female psyche and the interpellation of the female subject.[2]

Three-way Split

We can see in the extracts from Patricia Waugh and Kate Soper how feminism's concern with the female subject has often been conceptualized as a debate between feminism, humanism and postmodernism. Sometimes this is presented as an amicable three-way conversation; sometimes feminism adopts a strongly partisan position; on other occasions feminism is the uncomfortable mediator between two opponents. Waugh describes two classic positions on the subject – the humanist, 'a unitary self-directing, isolated ego', and the post-modernist, 'contradictory, non-unitary, and historically produced through "discursive" and ideological formations' – and, though her engagement in this book is with postmodernism, her overall proposition is that both liberal humanism and postmodernism have been problematic for women. Part of her argument defends feminism from accusations of a regressive adherence to humanism; part of it indicates how some of feminism's most 'postmodernist' views actually pre-date postmodernism. Like Rose, Waugh points out that the concept of a unitary subject understandably holds attraction to women who have never experienced the kind of presence and authority which such a subject-position implies: one can deconstruct only what one has, not that which, historically, has been withheld. Moreover, as with other radical political positions, feminism cannot afford to lose its commitment to 'agency', 'a belief that human beings *can* act upon the world as partially autonomous agents'. Without this view how could feminists ever effect change? Waugh links feminist political needs with a postmodernist understanding of the subject; each position qualifies the other. Hence, we can note her insistence that the feminist agent is constructed, not the product of 'a natural "self" outside, or prior to, the social' and, equally, her belief that the subject feminists seek is not the isolated achiever of bourgeois ideology but a collective subject, 'constructed through *relationship*'. In both these views feminism and postmodernism temper each other.

It is the point about relationship and collectivity that is central to Kate Soper's extract. Working with the same three 'isms' as Waugh, her conclusion is not Waugh's guarded alliance with postmodernism but a rejection of it; 'in short, feminism should be both "humanist" and "feminist" ', though this association with humanism is a significantly more self-conscious coalition than earlier, untheorized relationships between feminism and humanism.[3] Soper sees in postmodernism the danger of 'extreme particularism' that obliterates the possibility of a collective identity. To Soper the emphasis in postmodern-ist thought on difference renders invalid both the '*sameness* and "common cause" ' of the feminist movement and the right ' "to speak on behalf of" others'. The categories 'woman' and 'women' could be endlessly decons-tructed until, ultimately, each of us is uniquely and singly situated. Further-more, generalized descriptions of societies – patriarchal, capitalist – and of opposing forces – feminism, socialism – are also suspect in postmodernist thought as totalizing and homogenizing responses. Soper wonders about the status of feminism as a revolutionary movement if feminism becomes simply one more 'narrative' to set aside the 'narrative' of male oppression. What happens to the 'truth' of female subordination and resistance?

The Problem of Agency

The concept of 'agency', of women acting on their own behalf and in their own interests, has experienced the most radical deconstruction in the work of Judith Butler: it is unlikely that she would see either Soper's sophisticated version of feminist humanism or Waugh's concept of a collective, 'relational' subjectivity as adequate propositions. The extract included here is the final section of Butler's *Gender Trouble: Feminism and the Subversion of Identity* where she summarizes her questioning of binary oppositions which exemplify what she calls the '*foundational* restrictions' of Western epistemology, feminism included: I/self: Other; sex: gender; agency: construction; heterosexual: homosexual. In each case, Butler argues, the first term is conventionally seen as 'foundational', 'natural' or 'real' while Butler would view them as 'phantasmatic' constructions, produced in culture, with no special primacy or anterior status. Thus, with reference to agency, the agent, the 'doer' of feminist politics does not enjoy 'some stable existence prior to the cultural field it negotiates'; instead, 'the "doer" is variable constructed in and through the deed'. We could compare here Belsey's exposition of Saussure's theories: ' . . . the world is intelligible only through discourse: there is no unmediated experience, no access to the raw reality of self and others'.

Butler's contention is that 'the destruction of identity is not the destruction of politics'. On the contrary, she interprets the dispersal of identity as a liberating opportunity for the construction of new subjectivities and new political configurations and, conversely, she construes feminism's allegiance to identity politics as restrictive and limiting. The way forward from the old world to the new lies in the 'subversive' strategies of her subtitle, using the devices of performance, parody and pastiche to undermine the status of 'the real' and 'the natural'. As Butler remarks earlier in her study, 'There is no gender identity behind the expressions of gender; that identity is performatively constituted by the very "expressions" that are said to be its results'.[4] Thus, what our culture understands by feminine behaviour is not the consequence or the product of a feminine identity; instead, our understanding of a feminine identity is produced, within signification, through the repeated performance of words and actions which we code as 'feminine'. The role of 'agency' can be seen if we accept that the subject is not *determined* by the cultural norms of gender difference. For instance, the cultural construct of femininity I just mentioned is varied and disputed: there is no single, feminine identity. In this sense the subject is active within the 'regulated process of repetition' by which these norms are established. There is space for change, for the rules to be challenged or rewritten, for 'a variation on that repetition'.

Like Waugh, Seyla Benhabib believes that feminism has not been trotting behind postmodernism as a kind of younger sister but, independently, has been developing its own comparable or contradictory theses. Set alongside postmodernism's theories of the Death of Man, the Death of History and the Death of Metaphysics, Benhabib places certain feminist endeavours – the 'Demystification of the Male Subject of Reason', the 'Engendering of Historical Narrative' and 'Feminist Skepticism Towards the Claims of Transcendent Reason'. In the section from her essay included here, Benhabib looks at the first of these propositions, the Death of Man, and posits both a 'strong' and 'weak' version of the thesis. The strong version is concerned with the dissolution of the subject – 'The subject thus dissolves into the chain of significations of which it is supposed to be the initiator'. The weak version would challenge certain aspects of 'Man', the Western philosophical subject, and transform others. Particularly it would '*situate* the subject in the context of various social, linguistic and discursive practices' but it would not lose sight of the subject as rational, self-conscious, responsible. In comparison with earlier extracts we could view Benhabib's strong version as approximating Butler's argument and the weak version approximating Waugh's and Soper's. Benhabib's conviction is that 'the strong version of the Death of the Subject thesis is not compatible with the goals of feminism', in notable contrast to Butler's belief that the dissolution of the subject aids progressive politics.

On a series of points, Benhabib takes issue with Butler. Firstly, if subjectivity is constituted in performance, if we have 'deeds without the doer', then what happens to the concept of personal or collective responsibility? Secondly, what is the status of Butler's own text? Is it in any way her own; what is the nature of the control she has – if she has any – over the words on the page? Butler anticipates this question when, in using the pronoun 'I', she immediately introduces a parenthesis to account for the 'I' who is writing: 'I have argued ('I' deploy the grammar . . . etc.).[5] Thirdly, Benhabib believes we need a more subtle theory of both social and psychic forces to explain how the subject is constituted. For instance, if agency, as Butler argues, 'is to be located within the possibility of a variation on that repetition', how is this variation to be brought about? 'What psychic, intellectual or other sources of creativity and resistance must we attribute to subjects for such variation to be possible?' The key issue for Benhabib lies in the comment, 'the I although constituted by discourse is not determined by it'. For Benhabib the subject is not only the product of discursive practices and signification but retains a certain autonomy to act with, through and against those practices and signs. This is not the case for Butler for whom there is no such vantage point: '. . . there is no possibility of agency or reality outside of the discursive practices that give those terms the intelligibility that they have'. One interpretation of Butler's work might suggest that we are all endlessly condemned to shifting the pieces on the chess board without ever changing the game. Benhabib uses a different metaphor: '. . . is there ever any chance to stop the performance for a while, to pull the curtain down, and only let it rise if one can have a say in the production of the play itself?' Butler's answer to that question would be 'no' but she would say also that the negative reply does not prevent change or stop us from asking the most fundamental and necessary questions about gender and the sexed subject. Butler's own text gives ample illustration of that capacity.

The Problem of Essence

Just as problematic as agency has been the debate on 'essence' and the role of essentialism in feminist thinking and politics. Linda Alcoff explores two strands in feminism, cultural feminism and post-structuralist. She presents cultural feminists as concerned with the difference and uniqueness of women, the importance of feminine values, the need to valorize these qualities not dismiss them – in short, a female essence, perhaps biologically based, perhaps culturally produced. As we note from the start of Alcoff's extract, post-structuralist feminism sees 'woman' as a construct, a fiction with no essential characteristics.[6] Briefly surveying some of the views of Derrida, Foucault and Kristeva, Alcoff discusses two attractions for feminism in post-structuralist thought: firstly, the emphasis on difference allows women to think beyond the prescriptiveness of normative gender identity; secondly, Alcoff finds a potential in post-structuralism's questioning of the construction of the subject.[7]

As ever there are also problems. By now we can appreciate that Alcoff's interrogation of the 'undecidability' of both text and 'woman' is a recurrent anxiety in feminist debates on the subject, though her stress on the political goals which, of necessity, require the invocation of 'woman' cannot be mentioned too often: 'How can we demand legal abortions, adequate child care, or wages based on compatible worth without invoking the concept "woman"?' A further reservation concerns the possible alliance between post-structuralism and liberal humanism around concepts of the subject. Could post-structuralism's deconstruction of gender, race, class at some level coincide with humanism's view of a *common* humanity? In a post-structuralist argument these terms would be in inverted commas to indicate their contingency; in a humanist argument they could be seen as false distinctions imposed upon our essential, universal subjectivity. Though theoretically at odds, Alcoff fears that in practice both positions could efface the importance to women of gender identity; one presents the identity as fictive; the other as peripheral.

The extracts from Teresa de Lauretis and Diana Fuss offer two interesting responses on the issue of essence, de Lauretis's directly concerned with

Alcoff's argument, both concerned with deconstructing the familiar opposition of essence against construct. De Lauretis finds lacking Alcoff's formulation of the issues. Why construct the problem as a binary opposition ('Cultural Feminism versus Post-Structuralism' is Alcoff's title), especially as within the essay there is evidence that feminist positions are more numerous and that the oppositional way of presenting the case has been superseded? Both de Lauretis and Fuss challenge this binary approach. De Lauretis warns against hierarchical relationships – essentialism as naïve, a constructionist view as theoretically aware. With an equally deconstructive move, Fuss turns the theoretical spotlight away from essentialism to check the validity of the constructionist claims. Firstly, Fuss queries whether the specificity of constructionist identities avoids essence or merely multiplies essentialist definitions. Secondly, she collapses the division between essence and construct and, intriguingly, suggests that the very concept of essentialism could 'operate as a deconstructionist strategy', embodying 'some strategic or interventionary value'. Thirdly, she reminds the constructionists that essence is also a sign: paradoxically, essence is without an essence. To dismiss essence as always reactionary is a notably undeconstructive response, an inability to recognize the play of signification. In such ways Fuss recoups essentialism as a term to operate *within* deconstructionist debates.[8]

Who is the Subject?

One of the recurrent critiques of postmodernism concerns its élitism, its location in the rarefied corners of the university system, its distance from political realities and this criticism has been levelled at feminist appropriations of postmodernism as much as at postmodernism itself. Discussions of race have been important in this developing argument.[9] Given the historical dominance of white women in feminism, feminism could reproduce a white solipsism in its creation of female subjects. The problem lies in how we define our categories of feminism – white, Black, Western, 'third world', women of colour – and how each category constructs the other. Let us remind ourselves of some of the points we have considered hitherto on this question. As early as 1981, Gayatri Spivak was placing French feminism in 'an international frame' and asking 'not merely who am I? but who is the other woman? How am I naming her? How does she name me?' (chapter 1). This point is still relevant some years later when Trinh T. Minh-ha comments, 'Whether "Third World" sounds negative or positive also depends on *who* uses it. Coming from you Westerners, the word can hardly mean the same as when it comes from Us members of the Third World'. Since Spivak's essay, the expansion of 'third world' feminism, the importance, in the USA, of Chicana feminism, the changes in Eastern Europe, the growth of a European feminist consciousness, the impact of feminist work from Australia and the Pacific have all contributed to a proliferation of different understandings of that term, 'international feminism'. In chapter 4, we saw that Nancy Fraser and Linda Nicholson's contention that postmodernism was open to subordinated groups was challenged in bell hooks's extract. In this chapter, Soper compares the competing claims of particularism and collectivity while Fuss wonders if long lists of multiple identities, taking into account gender, race, class, sexuality . . . and more, break through essentialism or, simply redeploy it.

Chandra Talpade Mohanty is acutely aware of all these dilemmas. Her first footnote debates the description 'third world' and her opening page is alert to the danger of seeing both Western and 'third world' women in monolithic terms: to set up any categories, to make any generalized comment is to raise issues.[10] As in hooks's extract in chapter 4, Mohanty's emphasis is on a structural relationship, which as also a power relationship, and which positions the subordinated group as 'Other'. Thus, the Western woman, feminist or not, is the normative female subject; the 'third world' woman is the difference and the deviation. Or as Trinh puts the point, 'the generic "woman", like its counterpart, the generic "man", tends to efface difference within itself'. In such a way, the 'third world' woman is unrepresented. Mohanty's interest is in the textual strategies employed by Western feminists which reinscribe and legitimate this power imbalance. Despite protestations of global sisterhood, despite its position as a critical discourse within its own culture, Western feminism may be limiting and demarking 'third world' women in ways that reproduce colonialist attitudes. As Mohanty comments, '. . . it is both to the *explanatory potential* of particular analytic strategies employed by such writing, and to their *political effect* in the context of the hegemony of Western scholarship that I want to draw attention here'. Mohanty critically investigates three common modes of analysis – the construction of a universal female subject, cutting across or subordinating other forms of difference; the unsatisfactory manner in which 'proof' is provided to validate this subject; the construction of an 'average third world woman', an oppressed victim in comparison with the autonomous, achieving 'first world' woman. Trinh reinforces this final point in her reference to the Western feminist preoccupation with footbinding, genital mutilation and *suttee*. I suspect that Trinh would not see any of these as unproblematic practices beyond discussion. The question is how to understand them *without* constructing the 'third world' woman as 'ignorant, poor, uneducated, tradi-tion-bound, domestic, family-orientated, victimized' (Mohanty).

Trinh indicates additional ways in which the 'first world' academic feminist retains a superior position in relation to the 'third world'. The 'third world' woman becomes a subject of 'special' (for which read 'marginal') interest. Within the predominantly white academy she is the 'foreign worker' or the 'migrant'. Trinh quotes Kristeva's title, 'woman can never be defined' (see chapter 4) and illustrates with a range of examples the discursive play that surrounds the 'third world' woman. The glib distinction between 'first world' and 'third world' cannot be easily maintained: 'The Master is bound to recognize that His Culture is not as homogeneous, as monolithic as He believed it to be.' 'Third World Women in the U.S.', 'a Third world within the Third World' are further configurations within which the 'third world' woman situates herself or is situated. As in Mohanty's work, the complexity and power politics of these subject positions are central to Trinh's argument.[11]

New Subjectivities

Unsurprisingly, as feminists deconstruct existing female subjects they construct other, as yet mythic figures that offer possibilities for new, though already emerging, female subjectivities. The examples to consider here are Donna Haraway's 'cyborg', Gloria Anzaldúa's 'mestiza' and Monique Wittig's 'lesbian'.[12] Several factors are held in common: the idea of shifting, reformulated identities; the critique of dualistic thinking – the product of 'the straight mind' (Wittig) and in need of 'massive uprooting' (Anzaldúa); the political importance of language – 'we work also at the level of language/manifesto, of language/action' (Wittig); 'releasing the play of writing is deadly serious' (Haraway). The similarities and differences in Haraway's and Anzaldúa's use of language illustrate their constructions of approximate, but not identical, female subjectivities. Both make elaborate use of the concept of 'borders'. In one sense this is a literal, physical border, specifically the USA/Mexico border for Anzaldúa, more generally for Haraway, the many geographical borders crossed by 'women of colour'. But is also a metaphorical border. Above all, the new female subject is mobile and flexible, traversing all manner of psychological, linguistic and conceptual barriers. Along the way, she embraces contradiction, ambiguity, irony, revels in her illegitimacy. A difference in their use of language lies in Anzaldúa's attachment to organicist metaphors – seas, corn, roots of trees – to embody regeneration and a new, more inclusive sense of wholeness. Against this, Haraway expresses an openness to the technological and a greater suspicion than Anzaldúa concerning myths of origin and fulfilment: 'The cyborg does not dream of community on the model of the organic family, this time without the Oedipal project. The cyborg would not recognize the Garden of Eden; it is not made of mud and cannot dream of returning to dust.' Compare these words with Anzaldúa's conclusion: 'She becomes a *nahual*, able to transform herself into a tree, a coyote, into another person. She transforms the small 'I' into the total Self.'[13]

   The utopian projections of these authors are attempts to act/think beyond the dominant order while knowing, of course, the constraints that bind. There is an invigorating animation in this mode though some of the more euphoric parts of Haraway's work almost seem to suggest that one can 'internet' oneself to liberation or, as in fairy tales, that if one concentrates hard enough on an idea, it will come to pass.[14] Wittig wants to 'break off the heterosexual contract', to be free of the man/woman couple. She decries the 'heterosexual myths' circulating in psychoanalysis, the social sciences, anthropology with their aim 'to systematically heterosexualize that personal dimension. . . .'. Thus, the radical logic of Wittig's argument is that the categories 'man' and 'woman' must disappear and the astounding conclusion is that 'lesbians are not women' since to be a woman is to be caught in a heterosexual definition, 'woman' rather than 'man'. We could compare, here, Adrienne Rich's notion of the 'lesbian continuum' (see chapter 1) which in its wide definition of 'lesbian' seems to pose the opposite to Wittig – not that 'lesbians are not women' but that all women of a feminist or quasi-feminist consciousness are lesbian. What Wittig does not consider here is how the lesbian subject may construct herself outside the influence of 'the straight mind' given its pervasiveness.[15]

Like Haraway and Anzaldúa, Wittig is interested in the 'materiality' of language and 'a political semiology'. We have already seen how one term, 'woman' can be disputed, having an absolute meaning for some feminists, diverse and strategic meanings for other. Rosi Braidotti, conveniently covering several of the theorists mentioned in this chapter, summarizes: 'Woman therefore ceases to be the culturally dominant and prescriptive model for female subjectivity and turns instead into an identifiable topos for analysis: as a construct (de Lauretis); a masquerade (Butler); a positive essence (Irigaray); or an ideological trap (Wittig) . . . '. At least one of the terms Wittig dismisses as degraded and beyond redemption, 'nigger', has already returned to the political vocabulary – as have, 'bitch', 'dyke' and 'queer'. But, as critics such as Trinh and Spivak so necessarily remind us, who does the naming, in what context, for what purpose remain the operative questions. There is a world of difference between 'nigger' being used in a self-conscious way between Black friends and/or political allies and 'nigger' being used as a term of abuse by racist whites.

Conclusion

In Waugh's first paragraph she discusses feminism's relation to two subjectivities, the unitary and the postmodernist, and presents them as sequential, even to the extent of indicating dates: women in the sixties and seventies were involved with the unitary subject, later with the postmodernist. Whatever Waugh's intention, it is easy to read this schema in hierarchical terms. Waugh refers to the involvement with the unitary subject as 'an essential phase' which, while reinforcing its significance on one level, suggests, at another, that this 'phase' was followed by a subsequent, more subtle and elaborated position. It is precisely such a hierarchical relation to which de Lauretis objects in her remarks on Alcoff's essay. Braidotti also uses the term 'phase' and the equally problematic 'level' in her survey of the female subject, but she emphasizes that 'these levels are not meant to be approached sequentially and dialectically'; rather they 'occur simultaneously and . . . in everyday life, they coexist and cannot be easily distinguished'. I include Braidotti's 'scheme of feminist nomadism' as the final extract since it reviews many of the ideas covered in this chapter and also continues to ask questions about these issues and the way in which we conceptualize them. The first table focuses on feminism's critique of the universal subject and man's identification with the universal. An emphasis on sexual difference functions as an important resistance to this worldview. The second table is concerned with the multiplicity of female and feminist subjectivities, how to recognize this 'without falling into relativism'. The third links the psyche and the body, the corporeal. Braidotti comments, 'In my scheme of thought, identity bears a privileged bond to unconscious processes, whereas political subjectivity is a conscious and wilful position', a distinction between 'identity' and 'subjectivity' that could be usefully explored in many of the extracts in this chapter. Some pages on, she defines 'nomadism' as: 'sexual difference as providing shifting locations for multiple female feminist embodied voices'.[16] These voices and their creation are the subject and the subjects of feminism: they are both its subject-matter and its living practitioners. Braidotti's extract ends with a hopeful energy and optimism. A female feminist, she says is a woman who 'longs for, tends toward, is driven to feminism'. This passion, coupled with 'a healthy dose of the hermeneutics of suspicion' and a rediscovery of 'merrymaking' will liberate in women 'their desire for freedom, lightness, justice, and self-accomplishment'. I do hope so.

Notes

1 It would help here to look also at the extracts from Kaplan and Wilson in ch. 4.

2 For useful introductions to this material see Chris Weedon, *Feminist Practice and Poststructuralist Theory* (Oxford, Blackwell, 1987); Elizabeth Grosz, 'Contemporary Theories of Power and Subjectivity' in Sneja Gunew (ed.) *Feminist Knowledge: Critique and Construct* (London, Routledge, 1990); Grosz's entry on 'the subject' in Elizabeth Wright (ed.) *Feminism and Psychoanalysis: A Critical Dictionary* (Oxford, Blackwell, 1992); Jackie Stacey, 'Untangling Feminist Theory' in Diane Richardson and Victoria Robinson (eds) *Introducing Women's Studies: Feminist Theory and Practice* (London, Macmillan, 1993).

3 See, for example, Moi in ch. 4 for comments on unwitting links between feminism and humanism. The quotation here is taken from later in Soper's essay, anthologized in Mary Evans (ed.) *The Woman Question* (Second Edition), (London, Sage, 1994), p. 20.

4 See Judith Butler, *Gender Trouble: Feminism and the Subversion of Identity* (London, Routledge, 1990), p. 25. For a reading of Butler in light of gay theory see Biddy Martin, 'Sexual Practice and Changing Lesbian Identities' in Michèle Barrett and Anne Phillips (eds) *Destabilizing Theory: Contemporary Feminist Debates* (Oxford, Polity Press, 1992).

5 Peggy Kamuf's comments in ch. 5 are also part of this debate in contemporary theory about the status of the author.

6 You will notice that Alcoff is using here the term 'post-structuralist' to describe the characteristics which we have been discussing, hitherto, as 'postmodernist'. The arguments around terminology are many and complex. For an introduction see, Peter Brooker's 'Introduction' in his *Modernism/Postmodernism* (London, Longman, 1992). For the sake of clarity I shall use the same term as the author in discussing her essay.

7 I think Kristeva's argument is more conditional than Alcoff credits. See the extract in ch. 4 from 'Woman Can Never Be Defined' to which Alcoff refers here. Note how Kristeva qualifies the 'absurdity' of 'being a woman'.

8 You might want to look back here to the debates in ch. 5 on sexual difference where several commentators remark on the *strategic* and political importance of the concept. See also issues on issues of essentialism, Tania Modelski, *Feminism without Women: Culture and Criticism in a Postfeminist Age* (London, Routledge, 1991) and Naomi Schor and Elizabeth Weed (eds) *The Essential Difference* (Bloomington and Indianapolis, Indiana University Press, 1994).

9 bell hooks's extract in ch. 4 is also relevant here.

10 I am following Mohanty's lead in using the term 'third world' but using it with inverted commas. Trinh, as you will notice, writes the term without inverted commas but with initial capital letters (Third World). In quoting from her work I have retained her format.

11 A short introduction to Mohanty and 'third world' feminist criticism can be found in Maggie Humm, *A Reader's Guide to Contemporary Feminist Literary Criticism* (London, Harvester Wheatsheaf, 1994). For further examples of Mohanty's and Trinh's work see, Mohanty, 'Feminist Encounters: Locating the Politics of Experience' in Michèle Barrett and Anne Phillips (eds) op.cit.; Trinh, *When the Moon Waxes Red: Representation, Gender and Cultural Politics* (London, Routledge, 1992).

12 Other possibilities are Teresa de Lauretis's 'eccentric subjects' in 'Eccentric Subjects: Feminist Theory and Historical Consciousness', *Feminist Studies* vol. 16, no. 1 (Spring 1990) and Rosi Braidotti's 'nomadic subjects' in *Nomadic Subjects: Embodiment and Sexual Difference in Contemporary Feminist Theory* (New York, Columbia University Press, 1994). See also in these texts de Lauretis's comments on Wittig and Braidotti's comments on Haraway.

13 A further reference here would be to Irigaray's comments on 'language work' in ch. 5.

14 Haraway's essay has been variously anthologized. I would refer you particularly to its inclusion in Elizabeth Weed (ed.) *Coming to Terms: Feminism, Theory, Politics* (London, Routledge, 1989) as it is accompanied by a series of responses and an essay on related issues by Gayatri Chakravorty Spivak, 'The Political Economy of Women as Seen by a Literary Critic'. Haraway's essay is also readily available in Linda Nicholson (ed.) *Feminism/Postmodernism* (London, Routledge, 1990).

15 Diana Fuss develops this and other points in her commentary on Wittig in *Essentially Speaking: Feminism, Nature and Difference* (London, Routledge, 1989).

16 Rosi Braidotti, op.cit., p. 172.

JULIA KRISTEVA

'A Question of Subjectivity: An Interview'
Women's Review

Susan Sellers: As a professor of linguistics, and with publications on subjects ranging from philosophy to literary criticism, what led you also to train as a psychoanalyst?

Julia Kristeva: I don't believe one commits oneself to psychoanalysis without certain secret motivations . . . difficulties living, a suffering which is unable to express itself. I talked to my psychoanalyst about this aspect of things and so today can speak about these motives for my work.

I wanted to examine the states at the limits of language; the moments where language breaks up in psychosis for example, or the moments where language doesn't yet exist such as during a child's apprenticeship to language. It seemed to me to be impossible to content oneself with a description which held itself to be objective and neutral in these two cases, because already the selection of examples presupposes a particular type of contact with the people who talk to you.

Also the interpretation of people's speech presupposes that you apply yourself to the meaning of what they say. I saw that there was no neutral objectivity possible in descriptions of language at its limits and that we are constantly in what psychoanalysis calls a 'transfer'. It seemed to me dishonest to apply this transfer without having myself undergone the experience of psychoanalysis.

Susan Sellers: An important part of your psychoanalytic research has been the process by which the individual acquires language. What does this 'process' entail?

Julia Kristeva: I used the term 'process' whilst I was working on the texts of Antonin Artaud. Artaud is an extremely disturbing writer in modern French literature, partly because he underwent a dramatic experience of madness and partly because he thought carefully about the music in language. Anyone who reads Artaud's texts will realize that all identities are unstable: the identity of linguistic signs, the identity of meaning and, as a result, the identity of the speaker. And in order to take account of this de-stabilization of meaning and of the subject I thought the term 'subject in process' would be appropriate. 'Process' in the sense of process but also in the sense of a legal proceeding where the subject is committed to trial, because our identities in life are constantly called into question, brought to trial, over-ruled.

I wanted to examine the language which manifests these states of instability because in ordinary communication – which is organized, civilized – we repress these states of incandescence. Creativity as well as suffering comprises these moments of instability, where language, or the signs of language, or subjectivity itself are put into 'process'. And one can extrapolate this notion and use it not just for the texts of Artaud but for every 'proceeding' in which we move outside the norms.

Susan Sellers: Writing about this process, one of the distinctions you have drawn in order to chart the development from non-differentiated infant to speaking subject is the distinction between 'the semiotic' and 'the symbolic'. Can you explain this distinction?

Julia Kristeva: In order to research this state of instability – the fact that meaning is not simply a structure or process, or that the subject is not simply a unity but is constantly called into question – I proposed to take into account two modalities or conditions of meaning which I called 'the semiotic' and 'the symbolic'. What I call 'the semiotic' takes us back to the pre-linguistic states of childhood where the child babbles the sounds s/he hears, or where s/he articulates rhythms, alliterations, or stresses, trying to imitate her/his surroundings. In this state the child doesn't yet possess the necessary linguistic signs and thus there is no meaning in the strict sense of the term. It is only after the mirror phase or the experience of castration in the Oedipus complex that the individual becomes subjectively capable of taking on the signs of language, of articulation as it has been prescribed – and I call that 'the symbolic'.

Susan Sellers: What actually happens during the mirror phase and the Oedipus complex?

Julia Kristeva: Identification takes place. What I call 'the semiotic' is a state of disintegration in which patterns appear but which do not have any stable identity: they are blurred and fluctuating. The processes which are at work here are those which Freud calls 'primary': processes of transfer. We have an example of this if we refer once again to the melodies and babblings of infants which are a sound image of their bodily instability. Babies and children's bodies are made up of erotogenic zones which are extremely excitable, or, on the contrary, indifferent, in a state of constant change, of excitation, or extinction, without there being any fixed identity.

A 'fixed identity': it's perhaps a fiction, an illusion – who amongst us has a 'fixed' identity? It's a phantasm; we do nevertheless arrive at a certain type of stability. There are several steps which lead to this stability and one step which has been accentuated by the French psychoanalyst Jacques Lacan is the specular identification which he calls 'the mirror phase'. In this phase one recognizes one's image in a mirror as one's self-image. It is a first identification of the chaotic, fragmented body, and is both violent and jubilatory. The identification comes about under the domination of the maternal image, which is the one nearest to the child and which allows the child both to remain close and to distance itself.

I see a face. A first differentiation takes place, and thus a first self-identity. This identity is still unstable because sometimes I take myself to be me, sometimes I confuse myself with my mother. This narcissistic instability, this doubt persists and makes me ask 'who am I?', 'is it me or is it the other?' The confusion with the maternal image as first other remains.

In order for us to be able to get out of this confusion, the classical pattern of development leads us to a confrontation inside the Oedipal triangle between our desire for the mother and the process of loss which is the result of paternal authority. In the ideal case, this finishes by stabilising the subject, rendering her/him capable both of pronouncing sentences which conform to the rules, to the law, and of telling her/his own story – of giving her/his account.

These are symbolic acquisitions that are pre-conditioned by a certain psychic experience which is the stabilization of the self in relation to the other.

(1986)

JACQUELINE ROSE

'Femininity and its Discontents'
Feminist Review

Psychoanalysis has often been accused of 'functionalism'. It is accepted as a theory of how women are psychically 'induced' into femininity by a patriarchal culture, but is then accused of perpetuating that process, either through a practice assumed to be *prescriptive* about women's role (this is what women *should* do), or because the very effectiveness of the account as a *description* (this is what is demanded of women, what they are *expected* to do) leaves no possibility of change.

It is this aspect of Juliet Mitchell's pioneering book *Psychoanalysis and Feminism* which seems to have been taken up most strongly by feminists who have attempted to follow through the political implications of psychoanalysis as a critique of patriarchy.[1]

Thus Gayle Rubin, following Mitchell, uses psychoanalysis for a general critique of a patriarchal culture which is predicated on the exchange of women by men.[2] Nancy Chodorow shifts from Freud to later object relations theory to explain how women's childcaring role is perpetuated through the earliest relationship between a mother and her child, which leads in her case to a demand for a fundamental change in how childcare is organized between women and men in our culture.[3] Although there are obvious differences between these two readings of psychoanalysis, they nonetheless share an emphasis on the social exchange of women, or the distribution of roles for women, across cultures: 'Women's mothering is one of the few universal and enduring elements of the sexual division of labour'.[4]

The force of psychoanalysis is therefore (as Janet Sayers points out)[5] precisely that it gives an account of patriarchal culture as a trans-historical and cross-cultural force. It therefore conforms to the feminist demand for a theory which can explain women's subordination across specific cultures and different historical moments. Summing this up crudely, we could say that psycho-analysis adds sexuality to Marxism, where sexuality is felt to be lacking, and extends beyond Marxism where the attention to specific historical instances, changes in modes of production etc., is felt to leave something unexplained.

But all this happens at a cost, and that cost is the concept of the unconscious. What distinguishes psychoanalysis from sociological accounts of gender (hence for me the fundamental impasse of Nancy Chodorow's work) is that whereas for the latter, the internalization of norms is assumed roughly to work, the basic premise and indeed starting-point of psychoanalysis is that it does not. The unconscious constantly reveals the 'failure' of identity. Because there is no continuity of psychic life, so there is no stability of sexual identity, no position for women (or for men) which is ever simply achieved. Nor does psychoanalysis see such 'failure' as a special-case inability or an individual deviancy from the norm. 'Failure' is not a moment to be regretted in a process of adaptation, or development into normality, which ideally takes its course (some of the earliest critics of Freud, such as Ernest Jones, did, however, give an account of development in just these terms). Instead 'failure' is something endlessly repeated and relived moment by moment throughout our individual histories. It appears not only in the symptom, but also in dreams, in slips of the tongue and in forms of sexual pleasure which are pushed to the sidelines of the norm. Feminism's affinity with psychoanalysis rests above all, I would argue, with this recognition that there is a resistance to identity at the very heart of psychic life. Viewed in this way, psychoanalysis is no longer best understood as an account of how women are fitted into place (even this, note, is the charitable reading of Freud). Instead psychoanalysis becomes one of the few places in our culture where it is recognized as more than a fact of individual pathology that most women do not painlessly slip into their roles as women, if indeed they do at all. Freud himself recognized this increasingly in his work. In the articles which run from 1924 to 1931,[6] he moves from that famous, or rather infamous, description of the little girl struck with her 'inferiority' or 'injury' in the face of the anatomy of the little boy and wisely accepting her fate ('injury' as the *fact* of being feminine), to an account which quite explicitly describes the process of becoming 'feminine' as an 'injury' or 'catastrophe' for the complexity of her earlier psychic and sexual life ('injury' as its *price*).

Elizabeth Wilson and Janet Sayers are, therefore, in a sense correct to criticize psychoanalysis when it is taken as a general theory of patriarchy or of gender identity, that is, as a theory which explains how women wholly internalize the very mode of being which is feminism's specific target of attack; but they have missed out half the (psychoanalytic) story. In fact the argument seems to be circular. Psychoanalysis is drawn in the direction of a general theory of culture or a sociological account of gender because these seem to lay greater emphasis on the pressures of the 'outside' world, but it is this very pulling away from the psychoanalytic stress on the 'internal' complexity and difficulty of psychic life which produces the functionalism which is then critized.

The argument about whether Freud is being 'prescriptive' or 'descriptive' about women (with its associated stress on the motives and morals of Freud himself) is fated to the extent that it is locked into this model. Many of us will be familiar with Freud's famous pronouncement that a woman who does not succeed in transforming activity to passivity, clitoris to vagina, mother for father, will fall ill. Yet psychoanalysis testifies to the fact that psychic illness or distress is in no sense the prerogative of women who 'fail' in this task. One of my students recently made the obvious but important point that we would be foolish to deduce from the external trappings of normality or conformity in a woman that all is in fact well. And Freud himself always stressed the psychic cost of the civilizing process for all (we can presumably include women in that 'all' even if at times he did not seem to do so).

All these aspects of Freud's work are subject to varying interpretation by analysts themselves. The first criticism of Freud's 'phallocentrism' came from inside psychoanalysis, from analysts such as Melanie Klein, Ernest Jones and Karen Horney who felt, contrary to Freud, that 'femininity' was a quality with its own impetus, subject to checks and internal conflict, but tending ultimately to fulfilment. For Jones, the little girl was 'typically receptive and acquisitive' from the outset; for Horney, there was from the beginning a 'wholly womanly' attachment to the father.[7] For these analysts, this development might come to grief, but for the most part a gradual strengthening of the child's ego and her increasing adaptation to reality, should guarantee its course. Aspects of the little girl's psychic life which were resistant to this process (the famous 'active' or 'masculine' drives) were defensive. The importance of concepts such as the 'phallic phase' in Freud's description of infantile sexuality is not, therefore, that such concepts can be taken as the point of insertion of patriarchy (assimilation to the norm). Rather their importance lies in the way that they indicate, through their very artificiality, that something was being *forced*, and in the concept of psychic life with which they were accompanied. In Freud's work they went hand in hand with an increasing awareness of the difficulty, not to say impossibility of the path to normality for the girl, and an increasing stress on the fundamental divisions, or splitting, of psychic life. It was those who challenged these concepts in the

1920s and 1930s who introduced the more normative stress on a sequence of development, and coherent ego, back into the account.

I think we go wrong again, therefore, if we conduct the debate about whether Freud's account was developmental or not entirely in terms of his own writing. Certainly the idea of development is present at moments in his work. But it was not present *enough* for many of his contemporaries, who took up the issue and reinstated the idea of development precisely in relation to the sexual progress of the girl (her passage into womanhood).

'Psychoanalysis' is not, therefore, a single entity. Institutional divisions within psychoanalysis have turned on the very questions about the phallocentrism of analysts, the meaning of femininity, the sequence of psychic development and its norms, which have been the concern of feminists. The accusations came from analysts themselves. In the earlier delates, however, the reproach against Freud produced an account of femininity which was more, rather than less, normative than his own.

The politics of Lacanian psychoanalysis begin here. From the 1930s, Lacan saw his intervention as a return to the concepts of psychic division, splitting of the ego, and an endless (he called it 'insistent') pressure of the unconscious against any individual's pretension to a smooth and coherent psychic and sexual identity. Lacan's specific target was 'ego-psychology' in America, and what he saw as the dilution of psychoanalysis into a tool of social adaptation and control (hence the central emphasis on the concepts of the ego and identification which are often overlooked in discussions of his ideas). For Lacan, psychoanalysis does not offer an account of a developing ego which is 'not *necessarily* coherent',[8] but of an ego which is 'necessarily *not* coherent', that is, which is always and persistently divided against itself.

Lacan could therefore be picked up by a Marxist like Althusser not because he offered a theory of adaptation to reality or of the individual's insertion into culture (Althusser added a note to the English translation of his paper on Lacan criticizing it for having implied such a reading),[9] but because the force of the unconscious in Lacan's interpretation of Freud was felt to undermine the mystifications of a bourgeois culture proclaiming its identity, and that of its subjects, to the world. The political use of Lacan's theory therefore stemmed from its assault on what English Marxists would call bourgeois 'individualism'. What the theory offered was a divided subject out of 'synch' with bourgeois myth. Feminists could legitimately object that the notion of psychic fragmentation was of little immediate political advantage to women struggling for the first time to find a voice, and trying to bring together the dissociated components of their life into a political programme. But this is a very different criticism of the political implications of psychoanalysis than the one which accuses it of forcing women into bland conformity with their expected role.

(1983)

Notes

First published in *Feminist Review*, 14 (Summer 1983), pp. 5–21, this essay was originally requested by the editors of *Feminist Review* to counter the largely negative representation of psychoanalysis which had appeared in the journal, and as a specific response to Elizabeth Wilson's 'Psychoanalysis: psychic law and order', *Feminist Review*, 8 (Summer 1981). (See also Janet Sayers, 'Psychoanalysis and personal politics: a response to Elizabeth Wilson', *Feminist Review*, 10 (1982).) As I was writing the piece, however, it soon became clear that Elizabeth Wilson's article and the question of *Feminist Review*'s own relationship to psychoanalysis could not be understood independently of what has been – outside the work of Juliet Mitchell for feminism – a fairly consistent repudiation of Freud within the British Left. In this context, the feminist debate over Freud becomes part of a larger question about the importance of subjectivity to our understanding of political and social life. That this was in fact the issue became even clearer when Elizabeth Wilson and Angie Weir published an article 'The British women's movement' in *New Left Review*, 148 (November–December 1984), which dismissed the whole area of subjectivity and psychoanalysis from feminist politics together with any work by feminists (historians and writers on contemporary politics) who, while defining themselves as socialist feminists, nonetheless query the traditional terms of an exclusively class-based analysis of power.

1 Juliet Mitchell, *Psychoanalysis and Feminism* (Allen Lane, London, 1974).
2 See Gayle Rubin, 'The traffic in women'; and for a critique of the use of Lévi-Strauss on which this reading is based, Elizabeth Cowie, 'Woman as sign', *m/f*, 1978, pp. 49–63.
3 Nancy Chodorow, *The Reproduction of Mothering* (University of California Press, Berkeley, 1978).
4 Ibid., p. 3.
5 Janet Sayers, 'A response to Elizabeth Wilson', *Feminist Review*, 10 (1981), pp. 91–5.
6 Sigmund Freud, 'The dissolution of the Oedipus complex' (1924); 'Some psychical consequences of the anatomical distinction between the sexes' (1925); 'Female sexuality' (1931), *Standard Edition of Complete Psychological Works* (Hogarth, London, 1955–74), vol. 19.
7 Ernest Jones, 'The phallic phase', *International Journal of Psycho-Analysis*, 14 (1933), p. 265; Karen Horney, 'On the genesis of the castration complex in women' (1924), in *Feminine Psychology* (London, 1967), p. 53.
8 Elizabeth Wilson, 'Reopening the case – feminism and psychoanalysis', opening seminar presentation in discussion with Jacqueline Rose, London 1982. This was the first of a series of seminars on the subject of feminism and psychoanalysis which ran into 1983; see articles by Parveen Adams, Nancy Wood and Claire Buck, *m/f*, 8 (1983).
9 Louis Althusser, 'Freud and Lacan', see publisher's note in *Lenin and Philosophy and Other Essays* (London, 1971), pp. 189–90.

CATHERINE BELSEY

Critical Practice

The destination of all ideology is the subject (the individual in society) and it is the role of ideology to *construct people as subjects*:

> I say: the category of the subject is constitutive of all ideology, but at the same time and immediately I add that *the category of the subject is only constitutive of all ideology in so far as all ideology has the function (which defines it) of 'constituting' concrete individuals as subjects*. (ibid. [*Louis Althusser, Lenin and Philosophy*, London, Longman, 1971] p. 160)

Within the existing ideology it appears 'obvious' that people are autonomous individuals, possessed of subjectivity or consciousness which is the source of their beliefs and actions. That people are unique, distinguishable, irreplaceable identities is 'the elementary ideological effect' (*ibid*. p. 161).

The obviousness of subjectivity has been challenged by the linguistic theory which has developed on the basis of the work of Saussure. As Emile Benveniste argues, it is language which provides the possibility of subjectivity because it is language which enables the speaker to posit himself or herself as 'I', as the subject of a sentence. It is through language that people constitute themselves as subjects. Consciousness of self is possible only through contrast, differentiation: 'I' cannot be conceived without the conception 'non-I', 'you', and dialogue, the fundamental condition of language,[11] implies a reversible polarity between 'I' and 'you'. 'Language is possible only because each speaker sets himself up as a *subject* by referring to himself as *I* in his discourse' (Benveniste [*Problems in General Linguistics*, Miami University Press] 1971, p. 225). But if language is a system of differences with no positive terms, 'I' designates only the subject of a specific utterance. 'And so it is literally true that the basis of subjectivity is in the exercise of language. If one really thinks about it, one will see that there is no other objective testimony to the identity of the subject except that which he himself thus gives about himself (*ibid*, p. 226).

Within ideology, of course, it seems 'obvious' that the individual speaker is the origin of the meaning of his or her utterance. Post-Saussurean linguistics, however, implies a more complex relationship between the individual and meaning, since it is language itself which, by differentiating between concepts, offers the possibility of meaning. In reality, it is only by adopting the position of the subject within language that the individual is able to produce meaning. As Jacques Derrida puts it,

> what was it that Saussure in particular reminded us of? That 'language [which consists only of differences] is not a function of the speaking subject'. This implies that the subject (self-identical or even conscious of self-identity, self-conscious) is inscribed in the language, that he is a 'function' of the language. He becomes a *speaking* subject only by conforming his speech . . . to the system of linguistic prescriptions taken as the system of differences . . . (Derrida [*Speech and Phenomena*, Northwestern University Press] 1973, pp. 145–6)

Derrida goes on to raise the question whether, even if we accept that it is only the signifying system which makes possible the speaking subject, the signifying subject, we cannot nonetheless conceive of a non-speaking, non-signifying subjectivity, 'a silent and intuitive consciousness' (*ibid*, p. 146). The problem here, he concludes, is to define consciousness-in-itself as distinct from consciousness of something, and ultimately as distinct from consciousness of self. If consciousness is finally consciousness of self, this in turn implies that consciousness depends on differentiation, and specifically on Benveniste's differentiation between 'I' and 'you', a process made possible by language.

The implications of this concept of the primacy of language over subjectivity have been developed by Jacques Lacan's reading of Freud.[12] Lacan's theory of the subject as constructed in language confirms the *decentring* of the individual consciousness so that it can no longer be seen as the origin of meaning, knowledge and action. Instead, Lacan proposes that the infant is initially an 'hommelette' – 'a little man and also like a broken egg spreading without hindrance in all directions' (Coward and Ellis [*Language and Materialism*, London, Routledge and Kégan Paul] 1977, p. 101). The child has no sense of identity, no way of conceiving of itself as a unity, distinct from what is 'other', exterior to it. During the 'mirror-phase' of its development, however, it 'recognizes' itself in the mirror as a unit distinct from the outside world. This 'recognition' is an identification with an 'imaginary' (because imaged) unitary and autonomous self. But it is only with its entry into language that the child becomes a full subject. If it is to participate in the society into which it is born, to be able to act deliberately within the social formation, the child must enter into the symbolic order, the set of signifying systems of culture of which the supreme example is language. The child who refuses to learn the language is 'sick', unable to become a full member of the family and of society.

In order to speak the child is compelled to differentiate; to speak of itself it has to distinguish 'I' from 'you'. In order to formulate its needs the child learns to identify with the first person singular pronoun, and this identification constitutes the basis of subjectivity. Subsequently it learns to recognize itself in a series of subject-positions ('he' or 'she', 'boy' or 'girl', and so on) which are the positions from which discourse is intelligible to itself and others. 'Identity', subjectivity, is thus a matrix of subject-positions, which may be inconsistent or even in contradiction with one another.

Subjectivity, then, is linguistically and discursively constructed and displaced across the range of discourses in which the concrete individual participates. It follows from Saussure's theory of language as a system of differences that the world is intelligible only through discourse: there is no unmediated experience, no access to the raw reality of self and others. Thus,

> As well as being a system of signs related among themselves, language incarnates meaning in the form of the series of positions it offers for the subject from which to grasp itself and its relations with the real. (Nowell-Smith ['A Note on History/Discourse', *Edinburgh 76 Magazine* no. 1] 1976, p. 26)

The subject is constructed in language and in discourse and, since the symbolic order in its discursive use is closely related to ideology, in ideology. It is in this sense that ideology has the effect, as Althusser argues, of constituting individuals as subjects, and it is also in this sense that their subjectivity appears 'obvious'. Ideology suppresses the role of language in the construction of the subject. As a result, people 'recognize' (misrecognize) themselves in the ways in which ideology 'interpellates' them, or in other words, addresses them as subjects, calls them by their names and in turn 'recognizes' their autonomy.[13] As a result, they 'work by themselves' (Althusser 1971, p. 169), they 'willingly' adopt the subject-positions necessary to their participation in the social formation. In capitalism they 'freely' exchange their labour-power for wages, and they 'voluntarily' purchase the commodities produced. And it is here that we see the full force of Althusser's use of the term 'subject', originally borrowed, as he says, from law. The subject is not only a grammatical subject, 'a centre of initiatives, author of and responsible for its actions', but also a *subjected being* who submits to the authority of the social formation represented in ideology as the Absolute Subject (God, the king, the boss, Man, conscience):

> the individual *is interpellated as a (free) subject in order that he shall submit freely to the commandments of the Subject, i.e. in order that he shall (freely) accept his subjection. (ibid.,* p. 169)

(1980)

Notes

11 The signals emitted to each other by bees preclude the possibility of dialogue and are therefore not to be confused with language (Benveniste, pp 49–54; Lacan 1977a, pp. 84–5).

12 Work by and on Lacan is becoming increasingly available in English (see Notes on Further Reading, 1.3).

13 I have stressed the role of interpellation in the constitution of subjectivity, although Althusser himself also lays considerable emphasis on the metaphor of imaginary recognition in the mirror-structure of ideology (1971, pp 167–8). This concept, derived from Lacan's analysis of the mirror-phase, is open to criticism. The notion of recognition by the subject of itself and of the Absolute Subject implies a subject prior to ideology which does the recognizing – 'Something must recognize that which it is to be' (Hirst 1976, p. 404). As Hirst goes on to argue, Althusser's position compels him to argue that the child is 'always-already' a subject, awaited as a subject even before its birth, in the certainty that it will bear its Father's Name (Althusser 1971, pp. 164–5). But children do not possess subjectivity at birth; they are not ' "knowing" subjects independent of their formation and training as social beings' (Hirst 1976, p. 406). Subjectivity, I have suggested, is to be understood above all as a linguistic construct, and the recognition (misrecognition) performed by the subject is most usefully understood as its identification with the *I* of language and then with the I AM of the Absolute Subject to which it accepts its subjection (Althusser 1971, p. 169). The set of subject-positions which make action possible are products of discourse, and it is the network of discourses which is the site of ideology in its specificity.

PATRICIA WAUGH

Feminine Fictions: Revisiting the Postmodern

If women have traditionally been positioned in terms of 'otherness', then the desire to become subjects (which dominates the first phase of post-1960s feminism) is likely to be stronger than the desire to deconstruct, decentre, or fragment subjectivity (which dominates post-1960s postmodernist practice and post-structuralist theory). They have not yet *experienced* this 'whole' or 'unitary' or 'essential' subjectivity. However, it seems to me that it is the gradual recognition of the value of construing human identity in terms of relationship and dispersal, rather than as a unitary, self-directing, isolated ego, which has fundamentally altered the course of modern and contemporary women's writing concerned to challenge gender stereotypes. It is this recognition, brought to full consciousness, which has led feminist writing closer to a 'postmodernist' conception of subjectivity. However, the pursuit of just such a unitary, essential self was a necessary phase in order that women writers might fully understand the historical and social construction of gender and identity. Certainly, for women in the 1960s and early 1970s, 'unity' rather than dispersal seemed to offer more hope for political change. To believe that there might be a 'natural' or 'true' self which may be discovered through lifting the misrepresentations of an oppressive social system is to provide nurturance and fuel for revolutionary hope and practice. Woolf, of course, was among the first feminist writers to emphasize the inauthenticity and the danger, for women, in adhering to this belief.

In fact, insights gained as feminism passed through a *necessary* stage of pursuing unity have produced an alternative conception of the subject as constructed through *relationship*, rather than postmodernism/post-structuralism's anti-humanist *rejection* of the subject. In many ways postmodernists have developed the modernist aesthetic of impersonality along the lines of Lacanian alienation, Derridean assault on presence and origin, and an Althusserian refusal of agency and determination as located in the individual. Much contemporary feminist fictional writing, however, has accommodated humanist beliefs in individual agency and the necessity and possibility of self-reflection and historical continuity as the basis of personal identity. It has modified the traditional forms of such beliefs, however, in order to emphasize the provisionality and positionality of identity, the historical and social construction of gender, and the discursive production of knowledge and power. What many of these texts suggest is that it is possible to experience oneself as a strong and coherent agent in the world, *at the same time* as understanding the extent to which identity and gender are socially constructed and represented.

For, while feminists have come to recognize acutely the *impersonal* social and historical determinants of women's oppression, that experience has itself developed in them strongly 'humanist' or 'personal' qualities: co-operativeness, nurturance, an awareness of self-in-relationship and of the relativity of fields of knowledge and totalizing systems which attempt to systematize individual and concrete human actions. Much recent feminist fiction and theory does indeed reflect a rejection and deconstruction of humanism in terms of its liberal contradictions and illusions which perpetuate women's marginalization and exclusion. Such writing, however, also preserves a belief that human beings *can* act upon the world as partially autonomous agents who can thus determine to some extent what they shall be. Many of the novels examined later in this book affirm a belief in the need for 'strong' selves without presenting the self is an unchanging, ahistorical essence or as an isolated ego struggling aggressively and competitively to define itself as unique, different, separate.

Thus the 'postmodernist' moment of feminist writing has, it seems to me, developed but modified an adherence to a fundamentally humanist concern with the subject in relationship. One of the most vociferous objections to postmodernism from both right and left (Graff, Jameson, Eagleton, Habermas) is that it has eschewed any potential oppositional power and simply added itself to the forms, surfaces, and obsessions of an anti-humanist, consumerist, and alienated culture. One of the critiques of early feminist and New Left rhetoric is that it was premised on naïvely opposed, distinct, and unified realms of the 'personal' and the 'social'. The latter was seen simply to distort, oppress, and repress the former in order to displace it from its 'natural' state. My argument is that most contemporary feminisms have refused to espouse an extreme anti-humanism but they have also recognized the contradictions in that liberal-humanist theory which posits a natural 'self' outside, or prior to, the social. What they have articulated instead is a core belief in a self which, although contradictory, non-unitary, and historically produced through 'discursive' and ideological formations, nevertheless has a material existence and history in actual human relationships, beginning crucially with those between infant and caretakers at the start of life.

Even in its 'essentialist' modes, in fact, feminism has radicalized the subject at least as much as postmodernism/post-structuralism. Although early feminism situated resistance at the site of the 'personal' and the 'experiential', consciousness-raising developed a deep understanding of how 'consciousness' itself, that liberal centre of self, is produced within historically materialist practices and actual relations of power, and cannot therefore be seen as simply productive and determining of the social world. 'Inside' and 'outside' ceased to be discrete; subjectivity was recognized as a relative and shifting positionality. In these terms there are striking similarities between the 'subjects' of feminism and those of postmodernism, yet writers on each rarely make explicit connections between them. Rachael Blau DuPlessis, defining a feminist writing practice, argues, for example:

> One may assert that any female cultural practice that makes the 'meaning production process' itself 'the site of struggle' may be considered feminist. These authors are 'feminist' because they construct a variety of oppositional strategies to the depiction of gender institutions in narrative. A writer expresses dissent from an ideological formation by attacking elements of narrative that

repeat, sustain or embody the values and attitudes in question. So after breaking the sentence, a rupture with the internalization of the authorities and voices of dominance, the woman writer will create that further rupture . . . breaking the sequence – the expected order. (Blau DuPlessis [*Writing Beyond the Ending*, Indiana University Press] 1985, p. 34)

Her definition emphasizes the discursive production of meaning within institutionalized power relations and the need, therefore, to 'break the sentence', fragment the hierarchies of discourse which reproduce ideological formations. Her attack is clearly, though not explicitly, focused on what post-structuralists have referred to as the 'master narratives', the 'grand plots' of history which produce and legitimate social practices and relationships including those between men and women. Victor Burgin sees the political import of postmodernism in terms very similar to Blau DuPlessis's understanding of feminism. Criticizing left-oppositional criticism which develops out of Romanticism and is the culmination of liberal-humanist conceptions of the autonomously expressive individual and the 'people' as a projection of the dream of a pre-capitalist organic society, he sees the political value of postmodernism in its insight that:

What have expired are the absolute guarantees issued by overriding metaphysical systems. 'Certainties and necessities' are now seen as inescapably *positional*, derived from, and applied within, complex networks of mainly local and contingent conditions; it is thus that Lyotard sees the great legitimating narratives, 'good for all time', as having given way to a proliferation of smaller narratives, 'good for the moment', or at best 'for the foreseeable future'. (Burgin [*The End of Art Theory*, London, Macmillan] 1986, pp. 198–9)

These statements reveal the commitment of feminism *and* postmodernism to the project of deconstructing both the subject and the 'master narratives' of history. In each case there will be nostalgia for their loss: from 'neo-conservative' postmodernists perhaps, and from feminists who have remained rooted in the earlier essentialist understanding of the subject. Any account of the relation between feminism and postmodernism must, however, acknowledge their historical differences. Postmodernism assumes or even rejects relationships which, as feminists have rightly argued, women have *never* experienced as subjects in their own right: relationships to the dominant literary and political institutions which legitimate and reproduce the 'master narratives', for example. Furthermore, the obvious fact remains that, historically, men and women have experienced both the world and their own selves in very different ways, and it is the central argument of this book, therefore, that despite common concerns the postmodern deconstruction of subjectivity is as problematic for women as the liberal construction of self.

(1989)

KATE SOPER

'Feminism, Humanism and Postmodernism'
Radical Philosophy

On the other hand, if difference is not given this kind of anchorage in the feminine body and function, it is not clear why there is any reason, once set on the path of difference, for feminism to call a halt. In other words, if one disallows the feminine universal of a common bodily essence, then the commitment to difference ought to move into a deconstruction of feminine difference itself. Having exposed the 'masculinism' of humanism in the name of feminine difference, one must surely go on, by the same logic, to expose the generalizing and abstract (and quasi-humanist) appeal to feminine difference in the name of the plurality of concrete differences between women (in their nationality, race, class, age, occupation, sexuality, parenthood status, health, and so on.) For on this argument 'woman' can no more be allowed to stand for all women than can 'man' be allowed to stand for all members of the human species. The way then, of course, lies open to an extreme particularism in which all pretensions to speak (quasi-humanistically) in general for this or that grouping, or to offer an abstract and representative discourse on behalf of such putative groups, must give way to a hyper-individualism.[9] From this standpoint, any appeal to a collectivity would appear to be illegitimate – yet another case of 'logocentric imperialism', to use the inflated rhetoric of poststructuralism.

But at this point, one is bound to feel that feminism as theory has pulled the rug from under feminism as politics. For politics is essentially a group affair, based on the idea of making 'common cause', and feminism, like any other politics, has always implied a banding together, a movement based on the solidarity and sisterhood of women, who are linked by perhaps very little else than their *sameness* and 'common cause' as women. If this sameness itself is challenged on the grounds that there is no 'presence' of womanhood, nothing that the term 'woman' immediately expresses, and nothing instantiated concretely except particular women in particular situations, then the idea of a political community build around women – the central aspiration of the early feminist movement – collapses. I say the 'idea', for women do still come together in all sorts of groups for feminist purposes, and will doubtless continue to do so for a good while to come even if their doing so transgresses some Derridean conceptual rulings. But *theoretically*, the logic of difference tends to subvert the concept of a feminine political community of 'women' as it does of the more traditional political communities of class, party, trade union, etc. And theory does, of course, in the end get into practice, and maybe has already begun to do so; one already senses that feminism as a campaigning movement is yielding to feminism as discourse (and to discourse of an increasingly heterogeneous kind).

In the face of this dispersion, with its return from solidarity to individualism, it is difficult not to feel that feminism itself has lost its hold, or at any rate that much contemporary theory of the feminine is returning us full circle to those many isolated, and 'silent', women from which it started – and for whom it came to represent, precisely, a 'common voice'. It is a *renversement*, moreover, which leaves feminism exposed to the temptations of what are arguably deeply nostalgic and conservative currents of postmodernist thinking. It would seem quite complicit, for example, with the distaste for anything smacking of a militant feminist politics implicit in Baudrillard's suggestion that it is our very resistance to reactivating traditional feminine charms which is pre-empting cultural renewal. 'Only by the power of seduction does woman master the symbolic universe,' he tells us,[10] in a piece of rhetorical blandishment redolent with nostalgia for the good old days when men ruled and women cajoled. It is true that it is not officially as an ideologue of patriarchal culture that Baudrillard offers this Rousseauian advice. On the contrary, he would seduce us back into seduction with the altogether more respectable end, so he claims, of taking us beyond all sociality, sentimentality and sexuality.[11] But it is interesting, all the same, that it remains out of place for woman directly to contest the father's authority, and that our cultural duty requires us still to have recourse to the subtler arts of cajolery: to beguile the phallus round. By such means, so Baudrillard tempts us to think, women will readily contrive to wrap the symbolic order around her charming little finger.[12]

This kind of sophistry, in truth, is not very tempting and probably unimportant. But I think in a general way it is fair to claim that the same logic of 'difference' which ends up subverting the project of feminine emancipation by denying the validity of any political community in whose name it could be pursued also deprives feminist argument of recourse against such retrograde poststructuralist idealism.

In introducing the term 'emancipation', one opens the way to consideration of another aspect of the problem of the relations between feminism, humanism and postmodernism. For if the building of political collectivities becomes problematic in the light of anti-humanist critique, this also reflects a reluctance of these critiques 'to speak on behalf of' others: to say, in short, what others – in this case women – want. In other words, the observance of the logic of difference has also made feminist theorists reluctant utopians. This caution in speaking for others' desires is understandable against a background of so much claimed knowledge of the 'alienation' and 'true needs' of others (especially of that notorious 'universal subject' of humanity, the proletariat). It is a needed corrective to the enforced collectivizations of interests and needs which have been given theoretical legitimation in the past.

But again, the thinking which motivated this healthy resistance to glib pronouncements of solidarity and struggle has also in recent argument developed a momentum which begins to undermine the possibility of speaking of any kind of political collective and agreement at all. Foucault, for example, has denounced any totalizing attempt in theory (any attempt, that is, to offer general diagnoses and general remedies for the ills of society) as 'totalitarian'. Even Habermas, who is hardly a Stalinist in theory, and who argues no more than that people should be allowed to discover the truth of their interests in the free discussions of his 'ideal communication situation', has been denounced by Lyotard for aspiring to a consensus.[13]

In other words, the drift of such arguments would seem to rule out any holistic analysis of societies (any analysis of the kind that allows us to define them as 'capitalist' or 'patriarchal' or 'totalitarian'), together with the radically transformative projects which such analyses tend to recommend. Indeed, as Isaac Balbus has argued in his defence of object-relations feminism against Foucauldian logic, if we accept the claim that any continuous history or *longue durée* accounting is posturing as 'True' (and therefore dominating) discourse, then feminism itself becomes a form of totalitarianism. The very idea of a centuries-old subordination of women explicable by reference to transhistorical patriarchal structures becomes deeply problematic from the standpoint of the 'postmodernist' rejection of truth and scientific knowledge and of the continuities they posit. If all that we once called knowledge or theory is now mythopoeic 'narrative', then the narrative of male oppression is itself but one more myth of Knowledge generated in response to a 'Will to Power'. And, by the same token, 'progress' out of oppression becomes a meaningless aspiration.[14]

(1990)

Notes

9 Recent feminist self-criticism regarding the 'white middle- class' outlook of feminist politics reflects this anxiety about conceptual conflations, even if it does not collapse into the extreme particularism which would seem to be its ultimate logic.

10 Jean Baudrillard, *De la séduction* (Paris, 1979), p. 208; cf. Jardine, *Gynesis*, p. 67.

11 Jean Baudrillard, interview in *Marxism Today*, January 1989, p. 54.

12 There will be some, no doubt, who will come to Baudrillard's defence. They argue, perhaps, that he is in fact repaying the debt of patriarchy with a clear and self-confessed vagina envy. Or they may point out that Baudrillard is simply saying that the means must match the end, and that for women to use 'male' methods is to give themselves over to the masculine forms of power they wish to contest. Very well, then, let him for his part, show his good faith by yielding up the language of 'female sacrifice' and 'female seduction'. And let him ask men, too, to put a hand in the churn of cultural revolution. Or is the subversion of the Symbolic to be wholly women's work?

13 François Lyotard, *The Postmodern Condition* (Manchester, 1986), p. 66; cf. pp. 10–16; 25; 57–9; 63–5.

14 Isaac Balbus, 'Disciplining women', in Comell and Benhabib, *Feminism as Critique*, pp. 110–27.

JUDITH BUTLER

Gender Trouble: Feminism and the Subversion of Identity

I began with the speculative question of whether feminist politics could do without a "subject" in the category of women. At stake is not whether it still makes sense, strategically or transitionally, to refer to women in order to make representational claims in their behalf. The feminist "we" is always and only a phantasmatic construction, one that has its purposes, but which denies the internal complexity and indeterminacy of the term and constitutes itself only through the exclusion of some part of the constituency that it simultaneously seeks to represent. The tenuous or phantasmatic status of the "we," however, is not cause for despair or, at least, it is not *only* cause for despair. The radical instability of the category sets into question the *foundational* restrictions on feminist political theorizing and opens up other configurations, not only of genders and bodies, but of politics itself.

The foundationalist reasoning of identity politics tends to assume that an identity must first be in place in order for political interests to be elaborated and, subsequently, political action to be taken. My argument is that there need not be a "doer behind the deed," but that the "doer" is variably constructed in and through the deed. This is not a return to an existential theory of the self as constituted through its acts, for the existential theory maintains a prediscursive structure for both the self and its acts. It is precisely the discursively variable construction of each in and through the other that has interested me here.

The question of locating "agency" is usually associated with the viability of the "subject," where the "subject" is understood to have some stable existence prior to the cultural field that it negotiates. Or, if the subject is culturally constructed, it is nevertheless vested with an agency, usually figured as the capacity for reflexive mediation, that remains intact regardless of its cultural embeddedness. On such a model, "culture" and "discourse" *mire* the subject, but do not constitute that subject. This move to qualify and enmire the preexisting subject has appeared necessary to establish a point of agency that is not fully *determined* by that culture and discourse. And yet, this kind of reasoning falsely presumes (a) agency can only be established through recourse to a prediscursive "I," even if that "I" is found in the midst of a discursive convergence, and (b) that to be *constituted* by discourse is to be *determined* by discourse, where determination forecloses the possibility of agency.

Even within the theories that maintain a highly qualified or situated subject, the subject still encounters its discursively constituted environment in an oppositional epistemological frame. The culturally enmired subject negotiates its constructions, even when those constructions are the very predicates of its

own identity. In Beauvoir, for example, there is an "I" that does its gender,
that becomes its gender, but that "I," invariably associated with its gender, is
nevertheless a point of agency never fully identifiable with its gender. That
cogito is never fully *of* the cultural world that it negotiates, no matter the
narrowness of the ontological distance that separates that subject from its
cultural predicates. The theories of feminist identity that elaborate predicates
of color, sexuality, ethnicity, class, and able-bodiedness invariably close with
an embarrassed "etc." at the end of the list. Through this horizontal trajectory
of adjectives, these positions strive to encompass a situated subject, but
invariably fail to be complete. This failure, however, is instructive: what
political impetus is to be derived from the exasperated "etc." that so often
occurs at the end of such lines? This is a sign of exhaustion as well as of the
illimitable process of signification itself. It is the *supplément*, the excess that
necessarily accompanies any effort to posit identity once and for all. This
illimitable *et cetera*, however, offers itself as a new departure for feminist
political theorizing.

If identity is asserted through a process of signification, if identity is always
already signified, and yet continues to signify as it circulates within various
interlocking discourses, then the question of agency is not to be answered
through recourse to an "I" that preexists signification. In other words, the
enabling conditions for an assertion of "I" are provided by the structure of
signification, the rules that regulate the legitimate and illegitimate invocation
of that pronoun, the practices that establish the terms of intelligibility by
which that pronoun can circulate. Language is not an *exterior medium or
instrument* into which I pour a self and from which I glean a reflection of that
self. The Hegelian model of self-recognition that has been appropriated by
Marx, Lukács, and a variety of contemporary liberatory discourses presupposes a potential adequation between the "I" that confronts its world,
including its language, as an object, and the "I" that finds itself as an object
in that world. But the subject/object dichotomy, which here belongs to the
tradition of Western epistemology, conditions the very problematic of identity
that it seeks to solve.

What discursive tradition establishes the "I" and its "Other" in an
epistemological confrontation that subsequently decides where and how
questions of knowability and agency are to be determined? What kinds of
agency are foreclosed through the positing of an epistemological subject
precisely because the rules and practices that govern the invocation of that
subject and regulate its agency in advance are ruled out as sites of analysis
and critical intervention? That the epistemological point of departure is in no
sense inevitable is naively and pervasively confirmed by the mundane
operations of ordinary language – widely documented within anthropology –
that regard the subject/object dichotomy as a strange and contingent, if not
violent, philosophical imposition. The language of appropriation, instrumen-

tality, and distanciation germane to the epistemological mode also belong to a strategy of domination that pits the "I" against an "Other" and, once that separation is effected, creates an artificial set of questions about the knowability and recoverability of that Other.

As part of the epistemological inheritance of contemporary political discourses of identity, this binary opposition is a strategic move within a given set of signifying practices, one that establishes the "I" in and through this opposition and which reifies that opposition as a necessity, concealing the discursive apparatus by which the binary itself is constituted. The shift from an *epistemological* account of identity to one which locates the problematic within practices of *signification* permits an analysis that takes the epistemological mode itself as one possible and contingent signifying practice. Further, the question of *agency* is reformulated as a question of how signification and resignification work. In other words, what is signified as an identity is not signified at a given point in time after which it is simply there as an inert piece of entitative language. Clearly, identities *can* appear as so many inert substantives; indeed, epistemological models tend to take this appearance as their point of theoretical departure. However, the substantive "I" only appears as such through a signifying practice that seeks to conceal its own workings and to naturalize its effects. Further, to qualify as a substantive identity is an arduous task, for such appearances are rule-generated identities, ones which rely on the consistent and repeated invocation of rules that condition and restrict culturally intelligible practices of identity. Indeed, to understand identity as a *practice*, and as a signifying practice, is to understand culturally intelligible subjects as the resulting effects of a rule-bound discourse that inserts itself in the pervasive and mundane signifying acts of linguistic life. Abstractly considered, language refers to an open system of signs by which intelligibility is insistently created and contested. As historically specific organizations of language, discourses present themselves in the plural, coexisting within temporal frames, and instituting unpredictable and inadvertent convergences from which specific modalities of discursive possibilities are engendered.

As a process, signification harbors within itself what the epistemological discourse refers to as "agency." The rules that govern intelligible identity, i.e., that enable and restrict the intelligible assertion of an "I," rules that are partially structured along matrices of gender hierarchy and compulsory heterosexuality, operate through *repetition*. Indeed, when the subject is said to be constituted, that means simply that the subject is a consequence of certain rule-governed discourses that govern the intelligible invocation of identity. The subject is not *determined* by the rules through which it is generated because signification is *not a founding act, but rather a regulated process of repetition* that both conceals itself and enforces its rules precisely through the production of substantializing effects. In a sense, all signification takes place within the orbit of the compulsion to repeat; "agency," then, is to be located within the possibility of a variation on that repetition. If the rules governing signification not only restrict, but enable the assertion of alternative domains of cultural intelligibility, i.e., new possibilities for gender that contest the rigid codes of hierarchical binarisms, then it is only *within* the practices of repetitive signifying that a subversion of identity becomes possible. The injunction *to be* a given gender produces necessary failures, a variety of incoherent configurations that in their multiplicity exceed and defy the injunction by which they are generated. Further, the very injunction to be a given gender takes place through discursive routes: to be a good mother, to be a heterosexually desirable object, to be a fit worker, in sum, to signify a multiplicity of guarantees in response to a variety of different demands all at once. The coexistence or convergence of such discursive injunctions produces the possibility of a complex reconfiguration and redeployment; it is not a transcendental subject who enables action in the midst of such a convergence. There is no self that is prior to the convergence or who maintains "integrity" prior to its entrance into this conflicted cultural field. There is only a taking up of the tools where they lie, where the very "taking up" is enabled by the tool lying there.

What constitutes a subversive repetition within signifying practices of gender? I have argued ("I" deploy the grammar that governs the genre of the philosophical conclusion, but note that it is the grammar itself that deploys and enables this "I," even as the "I" that insists itself here repeats, redeploys, and – as the critics will determine – contests the philosophical grammar by which it is both enabled and restricted) that, for instance, within the sex/gender distinction, sex poses as "the real" and the "factic," the material or corporeal ground upon which gender operates as an act of cultural *inscription*. And yet gender is not written on the body as the torturing instrument of writing in Kafka's "In the Penal Colony" inscribes itself unintelligibly on the flesh of the accused. The question is not: what meaning does that inscription carry within it, but what cultural apparatus arranges this meeting between instrument and body, what interventions into this ritualistic repetition are possible? The "real" and the "sexually factic" are phantasmatic constructions – illusions of substance – that bodies are compelled to approximate, but never can. What, then, enables the exposure of the rift between the phantasmatic and the real whereby the real admits itself as phantasmatic? Does this offer the possibility for a repetition that is not fully constrained by the injunction to reconsolidate naturalized identities? Just as bodily surfaces are enacted *as* the natural, so these surfaces can become the site of a dissonant and denaturalized performance that reveals the performative status of the natural itself.

Practices of parody can serve to reengage and reconsolidate the very distinction between a privileged and naturalized gender configuration and one that appears as derived, phantasmatic, and mimetic – a failed copy, as it were. And surely parody has been used to further a politics of despair, one which affirms a seemingly inevitable exclusion of marginal genders from the territory of the natural and the real. And yet this failure to become "real" and to embody "the natural" is, I would argue, a constitutive failure of all gender enactments for the very reason that these ontological locales are fundamentally uninhabitable. Hence, there is a subversive laughter in the pastiche-effect of parodic practices in which the original, the authentic, and the real are themselves constituted as effects. The loss of gender norms would have the effect of proliferating gender configurations, destabilizing substantive identity, and depriving the naturalizing narratives of compulsory heterosexuality of their central protagonists: "man" and "woman." The parodic repetition of gender exposes as well the illusion of gender identity as an intractable depth and inner substance. As the effects of a subtle and politically enforced performativity, gender is an "act," as it were, that is open to splittings, self-parody, self-criticism, and those hyperbolic exhibitions of "the natural" that, in their very exaggeration, reveal its fundamentally phantasmatic status.

I have tried to suggest that the identity categories often presumed to be foundational to feminist politics, that is, deemed necessary in order to mobilize feminism as an identity politics, simultaneously work to limit and constrain in advance the very cultural possibilities that feminism is supposed to open up. The tacit constraints that produce culturally intelligible "sex" ought to be understood as generative political structures rather than natu-ralized foundations. Paradoxically, the reconceptualization of identity as an *effect*, that is, as *produced* or *generated*, opens up possibilities of "agency" that are insidiously foreclosed by positions that take identity categories as founda-tional and fixed. For an identity to be an effect means that it is neither fatally determined nor fully artificial and arbitrary. That the *constituted* status of identity is misconstrued along these two conflicting lines suggests the ways in which the feminist discourse on cultural construction remains trapped within the unnecessary binarism of free will and determinism. Construction is not opposed to agency; it is the necessary scene of agency, the very terms in which agency is articulated and becomes culturally intelligible. The critical task for feminism is not to establish a point of view outside of constructed identities; that conceit is the construction of an epistemological model that would disavow its own cultural location and, hence, promote itself as a global subject, a position that deploys precisely the imperialist strategies that feminism ought to criticize. The critical task is, rather, to locate strategies of subversive repetition enabled by those constructions, to affirm the local possibilities of intervention through participating in precisely those practices of repetition that constitute identity and, therefore, present the immanent possibility of contesting them.

This theoretical inquiry has attempted to locate the political in the very signifying practices that establish, regulate, and deregulate identity. This effort, however, can only be accomplished through the introduction of a set of questions that extend the very notion of the political. How to disrupt the foundations that cover over alternative cultural configurations of gender? How to destabilize and render in their phantasmatic dimension the "premises" of identity politics?

This task has required a critical genealogy of the naturalization of sex and of bodies in general. It has also also demanded a reconsideration of the figure of the body as mute, prior to culture, awaiting signification, a figure that cross-checks with the figure of the feminine, awaiting the inscription-as-incision of the masculine signifier for entrance into language and culture. From a political analysis of compulsory heterosexuality, it has been necessary to question the construction of sex as binary, as a hierarchical binary. From the point of view of gender as enacted, questions have emerged over the fixity of gender identity as an interior depth that is said to be externalized in various forms of "expression." The implicit construction of the primary heterosexual construction of desire is shown to persist even as it appears in the mode of primary bisexuality. Strategies of exclusion and hierarchy are also shown to persist in the formulation of the sex/gender distinction and its recourse to "sex" as the prediscursive as well as the priority of sexuality to culture and, in particular, the cultural construction of sexuality as the prediscursive. Finally, the epistemological paradigm that presumes the priority of the doer to the deed establishes a global and globalizing subject who disavows its own locality as well as the conditions for local intervention.

If taken as the grounds of feminist theory or politics, these "effects" of gender hierarchy and compulsory heterosexuality are not only misdescribed as foundations, but the signifying practices that enable this metaleptic misdescription remain outside the purview of a feminist critique of gender relations. To enter into the repetitive practices of this terrain of signification is not a choice, for the "I" that might enter is always already inside: there is no possibility of agency or reality outside of the discursive practices that give those terms the intelligibility that they have. The task is not whether to repeat, but how to repeat or, indeed, to repeat and, through a radical proliferation of gender, *to displace* the very gender norms that enable the repetition itself. There is no ontology of gender on which we might construct a politics, for gender ontologies always operate within established political contexts as normative injunctions, determining what qualifies as intelligible sex, invoking and consolidating the reproductive constraints on sexuality, setting the prescriptive requirements whereby sexed or gendered bodies come into cultural intelligibility. Ontology is, thus, not a foundation, but a normative injunction that operates insidiously by installing itself into political discourse as its necessary ground.

The deconstruction of identity is not the deconstruction of politics; rather, it establishes as political the very terms through which identity is articulated. This kind of critique brings into question the foundationalist frame in which feminism as an identity politics has been articulated. The internal paradox of this foundationalism is that it presumes, fixes, and constrains the very "subjects" that it hopes to represent and liberate. The task here is not to celebrate each and every new possibility *qua* possibility, but to redescribe those possibilities that *already* exist, but which exist within cultural domains designated as culturally unintelligible and impossible. If identities were no longer fixed as the premises of a political syllogism, and politics no longer understood as a set of practices derived from the alleged interests that belong to a set of ready-made subjects, a new configuration of politics would surely emerge from the ruins of the old. Cultural configurations of sex and gender might then proliferate or, rather, their present proliferation might then become articulable within the discourses that establish intelligible cultural life, confounding the very binarism of sex, and exposing its fundamental unnaturalness. What other local strategies for engaging the "unnatural" might lead to the denaturalization of gender as such?

(1990)

SEYLA BENHABIB

'Feminism and the Question of Postmodernism'
Situating the Self

I will now formulate two versions of the three theses enumerated above with the goal of clarifying once more the various conceptual options made available with the demise of the episteme of representations. Put in a nutshell, my argument is that strong and weak versions of the theses of the Death of Man, of History and of Metaphysics are possible. Whereas the weak versions of these theses entail premises around which critical theorists as well as postmodernists and possibly even liberals and communitarians can unite, their strong versions undermine the possibility of normative criticism at large. Feminist theory can ally itself with this strong version of postmodernism only at the risk of incoherence and self-contradictoriness.

1 Let us begin by considering the thesis of the Death of Man for a closer understanding of the conceptual option(s) allowed by the end of the episteme of representation. The weak version of this thesis would *situate* the subject in the context of various social, linguistic and discursive practices. This view would by no means question the desirability and theoretical necessity of articulating a more adequate, less deluded and less mystified vision of subjectivity than those provided by the concepts of the Cartesian cogito, the "transcendental unity of apperception," "Geist and consciousness," or "das Man" (the they). The traditional attributes of the philosophical subject of the West, like self-reflexivity, the capacity for acting on principles, rational accountability for one's actions and the ability to project a life-plan into the

future, in short, some form of autonomy and rationality, could then be reformulated by taking account of the radical situatedness of the subject.

The strong version of the thesis of the Death of Man is perhaps best captured in Flax's own phrase that "Man is forever caught in the web of fictive meaning, in chains of signification, *in which the subject is merely another position in language*." [*Psychoanalysis, Feminism and Postmodernism*, University of California Press.] The subject thus dissolves into the chain of significations of which it was supposed to be the initiator. Along with this dissolution of the subject into yet "another position in language" disappear of course concepts of intentionality, accountability, self-reflexivity and autonomy. The subject that is but another position in language can no longer master and create that distance between itself and the chain of significations in which it is immersed such that it can reflect upon them and creatively alter them.

The strong version of the Death of the Subject thesis is not compatible with the goals of feminism. Surely, a subjectivity that would not be structured by language, by narrative and by the symbolic codes of narrative available in a culture is unthinkable. We tell of who we are, of the "I" that we are, by means of a narrative. "I was born on such and such a date, as the daughter of such and such . . ." etc. These narratives are deeply colored and structured by the codes of expectable and understandable biographies and identities in our cultures. We can concede all that, but nevertheless we must still argue that we are not merely extensions of our histories, that *vis-à-vis* our own stories we are in the position of author and character at once. The situated and gendered subject is heteronomously determined but still strives toward autonomy. I want to ask how in fact the very project of female emancipation would be thinkable without such a regulative ideal of enhancing the agency, autonomy and selfhood of women.

Feminist appropriations of Nietzsche on this question can only be incoherent. In her recent book, *Gender Trouble: Feminism and the Subversion of Identity*, Judith Butler wants to extend the limits of reflexivity in thinking about the self beyond the dichotomy of "sex" and "gender." Her convincing and original arguments rejecting this dichotomous reasoning within which feminist theory has operated until recently get clouded, however, by the claim that to reject this dichotomy would mean subscribing to the view that the "gendered self" does not exist; all that the self is, is a series of performances. "Gender," writes Butler, "is not to culture as sex is to nature; gender is also the discursive/cultural means by which 'sexed nature' or a 'natural sex' is produced and established as 'prediscursive,' prior to culture, a politically neutral surface *on which* culture acts."[6] For Butler the myth of the already sexed body is the epistemological equivalent of the myth of the given: just as the given can only be identified within a discursive framework, so too it is the culturally available codes of gender that "sexualize" a body and that construct the directionality of that body's sexual desire.

But Butler also maintains that to think beyond the univocality and dualisms of gender categories, we must bid farewell to the "doer behind the deed," to the self as the subject of a life-narrative. "In an application that Nietzsche himself would not have anticipated or condoned, we might state as a corollary: There is no gender identity behind the expressions of gender; that identity is performatively constituted by the very 'expressions' that are said to be its results."[7] Yet if this view of the self is adopted, is there any possibility of transforming those "expressions" which constitute us? If we are no more than the sum total of the gendered expressions we perform, is there ever any chance to stop the performance for a while, to pull the curtain down, and only let it rise if one can have a say in the production of the play itself? Isn't this what the struggle over gender is all about? Surely we can criticize the "metaphysical presuppositions of identity politics" and challenge the supremacy of heterosexist positions in the women's movement. Yet is such a challenge only thinkable via a complete debunking of any concepts of selfhood, agency and autonomy? What follows from this Nietzschean position is a vision of the self as a masquerading performer, except of course we are now asked to believe that there is no self behind the mask. Given how fragile and tenuous women's sense of selfhood is in many cases, how much of a hit-and-miss affair their struggles for autonomy are, this reduction of female agency to a "doing without the doer" at best appears to me to be making a virtue out of necessity.

The view that gendered identity is constituted by "deeds without the doer," or by performances without a subject, not only undermines the normative vision of feminist politics and theory. It is also impossible to get rid of the subject altogether and claim to be a fully accountable participant in the community of discourse and inquiry: the strong thesis of the death of the subject undermines the discourse of the theorist herself. If the subject who produces discourse is but a product of the discourse it has created, or better still is but "another position in language," then the responsibility for this discourse cannot be attributed to the author but must be attributable to some fictive "authorial position," constituted by the intersection of "discursive planes." (I am tempted to add that in geometry the intersection of planes produces a line!) Butler entertains this possibility in the introduction to her work: "Philosophy is the predominant disciplinary mechanism that currently mobilizes this author-subject."[8] The "subject" here means also the "object of the discourse"; not the one who utilizes the discourse but the one who is utilized by the discourse itself. Presumably that is why Butler uses the language of "a discourse mobilizing an author/subject." The center of motility is not the thinking, acting and feeling self but "discourses," "systems of signification," "chains of signs," etc. But how then should we read Gender Trouble?

The kind of reading I am engaging here presupposes that there is a thinking author who has produced this text, who has intentions, purposes and goals in communicating with me; that the task of theoretical reflection begins with the attempt to understand what the author meant. Certainly, language always says much more than what the author means; there will always be a discrepancy between what we mean and what we say; but we engage in communication, theoretical no less than everyday communication, to gain some basis of mutual understanding and reasoning. The view that the subject is not reducible to "yet another position in language," but that no matter how constituted by language the subject retains a certain autonomy and ability to rearrange the significations of language, is a regulative principle of all communication and social action. Not only feminist politics, but also coherent theorizing becomes impossible if the speaking and thinking self is replaced by "authorial positions," and if the self becomes a ventriloquist for discourses operating through her or "mobilizing" her.

Perhaps I have overstated the case against Butler. Perhaps Butler does not want, any more than Flax herself, to dispense with women's sense of selfhood, agency and autonomy. In the concluding reflections to *Gender Trouble* Butler returns to questions of agency, identity and politics. She writes:

> The question of locating "agency" is usually associated with the viability of the "subject," where the subject is understood to have some stable existence prior to the cultural field that it negotiated. Or, if the subject is culturally constructed, it is nevertheless vested with an agency, usually figured as the capacity for reflexive mediation, that remains intact regardless of its cultural embeddedness. On such a model, "culture" and "discourse" *mire* the subject, but do not constitute that subject. This move to qualify and to enmire the preexisting subject has appeared necessary to establish a point of agency that is not fully *determined* by that culture and discourse. And yet, this kind of reasoning falsely presumes (a) agency can only be established through recourse to a prediscursive "I," even if that "I" is found in the midst of a discursive convergence, and (b) that to be *constituted* by discourse is to be *determined* by discourse, where determination forecloses the possibility of agency.[9]

Butler rejects that identity can only be established through recourse to an " 'I' that preexists signification."[10] She points out that "the enabling conditions for an assertion of 'I' are provided by the structure of signification, the rules that regulate the legitimate and illegitimate invocation of that pronoun, the practices that establish the terms of intelligibility by which that pronoun can circulate." The narrative codes of a culture then define the content with which this pronoun will be invested, the appropriate instances when it can be invoked, by whom and how. Yet one can agree with all that and still maintain that no individual is merely a blank slate upon whom are inscribed the codes of a culture, a kind of Lockean tabula rasa in latter-day Foucaultian garb! The historical and cultural study of diverse codes of the constitution of subjectivity, or the historical study of the formation of the individual, does not answer the question: what mechanisms and dynamics are involved in the developmental process through which the human infant, a vulnerable and dependent body, becomes a distinct self with the ability to speak its language and the ability to participate in the complex social processes which define its world? Such dynamics and mechanisms enabled the children of the ancient Egyptians to become members of that cultural community no less than they enabled Hopi children to become social individuals. The study of culturally diverse codes which define individuality is not the same as an answer to the question as to *how* the human infant becomes the social self, regardless of the cultural and normative content which defines selfhood. In the latter case we are studying *structural processes and dynamics of socialization and individuation*; in the former, historical processes of signification and meaning constitution. Indeed, as Butler observes, "to be constituted by discourse is not to be determined by discourse." We have to explain how a human infant can become the speaker of an infinitely meaningful number of sentences in a given natural language, how it acquires, that is, the competence to become a linguistic being; furthermore, we have to explain how every human infant can become the initiator of a unique life-story, of a meaningful tale – which certainly is only meaningful if we know the cultural codes under which it is constructed – but which we cannot predict even if we knew these cultural codes.

Butler writes "that 'agency' then is to be located within the possibility of a variation on that repetition" (the repetition of gender performances).[11] But where are the resources for that variation derived from? What is it that enables the self to "vary" the gender codes? to resist hegemonic discourses? What psychic, intellectual or other sources of creativity and resistance must we attribute to subjects for such variation to be possible?

The answers to these questions, even if they were fully available to me at this point, which they are not, would go beyond the boundaries of this analysis. Yet we have reached an important conclusion: the issues generated by the complex interaction between feminism and postmodernism around concepts of the self and subjectivity cannot be captured by bombastic proclamations of the "Death of the Subject." The central question is how we must understand the phrase: "the I although constituted by discourse is not determined by it." To embark upon a meaningful answer to this query from where we stand today involves not yet another decoding of metaphors and tropes about the self, but a serious interchange between philosophy and the social sciences like sociolinguistics, social interactionist psychology, socialization theory, psychoanalysis and cultural history among others. To put it bluntly: the thesis of the Death of the Subject presupposes a remarkably crude version of individuation and socialization processes when compared with currently available social science reflections on the subject. But neither the fundamentalist models of inquiry of the tradition, which privilege the reflective I reflecting upon the conditions of its reflexive or non-reflexive existence, nor the postmodernist decoding of the subject into bodily surfaces "that are enacted *as* the natural, so [that] these surfaces can become the site of a dissonant and denaturalized performance" (Butler) will suffice in the task of explaining how the individual can be "constituted by discourse and yet not be determined by it." The analysis of gender once more forces the boundaries of disciplinary discourses toward a new integration of theoretical paradigms.

(1992)

Notes

6 J. Butler, *Gender Trouble: Feminism and the Subversion of Identity* (Routledge, London, 1990), p. 7.
7 Ibid., p. 25.
8 Ibid., p. xiii.
9 Ibid., p. 143.
10 Ibid., p. 143.
11 Ibid., p. 145.

LINDA ALCOFF

'Cultural Feminism versus Post-structuralism: The Identity Crisis in Feminist Theory' Signs: Journal of Women in Culture and Society

Applied to the concept of woman the post-structuralist's view results in what I shall call nominalism: the idea that the category "woman" is a fiction and that feminist efforts must be directed toward dismantling this fiction. "Perhaps . . . 'woman' is not a determinable identity. Perhaps woman is not some thing which announces itself from a distance, at a distance from some other thing. . . . Perhaps woman – a non-identity, non-figure, a simulacrum – is distance's very chasm, the out-distancing of distance, the interval's cadence, distance itself."[27] Derrida's interest in feminism stems from his belief, expressed above, that woman may represent the rupture in the functional discourse of what he calls logocentrism, an essentialist discourse that entails hierarchies of difference and a Kantian ontology. Because woman has in a sense been excluded from this discourse, it is possible to hope that she might provide a real source of resistance. But her resistance will not be at all effective if she continues to use the mechanism of logocentrism to redefine woman: she can be an effective resister only if she drifts and dodges all attempts to capture her. Then, Derrida hopes, the following futuristic picture will come true: "Out of the depths, endless and unfathomable, she engulfs and distorts all vestige of essentiality, of identity, of property. And the philosophical discourse, blinded, founders on these shoals and is hurled down these depths to its ruin."[28] For Derrida, women have always been defined as a subjugated difference within a binary opposition: man/woman, culture/

nature, positive/negative, analytical/intuitive. To assert an essential gender difference as cultural feminists do is to reinvoke this oppositional structure. The only way to break out of this structure, and in fact to subvert the structure itself, is to assert total difference, to be that which cannot be pinned down or subjugated within a dichotomous hierarchy. Paradoxically, it is to be what is not. Thus feminists cannot demarcate a definitive category of "woman" without eliminating all possibility for the defeat of logocentrism and its oppressive power.

Foucault similarly rejects all constructions of oppositional subjects – whether the "proletariat," "woman," or "the oppressed" – as mirror images that merely recreate and sustain the discourse of power. As Biddy Martin points out, "The point from which Foucault deconstructs is off–center, out of line, apparently unaligned. It is not the point of an imagined absolute otherness, but an 'alterity' which understands itself as an internal exclusion."[29]

Following Foucault and Derrida, an effective feminism could only be a wholly negative feminism, deconstructing everything and refusing to construct anything. This is the position Julia Kristeva adopts, herself an influential French post-structuralist. She says: "A woman cannot be; it is something which does not even belong in the order of being. *It follows that a feminist practice can only be negative*, at odds with what already exists so that we may say 'that's not it' and 'that's still not it.'"[30] The problematic character of subjectivity does not mean, then, that there can be no political struggle, as one might surmise from the fact that post-structuralism deconstructs the position of the revolutionary in the same breath as it deconstructs the position of the reactionary. But the political struggle can have only a "negative function," rejecting "everything finite, definite, structured, loaded with meaning, in the existing state of society."[31]

The attraction of the post-structuralist critique of subjectivity for feminists is two-fold. First, it seems to hold out the promise of an increased freedom for women, the "free play" of a plurality of differences unhampered by any predetermined gender identity as formulated by either patriarchy or cultural feminism. Second, it moves decisively beyond cultural feminism and liberal feminism in further theorizing what they leave untouched: the construction of subjectivity. We can learn a great deal here about the mechanisms of sexist oppression and the construction of specific gender categories by relating these to social discourse and by conceiving of the subject as a cultural product. Certainly, too, this analysis can help us understand right-wing women, the reproduction of ideology, and the mechanisms that block social progress. However, adopting nominalism creates significant problems for feminism. How can we seriously adopt Kristeva's plan for only negative struggle? As the Left should by now have learned, you cannot mobilize a movement that is only and always against: you must have a positive alternative, a vision of a better future that can motivate people to sacrifice their time and energy toward its realization. Moreover, a feminist adoption of nominalism will be confronted with the same problem theories of ideology have, that is, Why is a right-wing woman's consciousness constructed via social discourse but a feminist's consciousness not? Post-structuralist critiques of subjectivity pertain to the construction of all subjects or they pertain to none. And here is precisely the dilemma for feminists: How can we ground a feminist politics that deconstructs the female subject? Nominalism threatens to wipe out feminism itself.

Some feminists who wish to use post-structuralism are well aware of this danger. Biddy Martin, for example, points out that "we cannot afford to refuse to take a political stance 'which pins us to our sex' for the sake of an abstract theoretical correctness. . . . There is the danger that Foucault's challenges to traditional categories, if taken to a 'logical' conclusion . . . could make the question of women's oppression obsolete."[32] Based on her articulation of the problem with Foucault we are left hopeful that Martin will provide a solution that transcends nominalism. Unfortunately, in her reading of Lou Andreas-Salome, Martin valorizes undecidability, ambiguity, and elusiveness and intimates that by maintaining the undecidability of identity the life of Andreas-Salome provides a text from which feminists can usefully learn.[33]

However, the notion that all texts are undecidable cannot be useful for feminists. In support of his contention that the meaning of texts is ultimately undecidable, Derrida offers us in *Spurs* three conflicting but equally warranted interpretations of how Nietzsche's texts construct and position the female. In one of these interpretations Derrida argues we can find purportedly feminist propositions.[34] Thus, Derrida seeks to demonstrate that even the seemingly incontrovertible interpretation of Nietzsche's works as misogynist can be challenged by an equally convincing argument that they are not. But how can this be helpful to feminists, who need to have their accusations of misogyny validated rather than rendered "undecidable"? The point is not that Derrida himself is antifeminist, nor that there is nothing at all in Derrida's work that can be useful for feminists. But the thesis of undecidability as it is applied in the case of Nietzsche sounds too much like yet another version of the antifeminist argument that our perception of sexism is based on a skewed, limited perspective and that what we take to be misogyny is in reality helpful rather than hurtful to the cause of women. The declaration of undecidability must inevitably return us to Kristeva's position, that we can give only negative answers to the question, What is a woman? If the category "woman" is fundamentally undecidable, then we can offer no positive conception of it that is immune to deconstruction, and we are left with a feminism that can be only deconstructive and, thus, nominalist once again.[35]

A nominalist position on subjectivity has the deleterious effect of de-gendering our analysis, of in effect making gender invisible once again. Foucault's ontology includes only bodies and pleasures, and he is notorious for not including gender as a category of analysis. If gender is simply a social construct, the need and even the possibility of a feminist politics becomes immediately problematic. What can we demand in the name of women if "women" do not exist and demands in their name simply reinforce the myth that they do? How can we speak out against sexism as detrimental to the interests of women if the category is a fiction? How can we demand legal abortions, adequate child care, or wages based on comparable worth without invoking a concept of "woman"?

Post-structuralism undercuts our ability to oppose the dominant trend (and, one might argue, the dominant danger) in mainstream Western intellectual thought, that is, the insistence on a universal, neutral, perspective-less epistemology, metaphysics, and ethics. Despite rumblings from the Continent, Anglo-American thought is still wedded to the idea(l) of a universalizable, apolitical methodology and set of transhistorical basic truths unfettered by associations with particular genders, races, classes, or cultures. The rejection of subjectivity, unintentionally but nevertheless, colludes with this "generic human" thesis of classical liberal thought, that particularities of individuals are irrelevant and improper influences on knowledge. By designating individual particularities such as subjective experience as a social construct, post-structuralism's negation of the authority of the subject coincides nicely with the classical liberal's view that human particularities are irrelevant. (For the liberal, race, class, and gender are ultimately irrelevant to questions of justice and truth because "underneath we are all the same." For the post-structuralist, race, class, and gender are constructs and, therefore, incapable of decisively validating conceptions of justice and truth because underneath there lies no natural core to build on or liberate or maximize. Hence, once again, underneath we are all the same.) It is, in fact, a desire to topple this commitment to the possibility of a worldview – purported in fact as the best of all possible worldviews – grounded in a generic human, that motivates much of the cultural feminist glorification of femininity as a valid specificity legitimately grounding feminist theory.[36]

(1988)

Notes

27 Jacques Derrida, *Spurs*, trans. Barbara Harlow (Chicago: University of Chicago Press, 1978), 49.
28 Ibid., 51.
29 Biddy Martin, "Feminism, Criticism, and Foucault," *New German Critique* 27 (1982): 11.
30 Julia Kristeva, "Woman Can Never Be Defined," in *New French Feminisms*, ed. Elaine Marks and Isabelle de Courtivron (New York: Schocken, 1981), 137 (my italics).
31 Julia Kristeva, "Oscillation between Power and Denial," in Marks and Courtivron, eds., 166.
32 Martin, 16–17.
33 Ibid., esp. 21, 24, and 28.
34 See Derrida, *Spurs*, esp. 57 and 97.

35 Martin's most recent work departs from this in a positive direction. In an essay coauthored with Chandra Talpade Mohanty, Martin points out "the political limitations of an insistence on 'indeterminacy' which implicitly, when not explicitly, denies the critic's own situatedness in the social, and in effect refuses to acknowledge the critic's own institutional home." Martin and Mohanty seek to develop a more positive, though still problematized, conception of the subject as having a "multiple and shifting" perspective. In this, their work becomes a significant contribution toward the development of an alternative conception of subjectivity, a conception not unlike the one that I will discuss in the rest of this essay ("Feminist Politics: What's Home Got to Do with It?" in Lauretis, ed. [n. 18 above], 191–212, esp. 194).

36 A wonderful exchange on this between persuasive and articulate representatives of both sides was printed in *Diacritics* (Peggy Kamuf, "Replacing Feminist Criticism," *Diacritics* 12 [1982]: 42–47; and Nancy Miller, "The Text's Heroine: A Feminist Critic and Her Fictions," *Diacritics* 12 [1982]: 48–53).

TERESA DE LAURETIS

'Upping the Anti (Sic) in Feminist Theory' Conflicts in Feminism

The title of Alcoff's essay, "Cultural Feminism versus Post-structuralism: The Identity Crisis in Feminist Theory," bespeaks some of the same problems: a manner of thinking by mutually oppositional categories, an agonistic frame of argumentation, and a focus on division, a "crisis in feminist theory" that may be read not only as a crisis *over* identity, a metacritical doubt and a dispute among feminists as to the notion of identity, but also as a crisis *of* identity, of self-definition, implying a theoretical impasse for feminism as a whole. The essay, however, is more discerning, goes much further than its title suggests, and even contradicts it in the end, as the notion of identity, far from fixing the point of an impasse, becomes an active shifter in the feminist discourse of woman.[5]

Taking as its starting point "the concept of woman," or rather, its redefinition in feminist theory ("the dilemma facing feminist theorists today is that our very self-definition is grounded in a concept that we must deconstruct and deessentialize in all of its aspects"), Alcoff finds two major categories of responses to the dilemma, or what I would call the paradox of woman (p. 406). Cultural feminists, she claims, "have not challenged the defining of woman but only that definition given by men" (p. 407), and have replaced it with what they believe a more accurate description and appraisal, "the concept of the essential female" (p. 408). On the other hand, the poststructuralist response has been to reject the possibility of defining woman altogether and to replace "the politics of gender or sexual difference . . . with a plurality of difference where gender loses its position of significance" (p. 407). A third category is suggested, but only indirectly, in Alcoff's unwillingness to include among cultural feminists certain writers of color such as Moraga and Lorde in spite of their emphasis on cultural identity, for in her view "their work has consistently rejected essentialist conceptions of gender" (p. 412). Why an emphasis on racial, ethnic, and/or sexual identity need not be seen as essentialist is discussed more fully later in the essay with regard to identity politics and in conjunction with a third trend in feminist theory which Alcoff sees as a new course for feminism, "a theory of the gendered subject that does not slide into essentialism" (p. 422).

Whereas the narrative structure underlying Weedon's account of feminist theories is that of a contest where one actor successively engages and defeats or conquers several rivals, Alcoff's develops as a dialectics. Both the culturalist and the poststructuralist positions display internal contradictions: for example, not all cultural feminists "give explicitly essentialist formulations of what it means to be a woman" (p. 411), and their emphasis on the affirmation of women's strength and positive cultural roles and attributes has done much to counter images of woman as victim or of woman as male when in a business suit; but insofar as it reinforces the essentialist explanations of those attributes that are part and parcel of the traditional notion of woman-hood, cultural feminism may, and for some women does, foster another form of sexist oppression. Conversely, if the post-structuralist critique of the unified, authentic subject of humanism is more than compatible with the feminist project to "deconstruct and de-essentialize" woman (as Alcoff puts it, in clearly poststructuralist terms), its absolute rejection of gender and its negation of biological determinism in favor of a cultural-discursive determi-nism result, as concerns women, in a form of nominalism. If "woman" is a fiction, a locus of pure difference and resistance to logocentric power, and if there are no women as such, then the very issue of women's oppression would appear to be obsolete and feminism itself would have no reason to exist (which, it may be noted, is a corollary of poststructuralism and the stated position of those who call themselves "post-feminists"). "What can we demand in the name of women," Alcoff asks, "if 'women' do not exist and demands in their name simply reinforce the myth that they do?" (p. 420).

The way out – let me say, the sublation – of the contradictions in which are caught these two mainstream feminist views lies in "a theory of the subject that avoids both essentialism and nominalism" (p. 421), and Alcoff points to it in the work of a few theorists, "a few brave souls," whom she rejoins in developing her notion of "woman as positionality": "woman is a position from which a feminist politics can emerge rather than a set of attributes that are 'objectively identifiable' " (pp. 134–435). In becoming feminist, for instance, women take up a position, a point of perspective, from which to interpret or (re)construct values and meanings. That position is also a politically assumed identity, and one relative to their sociohistorical location, whereas essentialist definitions would have woman's identity or attributes independent of her external situation; however, the positions available to women in any sociohis-torical location are neither arbitrary nor undecidable. Thus, Alcoff concludes,

> If we combine the concept of identity politics with a conception of the subject as positionality, we can conceive of the subject as nonessentialized and emergent from a historical experience and yet retain our political ability to take gender as an important point of departure. Thus we can say at one and the same time that gender is not natural, biological, universal, ahistorical, or essential and yet still claim that gender is relevant because we are taking gender as a position from which to act politically. (p. 433)

I am, of course, in agreement with her emphases on issues and arguments that have been central in my work, such as the necessity to theorize experience in relation to practices, the understanding of gendered subjectivity as "an emergent property of a historicized experience" (p. 431), and the notion that identity is an active construction and a discursively mediated political interpretation of one's history. What I must ask, and less as a criticism of Alcoff's essay than for the purposes of my argument here, is: why is it still necessary to set up two opposing categories, cultural feminism and poststructuralism, or essentialism and anti-essentialism, thesis and antithesis, when one has already achieved the vantage point of a theoretical position that overtakes them or sublates them?

Doesn't the insistence on the "essentialism" of cultural feminists reproduce and keep in the foreground an image of "dominant" feminism that is at least reductive, at best tautological or superseded, and at worst not in our interests? Doesn't it feed the pernicious opposition of low versus high theory, a low-grade type of critical thinking (feminism) that is contrasted with the high-test theoretical grade of a poststructuralism from which some feminists would have been smart enough to learn? As one feminist theorist who's been concurrently involved with feminism, women's studies, psychoanalytic theory, structuralism, and film theory from the beginning of my critical activity, I know that learning to be a feminist has grounded, or embodied, all of my learning and so en-gendered thinking and knowing itself. That engendered thinking and that embodied, situated knowledge (in Donna Haraway's phrase)[6] are the stuff of feminist theory, whether by "feminist theory" is meant one of a growing number of feminist critical discourses – on culture, science, subjectivity, writing, visual representation, social institutions, etc. – or, more particularly, the critical elaboration of feminist thought itself and the ongoing (re)definition of its specific difference. In either case, feminist theory is not of a lower grade than that which some call "male theory," but different in kind; and it is its essential difference, the essence of that triangle, that concerns me here as a theorist of feminism.

Why then, I ask again, continue to constrain it in the terms of essentialism and anti-essentialism even as they no longer serve (but did they ever?) to formulate our questions? For example, in her discussion of cultural feminism, Alcoff accepts another critic's characterization despite some doubt that the latter "makes it appear too homogeneous and . . . the charge of essentialism is on shaky ground" (p. 411). Then she adds:

> In the absence of a clearly stated position on the ultimate source of gender difference, Echols *infers* from their emphasis on building a feminist free-space and woman-centered culture that cultural feminists hold some version of essentialism. I share Echols's *suspicion*. Certainly, *it is difficult to render the views of Rich and Daly into a coherent whole without supplying a missing premise* that there is an innate female essence. (p. 412; emphasis added)

But why do it at all? What is the purpose, or the gain, of supplying a missing premise (innate female essence) in order to construct a coherent image of feminism which thus becomes available to charges (essentialism) based on the very premise that had to be supplied? What motivates such a project, the suspicion, and the inferences?

(1990)

Notes

5 Since Alcoff refers extensively to my own work, this essay is in a sense a dialogue with her and with myself – that dialogue in feminist critical writing which often works as a variation of consciousness raising or better, its transformation into a significant form of feminist cultural practice, and one not always reducible to "academic" activity.

6 Donna Haraway, "Situated Knowledges: The Science Question in Feminism and the Privilege of Partial Perspective," *Feminist Studies* 14, no. 3 (Fall 1988): 575–99.

DIANA FUSS

Essentially Speaking: Feminism, Nature and Difference

Despite the uncertainty and confusion surrounding the sign "essence," more than one influential theorist has advocated that perhaps we cannot do without recourse to irreducibilities. One thinks of Stephen Heath's by now famous suggestion, "the risk of essence may have to be taken" ("Difference" [*Screen* vol. 19, no. 3] 1978, 99). It is poststructuralist feminists who seem most intrigued by this call to risk essence. Alice Jardine, for example, finds Stephen Heath's proclamation (later echoed by Gayatri Spivak) to be "one of the most thought-provoking statements of recent date" ("Men in Feminism: Odor di Uomo Or Compagnons de Route?" in Jardine and Smith, [*Men in Feminism*, London, Methuen] 1987, 58). But not all poststructuralist feminists are as comfortable with the prospect of re-opening theory's Pandora's box of essentialism. Peggy Kamuf warns that calls to risk essentialism may in the end be no more than veiled defenses against the unsettling operations of decon-struction:

How is one supposed to understand essence as a *risk* to be run when it is by definition the non-accidental and therefore hardly the apt term to represent danger or risk? Only over against and in impatient reaction to the deconstruction of the subject can "essence" be made to sound excitingly dangerous and the phrase "the risk of essence" can seem to offer such an appealing invitation.... "Go for it," the phrase incites. "If you fall into 'essence,' you can always say it was an accident." ("Femmeninism," in Jardine and Smith 1987, 96)

In Kamuf's mind, risking essence is really no risk at all; it is merely a clever way of preserving the metaphysical safety net should we lose our balance walking the perilous tightrope of deconstruction.

But the call to risk essence is not merely an "impatient reaction" to deconstruction (though it might indeed be this in certain specific instances); it can also operate as a deconstructionist strategy. "Is not strategy itself the real risk?" Derrida asks in his seminar on feminism ("Women in the Beehive," in Jardine and Smith 1987, 192). To the deconstructionist, strategy of any kind is a risk because its effects, its outcome, are always unpredictable and undecidable. Depending on the historical moment and the cultural context, a strategy can be "radically revolutionary or deconstructive" or it can be "dangerously reactive" (193). What is risky is giving up the security – and the fantasy – of occupying a single subject-position and instead occupying two places at once. In a word, "we have to negotiate" (202). For an example of this particular notion of "risk" we can turn to Derrida's own attempts to dare to speak as woman. For a male subject to speak as woman can be radically de-essentializing; the transgression suggests that "woman" is a social space which any sexed subject can fill. But because Derrida never specifies *which* woman he speaks as (a French bourgeois woman, an Anglo-American lesbian, and so on), the strategy to speak as woman is simultaneously re-essentializing. The risk lies in the difficult negotiation between these apparently contradictory effects.

It must be pointed out here that the constructionist strategy of specifying more precisely these sub-categories of "woman" does not necessarily preclude essentialism. "French bourgeois woman" or "Anglo-American lesbian," while crucially emphasizing in their very specificity that "woman" is by no means a monolithic category, nonetheless reinscribe an essentialist logic at the very level of historicism. Historicism is not always an effective counter to essentialism if it succeeds only in fragmenting the subject into multiple identities, each with its own self-contained, self-referential essence. The constructionist impulse to specify, rather than definitively counteracting essentialism, often simply redeploys it through the very strategy of historicization, rerouting and dispersing it through a number of micropolitical units or sub-categorical classifications, each presupposing its own unique interior composition or metaphysical core.

There is an important distinction to be made, I would submit, between "deploying" or "activating" essentialism and "falling into" or "lapsing into" essentialism. "Falling into" or "lapsing into" implies that essentialism is inherently reactionary – inevitably and inescapably a problem or a mistake.[14] "Deploying" or "activating," on the other hand, implies that essentialism may have some strategic or interventionary value. What I am suggesting is that the political investments of the sign "essence" are predicated on the subject's complex positioning in a particular social field, and that the appraisal of this investment depends not on any interior values intrinsic to the sign itself but rather on the shifting and determinative discursive relations which produced it. As subsequent chapters will more forcefully suggest, the radicality or conservatism of essentialism depends, to a significant degree, on *who* is utilizing it, *how* it is deployed, and *where* its effects are concentrated.

It is important not to forget that essence is a sign, and as such historically contingent and constantly subject to change and to redefinition. Historically, we have never been very confident of the definition of essence, nor have we been very certain that the definition of essence is to *be* the definitional. Even the essence/accident distinction, the inaugural moment of Western metaphysics, is by no means a stable or secure binarism. The entire history of metaphysics can be read as an interminable pursuit of the essence of essence, motivated by the anxiety that essence may well be accidental, changing and unknowable. Essentialism is not, and has rarely been, monolithically coded. Certainly it is difficult to identify a single philosopher whose work does not attempt to account for the question of essentialism in some way; the repeated attempts by these philosophers to fix or to define essence suggest that essence is a slippery and elusive category, and that the sign itself does not remain stationary or uniform.

The deconstruction of essentialism, rather than putting essence to rest, simply raises the discussion to a more sophisticated level, leaps the analysis up to another higher register, above all, keeps the sign of essence in play, even if (indeed *because*) it is continually held under erasure. Constructionists, then, need to be wary of too quickly crying "essentialism." Perhaps the most dangerous problem for anti-essentialists is to see the category of essence as "always already" knowable, as immediately apparent and naturally transparent. Similarly, we need to beware of the tendency to "naturalize" the category of the natural, to see this category, too, as obvious and immediately perceptible *as such*. Essentialism may be at once more intractable and more irrecuperable than we thought; it may be essential to our thinking while at the same time there is nothing "quintessential" about it. To insist that essentialism is always and everywhere reactionary is, for the constructionist, to buy into essentialism in the very act of making the charge; *it is to act as if essentialism has an essence.*

(1989)

Note

14 Toril Moi's *Sexual/Textual Politics* provides a particularly good example of how this locution can
   be used to dismiss entire schools of feminist thought – in Moi's case, to discredit "Anglo-American" feminism. Moi's sweeping criticism of writers as diverse as Elaine Showalter, Myra Jehlen,
   Annette Kolodny, Sandra Gilbert, and Susan Gubar consists mainly in mapping out in detail the
   points in which their analyses "slip into" essentialism and therefore "reinscribe patriarchal
   humanism." Such an ostensibly anti-essentialist critique can only be built on the grounds of the
   twin assumptions that essentialism is, in essence, "patriarchal" and that "patriarchal humanism"
   has an essence which is inherently, inevitably reactionary.

CHANDRA TALPADE MOHANTY

'*Under Western Eyes: Feminist Scholarship and Colonial Discourses*'
Third World Women and the Politics of Feminism

Any discussion of the intellectual and political construction of "third world
feminisms" must address itself to two simultaneous projects: the internal
critique of hegemonic "Western" feminisms, and the formulation of autonomous, geographically, historically, and culturally grounded feminist concerns
and strategies. The first project is one of deconstructing and dismantling; the
second, one of building and constructing. While these projects appear to be
contradictory, the one working negatively and the other positively, unless
these two tasks are addressed simultaneously, "third world" feminisms run
the risk of marginalization or ghettoization from both mainstream (right and
left) and Western feminist discourses.

It is to the first project that I address myself. What I wish to analyze is
specifically the production of the "third world woman" as a singular
monolithic subject in some recent (Western) feminist texts. The definition of
colonization I wish to invoke here is a predominantly *discursive* one, focusing
on a certain mode of appropriation and codification of "scholarship" and
"knowledge" about women in the third world by particular analytic categories
employed in specific writings on the subject which take as their referent
feminist interests as they have been articulated in the U.S. and Western
Europe. If one of the tasks of formulating and understanding the locus of
"third world feminisms" is delineating the way in which it resists and *works
against* what I am referring to as "Western feminist discourse," an analysis of
the discursive construction of "third world women" in Western feminism is
an important first step.

Clearly Western feminist discourse and political practice is neither singular
nor homogeneous in its goals, interests, or analyses. However, it is possible to
trace a coherence of *effects* resulting from the implicit assumption of "the
West" (in all its complexities and contradictions) as the primary referent in

theory and praxis. My reference to "Western feminism" is by no means intended to imply that it is a monolith. Rather, I am attempting to draw attention to the similar effects of various textual strategies used by writers which codify Others as non-Western and hence themselves as (implicitly) Western. It is in this sense that I use the term *Western feminist*. Similar arguments can be made in terms of middle-class urban African or Asian scholars producing scholarship on or about their rural or working-class sisters which assumes their own middle-class cultures as the norm, and codifies working-class histories and cultures as Other. Thus, while this essay focuses specifically on what I refer to as "Western feminist" discourse on women in the third world, the critiques I offer also pertain to third world scholars writing about their own cultures, which employ identical analytic strategies.

It ought to be of some political significance, at least, that the term *colonization* has come to denote a variety of phenomena in recent feminist and left writings in general. From its analytic value as a category of exploitative economic exchange in both traditional and contemporary Marxisms (cf. particularly contemporary theorists such as Baran [*The Political Economy of Growth*, New York, Monthly Review Press] 1962, Amin [*Imperialism and Unequal Development*, New York, Monthly Review Press] 1977, and Gunder-Frank [*Capitalism and Underdevelopment in Latin America*, New York, Monthly Review Press] 1967) to its use by feminist women of color in the U.S. to describe the appropriation of their experiences and struggles by hegemonic white women's movements (cf. especially Moraga and Anzaldúa [*Back: Writings by Radical Women of Color*, New York, Kitchen Table Press] 1983, Smith [*Home Girls: A Black Feminist Anthology*, New York, Kitchen Table Press] 1983, Joseph and Lewis [*Common Differences: Conflicts in Black and White Feminist Perspectives*, Boston, Beacon Press] 1981, and Moraga [*Loving in the War Years*, Boston, South End Press] 1984), colonization has been used to characterize everything from the most evident economic and political hierarchies to the production of a particular cultural discourse about what is called the "third world."[1] However sophisticated or problematical its use as an explanatory construct, colonization almost invariably implies a relation of structural domination, and a suppression – often violent – of the heterogeneity of the subject(s) in question.

My concern about such writings derives from my own implication and investment in contemporary debates in feminist theory, and the urgent political necessity (especially in the age of Reagan/Bush) of forming strategic coalitions across class, race, and national boundaries. The analytic principles discussed below serve to distort Western feminist political practices, and limit the possibility of coalitions among (usually white) Western feminists and working-class feminists and feminists of color around the world. These limitations are evident in the construction of the (implicitly consensual) priority of issues around which apparently *all* women are expected to organize. The necessary and integral connection between feminist scholarship and feminist political practice and organizing determines the significance and status of Western feminist writings on women in the third world, for feminist scholarship, like most other kinds of scholarship, is not the mere production of knowledge about a certain subject. It is a directly political and discursive *practice* in that it is purposeful and ideological. It is best seen as a mode of intervention into particular hegemonic discourses (for example, traditional anthropology, sociology, literary criticism, etc.); it is a political praxis which counters and resists the totalizing imperative of age-old "legitimate" and "scientific" bodies of knowledge. Thus, feminist scholarly practices (whether reading, writing, critical, or textual) are inscribed in relations of power – relations which they counter, resist, or even perhaps implicitly support. There can, of course, be no apolitical scholarship.

The relationship between "Woman" – a cultural and ideological composite Other constructed through diverse representational discourses (scientific, literary, juridical, linguistic, cinematic, etc.) – and "women" – real, material subjects of their collective histories – is one of the central questions the practice of feminist scholarship seeks to address. This connection between women as historical subjects and the re-presentation of Woman produced by hegemonic discourses is not a relation of direct identity, or a relation of correspondence or simple implication.[2] It is an arbitrary relation set up by particular cultures. I would like to suggest that the feminist writings I analyze here discursively colonize the material and historical heterogeneities of the lives of women in the third world, thereby producing/re-presenting a composite, singular "third world woman" – an image which appears arbitrarily constructed, but nevertheless carries with it the authorizing signature of Western humanist discourse.[3]

I argue that assumptions of privilege and ethnocentric universality, on the one hand, and inadequate self-consciousness about the effect of Western scholarship on the "third world" in the context of a world system dominated by the West, on the other, characterize a sizable extent of Western feminist work on women in the third world. An analysis of "sexual difference" in the form of a cross-culturally singular, monolithic notion of patriarchy or male dominance leads to the construction of a similarly reductive and homogeneous notion of what I call the "third world difference" – that stable, ahistorical something that apparently oppresses most if not all the women in these countries. And it is in the production of this "third world difference" that Western feminisms appropriate and "colonize" the constitutive complexities which characterize the lives of women in these countries. It is in this process of discursive homogenization and systematization of the oppression of women in the third world that power is exercised in much of recent Western feminist discourse, and this power needs to be defined and named.

In the context of the West's hegemonic position today, of what Anouar Abdel-Malek ([*Social Dialectics*, State University of New York Press] 1981) calls a struggle for "control over the orientation, regulation and decision of the process of world development on the basis of the advanced sector's monopoly of scientific knowledge and ideal creativity," Western feminist scholarship on the third world must be seen and examined precisely in terms of its inscription in these particular relations of power and struggle. There is, it should be evident, no universal patriarchal framework which this scholarship attempts to counter and resist – unless one posits an international male conspiracy or a monolithic, ahistorical power structure. There is, however, a particular world balance of power within which any analysis of culture, ideology, and socioeconomic conditions necessarily has to be situated. Abdel-Malek is useful here again, in reminding us about the inherence of politics in the discourses of "culture":

> Contemporary imperialism is, in a real sense, a hegemonic imperialism, exercising to a maximum degree a rationalized violence taken to a higher level than ever before – through fire and sword, but also through the attempt to control hearts and minds. For its content is defined by the combined action of the military-industrial complex and the hegemonic cultural centers of the West, all of them founded on the advanced levels of development attained by monopoly and finance capital, and supported by the benefits of both the scientific and technological revolution and the second industrial revolution itself. (145–46)

Western feminist scholarship cannot avoid the challenge of situating itself and examining its role in such a global economic and political framework. To do any less would be to ignore the complex interconnections between first and third world economies and the profound effect of this on the lives of women in all countries. I do not question the descriptive and informative value of most Western feminist writings on women in the third world. I also do not question the existence of excellent work which does not fall into the analytic traps with which I am concerned. In fact I deal with an example of such work later on. In the context of an overwhelming silence about the experiences of women in these countries, as well as the need to forge international links between women's political struggles, such work is both pathbreaking and absolutely essential. However, it is both to the *explanatory potential* of particular analytic strategies employed by such writing, and to their *political effect* in the context of the hegemony of Western scholarship that I want to draw attention here. While feminist writing in the U.S. is still marginalized (except from the point of view of women of color addressing privileged white women), Western feminist writing on women in the third world must be considered in the context of the global hegemony of Western scholarship – i.e., the production, publication, distribution, and consumption of information and ideas. Marginal or not, this writing has political effects and implications beyond the immediate feminist or disciplinary audience. One such significant effect of the dominant "representations" of Western feminism is its conflation with imperialism in the eyes of particular third world women.[4] Hence the urgent need to examine the *political* implications of our *analytic* strategies and principles.

My critique is directed at three basic analytic principles which are present in (Western) feminist discourse on women in the third world. Since I focus primarily on the Zed Press Women in the Third World series, my comments on Western feminist discourse are circumscribed by my analysis of the texts in this series.[5] This is a way of focusing my critique. However, even though I am dealing with feminists who identify themselves as culturally or geographically from the "West," as mentioned earlier, what I say about these presuppositions or implicit principles holds for anyone who uses these methods, whether third world women in the West, or third world women in the third world writing on these issues and publishing in the West. Thus, I am not making a culturalist argument about ethnocentrism; rather, I am trying to uncover how ethnocentric universalism is produced in certain analyses. As a matter of fact, my argument holds for any discourse that sets up its own authorial subjects as the implicit referent, i.e., the yardstick by which to encode and represent cultural Others. It is in this move that power is exercised in discourse.

The first analytic presupposition I focus on is involved in the strategic location of the category "women" vis-à-vis the context of analysis. The assumption of women as an already constituted, coherent group with identical interests and desires, regardless of class, ethnic or racial location, or contradictions, implies a notion of gender or sexual difference or even patriarchy which can be applied universally and cross-culturally. (The context of analysis can be anything from kinship structures and the organization of labor to media representations.) The second analytical presupposition is evident on the methodological level, in the uncritical way "proof" of universality and cross-cultural validity are provided. The third is a more specifically political presupposition underlying the methodologies and the analytic strategies, i.e., the model of power and struggle they imply and suggest. I argue that as a result of the two modes – or, rather, frames – of analysis described above, a homogeneous notion of the oppression of women as a group is assumed, which, in turn, produces the image of an "average third world woman." This average third world woman leads an essentially truncated life based on her feminine gender (read: sexually constrained) and her being "third world" (read: ignorant, poor, uneducated, tradition-bound, domestic, family-oriented, victimized, etc.). This, I suggest, is in contrast to the (implicit) self-representation of Western women as educated, as modern, as having control over their own bodies and sexualities, and the freedom to make their own decisions.

The distinction between Western feminist re-presentation of women in the third world and Western feminist self-presentation is a distinction of the same order as that made by some Marxists between the "maintenance" function of the housewife and the real "productive" role of wage labor, or the characterization by developmentalists of the third world as being engaged in the lesser production of "raw materials" in contrast to the "real" productive activity of the first world. These distinctions are made on the basis of the privileging of a particular group as the norm or referent. Men involved in wage labor, first world producers, and, I suggest, Western feminists who sometimes cast third world women in terms of "ourselves undressed" (Michelle Rosaldo's [1980] term), all construct themselves as the normative referent in such a binary analytic.

(1991)

Notes

This essay would not have been possible without S. P. Mohanty's challenging and careful reading. I would also like to thank Biddy Martin for our numerous discussions about feminist theory and politics. They both helped me think through some of the arguments herein.

1 Terms such as *third* and *first world* are very problematic both in suggesting oversimplified similarities between and among countries labeled thus, and in implicitly reinforcing existing economic, cultural, and ideological hierarchies which are conjured up in using such terminology. I use the term "*third world*" with full awareness of its problems, only because this is the terminology available to us at the moment. The use of quotation marks is meant to suggest a continuous questioning of the designation. Even when I do not use quotation marks, I mean to use the term critically.

2 I am indebted to Teresa de Lauretis for this particular formulation of the project of feminist theorizing. See especially her introduction in de Lauretis, *Alice Doesn't: Feminism, Semiotics, Cinema* (Bloomington: Indiana University Press, 1984); see also Sylvia Wynter, "The Politics of Domination," unpublished manuscript.

3 This argument is similar to Homi Bhabha's definition of colonial discourse as strategically creating a space for a subject people through the production of knowledges and the exercise of power. The full quote reads: "[colonial discourse is] an apparatus of power. . . . an apparatus that turns on the recognition and disavowal of racial/cultural/historical differences. Its predominant strategic function is the creation of a space for a subject people through the production of knowledges in terms of which surveillance is exercised and a complex form of pleasure/unpleasure is incited. It (i.e. colonial discourse) seeks authorization for its strategies by the production of knowledges by coloniser and colonised which are stereotypical but antithetically evaluated" (1983, 23).

4 A number of documents and reports on the UN International Conferences on Women, Mexico City, 1975, and Copenhagen, 1980, as well as the 1976 Wellesley Conference on Women and Development, attest to this. Nawal el Saadawi, Fatima Mernissi, and Mallica Vajarathon (1978) characterize this conference as "American-planned and organized," situating third world participants as passive audiences. They focus especially on the lack of self-consciousness of Western women's implication in the effects of imperialism and racism in their assumption of an "international sisterhood." A recent essay by Valerie Amos and Pratibha Parmar (1984) characterizes as "imperial" Euro-American feminism which seeks to establish itself as the only legitimate feminism.

5 The Zed Press Women in the Third World series is unique in its conception. I choose to focus on it because it is the only contemporary series I have found which assumes that "women in the third world" are a legitimate and separate subject of study and research. Since 1985, when this essay was first written, numerous new titles have appeared in the Women in the Third World

series. Thus, I suspect that Zed has come to occupy a rather privileged position in the dissemination and construction of discourses by and about third world women. A number of the books in this series are excellent, especially those which deal directly with women's resistance struggles. In addition, Zed Press consistently publishes progressive feminist, antiracist, and antiimperialist texts. However, a number of the texts written by feminist sociologists, anthropologists, and journalists are symptomatic of the kind of Western feminist work on women in the third world that concerns me. Thus, an analysis of a few of these particular works in this series can serve as a representative point of entry into the discourse I am attempting to locate and define. My focus on these texts is therefore an attempt at an internal critique: I simply expect and demand more from this series. Needless to say, progressive publishing houses also carry their own authorizing signatures.

TRINH T. MINH-HA

Woman, Native, Other: Writing Postcoloniality and Feminism

Words manipulated at will. As you can see, "difference" is essentially "division" in the understanding of many. It is no more than a tool of self-defense and conquest. You and I might as well not walk into this semantic trap which sets us up against each other as expected by a certain ideology of separatism. Have you read the grievances some of our sisters express on being among the few women chosen for a "Special Third World Women's Issue" or on being the only Third World Woman at readings, workshops, and meetings? It is as if everywhere we go, we become Someone's private zoo. Gayatri Chakravorty Spivak spoke of their remarking "the maids upstairs in the guest quarters were women of color" in a symposium;[7] Gloria Anzaldúa, of their using her as a token woman and her friend Nellie Wong as a "purveyor of resource lists";[8] Mitsuye Yamada, of having to start from scratch each time, as if she were "speaking to a brand new audience of people who had never known an Asian Pacific woman who is other than the passive, sweet, etc., stereotype of the 'Oriental' woman";[9] Audre Lorde, of the lack of interracial cooperation between academic feminists whose sole explanation for the issue remains: "We did not know who to ask";[10] and Alice Walker, of the necessity of learning to discern the true feminist – "for whom racism is inherently an impossibility" – from the white female opportunist – "for whom racism, inasmuch as it assures white privilege, is an accepted way of life."[11] The decision you and I are called upon to make is fraught with far-reaching consequences. On the one hand, it is difficult for us to sit at table with them (the master and/or his substitutes) without feeling that our presence, like that of the "native" (who happens to be invited) among the anthropologists, serves to mask the refined sexist and/or racist tone of their discourse, reinforcing thereby its pretentions to universality. Given the permanent status of "foreign workers," we – like the South African blacks who are allowed to toil on white territories as "migrants," but are gotten rid of and resettled to the homeland area as soon as they become unprofitable labor units – continue in most cases to be treated as "temporary sojourners," even though we may spend our whole lifetime by their side pleading a common cause.

> the white rancher told Chato he was too old to work for him any more, and Chato and his old woman should be out of the shack by the next afternoon because the rancher had hired new people to work there. That had satisfied her. To see how the white man repaid Chato's years of loyalty and work. All of Chato's fine-sounding English didn't change things.[12]

The lines are an excerpt from Leslie Marmon Silko's "Lullaby." From the South African reserve to the American Laguna Pueblo Reservation, the story changes its backdrops but remains recognizable in the master's indifference to the lot of his non-European workers. Yet, on the other hand, you and I acquiesce in reviving the plot of the story, hoping thereby that our participation from the inside will empower us to act upon the very course of its events. Fools? It all depends on how sharply we hone ourselves on the edge of reality; and, I venture to say, we do it enough to never lose sight of our distinct actualities. Silence as a refusal to partake in the story does sometimes provide us with a means to gain a hearing. It is voice, a mode of uttering, and a response in its own right. Without other silences, however, my silence goes unheard, unnoticed; it is simply one voice less, or more point given to the silencers. Thus, no invitation is declined except in particular circumstances where we feel it is necessary to do so for our own well-being. What does it matter who the sponsor is? Every opportunity is fitted for consciousness raising; to reject it is almost tantamount to favoring apartheid ideology. White and black stand apart (armed legislation versus tribal law) and never the twain shall meet. There the matter rests. Crossed fears continue to breed wars, for they feed endlessly on each other until no conversation can possibly be carried out without heaping up misunderstandings. It is, indeed, much easier to dismiss or eliminate on the pretext of difference (destroy the other in our minds, in our world) than to live fearlessly with and within difference(s).

[. . .]

Woman can never be defined. Bat, dog, chick, mutton, tart. Queen, madam, lady of pleasure. MISTRESS. *Belle-de-nuit*, woman of the streets, girl. Lady and whore are both bred to please. The old Woman image-repertoire says She is a Womb, a mere baby's pouch, or "nothing but sexuality." She is a passive substance, a parasite, an enigma whose mystery proves to be a snare and a delusion. She wallows in night, disorder, and immanence and is at the same time the "disturbing factor (between men)" and the key to the beyond. The further the repertoire unfolds its images, the more entangled it gets in its attempts at capturing Her. "Truth, Beauty, Poetry – she is All: once more all under the form of the Other. All except herself,"[27] Simone De Beauvoir wrote. Yet, even with or because of Her capacity to embody All, Woman is the lesser man, and among male athletes, to be called a woman is still resented as the worst of insults. "Wo-" appended to "man" in sexist contexts is not unlike "Third World," "Third," "minority," or "*color*" affixed to *woman* in pseudo-feminist contexts. Yearning for universality, the generic "woman," like its counterpart, the generic "man," tends to efface difference within itself. Not every female is "a real woman," one knows this through hearsay . . . Just as "man" provides an example of how the part played by women has been ignored, undervalued, distorted, or omitted through the use of terminology presumed to be generic, "woman" more often than not reflects the subtle power of linguistic exclusion, for its set of referents rarely includes those relevant to Third World "female persons." "All the Women Are White, All the Blacks are Men, But Some of Us Are Brave" is the title given to an anthology edited by Gloria T. Hull, Patricia Bell Scott, and Barbara Smith. It is, indeed, somehow devious to think that WOMAN also encompasses the Chinese with bound feet, the genitally mutilated Africans, and the one thousand Indians who committed *suttee* for one royal male. Sister Cinderella's foot is also enviably tiny but never crooked! And, European witches were also burnt to purify the body of Christ, but they do not pretend to "self-immolation." "Third World," therefore, belongs to a category apart, a "special" one that is meant to be both complimentary and complementary, for First and Second went out of fashion, leaving a serious Lack behind to be filled.

Third World?

To survive, "Third World" must necessarily have negative *and* positive connotations: negative when viewed in a vertical ranking system – "underdeveloped" compared to over-industrialized, "underprivileged" within the already Second sex – and positive when understood sociopolitically as a subversive, "non-aligned" force. Whether "Third World" sounds negative or positive also depends on *who* uses it. Coming from you Westerners, the word can hardly mean the same as when it comes from Us members of the Third World. Quite predictably, you/we who condemn it most are both we who buy in and they who deny any participation in the bourgeois mentality of the West. For it was in the context of such mentality that "Third World" stood out as a new semantic finding to designate what was known as "the savages" before the Independences. Today, hegemony is much more subtle, much more pernicious than the form of blatant racism once exercised by the colonial West. I/i always find myself asking, in this one-dimensional society, where I/i should draw the line between tracking down the oppressive mechanisms of the system and aiding their spread. "Third World" commonly refers to those states in Africa, Asia and Latin America which called themselves "non-aligned," that is to say, affiliated with neither the Western (capitalist) nor the Eastern (communist) power blocs. Thus, if "Third World" is often rejected for its judged-to-be-derogative connotations, it is not so much because of the hierarchical, first-second-third order implied, as some invariably repeat, but because of the growing threat "Third World" consistently presents to the Western bloc the last few decades. The emergence of repressed voices into the worldwide political arena has already prompted her (Julia Kristeva) to ask: "How will the West greet the awakening of the 'third world' as the Chinese call it? Can we [Westerners] participate, actively and lucidly, in this awakening when the center of the planet is in the process of moving toward the East?"[28] Exploited, looked down upon, and lumped together in a convenient term that denies their individualities, a group of "poor" (nations), having once sided with neither of the dominating forces, has slowly learned to turn this denial to the best account. "The Third World to Third World peoples" thus becomes an empowering tool, and one which politically includes all non-whites in their solidarist struggle against all forms of Western dominance. And since "Third World" now refers to more than the geographically and economically determined nations of the "South" (versus "North"), since the term comprises such "developed" countries as Japan and those which have opted for socialist reconstruction of their system (China, Cuba, Ethiopia, Angola, Mozambique) as well as those which have favored a capitalist mode of development (Nigeria, India, Brazil), there no longer exists such a thing as a unified unaligned Third World bloc. Moreover, Third World has moved West (or North, depending on where the dividing line falls) and has expanded so as to include even the remote parts of the First World. What is at stake is not only the hegemony of Western cultures, but also their identities as unified cultures. Third World dwells on diversity; so does First World. This is our strength and our misery. The West is painfully made to realize the existence of a Third World in the First World, and vice versa. The Master is bound to recognize that His Culture is not as homogeneous, as monolithic as He believed it to be. He discovers, with much reluctance, He is just an other among others.

Thus, whenever it is a question of "Third World women" or, more disquietingly, of "Third World Women in the U.S.," the reaction provoked among many whites almost never fails to be that of annoyance, irritation, or vexation. "Why Third World in the U.S.?" they say angrily; "You mean those who still have relatives in South East Asia?" "Third World! I don't understand how one can use such a term, it doesn't mean anything." Or even better, "Why use such a term to defeat yourself?" Alternatives like "Western" and "non-Western" or "Euro-American" and "non-Euro-American" may sound a bit less charged, but they are certainly neither neutral nor satisfactory, for they still take the dominant group as point of reference, and they reflect well the West's ideology of dominance (it is as if we were to use the term "non-Afro-Asian," for example, to designate all white peoples). More recently, we have been hearing of the Fourth World which, we are told, "is a world populated by indigenous people who still continue to bear a spiritual relationship to their traditional lands." The colonialist creed "Divide and Conquer" is here again, alive and well. Often ill at ease with the outspoken educated natives who represent the Third World in debates and paternalistic-ally scornful of those who remain reserved, the dominant thus decides to weaken this term of solidarity, both by invalidating it as empowering tool and by inciting divisiveness within the Third World – a Third World within the Third World. Aggressive Third World (educated "savages") with its aware-ness and resistance to domination must therefore be classified apart from gentle Fourth World (uneducated "savages"). Every unaligned voice should necessarily/consequently be either a personal or a minority voice. The (impersonal) majority, as logic dictates, has to be the (aligned) dominant.

> It is, apparently, inconvenient, if not downright mind stretching [notes Alice Walker], for white women scholars to think of black women as women, perhaps because "woman" (like "man" among white males) is a name they are claiming for themselves, and themselves alone. Racism decrees that if they are now women (years ago they were ladies, but fashions change) then black women must, perforce, be something else. (While they were "ladies" black women could be "women" and so on.)[29]

Another revealing example of this separatist majority mentality is the story Walker relates of an exhibit of women painters at the Brooklyn Museum: when asked "Are there no black women painters represented here?" (none of them is, apparently), a white woman feminist simply replies "It's a *women's* exhibit!"[30] Different historical contexts, different semantic contents . . .

(1989)

Notes

7 Gayatri Chakravorty Spivak, "The Politics of Interpretations," *Critical Inquiry* 9, no. 1 (1982), p. 278.
8 Gloria Anzaldúa, "Speaking in Tongues: A Letter to 3rd World Women Writers," *This Bridge*, pp. 167–68.
9 Mitsuye Yamada, "Asian Pacific American Women and Feminism," *This Bridge*, p. 71.
10 Lorde, "The Master's Tools . . .," p. 100.
11 Alice Walker, "One Child of One's Own: A Meaningful Digression Within the Work(s)," *The Writer on Her Work*, ed. J. Sternburg (New York: W. W. Norton, 1980), p. 137.
12 Leslie Marmon Silko, "Lullaby," *The Ethnic American Woman*, ed. E. Blicksilver (Dubuque, Iowa: Kendall/Hunt, 1978), p. 57.

[. . .]

27 Simone De Beauvoir, *The Second Sex* (1952, rpt. New York: Bantam, 1970), p. 223.
28 Julia Kristeva, "Woman Can Never Be Defined," trans. Marilyn A. August, *New French Feminism*, ed. E. Marks & I. De Courtivon (Amherst: Univ. of Massachusetts Press, 1980), p. 139.
29 "One Child of One's Own . . .," pp. 133–34.
30 Ibid., p. 136.

DONNA HARAWAY

'A Manifesto for Cyborgs: Science, Technology, and Socialist Feminism in the 1980s' Socialist Review

The cyborg is a creature in a post-gender world; it has no truck with bisexuality, pre-Oedipal symbiosis, unalienated labor, or other seductions to organic wholeness through a final appropriation of all the powers of the parts into a higher unity. In a sense, the cyborg has no origin story in the Western sense; a "final" irony since the cyborg is also the awful apocalyptic *telos* of the "West's" escalating dominations of abstract individuation, an ultimate self untied at last from all dependency, a man in space. An origin story in the "Western," humanist sense depends on the myth of original unity, fullness, bliss and terror, represented by the phallic mother from whom all humans must separate, the task of individual development and of history, the twin potent myths inscribed most powerfully for us in psychoanalysis and Marxism. Hilary Klein has argued that both Marxism and psychoanalysis, in their concepts of labor and of individuation and gender formation, depend on the plot of original unity out of which difference must be produced and enlisted in a drama of escalating domination of woman/nature. The cyborg skips the step of original unity, of identification with nature in the Western sense. This is its illegitimate promise that might lead to subversion of its teleology as star wars.

The cyborg is resolutely committed to partiality, irony, intimacy, and perversity. It is oppositional, utopian, and completely without innocence. No longer structured by the polarity of public and private, the cyborg defines a technological polis based partly on a revolution of social relations in the *oikos*, the household. Nature and culture are reworked; the one can no longer be the resource for appropriation or incorporation by the other. The relationships for forming wholes from parts, including those of polarity and hierarchical domination, are at issue in the cyborg world. Unlike the hopes of Frankenstein's monster, the cyborg does not expect its father to save it through a restoration of the garden; i.e., through the fabrication of a heterosexual mate, through its completion in a finished whole, a city and cosmos. The cyborg does not dream of community on the model of the organic family, this time without the Oedipal project. The cyborg would not recognize the Garden of Eden; it is not made of mud and cannot dream of returning to dust. Perhaps that is why I want to see if cyborgs can subvert the apocalypse of returning to nuclear dust in the manic compulsion to name the Enemy. Cyborgs are not reverent; they do not re-member the cosmos. They are wary of holism, but needy for connection – they seem to have a natural feel for united front politics, but without the vanguard party. The main trouble with cyborgs, of course, is that they are the illegitimate offspring of militarism and patriarchal capitalism, not to mention state socialism. But illegitimate offspring are often exceedingly unfaithful to their origins. Their fathers, after all, are inessential.

[. . .]

I want to conclude with a myth about identity and boundaries which might inform late twentieth-century political imaginations. I am indebted in this story to writers like Joanna Russ, Samuel Delany, John Varley, James Tiptree, Jr., Octavia Butler, Monique Wittig, and Vonda McIntyre.[29] These are our storytellers exploring what it means to be embodied in high-tech worlds. They are theorists for cyborgs. Exploring conceptions of bodily boundaries and social order, the anthropologist Mary Douglas should be credited with helping us to consciousness about how fundamental body imagery is to world view, and so to political language.[30] French feminists like Luce Irigaray and Monique Wittig, for all their differences, know how to write the body; how to weave eroticism, cosmology, and politics from imagery of embodiment, and especially for Wittig, from imagery of fragmentation and reconstitution of bodies.[31]

American radical feminists like Susan Griffin, Audre Lorde, and Adrienne Rich have profoundly affected our political imaginations – and perhaps restricted too much what we allow as a friendly body and political language.[32] They insist on the organic, opposing it to the technological. But their symbolic systems and the related positions of ecofeminism and feminist paganism, replete with organicisms, can only be understood in Sandoval's terms as oppositional ideologies fitting the late twentieth century. They would simply bewilder anyone not preoccupied with the machines and consciousness of late capitalism. In that sense they are part of the cyborg world. But there are also great riches for feminists in explicitly embracing the possibilities inherent in the breakdown of clean distinctions between organism and machine and similar distinctions structuring the Western self. It is the simultaneity of breakdowns that cracks the matrices of domination and opens geometric possibilities. What might be learned from personal and political "technological" pollution? I will look briefly at two overlapping groups of texts for their insight into the construction of a potentially helpful cyborg myth: constructions of women of color and monstrous selves in feminist science fiction.

Earlier I suggested that "women of color" might be understood as a cyborg identity, a potent subjectivity synthesized from fusions of outsider identities and in the complex political-historical layerings of her (Audre Lorde) "biomythography," *Zami*.[33] There are material and cultural grids mapping this potential. Audre Lorde captures the tone in the title of her *Sister Outsider*. In my political myth, Sister Outsider is the offshore woman, whom U.S. workers, female and feminized, are supposed to regard as the enemy preventing their solidarity, threatening their security. Onshore, inside the boundary of the United States, Sister Outsider is a potential amidst the races and ethnic identities of women manipulated for division, competition, and exploitation in the same industries. "Women of color" are the preferred labor force for the science-based industries, the real women for whom the world-wide sexual market, labor market, and politics of reproduction kaleidoscope into daily life. Young Korean women hired in the sex industry and in electronics assembly are recruited from high schools, educated for the integrated circuit. Literacy, especially in English, distinguishes the "cheap" female labor so attractive to the multinationals.

Contrary to orientalist stereotypes of the "oral primitive," literacy is a special mark of women of color, acquired by U.S. black women as well as men through a history of risking death to learn and to teach reading and writing. Writing has a special significance for all colonized groups. Writing has been crucial to the Western myth of the distinction of oral and written cultures, primitive and civilized mentalities, and more recently to the erosion of that distinction in "post-modernist" theories attacking the phallogocentrism of the West, with its worship of the monotheistic, phallic, authoritative, and singular work, the unique and perfect name.[34] Contests for the meanings of writing are a major form of contemporary political struggle. Releasing the play of writing is deadly serious. The poetry and stories of U.S. women of color are repeatedly about writing, about access to the power to signify; but this time that power must be neither phallic nor innocent. Cyborg writing must not be about the Fall, the imagination of a once-upon-a-time wholeness before language, before writing, before Man. Cyborg writing is about the power to survive, not on the basis of original innocence, but on the basis of seizing the tools to mark the world that marked them as other.

The tools are often stories, retold stories, versions that reverse and displace the hierarchical dualisms of naturalized identities. In retelling origin stories, cyborg authors subvert the central myths of origin of Western culture. We have all been colonized by those origin myths, with their longing for fulfillment in apocalypse. The phallogocentric origin stories most crucial for feminist cyborgs are built into the literal technologies – technologies that write the world, biotechnology and microelectronics – that have recently textualized our bodies as code problems on the grid of C³I. Feminist cyborg stories have the task of recoding communication and intelligence to subvert command and control.

Figuratively and literally, language politics pervade the struggles of women of color; and stories about language have a special power in the rich contemporary writing by U.S. women of color. For example, retellings of the story of the indigenous woman Malinche, mother of the mestizo "bastard" race of the new world, master of languages, and mistress of Cortés, carry special meaning for Chicana constructions of identity. Cherríe Moraga in Loving in the War Years explores the themes of identity when one never possessed the original language, never told the original story, never resided in the harmony of legitimate heterosexuality in the garden of culture, and so cannot base identity on a myth or a fall from innocence and right to natural names, mother's or father's.[35] Moraga's writing, her superb literacy, is presented in her poetry as the same kind of violation as Malinche's mastery of the conquerer's language – a violation, an illegitimate production, that allows survival. Moraga's language is not "whole"; it is self-consciously spliced, a chimera of English and Spanish, both conquerer's languages. But it is this chimeric monster, without claim to an original language before violation, that crafts the erotic, competent, potent identities of women of color. Sister Outsider hints at the possibility of world survival not because of her innocence, but because of her ability to live on the boundaries, to write without the founding myth of original wholeness, with its inescapable apocalypse of final return to a deathly oneness that Man has imagined to be the innocent and all-powerful Mother, freed at the End from another spiral of appropriation by her son. Writing marks Moraga's body, affirms it as the body of a woman of color, against the possibility of passing into the unmarked category of the Anglo father or into the orientalist myth of "original illiteracy" of a mother that never was. Malinche was mother here, not Eve before eating the forbidden fruit. Writing affirms Sister Outsider, not the Woman-before-the-Fall-into-Writing needed by the phallogocentric Family of Man.

Writing is pre-eminently the technology of cyborgs, etched surfaces of the late twentieth century. Cyborg politics is the struggle for language and the struggle against perfect communication, against the one code that translates all meaning perfectly, the central dogma of phallogocentrism. That is why cyborg politics insist on noise and advocate pollution, rejoicing in the illegitimate fusions of animal and machine. These are the couplings which make Man and Woman so problematic, subverting the structure of desire, the force imagined to generate language and gender, and so subverting the structure and modes of reproduction of "Western" identity, of nature and culture, of mirror and eye, slave and master, body and mind. "We" did not originally choose to be cyborgs, but choice grounds a liberal politics and epistemology that imagines the reproduction of individuals before the wider replications of "texts."

From the perspective of cyborgs, freed of the need to ground politics in "our" privileged position of the oppression that incorporates all other dominations, the innocence of the merely violated, the ground of those closer to nature, we can see powerful possibilities. Feminisms and Marxisms have run aground on Western epistemological imperatives to construct a revolutionary subject from the perspective of a hierarchy of oppressions and/or a latent position of moral superiority, innocence, and greater closeness to nature. With no available original dream of a common language or original symbiosis promising protection from hostile "masculine" separation, but written into the play of a text that has no finally privileged reading or salvation history, to recognize "oneself" as fully implicated in the world, frees us of the need to root politics in identification, vanguard parties, purity, and mothering. Stripped of identity, the bastard race teaches about the power of the margins and the importance of a mother like Malinche. Women of color have transformed her from the evil mother of masculinist fear into the originally literate mother who teaches survival.

This is not just literary deconstruction, but liminal transformation. Every story that begins with original innocence and privileges the return to wholeness imagines the drama of life to be individuation, separation, the birth of the self, the tragedy of autonomy, the fall into writing, alienation; i.e., war, tempered by imaginary respite in the bosom of the Other. These plots are ruled by a reproductive politics – rebirth without flaw, perfection, abstraction. In this plot women are imagined either better or worse off, but all agree they have less selfhood, weaker individuation, more fusion to the oral, to Mother, less at stake in masculine autonomy. But there is another route to having less at stake in masculine autonomy, a route that does not pass through Woman, Primitive, Zero, the Mirror Stage and its imaginary. It passes through women and other present-tense, illegitimate cyborgs, not of Woman born, who refuse the ideological resources of victimization so as to have a real life. These cyborgs are the people who refuse to disappear on cue, no matter how many times a "Western" commentator remarks on the sad passing of another primitive, another organic group done in by "Western" technology, by writing.[36] These real-life cyborgs (e.g., the Southeast Asian village women workers in Japanese and U.S. electronics firms described by Aihwa Ong), are actively rewriting the texts of their bodies and societies. Survival is the stakes in this play of readings.

(1985)

Notes

29 Katie King, "The Pleasure of Repetition and the Limits of Identification in Feminist Science Fiction: Reimaginations of the Body after the Cyborg," California American Studies Association, Pomona, 1984. An abbreviated list of feminist science fiction underlying themes of this essay: Octavia Butler, *Wild Seed, Mind of My Mind, Kindred, Survivor*, and *Dawn*; Suzy McKee Charnas, *Motherliness*; Samuel Delany, *Tales of Neveryon*; Anne McCaffrey, *The Ship Who Sang*, and *Dinosaur Planet*; Vonda McIntyre, *Superluminal* and *Dreamsnake*; Joanna Russ, *Adventures of Alyx, The Female Man*; James Tiptree, Jr., *Star Songs of an Old Primate*, and *Up the Walls of the World*; John Varley, *Titan, Wizard*, and *Demon*.

30 Mary Douglas, *Purity and Danger* (London: Routledge & Kegan Paul, 1966) and *Natural Symbols* (London: Cresset Press, 1970).

31 French feminisms contribute to cyborg heteroglossia. Carolyn Burke, "Irigaray through the Looking Glass," *Feminist Studies*, vol. 7, no. 2 (Summer 1981): 288–306; Luce Irigaray, *Ce sexe qui n'en est pas un* (Paris: Minuit, 1977); Luce Irigaray, *Et l'une ne bouge pas sans l'autre* (Paris: Minuit, 1979); Elaine Marks and Isabelle de Courtivron, eds., *New French Feminisms* (Amherst: University of Massachusetts Press, 1981); *Signs*. vol. 7, no. I (Autumn, 1981), special issue on French feminism; Monique Wittig, *The Lesbian Body*, trans. David Le Vay (New York: Avon, 1975; *Le*

corps lesbien, 1973). See especially *Feminist Issues: A Journal of Feminist Social and Political Theory* (1980 ff); and Claire Duchen, *Feminism in France: From May '68 to Mitterand* (London: Routledge & Kegan Paul, 1986).

32 But all these poets are very complex, not least in treatment of themes of lying and erotic, decentered collective and personal identities. Susan Griffin, *Women and Nature: The Roaring Inside Her* (New York: Harper & Row, 1978); Audre Lorde, *Sister Outsider* (New York: Crossing Press, 1984); Adrienne Rich, *The Dream of a Common Language* (New York: Norton, 1978).

33 Audre Lorde, *Zami, a New Spelling of my Name* (New York: Crossing Press, 1982); Katie King, "Audre Lorde: Layering History/Constructing Poetry," in "Canons without Innocence," Ph.D. dissertation, UCSC, 1987.

34 Jacques Derrida, *Of Grammatology*, trans. and Introd. Gayatri Chakravorty Spivak (Baltimore: Johns Hopkins University Press, 1976), esp. part II, "Nature, Culture, Writing"; Claude Lévi-Strauss, *Tristes Tropiques*, trans. John Russell (New York, Atheneum, 1961), esp. "The Writing Lesson"; Henry Louis Gates, Jr., "Writing 'Race' and the Difference It Makes," in " 'Race,' Writing and Difference," special issue of *Critical Inquiry*, ed. Gates, vol. 12, no. 1 (Autumn 1985): 1–20; Douglas Kahn and Diane Neumaier, eds., *Cultures in Contention* (Seattle: Real Comet Press, 1985); Walter Ong, *Orality and Literacy: The Technologizing of the Word* (New York: Methuen, 1982); Cheris Kramarae and Paula Treichler, *A Feminist Dictionary* (Boston: Pandora, 1985).

35 Cherrie Moraga, *Loving in the War Years* (Boston: South End Press, 1983). The sharp relation of women of color to writing as theme and politics can be approached through: "The Black Woman and the Diaspora: Hidden Connections and Extended Acknowledgements," An International Literacy Conference, Michigan State University, October 1985; Mari Evans, ed., *Black Women Writers: A Critical Evaluation* (Garden City, N.Y.: Doubleday/Anchor, 1984); Barbara Christian, *Black Feminist Criticism* (New York: Pergamon, 1985); Dexter Fisher, ed., *The Third Woman: Minority Women Writers of the United States* (Boston: Houghton Mifflin, 1980); several issues of *Frontiers*, esp. vol. 5 (1980), "Chicanas en el Ambiente Nacional" and vol. 7 (1983), "Feminisms in the Non-Western World"; Maxine Hong Kingston, *China Men* (New York: Knopf, 1977); Gerda Lerner, ed., *Black Women in White America: A Documentary History* (New York: Vintage, 1973); Paula Giddings, *When and Where I Enter: The Impact of Black Women on Race and Sex in America* (Toronto: Bantam, 1985); Cherrie Moraga and Gloria Anzaldua, eds., *This Bridge Called My Back: Writings by Radical Women of Color* (Watertown, Mass.: Persephone, 1981); Robin Morgan, ed., *Sisterhood Is Global* (Garden City, N.Y.: Anchor/Doubleday, 1984). The writing of white women has had similar meanings: Sandra M. Gilbert and Susan Gubar, *The Madwoman in the Attic* (New Haven: Yale University Press, 1979); Joanna Russ, *How to Suppress Women's Writing* (Austin: University of Texas Press, 1983).

36 James Clifford argues persuasively for recognition of continuous cultural reinvention, the stubborn non-disappearance of those "marked" by Western imperializing practices. See Clifford's "On Ethnographic Allegory" in Clifford and Marcus, *Writing Culture*, and his "On Ethnographic Authority," *Representations*, vol. 1, no. 2 (1983): 118–146.

GLORIA ANZALDUA

Borderlands / La Frontera: The New Mestiza

These numerous possibilities leave *la mestiza* floundering in uncharted seas. In perceiving conflicting information and points of view, she is subjected to a swamping of her psychological borders. She has discovered that she can't hold concepts or ideas in rigid boundaries. The borders and walls that are supposed to keep the undesirable ideas out are entrenched habits and patterns of behavior; these habits and patterns are the enemy within. Rigidity means death. Only by remaining flexible is she able to stretch the psyche horizontally and vertically. *La mestiza* constantly has to shift out of habitual formations; from convergent thinking, analytical reasoning that tends to use rationality to move toward a single goal (a Western mode), to divergent thinking,[4] characterized by movement away from set patterns and goals and toward a more whole perspective, one that includes rather than excludes.

The new *mestiza* copes by developing a tolerance for contradictions, a tolerance for ambiguity. She learns to be an Indian in Mexican culture, to be Mexican from an Anglo point of view. She learns to juggle cultures. She has a plural personality, she operates in a pluralistic mode – nothing is thrust out, the good the bad and the ugly, nothing rejected, nothing abandoned. Not only does she sustain contradictions, she turns the ambivalence into something else.

She can be jarred out of ambivalence by an intense, and often painful, emotional event which inverts or resolves the ambivalence. I'm not sure exactly how. The work takes place underground – subconsciously. It is work that the soul performs. That focal point or fulcrum, that juncture where the mestiza stands, is where phenomena tend to collide. It is where the possibility of uniting all that is separate occurs. This assembly is not one where severed or separated pieces merely come together. Nor is it a balancing of opposing powers. In attempting to work out a synthesis, the self has added a third element which is greater than the sum of its severed parts. That third element is a new consciousness – a mestiza consciousness – and though it is a source of intense pain, its energy comes from continual creative motion that keeps breaking down the unitary aspect of each new paradigm.

En unas pocas centurias, the future will belong to the mestiza. Because the future depends on the breaking down of paradigms, it depends on the straddling of two or more cultures. By creating a new mythos – that is, a change in the way we perceive reality, the way we see ourselves, and the ways we behave – *la mestiza* creates a new consciousness.

The work of *mestiza* consciousness is to break down the subject-object duality that keeps her a prisoner and to show in the flesh and through the images in her work how duality is transcended. The answer to the problem between the white race and the colored, between males and females, lies in healing the split that originates in the very foundation of our lives, our culture, our languages, our thoughts. A massive uprooting of dualistic thinking in the individual and collective consciousness is the beginning of a long struggle, but one that could, in our best hopes, bring us to the end of rape, of violence, of war.

La encrucijada / The Crossroads

> A chicken is being sacrificed
> at a crossroads, a simple mound of earth
> a mud shrine for *Eshu*,

> *Yoruba* god of indeterminacy,
> who blesses her choice of path.
> She begins her journey.

Su cuerpo es una bocacalle. La mestiza has gone from being the sacrificial goat to becoming the officiating priestess at the crossroads.

As a mestiza I have no country, my homeland cast me out; yet all countries are mine because I am every woman's sister or potential lover. (As a lesbian I have no race, my own people disclaim me; but I am all races because there is the queer of me in all races.) I am cultureless because, as a feminist, I challenge the collective cultural/religious male-derived beliefs of Indo-Hispanics and Anglos; yet I am cultured because I am participating in the creation of yet another culture, a new story to explain the world and our participation in it, a new value system with images and symbols that connect us to each other and to the planet. *Soy un amasamiento,* I am an act of kneading, of uniting and joining that not only has produced both a creature of darkness and a creature of light, but also a creature that questions the definitions of light and dark and gives them new meanings.

We are the people who leap in the dark, we are the people on the knees of the gods. In our very flesh, (r)evolution works out the clash of cultures. It makes us crazy constantly, but if the center holds, we've made some kind of evolutionary step forward. *Nuestra alma el trabajo,* the opus, the great alchemical work; spiritual *mestizaje,* a "morphogenesis,"[5] an inevitable unfolding. We have become the quickening serpent movement.

Indigenous like corn, like corn, the *mestiza* is a product of crossbreeding, designed for preservation under a variety of conditions. Like an ear of corn – a female seed-bearing organ – the *mestiza* is tenacious, tightly wrapped in the husks of her culture. Like kernels she clings to the cob; with thick stalks and strong brace roots, she holds tight to the earth – she will survive the crossroads.

Lavando y remojando el maíz en agua de cal, despojando el pellejo. Moliendo, mixteando, amasando, haciendo tortillas de masa.[6] She steeps the corn in lime, it swells, softens. With stone roller on *metate,* she grinds the corn, then grinds again. She kneads and moulds the dough, pats the round balls into *tortillas.*

> We are the porous rock in the stone *metate*
> squatting on the ground.
> We are the rolling pin, *el maíz y agua,*
> *la masa harina. Somos el amasijo.*
> *Somos lo molido en el metate.*

We are the *comal* sizzling hot,
the hot *tortilla*, the hungry mouth.
We are the coarse rock.
We are the grinding motion,
the mixed potion, *somos el molcajete*.
We are the pestle, the *comino, ajo, pimienta*,
We are the *chile colorado*,
the green shoot that cracks the rock.
We will abide.

El camino de la mestiza / The Mestiza Way

Caught between the sudden contraction, the breath sucked in and the endless space, the brown woman stands still, looks at the sky. She decides to go down, digging her way along the roots of trees. Sifting through the bones, she shakes them to see if there is any marrow in them. Then, touching the dirt to her forehead, to her tongue, she takes a few bones, leaves the rest in their burial place.

She goes through her backpack, keeps her journal and address book, throws away the muni-bart metromaps. The coins are heavy and they go next, then the greenbacks flutter through the air. She keeps her knife, can opener and eyebrow pencil. She puts bones, pieces of bark, *hierbas*, eagle feather, snakeskin, tape recorder, the rattle and drum in her pack and she sets out to become the complete *tolteca*.[7]

Her first step is to take inventory. *Despojando, desgranando, quitando paja.* Just what did she inherit from her ancestors? This weight on her back – which is the baggage from the Indian mother, which the baggage from the Spanish father, which the baggage from the Anglo?

Pero es difícil differentiating between *lo heredado, lo adquirido, lo impuesto.* She puts history through a sieve, winnows out the lies, looks at the forces that we as a race, as women, have been a part of. *Luego bota lo que no vale, los desmientos, los desencuentos, el embrutecimiento. Aguarda el juicio, hondo y enraizado, de la gente antigua.* This step is a conscious rupture with all oppressive traditions of all cultures and religions. She communicates that rupture, documents the struggle. She reinterprets history and, using new symbols, she shapes new myths. She adopts new perspectives toward the darkskinned, women and queers. She strengthens her tolerance (and intolerance) for ambiguity. She is willing to share, to make herself vulnerable to foreign ways of seeing and thinking. She surrenders all notions of safety, of the familiar. Deconstruct, construct. She becomes a *nahual*, able to transform herself into a tree, a coyote, into another person. She learns to transform the small "I" into the total Self. *Se hace moldeadora de su alma. Según la concepción que tiene de sí misma, así será.*

(1987)

Notes

4 In part, I derive my definitions for "convergent" and "divergent" thinking from Rothenberg, 12–13.

5 To borrow chemist Ilya Prigogine's theory of "dissipative structures." Prigogine discovered that substances interact not in predictable ways as it was taught in science, but in different and fluctuating ways to produce new and more complex structures, a kind of birth he called "morphogenesis," which created unpredictable innovations. Harold Gilliam, "Searching for a New World View," *This World* (January, 1981), 23.

6 *Tortillas de masa harina*: corn tortillas are of two types, the smooth uniform ones made in a tortilla press and usually bought at a tortilla factory or supermarket, and *gorditas*, made by mixing *masa* with lard or shortening or butter (my mother sometimes puts in bits of bacon or *chicharrones*).

7 Gina Valdés, *Puentes y Fronteras: Coplas Chicanas* (Los Angeles, CA: Castle Lithograph, 1982), 2.

MONIQUE WITTIG

'The Straight Mind'
Feminist Issues

Yes, straight society is based on the necessity of the different/ other at every level. It cannot work economically, symbolically, linguistically, or politically without this concept. This necessity of the different/other is an ontological one for the whole conglomerate of sciences and disciplines that I call the straight mind. But what is the different/other if not the dominated? For heterosexual society is the society which not only oppresses lesbians and gay men, it oppresses many different/others, it oppresses all women and many categories of men, all those who are in the position of the dominated. To constitute a difference and to control it is an "act of power, since it is essentially a normative act. Everybody tries to show the other as different. But not everybody succeeds in doing so. One has to be socially dominant to succeed in it."[7]

For example, the concept of difference between the sexes ontologically constitutes women into different/others. Men are not different, whites are not different, nor are the masters. But the blacks, as well as the slaves, are. This ontological characteristic of the difference between the sexes affects all the concepts which are part of the same conglomerate. But for us there is no such thing as being-woman or being-man. "Man" and "woman" are political concepts of opposition, and the copula which dialectically unites them is, at the same time, the one which abolishes them.[8] It is the class struggle between women and men which will abolish men and women.[9] The concept of difference has nothing ontological about it. It is only the way that the masters interpret a historical situation of domination. The function of difference is to mask at every level the conflicts of interest, including ideological ones.

In other words, for us, this means there cannot any longer be women and men, and that as classes and categories of thought or language they have to disappear, politically, economically, ideologically. If we, as lesbians and gay men, continue to speak of ourselves and to conceive of ourselves as women and as men, we are instrumental in maintaining heterosexuality. I am sure that an economic and political transformation will not dedramatize these categories of language. Can we redeem *slave?* Can we redeem *nigger, negress?* How is *woman* different? Will we continue to write *white, master, man?* The transformation of economic relationships will not suffice. We must produce a political transformation of the key concepts, that is of the concepts which are strategic for us. For there is another order of materiality, that of language, and language is worked upon from within by these strategic concepts. It is at the same time tightly connected to the political field, where everything that concerns language, science and thought refers to the person as subjectivity and to her/his relationship to society. And we cannot leave this within the power of the straight mind or the thought of domination.

If among all the productions of the straight mind I especially challenge the models of the Structural Unconscious, it is because: at the moment in history when the domination of social groups can no longer appear as a logical necessity to the dominated, because they revolt, because they question the differences, Lévi-Strauss, Lacan, and their epigones call upon necessities which escape the control of consciousness and therefore the responsibility of individuals.

They call upon unconscious processes, for example, which require the exchange of women as a necessary condition for every society. According to them, that is what the unconscious tells us with authority, and the symbolic order, without which there is no meaning, no language, no society, depends on it. But what does women being exchanged mean if not that they are dominated? No wonder then that there is only one Unconscious, and that it is heterosexual. It is an Unconscious which looks too consciously after the interests of the masters[10] in whom it lives for them to be dispossessed of their concepts so easily. Besides, domination is denied; there is no slavery of women, there is difference. To which I will answer with this statement made by a Rumanian peasant at a public meeting in 1848: "Why do the gentlemen say it was not slavery, for we know it to have been slavery, this sorrow that we have sorrowed." Yes, we know it, and this science of oppression cannot be taken away from us.

It is from this science that we must track down the "what-goes-without-saying" heterosexual, and (I paraphrase the early Roland Barthes) we must not bear "seeing Nature and History confused at every turn."[11] We must make it brutally apparent that psychoanalysis after Freud and particularly Lacan have rigidly turned their concepts into myths – Difference, Desire, the Name-of-the-father, etc. They have even "over-mythified" the myths, an operation that was necessary for them in order to systematically hetero-sexualize that personal dimension which suddenly emerged through the dominated individuals into the historical field, particularly through women, who started their struggle almost two centuries ago. And it has been done systematically, in a concert of interdisciplinarity, never more harmonious than since the heterosexual myths started to circulate with ease from one formal system to another, like sure values that can be invested in anthropology as well as in psychoanalysis and in all the social sciences.

This ensemble of heterosexual myths is a system of signs which uses figures of speech, and thus it can be politically studied from within the science of our oppression; "for-we-know-it-to-have-been-slavery" is the dynamic which introduces the diachronism of history into the fixed discourse of eternal essences. This undertaking should somehow be a political semiology, although with "this sorrow that we have sorrowed" we work also at the level of language/manifesto, of language/action, that which transforms, that which makes history.

In the meantime, in the systems that seemed so eternal and universal that laws could be extracted from them, laws that could be stuffed into computers, and in any case for the moment stuffed into the unconscious machinery, in these systems, thanks to our action and our language, shifts are happening. Such a model, as for example, the exchange of women, reengulfs history in so violent and brutal a way that the whole system, which was believed to be formal, topples over into another dimension of knowledge. This dimension of history belongs to us, since somehow we have been designated, and since, as Lévi-Strauss said, we talk, let us say that we break off the heterosexual contract.

So, this is what lesbians say everywhere in this country and in some others, if not with theories at least through their social practice, whose repercussions upon straight culture and society are still unenvisionable. An anthropologist might say that we have to wait for fifty years. Yes, if one wants to universalize the functioning of these societies and make their invariants appear. Meanwhile the straight concepts are undermined. What is woman? Panic, general alarm for an active defense. Frankly, it is a problem that the lesbians do not have because of a change of perspective, and it would be incorrect to say that lesbians associate, make love, live with women, for "woman" has meaning only in heterosexual systems of thought and heterosexual economic systems. Lesbians are not women.

(1980)

Notes

7 Claude Faugeron and Philippe Robert, *La Justice et son public et les représentations sociales du système pénal* (Paris: Masson, 1978).

8 See, for her definition of "social sex," Nicole-Claude Mathieu, "Notes pour une définition sociologique des catégories de sexe," *Epistémologie Sociologique* 11 (1971). Translated as *Ignored by Some, Denied by Others: The Social Sex Category in Sociology* (pamphlet), Explorations in Feminism 2 (London: Women's Research and Resources Centre Publications, 1977), pp. 16–37.

9 In the same way that in every other class struggle the categories of opposition are "reconciled" by the struggle whose goal is to make them disappear.

10 Are the millions of dollars a year made by the psychoanalysts symbolic?

11 Roland Barthes, *Mythologies* (New York: Hill and Wang, 1972), p. 11.

ROSI BRAIDOTTI

Nomadic Subjects: Embodiment and Sexual Difference in Contemporary Feminist Theory

The starting point, for my scheme of feminist nomadism, is that feminist theory is not only a movement of critical opposition of the false universality of the subject, it is also the positive affirmation of women's desire to affirm and enact different forms of subjectivity. This project involves both the critique of existing definitions and representations of women and also the creation of new images of female subjectivity. The starting point for this project (both critical and creative) is the need to have real-life women in positions of discursive subjectivity. The key terms here are embodiment and the bodily roots of subjectivity and the desire to reconnect theory to practice.

For the sake of clarity, I will divide the project of feminist nomadism into three phases, all of which will be linked to sexual difference. I want to stress the fact that these three different levels are not dialectically ordained phases but rather that they can coexist chronologically and that each and every one continues to be available as an option for political and theoretical practice. The distinction I will consequently draw between "difference between men and women," "differences among women," and "differences within each woman" is not to be taken as a categorical distinction but as an exercise in naming different facets of a single complex phenomenon.

Nor is this diagram a paradigmatic model: it is a map, a cartography that depicts the different layers of complexity involved in a nomadic epistemology from the perspective of sexual difference. These levels can be viewed spatially, as well as temporally; they spell out different structures of subjectivity but also different moments in the process of becoming-subject. Consequently, these levels are not meant to be approached sequentially and dialectically. Following the nomadic approach that I am defending in this book, the cartography can be entered at *any level* and at *any moment*. I want to stress in fact that these layers occur simultaneously and that, in daily life, they coexist and cannot be easily distinguished. I would even argue that it is precisely the

capacity to transit from one level to another, in a flow of experiences, time
sequences, and layers of signification that is the key to that nomadic mode I
am defending, not only intellectually but also as an art of existence.

TABLE 1

Sexual Difference Level 1: Difference Between Men and Women

SUBJECTIVITY AS	VERSUS	WOMAN AS
• phallogocentric		• the lack/excess/"other-than"/ subject
• universal notion of the subject		• devalorized difference
• coinciding with consciousness		• non consciousness
• self-regulating		• uncontrolled
• rational agency		• irrational
• entitled to rationality		• in excess of rationality
• capable of transcendence		• confined to immanence
• denying corporal origins orobjectifying the body		• Identified with the body – corporeality that is both exploited and reduced to silence

The central issue at stake at this level of analysis is the critique of
universalism as being male-identified and of masculinity as projecting itself as
a pseudo-universal. This also accompanies the critique of the idea of otherness
as devalorization. In a very Hegelian framework, Simone de Beauvoir
formulated fifty years ago a path-breaking analysis of the universalism of the
subject. Confronted with this scheme, she asserted as the theoretical and
political option for women the struggle to attain transcendence and thereby
acquire the same entitlement to subjectivity as men. As Judith Butler points
out in her lucid analysis[43] of this Hegelian moment of feminist theory,
Beauvoir sees the difference that women embody as something that is as yet
unrepresented. Beauvoir consequently concludes that this devalorized and
misrepresented entity can and must be brought into representation, and that
this is the main task of the women's movement.

In a poststructuralist perspective, however, contemporary theorists of difference, like Luce Irigaray, move beyond dialectics. Irigaray evaluates women's
"otherness" not merely as that which is not yet represented but rather as that
which remains *unrepresentable* within this scheme of representation. Woman as
the other remains in excess of or outside the phallogocentric framework that
conflates the masculine with the (false) universalist position. The relationship

between subject and other, therefore, is not one of reversibility; on the contrary, the two poles of the opposition exist in an asymmetrical relationship. Under the heading of "the double syntax" Irigaray defends this irreducible and irreversible difference and proposes it as the foundation for a new phase of feminist politics. In other words, Luce Irigaray stresses the need to recognize as a factual and historical reality that there is no symmetry between the sexes and that this asymmetry has been organized hierarchically by the phallogocentric regime. Recognizing that difference has been turned into a mark of pejoration, the feminist project attempts to redefine it in terms of positivity.

The starting point for the project of sexual difference – level one – remains the political will to assert the specificity of the lived, female bodily experience; the refusal to disembody sexual difference into a new allegedly "postmodern" and "antiessentialist" subject, and the will to reconnect the whole debate on difference to the bodily existence and experience of women.

Politically, the project amounts to the rejection of emancipationism as leading to homologation, that is to say the assimilation of women into masculine modes of thought and practice and consequently sets of values. Recent socioeconomic developments in the status of women in Western, postindustrial societies have in fact shown – besides the persistence of classical forms of discrimination leading to the feminization of poverty – that female emancipation can easily turn into a one-way street into a man's world. This warning has been issued very strongly by feminists as different from each other as Luce Irigaray,[44] Antoinette Fouque,[45], and Marguerite Duras,[46] who warn women against investing all of their time and energy in correcting the errors and mistakes of male culture. A better and politically more rewarding investment consists in trying to elaborate alternative forms of female subjectivity, in a process that is also described as asserting the positivity of sexual difference.

This shift in perspective turned out to be a far from easy moment in feminist practice. In fact, it led to a wave of polemics and, often, to conflicts among women, made all the more acute by the differences of generation.[47] The more lasting aspect of the polemic concerned an opposition between on the one hand the antiemancipationism of the sexual difference theorists and, on the other, the charges of "essentialism" made by the equality-minded thinkers against the sexual difference feminists. I deal with this debate on equality-versus-difference in chapter 15 ("Theories of Gender; or, Language is a Virus").

Far from separating the struggle for equality from the affirmation of difference, I see them as complementary and part of a continuous historical evolution. The women's movement is the space where sexual difference becomes operational, through the strategy of fighting for equality of the sexes in a cultural and economic order dominated by the masculine homosocial bond. What is at stake is the definition of woman as other-than a nonman.

One of the crucial questions of this project is how one can argue both for the loss of the classical paradigm of subjectivity and for the specificity of an alternative female subject. Given that the reaffirmation of sexual difference by feminists dates to the same moment in history as modernity itself, that is to say the moment of loss of the rationalist and naturalistic paradigm, feminists have the double task of stressing the need for a new vision of subjectivity at large, and of a sex-specific vision of female subjectivity in particular.

The analysis of the first level of sexual difference came to be challenged not only because of changing political and intellectual contexts but also because of evolutions internal in the feminist movement itself. On the one hand the existentialist ethics of solidarity was also challenged by psychoanalytic and poststructuralist claims about the coexistence of knowledge and power, which have changed the understanding of phenomena such as oppression and liberation.[48] On the other hand, a new generation of feminists grew frustrated with Beauvoir's sweeping generalizations about "women" as the "second sex." The political and theoretical emphasis since the seventies has been shifting from the

TABLE 2

Sexual Difference Level 2: Differences among women

WOMEN AS THE OTHER	VERSUS	REAL-LIFE WOMEN
– as institution and representation	critical hiatus between them – feminist subjectivity	• experience • embodiment • situated knowledges • women-based knowledges • empowerment
(see level 1)	• positivity of sexual difference as political project • female feminist genealogies, or countermemory • politics of location and resistance • dissymmetry between the sexes	• multiplicity of differences (race, age, class, etc.) or diversity

asymmetry between the sexes to the exploration of the sexual difference embodied and experienced by women.

The central issue at stake here is how to create, legitimate, and represent a multiplicity of alternative forms of feminist subjectivity without falling into relativism. The starting point is the recognition that *Woman* is a general umbrella term that brings together different kinds of women, different levels of experience and different identities.

The notion of *Woman* refers to a female, sexed subject that is constituted, as psychoanalysis convincingly argues, through a process of identification with culturally available positions organized in the dichotomy of gender. As the "second sex" of the patriarchal gender dichotomy, *Woman* is inscribed in what Kristeva calls the longer, linear time of history.[49] As the starting point for feminist consciousness, however, female identity pertains also and simultaneously to a different temporality: a deeper and more discontinuous sense of time that is the time of transformation, resistance, political genealogies, and becoming. Thus, we have on the one hand teleological time and on the other the time of consciousness-raising: history and the unconscious.

I call feminism the movement that struggles to change the values attributed to and the representations made of women in the longer historical time of patriarchal history (*Woman*) as well as in the deeper time of one's own identity. In other words, the feminist project encompasses both the level of subjectivity in the sense of historical agency, and political and social entitlement, and the level of identity that is linked to consciousness, desire, and the politics of the personal; it covers both the conscious and the unconscious levels.

The feminist subject is historical because it is involved in patriarchy by negation; but it is also linked to female identity, to the personal. In other words, the "woman" is to be situated in a structurally different position from the feminist because, being structured as the referent of otherness, it is opposed specularly to the masculine as referent of subjectivity. The second sex is in a dichotomous opposition to the male as representative of the universal. Consequently, feminism requires both an epistemological and a political distinction between *woman* and *feminist*. What is feminist is both the push toward the insertion of women into patriarchal history (the emancipatory moment, or, sexual difference level one) and the questioning of personal identity on the basis of power relations, which is the feminism of difference (sexual difference level two).

Let me repeat the same point from a different angle: critical distance from the institution and representation of "*Woman*" is the starting point for feminist consciousness; the women's movement rests on a consensus that all women partake of the condition of "the second sex." This can be seen as the sufficient condition for the elaboration of a feminist subject position; the recognition of a bond of commonality among women is the starting point for feminist consciousness in that it seals a pact among women. This moment is the foundation stone that allows for the feminist position or standpoint to be articulated.

But this recognition of a common condition of sisterhood in oppression cannot be the final aim; women may have common situations and experiences, but they are not, in any way, *the same*. In this respect, the idea of the politics of location is very important. This idea, developed into a theory of recognition of the multiple differences that exist among women, stresses the importance of rejecting global statements about all women and of attempting instead to be as aware as possible of the place from which one is speaking. Attention to the *situated* as opposed to the universalistic nature of statements is the key idea. In its political applications, the politics of location determines one's approach to time and history; the sense of location, for me, has to do with countermemory, or the development of alternative genealogies. It means that it does make a difference to have the historical memory of oppression or exclusion, as women, rather than being the empirical referent for a dominant group, like men.

Thus, we need to rephrase the point about the relation between *woman* and *feminist*. As Teresa De Lauretis argued, all women are implicated in the confrontation with a certain image of "*Woman*" that is the culturally dominant model for female identity. The elaboration of a political subjectivity as feminist, therefore, requires as its precondition the recognition of a distance between "*Woman*" and real women. Teresa De Lauretis has defined this moment as the recognition of an "essential difference" between woman as representation ("*Woman*" as cultural imago) and woman as experience (real women as agents of change).

In other words, with the help of semiotic and psychoanalytic theories, a foundational distinction is drawn between "*Woman*" as the signifier that is codified in a long history of binary oppositions and the signifier "feminist" as that which builds upon the recognition of the constructed nature of *Woman*. The recognition of the hiatus between *Woman* and women is crucial, as is the determination to seek for adequate representations of it, both politically and symbolically.

Before this development of the philosophy of sexual difference becomes at all possible, however, it is necessary to posit the distinction between *Woman* and women as the foundational gesture for feminist thought to exist at all. This initial step is the assertion of an essential and irreconcilable difference, which I call sexual difference level two, or, differences among women.

Thus, to return to my opening remarks on feminism and modernity: feminist theory as the philosophy of sexual difference identifies as a historical essence the notion of *Woman* at the exact period in history when this notion is deconstructed and challenged. The crisis of modernity makes available to feminists the essence of femininity as an historical construct that needs to be worked upon. Woman therefore ceases to be the culturally dominant and prescriptive model for female subjectivity and turns instead into an identifiable topos for analysis: as a construct (De Lauretis); a masquerade (Butler); a positive essence (Irigaray); or an ideological trap (Wittig) – to mention only a few.

It seems to me that a feminist nomadic position can allow for these different representations and modes of understanding of female subjectivity to coexist and to provide material for discussion. Unless a position of nomadic flexibility comes into being, these different definitions and understandings will have a divisive effect on feminist practice.

Another problem that emerges here is the importance of finding adequate forms of representation for these new figurations of the female subject. As I have argued elsewhere, alternative figurations are crucial at this point and great creativity is needed to move beyond established conceptual schemes. To achieve this, we need not only a transdisciplinary approach but also more effective exchanges between theorists and artists, academics and creative minds. But more on this later.

TABLE 3
Sexual Difference Level 3: Differences
Within Each Woman

Each Real-Life Woman (n.b. *Not "Woman"*) or
Female Feminist Subject is

- a multiplicity in herself: slit, fractured
- a network of Levels of experience (as outlined on levels 2 and 1)
- a living memory and embodied genealogy
- not one conscious subject, but also the subject of her unconscious: identity as identifications
- in an imaginary relationship to variables like class, race, age, sexual choices

This third level of analysis highlights the complexity of the embodied structure of the subject. The body refers to a layer of corporeal materiality, a substratum of living matter endowed with memory. Following Deleuze, I understand this as pure flows of energy, capable of multiple variations. The "self," meaning an entity endowed with identity, is anchored in this living matter, whose materiality is coded and rendered in language. The postpsychoanalytic vision of the corporeal subject that I propose here implies that the body cannot be fully apprehended or represented: it exceeds representation. A difference within each entity is a way of expressing this condition. Identity for me is a play of multiple, fractured aspects of the self; it is relational, in that it requires a bond to the "other"; it is retrospective, in that it is fixed through memories and recollections, in a genealogical process. Last, but not least, identity is made of successive identifications, that is to say unconscious internalized images that escape rational control.

This fundamental noncoincidence of identity with consciousness implies also that one entertains an imaginary relationship to one's history, genealogy, and material conditions.

I stress this because far too often in feminist theory, the level of identity gets merrily confused with issues of political subjectivity. In my scheme of thought, identity bears a privileged bond to unconscious processes, whereas political subjectivity is a conscious and willful position. Unconscious desire and willful choice do not always coincide.

Paying attention to the level of identity as complexity and multiplicity would also encourage feminists to deal with their own internal contradictions and discontinuities – if possible with humor and lightness. As I suggest in the introduction to this book, I do think it important to leave room for contradictory moments, for confusions and uncertainties, and not to see them as defeats or lapses into "politically incorrect" behavior. In this respect, nothing could be more antithetical to the nomadism I am advocating than feminist moralism.

The central issue at stake here is how to avoid the repetition of exclusions in the process of legitimating an alternative feminist subject? How to avoid hegemonic recodification of the female subject, how to keep an open-ended view of subjectivity, while asserting the political and theoretical presence of another view of subjectivity?

According to this vision of a subject that is both historically anchored and split, or multiple, the power of synthesis of the "I" is a grammatical necessity, a theoretical fiction that holds together the collection of differing layers, the integrated fragments of the ever-receding horizon of one's identity. The idea of "differences within" each subject is tributary to psychoanalytic theory and practice in that it envisages the subject as the crossroads of different registers of speech, calling upon different layers of lived experience.

To translate this standpoint back into the debate on the politics of subjectivity within the feminist practice of sexual difference, I would ask the following question: What is the technology of the self at work in the expression of sexual difference?

In this scheme of thought, following the distinction of levels I am proposing, it is also plausible to posit feminist subjectivity as an object of desire for women. A female feminist could consequently be seen as someone who longs for, tends toward, is driven to feminism. I would call this an "intensive" reading of the feminist position, which then comes to be understood not merely in terms of willful commitment to a set of values or political beliefs but also in terms of the passions or desires that sustain it and motivate it.[50] This "topology" of passion is an approach inspired by Nietzsche via Deleuze; it allows us to see volitional choices not as transparent, self-evident positions but rather as multilayered ones. A healthy dose of a hermeneutics of suspicion toward one's beliefs is no form of cynicism, or nihilism; on the contrary, it is a way of returning political beliefs to their fullness, their embodiedness, and consequently their partiality.

As Maaike Meijer observes,[51] a psychoanalytic, "intensive" approach is seldom applied to the analysis of politics. If it ever is, as in the case of Nazism, it usually aims at explaining dark and terrifying motivating forces. It is as if reference to a topology of political passions could only carry negative connotations. In response to this, I would turn to Deleuze's idea of the positivity of passions – a notion that he explores with Nietzsche and Spinoza – in order to account for a "desire for feminism" as a joyful, affirmative passion. What feminism liberates in women is also their desire for freedom, lightness, justice, and self-accomplishment. These values are not only rational political beliefs, they are also objects of intense desire. This merry spirit was quite manifest in the earlier days of the women's movement, when it was clear that joy and laughter were profound political emotions and statements. Not much of this joyful beat survives in these days of postmodernist gloom, and yet we would do well to remember the subversive force of Dionysian laughter. I wish feminism would shed its saddening, dogmatic mode to rediscover the merrymaking of a movement that aims to change life.[52]

As Italo Calvino points out,[53] the key words to help us to move out of the postmodernist crisis are: lightness, quickness, and multiplicity. The third level of sexual difference alerts us to the importance of a certain lightness of touch to accompany the complexity of the political and epistemological structures of the feminist project.

(1994)

Notes

43 Judith Butler, *Subjects of Desire: Hegelian Reflections in Twentieth-Century France* (New York: Columbia University Press, 1987; *Gender Trouble* (New York and London: Routledge, 1990). See especially chapter one.

44 Luce Irigaray, "Equal to whom," pp. 59–76.

45 Antoinette Fouque, "Women in Movements: Yesterday, Today, and Tomorrow," *differences* 13, no. 3 (1991): 1–25.

46 Marguerite Duras, an interview, in *Shifting Scenes: Interviews on Women, Writing and Politics in Post-68 France*, p. 74.

47 Dorothy Kaufmannn, "Simone de Beauvoir: Questions of Difference and Generation," in *Yale French Studies*, no. 72 (1986). See also, Marianne Hirsch and Evelyn Fox Keller, eds., *Conflicts in Feminism*.

48 Emblematic of this change of perspective is the polemic that opposed Foucault to Sartre on the issue of the role of the intellectuals and Beauvoir to Cixous and Irigaray on the "liberation" of women. For a summary of these debates, see my *Patterns of dissonance*.

49 Julia Kristeva, "Women's Time," in N. O. Keohane, ed., *Feminist Theory: A Critique of Ideology* (Chicago: University of Chicago Press, 1988).

50 On this point, I am indebted to the discussion on feminism and psychoanalysis that took place in the graduate seminar of the Women's Studies program in Utrecht in March/April 1993, especially remarks made by Maaike Meijer and Juliana de Novellis.

51 Ibid.

52 This was a famous slogan during the May 1968 riots in Paris.

53 Italo Calvino, *Lezioni americane: Sei proposte per il prossimo millennio* (Milan: Garzanti, 1988).

Bibliography of Extracts

The following list gives bibliographical information on all the extracts included in this *Reader* To help in locating the material, I have given supplementary information for other sources. I refer you particularly to well-known, and hence readily accessible, collections of feminist literary theory.

ALCOFF, Linda 'Cultural Feminism versus Post-structuralism: The Identity Crisis in Feminist Theory', *Signs: Journal of Women in Culture and Society*, vol. 13, no. 3 (1988).

ANZALDUA, Gloria *Borderlands/ La Frontera: The New Mestiza* (San Francisco, Spinsters/Aunt Lute, 1987). The relevant chapter is included in Linda S. Kauffman, *American Feminist Thought At Century's End: A Reader* (Oxford, Basil Blackwell, 1993).

ARMSTRONG, Isobel 'Christina Rossetti: Diary of a Feminist Reading' in Sue Roe (ed.) *Women Reading Women's Writing* (Sussex, Harvester Press, 1987).

ARMSTRONG, Nancy *Desire and Domestic Fiction: A Political History of the Novel* (Oxford, Oxford University Press, 1987).

ATWOOD, Margaret 'Paradoxes and Dilemmas, the Woman as Writer', in Gwen Matheson (ed.) *Women in the Canadian Mosaic* (Toronto, Peter Martin Associates, 1976). Anthologized in Jeannette L. Webber and Joan Grumman (eds.), *Woman as Writer* (Boston, Houghton Mifflin Co., 1978).

BAINES, Elizabeth 'Naming the Fictions' (1985) commissioned for the first edition of *Feminist Literary Theory: A Reader*.

BARR SNITOW, Ann 'Mass Market Romance: Pornography for Women is Different', *Radical History Review*, no. 20 (Spring/Summer, 1979). Anthologized in Ann Snitow et al. (eds), *Powers of Desire: The Politics of Sexuality* (New York, New Feminist Library, 1983).

BARRETT, Michèle *Women's Oppression Today: Problems in Marxist Feminist Analysis* (London, Verso and NLB, 1980). The relevant chapter can also be found in Judith Newton and Deborah Rosenfelt (eds) *Feminist Criticism and Social Change: Sex, Class and Race in Literature and Culture* (New York and London, Methuen, 1985).

BARRETT, Michèle 'Feminism and the Definition of Cultural Politics', in Rosalind Brunt and Caroline Rowan (eds) *Feminism, Culture and Politics* (London, Lawrence and Wishart, 1982).

BELSEY, Catherine *Critical Practice* (London, Methuen, 1980. Revised version in Judith Newton and Deborah Rosenfelt (eds) *Feminist Criticism and Social Change: Sex, Class and Race in Literature and Culture* (New York and London, Methuen,

1985); Robyn R. Warhol and Diane Price Herndl (eds.), *Feminisms: An Anthology of Literary Theory and Criticism* (New Jersey, Rutgers University Press, 1991).

BENHABIB, Seyla 'Feminism and the Question of Postmodernism', *Situating the Self* (Cambridge, Polity Press, 1992). Included in *The Polity Reader in Gender Studies* (Cambridge, Polity Press, 1994).

BERG, Christine and BERRY, Philippa ' "Spiritual Whoredom": An Essay on Female Prophets in the Seventeenth Century' in Frances Barker et al. (eds) *1642: Literature and Power in the Seventeenth Century* (Essex, University of Essex, 1980).

BLACK WOMAN TALK COLLECTIVE 'Black Woman Talk', *Feminist Review*, no. 17 (1984).

BOWLBY, Rachel 'Flight Reservations: The Anglo-American/French Divide in Feminist Criticism' (first published 1988) in *Still Crazy After All These Years: Women, Writing and Psychoanalysis* (London and New York, Routledge, 1992).

BRAIDOTTI, Rosi *Nomadic Subjects: Embodiment and Sexual Difference in Contemporary Feminist Theory* (New York, Columbia University Press, 1994).

BUTLER, Judith *Gender Trouble: Feminism and the Subversion of Identity* (London, Routledge, 1990).

CHRISTIAN, Barbara 'The Race for Theory' in Linda Kauffman (ed.) *Gender and Theory: Dialogues on Feminist Criticism* (Oxford, Basil Blackwell, 1989). An earlier version can be found in *Cultural Critique* 6 (Spring, 1987).

CIXOUS, Hélène 'Castration or Decapitation?', *Signs: Journal of Women in Culture and Society* vol. 7, no. 1 (Autumn, 1981).

CIXOUS, Hélène 'The Laugh of the Medusa' in Elaine Marks and Isabel de Courtivron (eds) *New French Feminisms: An Anthology* (Sussex, Harvester Press, 1981). Also available in *Signs: Journal of Women in Culture and Society*, vol. 1, no. 4 (Autumn, 1976); Dennis Walder (ed.) *Literature in the Modern World* (Oxford, Oxford University Press and The Open University, 1990); Robyn R. Warhol and Diane Price Herndl (eds) *Feminisms: An Anthology of Literary Theory and Criticism* (New Jersey, Rutgers University Press, 1991).

CIXOUS, Hélène et al. 'Conversations' in Susan Sellars (ed.) *Writing Differences: Readings from the Seminar of Hélène Cixous* (Milton Keynes, The Open University Press, 1988).

CLEMENT, Catherine 'Enslaved Enclave' in Elaine Marks and Isabel de Courtivron (eds) *New French Feminisms: An Anthology* (Sussex, Harvester Press, 1981).

COWARD, Rosalind *Female Desire: Women's Sexuality Today* (London, Paladin, 1984).

COWARD, Rosalind ' "This Novel Changes Lives": Are Women's Novels Feminist Novels? A Response to Rebecca O'Rourke's Article "Summer Reading" ' *Feminist Review*, no. 5 (1980). Anthologized in Elaine Showalter (ed.) *The New Feminist Criticism: Essays on Women, Literature and Theory* (London, Virago, 1986).

COWIE, Elizabeth et al. 'Representation vs. Communication' in Feminist Anthology Collective, *No Turning Back: Writings from the Women's Liberation Movement 1975–80* (London, The Women's Press, 1981).

CRANNY-FRANCIS, Anne *Feminist Fiction: Feminist Uses of Generic Fiction* (Oxford, Polity Press, 1990).

CULLER, Jonathan 'Reading as a Woman' in *On Deconstruction: Theory and Criticism after Structuralism* (London, Routledge, 1983) (first published 1982). The relevant section is included in Robyn R. Warhol and Diane Price Herndl (eds)

Feminisms: An Anthology of Literary Theory and Criticism (New Jersey, Rutgers University Press, 1991).

DE LAURETIS, Teresa 'Upping the Anti (sic) in Feminist Theory' in Marianne Hirsch and Evelyn Fox Keller (eds) *Conflicts in Feminism* (London, Routledge, 1990).

EDITORIAL COLLECTIVE OF QUESTIONS FEMINISTES 'Variations on Common Themes' in Elaine Marks and Isabel de Courtivron (eds) *New French Feminisms: An Anthology* (Sussex, Harvester Press, 1981).

ELLMANN, Mary *Thinking About Women* (London, Virago, 1979) (first published 1968).

FARLEY KESSLER, Carol Introduction to *Daring to Dream: Utopian Stories by United States Women, 1836–1919* (London, Routledge and Kegan Paul, 1984).

FELMAN, Shoshana 'Women and Madness: The Critical Phallacy', *Diacritics*, vol. 5, no. 4 (1975). Anthologized in Robyn R. Warhol and Diane Price Herndl (eds) *Feminisms: An Anthology of Literary Theory and Criticism* (New Jersey, Rutgers University Press, 1991) and Catherine Belsey and Jane Moore (eds) *The Feminist Reader: Essays in Gender and the Politics of Literary Criticism* (London, Macmillan, 1989).

FELSKI, Rita *Beyond Feminist Aesthetics: Feminist Literature and Social Change* (Cambridge Mass., Harvard University Press, 1989).

FETTERLEY, Judith *The Resisting Reader* (Bloomington, Indiana University Press, 1978). The relevant chapter is included in Robyn R. Warhol and Diane Price Herndl (eds) *Feminisms: An Anthology of Literary Theory and Criticism* (New Jersey, Rutgers University Press, 1991).

FORRESTER, Viviane 'What Women's Eyes See' (first published 1976) in Elaine Marks and Isobelle de Courtivron (eds) *New French Feminisms: An Anthology* (Sussex, Harvester Press, 1981).

FRASER, Nancy and NICHOLSON, Linda J. 'Social Criticisms Without Philosophy: An Encounter Between Feminism and Postmodernism' in Linda J. Nicholson (ed.) *Feminism/Postmodernism* (New York and London, Routledge, 1990).

FUSS, Diana *Essentially Speaking: Feminism, Nature and Difference* (London, Routledge, 1989).

GATES Jr, Henry Louis 'Introduction: Writing "Race" and the Difference it Makes', Gates (ed.) *"Race", Writing and Difference* (Chicago and London, University of Chicago Press, 1986).

GILBERT, Sandra M. and GUBAR, Susan *The Madwoman in the Attic: The Woman Writer and the Nineteenth-Century Literary Imagination* (New Haven and London, Yale University Press, 1979).

GILBERT, Sandra M. and GUBAR, Susan (eds) *Shakespeare's Sisters: Feminist Essays on Women Poets* (Bloomington and London, Indiana University Press, 1979).

HARAWAY, Donna 'A Manifesto for Cyborgs: Science, Technology, and Socialist Feminism in the 1980s', *Socialist Review*, vol. 15, no. 18 (1985). Included in Elizabeth Weed (ed.) *Coming to Terms: Feminism, Theory, Politics* (London, Routledge, 1989) and Linda J. Nicholson (ed.) *Feminism/Postmodernism* (London, Routledge, 1990).

HEATH, Stephen *The Sexual Fix* (London, Macmillan, 1982).

hOOKS, bELL 'Postmodern Blackness' in *Yearning: Race, Gender and Cultural Politics* (London, Turnaround, 1991).

IRIGARAY, Luce 'The Powers of Discourse and the Subordination of the Feminine', (first published, in French in 1977) *This Sex Which Is Not One* (Ithaca, New York, Cornell University Press, 1985). Included in Margaret Whitford (ed.) *The Irigaray Reader* (Oxford, Basil Blackwell, 1991).

JACKSON, Cath 'A Press of One's Own', *Trouble and Strife*, no. 26 (Summer, 1993).

JACKSON, Rosemary *Fantasy: The Literature of Subversion* (London, Methuen, 1981).

JACOBUS, Mary 'The Buried Letter: Feminism and Romanticism in *Villette*', Jacobus (ed.) *Women Writing and Writing About Women* (London, Croom Helm, 1979).

JACOBUS, Mary *Reading Woman: Essays in Feminist Criticism* (London, Methuen, 1986).

JAFFER, Frances Quoted in Rachel Blan DuPlessis, 'For the Etruscans: Sexual Difference and Artistic Production – The Debate over a Female Aesthetic' in Hester Eisenstein and Alice Jardine (eds) *The Future of Difference* (Boston, G. K. Hall, 1980). A revised version became part of DuPlessis's collection, *The Pink Guitar: Writing as Feminist Practice* (New York, Routledge, 1990). The revised version is also included in Elaine Showalter (ed.) *The New Feminist Criticism: Essays on Women, Literature and Theory* (London, Virago, 1986) and Rick Rylance (ed.) *Debating Texts: A Reader in 20th Century Literary Theory and Method* (Milton Keynes, The Open University Press, 1987).

JARDINE, Alice A. *Gynesis: Configurations of Woman and Modernity* (Ithaca and London, Cornell University Press, 1985).

JONES, Ann Rosalind 'Writing the Body: Toward An Understanding of "L'Ecriture Féminine"', *Feminist Studies*, vol. 7, no. 2 (Summer, 1981). Also available in Elaine Showalter (ed.) *The New Feminist Criticism: Essays on Women, Literature and Theory* (London, Virago, 1986); Judith Newton and Deborah Rosenfelt (eds.), *Feminist Criticism and Social Change: Sex, Class and Race in Literature and Culture* (New York and London, Methuen, 1985); Robyn R. Warhol and Diane Price Herndl (eds.) *Feminisms: An Anthology of Literary Theory and Criticism* (New Jersey, Rutgers University Press, 1991).

KANNEH, Kadiatu 'Love, Mourning and Metaphor: Terms of Identity' in Isobel Armstrong (ed.) *New Feminist Discourses: Critical Essays on Theories and Texts* (London, Routledge, 1992).

KAMUF, Peggy 'Writing Like a Woman' in Sally McConnell-Ginet et al. (eds) *Women and Language in Literature and Society* (New York, Praeger Publishers, 1980).

KAPLAN, Cora (ed.) Elizabeth Barrett Browning, *Aurora Leigh and Other Poems* (London, The Women's Press, 1978).

KAPLAN, Cora 'Speaking/Writing/Feminism' in Michelene Wandor (ed.) *On Gender and Writing* (London, Routledge and Kegan Paul, 1983). Now included in Kaplan's own collection *Sea Changes: Essays on Culture and Feminism* (London, Verso, 1986).

KOLODNY, Annette 'Dancing Through the Minefield: Some Observations on the Theory, Practice and Politics of a Feminist Literary Criticism', *Feminist Studies*, vol. 6, no. 1 (Spring, 1980). Included in Elaine Showalter (ed.) *The New Feminist Criticism: Essays on Women, Literature and Theory* (London, Virago, 1986) and

Robyn R. Warhol and Diane Price Herndl (eds) *Feminisms: An Anthology of Literary Theory and Criticism* (New Jersey, Rutgers University Press, 1991).

KRISTEVA, Julia 'Woman Can Never Be Defined' (first published 1974) in Elaine Marks and Isabelle de Courtivron (eds) *New French Feminisms: An Anthology* (Sussex, Harvester Press, 1981).

KRISTEVA, Julia 'A Question of Subjectivity: An Interview', *Women's Review*, no. 12 (Oct., 1986). Included in Philip Rice and Patricia Waugh (eds) *Modern Literary Theory: A Reader* (London, Edward Arnold, 1989).

KRISTEVA, Julia 'Talking about *Polylogue*' (first published 1977) in Toril Moi (ed.) *French Feminist Thought: A Reader* (Oxford, Basil Blackwell, 1987).

LAUTER, Paul 'Race and Gender in the Shaping of the American Literary Canon: A Case Study from the Twenties', (first published 1983) in Judith Newton and Deborah Rosenfelt (eds) *Feminist Criticism and Social Change: Sex, Class and Race in Literature and Culture* (New York and London, Methuen, 1985).

LEFANU, Sarah *In the Chinks of the World Machine: Feminism and Science Fiction* (London, The Women's Press, 1988).

LIGHT, Alison 'Feminism and the Literary Critic', *LTP: Journal of Literature, Teaching, Politics* (Sussex, University of Sussex, 1983).

LIGHT, Alison *Forever England: Femininity, Literature and Conservatism Between the Wars* (London, Routledge, 1991).

LOVELL, Terry 'Writing Like a Woman: A Question of Politics' in Frances Barker et al. (eds) *The Politics of Theory* (Essex, The University of Essex, 1983).

LOVELL, Terry *Consuming Fiction* (London, Verso, 1987).

McDOWELL, Deborah E. 'New Directions for Black Feminist Criticism', *Black American Literature Forum*, 14 (1980). Included in Elaine Showalter (ed.) *The New Feminist Criticism: Essays on Women, Literature and Theory* (London, Virago, 1986).

MILLER, Nancy K. 'Parables and Politics: Feminist Criticism in 1986', *Paragraph*, vol. 8 (Oct., 1986).

MITCHELL, Juliet 'Femininity, Narrative and Psychoanalysis' in *Women: The Longest Revolution* (London, Virago, 1984).

MOERS, Ellen *Literary Women* (London, The Women's Press, 1978) (first published in the UK 1977).

MOHANTY, Chandra Talpade 'Under Western Eyes: Feminist Scholarship and Colonial Discourses' in Mohanty, Ann Russo and Lourdes Torres (eds) *Third World Women and the Politics of Feminism* (Bloomington and Indianapolis, Indiana University Press, 1991). Earlier versions are to be found in *Boundary 2*, vol. 12, no. 3/vol 13, no. 1 (Spring/Fall, 1984) and *Feminist Review*, no. 30 (Autumn, 1988).

MOI, Toril *Sexual/Textual Politics: Feminist Literary Theory* (London, Methuen, 1985).

NGCOBO, Lauretta 'Editor's Introduction' to *Let It Be Told: Essays by Black Women in Britain* (London, Virago, 1988) (first published 1987).

OATES, Joyce Carol 'Is There a Female Voice? Joyce Carol Oates Replies' in Janet Todd (ed.) *Women and Literature Vol. 1, Gender and Literary Voice* (New York, Holmes and Meier, 1980).

OHMANN, Carol 'Emily Brontë in the Hands of Male Critics', *College English*, vol. 32, no. 8 (May, 1971).

OLSEN, Tillie *Silences* (London, Virago, 1980) (first published 1978).

POOVEY, Mary 'Feminism and Deconstruction', *Feminist Studies*, vol. 14, no. 1 (Spring, 1988).

RADWAY, Janice 'Women Read the Romance: The Interaction of Text and Context', *Feminist Studies*, vol. 9, no. 1 (1983). This essay subsequently became part of *Reading the Romance: Women, Patriarchy, and Popular Literature* (Chapel Hill, University of North Carolina Press, 1984). The relevant chapter is anthologized in Robyn R. Warhol and Diane Price Herndl (eds) *Feminisms: An Anthology of Literary Theory and Criticism* (New Jersey, Rutgers University Press, 1991).

REGISTER, Cheri 'American Feminist Literary Criticism: A Bibliographical Introduction' in Josephine Donovan (ed.) *Feminist Literary Criticism: Explorations in Theory* (Kentucky, University Press of Kentucky, 1975).

RICH, Adrienne 'When We Dead Awaken: Writing as Re-Vision', (first published 1972) *On Lies, Secrets, and Silence: Selected Prose 1966–1978* (New York and London, W. W. Norton and Co., 1979).

RICH, Adrienne 'Compulsory Heterosexuality and Lesbian Existence', Elizabeth Abel and Emily K. Abel (eds), *The Signs Reader: Women, Gender and Scholarship* (Chicago, University of Chicago Press, 1983). This essay has been widely anthologized. It is most readily available in Rich's collection *Blood, Bread, and Poetry: Selected Prose 1979–1985* (London, Virago, 1987).

ROSE, Jacqueline 'Femininity and Its Discontents', *Feminist Review*, no. 14 (1983). Revised in Rose's *Sexuality in the Field of Vision* (London, Verso, 1986). Included in Terry Lovell (ed.) *British Feminist Thought: A Reader* (Oxford, Basil Blackwell, 1990).

RUTHVEN, K. K. *Feminist Literary Studies: An Introduction* (Cambridge, Cambridge University Press, 1984).

SCANLON, Joan and SWINDELLS, Julia 'Bad Apple', *Trouble and Strife*, no. 28 (Spring, 1994).

SCHOLES, Robert 'Reading Like a Man' in Alice Jardine and Paul Smith (eds) *Men in Feminism* (London and New York, Methuen, 1987).

SHOWALTER, Elaine *A Literature of Their Own: British Women Novelists from Brontë to Lessing* (London, Virago, 1978) (first published 1977). The relevant chapter is anthologized in Robyn R. Warhol and Diane Price Herndl (eds) *Feminisms: An Anthology of Literary Theory and Criticism* (New Jersey, Rutgers University Press, 1991).

SHOWALTER, Elaine 'Toward a Feminist Poetics' in Mary Jacobus (ed.) *Women Writing and Writing About Women* (London, Croom Helm, 1979). Included in Showalter's edited volume, *The New Feminist Criticism: Essays on Women, Literature and Theory* (London, Virago, 1986) (first published 1985); Rick Rylance (ed.) *Debating Texts: A Reader in 20th Century Literary Theory and Method* (Milton Keynes, The Open University Press, 1987); Philip Rice and Patricia Waugh (eds) *Modern Literary Theory: A Reader* (London, Edward Arnold, 1989).

SMITH, Barbara 'Toward a Black Feminist Criticism', *Conditions: Two*, vol. 1, no. 2 (Oct., 1977). Anthologized in Judith Newton and Deborah Rosenfelt (eds) *Feminist Criticism and Social Change: Sex, Class and Race in Literature and Culture* (New York and London, Methuen, 1985) and Elaine Showalter (ed.) *The New Feminist Criticism: Essays on Women, Literature and Theory* (London, Virago, 1986).

SOPER, Kate 'Feminism, Humanism and Postmodernism', *Radical Philosopy*, 55 (Summer, 1990). Anthologized in Mary Evans (ed.) *The Woman Question* (Second Edition), (London, Sage, 1994).

SPENCER, Jane *The Rise of the Woman Novelist: From Aphra Behn to Jane Austen* (Oxford, Basil Blackwell, 1986).

SPIVAK, Gayatri Chakravorty 'French Feminism in an International Frame', *Yale French Studies*, 62 (1981). Included in Spivak's collection, *In Other Worlds: Essays in Cultural Politics* (New York and London, Methuen, 1987) and Mary Eagleton (ed.) *Feminist Literary Criticism* (London, Longman, 1991).

STANTON, Domna C. 'Language and Revolution: The Franco-American Dis-Connection' in Hester Eisenstein and Alice Jardine (eds) *The Future of Difference* (Boston, G. K. Hall, 1980).

STILL, Judith 'A Feminine Economy: Some Preliminary Thoughts' in Helen Wilcox et al. (eds) *The Body and the Text: Hélène Cixous, Reading and Teaching* (Hertfordshire, Harvester Wheatsheaf, 1990).

TODD, Janet *Feminist Literary History: A Defence* (Oxford, Polity Press, 1988).

TRINH T. Minh-ha *Woman, Native, Other: Writing Postcoloniality and Feminism* (Bloomington and Indianapolis, Indiana University Press, 1989).

WALKER, Alice 'Saving the Life That Is Your Own: The Importance of Models in the Artist's Life' (first published 1976) and 'In Search of Our Mothers' Gardens', (first published 1974) *In Search of Our Mothers' Gardens* (London, The Women's Press, 1984).

WANDOR, Michelene 'The Impact of Feminism on the Theatre', *Feminist Review*, no. 18 (1984).

WATT, Ian *The Rise of the Novel: Studies in Defoe, Richardson and Fielding* (London, Chatto and Windus, 1957).

WAUGH, Patricia *Feminine Fictions: Revisiting the Postmodern* (London, Routledge, 1989).

WEEDON, Chris *Feminist Practice and Poststructuralist Theory* (Oxford, Basil Blackwell, 1987).

WILLIAMS, Linda R. 'Happy Families? Feminist Reproduction and Matrilineal Thought', in Isobel Armstrong (ed.) *New Feminist Discourses: Critical Essays on Theories and Texts* (London, Routledge, 1992).

WILSON, Elizabeth *Mirror Writing: An Autobiography* (London, Virago, 1982).

WITTIG, Monique 'The Straight Mind', *Feminist Issues* vol. 1, no. 1 (Summer, 1980). Collected in *The Straight Mind and Other Essays* (London, Harvester Wheatsheaf, 1992).

WOMEN IN PUBLISHING *Reviewing the Reviews: A Woman's Place on the Book Page* (London, The Journeyman Press, 1987).

WOOLF, Virginia *A Room of One's Own* (1929). There are several editions of *A Room of One's Own*. The two most useful are the combined volume of *A Room of One's Own* and *Three Guineas* (ed.) Michèle Barrett (London, Penguin, 1993) and the World's Classics combined volume (ed.) Morag Shiach (Oxford, Oxford University Press, 1992).

WOOLF, Virginia 'Professions for Women', *The Death of the Moth* (1942). Included in Michèle Barrett (ed.), *Virginia Woolf: Women and Writing* (London, The Women's Press, 1975:1992).

ZIMMERMAN, Bonnie 'What Has Never Been: An Overview of Lesbian Feminist Literary Criticism', *Feminist Studies* vol. 7, no. 3 (Autumn, 1981). Anthologized in Elaine Showalter (ed.) *The New Feminist Criticism: Essays on Women, Literature and Theory* (London, Virago, 1986); Robyn R. Warhol and Diane Price Herndl (eds) *Feminisms: An Anthology of Literary Theory and Criticism* (New Jersey, Rutgers University Press, 1991); Gayle Green and Coppélia Khan (eds) *Making a Difference: Feminist Literary Criticism* (London, Methuen, 1985).

Index

Page numbers in italics refer to extracts from authors